Threads of Arctic Prehistory: Papers in honour of William E. Taylor, Jr.

edited by David Morrison
and Jean-Luc Pilon

Archaeological
Survey of Canada

Mercury Series
Paper 149

CANADIAN MUSEUM OF CIVILIZATION

© Canadian Museum of Civilization 1994

CANADIAN CATALOGUING IN PUBLICATION DATA

Threads of Arctic prehistory : papers in honour of
William E. Taylor, Jr.

(Mercury series, ISSN 0316-1854)
(Paper / Archaeological Survey of Canada, ISSN 0317-2244 ;
no. 149)
Includes an abstract in French.
ISBN 0-660-50751-X

1. Taylor, William E., 1927-
2. Archaeologists – Canada – Biography.
3. Arctic regions – Antiquities.
4. Excavations (Archaeology) – Arctic regions.
5. Indians of North America – Antiquities.
I. Morrison, David A.
II. Pilon, J.-L. (Jean Luc)
III. Canadian Museum of Civilization.
IV. Title : Papers in honour of William E. Taylor, Jr.
V. Series.
VI. Series: Paper (Archaeological Survey of Canada) ; no. 149.

E78.C2T47 1994   971.9'01   C94-980291-3

 PRINTED IN CANADA

Published by
Canadian Museum of Civilization
100 Laurier Street
P.O. Box 3100, Station B
Hull, Quebec
J8X 4H2

HEAD OF PRODUCTION: Deborah Brownrigg

COVER DESIGN: Purich Design Studio

PAPER COORDINATOR: Richard E. Morlan

COVER PHOTO: William E. Taylor, Jr., at the site of a Thule
culture dwelling at Pearce Point on the Amundsen Gulf coast that
was excavated in 1990. (The stepladder allowed the team to take
oblique-angle photographs.) This work was part of Bill's third
season of research along the Amundsen Gulf shores following his
retirement as President of the Social Sciences and Humanities
Research Council of Canada. Bill's scientific interests in the area
began with a survey in 1963.

OBJECT OF THE MERCURY SERIES

The Mercury Series is designed to permit the rapid
dissemination of information pertaining to the disciplines
in which the Canadian Museum of Civilization is active.
Considered an important reference by the scientific
community, the Mercury Series comprises over three
hundred specialized publications on Canada's history and
prehistory.

Because of its specialized audience, the series consists
largely of monographs published in the language of the
author.

In the interest of making information available quickly,
normal production procedures have been abbreviated. As
a result, grammatical and typographical errors may occur.
Your indulgence is requested.

Titles in the Mercury Series can be obtained by writing to:

Mail Order Services
Canadian Museum of Civilization
100 Laurier Street
P.O. Box 3100, Station B
Hull, Quebec
J8X 4H2

BUT DE LA COLLECTION MERCURE

La collection Mercure vise à diffuser rapidement le résultat
de travaux dans les disciplines qui relèvent des sphères
d'activités du Musée canadien des civilisations.
Considérée comme un apport important dans la
communauté scientifique, la collection Mercure présente
plus de trois cents publications spécialisées portant sur
l'héritage canadien préhistorique et historique.

Comme la collection s'adresse à un public spécialisé,
celle-ci est constituée essentiellement de monographies
publiées dans la langue des auteurs.

Pour assurer la prompte distribution des exemplaires
imprimés, les étapes de l'édition ont été abrégées. En
conséquence, certaines coquilles ou fautes de grammaire
peuvent subsister : c'est pourquoi nous réclamons votre
indulgence.

Vous pouvez vous procurer la liste des titres parus dans la
collection Mercure en écrivant au :

Service des commandes postales
Musée canadien des civilisations
100, rue Laurier
C.P. 3100, succursale B
Hull (Québec)
J8X 4H2

FOREWORD

George MacDonald
Executive Director
Canadian Museum of Civilization

The many contributors to this volume pay tribute to Bill Taylor's achievements as an Arctic archaeologist. Here, I would like to focus on another major area of accomplishment, that is, Bill's long career as Director of the National Museum of Man (now the Canadian Museum of Civilization).

It is not unusual for museum directors to rise through the ranks of archaeology, where they receive early training in interdisciplinary and labour-intensive activities. Field archaeologists have to spend much of their time honing their skills in budgetary, administrative and human resources issues. In Canada they also have to negotiate with a wide cross-section of farmers, Native peoples, the resource industry, and a variety of government agencies in order to obtain the access rights and permits they need to pursue their excavation plans.

Bill Taylor faced other administrative challenges not only in his field programme but also at the Museum, where he began work in 1956 under Richard (Scotty) MacNeish, the first post-war head of the Archaeology Section (within the Anthropology Division) at the National Museum of Canada (NMC). During the boom-time economy of the sixties, Scotty's fieldwork took him to the Yukon and the Northwest Territories in the summer, and to Mexico in the winter. He left Bill Taylor to cope with the difficulties of managing a rapidly expanding research team. In 1964 Bill was made the first Chief of the newly created Archaeology Division. He was the perfect candidate for the position.

In those buoyant times, Bill was quick to grasp the opportunities available. He recruited bright young staff — particularly at the memorable Canada House parties he always arranged at annual meetings of the Society for American Archaeology (SAA). His intent behind those parties was to give Canada some profile while allowing him and his growing number of colleagues at NMC to review the latest crop of graduating archaeologists. As I recall, Bill assigned each staff member who attended an SAA meeting to interview, informally, one or more budding archaeologists for the new posts opening in his division. Bill Taylor deserves much of the credit for expanding the Archaeology Division from a two-person to a ten-person operation in that halcyon decade.

In the late sixties, the growth of postgraduate programmes in archaeology and anthropology at Canadian universities set the stage for Bill's next initiative, which was to create a Canadian Archaeological Association. Again, we all received our assignments: to serve on the executive and committees of the Association, as well as to organize and chair sessions and edit the resulting publications. Bill always created new challenges for his research staff.

By current standards, it was a very macho environment within the Archaeology Division at NMC, accented by the language and humour of the day; but there was also a discipline, inspired by the military motto that every man was expected to do his duty. This environment served to create a close-knit cadre of archaeologists who were very productive and who were encouraged to strive for excellence in their research fields. From the Maritimes to the Yukon, field parties were sent out every year, and were expected not only to "fill in the missing gaps in Canada's archaeological map" but also to nurture the fledgling archaeological programmes that were emerging across the country.

The incubation period of the sixties brought forth in Bill a vigorous organizer and a visionary who was to steer the newly created (1968) National Museum of Man (NMM) through a remarkably rapid and dramatic series of changes. Bill Taylor became the first director of what was to be a completely separate human history museum; the NMM continued, however, to share the old Victoria Memorial Museum Building (VMMB) in Ottawa with the National Museum of Natural Science.

Under the new corporate structure of the National Museums of Canada, Bill Taylor was a skilful fighter for resources, which meant that the Museum of Man flourished. As director, Bill's interests — or, rather, his passion — expanded ambitiously. One result was the creation of a Folk Culture Division (under Carmen Roy), for which Bill found major new funding. Another was the establishment of research and publishing activities within the Canadian War Museum, an affiliate of the National Museum of Man. Nor was archaeology neglected: as Bill's successor as Chief of the Archaeology Division, I was encouraged (with the increased funding he found in 1971) to reorganize it into the Archaeological Survey of Canada.

Another tribute to Bill's leadership is the Mercury Series of publications, instituted to complement the former annual reports and monographs in archaeological research. The Mercury Series was soon extended to the other areas of research in the Museum. Bill tapped new sources of money — including private funds from generous patrons such as Dr. Margaret Hess of Calgary — to produce more than a hundred titles in prehistoric archaeology, and close to 500 Mercury titles from the combined efforts of all Museum divisions. In this period, under Bill's tutelage, more Museum-based research was published at the National Museum of Man than by all other Canadian museums and universities combined. He took great delight in these statistics and, through his active contacts with universities across the country, constantly monitored recent graduates in order to garner the best work for the series. The careers of many young scholars have been affected by this process.

Perhaps the most dramatic initiative during Bill's directorship was the refurbishment of the Museum of Man exhibitions in the seventies; the Victoria Memorial Museum Building was closed in 1972 for this purpose. Bill's aim was to transform the exhibitions from an outdated state to one that responded to the tenets of the new museology: that is, exhibits that were thematically organized, employed contextual settings, and were as rich in information as possible. This stemmed from Bill's vision of museums as, first and foremost, institutions with an educational mission.

Public education through museums was a passion for Bill throughout the seventies, but the task of funding his vision became increasingly formidable, as his requirements vaulted from the thousands of dollars required by research projects to the millions required by museological ones. The VMMB was completely gutted and renovated in less than five years, which involved developing some 40,000 square feet of new exhibitions. Bill tapped into the new group of young designers who had proved their mettle at Expo 67 in Montreal, in order to create exhibits at NMM that would push the boundaries of museology to new levels. Bill's reaction to my proposal for an exhibit inside the VMMB, entailing reconstruction of a shell midden excavation in a west-coast rain forest, was characteristic of his outlook: "Geordie, if you think you can deliver this kookie idea," he said, "I'll find the money." As a director, Bill never discouraged a curator from, as he put it, "dreaming in technicolour." As Bill's successor, it's a tradition I have been proud to follow.

While Bill competed with the directors of the other three National Museums for corporate resources, he also cooperated with these colleagues in equal measure. One of his first challenges, on taking up the director's post, was to manage the transfer of extensive collections from his museum to provide a foundation for the newly created National Museum of Science and Technology (which took over all of the NMM's farm machinery, wheeled vehicles, etc.), as well as the transfer of all aircraft from the Canadian War Museum to the new National Aviation Museum (at that time without its own home).

While the VMMB was closed, Bill challenged the sedate National Gallery of Canada to mount its first large show of Indian and Inuit prehistoric and contemporary art. Another such exhibit was shipped to Paris; the impact it made on European sensibility to Canadian Native art was profound and lasting. In fact, it was Bill's recognition of the importance of contemporary Inuit art that provided the impetus to build, at the NMM, what has become the best and most comprehensive collection in the world. He encouraged field researchers to send to the Museum any Inuit art works that they felt belonged among the national treasures — in this piecemeal way the collection grew.

Even before the new exhibits were opened at the refurbished VMMB, Bill was aware of the shortfalls of the old building, in terms of exhibit space and conservation standards. So he set his sights higher. This time Bill's dream of a new museum would cost hundreds of millions of dollars to achieve.

At the point when that dream became a possibility, with the government's commitment in 1982 to build a new home for the NMM, I was enjoying a two-year work assignment at the University of British Columbia Museum of Anthropology — a project Bill had provided as part of the Museum's outreach plans. Halfway through that assignment, I received a call from him: "Geordie, we got the money, and I want you back here to lead the new museum project." I recoiled from the phone, with visions of *Paradise Lost* and having to enter the slough of public works bureaucracy. For a few days I cursed Bill's enthusiasm and his museological visions; but, as we travelled together across the country in the months that followed, interviewing Canada's top architects, I once again caught his infectious fever of enthusiasm, against which few have immunity.

When I showed Bill an article illustrating the works of a little-known architect of Native heritage from Alberta, whose wildly innovative architecture seemed to capture the landscape and rugged essence of our country, Bill's response was, again, supportive: "Geordie, I trust your judgement, but how much money do I gotta find?" Bill found some $300 million before he was called to take the helm as President of the Social Sciences and Humanities Research Council of Canada (SSHRC). While he embraced that opportunity to turn his vision to the broader scope of social science research, and into every university in the country, he clearly regretted having to leave the new museum project that he had so successfully launched.

The five years that Bill Taylor spent at the SSHRC were characteristically innovative and vigorous. He took every opportunity provided at the end of the boom-time economy to foster research in Canada, and to encourage interest in Canadian Studies abroad. But eventually, the call of his own personal research, which had had to be set aside by his museological and research management duties, lured him back to the honorary post of Director Emeritus of his old institution, now the Canadian Museum of Civilization. Even then, Bill devoted much of his time unstintingly to the coordination of an international research project involving scholars and institutions in Canada, the United States and Britain — a multidisciplinary project encompassing the archival records of Elizabethan Europe, the memories of Inuit elders, and archaeological remains on a remote Arctic island. This project too, like the tasks he undertook in previous roles, benefited from his negotiation skills and his careful attention to the highest principles and standards of research.

I am delighted to take this opportunity to pay tribute to a few of Dr. William Taylor's myriad contributions to the field of Canadian Studies: contributions not only to archaeological research in Canada but to many fields of investigation and to the careers of many investigators — not least my own — that he has affected so positively.

PREFACE

Dr. William E. Taylor, Jr., Arctic archaeologist, former director of the National Museum of Man (now the Canadian Museum of Civilization), and past president of the Social Sciences and Humanities Research Council of Canada, officially retired in the summer of 1991. His career has been a long and productive one, spanning six decades from his first fieldwork in 1949, to the 1990s. Indeed, Bill has had a pivotal role in the development of Arctic archaeology, providing the generational link between pioneer Arctic archaeologists, like his friend and mentor Henry Collins, and a raft of younger scholars. For years Bill was the only Canadian in the field. One of his favourite claims to fame is his authorship of the first monograph on Canadian Arctic prehistory written by a Canadian: The Arnapik and Tyara Sites (1968).

As an insightful and productive scholar, during the 1950s and early 1960s Bill made major contributions to the two outstanding issues of the day; the so-called "Dorset problem" and the question of the origin of historic Inuit culture. With Arnapik and Tyara he successfully dissipated Meldgaard's "smell of the forest" by demonstrating the local Pre-Dorset origins of Dorset culture. And in innumerable journal articles he hammered away at the "Birket-Smith" model of Inuit prehistory, arguing persuasively that the origin of the historic Inuit was to be found in coastal Thule culture and not among hypothetical inland Proto-Eskimos.

With his elevation into the higher ranks of bureaucracy in 1967, Bill Taylor assumed something of a godfather role in Canadian archaeology. It was he who presided over the glory days at the National Museum of Man in the 1970s, when there was, seemingly, enough money and optimism to solve any problem. His enthusiasm for the discipline was infectious, and he did his utmost to promote research and researchers. One of the editors of this volume credits his psychological survival of graduate school in part to the kindly interest that Bill Taylor took in his work. Countless other students have benefited from Bill's favourable grant reviews and unsolicited testimonials of support.

It was Chuck Arnold who first suggested that a session of the Canadian Archaeological Association be held in honour of Bill Taylor's retirement. The call for papers was enthusiastically received, and 19 presentations were made over a two-day session held on May 7 and 8, 1992 in London, Ontario. The present festschrift volume closely reflects that session. Three original participants were unable to contribute (Steven Cox, Ian Badgley and Jack Brink), and two new papers (by Carole Stimmell and Bjarne Grønnow) have been added. Otherwise, with minor amendments, the papers appear here as they were given in London. The success of the session and of the viciously funny "roast" that accompanied it testify to the warm regard in which Bill Taylor is held by his many friends and colleagues.

Let those of us who aspire to his eminence in the profession consider the motto engraved in Gaelic on the ice axe presented to him by Henry Collins: "*i dtir na ndall is ri feare na leathshuile*" ("in the land of the blind, the one-eyed man is king"). In any land, Bill Taylor is a gentleman and a scholar.

David Morrison and Jean-Luc Pilon
Canadian Museum of Civilization

AVANT-PROPOS

William E. Taylor, archéologue de l'Arctique, ancien directeur du Musée national de l'Homme (l'actuel Musée canadien des civilisations) et ancien président du Conseil de recherches en sciences humaines, a pris officiellement sa retraite à l'été 1991. Sa carrière, longue et féconde, s'est étalée sur six décennies, depuis ses premiers travaux sur le terrain en 1949 jusqu'aux années 1990. En effet, Bill Taylor a joué un rôle central dans l'évolution de l'archéologie de l'Arctique, puisqu'il a été le lien entre les premiers archéologues de l'Arctique, tel son ami et mentor Henry Collins, et les chercheurs qui l'ont suivi. Pendant des années, M. Taylor a été le seul Canadien dans ce domaine. Il est tout particulièrement connu comme l'auteur de la première monographie sur la préhistoire de l'Arctique canadien rédigée par un Canadien, The Arnapik and Tyara Sites (1968).

Spécialiste pénétrant et fécond, il a, au cours des années 1950 et au début des années 1960, fait d'importantes contributions aux deux problèmes non résolus de la préhistoire de l'Arctique, ce qu'on appelle le «problème dorsétien» et la question de l'origine de la culture inuit historique. Avec Arnapik and Tyara, il a réussi a dissiper l'«odeur de la forêt» de Meldgaard en démontrant l'origine locale prédorsétienne de la culture dorsétienne. Et, dans d'innombrables articles de revue, il s'est attaqué au «modèle de Birket-Smith» de la préhistoire inuit, faisant valoir de façon convaincante que l'origine des Inuit de la période historique devait se trouver du côté de la culture thuléenne côtière et non chez d'hypothétiques Proto-Esquimaux de l'intérieur des terres.

Promu au sommet de la bureaucratie en 1967, Bill Taylor a joué en quelque sorte un rôle de parrain dans le monde de l'archéologie canadienne. C'est lui qui a présidé la période glorieuse du Musée national de l'Homme, dans les années 1970, où il semblait y avoir assez d'argent et d'optimisme pour résoudre tous les problèmes. Son enthousiasme pour la discipline était contagieux, et il a tout mis en œuvre pour favoriser la recherche et les chercheurs. Un des rédacteurs de cet ouvrage affirme que, au cours de ses études de troisième cycle, s'il a réussi à tenir le coup sur le plan psychologique, c'est en grande partie à cause de l'intérêt bienveillant manifesté par Bill pour son travail. D'innombrables autres étudiants se sont vu accorder des bourses grâce à son appréciation de leur travail ou ont profité de son soutien sans l'avoir sollicité.

C'est Chuck Arnold qui a suggéré le premier qu'une session de l'Association canadienne d'archéologie ait lieu pour rendre hommage à Bill Taylor à l'occasion de sa retraite. La demande de communications a été reçue avec enthousiasme, et 19 exposés ont été faits au cours d'une session de deux jours tenue les 7 et 8 mai 1992 à London (Ontario). Le présent volume d'articles se veut le reflet de cette session. Trois participants n'ont pu contribuer (Steven Cox, Ian Badgly et Jack Brink) et deux nouvelles communications (par Carole Stimmell et Bjarne Grønnow) ont été ajoutées. Sinon, avec quelques changements mineurs, les communications sont reproduites telles qu'elles ont été faites à London. Le succès de la session et du «bien cuit» follement drôle qui l'a accompagnée témoigne de la chaleureuse estime que portent à Bill Taylor ses nombreux amis et collègues.

Que ceux d'entre nous qui aspirent à l'éminence de William Taylor dans la profession se penchent sur la devise gravée en gaélique sur le piolet qui lui a été présenté par Henry Collins : «i dtir na ndall is ri feare na leathshuile» («au royaume des aveugles, le borgne est roi»). Dans tout royaume, Bill Taylor est un gentleman et un érudit.

David Morrison et Jean-Luc Pilon
Musée canadien des civilisations

ACKNOWLEDGEMENTS

Compiling a volume such as this one requires the help of a number of people. Editing duties were divided by culture period, with Jean-Luc Pilon handling the Palaeoeskimo papers (Nagy, Helmer, Stimmell, Pilon, Le Blanc, Plumet, Pintal, Renouf, and Grønnow) and David Morrison dealing with those concerned with Neoeskimo topics (Fitzhugh, Arnold, Savelle and McCartney, Morrison, Gordon, Friesen and Stewart, Rowley, Hallendy, and Stenton and Park). We wish to thank our very prompt and professional reviewers: Don Clark, Bill Fitzhugh, Karen McCullough, Bob McGhee and Pat Sutherland. Neal Ferris and Bill Finlayson helped organize the London Canadian Archaeological Association session and roast, and Allen McCartney and Moreau Maxwell served as session discussants. We also gratefully acknowledge the help of Luc Nolin and Lucie Johanis in reviewing the French-language abstracts.

CONTENTS

A Critical Review of the Pre-Dorset/Dorset Transition

Murielle Nagy
University of Alberta
Edmonton, Alberta

Abstract

In a study of the origins of Dorset culture published in 1968, William E. Taylor Jr. concluded that there is a cultural continuity from Pre-Dorset to Dorset culture in the Canadian eastern Arctic and, within this area, the Dorset culture developed *in situ*. What is remarkable about Taylor's work is that although he was using very small samples, his conclusions are still accepted by most eastern Arctic archaeologists. However, despite a discourse that describes Pre-Dorset and Dorset as parts of a cultural continuum, these two concepts are used primarily to contrast and accentuate cultural differences rather than to stress similarities between these two periods. Furthermore, the identification of so-called "Pre-Dorset/Dorset transitional" sites is not obvious. One might even ask if substantial cultural changes really took place between the Pre-Dorset and the Dorset periods. This paper will discuss several issues linked to the Pre-Dorset/Dorset transitional period in the Eastern Arctic.

Résumé

Dans une étude sur les origines de la culture dosétienne parue en 1968, William E. Taylor Jr. concluait qu'il existe une continuité culturelle entre le Prédorsetien et le Dorsétien de l'Arctique oriental canadien et que la culture dorsétienne s'y était développée *in situ*. Ce qu'il y a de remarquable dans le travail de Taylor c'est que ce dernier se basait sur de petits échantillonnages pour arriver à des conclusions qui sont toujours acceptées par la majorité des archéologues travaillant dans l'Arctique oriental. Cependant, malgré un discours qui décrit le Prédorsetien et le Dorsétien comme faisant partie d'un continuum culturel, ces deux concepts sont surtout utilisés pour contraster et accentuer des différences culturelles et non pour souligner les similarités entre ces deux périodes. De plus, l'identification de sites dits de "transition" entre le Prédorsetien et le Dorsétien n'est pas évidente. On peut même se demander s'il y a vraiment eu des changements culturels substantiels entre le Prédorsetien et le Dorsétien. Cet article discutera des problèmes relatifs à la période de transition entre le Prédorsetien et le Dorsétien dans l'Arctique oriental.

Introduction

Over the last twenty years, two major criticisms have been levelled at Arctic archaeology. The first concerns the limitations of the culture-historical approach to explain, rather than describe, culture

Threads of Arctic Prehistory: Papers in Honour of William E. Taylor Jr., David Morrison and Jean-Luc Pilon, eds. Canadian Museum of Civilization, Mercury Series, Archaeological Survey of Canada Paper 149. 1994.

change (Bielawski 1983; Dekin 1976; Schindler 1985). The main argument expressed by Arctic archaeologists for using a culture-historical approach is the need to gather more data to integrate into a chronological framework before addressing explanatory questions (e.g. Auger 1986; Helmer 1991; Schledermann 1990; Taylor and McGhee 1979). The second criticism concerns the confusing and inadequate conceptual jargon used by Arctic archaeologists (see criticisms by Elling 1992; Helmer 1987, this volume; McGhee 1982; Plumet 1982, 1987; Tuck and Fitzhugh 1986; Tuck and Ramsden 1990). For example, when referring to Pre-Dorset and Dorset, archaeologists use terms such as "culture", "period", "complex", "phase", "tradition" and "stage" in a rather cavalier manner. Other problems concern the methods and theories used in Palaeoeskimo archaeology. In her discussion of such issues, Bielawski (1988: 72) concludes that "neither general evolutionary nor cultural ecological theory seem specific nor strong enough at present to order the data, much less to explain them". She further argued that if stylistic types are assigned appropriate historical meaning, then interpretation based on historical particularism need not be rejected in favour of that based on systemic causation. However, despite the fact that Arctic archaeologists are well aware of the limitations inherent in the use of fossil guides to establish chronological control of their collections (see McGhee 1983), they still rely almost exclusively on interpretations based upon the analysis of distinct artifact styles. As Elling (1992: 2) noted in the context of Greenland archaeology, "culture classificatory terminology holds a danger of turning into doctrines that predefine the structure in which new archaeological results have to fit".

A good example of the lack of consistency associated with the identification of cultural affiliation of Palaeoeskimo sites can be found in the so-called "Pre-Dorset/Dorset Transition". The identification of Pre-Dorset/Dorset transitional sites is far from obvious, and it can be asked if substantial cultural changes really took place between the Pre-Dorset and the Dorset periods. This paper will present several issues linked to the Pre-Dorset/Dorset transitional period in the Eastern Arctic. I will then use a model to explain how Arctic archaeologists have come to accept and uncritically use the concept of transition. I will conclude with a discussion of the concept of the Pre-Dorset/Dorset Transition.

Pre-Dorset to Dorset Transition

Pre-Dorset and Dorset are terms used by Arctic archaeologists to distinguish between two chronological and cultural periods of a broader Palaeoeskimo culture known as the Arctic Small Tool tradition (ASTt). Although the terms Pre-Dorset and Dorset are well entrenched in Arctic archaeological literature, the transition between these two periods is poorly known and problematical. It has been said (e.g. Maxwell 1984, 1985) that during the transition from Pre-Dorset to Dorset (ca. 800 to 500 B.C.), many cultural traits emerged while others disappeared. The causes of such cultural transformations have been mostly linked to environmental changes leading to new technological and economic adaptations of the later Dorset people (e.g. Maxwell 1985; McGhee 1988).

Pre-Dorset/Dorset transitional sites have been identified on the southeastern coast of Baffin Island (Maxwell 1985: 111) and west of Ungava Bay (e.g. Nagy 1993; Plumet this volume). On the

Labrador Coast, the eastern Lower North Shore (*Basse-Côte-Nord*) of Quebec and in Newfoundland, transitional sites are associated with the Groswater Dorset complex (Auger 1986; Fitzhugh 1972, 1976, 1980; Pintal this volume; Renouf this volume; Tuck and Fitzhugh 1986). In the High Arctic such sites are classified as part of the Independence II complex by McGhee (1981), but as transitional by Helmer (1991) and Schledermann (1990). Although the cultural changes between Pre-Dorset and Dorset periods have been contrasted in terms of structural remains, tool styles, use of different raw materials and subsistence patterns (Maxwell 1985; McGhee 1978), the definition of the transitional period is less clear. Thus, unless sites are thought to be contaminated through re-occupation, those containing traits from both Pre-Dorset and Dorset periods are identified as transitional ones. However, since the differences in material culture are not extreme, and because dating of sites is often lacking, archaeologists seem to rely primarily on subjective criteria to identify what they call "Late Pre-Dorset", "Transitional" and "Early Dorset" sites. As Park (1992: 122) noted about Schledermann's (1990) distinction between "Transitional" and "Early Dorset" sites on Ellesmere Island: "the categorization appears to have been largely intuitive on Schledermann's part".

Pre-Dorset to Dorset Cultural Continuum

To appreciate how archaeologists perceive the nature of the transition between the Pre-Dorset and the Dorset periods, it is necessary to go back to the research concerning the origins of the Dorset culture. During the summers of 1957 to 1959, William E. Taylor Jr. excavated archaeological sites on Mansel Island, and at Ivujivik and Sugluk (Salluit) in Nouveau-Québec. The results of this work can be found in several published articles (e.g. Taylor 1958, 1962) and especially in a study of the origins of the Dorset culture published in 1968. Taylor's conclusions were as follows: there is a cultural continuity from Pre-Dorset to Dorset in the Canadian Eastern Arctic and, within this area, the Dorset culture developed *in situ*. What is remarkable about Taylor's work is that although he was using very small samples, his conclusions are still accepted by most Eastern Arctic archaeologists.

Some researchers think that the Dorset culture developed locally and simultaneously throughout the Eastern Arctic (Maxwell 1985: 121-125). Others prefer an explanation based upon diffusion from a so-called "core area", a rough circle of some 1,000 km diameter including the coasts of Fury and Hecla Straits, Hudson Bay and Hudson Strait (McGhee 1976: 15). However, there is no consensus on the nature and direction of such diffusion. Schledermann (1990: 166) warns that "the transition cannot be conceived of as being smooth and uniform" and adds that, "although the core area played a major role in the Pre-Dorset/Dorset transition, the evidence from Labrador, southern Baffin Island and the Bache Peninsula region strongly indicates that the transition was considerably more complex and regionally distinctive than originally envisaged" (Schledermann 1990: 325).

Explanations of the causes of cultural changes between Pre-Dorset and Dorset periods have been diverse. Fitzhugh (1976) postulates that it was a time of population response to a diminution of caribou herds in Nouveau-Québec. McGhee (1981) describes the beginning of the Dorset culture as one of population expansion. The most common interpretation is that economic and technological changes gave rise to the Dorset period. Maxwell (1976, 1985) sees the Dorset culture as the merging of two lifeways (land-mammal hunting and sea-mammal hunting) that were in a state of relative equilibrium. All these explanations are based on the premise that there was a change in the environment. During the Pre-Dorset period, the climate was apparently warmer than during the Dorset period (Maxwell 1985: 107). Climatic changes affected the existing culture, which in turn had to change in order to survive (Maxwell 1985; Schledermann 1990). Another possibility, although less explored, is that some aspects of the Dorset culture were originally influenced by the Norton culture of Alaska (see Arnold 1981).

As we have seen, the Pre-Dorset and Dorset periods could be interpreted as elements of a relatively stable system that was punctuated by a period of change identified as the "transitional period". By contrast, it is also possible that this period reflects only one chronological segment, without important cultural changes, in a Palaeoeskimo continuum. Some of the stylistic differences that have been observed between Pre-Dorset and Dorset collections may be only functional ones, and what has been attributed to cultural change could be explained by the remains of specific activities occurring within one site (see Binford and Binford 1966; Dunnel 1978; Sackett 1986). It is also possible that the presence of cultural traits belonging to the two periods at any specific site are the result of the re-occupation of a Pre-Dorset site during the Dorset period.

Despite a discourse that describes Pre-Dorset and Dorset as parts of a cultural continuum (Maxwell 1976, 1985), these two concepts are primarily used to contrast and accentuate cultural differences rather than to stress similarities between these two periods (on this issue see also Møbjerb 1988; Plumet 1987). Furthermore, opinions differ over whether transitional assemblages are more similar to Pre-Dorset or to Dorset material. For example, Cox (1978: 104) described the "Terminal Pre-Dorset/Groswater Dorset" as a "transitional stage" that is "essentially the final stage of Pre-Dorset cultural evolution in Labrador". Such a view is shared by Pintal (this volume) who excavated Groswater material from the Lower North Shore (*Basse-Côte-Nord*) of Quebec. Recently, Tuck and Ramsden (1990) have argued that Early Dorset (which they group along with Groswater and Independence II complexes) is in fact the end of the Pre-Dorset continuum. On the other hand, working on material from Devon Island in High Arctic, Helmer (this volume) linked the transitional "horizon" under the "cultural tradition" of the Dorset culture. Such contrasting views raise the question of whether archaeologists' perceptions of cultural transitions are influenced by regional variability in material culture.

What is Meant by "Transition"?

Although it is a term widely used by archaeologists to describe cultures undergoing change, it is extremely difficult to find a clear definition of "transition". In Europe, archaeologists studying Mesolithic societies still disagree on the meaning of the transition from Palaeolithic hunting and gathering to Neolithic farming. The different definitions of the Mesolithic listed by Zvelebil (1986: 7) provide a case in point. Depending on the researcher, the term "Mesolithic" represents a strictly chronological period, a cultural adaptation or a different economy linked to environmental changes. However, as Zvelebil (1986: 6) noted, the cultural variability of the Mesolithic should not be forced into a shopping list definition of a period characterized on a presence/absence basis. Such a warning could easily be transplanted to Arctic prehistory, particularly in regard to the transition between the Pre-Dorset and Dorset periods. In fact, although most Arctic archaeologists view this transition as part of a cultural continuum, they still treat it as a strange cultural hybrid.

Problems With The Pre-Dorset/Dorset Transition

Transitional sites have not been the focus of a systematic study. They are described in the archaeological literature more on an opportunistic basis (i.e. when they are found) rather than with an appropriate set of questions regarding their nature. As a result, problems with the data are often overlooked. For example, many Dorset sites have excellent preservation of organic remains compared to the earlier Pre-Dorset sites. Such a different state of organic material preservation has important repercussions in contrasting Pre-Dorset with Dorset periods, and in identifying transitional sites. The trait list that Maxwell (1985: 123) uses to distinguish the Dorset period from the preceding one includes the following organic artifacts: sled shoes and sled models, ice creepers, snow knives, and a rich, presumably magic-related art. These items are not found in Pre-Dorset sites. More intensive occupation of sites by the Dorset people leading to the development of frozen middens of organic materials, and the presence of an active layer of permafrost during the Dorset period may be responsible for the preservation of artifacts which were, until then, not found in archaeological sites. It might very well be that the above-mentioned articles were used during the Pre-Dorset period, but were simply not preserved.

The dating of transitional sites is another problem. In many cases, these sites are dated solely by reference to the types of artifacts they contain (e.g. Helmer 1991; Schledermann 1990). Transitional sites are generally dated to between 800 and 500 B.C., but many of the published radiocarbon dates are problematic since they were obtained from samples containing sea mammal bones and/or burned fat. These may be contaminated due to the "reservoir effect" (see Arundale 1980; McGhee and Tuck 1976; Morrison 1989; Taylor 1987). Although radiocarbon dates obtained from driftwood are still used by Arctic archaeologists (e.g. Helmer 1991; Schledermann 1990), these too should be considered with caution since it it impossible to determine the age of the wood when it started to travel the Arctic waters, how long it drifted, or how long it may have lain on a beach before being used by humans. Thus, an error of 200 years might attribute a site to the Late Pre-Dorset or Early Dorset rather than a Pre-Dorset/Dorset Transition temporal affiliation.

Another method used by Arctic archaeologists to assign ages to sites relies on the different elevations of the beach ridges on which sites are located (e.g. Bielawski 1988: 64; Maxwell 1976: 70). Archaeologists assume that people choose to settle near the shore, and that sites found on higher terraces should be older than those on lower ones. This, of course, is not always the case. For example, Harp (1976: 120) has noted that in the Dorset site of Port au Choix, the oldest house was found on the lower terrace while the younger houses were found on the higher terrace. This, according to Harp (ibid.), represents "another apparent example of aboriginal disregard for cherished modern notions about beachridge dating". Another problem concerns the use of isostatic rebound rates for inferring site chronology (e.g. Badgley 1980; Lewis Johnson and Stright 1992). Finally, when sites contain a cultural mixture resembling both Pre-Dorset and Dorset assemblages and dates are not available, the sites are often ascribed a date between 800 and 500 B.C., since this is when the transition is thought to have occurred.

As mentioned earlier, archaeologists distinguish two complexes (or "traditions") in this transitional period (Independence II and Groswater), both of which have dates that overlap with the beginning of the Dorset period. Independence II sites are located in Greenland and the High Arctic while Groswater sites were originally found in Labrador and Newfoundland, but have also recently been found west of Ungava Bay in Nouveau-Québec (Gendron 1990; Plumet this volume). Groswater occupations seem to be perceived by archaeologists as a distinct cultural entity that disappeared shortly after the arrival of an Early Dorset population around 2500 BP, but which persisted on the Labrador coast until ca. 2200 BP (Cox 1978: 104; Fitzhugh 1976; Tuck 1975, 1976). However, it remains unclear whether the Independence II and Groswater complexes are ancestral to the Dorset culture or independent and unrelated (e.g. Auger 1986; Cox 1978). In a recent critique on the classification of Palaeoeskimo cultures in Greenland, Elling (1992: 1) insisted that the "Independence II group must be seen as an Early Dorset phase/Late Pre-Dorset phase adapted to the environmental conditions of Northern Greenland", thus stressing the transitional nature of the such material. In contrast, Tuck and Fitzhugh (1986) have argued that the designation of Groswater "traditions" should be extended to a number of sites previously termed "Early Dorset" in Newfoundland, and that these are more closely related to the Late Pre-Dorset than the Early Dorset. If this is the case, Hood's (1986) conclusions on the similarities between Groswater and Early Dorset habitation structures from the Nain Region in Labrador should be interpreted as continuity within Pre-Dorset, but not with Dorset.

Other archaeologists have expressed doubts about the cultural continuity between Pre-Dorset and Dorset material. Working on archaeological sites from Port au Choix on the west shore of Newfoundland, Renouf (this volume) questioned the continuity between Groswater and Dorset on the island. Loring and Cox (1986) placed the "Late Groswater" lithic assemblages of Kaipokok Bay in Labrador as transitional between Pre-Dorset and Dorset forms. They even found technological and stylistic similarities between the burin-like tools of their Groswater assemblages with those of Early Dorset sites from Southampton Island. However, despite their discussion of such similarities, they insisted that Early Dorset occupations on the north Labrador coast were the result of a new population in Labrador, and not an *in situ* development from Groswater ancestry. Their argument was that there were significant changes in the subsistence-settlement and technological systems of Early Dorset people, and because Groswater remained on the central coast of Labrador while it had been replaced by Early Dorset on the north coast.

The very foundation of Palaeoeskimo prehistory, that is the cultural continuity between Pre-Dorset and Dorset cultures, might not be as valid as has been assumed. Thus, Tuck and Ramsden (1990) have recently challenged what they called the "Taylor-made" solution to cultural continuity between Pre-Dorset and Dorset cultures. They concluded that such continuity can only be found between Early Pre-Dorset and Early Dorset. They also noted that the use of "Early Dorset" is misleading since it implies further continuity with the Middle and Late Dorset, for which they felt evidence was lacking. According to them, cultural changes started only with the Middle Dorset at about 500 B.C. If such is the case, there is no need to talk about a "Pre-Dorset/Dorset Transition" but rather about an "Early Dorset/Middle Dorset Transition". Or, if one follows their argument that Early Dorset is Late Pre-Dorset (see also Tuck and Fitzhugh 1986) and Middle Dorset is the beginning of Dorset, and if there was a cultural continuity, then the "Pre-Dorset/Dorset Transition" happened later than originally proposed. However, if there is no cultural continuity between Early Dorset and Middle Dorset, as they also argued, then the whole idea of Pre-Dorset/Dorset Transition falls apart.

In short, the nature of the transition from Pre-Dorset to Dorset remains ambiguous and much in need of refined archaeological study. If archaeologists agree that Pre-Dorset and Dorset are part of the same cultural continuum, those terms should not be used with strong ethnic connotations (see Plumet 1987). The use of a term such as "transition" implies that there were cultural changes within the same culture. However, evidence of significant transformations within the so-called Pre-Dorset/Dorset Transition has yet to be produced. Two important questions are still to be answered about this period. First, are we seeing continuity and gradual change, or is there a sharp cultural break in the technology and economy of the people who lived in the Eastern Arctic around 800 to 500 B.C.? Secondly, is there a distinctive archaeological signature that can be used to define transitional sites?

Toward a Model of Archaeological Perception

So far, my intention has been to stress the deficiencies associated with the use of the Pre-Dorset/Dorset Transition concept. I am afraid that the Pre-Dorset/Dorset Transition is taking a life of its own and that archaeologists will (if they haven't already) treat it as a cultural (if not "ethnic") entity. Yet the concept is far from being clearly defined or even tested. My apprehensions are based on the fact that such behaviour (i.e. ready acceptance and use of taxonomic labels) has been common among Arctic archaeologists. To make my point I will now present a model of perception which was originally designed by van der Leeuw (1989) to explain the process of innovation.

In his model, van der Leeuw (1989: 311-314) explains that perception is based on the comparison of perceived patterns. At first, comparison takes place outside of any applicable context, so that there is no referent, no specific bias toward similarity or dissimilarity. Once an initial comparison has led to the establishment of a patterning of similarity and dissimilarity, this context is tested against other phenomena to establish the limits of its applicability. There is now a distinct bias to look for similar elements. Here we can think of Diamond Jenness sorting the collection that was shipped to him from Cape Dorset and his later identification of the Cape Dorset Culture in the 1920s (see Jenness 1925). The notion of Pre-Dorset/Dorset continuity stressed by Taylor (1968) can also be associated with this stage of "archaeological perception".

After the context has been well established and is no longer scrutinized, new elements are compared. The comparisons are now biased towards the individuality of new elements and dissimilarity is accentuated. At this stage, we can think of the recognition and definition of the Pre-Dorset culture by Collins (1951), or the Sarqaq culture by Larsen and Melgaard (1958) as different from the homogeneous whole that once characterized the Dorset culture in the minds of Arctic archaeologists.

The model then predicts that once other elements have been judged in this way, the initial bias toward similarity is neutralized, and the context is no longer considered relevant. More comparisons will then create another context. This process can be applied to the present-day perception of discontinuity between Early Dorset and Middle Dorset as underlined by Tuck and Ramsden (1990). It can also be linked to the categorization of the Pre-Dorset/Dorset Transition as belonging to neither period, but rather representing a *mélange* of both Pre-Dorset and Dorset. An original category like "Dorset" is easily recognized because one can discriminate between the elements that belong to it and those that do not. However, a new category like the "Pre-Dorset/Dorset Transition" is only defined by elements which belong to it because similarities are still being stressed, but elements which eventually will not are yet to be recognized. The perception of the "Pre-Dorset/Dorset Transition" remains "fuzzy and open-ended", to use van der Leeuw's (1989: 315) qualifications of a new category.

By using van der Leeuw's model, I have tried to underline that it is not an accident that transitional sites are now a common component of the Arctic literature (e.g. Helmer 1991; Maxwell 1985; Schledermann 1990). This was not the case 30 years ago because Pre-Dorset and Dorset cultures were still being compared and considered as homogeneous entities. As more archaeological research took place in the Arctic, the range of variability between sites increased, broad generalizations became more refined, and new categories emerged. The notion of transition from Pre-Dorset to Dorset was discussed (e.g. Maxwell 1973; Melgaard 1962; Taylor 1968), but transitional sites were not recognized as such, and sites were considered to belong to either "Late Pre-Dorset" or "Early Dorset" cultures. The notion of "Pre-Dorset/Dorset Transitional sites" started to appear in the Arctic literature only in the 1970s (e.g. Cox 1978; Maxwell 1976). However, as I have tried to demonstrate with this model, and as I have stressed many times in this paper, the recognition of such sites is still in a "fuzzy" stage and in need of refinement.

Discussion

The Pre-Dorset/Dorset transitional period is identified by most archaeologists as the beginning of cultural modifications that were accentuated during the Dorset period. As we have seen, other archaeologists (e.g. Tuck and Ramsden 1990) interpret this time period as the end of the Pre-Dorset culture, and not as a period of transition. Furthermore, the contrasting views of archaeologists on transitional sites raise the possibility that the specificity of the assemblages they analyze bias their view toward cultural continuity or discontinuity. Archaeologists should remember that the sites they excavate represent only one segment of a greater picture. By focusing on that segment they may loose the perspective of the whole picture and, as in van der Leeuw's model, thus emphasize discontinuity rather than continuity in their data.

Before even talking about a cultural transition, it is necessary to ask if changes in the material culture of the Dorset people were profound enough to constitute a cultural transformation. When microblades and burin-like tool frequencies increase, as they do in Dorset assemblages (e.g. Maxwell 1985: 108-109; Schledermann 1990: 182-183), do they reflect cultural changes or do they witness the kind of activities that took place in specific sites? Since the function of burin-like tools is still debated among archaeologists (see Maxwell 1985: 142), how can we even begin to understand the reasons for an increase in their use? One may also wonder if by using new types of harpoons, people become different from their predecessors. To take a more recent example, were the first Inuit who hunted with rifles culturally different from their grandparents? Furthermore, were there really major changes in the economy of the Dorset people? After all, both Pre-Dorset and Dorset people exploited sea and land resources. Even if sea mammal hunting was emphasized to a greater degree by the Dorset people (e.g. Maxwell 1984, 1985), it does not necessarily mean that their subsistence-settlement system was completely altered. Archaeologists are quick to equate culture with material culture since lithic tools are often the only data they are studying. However, people are more than the technology or the organic midden they left behind. Archaeologists should be more concerned with the meaning of observed changes in material culture and subsistence-settlement patterns than with taxonomy. They still need to verify whether there were gradual changes or a sharp cultural break in the technology and economy of the people who lived in the Eastern Arctic around 800 to 500 B.C.

It is possible that what researchers have described as discontinuities are actually regional variations and the idea of a cultural transition is still helpful. In fact, the term transition infers, as Taylor (1968) concluded, that there is cultural continuity between Pre-Dorset and Dorset. In other words, one culture did not replace another, but rather cultural changes occurred within the same culture. Thus, Pre-Dorset and Dorset should refer to different chronological segments of one people's history through time. Each period had its own characteristics but overall evidence suggests that these were the same people. Accordingly, regional variations within each period are only that, and should not be equated with different cultures (see also Elling 1992).

If the Pre-Dorset/Dorset Transition is a viable and workable concept, it should be possible to define and test it. The term transition implies changes and these changes need to be identified. Archaeologists should use a comparative set of attributes that would justify their identification of transitional sites, rather than relying on subjective criteria. They should also identify some of the key elements that were part of the Pre-Dorset to Dorset cultural transformation. Rather than simply identifying the chronological order of cultural material, one has to find what elements developed from the Pre-Dorset period and those that emerged during the transitional period. In the case of cultural elements that came out strictly during the Dorset period, there is little need to refer to a cultural transition with the Pre-Dorset. For example, rectangular semi-subterranean houses have been associated with the Dorset period (Maxwell 1985), and if there was Pre-Dorset/Dorset continuity in this cultural aspect, prototypes of such dwelling can be expected in the context of at least some transitional sites. If these constructions are not found, this can be taken as evidence that such structures emerged only during the Dorset period. Taking such a point of view might reconcile the dichotomy between Early Dorset and Middle Dorset described by Tuck and Ramsden (1990), or that between Groswater and Dorset (Renouf this volume) with the notion of Pre-Dorset to Dorset cultural continuity proposed by Taylor (1968). In other words, some cultural changes associated with the Dorset period were already taking place during the Late Pre-Dorset and transitional periods while others bear no link with Pre-Dorset culture.

Conclusion

In this paper, I have examined some of the issues related to the Pre-Dorset/Dorset Transition in the Eastern Arctic. I have used a model of perception to explain how archaeologists came to use the concept of Pre-Dorset/Dorset Transition and I have questioned whether it is an "artifact" of archaeological methods. Archaeologists still need to verify if significant cultural changes occurred during the so-called "transitional" period. If such changes are recorded, it will still be necessary to define their nature. That is, are we looking at continuity and gradual change, or at a sharp cultural break in the technology and economy of people who lived in the Eastern Arctic around 800 to 500 B.C.?

Assuming that the concept of transition proves to be viable, researchers should focus on cultural elements that developed during the Pre-Dorset period and those that emerged from the transitional period, in contrast to those that came out of the Dorset period. Such an approach might reconcile the view of Pre-Dorset to Dorset cultural continuity originally stressed by Taylor (1968) with that of discontinuity described recently by other archaeologists. Ultimately, the observation of any lithic, subsistence and/or settlement patterns associated with transitional sites should not be limited to a simple description. The real objective will be to find an explanation for such patterns associated with Palaeoeskimo culture change.

Acknowledgements

Thanks to Raymond Le Blanc, Moreau Maxwell and one anonymous reviewer for their comments. Many thanks to Jack Brink and especially to Shirleen Smith for editorial advises and suggestions. I also wish to thank Bill Taylor for sending me a copy of Henrik Elling's paper.

References

Arnold, C.D.1981. The Lagoon site (OjRl-3): Implications for Paleoeskimo Interactions. National Museum of Man, Mercury series, Archaeological Survey of Canada Paper 107.

Arundale, W.H. 1980. Functional Analysis of Three Unusual Assemblages from the Cape Dorset Area, Baffin Island. Arctic, 33(3): 464-486.

Auger, R. 1986. Factory Cove: An Early Palaeo-Eskimo Component from the West Coast of Newfoundland. In, Palaeo-Eskimo Cultures in Newfoundland, Labrador and Ungava. Memorial University of Newfoundland, Reports in Archaeology, 1: 111-118.

Badgley, I. 1980. Stratigraphy and Habitation Features at DIA. 4 (JfEl-4), a Dorset Site in Arctic Québec. Arctic, 33(3): 569-584.

Bielawski, E. 1983. Northern Archaeology to 1983: a Perspective from Arctic Prehistory. The Musk-Ox, 33: 37-41.

Bielawski, E. 1988. Paleoeskimo Variability: The Early Archaic Small-Tool Tradition in the Central Canadian Arctic. American Antiquity, 53: 52-74.

Binford, L.R. and S. Binford. 1966. A preliminary Analysis of Functional Variability in the Mousterian of Levallois Facies. American Anthropologist, 68: 239-259.

Collins, H. 1951. The Origin and Antiquity of the Eskimo. Washington: Smithsonian Report for 1950.

Cox, S.L. 1978. Paleo-Eskimo occupations of the north Labrador coast. Arctic Anthropology, 15: 96-118

Denkin, A.A., Jr. 1976. Elliptical Analysis: An Heuristic Technique for the Analysis of Artifact Clusters. In, Eastern Arctic Prehistory: Paleoeskimo Problems, M.S. Maxwell, ed. Memoirs of the Society for American Archaeology, 31: 79-88 .

Dunnel, R.C. 1978. Style and Function: A Fundamental Dichotomy. American Antiquity, 43: 192-202.

Elling, H. 1992. The Paleo-Eskimo Cultures in Northern Greenland and Northeastern Greenland in Relation to the West Greenland Cultures. Paper presented at "The Paleo-Eskimo Cultures of Greenland-New Perspectives in Greenlandic Archaeology". Symposium at the Institute of Prehistoric and Classical Archaeology, University of Copenhagen.

Fitzhugh, W.W. 1972. Environmental Archaeology and Cultural Systems in Hamilton Inlet, Labrador. Smithsonian Contributions to Anthropology, 16.

Fitzhugh, W.W. 1976. Environmental Factors in the Evolution of Dorset Culture: A Marginal Proposal for Hudson Bay. In, Eastern Arctic Prehistory: Paleoeskimo Problems, M.S. Maxwell, ed. Memoirs of the Society for American Archaeology, 31: 139-149.

Fitzhugh, W.W. 1980. Review of Paleo-Eskimo culture history in southern Quebec-Labrador and Newfoundland. Etudes/Inuit/Studies, 4: 21-31.

Gendron, D. 1990. The JgEj-3 site: A Groswater occupation in Northwestern Ungava Bay. Paper presented at the 23rd Annual Meeting of the Canadian Archaeological Association, Whitehorse, Yukon.

Harp, E., Jr. 1976. Dorset Settlement Patterns in Newfoundland and Southeastern Hudson Bay. In, Eastern Arctic Prehistory: Paleoeskimo Problems, M.S. Maxwell, ed. Memoirs of the Society for American Archaeology, 31: 119-138.

Helmer, J.W. 1987. Cultural Classificatory Terminology in Eastern Arctic Prehistory: The Horse isn't Dead Yet! Paper presented at the 20th Annual Meeting of the Canadian Archaeological Association, Calgary, Alberta.

Helmer, J.W. 1991. The Palaeo-Eskimo Prehistory of the North Devon Lowlands. Arctic, 44(4): 301-317.

Hood, B. 1986. Nukasusutok-12: Early/Middle Dorset Axial Structures from the Nain Region, Labrador. In, Palaeo-Eskimo Cultures in Newfoundland, Labrador and Ungava, Memorial University of Newfoundland, Reports in Archaeology, 1: 49-64.

Jenness, D. 1925. A new Eskimo culture in Hudson Bay. The Geographical Review, 15: 428-37.

Larsen, H. and J. Melgaard. 1958. Paleo-Eskimo cultures in Disko Bay, West Greenland. Medelelser om Grønland, 161: 1-75.

Lewis Johnson, L. and M. Stright. 1992. Paleoshorelines and Prehistory: An Investigation of Method. Boca Raton: CRC Press.

Loring, S. and S. Cox. 1986. The Postville Pentecostal Groswater Site, Kaipokok Bay, Labrador. In, Palaeo-Eskimo Cultures in Newfoundland, Labrador and Ungava, Memorial University of Newfoundland, Reports in Archaeology, 1: 65-94.

Maxwell, M.S. 1973. Archaeology of the Lake Harbour District, Baffin Island. National Museum of Man, Mercury Series, Archaeological Survey of Canada Paper 6.

Maxwell, M.S. 1976. Pre-Dorset and Dorset Artifacts: The View from Lake Harbour. In, Eastern Arctic Prehistory: Paleoeskimo Problems, M.S. Maxwell, ed.. Memoirs of the Society for American Archaeology, 31: 58-78.

Maxwell, M.S. 1984. Pre-Dorset and Dorset Prehistory of Canada. In, Handbook of North American Indians, Vol. 5, Arctic, D. Damas, ed. Washington: Smithsonian Institute, pp. 359-368.

Maxwell, M.S. 1985. Prehistory of the Eastern Arctic. New York: Academic Press.

McGhee, R. 1976. Paleoeskimo Occupations of Central and High Arctic Canada. In, Eastern Arctic Prehistory: Paleoeskimo Problems, M.S. Maxwell, ed. Memoirs of the Society for American Archaeology, 31: 15-38.

McGhee, R. 1978. Canadian Arctic Prehistory. Toronto: Van Nostrand Reinhold Ltd.

McGhee, R. 1981. The Dorset Occupations in the Vicinity of Port Refuge, High Arctic Canada. National Museum of Man, Mercury Series, Archaeological Survey Canada Paper 105.

McGhee, R. 1982. Comment on P. Plumet's paper. Etudes/Inuit/Studies, 6(1): 155-157.

McGhee, R. 1983. Eastern Arctic Prehistory: The Reality of a Myth? The Musk-Ox, 33: 21-25.

McGhee, R. 1988. The Prehistory and Prehistoric Art of the Canadian Inuit. In, Inuit Art: An Anthology, A. Houston, ed. Altona: D.W. Freisen & Sons, pp. 12-20.

McGhee, R. and Tuck, J. A. 1976. Un-dating the Arctic. In, Eastern Arctic Prehistory: Paleoeskimo Problems, M. S. Maxwell, ed. Memoirs of the Society for American Archaeology, 31: 6-14.

Melgaard, J. 1962. On the Formative Period of the Dorset Culture. In, Prehistoric Cultural Relation Between the Arctic and the Temperate Zone of North America, J.M. Campbell, ed. The Arctic Institute of North America, Technical Paper, 11: 92-95.

Møbjerg, T. 1988. Préhistoire du Gröenland. L'Anthropologie, 92(3): 945-968

Morrison, D. 1989. Radiocarbon dating Thule Culture. Arctic Anthropology, 26(2): 48-77.

Nagy, M. 1993. Fouilles archéologiques du site Pita (KcFr-5), Ivujivik, Nouveau-Québec. MS on file with the Ministère des Affaires Culturelles du Québec.

Park, R.W. 1992. Review of "Crossroads to Greenland: 3000 Years of Prehistory in the Eastern Arctic" by Peter Schledermann. Canadian Journal of Archaeology, 16: 121-122.

Plumet, P. 1982. Pour une révision du cadre conceptuel utilisé en préhistoire de l'Arctique central et oriental. Etudes/Inuit/Studies 6(1): 130-139.

Plumet, P. 1987. Le développement de l'approche archéologique dans l'Arctique. L'Anthropologie, 91(4): 859-872.

Sackett, J. R. 1986. Isochrestism and Style: A Clarification. Journal of Anthropological Archaeology, 5: 266-277.

Schindler D. L. 1985. Anthropology in the Arctic: A Critique of Racial Typology and Normative Theory. Current Anthropology, 26(4): 475-499.

Schledermann, P. 1990. Crossroads to Greenland. The Arctic Institute of North America, Komatic Series, 2.

Taylor, R.E. 1987. Radiocardon Dating: An Archaeological Perspective. Orlando: Academic Press.

Taylor, W.E., Jr. 1958. Archaeological work in Ungava, 1957. Arctic Circular, 10: 25-27.

Taylor, W.E., Jr. 1962. Pre-Dorset Occupations at Ivugivik in Northwestern Ungava. In, Prehistoric Cultural Relation Between the Arctic and the Temperate Zone of North America, J.M. Campbell, ed. The Arctic Institute of North America, Technical Paper, 11: 80-91.

Taylor, W.E., Jr. 1968. The Arnapik and Tyara sites: an Archaeological Study of Dorset Culture Origins. Memoirs of the Society for American Archaeology , 22.

Taylor, W.E., Jr. and McGhee, R. 1979. Archaeological material from Creswell Bay, N.W.T., Canada. National Museum of Man, Mercury Series, Archaeological Survey of Canada Paper 85.

Tuck, J.A. 1975. Prehistory of Saglek Bay, Labrador: Archaic and Palaeo-Eskimo Occupations. National Museum of Man Mercury Series, Archaeological Survey of Canada Paper 32.

Tuck, J.A. 1976. Paleoeskimo Cultures of Northern Labrador. In, Eastern Arctic Prehistory: Paleoeskimo Problems, M.S. Maxwell, ed. Memoirs of the Society for American Archaeology, 31: 89-102.

Tuck J.A. and W.W.Fitzhugh. 1986. Palaeo-Eskimo Traditions of Newfoundland and Labrador: A Re-Appraisal. In, Palaeo-Eskimo Cultures in Newfoundland, Labrador and Ungava, Memorial University of Newfoundland, Reports in Archaeology, 1: 161-168.

Tuck, J.A. and P.G. Ramsden. 1990. Continuities in Paleoeskimo Prehistory. Paper presented at the 23rd Annual Meeting of the Canadian Archaeological Association, Whitehorse, Yukon.

Van der Leeuw, S.E. 1989. Risk, perception and innovation. In, What's New? A Closer Look at the Process of Innovation, S.A. Van der Leeuw and R. Torrence, eds. London: Unwin Hyman, One World Archaeology 14: 300-329.

Zvelebil, Marek III. 1986. Mesolithic Prelude and Neolithic Revolution. In, Hunters in Transition: Mesolithic Societies of Temperate Eurasia and their Transition to Farming. Marek Zvelebil III, ed. Cambridge: Cambridge University Press, pp. 5-16.

Resurrecting the Spirit(s) of Taylor's "Carlsberg Culture": Cultural Traditions and Cultural Horizons in Eastern Arctic Prehistory

James W. Helmer
University of Calgary
Calgary, Alberta

Abstract

Following the lead (though late by some 23 years) of William E. Taylor Jr. who once argued that "Eastern Arctic archaeology is still in its infancy....The laissez-faire attitude towards its terminology reflects this." (Taylor 1968: 38), this paper calls for the standardization of Eastern Arctic culture-classificatory terminology. Focusing specifically on the period ca. 4500-1000/500 B.P., a pan-Eastern Arctic Dorset Cultural Tradition sub-divided into five Cultural Horizons—Transitional, Early, Middle, Late and Terminal—and a Pre-Dorset Cultural Tradition sub-divided into four Cultural Horizons—Initial, Early, Middle and Late Pre-Dorset—are defined. The advantages of this system for describing the major spatio-temporal divisions of the Arctic Small Tool tradition in the Eastern Arctic are discussed. The logical framework of a complementary culture classificatory taxonomy—the goal of which is to measure culture historically meaningful patterning and variation in Eastern Arctic Palaeoeskimo assemblages through both time and space—is also described.

Résumé

À l'instar de William E.Taylor Jr. qui, il y a 23 ans, soulignait que "L'archéologie de l'Arctique oriental est encore à ses débuts…l'attitude de laissez-faire en regard de la terminologie en est le reflet" (Taylor 1968: 38, traduction de l'éditeur), le présent article lance un appel à la standardisation de la terminologie utilisée pour classifier les cultures archéologiques de l'Arctique oriental. Portant particulièrement sur la période qui s'échellonne d'environ 4500-1000/500 avant aujourd'hui, l'auteur propose une Tradition culturelle dorsétienne subdivisée en cinq Horizons culturels, à savoir le transitionnel, l'inférieur, le moyen, le supérieur et le terminal. Celle-ci aurait été précédée par la Tradition culturelle prédorsétienne, à l'intérieure de laquelle on reconnaîtrait quatre Horizons culturels, c'est-à-dire l'initial, l'ancien, le moyen et le supérieur. Cet article discute des avantages d'un tel système terminologique pour décrire les grandes divisions spatio-temporelles de la Tradition microlithique de l'Arctique trouvée dans l'Arctique oriental. Nous y décrivons aussi la structure logique d'une taxonomie classificatoire de ces cultures, dont le but est de mesurer les ressemblances et les variations de nature historico-culturelle des assemblages paléoesquimaudes à travers le temps et l'espace dans l'Arctique oriental.

Threads of Arctic Prehistory: Papers in Honour of William E. Taylor Jr., David Morrison and Jean-Luc Pilon, eds. Canadian Museum of Civilization, Mercury Series, Archaeological Survey of Canada Paper 149. 1994.

Introduction

Culture classificatory schemes for the North American Arctic abound. Far from imposing order on the variety of recognized Arctic prehistoric complexes, however, the proliferation of such schemes has resulted in a palimpsest of terminological ambiguities and conceptual contradictions that obfuscates even the most elementary cultural historical relationships in Far Northern prehistory.

The problem of terminological confusion in Arctic archaeology is not a recent phenomenon. In 1968, William E. Taylor Jr. (1968: 38) noted that:

"Eastern Arctic archaeology is in its infancy... The laissez-faire attitude towards its terminology reflects this. The Pre-Dorset term appears often as an independent noun and at other times as an adjective for stage, period, culture, provenience, occupation and type."

Taylor (1968: 85) went on to suggest that:

"...(since) Pre-Dorset is such a crude and awkward term. Surely a new name should be adopted for the Canadian-Greenland branch of the Arctic Small Tool tradition. Could "Carlsberg Culture" be accepted ?"

To his lasting chagrin, Taylor's "Carlsberg" label has never caught on as a cure-all for what ails Eastern Arctic culture-historical taxonomy.

Contrary to the old axiom, things have not improved with time. Over the last 15 years, several noteworthy attempts have been made to revise, and thus to clarify, Eastern Arctic culture-classificatory terminology (e.g. Dekin 1978; Dumond 1987; Knuth 1977/78, Maxwell 1985; McGhee 1978, 1982; Plumet 1982, 1987; Schledermann 1990; Tuck and Fitzhugh 1986). Unfortunately, each such effort has been compromised by a common set of conceptual flaws that seriously limits, if not invalidates, its potential contribution (Helmer 1987; Helmer and Plumet n.d.).

Since 1985, I have been grappling with the often frustrating problem of developing a viable approach to Eastern Arctic cultural taxonomy that avoids the kinds of methodological and theoretical errors that have marred earlier such attempts. The first stage in this on-going endeavor involved a comprehensive review of the many disparate versions of Far Northern cultural nomenclature published over the past 10 to 15 years (Helmer 1987; Helmer and Plumet n.d.). The primary goal of this survey was to identify the terminological ambiguities and logical inconsistencies inherent in each such scheme. Informed by this review, the next stage in this exercise involved (and indeed still involves) the formulation of a coherent taxonomic strategy for classifying Eastern Arctic prehistoric cultural manifestations—a strategy that is firmly grounded in sound and broadly accepted principles of typology and classification (Helmer 1992a, 1992b).

In the following paper, I outline an alternative approach to Far Northern culture classification. This scheme, I shall argue, not only provides a consistent conceptual framework for identifying the broad spatio-temporal parameters of Far Northern culture history but also has the potential to contribute a legitimate taxonomic strategy for isolating and ultimately identifying regional cultural variants and developing regional sub-traditions within the Eastern Arctic. A few brief comments on what I perceive to be some of the important priorities of future goal-oriented research into Eastern Arctic prehistory are offered by way of a conclusion to this presentation.

An Alternative Approach to Eastern Arctic Culture-Classificatory Terminology

The alternative approach to the culture-historical taxonomy of Eastern Arctic prehistory which I advocate in this paper rests on the definition of two discrete, though conceptually-linked, hierarchical classificatory systems. The first of these systems provides a broad spatio-temporal framework for describing Eastern Arctic prehistory. The second scheme, as yet incomplete, offers a formal, but flexible, structure for identifying and ultimately interpreting culture-historical relationships within and between Far Northern occupational sequences.

Both complementary classificatory systems draw heavily on the paradigmatic structure of Willey and Phillips' (1958) model of culture-historical integration (something most prior Eastern Arctic cultural classifications have failed to do) and upon the logical extensions of this construct posited by Krause (1977) and Zeier (1982). Further inspiration has been derived from parallel attempts to create order out of the chaos of prior culture-historical reconstructions in the Northeastern Woodlands (Stoltman 1978), the Northwestern Plains (Foor 1985) and the Canadian Interior Plateau (Richards and Rousseau 1987).

The following review outlines the main features of this alternative approach as applied to the classification of prehistoric cultural manifestations from the Eastern Arctic (as defined in Damas 1984 and Maxwell 1985) dating to between ca. 4500 and 1000/500 B.P. This scheme can, of course, easily be extended to accommodate other geographic loci and temporal parameters.

A Spatio-Temporal Classification of Eastern Arctic Prehistory

The spatio-temporal component of my proposed culture-classificatory scheme for Eastern Arctic prehistory is summarized in Figure 1. The underlying logic of this culture chronological taxonomy stresses patterning through space and shared patterns of variation through time in the formal dimensions of archaeological assemblages from the Eastern Arctic dating, as noted above, to between ca.4500 B.P. and 1000/500 B.P. The omnipresent "noise" of regional and non-shared temporal variability is, therefore, deliberately suppressed.

The primary goal of this spatio-temporal taxonomy is to provide a consistent conceptual framework for classifying Eastern Arctic prehistoric cultural manifestations. Towards this end, many elements of existing terminologies are retained, but only in cases where the potential exists for consensus. To avoid unnecessary ambiguity, the hierarchical level and scale of measurement applied to each of the following taxonomic units is clearly defined herein.

Technological Tradition

The broadest analytical unit in the spatio-temporal taxonomy outlined in Figure 1 is the Technological Tradition. In contemporary North American archaeological literature, the concept of the "technological tradition" is most commonly equated with Willey and Phillips' (1958: 41) diagrammatic conceptualization of the relationships between component, phase, horizon and tradition.

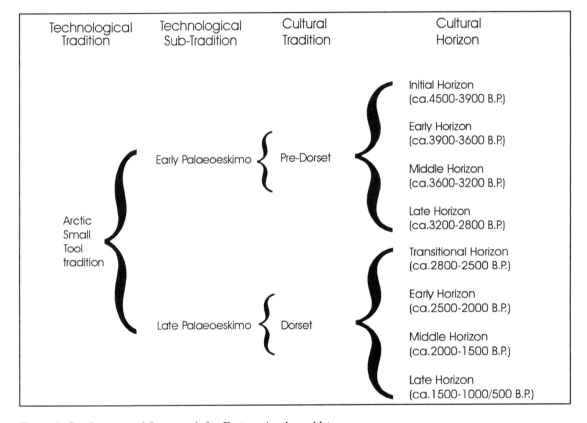

Figure 1 Spatio-temporal framework for Eastern Arctic prehistory.

Willey and Phillips (1958: 37) define "tradition" as a logical construct reflecting long temporal duration but finite spatial extent. Its primary purpose is to link, through time, assemblages and groups of assemblages (i.e. phases) within relatively closely circumscribed geographic localities or regions. As employed herein, the category of Technological Tradition groups those archaeological assemblages from throughout the North American Arctic (including both the Western Arctic and the Eastern Arctic) that share a constellation of specific technological attributes that can be demonstrated to have persisted over a relatively long period of time.

The Arctic Small Tool tradition, or ASTt, as defined by Irving (1957, 1962), and elaborated upon by MacNeish (1959), Maxwell (1973: 346-52) and Taylor (1968) among others, has been described as a polythetic set—in the sense used by Clarke (1968)—of lithic artefact types that distinguishes arctic archaeological assemblages dating to the interval between ca. 4500 to 1000/500 B.P. (Maxwell 1973, 1985; Taylor 1968). The list includes microblades struck from prepared cores, flake burins (with either spalled or ground working edges), and a wide variety of very small, finely made knives, scrapers, sideblades and stemmed, triangular and/or notched bifaces and endblades. This constellation of attributes clearly has broad formal, temporal and spatial parameters, yet it remains a useful, integrative device for linking historically-related material cultural manifestations from the Bering Straits to Greenland. As such, it is consistent with the taxonomic principles of a Technological Tradition as defined herein.

Table 1 Partial list of attributes characterizing the Early and Late Palaeoeskimo Technological Sub-Traditions.

EARLY PALAEOESKIMO	LATE PALAEOESKIMO
Spalled flake burins	Ground and polished burins
Unnotched bifaces and projectile points	Side-notched bifaces and projectile points
Barbed non-toggling harpoon heads Open-socketed toggling harpoon heads	Partially or completely closed-socketed harpoon heads
Bi-pointed needles with round cross-sections and circular eyelets	Uni-pointed needles with flat cross-sections and elongated gouged, eyelets

Technological Sub-Traditions

The next unit in my proposed spatio-temporal taxonomic scheme is the Technological Sub-Tradition. As the name suggests, a Technological Sub-Tradition represents a unique sub-set of attributes drawn from a specific Technological Tradition. By definition, these attributes persist through a more limited span of time than the original higher order taxonomic unit. This construct retains the broad spatial parameters of the Technological Tradition, but recognizes more precise chronological relationships.

In northern North America, two such Technological Sub-Traditions can be subsumed under the broader definition of the Arctic Small Tool tradition. These taxa are identified in Figure 1 as the Early Palaeoeskimo and the Late Palaeoeskimo Technological Sub-Traditions.

The Early and Late Palaeoeskimo Sub-Traditions can be distinguished on the basis of two mutually exclusive sub-sets of formal attributes occurring within the broader definitional parameters of the Arctic Small Tool tradition. A partial listing of these attributes is provided in Table 1.

Cultural Traditions

Technological Traditions and Technological Sub-Traditions emphasize the persistence of specific technological attributes over long periods of time and, as employed herein, over broad, but clearly defined geographic areas. Cultural taxonomists, however, have long recognized the need for a complementary analytical unit that measures the temporal persistence of specific patterns of material culture, economic adaptations, settlement strategies and social organization within a clearly definable culture-environmental area (e.g. Caldwell 1958; Goggin 1949; Lehmer and Caldwell 1966; Richards and Rousseau 1987; Sanger 1969; Willey and Phillips 1958; Zeier 1982). The concept of the Cultural Tradition, first introduced by Goggin (1949) and more recently applied with some success by Lehmer and Caldwell (1966) and by Sanger (1969) and Richards and Rousseau (1987) in their syntheses of Northern Plains and B.C. Interior Plateau prehistory respectively, satisfies these requirements.

As employed herein, the concept of Cultural Tradition groups cultural manifestations from within the Eastern Arctic study area exhibiting common social, economic and/or ideological characteristics. It is assumed that archaeological components so grouped share common historical bonds beyond those implied by their participation in a single Technological Sub-Tradition.

A minimum of two chronologically discrete Cultural Traditions are readily recognizable in the archaeological record of the Eastern Arctic dating to the period between ca. 4500 and 1000/500 B.P. These traditions are identified in Figure 1 as the Pre-Dorset Cultural Tradition and the Dorset Cultural Tradition.

It should be noted here that, although only two Cultural Traditions in the Eastern Arctic dating to the period between ca. 4500-1000/500 B.P. are identified in Figure 1, this does not preclude the possibility that additional Cultural Traditions—perhaps regional refinements of the two traditions identified herein—may, at some point, be identified.

My decision to retain the terms Dorset and especially Pre-Dorset—both of which carry manifold connotations in other Eastern Arctic cultural classificatory systems—is likely to prove controversial. In defense of this position, I would like to point out that implicit usage of the term "Dorset Culture" in contemporary Eastern Arctic archaeological literature, has by and large been consistent with the definition of a Cultural Tradition provided above. Adoption of the more rigorously defined taxon the "Dorset Cultural Tradition", therefore, is unlikely to prove too problematical. Admittedly, the same cannot be said of my decision to apply the much maligned label of "Pre-Dorset" to the Eastern Arctic cultural manifestation of the Early Palaeoeskimo Technological Sub-Tradition.

My reasons for retaining the term Pre-Dorset in this instance are largely historical. The term "pre-Dorset" was introduced by Henry Collins (1954) to describe a broad spatio-temporal construct roughly comparable to the category of Cultural Tradition (e.g. Collins 1954; Taylor 1968). That this was Collins' intent is clearly illustrated in a quotation from Taylor (1968: 43,88) who, following Collins (1954), states that:

> "Pre-Dorset" refers to a culture .... that occurred in the central and eastern North American Arctic ..... derived from the Arctic Small Tool tradition of the western Arctic .... (it was) ... an arctic-adapted culture with a sea-mammal economy whose people were organized in small seasonally, nomadic hunting bands."

Indeed, it has only been relatively recently that **implicit** definitions of the term Pre-Dorset have been extended beyond the conceptual constraints of a middle-range spatio-temporal taxon (which is what the Cultural Tradition—as it is employed herein—is) to include connotations presuming far more precise levels of culture-historical patterning and variability (e.g. Maxwell 1973; McGhee 1974, 1976, 1978, 1979; Schledermann; 1990 among others).

In my taxonomic strategy I have adopted the unambiguous position that the goals of a broad spatio-temporal cultural classification, by their very definition, differ from those of a specific culture historical classification. The hierarchical structures of both classificatory strategies—including the taxonomic units employed and the labels ascribed to them—should, therefore, also differ. In my view, the original definition of Pre-Dorset—that is as a broadly applicable label for various cultural expressions of the Early Palaeoeskimo Sub-Tradition in the Eastern Arctic—has historical precedence over its more recent use (or misuse) as a term implying specific inter-regional and historical variability through time and/or space. In a sense then, my definition of Pre-Dorset as an Eastern Arctic Cultural Tradition retains the spirit, if not the substance, of Taylor's "Carlsberg Culture" designation.

In the final analysis, assignation of any label to a specific Cultural Tradition is an arbitrary process. An alternative nomenclature (even Taylor's "Carlsberg Culture") could, by consensus, be adopted in place of "Pre-Dorset". Of far greater importance to the proposed culture-classificatory scheme is recognition and acceptance of the concept of Cultural Tradition itself.

Cultural Horizons

The final taxonomic unit in the spatio-temporal classificatory scheme outlined in Figure 1 is the Cultural Horizon. As employed herein, the Cultural Horizon can be considered a logical extension of Willey and Phillips' (1958) Horizon concept (Richards and Rousseau 1987; Zeier 1982). It expands on the formal (i.e. cultural) dimension of Willey and Phillips' taxon by emphasizing the wide spread spatial distribution, over a relatively brief period of time, of a unique segment of a Cultural Tradition (Bicchieri 1975; Lehmer and Caldwell 1966; Richards and Rousseau 1987). The Cultural Horizon thereby becomes a useful taxonomic mechanism for recognizing significant temporal changes in material culture, settlement patterns, subsistence strategies and/or social organization within a single Cultural Tradition.

Division of a Cultural Tradition into Cultural Horizons must, by definition, be based on a reasoned assessment of significant thresholds of change within the broader parameters of variation characteristic of the larger continuum. Theoretically, there is no set limit to the number of horizons recognized. Depending on the criteria selected, fewer or more legitimate sub-divisions of a cultural tradition can be made. Suggested preliminary divisions of the Eastern Arctic Pre-Dorset and Dorset Cultural Traditions are presented in Figure 1.

The designations used in Figure 1 should be regarded as temporary labels only. Alternative more descriptive, or historically relevant labels (i.e. the Independence Horizon instead of the Initial Horizon of the Pre-Dorset Cultural Tradition) could easily be adopted (through broad consensus). It is not the labels *per se* that are of importance but the taxonomic unit(s) of the Cultural Horizon itself that is of primary significance.

Dorset Tradition Cultural Horizons

Sub-division of the Dorset Cultural Tradition into discrete Cultural Horizons is discussed here first, as these taxa should prove less controversial than will certainly be the case with the Cultural Horizons proposed for the Pre-Dorset Cultural Tradition.

For nearly 30 years, Eastern Arctic archaeologists have used a series of informal constructs closely analogous to Cultural Horizons to sub-divide the Dorset Cultural Tradition (Maxwell 1973, 1984, 1985; McGhee 1976, 1979, 1981; Meldgaard 1960b; Schledermann 1990; Taylor 1968). In his seminal volume on Eastern Arctic prehistory, for example, Maxwell (1985), following Meldgaard (1960b), recognizes five major sub-divisions of the Dorset "Culture." These include: 1) the Pre-Dorset to Dorset Transition 2) Early Dorset 3) Middle Dorset, 4) Late Dorset and 5) the Terminal Dorset "stages". Each taxon, Maxwell (1985: 111-245) argues, is distinguished by typological changes in artifacts, shifting trends in economic adaptations, variations in settlement pattern characteristics and developing expressions of art and ideology. Though he never uses the term, Maxwell's "stages" of the Dorset "Culture" are entirely consistent with the concept of Cultural Horizon as defined herein.

Of particular relevance to the position adopted here is the fact that Eastern Arctic archaeologists seldom have any difficulty applying Maxwell's units to their own local sequences—regardless of where these may occur in the Eastern Arctic. In other words, when one refers to the Early Dorset occupation of Karluk Island in the central Canadian High Arctic (e.g. Helmer 1979, 1980, 1981) one is referring to much the same thing as scholars working on contemporary components from, for example, Victoria Island (Taylor 1967, 1972), Southampton Island (Collins 1956a, 1956b), Northern Labrador (Cox 1978) or the Melville Peninsula (Meldgaard 1960b, 1962). As noted by Schledermann (1990: 328):

"Perhaps the most important reason for isolating an Early Dorset component in the Bache Peninsula region is to illustrate that the activities of the Palaeoeskimos in the Canadian High Arctic and at least northern Greenland were very much part of the overall ASTt developments in Central and Eastern Canada. Considering the vast geographical distances involved, the stylistic similarities between these assemblages are perhaps more striking than their differences."

Pre-Dorset Tradition Horizons

In contrast to the situation with the Dorset Cultural Tradition, few, if any, attempts have been made to sub-divide formally the Pre-Dorset Cultural Tradition—or any comparable broad culture-historical construct—into units even remotely analogous to Cultural Horizons. It has been common practice in Early Palaeoeskimo studies to regard regional variation as the basic unit of analysis, irrespective of chronological considerations. Thus, the most frequently recognized culture-historical sub-divisions of the Early Palaeoeskimo Technological Sub-Tradition in the Eastern Arctic—i.e. "Independence I", "Saqqaq", "Barrenground Pre-Dorset", "Core Area Pre-Dorset", etc.—emphasize perceived quantitative and/or stylistic differences between geographically discrete groups of assemblages. They are categorically not based on the broad similarities shared by analogous components from across the Far North. (see Bielawski 1988; Elling 1992).

As defined herein, the Pre-Dorset Cultural Tradition encompasses the entire range of material cultural, economic and social variability—both spatial and temporal—inherent in all Eastern Arctic manifestations of the Early Palaeoeskimo Sub-Tradition. Sub-division of the Pre-Dorset Cultural tradition into Cultural Horizons must, therefore, be based on the recognition of trends—including continuities and changes—held in common throughout the study area.

It is interesting to note that although Early Palaeoeskimo specialists working in the Eastern Arctic have been reluctant to identify anything comparable to Cultural Horizons, individual researchers have frequently recognized two or more chronological "stages", "phases" or "complexes" of Early Palaeoeskimo occupations in their study areas. Taylor (1962, 1968: 40-41), for example, argues on taxonomic grounds, that three or more "episodes" of Pre-Dorset occupation can be identified in the archaeological sequence from northwestern Ungava. In a similar vein, Gordon (1975), McGhee (1970, 1971, 1976), Müller-Beck (1977) and Taylor (1967, 1972) have all acknowledged that the Pre-Dorset occupations of the west-central Canadian Arctic can be divided into the "middle to late stages" of Pre-Dorset. Finally, Schledermann (1990) and Helmer (1991) have independently provided solid artifactual, elevational and radiometric evidence for a minimum of four chronologically and stylistically discrete Early Palaeoeskimo occupations in the Bache Peninsula and North Devon Lowlands areas of the Canadian High Arctic respectively.

The preceding informal sub-divisions are all based on the recognition of internal patterning and variation in a combination of artifactual, economic and settlement pattern criteria. Furthermore, corroboration of specific stages, phases or complexes, has often been achieved through cross-comparison with other, similarly conceived, local sequences. That legitimate cross-comparisons can be made across vast areas of the Eastern Arctic suggests to me that these local sub-divisions, as a group, come close to fulfilling the criteria of Cultural Horizons.

Perhaps prematurely anticipating the results of future research efforts, I would like to suggest here that the Eastern Arctic Pre-Dorset Cultural Tradition be sub-divided into a minimum of four Cultural Horizons: 1) an Initial Pre-Dorset Horizon, 2) an Early Pre-Dorset Horizon, 3) a Middle Pre-Dorset Horizon and 4) a Late Pre-Dorset Horizon (Figure 1).

As yet, these divisions of the Pre-Dorset Cultural Tradition remain hypothetical. There is good preliminary evidence, however, to suggest the legitimacy of at least one of these Cultural Horizons.

Archaeological evidence pertaining to the earliest Early Palaeoeskimo occupation of the Eastern Arctic has been reported from, among other areas, northeastern Greenland (Andreasen 1992; Knuth 1967), northern Ellesmere Island (Knuth 1967; Sutherland 1992), eastern Ellesmere Island (Schledermann 1978a, 1990), western Greenland (Grønnow 1988, Grønnow and Meldgaard 1988; Meldgaard 1983), northeastern Devon Island (Helmer 1986, 1991), the McDougall Sound region (Schledermann 1978b), northern Baffin Island (Mary-Rousellière 1964), southeastern Baffin Island (Maxwell 1973, 1985), the Foxe Basin and Hudson Straits area (Bielawski 1985; Meldgaard 1960a, 1960b, 1962; Taylor 1962) and northern Labrador (Cox 1978). Radiocarbon estimates obtained from a majority of these occupations fall between ca. 4500 and 3900 radiocarbon years before present (not calibrated).

As noted earlier, it has been common practice for Eastern Arctic prehistorians (see Maxwell

1985; Schledermann 1990 for recent examples) to identify three (or four if Knuth's (1977/78) "Old Nugdlit Culture" is included) discrete "cultural" divisions within this sample of early assemblages—"Independence I", early "Pre-Dorset" and early "Saqqaq". If the criteria used to describe each of these constructs are examined closely, however, it becomes readily apparent that a majority of traits claimed to distinguish between these constructs—serrated edge bi-points and tapered stem bifaces, large burins, microblades and mid-passage tent rings, for example—is, in fact, shared by most, if not all, of them (see also Elling 1992). There are, therefore, more (and better in my opinion) reasons to group these early occupations together into an Initial Pre-Dorset Horizon taxon, than there are (at least at present) to distinguish between them.

I do not mean to imply that "Independence I", early "Pre-Dorset" and early "Saqqaq" are identical or that, over time, evidence indicating culture-historically significant differences between them will never be found—though this evidence will only come to the fore through explicit culture-historically relevant typological analysis. My point is that, in broad spatio-temporal terms, these early Early Palaeoeskimo assemblages are more like each other than they are like later manifestations of the Pre-Dorset Cultural Tradition.

I also suspect that, in the foreseeable future, we will find comparable evidence of similar broad patterns of association exhibited between Eastern Arctic Early Palaeoeskimo cultural manifestations at other points in both time and space.

A Culture-Historical Taxonomic Strategy for Eastern Arctic Prehistory

To this point, I have focused attention on the logical structure of an alternative spatio-temporal classification of Eastern Arctic cultural manifestations. In my view, the hierarchical units of Technological Tradition, Technological Sub-Tradition, Cultural Tradition and Cultural Horizon, as described herein, offer much needed consistency to Eastern Arctic prehistory. They also provide useful tools for describing broad patterns of shared variability in the Far North through both time and space. It should be made clear once more, however, that this taxonomic scheme does not address, nor is it intended to address, issues relating to the dynamics of inter-regional and extra-regional cultural interactions.

In keeping with the theme stressed throughout this paper, the logical structure of a classificatory system dedicated to measuring and interpreting specific culture-historical relationships must, by definition, differ from that of a spatio-temporal classification. In spatio-temporal taxonomies, classificatory units are largely divisive in nature. That is to say, hierarchical relationships proceed from the general (i.e. Technological Tradition) to the specific (i.e. Cultural Horizons). Culture-historical taxonomies, on the other hand, should be cumulative. In other words, such taxonomies should proceed from the specific (i.e. individual cultural assemblages), to the general (i.e. regional phases or regional cultural sub-traditions).

For the past several years I have been struggling to develop a workable culture-historical classificatory system for Eastern Arctic prehistory. A first approximation of the logical structure of such a taxonomic strategy is outlined in Figure 2.

Components and Localities

The primary cultural unit in my proposed culture-historical taxonomic scheme is the Component. A Component can be broadly defined as the physical manifestation of a discrete occupation at a given site (Willey and Phillips 1958: 21).

The primary spatial unit employed in this complementary taxonomy—the unit within which groups of components can be geographically bounded—is the Locality, defined as "a geographical space small enough to permit the working assumption of ... cultural homogeneity at any given point in time" (1958: 18-19). In particular reference to hunter-gatherers, this construct pertains to the geographical span within which a group would normally conduct its seasonal subsistence-settlement round (Willey and Phillips 1958: 18).

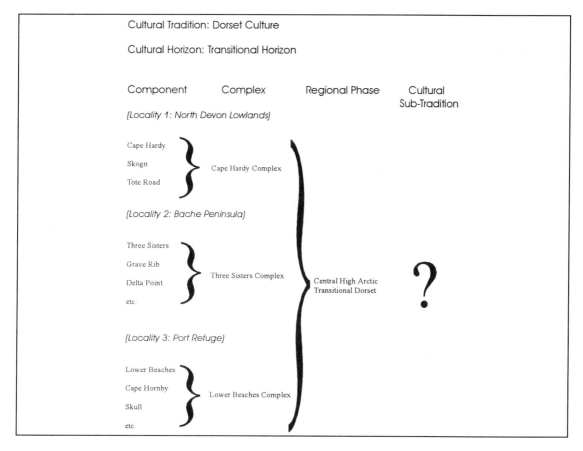

Figure 2 Culture-historical framework for Eastern Arctic prehistory: A tentative example.

It is important to bear in mind that this definition of Locality is not meant to imply any necessary degree of permanence in terms of the human occupation of a given Locality. Specific hunter-gather groups—both ethnographical and archaeological—could and did practice a high degree of settlement mobility which could have seen them shift their territorial focus, over time, to two or more spatially discrete Localities. I believe this to be particularly true of High Arctic-adapted Palaeoeskimo peoples (see Helmer 1991, 1992c; McCartney 1989; McCartney and Helmer 1989). Similarly, over time, a given Locality could have been occupied by different social or culture-chronological groups.

The Locality, in context with the proposed culture-historical taxonomy, represents the inferred zone of exploitation likely utilized (at least seasonally) by a given social group (as represented by a component or group of related components) at a given point in time.

Complexes

Complexes (see Rouse 1972: 238) are the first truly typological taxa in my alternative culture-historical taxonomy. Such constructs are (or will be) defined on the basis of rigorous inter-assemblage comparisons of all cultural Components associated with a specific Cultural Horizon identified within a given geographic Locality. The relationship between cultural Complexes and the Cultural Horizon in this taxonomy, it should be noted, is explicit—the Cultural Horizon is to be understood and locally interpreted within the context of its constituent Components. As a result, a conceptual link is maintained between the Culture-Historical and Spatio-Temporal taxonomic schemes proposed in my alternative approach to Eastern Arctic cultural classification.

Regional Phases

The Regional Phase is the second typological unit in my proposed culture-historical taxonomic scheme. Regional Phases will be defined on the basis of the comprehensive comparison of the material cultural, economic and/or settlement pattern attributes of specific Complexes defined from two or more spatially proximate Localities from within a defined Region (defined by Willey and Phillips [1958: 19-20] as a "minor physiographic unit " corresponding to the territory occupied by "a social unit larger than the community") through time. The High Arctic Islands or Western Greenland come to mind as examples of what **might** ultimately prove to be legitimate archaeological Regions.

Cultural Sub-Traditions

The final hierarchical taxonomic unit identified in Figure 2 is the Cultural Sub-Tradition. Cultural Sub-Traditions in Eastern Arctic prehistory will (ultimately) be identified through the rigorous study of patterned variations (if any can be shown to exist) linking discrete Regional Phases through both time and space.

At the level of the Cultural Sub-Tradition it should be possible to trace the development of distinctive regional variants within a Cultural Tradition. For example, recent work by Grønnow (1992) appears to indicate that Saqqaq—a regional manifestation of the Pre-Dorset Cultural Tradition—tools found in stratigraphic context at the West Greenland Qeqertassusuq site (see Grønnow 1988, Grønnow and Meldgaard 1988) exhibits little or no variation in specific qualitative stylistic attributes over an extended span of time. Saqqaq may, therefore, be a good candidate for future recognition as a distinctive Cultural Sub-Tradition.

Discussion

To better illustrate the mechanics of the preceding culture-historical taxonomic scheme, details of a very preliminary—and very speculative !—application of this strategy to selected Transitional Dorset Horizon components from three Localities in the Canadian High Arctic—the North Devon Lowlands region of northeastern Devon Island (Helmer 1991), the Bache Peninsula area of eastern Ellesmere Island (Schledermann 1990) and Port Refuge, on northwestern Devon Island (McGhee 1981)—have been incorporated into Figure 2. The reader is cautioned that this example is for illustrative purposes only and should not be taken as a formal culture-historical interpretation of the cited data.

For the North Devon Lowlands locality, three small assemblages corresponding to the Transitional Dorset Horizon (Helmer 1991) have been loosely grouped into what I have referred to as the Cape Hardy Complex: the local manifestation of the Transitional Dorset Cultural Horizon (Helmer 1991: 313-14). Peter Schledermann (1990) has similarly associated assemblages from nine sites on the Bache Peninsula to the Transitional Dorset "Phase". In my proposed culture-historical taxonomy, these assemblages **could** represent the local manifestation of the Transitional Dorset Cultural Horizon in the Bache Peninsula area. For the sake of argument, this aggregate of components has been identified in Figure 2 as the Three Sisters Complex (named after the Three Sisters Site which is the first component Schledermann describes in his 1990 publication). Finally, Bob McGhee (1981) has assigned eight discrete components he discovered in the Port Refuge area to the Transitional Dorset "Independence II Culture". In Figure 2 these components comprise the empirical basis for defining the Lower Beaches Complex (named after the first "Independence II" site McGhee (1981) describes in his monograph on the "Dorset" occupations of the Port Refuge area). In the context of the alternative taxonomic scheme proposed in this paper, the Lower Beaches Complex would (or could) be the local (to NW Devon Island) manifestation of the Transitional Dorset Horizon.

Formal definition of the preceding "complexes" would ideally be based on the statistical comparison of their constituent assemblages to demonstrate significant quantitative and qualitative associations (or differences!) between them. It is entirely conceivable, of course, that there may be more than one "complex" associated with a specific Cultural Horizon in a local area. In other words, the simple fact that two components associated with a Cultural Horizon occur in the same locality doesn't necessarily mean they belong to the same "complex".

At the next level in my proposed culture-historical taxonomy, the above complexes would be qualitatively and quantitatively compared and grouped (or sub-divided) into Regional Phases based again, on shared constellations of attributes. In the case of the North Devon Lowlands, Bache Peninsula and Port Refuge complexes, the three "complexes" identified in Figure 2 might, after detailed analysis, be found to be sufficiently alike to identify a regional Central High Arctic Transitional Dorset Phase. Extending this example a little further, Transitional Dorset complexes from Ungava, Labrador and Newfoundland may—and I suspect ultimately will—be found to be qualitatively distinct from this Central High Arctic Transitional Dorset Phase and could be grouped into an Eastern Canadian Arctic Transitional Dorset Phase.

The final step in my proposed culture-historical taxonomic strategy would be to examine the relationships between local complexes and earlier and later occupations (belonging to earlier or later Cultural Horizons) to determine temporal continuity or discontinuity. At this level we will likely find very interesting patterns of widening and/or shrinking regional interactions. However, attainment of this level is a long way off and we can only speculate about what associations we will ultimately be able to find.

Concluding Remarks

The approaches to Eastern Arctic culture-classification detailed in this paper are, in my opinion, both internally consistent and well grounded in typological theory. Unfortunately, we do not, as yet, have sufficiently detailed assemblage data from anywhere in the Eastern Arctic to effectively apply this culture-historical taxonomic strategy beyond the local level (i.e. the definition of "Complexes"). A full implementation of the preceding complementary approach to Eastern Arctic culture-classification will require, at the very least, a significant increase in the number of available, large and statistically representative, Palaeoeskimo artifact assemblages. As such assemblages are exceedingly rare—partly because of the sparseness of the archaeological record itself but also because of the way archaeological work has been conducted up to this point in time—we may have to wait a long time before it will be possible to fully exploit the benefits of this strategy. The challenge that lays before us all, therefore, is to devote our energies to the systematic and comprehensive acquisition and publication of primary material cultural, economic and settlement pattern information from local areas so that we can begin to pursue more detailed analyses of Eastern Arctic culture-historical dynamics.

References Cited

Andreasen C. 1992. A survey of Paleo-Eskimo sites in North East Greenland. Paper presented at the Paleo-Eskimo Cultures of Greenland - New Perspectives in Greenlandic Archaeology Archaeology Symposium, May 1992, Copenhagen.

Bicchieri, B. 1975. Units of culture and units of time: periodization and its use in syntheses of Plateau prehistory. Northwest Anthropological Research Notes, 9(2): 246-265.

Bielawski, E.E. 1985. Paleoeskimo Archaeology at Roche Bay, N.W.T. 1984 Field Work and Preliminary Analysis. MS on file at the Prince of Wales Northern Heritage Centre, Yellowknife.

Bielawski, E.E. 1988. Paleoeskimo variability: The Arctic Small Tool tradition in the Central Canadian Arctic. American Antiquity, 53(1): 52-74.

Caldwell, J. R. 1958. Trend and tradition in the history of the Eastern United States. American Anthropological Association Memoir 88.

Clarke, D.L. 1968. Analytical Archaeology. London: Methuen.

Collins, H.B. 1954. Archaeological research in the North American Arctic. Arctic, 7(3-4): 296-306.

Collins, H.B. 1956a. Archaeological Investigations on Southampton and Coats Islands, N.W.T. National Museums of Canada Bulletin, 142: 82-113.

Collins, H.B. 1956b. The T-1 Site at Native Point, Southampton Island, N.W.T. University of Alaska Anthropological Papers, 4(2): 63-89.

Cox, S.L. 1978. Paleoeskimo Occupations of the North Labrador Coast. Arctic Anthropology, 15(2): 96-118.

Damas, D., ed. 1984. Handbook of North American Indians Volume 5: Arctic. Washington: Smithsonian Institution.

Dekin, A.A., Jr. 1975. Models of Pre-Dorset Culture:Toward an Explicit Methodology. Unpublished Ph.D. Dissertation, Department of Anthropology, Michigan State University, East Lansing.

Dekin, A.A., Jr. 1978. Arctic Archaeology: A Bibliography. New York: Garland Press.

Dumond, D. 1987. The Eskimos and Aleuts. London: Thames and Hudson.

Elling, H. 1992. The Palaeo-Eskimo Cultures in Northern Greenland and Northeastern Greenland in Relation to West Greenland Cultures. Paper presented at the Paleo-Eskimo Cultures of Greenland - New Perspectives in Greenlandic Prehistory Symposium May 1992, Copenhagen.

Foor, T.A. 1985. Archaeological Classification in the Northwestern Plains. Plains Anthropologist, 30-108: 123-135.

Goggin, J.M. 1949. Cultural Traditions in Florida Prehistory. In, The Florida Indian and his Neighbors, J.W. Griffin, ed., pp.13-44.

Gordon, B.H.C. 1975. Of Men and Herds in Barrenland Prehistory. National Museum of Man, Mercury Series, Archaeological Survey of Canada Paper 28.

Grønnow, B. 1988. Prehistory in permafrost: investigations at the Saqqaq site Qeqetasussuk, Disco Bay, West Greenland. Journal of Danish Archaeology, 7: 24-39.

Grønnow, B. 1992. The Stone Tools of Qeqertasussuq - Aspects of function, Raw Material Utilization and Chronology. Paper presented at the Paleo-Eskimo Cultures of Greenland - New Perspectives in Greenlandic Archaeology Symposium, May 1992, Copenhagen.

Grønnow, B. and M. Meldgaard 1988. Boplads i dybfrost - - Fra Christianshab Museums ubgravninger pa   Vestgronlands aeldste boplads. Naturens Verden, 11-12: 409 -440.

Helmer, J.W. 1979. Paleoeskimo occupations at Markham Point, N.W.T.: Implications for High Arctic prehistory. Paper presented at the 12th Annual Archaeology Association Conference, Calgary, Alberta.

Helmer, J.W. 1980. Early Dorset in the High Arctic: A Report from Karluk Island, N.W.T. Arctic, 33: 427-442.

Helmer, J.W. 1981 Climate Change and Dorset Culture Change in the Crozier Strait Region, NWT: A Test of the Hypothesis. Unpublished Ph.D. dissertation, Department of Archaeology, University of Calgary.

Helmer, J.W. 1986. A face from the Past: An Early Pre-Dorset ivory maskette from North Devon Island N.W.T. Etudes/Inuit Studies, 10(1-2): 179-202.

Helmer, J.W. 1987 Cultural classificatory terminology in Eastern Arctic prehistory. Paper presented at the 20th Annual Meetings of the Canadian Archaeological Association, Calgary, Alberta.

Helmer, J.W. 1991 The Palaeo-Eskimo prehistory of the North Devon Lowlands. Arctic, 44(4): 301-317.

Helmer, J.W. 1992a. Resurrecting the Spirit(s) of Taylor's Carslberg Tradition: Cultural Traditions and Cultural Horizons in Eastern Arctic Prehistory. Paper presented at the 25th Annual Meeting of the Canadian Archaeological Association Meeting, May 1992, London.

Helmer, J.W. 1992b. What's in a Name ?: A Proposal for the Revision of Eastern Arctic Culture Classificatory Terminology. Paper presented at the Paleo-Eskimo Cultures of Greenland - New Perspectives in Greenlandic Archaeology Symposium, May 1992, Copenhagen.

Helmer, J.W. 1992c. Prehistoric Site Location Strategies in the North Devon Lowlands, High Arctic Canada. Journal of Field Archaeology, 19: 291-313.

Helmer, J.W. and P. Plumet n.d. What's in a name ?: Standardizing Eastern Arctic culture-classificatory terminology. MS on file in the Department of Archaeology, University of Calgary.

Irving, W.N. 1957. An Archaeological Survey of the Susitna Valley. <u>Anthropological Papers of the University of Alaska</u>, 6(1): 37-52.

Irving, W.N. 1962. A Provisional Comparison of Some Alaska and Asian Stone Industries. In, <u>Prehistoric Culture Relations between the Arctic and Temperate Zones of North America</u>, J.M. Campbell, ed. Arctic Institute of North America Technical Paper, 11: pp. 55-68.

Knuth, E. 1967. <u>Archaeology of the Musk-ox Way.</u> Ecoles Practiques des Hautes Etudes, Centre d'Etudes Arctiques et Finno-Scandinaves, Contributions 5.

Knuth, E. 1977/78. The "Old Nugdlit Culture" site at Nugdlit Peninsula, Thule District and the "Meso-Eskimo" site below it. <u>Folk</u>, 19/20: 15-47.

Krause, R.A. 1977. Taxonomic Practice and Middle Missouri Prehistory: A Perspective on Donald J. Lehmer's Contributions. <u>Plains Anthropologist</u>. 22-78(2): 5-13.

Lehmer, D.J. and W.W. Caldwell 1966. Horizon and Tradition in the Northern Plains. <u>Plains Anthropologist</u>, 31(4): 511-516.

MacNeish, R.S. 1959. A speculative framework of northern North American Prehistory as of April, 1959. <u>Anthropologica</u>, 1: 1-17.

Mary-Rousselière, G. 1964. The Paleo-Eskimo Remains in the Pelly Bay Region, N.W.T. National Museum of Canada Contributions to Anthropology 1961-1962. <u>National Museum of Canada Bulletin</u>, 193: 62-183.

Maxwell, M.S. 1973. <u>Archaeology of the Lake Harbour District, Baffin Island.</u> National Museum of Man, Mercury Series, Archaeological Survey of Canada Paper 6.

Maxwell, M.S. 1984. Pre-Dorset and Dorset Prehistory of Canada. In, <u>Handbook of North American Indians, Vol. 5, Arctic,</u> D. Damas, ed. Washington: Smithsonian Institute, pp.359-368.

Maxwell, M.S. 1985. <u>Prehistory of the Eastern Arctic.</u> New York: Academic Press.

McCartney, P.H. 1989. Paleoeskimo Subsistence and Settlement in the High Arctic. Unpublished Ph.D. Dissertation, University of Calgary, Calgary.

McCartney, P.H. and J.W. Helmer. 1989. Marine and Terrestrial Mammals in High Arctic Paleoeskimo Economy. <u>Archaeozoologia</u>, 3(1-2): 143-160.

McGhee, R. 1970. Excavations at Bloody Falls, N.W.T., Canada. <u>Arctic Anthropology</u>, 6(2): 53-72.

McGhee, R. 1971. An Archaeological Survey of Western Victoria Island, N.W.T., Canada. National Museum of Canada Bulletin, 232: 158-191.

McGhee, R. 1974. A current interpretation of central Canadian Arctic prehistory. Internord, 13/14: 171-80.

McGhee, R. 1976. Paleoeskimo Occupations of Central and High Arctic Canada. In, Eastern Arctic Prehistory: Paleoeskimo Problems, M.S. Maxwell, ed. Memoirs of the Society for American Archaeology, 31, pp. 15-39.

McGhee, R. 1978. Canadian Arctic Prehistory. Toronto: Van Nostrand Reinhold Ltd.

McGhee, R. 1979. The Palaeoeskimo Occupations at Port Refuge, High Arctic Canada. National Museum of Man, Mercury Series, Archaeological Survey of Canada Paper 92.

McGhee, R. 1981. The Dorset Occupations in the Vicinity of Port Refuge, High Arctic Canada. National Museum of Man, Mercury Series, Archaeological Survey of Canada Paper 105.

McGhee, R. 1982. Comment on P. Plumet's paper "Pour une révision du cadre conceptual utilisé en préhistoire de l'Arctiques central et oriental". Etudes/Inuit/Studies, 6(2): 155-157.

Meldgaard, J. 1960a. Origin and Evolution of Eskimo Cultures in the Eastern Arctic. Canadian Geographic Journal, 60(2): 64-75.

Meldgaard, J. 1960b. Prehistoric Sequences in the Eastern Arctic as Elucidated by Stratified Sites at Igloolik. In, Selected Papers of the Fifth International Congress Of Anthropological and Ethnological Sciences, A.F.C. Wallace, ed. Philadelphia: University of Pennsylvania Press, pp.588-595.

Meldgaard, J. 1962. On the Formative Period of the Dorset Culture. In, Prehistoric Cultural Relations Between the Arctic and Temperate Zones of North America, J.M. Campbell, ed. Arctic Institute of North America Technical Paper, 11: 92-95.

Meldgaard, J. 1983. Qaja, en kokkenmodding i dybfrost. Feltrapport fra arbejdsmarken i Grønland, Saertryk af National Museet, Arbejdsmark, Copenhagen.

Müller-Beck, H.J., ed. 1977. Excavations at Umingmak on Banks Island, N.W.T., 1970 and 1973: preliminary report. Institut für Urgeschichte der Universitat Tübingen. Urgeschichtliche Materialhefte 1.

Plumet, P. 1982. Pour une révision du cadre conceptual utilisé en préhistoire de l' Arctique central et oriental. Etudes/Inuit/Studies, 6(1): 130-139.

Plumet, P. 1987. Le Développement de l'Approach Archéologique dans l'Arctique. L' Anthropologie, 91(4): 859-872.

Richards, T. and M. Rousseau 1987. Late Prehistoric Cultural Horizons on the Canadian Plateau. Simon Fraser University, Department of Archaeology Paper16.

Rouse, I. 1972. Introduction to Prehistory: A Systemic Approach. New York: McGraw-Hill Book Company.

Sanger, D. 1969. Cultural traditions in the interior of British Columbia. Syesis, 2: 189-200.

Schledermann, P. 1978a. Preliminary Results of Archaeological Investigations in the Bache Peninsula Region, Ellesmere Island, N.W.T. Arctic, 31: 459-474.

Schledermann, P. 1978b. Prehistoric Demographic Trends in the Canadian High Arctic. Canadian Journal of Archaeology, 2: 43-58.

Schledermann, P. 1990. Crossroads to Greenland. Arctic Institute of North America, Komatik Series, 2.

Stoltman, J.B. 1978. Temporal models in prehistory: An example from eastern North America. Current Anthropology, 19(4): 703-747.

Sutherland, P.D. 1992. Continuity and change in the Paleo-Eskimo prehistory of northern Ellesmere Island. Paper presented at the Paleo-Eskimo Cultures of Greenland - New Perspectives in Greenlandic Archaeology Symposium. May 1992, Copenhagen.

Taylor, W.E., Jr. 1962 Prehistoric Occupations at Ivugivik in Northwest Ungava. In, Prehistoric Cultural Relations between the Arctic and Temperate Zones of North America, J.M. Campbell, ed. Arctic Institute of North America Technical Paper, 11: pp. 80-91.

Taylor, W.E., Jr. 1967. Summary of Archaeological Fieldwork on Banks and Victoria Islands, Arctic Canada, 1965. Arctic Anthropology, 4(1): 221-243.

Taylor, W.E., Jr. 1968. The Arnapik and Tyara Sites: An Archaeological Study of Dorset Culture Origins. Memoirs of the Society for American Archaeology, 22.

Taylor, W.E., Jr. 1972. An Archaeological Survey Between Cape Parry and Cambridge Bay, N.W.T., Canada. National Museum of Man, Mercury Series, Archaeological Survey of Canada Paper 1.

Tuck, J. and W. Fitzhugh. 1986. Paleo-Eskimo Traditions of Newfoundland and Labrador: a Re-appraisal. In, Palaeo-Eskimo Cultures in Newfoundland, Labrador and Ungava. Memorial University of Newfoundland, Reports in Archaeology, 1.

Willey, G.R. and P. Phillips.1958. Method and Theory in American Archaeology. Chicago: The University of Chicago Press.

Zeier, C. 1982. The Willey and Phillips System Revisited: A proposed Expansion of the Paradigm. Plains Anthropologist, 27(95): 29-36.

Going To Pot:
A Technological Overview of North American Arctic Ceramics

Carole Stimmell
Archaeological Resource Centre
Toronto Board of Education
Toronto, Ontario

Abstract

Analysis of ceramic found on North American Arctic sites demonstrates the presence of two distinct pottery making traditions, Palaeoeskimo and Neoeskimo. Within each of these traditions, regional, temporal and cultural groups existed. Regardless of the final assessment of the artifacts from aesthetic and functional perspectives, their existence in such a harsh environment is testimony to the ingenuity of prehistoric Arctic peoples.

Résumé

Les résultats d'analyse de poterie provenant de sites archéologiques de l'Arctique nord-américain, indiquent la présence de deux traditions de fabrication de la céramique, à savoir la tradition paléoesquimaude et la tradition néoesquimaude. Chacune de celles-ci peut être aussi sous-divisées selon des critères chronologiques, géographiques et culturels. Mis à part notre évaluation de leur valeur fonctionnelle ou esthétique, le simple fait d'avoir fabriqué des vases en céramique dans un environnement aussi rude, en dit long sur l'ingéniosité de ces cultures préhistoriques.

Introduction

Broken pot-sherds found on archaeological sites in North America are all that remain as evidence of an important prehistoric industry. These bits and pieces of the past were manufactured by potters who, over countless generations, experimented with many types of new materials and technologies in an attempt to produce improved ceramic products. Pottery from the North American Arctic, however, has long been considered an exception to this process, perhaps because the Eastern Arctic is one of the few areas in the world where the production of ceramics was abandoned and subsequently replaced by stone vessel technology.

Unfortunately very little is known about ceramic traditions in the North American Arctic. Pottery is a relatively recent and somewhat irregular addition to the cultural inventory of the North American Arctic. Early Arctic pottery is relatively scarce and Neoeskimo ceramics have been largely ignored by archaeologists because the pottery found on most late prehistoric Arctic sites does not lend

Threads of Arctic Prehistory: Papers in Honour of William E. Taylor Jr., David Morrison and Jean-Luc Pilon, eds. Canadian Museum of Civilization, Mercury Series, Archaeological Survey of Canada Paper 149. 1994.

itself to traditional methods of rim sherd classification and decorative element attribute analysis.

This paper will present a technological approach to ceramics traditions from Northern Alaska and the Canadian Arctic using data derived from technological and stylistic attributes. Pottery from over 25 sites was examined for this study (Figure 1). Additional clay samples, both from archaeological sites and adjacent areas, were also included in some of the analysis.

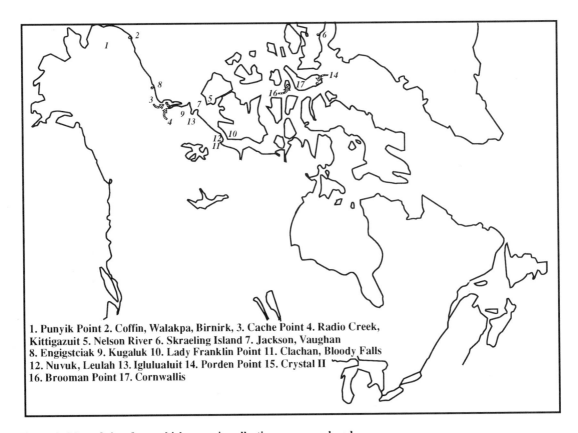

1. Punyik Point 2. Coffin, Walakpa, Birnirk, 3. Cache Point 4. Radio Creek, Kittigazuit 5. Nelson River 6. Skraeling Island 7. Jackson, Vaughan 8. Engigstciak 9. Kugaluk 10. Lady Franklin Point 11. Clachan, Bloody Falls 12. Nuvuk, Leulah 13. Iglulualuit 14. Porden Point 15. Crystal II 16. Brooman Point 17. Cornwallis

Figure 1 Map of sites from which ceramic collections were analyzed.

This research has led the author to conclude that the study of differences in ceramic technologies in this region may offer insights into prehistoric environmental adaptations and culture history. Furthermore, it is proposed that changes in the ceramic industry of late prehistoric Neoeskimo peoples are a reflection of technological flexibility in an area which was marginal for the production of pottery.

Methodology

Both traditional archaeological methods of analysis and laboratory techniques adapted for archaeological materials were used to examine a wide spectrum of technical and stylistic ceramic elements. Initial identification of the mineral temper, and gross estimation of the size and amount of mineral and fibre temper were done using a binocular microscope. Certain sherds were selected for additional laboratory testing. The sherds were chosen to constitute representative samples of the collections wherever possible. Twenty-eight petrographic thin-sections were analyzed from ten different sites. Petrographic analysis facilitates the identification and quantification of mineral temper, paste varieties and porosity.

One hundred-and-eight samples of pottery and clay were analyzed by Instrumental Neutron Activation Analysis (INAA) using the SLOWPOKE facility at the University of Toronto. Twelve short-lived isotopes were examined including a representation of major, minor and trace elements. INAA can provide highly accurate and detailed data on elemental composition, and has been used successfully in a number of archaeological contexts (Stimmell et al. 1986).

A number of replication experiments were conducted to test assumptions about the production of Thule pottery, and to test Arctic clay sources for their suitability as pottery clays. Experiments on the use of organic materials in the manufacture of pottery was done by Karen Edwards, a master's degree candidate from the Museum Studies program at the University of Toronto.

Sixty-seven samples of pottery, clay and soil were tested for the presence of organic materials, particularly blood. Determining the presence of blood in pottery samples focused on the detection of the major constituent of blood, hemoglobin, using colourmetric tests and electrophoresis (Gurfinkel and Franklin 1988). The results of these tests will be discussed later.

The Palaeoeskimo Pottery Tradition

Denbigh wares

Current evidence indicates that pottery was introduced into Alaska around 1500 B.C. from Late Neolithic Siberian complexes. Ackerman (1982: 32) suggests that the Chukotka region of Siberia is the most probable source for early Alaska wares. This area, however, was peripheral to the developments happening elsewhere in major Asian ceramic industries. Recent changes in the access to Siberian collections should help researchers gain a better understanding of the relationships between Siberian wares and early Alaskan material.

The earliest ceramic finds are associated with late Denbigh components of the Arctic Small Tool tradition in northwestern Alaska. While pottery is not commonly found on Denbigh sites, a few, small collections of sherds have been excavated.

Stanford (1971, 1976) recovered pottery from two components of his Walakpa phase of the Arctic Small Tool tradition south of Point Barrow (Figure 1). This phase has been dated by ^{14}C to 1450 B.C. (Stanford 1976: 16). Over 150 sherds were found in association with Denbigh artifacts at

Coffin and Walakpa.

Most of the collection is made up of very small (under 2 cm), thin (average around 8 mm in thickness) sherds. Sherds are generally soft and low-fired. Their reddish-brown colour suggests that the sherds were fired in an oxidizing atmosphere. They are predominately tempered with round, coarse sand (temper here refers to purposeful additions to the paste rather than aplastics which occur naturally in the clay). Almost 50% of the sherds also have small amounts of fibre temper whose impressions suggest hair was used. Feather impressions are visible in a very small number of sherds.

Almost half of the exterior surfaces are undecorated and exhibit plain, unburnished finishes. The remaining exterior surfaces are covered with linear impressions. The linear impressions were applied either in a parallel, crossed-hatched or herring-bone pattern (Figure 2), and many of these have been partly smoothed over. Some interior walls were also imprinted.

Figure 2 Late Denbigh pottery sherds, Coffin Site.

Hurley et al. (In Press) has identified the linear decorations as fine engraved-dowel rouletting rather than stamped designs. Some of the engraved-dowel decoration resembles close, simple-twined basketry. However, the sherds were too small to make a positive identification. Two sherds have smoothed-over, large (5 mm x 3 mm) check impressions.

Because of the limited number of samples and the small size of most sherds, it is difficult to gauge overall vessel shape or size. However, two sherds from near the base suggest that vessel bottoms were rounded. Three sherds had repair holes drilled from the exterior, adjacent to a fracture. No ceramic lamps were noted in any ASTt assemblage.

Irving recovered a small amount of pottery from "site Nine, at North Point (Punyik Point)" associated with the Arctic Small Tool tradition component (Irving 1962: 78 and pers. comm.). The sherds are very thin (3-5 mm), and have very little visible mineral temper although fibre temper is present in small quantities. The exterior of the sherds are impressed with either cord-marks or rouletting (Hurley et al. In Press). The cord-marks are caused by impressing a simple twined basket onto the surface of an unfired vessel. Two types of engraved-dowel rouletting were identified (Hurley et al. In Press).

Hurley noted similarities between the rouletting found on the early Alaskan samples he examined and pottery from Japanese Middle Jomon sites of approximately the same age. While these ceramic decorative attributes do not indicate a direct relationship between Alaskan and Jomon pottery, they suggest a common Asian root for this trait.

Pottery has also been attributed to ASTt components at Engigstciak (Clark 1976; MacNeish 1959), although no detailed analysis of this material is as yet available. A superficial examination of the Engigstciak collection noted many similarities to the Coffin and Punyik Point assemblages.

However, a large portion of the Engigstciak material is in such poor condition that it will be difficult to analyze.

Unfortunately, most of the late Denbigh pottery is in a very poor state of preservation, often with either interior or exterior surfaces missing. There appears to be a direct relationship between the state of oxidation of the sherds, and their condition. Sherds which have been totally oxidized, either in their initial firing or in subsequent use, are smaller and more exfoliated than sherds still retaining a grey, carbon core. The poor condition of most Denbigh sherds may explain why so little pottery has been recovered from ceramic Denbigh sites. This is not to suggest, however, that pottery was necessarily present on most ASTt components.

Choris wares

After 1600 B.C., another Arctic Small Tool Tradition complex called Choris emerges (Anderson 1984: 85). Pottery very similar to the earlier Denbigh material is found on some, but not all Choris sites. As would be expected, ceramics from Choris (Giddings 1957, 1968), closely resemble the late Denbigh wares in decorative style and surface treatment, although Denbigh sites produced higher percentages of plain pottery. Unlike the Denbigh pottery, however, the Choris material is tempered exclusively with feathers, and mineral temper is uncommon. Because later Norton wares can contain significant amounts of mineral temper, it is most likely that these differences in tempering material relate to local resource utilization rather than a temporal trend.

It is interesting to note that experiments by Skibo et al. (1988) suggest that there is a relationship between the use of fibre temper and a population's mobility. Fibre temper vessels are about 30% lighter, making them easier to transport. Furthermore, the addition of fibre allows the potter to work with wetter, more plastic clays and adds green-strength to the vessel before it is fired. There may be a correlation between the differential use of fibre and mineral temper in Choris and Norton ceramics, and seasonal movement to capitalize on differing local resources. The production of pottery on Choris sites does not appear to be linked to other cultural innovations, because the time and sequence of its introduction varied by region.

Norton wares

Norton is the first North American Arctic culture for which there is evidence of a well-established ceramic industry. Norton sites are concentrated in western Alaska with a distribution ranging from the Alaskan Peninsula in the south to Point Barrow and the northern Yukon Territory in the north. Norton sites were occupied from about 500 B.C. to A.D.400 (Dumond 1977: 106), and much of Norton stone technology is derived from Denbigh and Choris (Anderson 1984: 88).

Because Norton ceramics have been described extensively elsewhere (Ackerman 1982; Griffin 1953; Griffin and Wilmeth 1964; Oswalt 1955), they will only be characterized briefly here. Norton pottery is generally divided into three basic types: Norton Plain, Norton Check Stamp, and Norton Linear Stamp. The check and linear impressions may have been applied to the pottery with either a carved paddle, a stamp or by rouletting (Hurley et al. In Press) and occur in a variety of patterns.

Cord-marked pottery is found but has a limited temporal and areal distribution (Ackerman 1982: 19).

Norton ceramics are predominantly tempered with feathers. However, pottery from both the southern and northern limits of the Norton range do contain higher percentages of sand and grit temper (Ackerman 1982: 17-18). Norton pots have flat bottoms and straight sides, and were made using the paddle-and-anvil method. Pottery lamps are oval or round bowl-like forms with plain surfaces (Giddings 1964: 169-70).

Although, Norton ceramics show a close continuity with earlier Denbigh and Choris materials, some differences are apparent. On many Norton sites such as Iyatayet (Griffin and Wilmeth 1964) and Unalakleet (Lutz 1970), the pottery contains a much higher percentage of fibre temper than was noted in the Denbigh wares examined. Conversely, the Norton wares have only half as much mineral temper as the Coffin and Walakpa sherds (31% at Coffin as apposed to 15% at Iyatayet) (Wilmeth, n.d.). The Punyik Point materials also have very little mineral temper, again suggesting that this attribute may not be directly related to temporal differences.

Check stamping appears to be rare on Denbigh sites and was not noted in the Choris collection. Norton Check Stamp, however, is a common decorative form on Norton sites. The check-stamp impressions on sherds from the Coffin site are significantly larger than the normal Norton check stamp impressions. Dentate stamp, which is also rare on Norton sites, was not noted in either the Denbigh or Choris collections I examined.

Cord-marking on pottery is the oldest decorative form in the world, and it would appear to be a horizon marker for early pottery in Alaska as well. In addition to the Denbigh sites, early Norton pottery with cord-marking has been identified from the Brooks River (Dumond 1969), Choris (Anderson 1980), Kotzebue Sound, Kuskokwim-Bristol (Ackerman 1982: 19) and Firth River areas (MacNeish 1956: 100). Hurley et al. (In Press) has identified the cord-marking on some of the early Arctic ceramics as basketry impressions.

It seems likely that cord-marked and linear-stamped (rouletted) pottery is earlier than check-stamping in Norton assemblages. These decorative treatments appear to have been gradually replaced by check-stamped wares. There also appears to be a corresponding reduction in the amount of undecorated pottery over time. However, these trends also have an areal component. For example, check-stamping is early south of Norton Sound.

While pottery is a common feature of Norton sites, the production of ceramics did not spread into all contemporary Arctic cultures. Ipiutak, while noted for the beauty and elaborateness of its art styles, did not produce ceramics although many other Ipiutak artifacts are similar to Norton types (Anderson 1984: 88).

The Neoeskimo Pottery Tradition

Birnirk wares

Around A.D.500, on the northern coast of Alaska, a new Arctic culture was introduced. Birnirk shares a number of characteristics with cultures which developed on the Siberian coast and

Saint Lawrence Islands, such as Early Punuk, Old Bering Sea and Okvik (Anderson 1984: 91).

While Birnirk pottery ultimately may be derived from the Norton tradition, it is quite distinct in its manufacturing techniques and decorative styles, and represents the emergence of a new ceramic technology in the Arctic. Griffin and Wilmeth (1964: 287) characterized these changes as "a trend toward increasing vessel wall thickness, increasing coarseness of paste, and increasing size and abundance of sand and pebble temper". Other differences between Birnirk and Norton pottery include firing atmosphere and method of decoration.

Birnirk vessels have walls almost twice as thick as Norton pottery; walls of both pots and lamps average around 14mm in thickness. Rims and bases of both vessel types, however, are thicker than body sherds, ranging from 18 to 26 mm.

Birnirk pottery is also very heavily tempered compared to earlier Norton materials. Mineral temper—very coarse sand or beach gravel less than 1 cm in size—can form up to 40% of the paste. The choice of temper size appears to be related to vessel wall thickness, although this distinction is not absolute. Thinner walled vessels generally had the smaller size temper. This temper size/wall thickness relationship had been previously noted on Thule sites from Banks Island (Arnold and Stimmell 1983).

About 60% of the sherds also contain feather or fibre temper. However, this organic material only represents between 2 and 10% of the paste. While Birnirk wares are low-fired and heavily reduced, they are usually well preserved. The pottery itself is carefully made, often with skilfully executed decorative designs.

Exterior surfaces are either plain or covered with curvilinear paddle impressions (Barrow Curvilinear). A number of whale bone paddles with concentric circle designs which could have produced such patterns have been excavated from Birnirk sites (B. Carter 1985: pers. comm.; Ford 1959: 205).

It was difficult to determine the exact amounts of decorated and plain pottery because many sherds are covered with thick carbon encrustations. Ford (1959: 200-201) reported that in the collection he studied, about 25% of the pottery was enhanced with curvilinear impressions. In addition to the paddle impressions, some rims are decorated with incised linear or diagonal lines or punctations (Figure 3). The diagonal lines were produced by rocker stamping. Observations on a limited sample suggest that rims are predominantly flat in shape. All pottery vessels have vertical walls and some have thickened conchoidal bases.

Figure 3 Birnirk sherd, Point Barrow.

Ford describes the pots as "bag-shaped vessels" (1959: 204).

A small percentage of sherds also have exterior cord or fibre impressions (basketry or textile). Interior cord-marking was noted on a few lamps. Plain sherds are occasionally lightly burnished.

Pottery lamps are numerous. Two general types of lamps were noted in the Birnirk site collection at Harvard's Peabody Museum: a shallow, saucer-shaped bowl which is either oval to round in shape, and a deeper vessel with a stepped profile, perhaps forming a small wick ledge. This second form was not observed by Ford (1959) at Point Barrow. Those he did find range in size from 25 to 35 cm in diameter (Ford 1959: 202).

Late Neoeskimo wares

While late Neoeskimo wares shares a number of characteristics with earlier Birnirk material, including the use of the Barrow Curvilinear paddle designs, they are coarser, less well-made, thicker and have fewer decorative modes. Late Neoeskimo pottery has been generally characterized as

> very thick, crumbles easily, and has a marked tendency to exfoliate. It is tempered with a very coarse gravel, and is poorly fired. It is black throughout, and is coated with burned grease and permeated with fat (de Laguna 1947: 233).

In fact, most late Neoeskimo artifacts are neither as carefully made, nor as aesthetically pleasing as Birnirk forms. However, late Neoeskimo artifacts types tend to be more versatile and utilitarian (B. Carter 1985: pers. comm.).

The one major late Neoeskimo ware type that is recognized—Barrow—is divided into plain and decorated forms. The decorated type is identical to the plain, with the exception that exteriors are stamped with curvilinear designs made with a carved paddle (Figure 4). Barrow Curvilinear wares are very similar to Birnirk wares. However, Barrow Curvilinear sherds normally form only a very small percentage of the pottery found on late Neoeskimo sites (under 5%). Many late Neoeskimo sites contain no Barrow Curvilinear pottery at all.

There are two major functional types of late Neoeskimo ceramics, lamps and cooking pots. Ethnographic reports suggest that pots were used primarily for cooking by the stone-boiling method. Some ceramic vessels have suspension holes indicating that they may have been hung over a fire, although Morrison (1990) noted that holes in a vessel from the late pre-contact site of Iglulualuit could not have been used for either suspension or repair holes because of their location and size. But it should be pointed out that ceramics from Iglulualuit were not necessarily typical of late Neoeskimo wares, as a number of unusual vessel forms were recovered including bowls and plates (Morrison 1990).

The poor condition of most of the excavated material makes vessel reconstruction very difficult. However, measurements indicate that a large majority of pots were the same size with rim diameters around 26 cm. Two different cooking vessel shapes have been identified: a situla type with angled shoulders, constricting neck and flaring mouth (Vanstone 1968: 280), and a barrel type with straight sides (Figure 5). Both flat and gently rounded bottoms are found, but the type of narrow pointed bottom described by Ford (1959) from Birnirk has not been reported. The regional significance of vessel shape will be discussed later.

The thickness of a late Neoeskimo vessel varies considerably from the rim to the base. The thickness of the average cooking pot wall is around 14 mm. Vessel bases are often over 40 mm thick. Lamp walls are generally thicker averaging around 26 cm.

Ceramic oil lamps have flat to gently sloping bottoms with short, curved, shallow walls. Rims occasionally have massive lips made of additional wedges of clay folded around the exterior. The heavier edges may have served as handles or been designed to provide vessel stability.

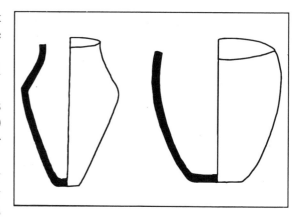

Figure 4 Typical Thule vessel shapes; *l*-situla-shaped, *r*-barrel-shaped.

"Baked ware" has been reported from a number of late Neoeskimo sites (McGhee 1974; Morrison 1983; Yorga 1980). Baked wares are either untempered or contain small amounts of sand and fibre. The sherds are thin (4-6 mm), and often cracked during manufacture and firing. Unlike almost all other late Neoeskimo pottery, the baked ware is oxidized and not coated in oil which suggests that it was probably never used for either cooking or heating. Some of the baked ware sherds appear to have come from small bowls and may be examples of pottery produced for special purposes such as ceremonial use or experiments by apprentice potters. They do not appear to be related to earlier Palaeoeskimo wares.

Only a few cases of non-vessel use of ceramic materials were observed. At the Nelson River sites on Banks Island, two sherds were discovered which had been polished on at least two adjacent surfaces. It is possible that these sherds were used as boot sole creasers (Arnold and Stimmell 1983: 8). I have identified similar specimens from Norton sites in Alaska. At the Kugaluk site, just east of the Mackenzie Delta, a small (30 mm diameter) unfired pottery ball was excavated (Morrison 1988). While it is possible that this object was wastage from the production of pottery, its carefully smoothed surface suggests that its shape was intentional.

The majority of late Neoeskimo pottery

Figure 5 Barrow Curvilinear pattern in Thule sherd.

is tempered with large amounts of mineral inclusions. The amount, size and type of temper has technological significance and discrete regional distribution: these will be discussed later.

A large percentage of the pottery also contains a variety of fibrous material. Feathers are the most common form of fibre, but animal hair, plants such as grasses and sedges, wood and even baleen (a keratin product of whales) are present in some assemblages. The amount of fibre temper in late Neoeskimo pottery varies from vessel to vessel, but is generally less than 20% by volume. Pots with larger amounts of fibre (in excess of 15%) have a tendency to exfoliate. Fibre-temper improves the dry-strength, and would have considerably reduced the time needed to dry the vessel before firing. It would also reduce the tendency of the thick-walled late Neoeskimo vessels to crack while drying and firing. Fibre-temper is believed to reduce thermally created stress by dissipating the stress through crack-arresting pores (Rye 1981: 114-116).

A large number of late Eskimo sherds are encrusted with a thick deposit of carbonized food residues (Figure 6). The surface carbon deposits make it difficult to determine the vessel's surface treatment, so that decorated pottery may be under-reported. The heavy covering also has an influence on porosity, reducing it by at least 40%. Porosity can be further lowered by post-burial alterations.

Petrographic thin sections from a number of western late Neoeskimo sites reveal that an iron-based mineral closely related to hematite had been deposited in many of the available pores. In addition, a small number of sherds have a deposit of vivianite on exterior surfaces. Vivianite is an iron phosphate compound which appears as a white to bluish-white fine-grained coating, and is also common on other artifacts excavated in the Arctic (Morlan 1980: 55-56).

An extremely high percentage of all late Neoeskimo pottery is heavily reduced. The unoxidized state of the pottery is due to a number of factors, including the short firing regime and the amount of organic material in the original paste. Exterior surfaces are further reduced through their use as cooking or heating vessels. Ethnographic reports suggest that pots may have been purposefully coated with grease or oil before each use to reduce porosity (Spencer 1959: 472). Just as with the Norton materials, the sherds which are either fully or partly oxidized, are in poorer condition than typical late Neoeskimo sherds.

After examining pottery from a number of late Neoeskimo sites, it became apparent

Figure 6 Typical Thule sherd from barrel-shaped vessel.

that, while all late Neoeskimo pottery shares a number of characteristics, it can divided into three major groups which have definite regional distributions: Western, Eastern and Mackenzie Delta. The attributes which seem to have the most significance in defining these groups include mineral temper type, vessel shape (including rim profile), firing regime and manufacturing techniques.

Western Late Neoeskimo

The Western late Neoeskimo ceramic complex is found on sites in Northern Alaska and Canada, west of, and including, Coronation Gulf. Western late Neoeskimo is perhaps closest to what is generally considered to be 'typical' late Neoeskimo pottery. Pottery from Banks Island (Nelson River sites), Jackson, Vaughan, Walakpa, and Coronation Gulf sites (Bloody Falls, Lady Franklin Point, Beulah, Clachan, Nuvuk) was used in characterizing the Western late Neoeskimo ceramic complex (Figure 1). This group encompasses both Western Thule and later Clachan Phase sites.

The most commonly utilized mineral temper was sedimentary-derived coarse sand and gravel. This material can form up to 50% of the paste in some vessels. Quartz sandstone, potassium feldspars and chert were the most abundantly identified minerals in petrographic thin sections. Chalcedony, siltstone, quartzite, biotite and shale were also observed. Siltstones showed bedding marks and cherts retained oolitic structures. In some samples, significant amounts of rounded limestone fragments were identified. The tempers were probably all locally obtained from sorted river or beach gravels. Fibre temper is also common in Western Thule pottery. Plants, feathers, wood and baleen were all utilized.

A thin-section of a sherd from Bloody Falls revealed evidence of the use of grog (sherd) temper. Grog temper is common in late prehistoric pottery from the southcentral and southwestern United States, but has not been previously reported from the Arctic. Grog temper is undoubtedly under-reported in other areas as well because it can often only be identified in thin-section. The Bloody Falls sherd was identical to other late Neoeskimo sherds in all other respects. This may be an example of late Neoeskimo potters experimenting with new tempering materials and pottery techniques. On some western late Neoeskimo sites, the size and amount of mineral temper varies according to the function of the vessel. For example, at the Nelson River Thule sites on Banks Island (A.D.1000), two sizes of rounded beach gravel were utilized for temper (Arnold and Stimmell 1983). The smaller temper (5-10 mm) was only used in smaller, thinner-walled vessels. The larger temper (10-15 mm) was associated with pottery lamps and the largest, thick-walled pots. This variation in temper was alsonoted in the Birnirk material.

The reason for the use of two different temper sizes may be technological. Lamps with their thicker walls and gently rounded shape would have greater resistance to thermal shock (Rye 1981), while cooking pots with their finer textured paste would have greater mechanical strength (Steponaitis 1980) allowing them to be moved with greater safety.

From Instrumental Neutron Activation Analysis (INAA) and comparative refiring data done on the Banks Island assemblage, it appears that all of the lamps and pots were manufactured using the same clay; only the tempering material was altered.

X-ray diffraction patterns of pottery from Banks Island suggests that the pottery was very low-fired, i.e. under 650° C. This temperature is not high enough to chemically alter clay minerals into a permanent ceramic product (750° C). The poor condition of most late Neoeskimo pottery is most likely the result of consistent under-firing. This would not have affected the usefulness of the vessel, but it does complicate the work of archaeologists considerably.

About 5% of Western late Neoeskimo pottery is decorated with curvilinear paddle impressions. The decorated pottery is similar in all other respects to plain pottery, although very few lamps are decorated.

While both barrel and situla-shaped vessels occur, Western late Neoeskimo sites contain a high proportion of straight-sided cooking pots. Rims are predominantly straight or simple convex in profile, and some have a small interior channel. Vessel wall thickness averages 13 mm. Bases are thicker (21 mm), and either flat or gently rounded in shape. However, both Cape Perry sites (Jackson and Vaughan) have higher percentages of the situla-shaped vessels with channelled rims. This may reflect their location close to the Mackenzie Delta where situla-shaped vessels are common. Both Jackson and Vaughan also have a higher percentage of Barrow Curvilinear wares than most Western late Neoeskimo sites.

Pottery lamps are circular or oval in shape. While it is difficult to estimate vessel counts, it would appear that ceramic lamps form about 5 - 10% of the assemblage on Western late Neoeskimo sites.

Western late Neoeskimo pottery is very similar in technology and style to its Birnirk predecessor. Similarly, there are few differences in the pottery from early and late Western late Neoeskimo sites, although later sites have far fewer examples of pottery lamps.

Mackenzie Delta

The second Neoeskimo pottery complex is centred in the Mackenzie Delta. Pottery from four sites was examined: Kittigazuit, Cache Point, Radio Creek, and the historic Kugaluk site (Figure 1). Unlike the Western and Eastern late Neoeskimo pottery complexes, the late Neoeskimo ceramics from the Mackenzie Delta region are generally later in time. While in adjacent areas, the sites which provided the late Neoeskimo ceramics are of Thule cultural affiliation, those of the Mackenzie Delta region are better described as post-Thule, Inuvialuit sites.

Mackenzie Delta pottery differs from the Western late Neoeskimo ceramic complex in two major aspects: use of tempering material and vessel shape.

While beach gravel and limestone was used as a tempering material in the Mackenzie Delta, the most common mineral temper is freshly fractured granite cobbles. Experimental evidence indicates that in coarse aggregates, the roughness of the surface texture increases tensile and flexural strength by improving the bond between the paste and the aggregate (Popovics 1979: 230). The angular grains of freshly-fractured granite have better cohesive properties than the water-worn beach gravel commonly used in Western late Neoeskimo pottery. Granite cobbles are common in the Delta. After extensive use as boiling stones, the cobbles would degrade, providing a practical source of tempering material for the potter.

There is a much greater variety of vessel shapes and rim profiles on Mackenzie Delta sites than from Western late Neoeskimo assemblages. The most common type of vessel shape is the situla with angular shoulders (Figure 5). Rim profiles of situla-shaped vessels include constricted neck with flaring rim, and both single and double exterior channels (Sutton and Stimmell 1985). Barrel or straight-sided vessels do occur, but are much less common than on Western late Neoeskimo sites. Bases are flat or pedestal in shape, and no round bottom vessels were noted. Between five and ten percent of the sherds in the Mackenzie Delta are decorated with a curvilinear paddle.

Over seventy percent of the vessels from Cache Point and Radio Creek are situla-shaped. However, vessels from Kittigazuit, which date somewhat later, are almost equally split between situla and straight-sided forms. There are similarities between the vessel shapes and rim profiles found on Mackenzie Delta wares and interior Alaska pottery (Sutton and Stimmell 1985). McGhee (1974: 87) has suggested that there is a "general similarity" between the Mackenzie Delta late Neoeskimo material culture, and that from the Kobuk and Noatak Rivers in northwestern Alaska. However, there are also examples of ceramics, such as a vessel from Kittigazuit with a triangular shaped rim-profile, which show affinities to Birnirk and north Alaskan material. Morrison (1990) suggests that the Mackenzie Delta Inuit had trade networks with a number of areas to the west, and this may be a factor in the development of such "foreign" traits.

Lamps are not as common in the Mackenzie Delta as on early Western late Neoeskimo sites, and there is not a clear-cut differentiation in the amount and size of mineral temper used in the manufacture of pots and lamps. There does seem to be some correlation between vessel shape and temper type, however. While situla-shaped vessels can contain either granite or beach gravel temper, the straight-sided vessels are tempered only with granite.

Most of the sites in the Mackenzie Delta share stylistic elements. However, pottery from the historic Kugaluk site has a number of anomalous characteristics (Morrison 1988). The sherds are thinner (9 mm) and have less mineral temper. The rim sherd profiles are not typical of other late Neoeskimo types, and two sherds are coated with a black organic slip or paint on the exterior surface. The slipped surface was also burnished.

Eastern Late Neoeskimo

Pottery is extremely rare on late Neoeskimo sites in the Eastern Arctic. Even those sites which have produced pottery (all Thule culture sites), rarely produce more than a handful of sherds, and 90% of these come from lamps. Pottery samples from Skraeling Island, Brooman Point, Porden Point, Crystal II and Cornwallis Island were used in this analysis (Figure 1).

A number of factors may have contributed to the dearth of eastern pottery. There are very few workable clay deposits in the Canadian Shield geological province which forms the bedrock in the eastern Arctic. Scarcity of fuel would also have been a major problem in the production of pottery. Driftwood, which is abundant in western coastal regions, is at a premium further north and east. Soapstone vessels are also much better suited for cooking over a seal oil fire then are friable clay pots.

Perhaps because of these limitations and the availability of alternate materials for vessels—limestone and soapstone—very few ceramic cooking pots were manufactured. Pottery lamps were produced, but are very different from their western counterparts. While the overall shape is similar, eastern lamps are generally larger and shaped like very shallow saucers. The lamps are tempered with large amounts of hair or plant fibre (over 25%). Mineral temper is often sand or small gravel and may, in some instances, be detrital to a very poor quality clay.

The lamps were manufactured by loosely joining overlapping coils together. The poor quality of the clay often prevented the coils from bonding properly and coil fractures are very common. This method of producing pottery is characteristic of Eastern late Neoeskimo sites. However, the Cape Perry sites of Vaughan and Jackson have examples of lamps made in a similar manner.

On a number of eastern sites, lamps were made of a combination of materials. The walls would be constructed of pottery, while the base was a soapstone or limestone slab. In these cases, the shape of the vessel was more similar to soapstone lamps than to ceramic lamps. Pottery was also commonly used to repair soapstone vessels which had broken (McGhee 1984: 69) or as a cement to hold limestone slabs together (Mathiassen 1927: 99,231).

One of the most interesting discoveries about the Eastern late Neoeskimo ceramic complex is that a large number of pottery lamps had never been fired (Figure 7). Uncarbonized plant fibre and animal hair is present throughout the fabric of the sherds, even on exterior surfaces. Lamps would not necessarily ever come in contact with a direct flame during normal usage, and so the fibre would never be burnt off.

The ethnographic literature does cite instances where some Inuit pottery was baked rather than fired. In an account of pottery manufacture in Kotzebue Sound, Stefansson (1914: 312) states that "pots were never burned, nor even allowed to get very hot on drying". Mathiassen (1927: 67) reports in a chemical analysis of sherds from the Naujan site on Repulse Bay: "The whole chemical composition of the sample showed that the vessel cannot have been subjected to any actual baking operation." Bogoras noted that historic pottery made on the Siberian coast was simply dried and soaked in oil before use (cited in Mathiassen 1927: 106).

Figure 7 Unfired pottery lamp section, Skraeling Island.

Sun-dried or baked clay vessels will deteriorate when wet and have little mechanical strength. It was hypothesized that late Neoeskimo potters were able to produce durable unfired pottery lamps by adding organic liquids, particularly blood, to the clay body during manufacture. This process would have created a grit-and-fibre reinforced polymer composite material (Arnold and Stimmell 1983; Stimmell and Stromberg 1986).

Polymers, such as blood, are strongly attracted to the lattice structure of clay minerals. When blood is added to a pottery mixture, the particles of clay act like a filler to stiffen the polymer chains and produce a crystallization of the system (Mark 1967: 92). This 'cementation' process can be made more permanent by heat-setting or baking the mixture.

To test whether any trace of blood could be detected in late Neoeskimo pottery, 67 samples of pottery, soil and clay were subject to colourmetric and electrophoresis analysis (Gurfinkel and

Franklin 1988). Because replication experiments indicated that blood residue is totally destroyed at temperatures over 100° C, only unfired pottery was tested. Other researchers working with spectrographic analysis have also failed to establish the presence of blood in fired ceramics (Duma and Lengyel 1969).

Clay and soil samples from the Arctic tested negative for protein in all cases, although some clay samples were weakly positive for heme—both the heme group and the protein must test positive for the presence of blood to be absolutely confirmed. Almost all samples of unfired pottery tested positive for both heme and protein, although the protein could not be identified as globin. It is likely that globin is too fragile to survive after long burial in Arctic conditions. This strongly suggests that blood was used in the production of Eastern late Neoeskimo pottery.

Examples of unfired pottery outside of the Eastern Arctic are rare. Two samples of unfired pottery from the Mackenzie Delta (one each from Kugaluk and Cache Point) and one lamp from Vaughan were analyzed. The Kugaluk sample (an unfired clay ball) tested negative for both heme and protein, while the Cache Point sherd tested weakly positive for heme. The Vaughan lamp sample, although very similar to Eastern late Neoeskimo lamps in appearance, failed to test positive for blood. While it is possible that blood may have been used in the manufacture of western and Mackenzie Delta pottery, these results suggest that this technology was restricted to eastern sites.

In addition to blood, the ethnographic literature lists a number of ingredients which Inuit informants considered essential to the manufacturing process, including feathers, hair, grease, and fish oil (Gordon 1906: 84; Mathiassen 1927: 231 and 271). While animal blood was the most commonly mentioned additive, replication studies indicated that fat, blood and fibre temper were equally important elements in creating a durable low or unfired pot. Test tiles made with blood, or blood and fibre alone, were not as durable as those with all three components (K. Edwards, pers. comm.).

Organic fluids such as blood are useful as pepisators to increase the workability of a poor quality clay. Animal blood can also be used as a glue or cement. Glues made of blood were commonly used until the 1930s in the manufacture of plywood (Bogue 1922: 347). Mathiassen (1927: 231) reported that the Sadlermiut of Hudson Bay used a mixture of blood, soot and dog hair to cement limestone slabs together. Soapstone vessels were repaired with a similar adhesive (Anderson 1857: 328; Birket-Smith 1929, Part 1: 236; Hough 1898: 1032 cited in deLaguna 1947: 235). Composite wood artifacts such as bows were also glued together with blood (C. Arnold pers. comm.).

The only eastern site from which a large amount of pottery, both lamps and cooking-pots, has been excavated, is Skraeling Island. The lamps from Skraeling are similar to other Eastern late Neoeskimo pottery lamps. However, the cooking vessels are most comparable to Western late Neoeskimo pots. Schledermann and McCullough (1980) see an affinity between the Ruin Island phase architecture and material culture, and early Western late Neoeskimo in the Kotzebue Sound/Bering Strait region.

To test for the possibility that the Barrow Curvilinear essels may have been imported, sherds from Skraeling Island were subjected to INAA. Three groups of pottery were distinguishable (Table 1).

Table 1 INAA results from Skraeling Island pottery.

	BARROW CURVILINEAR	BARROW PLAIN POTS	LAMPS
U ppm	2.50±.8	2.77±.7	1.51±.3
Dy ppm	2.79±.6	3.77±.4	2.27±.6
Ba ppm	466±183	554±99	580±96
Ti ppm	2638±390	2629±357	3516±637
Mg %	3.24±.8	2.77±.7	2.57±.6
Na ppm	7787±1132	9245±4739	17389±2633
V ppm	107±27	60±22	80±13
Al %	9.14±1.3	8.11±1.3	6.03±.7
Mn ppm	709±194	512±118	514±102
Cl ppm	155±45	254±38	231±92
Ca %	4.4±2.1	3.0±1.0	4.4±.7
	N=4	N=5	N=8

The pottery lamps have low values of Al, but high concentrations of Na, Ca and Ti. The decorated cooking pots (Barrow Curvilinear) have high elemental concentrations of Al and Ca, but are low in Na and Cl. The plain cooking pots are low in Na and Ca, and high in Cl. Some of the elemental variation between the plain and decorated pots could be due to differences in tempering material, but it appears that the pots and lamps were made from very different clay sources, increasing the likelihood that the pots may have been imported.

Summary and Conclusions

There are two distinct prehistoric pottery traditions found in the North American Arctic. Pottery was introduced into the North American Arctic around 1500 B.C., and found on a few late Denbigh components of the Arctic Small Tool tradition. Characteristics of this ceramic tradition, which are better known from Norton sites, include thin-walled vessels tempered with small amounts of either fibre or grit. The pottery was fired in an oxidizing atmosphere. Pots are straight-sided with either flat or gently rounded bases. Decorative modes include check or linear stamping (rouletting) and cord-marking (basketry). This tradition is centred in Alaska and the western Yukon.

After A.D.500, Norton ceramics are replaced by a very different ware type. Birnirk and late Neoeskimo pottery is thick-walled and tempered with large amounts of both grit and fibre. Most sherds are covered with a thick coating of carbon encrustations and are heavily reduced. Only one ware type is defined: Barrow.

During the late Neoeskimo period, the pottery can be divided into three regional groupings: Western, Mackenzie Delta and Eastern. The Western ceramic complex represents the most typical late Neoeskimo ceramics. The Mackenzie Delta pottery is very similar to Western late Neoeskimo technologically, but stylistically has a greater variety of vessel shapes. The Eastern complex represents a totally new innovation to ceramic technology. Pottery lamps are produced without firing through the use of organic cements. Ceramics are sporadically manufactured until the early historic period, at which time soapstone—abundant in the Eastern Arctic, easily worked and available either locally or through trade—supplants pottery.

Table 2 INAA results from Point Barrow, Alaska.

	BIRNIRK	WALAKPA (THULE)	COFFIN (DENBIGH)
U ppm	3.55±.4	3.40±.4	4.27±.9
Dy ppm	3.96±.5	3.48±.9	4.37±.7
Ba ppm	824±92	705±86	768±157
Ti ppm	3913±705	4065±685	5161±669
Mg %	1.31±.7	1.47±.7	1.58±.7
Na ppm	10536±7443	6784±3626	7972±854
V ppm	146±17	167±18	170±27
Al %	6.53±.8	7.28±.7	7.71±.7
Mn ppm	364±178	317±82	501±211
Cl ppm	1871±506	846±437	NA
Ca %	1.1±.9	.6±.1	.3±.1
	N=8	N=11	N=6

Late Neoeskimo pottery has often been assumed to be an archetype of technological "degeneration". I would suggest, however, that late Neoeskimo ceramics are a better example of the ability of craftsmen to modify known techniques to suit local environmental situations.

However, not all changes in Arctic pottery technology can be attributed to environmental adaptation. In Northern Alaska, INAA results suggest that the raw materials used in the production of pottery remained unchanged from late ASTt times through the Neoeskimo period (Table 2). Factors such as changes in social patterns and scheduling may have played a part in changing pottery production techniques. Here it is interesting to note that, at least in the historic period, there was a sexual element in the production of different types of vessels: men worked with soapstone and women manufactured pottery. Fluctuations in seasonal mobility could also have an effect on the ability to manufacture pottery in a region where the amount of time in which ceramics can be produced successfully is very short.

Conditions faced by prehistoric potters in the Canadian Arctic must be close to the ultimate 'bottom line' for the production of ceramics. The climate, scarcity of resources and prehistoric lifestyle, all mitigate against the development of a thriving pottery industry. Nevertheless, for over 3000 years, potters were able to produce a durable, useful product which served the needs of their community, a testament to the ingenuity of prehistoric Arctic peoples.

Acknowledgements

I would like to acknowledge all of the researchers who allowed me to not only examine their ceramics, but destroy bits and pieces in the name of science. Many thanks to Chuck Arnold, Dennis Stanford, David Morrison, Richard Stromberg, Robert Park, William Irving, Karen McCullough, Robert McGhee, and William Taylor. Ellen Blaubergs and Jean-Luc Pilon, who served as proof readers, and Michèlle Tremblay, who provided the illustrations also made important contributions.

I would also like to acknowledge Chuck Arnold and William Irving who were very supportive of my original research proposal. A large portion of this work was made possible by a Social Science and Humanities Research Council Grant.

References

Ackerman, R.E. 1982. The Neolithic-Bronze Age Cultures of Asia and the Norton Phase of Alaskan prehistory. Arctic Anthropology, 19(2): 11-38.

Anderson, D.D. 1980. Continuity and change in the Prehistoric Record from North Alaska. In, Alaska Native Culture and History, Y. Kotani and W.B. Workman, eds. Senri Ethnological Series No. 4: 233-251.

Anderson, D.D. 1984. Prehistory of North Alaska. In, Handbook of North American Indians, Vol. 5, Arctic, D. Damas, ed. Washington: Smithsonian Institute, pp. 80-93.

Anderson, J. 1857. Extracts from Chief Factor Anderson's Journal. Communicated by Sir John Richardson. Royal Geographical Society Journal, 27: 321-28

Arnold, C. and C. Stimmell. 1983. An analysis of Thule pottery. Canadian Journal of Archaeology, 7(1): 1-21.

Birket-Smith, K. 1929. The Caribou Eskimo; Material and Social Life and Their Cultural Position. Report of the 5th Thule Expedition 1921-24, 5 (1-2). Copenhagen: Gyldendal.

Bogue, R. 1922. The Chemistry and Technology of Gelatin and Glue. New York: McGraw-Hill.

Clark, D. 1976. Progress report on a re-examination of the Engigstciak Site collections. MS on file with the Canadian Museum of Civilization. Hull.

Duma, U.G. and I. Lengyel. 1969. Floureszenzonalytische utersuchungen aus bluthaltigen ton hergenstellter urzeitlicher gefusse. Archaeoligia Austrica, XLV: 1-17

Dumond, D.E. 1969. The prehistoric pottery of Alaska. Anthropological Papers of the University of Alaska, 14: 19-42.

Dumond, D.E. 1977. The Eskimos and Aleuts. London: Thames and Hudson.

de Laguna, F. 1947. The prehistory of northern North America as seen from the Yukon. Memoir of the Society for American Archaeology, 3.

Ford, J.A. 1959. Eskimo Prehistory in the Vicinity of Point Barrow, Alaska. Anthropological Papers of the American Museum of Natural History, 47(1).

Giddings, J.L. 1957. Round Houses in the Western Arctic. American Antiquity, 23: 125-135

Giddings, J.L.1964. The Archaeology of Cape Denbigh. Providence: Brown University Press.

Giddings, J.L.1967. Ancient Men of the Arctic. New York: Alfred A. Knopf.

Giddings, J.L.1968. Archaeological and physiographic investigations in the Kotzebue Sound. MS on file with the Arctic Institute of North America. Calgary.

Gordon, G.B. 1906. Notes on the western Eskimo. Transactions of the Department of Archaeology, Free Museum of Science and Art, II(1): 69-102.

Griffin, J.B. 1953. A Preliminary Statement on the Pottery from Cape Denbigh, Alaska. In, Asia and North America: Trans-Pacific Contacts. M.W. Smith, ed. Memoirs of the Society for American Archaeology, 9: 40-42.

Griffin, J.B. and R.H. Wilmeth, Jr. 1964. Appendix 1: The Ceramic Complexes at Iyatayet. In, The Archaeology of Cape Denbigh, by J. L. Giddings. Providence: Brown University Press, pp. 271-303.

Gurfinkel, D.M. and U.M. Franklin. 1988. A Study of the Feasibility of Detecting Blood Residue on Artifacts. Journal of Archaeological Science, 15: 83-97.

Hurley, W., H. Takamiya, D. Johnson and J.-L. Pilon. In Press. A Re-examination of Ceramic Decoration. In, Eastern Fibre Perishables, Jim Peterson, ed. University of Tennessee Press.

Irving, W.N. 1962. 1961 Field Work in the Western Brooks Range, Alaska: Preliminary Report. Arctic Anthropology, 1(1): 76-83.

Irving, W.N. 1964. Punyik Point and the Arctic Small Tool Tradition. Unpublished Ph.D. Dissertation in Anthropology, University of Wisconsin, Madison.

Lutz, B. 1970. Variations in Checked Pottery from an Archaeological Site near Unalakleet, Alaska. Anthropological Papers of the University of Alaska, 15(1): 33-48.

MacNeish, R.S. 1956. The Engigstciak Site on the Yukon Arctic Coast. Anthropological Papers of the University of Alaska, 4(2): 91-111.

MacNeish, R.S. 1959. Men Out of Asia, as Seen from Northwest Yukon. Annual Papers of the University of Alaska, 7 (2): 41-70.

Mark, H 1967. The nature of polymeric materials. In, Materials. New York: W.H. Freeman, pp. 85-96.

Mathiassen, T. 1927. Archaeology of the Central Eskimo: descriptive part. Report of the Fifth Thule Expedition 1921-24, 4(1). Copenhagen: Gyldendal.

McGhee, R. 1974. Beluga Hunters; An archaeological reconstruction of the history and culture of the Mackenzie Delta Kittegaryumiut. Memorial University of Newfoundland. Newfoundland Social and Economic Studies No. 13.

McGhee, R. 1984. Thule Prehistory of Canada. In, Handbook of North American Indians, Arctic. Vol. 5, Arctic, D. Damas, ed. Washington: Smithsonian Institute, pp. 369-376.

Morlan, R. 1980. Taphonomy and Archaeology in the Upper Pleistocene of the Northern Yukon Territory: A Glimpse of the Peopling of the New World. National Museum of Man, Mercury Series, Archaeological Survey of Canada Paper 94.

Morrison, D. 1983. Thule Culture in Western Coronation Gulf, N.W.T. National Museum of Man, Mercury Series, Archaeological Survey of Canada Paper 116.

Morrison, D. 1988. The Kugaluk site and the Nurvorugmiut: the archaeology and history of a nineteenth-century Mackenzie Inuit society. Canadian Museum of Civilization, Mercury Series, Archaeological Survey of Canada Paper 137.

Morrison, D. 1990. Iglulualumiut prehistory: the lost Inuit of Franklin Bay, N.W.T. Canadian Museum of Civilization, Mercury Series, Archaeological Survey of Canada Paper 142.

Oswalt, W. 1955. Alaskan Pottery: A Classification and Historical Reconstruction. American Antiquity, 21(1): 32-43.

Popovics, S. 1979. Concrete-making Materials. New York: McGraw-Hill.

Rye, O. 1981. Pottery Technology: Principles and Reconstruction. Washington: Taraxacum.

Schledermann, P. and K. McCullough. 1980. Western elements in the early Thule culture of eastern High Arctic. Arctic, 33: 833-41.

Skibo, James., M. Schiffer and K. Reid. 1988. Organic Tempered Pottery: An Experimental Study. Unpublished Manuscript.

Spencer, R. 1959. The North Alaskan Eskimo: a study in ecology and society. Bureau of American Ethnology Bulletin, 171.

Stanford, D. 1971. Evidence of Paleo-Eskimos on the North Coast of Alaska. Paper presented to the 36th Annual Meeting of the Society for American Archaeology. Norman, Oklahoma.

Stanford, D. 1976. The Walakpa site, Alaska. Smithsonian Contributions to Anthropology 20.

Stefansson, V. 1914. The Stefansson-Anderson Arctic Expedition of the American Museum: preliminary ethnographic report. Anthropological Papers of the American Museum of Natural History, 14(1).

Steponaitis, V. 1980. Ceramics, Chronology and Community Patterns at Moundville, a late prehistoric site in Alabama. Unpublished PhD dissertation, University of Michigan.

Stimmell. C.A., J. Pilon and R.G.V. Hancock. 1986. Problems in Coarse Ware Analysis. In, Proceedings of the 24th International Archaeometry Symposium, J.S. Olin and M. J. Blackman, ed. Washington, D.C.:Smithsonian Institution Press, pp. 407-418.

Stimmell, C. and R. Stromberg. 1986. A Reassessment of Thule Eskimo Ceramic Technology. In, Ceramics and Civilization, Vol. 2., W.D. Kingery, ed. American Ceramic Society.

Sutton, R. and C. Stimmell. 1985. A Typological Reassessment of Mackenzie Eskimo Ceramics. Paper presented at the 18th Annual meeting of the Canadian Archaeological Society, Winnipeg.

Vanstone, J. 1968. Tikchik Village, a Nineteenth Century Riverine Community in Southwestern Alaska. Fieldiana: Anthropology, 56 (3).

Wilmeth, R. n.d. Ceramic Collection from the Coffin Site. Unpublished manuscript.

Yorga, B. 1980. Washout: A Western Thule Site on Herschel Island, Yukon Territory. National Museum of Man, Mercury Series, Archaeological Survey of Canada Paper 98.

The Inuvik Phase of the Arctic Small Tool Tradition

Jean-Luc Pilon
Canadian Museum of Civilization
Hull, Quebec

Abstract

Sixteen centuries ago, Palaeoeskimos lived in the southwest Anderson Plain area of Canada's Northwest Territories. Their archaeological remains exhibit links with other sites in the Beaufort Sea-Amundsen Gulf region. These sites of the Inuvik Phase of the Arctic Small Tool tradition are clearly different from the Pre-Dorset sites of the Barrenlands, and much more closely related to the Denbigh Flint Complex of Alaska and Independence I of High Arctic Canada.

Résumé

Seize siècles avant notre ère, des Paléoesquimaux fréquentaient le sud-ouest de la plaine d'Anderson, aux Territoires du Nord-Ouest canadiens. Les restes archéologiques laissés par leur passage nous permettent d'établir des liens avec d'autres sites paléoesquimaux de la région de la mer de Beaufort et du golfe d'Amundsen. Ces sites de la phase Inuvik de la tradition microlithique de l'Arctique se différencient du Prédorsetien des Barrenlands et s'apparentent plutôt au Complexe Denbigh Flint de l'Alaska et à l'Indépendancien I du Haut-Arctique canadien.

Introduction

In the recent past, the Beaufort littoral has suffered greatly from the effects of the relative rise in sea level. Numerous instances can be cited of historic period archaeological sites being totally washed away or well on their way to being so (Le Blanc 1986; McGhee 1969). Present erosion rates vary widely from the Alaska border to the tip of Cape Bathurst Peninsula. The actual annual rates are not only controlled by the eustatic sea level rise, but also by the amount of ground ice present in the coastal zone and the direction of storm winds. Recently recorded coastal erosion rates are on the order of metres per year. For the Liverpool Bay-west Cape Bathurst Peninsula region, estimates average -1 to -2 m/yr, with maximum documented retreat rates of up to -7 m/yr (Harper et al. 1985).

It is generally assumed that such erosion, if it has persisted for any significant time, would have destroyed most or all of the sites associated with the passage of people from Alaska into the Canadian Arctic. Such a west to east route is currently held to have been followed by the first people known to have inhabited the Arctic Archipelago, the early Palaeoeskimos. While archaeological remains of this culture have been found in the Beaufort Sea coastal zone (Gordon 1970; MacNeish 1956), they are few in number, they have not been well studied, and their significance in terms of the

Threads of Arctic Prehistory: Papers in Honour of William E. Taylor Jr., David Morrison and Jean-Luc Pilon, eds. Canadian Museum of Civilization, Mercury Series, Archaeological Survey of Canada Paper 149. 1994.

peopling of the Canadian Arctic has yet to be determined.

During the field activities of the Canadian Museum of Civilization's Northern Oil and Gas Action Plan (NOGAP) Archaeology Project, Arctic Small Tool tradition (ASTt) artifacts were recovered at four different localities in the lower Mackenzie Valley of the Northwest Territories, more than 250 km from the Beaufort Sea coast. This article's primary aim is to describe the ASTt collections from the lower Mackenzie and to attempt to place them in the context of the complex picture of the early peopling of the Canadian Arctic.

Overview of Early Palaeoeskimo Prehistory

Numerous syntheses have brought together data relating to early Palaeoeskimo sites in Alaska and throughout the Canadian Arctic and Greenland (Arnold 1981; Dumond 1977; Maxwell 1985; McGhee 1976; Schledermann 1990). All are in general agreement that the earliest archaeological remains in the Canadian Arctic Islands and Greenland—materials ascribed to the Arctic Small Tool tradition—appeared around 4000 years ago.

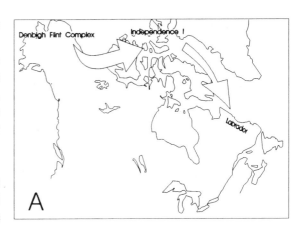

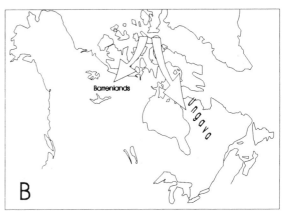

Figure 1 Major hypothesised Early Palaeoeskimo movements: A-4100 B.P., B-3500 B.P.

An important amount of uncertainty exists, however, over the mechanisms of human movements in the Arctic at this time. Much of this confusion stems in part from the dating of these early sites in different regions of the Arctic. While Proto-Denbigh materials at the Onion Portage site of Alaska are estimated to be 4100 years old (Anderson 1988: 89), accepted Denbigh Flint Complex dates at Cape Denbigh Alaska are on the order of 4000 to 3500 years old (Anderson 1988: 89; Dumond 1977: 86). The ealiest archaeological remains in the Canadian High Arctic and adjacent Greenland (Figure 1), artifacts of the Independence I culture, have been dated to about the same time period, and the earliest Arctic Small Tool tradition sites of the Labrador coast are contemporaneous with these or only slightly later (Tuck 1975: 137; Tuck and Fitzhugh 1986: 161). At Saglek Bay in Labrador, Tuck saw strong similarities with Independence I assemblages of the Canadian High Arctic.

The early Palaeoeskimo situation in the neighbouring Ungava Peninsula is complicated. Badgley has documented numerous Pre-Dorset sites on the west coast of the Ungava Peninsula in Hudson Bay, where the earliest date there is 3800 B.P. (I. Badgley 1993: pers. comm.). Related, but clearly different sites, described as reminiscent of Independence I, have been documented along the east shore of the peninsula.

The initial settlement of the Canadian Arctic involved very mobile groups who rapidly occupied much of the coastal reaches of the Canadian Arctic and Greenland. Whether the colonization of these different regions occurred sequentially, or whether a number of small groups moved out from an initial centre more or less simultaneously, remains to be adequately determined.

Notwithstanding the problems inherent with the radiocarbon dating of organic remains from the Arctic (McGhee and Tuck 1976; Morrison 1989) it is apparent that there is little chronological difference between the earliest Canadian and Greenland dates, and the purported Alaskan source of these migrants. Indeed, the closeness of available Alaskan Denbigh Flint Complex and related High Arctic Independence I radiocarbon dates has led McGhee (1987) to entertain the idea of a migration from the east, through central Siberia and Greenland to the Canadian High Arctic. Supporting evidence for this hypothesis remains, however, to be found.

With the possible exception of the Quebec-Labrador Peninsula, much of the Low Arctic appears to have been populated by the Arctic Small Tool tradition in later movements of people derived from the first migrants. This second migration may have been precipitated by harsher climatic conditions which occasionned a shift in the early ASTt range. By 3500 B.P., the High Arctic may have been depopulated, while Pre-Dorset groups shifted their range into the Barrenlands of the Northwest Territories and adjacent portions of the boreal forest. Although a more complex model has been assumed (McGhee 1976) a correlation with general climatic trends is nonetheless apparent.

The economic correlates of the movements into the different parts of the Canadian Arctic and Greenland have been determined or estimated to be similarly complex. Settlement/subsistence patterns in northern Alaska seem to have involved the seasonal use of a wide variety of ecological niches and resources (Anderson 1988: 149; Stewart 1989). Sea mammals were taken along the coastal tundra of northern and northwestern Alaska. Caribou were also hunted in these coastal areas as well as in the forested interior along rivers and lakes. The use of fish resources is also inferred by riparian and lacustrian locations throughout the Denbigh Flint Complex range.

In the High Arctic, various resources were exploited depending upon their availability. The adaptative strategies of the High Arctic Independence and Pre-Dorset groups were similar to the generalized Alaskan model in their flexibility. Musk-oxen were heavily depended upon in northern Greenland, on Ellesmere Island (Knuth 1967; Schledermann 1990) and on Banks Island (Arnold 1981), while seals and caribou were exploited on Devon Island (McCartney and Helmer 1989; McGhee 1979).

The situation in the Barrenlands is markedly different. Gordon (1975) has proposed a discrete association between human groups and caribou herds. This proposition, based on extensive field work, assumes that caribou herds have used essentially the same migration routes over several thousand years, between their wintering ranges within the boreal forest and their widely separated, distant calving grounds on the open tundra. With few other viable resources to exploit, Pre-Dorset groups developed a transhumant pattern which allowed them to exploit caribou during the full yearly cycle, over the course of which hundreds of kilometres of open terrain had to be traversed. Given widely separated calving grounds and migration routes, Gordon has proposed an entrenched relationship

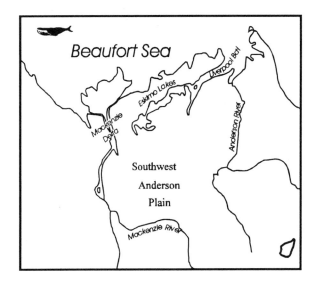

Figure 2 The lower Mackenzie Valley/Beaufort Sea study area.

whereby discrete hunting groups or bands were associated with discreet caribou herds. A corollary to this hypothesis is that over time communications between adjacent human groups was reduced, leading to lithic tool stylistic variants being associated with each of the four major Barrenlands caribou herd hunting bands.

To summarize, it is clear that present knowledge concerning the first people to inhabit the Canadian Arctic is not, considering the size of area involved, as complete as could be hoped for. However, the economic versatility and adaptability of the Arctic Small Tool tradition is well-known. Furthermore, their capacity to quickly come to know the resources of new regions has been well attested to. In short, they were a highly flexible group who adapted efficiently to new regions, while maintaining long-distance communication networks which covered several hundred kilometres in one of the harshest environmental zones of the world.

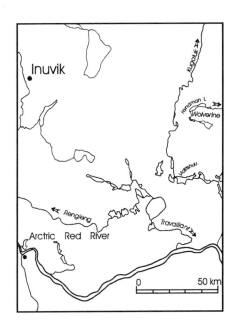

Figure 3 The southwest Anderson Plain.

The Study Area

The four ASTt collections described herein were found in the southwest Anderson Plain, a portion of the lower Mackenzie Valley of the Northwest Territories bounded on the south by the Mackenzie River, on the east by the Anderson River, on the north by the Eskimo Lakes and Liverpool Bay, and on the west by the Mackenzie Delta (Figure 2).

The area is marked by moderate relief, rolling hills and numerous large lakes. These water bodies form the headwaters of secondary drainage systems which lead north to the Beaufort Sea (Kugaluk River), east to the Anderson River (Wolverine and Carnwath Rivers), and south and east to the Mackenzie River (Travaillant and Rengleng Rivers).

Three of the four ASTt assemblages were found on Hyndman Lake, the headwater lake of the east-flowing

Wolverine River (Figure 3). The fourth ASTt-yielding site is the complex Vidiitshuu site on *Vidiitshuu* or Trout Lake, the headwater lake of the north-flowing Kugaluk River (Figure 3). These two water bodies lie within 50 km of each other.

The area is today well within the limits of the boreal forest, albeit one characterized as an open spruce-lichen forest. The faunal resources found here reflect the ecotonal situation it occupies. There are good fisheries of whitefish, lake trout and pike. The lakes are used as staging areas for migrating waterfowl, especially in the spring. A wide variety of mammals provide ample supplies of furs and food. The area today supports both woodland caribou and wintering members of the Bluenose barrenlands caribou herd. Moose are also found and have been present here for at least the last 6 centuries (Pilon 1989: 30).

Verna Mae Firth Site (NbTj-8)

The Verna Mae Firth site (NbTj-8) occupies a broad point jutting out from the middle of Hyndman Lake's north shore (Figure 4). This point, along with a less pronounced point directly opposite on the south shore, forms a narrows in the elongated water body. Our experience there in 1987 suggests that this is a strategic crossing for migrating caribou and even moose.

The interior of the point is relatively denuded of any arboreal species except for dwarf birch and willows. Thick sphagnum and poor drainage conditions prevail here as well. Spruce and willow are found at the back of the modern beach. An open spruce lichen forest begins at the base of the point and covers the slope leading up to the high plateau further to the north.

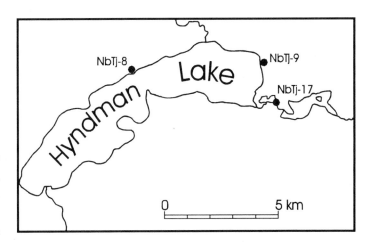

Figure 4 Hyndman Lake ASTt site locations.

The site was first discovered and tested in 1987 (Pilon 1988: 26-36). At that time the focus of the investigations was a large late prehistoric semi-subterranean structure located near the base of the point. In constructing this feature, archaeological specimens from an earlier occupation had been incorporated into the dwelling's roof. One such item was a spalled burin (Figure 5c) which compares quite well with Arctic Small Tool tradition specimens (Giddings 1951). We returned to the site in 1988, continuing our excavation of the house feature. In doing so, we also uncovered remains of an *in situ* ASTt occupation.

With the exception of specimens found in the roof debris of the late prehistoric dwelling, all of the artifacts which can be attributed to the Arctic Small Tool tradition (Table 1) were found in association with an elongated hearth feature just outside the limits of the house. Stratigraphically, the artifacts occurred in the thin humus which lay at the base of the vegetation mat, or in the upper few centimetres of the underlying sand matrix of the terrace. However, closer to the late prehistoric dwelling, the ASTt artifact-bearing humus had become buried by soil used in the construction of the 14th or 15th century roof.

Table 1 Tool frequencies and raw materials, NbTj-8.

	CH		SA	
	B	U	B	U
BURIN	-	1	1	-
PIÈCE ESQUILLÉE	1	-	4	-
PROJECTILE POINT	-	-	1	-
SCRAPER	-	-	-	-
BLANK/PREFORM	-	-	-	-
RETOUCHED/USED FLAKE	-	3	-	1
RETOUCHED BURIN SPALL	-	-	-	2
OTHER	-	-	1*	1**
TOTAL	1	4	7	4

CH-chert   SA-siliceous argillite   B-biface   U-uniface
* marginally retouched tablet edge fragment
** spokeshave fragment

Artifacts

The artifact assemblage includes a number of highly diagnostic items along with more ubiquitous implements (see Tables 1 and 6). The most easily identifiable tools are the single bipointed projectile point and the three burins (Figure 5).

The projectile point exhibits fine, parallel, oblique, collateral flaking typical of early Palaeoeskimo cultures such as the Denbigh Flint Complex and Independence I.

Two of the three burins are of the "mitten-shaped" variety—only one is included in Table 1 since the second was found in a disturbed context—while the third is a double-spalled, straight-between example. Modification of the distal portions of the burins for use is evident on all three specimens. This entailed the removal of short flakes from the dorsal surface of the implements, using the burin facets as striking platforms. This retouching resulted in the systematic thinning of the tool bits.

Truncated flake scars, resulting from the use of the burin spall facet as a striking platform to remove flakes from the burin's dorsal surface were observed on the edges (originally part of the burin's dorsal surface) of 6 of the 11 burin spalls found. Two of these spalls (Figure 5*f* and Figure 11*b*) were distally retouched and conform quite well to burin spall tools reported in Alaska (Giddings 1964: 220-222).

Although there were no scrapers found in proximity to the ASTt hearth feature, a small scraper found in Test Pit I, located some 7 m to the southwest may relate to the ASTt occupation. It is a simple end scraper noteworthy by its relatively small size (see Clark 1987 for a discussion of small end scrapers).

Three principal raw materials were represented in proximity to the ASTt hearth feature (see Tables 1 and 7). The first consists of siliceous argillite which is visually indistinguishable from the siliceous argillite which outcrops at the mouth of the Thunder River (Pilon 1990). However, the presence of numerous siliceous argillite cortex flakes indicates that local cobble beaches were the sources of a good proportion of this lithic type.

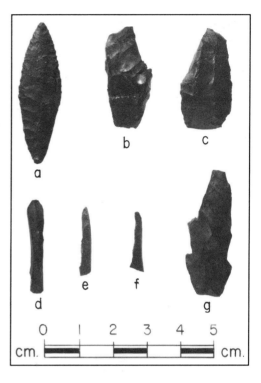

Figure 5 NbTj-8: *a*-bipoint, *b,c,g*-burins, *d,e*-burin spall, *f*-burin spall tool.

The next most frequent raw material is a coarse-grained quartzite found throughout the southwest Anderson Plain, and on a variety of sites in the Great Bear Lake and Colville Lake areas. Additionally, this material resembles the raw material utilized extensively by the late Arctic Small Tool tradition on Banks Island (Arnold 1981). It is undoubtedly common in the glacial deposits of the northwestern portion of the District of Mackenzie.

Other than the black or grey chert cobbles and miscellaneous crystalline rocks which were occasionally used, there is one other distinctive raw material which warrants comment. This material is identical to one of the predominant raw materials found on sites along the Old Horton River Channel by Le Blanc (1991a: 70), which include an early ASTt occupation (ObRw-11) and a later Lagoon Complex occupation (ObRv-1). Le Blanc (1991b) has shown that the source of this distinctive raw material, referred to as vesicular clinker, is along the lower Horton River, in the Cape Bathurst Peninsula region.

Dating

Charcoal was gathered from within the ASTt hearth deposits at a depth of approximately 15-20 cm below the original surface, and dated to 3390±255 B.P. (S-3000). A second charcoal sample obtained along the periphery of the hearth feature yielded an age of 2650±80 years B.P.(S-3363). This additional sample was gathered from a stratigraphically higher position, about 10 cm below surface. Its relatively younger age more than likely reflects its greater vulnerability to contamination with younger, downward moving carbon that such a stratigraphic position entails.

NbTj-9

Sandy beaches are rare along the perimeters of most of the lakes in the southwest Anderson Plain. One such beach, albeit a short one, is located in the north-east sector of Hyndman Lake (Figure 4). In addition to probable late prehistoric remains on a low terrace behind the modern sandy beach artifacts were found on a relic beach approximately 100 m from the lake shore. This discontinuous feature consists of a ridge of coarse sand and gravel which rises slightly above the surrounding poorly-drained terrain. It measures no more than 20 m at its widest point and roughly 70 m in length. The vegetation cover on this ridge is predominantly caribou moss with a few spruce trees, especially along its eastern perimeter. The terrain on either side of this ridge is characterized by hummocky muskeg. Fifty metres to the east a steep, high hill defines the edge of a plateau which appears to be part of a complex of glacial deposits which includes eskers. Today, the narrow corridor, formed by the lake shore on one side and the steep hill on the other, serves as a route for caribou moving along the east end of Hyndman Lake. In fact, a well-worn caribou trail runs down the centre of the relic beach.

Excavations took place in the inland area of the site over the course of the 1990 field season (Pilon 1991) and again in 1992 (Pilon 1992). As a result, three separate distributions were sampled. Artifacts were found immediately under the surface vegetation. The coarseness of the terrace matrix was such that a distinct humus layer had not formed. Rather, the upper 5 cm of this gravelly sand had a higher than usual humic content. Artifacts had managed to move into this layer as well.

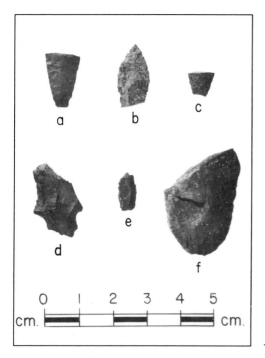

Figure 6 NbTj-9, Area A: *a-c*-bipoint fragments, *d*-burin, *e*-uniface, *f*-biface.

Area A (6 m²)

This area consists of a 2 m x 3 m block excavated in 1990. A very dense, but well-delimited concentration of lithic remains was found centred on a combustion zone. The feature was comprised of a basal layer of bright-orange oxidized sandy gravel (basically the upper portion of the relic beach deposits) which contained, in its uppermost few centimetres, charcoal flecks, numerous minute pieces of calcined bone and many fire-cracked rocks.

The associated lithic scatter was comprised of just under 3000 pieces and was made up of a very large proportion of primary debitage (see Table 6). The distribution of this large quantity of material suggests that an actual physical barrier, such as a skin tent, was involved rather than simply the vagaries of events during and following occupation.

Distinctive artifacts include four incomplete, delicately flaked bipointed projectile point fragments (Figure 6a-c), a badly heat-spalled "mitten-shaped" burin with a notch on either proximal edge (Figure 6d) which may indicate its method of hafting, along with the mid-section from a second burin, and microblades (10). Only two possible burin spalls—they may be microblades—were found.

A single stemmed biface was recovered (Figure 6f). The stem is lobate or lingual in shape. The remains of the triangular blade of the biface is separated from the stem element by a point of inflection which forms a slight shoulder. Judging from its size, the implement more than likely was designed as a hafted knife.

One complete uniface was recovered which warrants detailed description. Its length is 1.12 cm and its maximum width is 0.56 cm. In outline the implement is lanceolate with a slightly asymetric point (Figure 6e and Figure 9a). The edges are formed by carefully and steeply retouching the edges along both lateral margins while the basal edge is a snap. If shape were the only criteria necessary for attributing a possible function to this artifact, one might be tempted to refer to it as a point or a knife. However, given its reduced size, I am more inclined to assume that 1) the tool was hafted, and 2) such hafting would leave very little of it protruding. Therefore I propose that this implement functioned as a hafted graver.

Two implements were found which exhibit intentional grinding. One is nothing more than a large flake with a bifacially ground, convex edge. The second is the extremity of a large chipped biface. Grinding was then used to alter the edge of the implement as well as portions of its faces. At least four flakes were recovered which exhibited some limited dorsal grinding, and one of the unifaces, a notched flake, also has evidence of grinding on its dorsal surface.

Even though an overwhelming proportion of the debitage collection consisted of siliceous argillite (see Table 7), most of the lithic implements were manufactured from fine-grained cherts (see Table 2). Both the siliceous argillite and the cherts appear to have been derived from local secondary deposits.

Figure 7 NbTj-9, Area A: a-ground stone implement, b-biface exhibiting extensive grinding.

Table 2 Tool frequencies and raw materials, NbTj-9-Area A.

	CH		SA	
	B	U	B	U
BURIN	2	-	-	-
PIÈCE ESQUILLÉE	-	-	3	3
PROJECTILE POINT	4	-	-	-
SCRAPER	-	2	-	-
BLANK/PREFORM	4	-	1	-
RETOUCHED/USED FLAKE	-	4	-	12
RETOUCHED BURIN SPALL	-	-	-	-
OTHER	-	1*	-	5**
TOTAL	10	7	4	20

CH-chert   SA-siliceous argillite   B-biface   U-uniface
* notch ** 1-retouched microblade, 1-perforator, 3-notches

Figure 8 NbTj-9, Areas B & C: *a,c*-bifaces, *b*-bipoint.

Area B (4.5 m²) and Area C (6 m²)

Both Area B and Area C were initially identified on the basis of the presence of fire-cracked rock clusters (Pilon 1991: 24). These are located within 15 m of Area A and are presumed to be related to its occupation.

The artifacts from both areas confirmed the original suspicion that the fire-cracked rock clusters were indeed centres of activity by bearers of the Arctic Small Tool tradition. A number of important similarities can be described, yet there are some significant differences.

The collections from these two Areas are relatively small, not only in terms of their respective totals, but especially with regards the number of implements recovered (Table 6). Additionally, few of the tools are complete.

Only four artifacts warrant specific mention. The first, found in Area C, is a small bifacial bipoint manufactured of fine-grained chert (Figure 8*b*). Although the flaking exhibits refinement, the classic ripple effect is lacking. However, the craftsman may have experienced difficulty in thinning the piece which remained quite thick in the lower half of the tool.

A second biface of note was also recovered in Area C. It appears to be manufactured from a large cortical flake of poor-grade siliceous argillite (Figure 8*a*). It has a marked plano-convex cross-section resulting from most of the shaping having been perfored on one face, but the edges are bifacially retouched. The implement is lanceolate in shape with a straight, thick base, and a rounded distal tip. The tip thus confers an apparent asymetric plan to the implement. Both faces of the tool exhibit extensive wear of all arrisses. Rather than being indicative of use or even the intentional grinding by the artisan, this attrition has the appearance of having been produced by water tumbling or perhaps simply as a result of having been carried around in a skin bag for quite some time. As undiagnostic as it may be, the association with the Arctic Small Tool tradition occupation is good and there is no evidence to suggest occupation by any other cultural tradition at this specific locality.

Finally, there is a complete artifact which is similar to diminutive graver found in Area A (Figure 8*c* and Figure 9*b*). It appears to have been made from a fine chert burin spall. Its plan is lanceolate with steep ventral edge retouch. However, the edges adjacent to the pointed tip can be said to be bifacially retouched. It measures 1.18 cm x 0.4 cm x 0.16 cm. Another burin spall exhibits bifacial distal retouch at its tip, but lacks the lateral retouching. It also suggests use as an engraving tool.

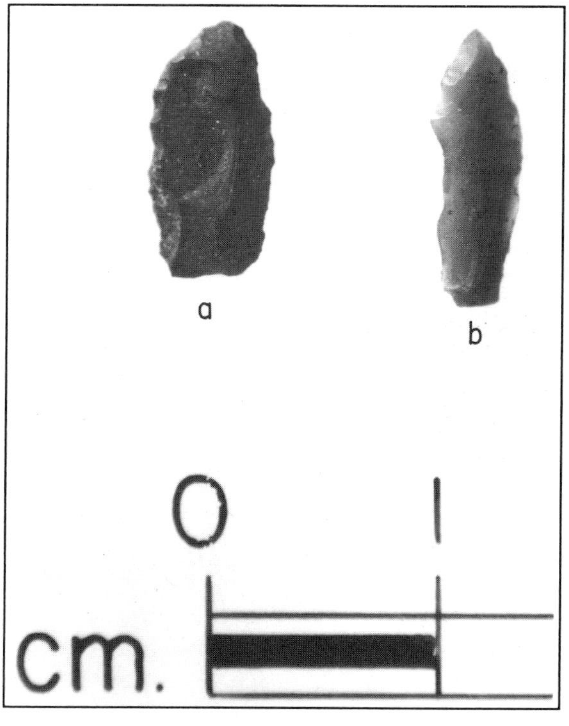

Burin spalls and burin fragments, as well as microblades were present in both areas and demonstrate that these items were part of the inventory of implements and technologies employed by the occupants in both areas.

As in Area A, raw materials are dominated by locally derived types (see Table 3 and 7), but fine-grained cherts were by far preferred for the manufactured of formal implements such as projectile points and burins. All but one of the large metamorphic rock

Figure 9 NbTj-9: engraving tools.

flakes, which have been tentatively identified as greywake, were recovered from Area B, where they occurred in good association with ASTt material. Many cortex flakes were found which show that the occupants were reducing local cobbles. A number of biface thinning flakes of this material were found which demonstrate that it was also being used to produce more refined, albeit large, implements.

Table 3 Tool frequencies and raw materials, NbTj-9-Areas B & C.

	CH		SA	
	B	U	B	U
BURIN	-	2**	-	-
PIÈCE ESQUILLÉE	-	-	-	-
PROJECTILE POINT	1	-	-	-
SCRAPER	-	1	-	-
BLANK/PREFORM	-	-	4***	-
RETOUCHED/USED FLAKE	-	1	-	1
RETOUCHED BURIN SPALL	-	-	-	1
OTHER	2*	-	-	-
TOTAL	3	4	4	2

CH-chert   SA-siliceous argillite   B-biface   U-uniface

* both appear to be retouched burin spalls and were likely used as gravers
** one is definitely a burin fragment while the second is questionable
*** three of these conjoined to form the lanceolate biface

Dating

Two wood charcoal samples, taken from the hearth feature in Area A, were submitted for radiocarbon dating. The results were 820±70 B.P. (S-3362) and less than 100 B.P. (S-3378) respectively. In spite of good context, the dates are obviously wrong. Three considerations might explain these results. Firstly, the soil which contained the charcoal consisted of a coarse sand with fine gravel. Such a porous soil could allow the downward movement of carbon deposited more recently. Secondly, the modern vegetation cover was made up primarily of caribou moss, which, when dry, shrinks and thereby exposes the underlying mineral soil to contamination. Lastly, the relic beach has been used by migrating caribou within the recent past. These animals have left a well-marked trail which coincidentally crosses the site. This prominent feature may well have been used over centuries. Such traffic could easily account for surface disturbances which in turn would lead to contaminating carbon.

NbTj-17

This site, discovered in 1988 (Pilon 1989), is located on the edge of the highest of two low terraces overlooking at once a small lake and the head of this lake's outlet stream, what is essentially the beginning of the east-flowing Wolverine River (Figure 4). The modern vegetation consists of an open spruce-lichen forest with some willow thickets. When revisited in 1990 (Pilon 1991), 11 m² were excavated.

The stratigraphy within the excavated area was relatively straightforward with an uppermost vegetation layer with its associated root mat and a thin humus layer overlying the terrace deposits of sand and occasional cobbles. Artifacts were clearly associated with the humus layer. Additionally, a small proportion of artifacts was also recovered from the top few centimetres of the sand.

A hearth area situated in the centre of the lithic scatter was uncovered by our excavations. It consists of an oval area (30 cm x 20 cm) of fire-reddened sand which in profile was saucer-shaped. The maximum depth of this reddened sand was found at the centre and reached up to 10 cm thick.

A few fire-cracked rocks were found in the vicinity of the oxidized sand and were clearly associated with the combustion feature. No faunal remains were recovered, but charcoal, found deep within the oxidized sand was collected.

Table 4 Tool frequencies and raw materials, NbTj-17.

	CH		SA		VC		MM	
	B	U	B	U	B	U	B	U
BURIN	1	3*	-	-	-	-	-	-
PIÈCE ESQUILLÉE	2	1	3	1	-	-	-	-
PROJECTILE POINT	-	-	1	-	-	-	-	-
SCRAPER	-	-	-	-	-	1	-	-
BLANK/PREFORM	2	-	-	-	-	-	1	-
RETOUCHED /USED FLAKE	-	1	1	-	-	-	-	-
RETOUCHED BURIN SPALL	-	4	-	1	-	-	-	-
Other	-	-	-	-	-	-	-	-
TOTAL	5	9	5	2	-	1	1	-

CH-chert   SA-siliceous argillite   VC-vesicular clinker   MM-metamorphic
B-biface   U-uniface
* one of these is a burin blank

Artifacts

The artifact collection recovered from NbTj-17 is surprizingly varied both in terms of raw materials and the array of lithic implements (see Tables 4 and 6).

Only one probable projectile point was found. Manufactured of siliceous argillite, this bipointed specimen lacks the fine flaking evident on projectile points from other ASTt sites in the area. This characteristic appears to stem from the lithic craftsperson's inability to thin a central mass which covers much of one face.

Figure 10 NbTj-17: *a*-bipoint, *b,c*-burins, *d*-burin blank, *e*-burin spall tool.

A burin, burin fragments (2) and a burin blank, along with burin spalls (13) attest to the importance of this functional class at NbTj-17 (Figure 10). Refits were possible in a number of instances, and show that not only were lithic implements being manufactured and rejunivated around this small hearth area, but these tools were also being used in the immediate vicinity. In one case, three black chert burin spalls—the primary and succeeding two rejuvinations spalls—could be fitted together. Of interest was the fact that two of these were distally retouched. As well, by refitting these implements, it was possible to observe the incremental reduction in the length of the tool between rejunivations. And finally, it was possible to observe the systematic use of the burin scar as a platform for the removal of small flakes from the burin's dorsal surface on 6 of the 13 burin spalls—5 of these were distally retouched (Figure 10*e* and Figure 11*a*)—as well as on two of the extant burin bits. These burins and the burin blank all appear to be of the "mitten-shaped" variety.

Microblades were found, albeit in very low numbers.

Although no implements were found which exhibited grinding, grinding as a shaping technique was known to the site occupants. A total of 11 flakes were found made of either some form of fine-grained, possibly sedimentary stone, or of a poor-grade siliceous argillite, which exhibited extensively ground platforms or facets on their dorsal surfaces.

One last artifact warrants mention. It is the mid-section of a large biface made of a coarse-grained metamorphic rock. Extrapolating from this section, the biface must have been on the order of 15 cm in total length and the fragment's width is 6.32 cm. If we also consider the presence of 11 flakes of a similar grade of raw material in the debitage collection, we must conclude that large, coarse-grained implements were part of the lithic inventory of the site's occupants.

Dating

A single wood charcoal sample was submitted for radiocarbon dating. It was obtained from deep within the deposits of the circular hearth feature, at a depth of approximately 10 centimetres below the feature's surface. The result was 3470 ± 430 B.P. (S-3377), which lies well within the range of early ASTt.

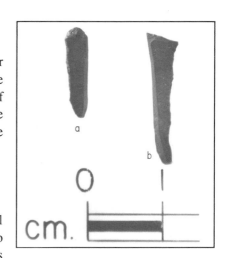

Figure 11 ASTt burin spall tools: *a*-NbTj-17, *b*-NbTj-8.

Vidiitshuu (MlTk-2)-East Point

MlTk-2 is the largest and most complex archaeological site identified on *Vidiitshuu* (Trout Lake or *lac à la Truite*) to date, if not in the entire southwest Anderson Plain. It is located on the west side of the Kugaluk River where it leaves the lake to begin its 150 km run to Liverpool Bay, at the outlet of the Eskimo Lakes (Figure 3). The site occupies a long point bounded on two sides by the lake and the river respectively and at the point's base there is a low, wet area which forms the effective western limit of the archaeological site.

Table 5 Tool frequencies and raw materials, MlTk-2, East Point-Area B.

| | CH | | SA | | MM | |
	B	U	B	U	B	U
BURIN	-	3	-	2	-	-
PIÈCE ESQUILLÉE	2	1	-	-	-	-
PROJECTILE POINT	1	-	2	-	-	-
SCRAPER	-	3	-	1	-	-
BLANK/PREFORM	2	-	-	-	1	-
RETOUCHED/USED FLAKE	-	6	1	-	-	1
RETOUCHED BURIN SPALL	-	-	-	-	-	-
OTHER	1*	2**	1***	-	-	-
TOTAL	4	15	4	3	1	1

CH-chert   SA-siliceous argillite   MM-metamorphic
B-biface   U-uniface
* flaked adze,   ** one miscellaneous uniface fragment, one perforator,   *** biface knife

Figure 12 MITk-2, East Point: *a-c,e*-projectile points, *d,f*-bifaces.

The site is located at a strategic narrows in the more than five kilometre long lake. At this point, the lake is less than 250 m across. In the recent past, caribou were quite often hunted here as these crossed to the south shore of Vidiitshuu.

Archaeological testing and excavations have been carried out at this extensive site over the course of five field seasons (Pilon 1985, 1987, 1988, 1991, 1992). Each time, different aspects of this site were focussed upon and investigated. In 1991, secondary testing took place at the easternmost extremity of the point (Nolin 1992). Excavations in this area, known as East Point, took place in two nearby blocks. While the smaller of the two blocks (Area B-5 m²) produced evidence of an Arctic Small Tool tradition occupation, the identify of those who left the artifacts in the second area (Area A-8 m²) was less clear.

Artifacts-Area B

The inventory of implements from Area B (Table 5) includes the usual variety of ASTt stone tools with at least one notable addition. It is a finely crafted, thin biface made of a fine-grained chert. It is triangular in shape with a convex base. The basal edge exhibits extensive use wear and polishing which extends somewhat onto one of the surfaces adjacent to the working edge. The implement, which was doubtless hafted, might have been a scraping tool or perhaps even a wood working tool.

The projectile points associated with this predominantly ASTt occupation area include one complete and two fragmentary specimens. The complete example is a diminutive lanceolate specimen with a narrow, slightly concave base (Figure 12*b*). One of the projectile point fragments appears to be the base of a diagonally flaked bipoint (Figure 12*c*) while the third, near-complete projectile point is also likely a bipointed variety (Figure 12*a*).

Three of the five burins found are of the mitten-shaped variety (Figure 13*a,b*). A fourth is a base fragment and the fifth is a burinated flake. Of note are two specimens which, while complete, are remarkably short and stocky. Were it not for the distinctive burin facets on these tools, it is quite conceivable that fragments from them would otherwise be classed as scrapers.

Another distinctive feature of at least two of the burins is the use of the burin scar as a platform from which to remove short flakes from the dorsal side of the distal end of the tool. In one case heavy crushing is noted along this platform edge as well. Dorsal retouching is also evident on

5 of the 6 the burin spalls. None of the burin spalls recovered (6) showed any sign of having been used or modified.

Although very few microblades (5) were recovered, those that were are good examples of such controlled and specialized core reduction as to leave no doubt that the technology was known and practiced to some extent by the site occupants.

The medio-proximal portion of a lingual or contracting stem biface (Figure 12*d*) was recovered which is similar to that found in Area A of NbTj-9. The stem element exhibits grounds edge which extend up to the point of inflection at the base of the biface's blade element. The actual tip of the base is rounded. The tool may have been a lance point or even a knife blade.

A tear drop-shaped fine chert biface exhibits extensive edge rounding and slight polish on its flake scars adjacent to the concave working edge (Figure 13*c*). The implement likely functioned as a scraping tool.

The debitage collection is dominated by local raw materials, especially siliceous argillite (see Table 7), although cherts are by far the raw materials preferred in the manufacture of stone tools. Also relatively important is the presence of a significant quantity of a coarse-grained raw material of local cobble beach origin, tentatively identified as greywake. No tools of this raw material were found, but the flakes of this rock indicate the manufacture of large bifaces.

As with the siliceous argillite, fine-grained cherts, quartzite and greywake can all be found on the cobble and boulder beach at the water's edge along the sides of the point. However, the distinctive vesicular clinker represented by a single piece of debitage and a lanceolate/triangular projectile point—recovered in Area A and described below—does not occur locally. Rather, its geological source is in the Cape Bathurst Peninsula region (Le Blanc 1991b) and its only means of transport to this site is by human agency.

Selected Artifacts-Area A

Although there are indications of reuse of the excavated areas of East Point, three items found in the Area A block can be tentatively ascribed to an Arctic Small Tool tradition occupation.

The first artifact is the proximal portion of what was likely a chert burin. Its extant edge received steep unifacial retouch on its dorsal face. A second, but complete mitten-shaped burin does not exhibit dorsal thinning.

The third object which is likely related to an ASTt occupation is a short lanceolate or triangular projectile point (Figure 12*e*). It is manufactured of vesicular clinker from the Cape Bathurst Peninsula region and ressembles projectile points which have been recovered from Pre-Dorset contexts further east in the Barrenlands (Clark 1987; Gordon 1975).

Dating

Faunal remains from Area B were present in both calcined and non-calcined states. One particularly weathered caribou longbone specimen was submitted for AMS dating and yielded a date 380±50 B.P. (Beta-51302). In addition to this obviously unassociated date, a second element was

Figure 13 MITk-2, East Point: *a,b*-burins, *c*-biface.

found in Area A which further suggests that the East Point was occupied by cultural groups other than the ASTt. In particular, the base of a lanceolate point made of sugary quartzite certainly indicates a distinctly different cultural manifestation (Figure 12*f*). The specimen could just as easily be ascribed a Plano origin as it could a Middle Taltheilei dating (Stewart 1991).

Summary of the Southwest Anderson Plain ASTt

Before attempting to summarize the southwest Anderson Plain Arctic Small Tool tradition, it is appropriate to address the question of sample size as represented by the ASTt assemblages from this area. Although they do not lend themselves to statistical manipulation, all four sites share a basic, unique and exceedingly rare feature for ASTt sites in the District of Mackenzie; they show no signs of multiple occupation—more than likely each one represents a single ASTt occupational event. They reflect something very real, rather than the result of repeated occupations over long periods of time by potentially different but related groups.

It should be apparent that the four Anderson Plain ASTt sites share a number of distinctive characteristics (Table 6). Some of these may allow us to reconcile these occupations to the prevailing theories regarding the presence of the Arctic Small Tool tradition in the region generally.

A first unifying trait is the fact that the predominant projectile point style by far is the bipointed variety. Flaking is most often parallel, oblique and collateral. The quality of workmanship is quite delicate and precise.

Burins of the classic "mitten-shaped" variety have been found at all four sites. In general they tend to be made on relatively long flake blanks, except at Vidiitshuu where some thick, stubby blanks were also employed. However, they are consistently made from unifacially shaped blanks. In virtually all cases, a distinctive thinning technique was used, apparently to adjust the width of the "bit". Grinding was restricted to the distal edge of the burin and appears to have been the most expedient way of creating a platform for burin spall removal. Facial grinding of burins was not recorded in the southwest Anderson Plain.

Grinding, as a technique intended to modify the overall shape of implements other than burins is, however, present at two of the southwest Anderson Plain ASTt sites (NbTj-9,17). Unfortunately these tools are fragmentary and their functions have yet to be determined.

Table 6 Assemblage summaries of the southwest Anderson Plain ASTt sites.

	NbTj-8	NbTj-9 Area A	NbTj-9 Area B	NbTj-9 Area C	NbTj-17	MlTk-2 East Point
DEBITAGE	1395	2984	357	30	730	1344
TOOLS	16	41	5	8	23	29
MICROBLADES	0	10	5	1	8	5
BURIN SPALLS	11	0	5	1	13	6
CORES	4	23	3	0	2	4

Although microblades were found at three of the four ASTt sites, they are present in very low numbers and microblade cores were not recovered. It seems reasonable to conclude that microblades did not play a very important role in the material culture of the southwest Anderson Plain ASTt. Might there be some seasonal or task specific use of microblades which could help explain the apparent importance of microblades at some sites and their relative unimportance at others? At present we would do well to remember that the relative unimportance of microblades at one site simply means they were not recovered in the same numbers compared to the total collection size as at another. This factor should be kept in mind since we did not completely excavate the sites we studied.

Evidence for the manufacture of large bifaces from coarse-grained raw materials such as greywake has been recovered from three of the four sites. Although not usually thought of as part of the finely-crafted lithic inventory of the Arctic Small Tool tradition, quite obviously such implements were well suited to the special needs of their inland adaptation (Gordon 1975: 263; Taylor 1972: 68).

Raw material use provides some useful insights into the ASTt presence in the region. By far the most prevalent raw material represented in the debitage collection was a distinctive siliceous argillite (Table 6). Although a primary geological extraction site has been identified at the mouth of the Thunder River (Pilon 1990), in the southern part of the study area, an abundance of cortex flakes on all ASTt sites attests to the use of local secondary sources; storm beaches and eroding moraine deposits. Other locally derived raw materials used in lesser quantities include a sugary white quartzite, wide-spread throughout the northwestern portion of the District of Mackenzie, coarse-grained metamorphic rock types, and a variety of fine-grained cherts.

Although siliceous argillite predominates in the debitage collections, points and burins are most often made of fine-grained cherts (Table 6). In contrast, pièces esquillées and scrapers—more expedient tools—are almost always made of siliceous argillite.

Only one raw material appears to be truly exotic to the southwest Anderson Plain; vesicular clinker whose geological source is the Cape Bathurst Peninsula region (Le Blanc 1991b). The discovery of this raw material in three of the four Anderson Plain ASTt sites indicates some kind of sustained contact with the coastal zone. Although unequivocal evidence of the exploitation of sea mammal resources has not yet been found in the early ASTt sites of the Cape Bathurst Peninsula, the

Table 7 Debitage raw materials of the southwest Anderson Plain ASTt sites.

	NbTj-8	NbTj-9 Area A	NbTj-9 Area B	NbTj-9 Area C	NbTj-17	MlTk-2 East Point
CHERT	212	400	141	10	300	80
SILICEOUS ARGILLITE	1119	2582	155	12	322	867
VESICULAR CLINKER	55	0	0	0	86	1
METAMORPHIC	0	1	45	1	11	97
SUGARY QUARTZITE	0	0	8	1	11	0
QUARTZITE	9	0	6	6	0	37
OTHER	0	1	2	0	0	262*

*mudstone

presence there of a people who elsewhere carried out this activity lends credence to the probability that such activities took place. Thus, we may posit a coastal-inland seasonal round or at the least, maintenance of close ties with coastal groups.

The chronology of the Arctic Small Tool tradition presence in the southwest Anderson Plain is an important one and at present rests upon a series of six radiocarbon dates obtained from the four ASTt sites (Table 7).

When the individual dates were presented earlier, it was made clear that a number of considerations must be weighed in assessing the reliability of samples, even before they are submitted for radiocarbon dating. Clearly, the three younger dates must be rejected, as the oldest of these is two millenia younger than any other known dated site of this type. Of the remaining three dates, two are quite similar while a second from NbTj-8 is six centuries younger. This divergence can be understood by the fact that the younger sample, although from the same feature as the 3390 B.P. date was collected closer to the surface and was thus more exposed to possible contamination from more recent carbon.

The boreal environment has a very dynamic carbon regimen. Forest fires are an important component of the ecology and occur with regularity. There is thus a constant source of new carbon being added to the uppermost part of a soil column every few centuries. As shown at NbTj-8 and NbTj-9, a number of factors can affect the potential rate of contamination; type of matrix and porosity, surface vegetation type and depth of permafrost.

Only two of the six ASTt dates fall within the accepted range for the existence of this cultural tradition, and coincidentally, both are on the order of 3400 B.P. Their relatively large sigma values are a reflection of the particular counter used rather than a true indication of the reliability of the dates (J. Wittenburg 1988: pers. comm.). Considering the potential problems with charcoal from the boreal forest, if anything, the central values for these dates should likely be somewhat older.

Other ASTt Sites in the Beaufort-Amundsen Region

A brief survey of other ASTt sites in the greater Beaufort Sea-Amundsen Gulf Region will now be undertaken. This overview will proceed from east to west along the Beaufort Sea coastal area and continue east to the Coppermine region. This will be followed by consideration of sites within the interior areas south of the Beaufort-Amundsen Region.

Sites of a similar age and cultural affiliation as the ASTt components of the southwest Anderson Plain are not numerous in the western Canadian Arctic. Early ASTt remains have been described from the Engigstciak site, NiVk-1, (MacNeish 1956) and Trout Lake (Gordon 1970) in Yukon. Recent studies of the collections from both these localities (Clark 1976; Greer 1991; see also Cinq-Mars et al. 1991) have outlined the severe provenance problems which existed at these sites; difficulties not always apparent to the original excavators. Enough questions exist surrounding associations and assemblage integrities so that beyond noting the presence of "*fossils indicateurs*", no more can be said, at this point, concerning the ASTt tool kits at these sites. Comparisons are thus severely limited.

At the Engigstciak site (NiKv-1) located near the mouth of the Firth River in the North Yukon coastal plain, the New Mountain Phase (MacNeish 1956) of the Arctic Small Tool tradition contained a number of bipointed projectiles. Some exhibit extremely fine edge serration and oblique, parallel flaking, while others are much less finely manufactured, yet they share the same general outline. Quite obvious ASTt-style of "mitten-shaped" burins also fill many specimen boxes in this collection. While the present author did not systematically examine these, some burins did exhibit the burin thinning described for most of the Anderson Plain specimens. However, the relative importance of this feature is unknown. Further, there is a strong possibility that the Engigstciak collection contains later, non-Denbigh, ASTt materials. A recently obtained AMS date from an ASTt context at this site yielded a date of 4280 ± 200 (RIDDL-320) (Vogel et al. 1991: 149). An earlier date of 1250 B.C. ± 156 (Rainey and Ralph 1959: 371) suggests a broad span for the ASTt presence at this site.

The Trout Lake sites of the north Yukon coastal plain (Gordon 1970) have far fewer specimens easily attributable to the Denbigh-related ASTt. Nonetheless, Greer (1991) has demonstrated the presence of a number of western-oriented (i.e. Alaskan-derived) cultural entities including Denbigh, Norton and Choris.

A small number of possible Arctic Small Tool tradition artifacts were recovered by McGhee (1969) from Atkinson Point (NlTk-5). Unfortunately, this site has since been completely destroyed by erosion. Further, its small collection lacks implements which would allow a specific cultural attibution within the tradition. Of note, however, is the presence of the extremity of a finely-crafted projectile point. It shows a highly controlled pattern of oblique, parallel, collateral flake removal. It could relate to a Denbigh or a later ASTt occupation.

More recently an early ASTt site (ObRw-11) was tested on the former banks of the Old Horton River (Le Blanc 1991a), 240 km N-NE of Hyndman Lake. The assemblage included unground burins, microblades and microblade cores, as well as finely serrated end-blades, one of which appears to be a bipointed variety (Le Blanc 1991a: Figure 11-h). Le Blanc posits that this collection "may be a link in the delicate thread of Independence I migration to the High Arctic at ca. 2000 B.C."(ibid.: 73).

During the 1992 field season K. Swayze found chipped mitten-shaped burins at two inland lake fishing sites in the interior of the Tuktoyaktuk Peninsula (Swayze 1993). While his prime objective was to sample late prehistoric/historic Inuvialuit middens associated with fish camps, the presence of what are clearly Denbigh burins in the basal layers of these middens shows that these localities were visited during much earlier times by members of the Arctic Small Tool tradition.

Further afield, ASTt remains have been identified in the lower Coppermine River region, notably at Dismal Lake (Harp 1958) and at Bloody Falls (McGhee 1970).

The site at Bloody Falls is particularly important since it is radiocarbon dated to 3300±90 B.P.(McGhee 1970: 58). In terms of comparisons with the Anderson Plain ASTt sites, the Bloody Falls projectile points are dominated by concave-based, lanceolate forms. The burins are comprised of both unifacial and bifacially prepared specimens. Although flake scars emanating from the burin facet are present, the great majority of the burin bits are either unmodified, or have received facial grinding in an apparent effort to modify the thickness of the bit. The use of grinding as a thinning and even a shaping technique is found in other lithic tool categories as well, and a number of basalt and metamorphic rock flakes (58) retain grinding on their dorsal surfaces.

McGhee (1970) pointed out some of the marked differences between the Bloody Falls ASTt collection and that found at the undated Dismal-2, a site whose occupation McGhee estimated to be several centuries earlier than the ASTt occupation at Bloody Falls.

At Dismal-2, projectile points are comprised of fragments which suggest bipointed varieties. Moreover, many of these exhibit fine edge serration and parallel, oblique, collateral flaking. The burins, like those from Bloody Falls, are made on either unifacially or bifacially prepared blanks, and are often thick. No grinding is apparent on any of the burins, or any of the other implements. Further, thinning of the burin bit faces by chipping is not a characteristic feature of these burins. Where noted, it appeared to be use-related rather than intentional.

Arctic Small Tool tradition sites have also been discovered in the interior of the District of Mackenzie, most notably between Great Bear Lake and Great Slave Lake (Noble 1971), to the north of the Great Bear Lake and in the vicinity of Colville Lake (Clark 1987), and further east throughout the District of Keewatin (Gordon 1975).

Most of the ASTt artifacts described by both Noble and Clark were collected from surface contexts, which in many instance contained artifacts attributable to other cultural traditions. This potential for assemblage mixing, as well as the total lack of radiometric assays, prevented Clark from atttempting to periodize the ASTt occupations north of Great Bear Lake. However, Noble proposed four distinct, yet clearly related phases to his Canadian Tundra Tradition.

Throughout the time spanned by Noble's so-called "Canadian Tundra Tradition", the dominant projectile point is the small, straight or concave-based triangular form. The polishing of burins is another trait which persists throughout the Canadian Tundra Tradition. Grinding and polishing is also a technique applied to other artifact categories such as adzes. Microblades are apparently rare in the early phases and more numerous in the later phases.

Like the sites of the Canadian Tundra Tradition, predominant point styles to the north of Great Bear Lake are similarly small, straight or concave-based triangular varieties. Burins often exhibit facial grinding and other ground tool categories were recovered (Clark 1987:129). Microblades are generally not numerous.

Clark estimates the ASTt presence in the area to begin about 1500 B.C. based on the dating of events in the District of Keewatin. Indeed, strong parallels are suggested with the Keewatin Pre-Dorset occupation and generally, the ASTt presence in the Great Bear region is seen as part of that same phenomenon (Gordon 1975:175).

Southwest Anderson Plain ASTt in the Regional Context

The southwest Anderson Plain ASTt sites lie well within the interior and might appear to be part of the inland ASTt distribution so well documented further east in the Colville Lake region, to the north and south of Great Bear Lake and into the District of Keewatin. Not only is there a semblance of geographic unison, but radiocarbon dates from the southwest Anderson Plain and chronological estimates for the onset of the ASTt occupation of the interior are similar.

However, there are key elements which do not articulate well with this hypothesis and suggest an alternate view of the southwest Anderson Plain ASTt occupation.

Between Great Slave and Great Bear Lakes and even further east in the Keewatin, bipointed projectile points are virtually absent. Instead, there is a fairly homogenous distribution of straight or concave-based triangular points to be found throughout those areas. North of Great Bear Lake and in the Colville Lake region, these varieties are also the principal ASTt styles with the possible addition of rare bipointed examples. However, these have been described as "asymetric side-blades". Projectile point styles within the southest Anderson Plain ASTt sites are almost always bipointed varieties. Bipointed projectiles were also found at Dismal-2, on the Old Horton Channel at ObRw-11, and at the Engigstciak site at the mouth of the Firth River on the north Yukon coast.

Along with the obvious differences in projectile point styles, we must also wonder about the shafts to which these implements were connected and their manner of hafting. This in turn might indicate significant differences in the weaponry employed and the kinds of hunting strategies used. In the Arctic Islands, there is no question that the small triangular projectiles were inset into the ends of harpoon sockets. Did the Barrenlands Pre-Dorset continue to use harpoon-related technology inland?

So-called "mitten-shaped" burins are not only a hallmark of the Denbigh Flint Complex, but they have also been found in related cultural expressions such as Independence I and Pre-Dorset. On their own, they can simply serve to identify the cultural tradition and not the specific regional phase or sub-tradition. Burins have been described in a myriad of ways; handedness, faciality, and number and orientation of burin facets to name but a few. In the southwest Anderson Plain, there seems to be a marked selection for thin unifacial blanks. Both left and righ-handed varieties are produced. However, as noted earlier, a distinctive thinning technique is characteristic of the Anderson Plain burins. This technique may also be present elsewhere but nowhere in the same proportion. However, the Dismal-2, ObRw-11, Engigstciak and southwest Anderson Plain sites stand in contrast to the Great Slave Lake, Great Bear Lake, and Keewatin ASTt sites where facial grinding appears to be the technique commonly employed to thin the bit of the burin. Grinding as a techique is present on other artifact forms in the southwest Anderson Plain, but is not applied to the thinning of burins. Similarly, ground stone tools occur north of Great Bear Lake and at Bloody Falls. There also we find facial grinding of burins to be a common trait.

Table 8 Radiocarbon dates from the southwest Anderson Plain ASTt sites.
(Calibrated using CALIB-3, Stuiver and Reimer 1993)

SITE	LABORATORY NUMBER	MATERIAL DATED	RADIOCARBON AGE B.P.	CALIBRATED AGE	ONE SIGMA RANGE
NbTj-8	S-3000	wood charcoal	3390±255	1680 B.C.	2015-1407 B.C.
	S-3363	wood charcoal	2650±80	810 B.C.	843-790 B.C.
NbTj-17	S-3377	wood charcoal	3470±430	1750 B.C.	2450-1267 B.C.
NbTj-9	S-3362	wood charcoal	820±70	A.D. 1230	A.D. 1167-1282
	S-3378	wood charcoal	<100	modern	
MITk-2	BETA-51302	caribou bone	380±50	A.D.1483	A.D. 1448-1648

The chronological placements of sites in the western Canadian Arctic is problematical and for the most part rests upon estimates arrived at through stylistic comparisons. The initial movement of the ASTt into the Barrenlands is generally agreed to be about 1500 B.C. Coincidentally, available radiocarbon dates from the southwest Anderson Plain are contemporaneous with this initial shift into the Barrenlands. As well, estimates for ObRw-11 and Dismal-2, as well as a radiocarbon date from Engigstciak range from 1500 B.C. to 2000 B.C., or sometime before the southern shift of ASTt people into the interior.

To summarize, it appears that the Arctic Small Tool tradition sites of the Beaufort-Amundsen region—Engigstciak in the north Yukon, ObRw-11 on Cape Bathurst Peninsula, the four southwest Anderson Plain and perhaps Dismal-2 near Coppermine—share a number of traits which set them apart from the Pre-Dorset who moved into the Barrenlands about 1500 B.C. These include projectile point styles and possibly the equipment to which the points were attached, as well as the attendant techniques and strategies surrounding their use. Similarities also include techniques for thinning burin bits, the general use of grinding as a shaping technique, and the dating of the occupations themselves.

The Inuvik Phase of the Arctic Small Tool Tradition

The above discussion clearly shows that the ASTt remains from the Beaufort-Amundsen region, with the exception of Bloody Falls, cannot be lumped with those described by Gordon in the Keewatin, and by Noble and Clark in the Great Slave and Great Bear Lakes regions. Although both groups are easily ascribed to the technological tradition that is the ASTt, elements of their material culture argue for distinguishing the two.

The group of sites which includes those of the southwest Anderson Plain shares some important elements with two previously described early Palaeoeskimo cultural constructs, namely the Denbigh Flint Complex of Alaska and the High Arctic Independence I. In both instances, bipointed projectile points are common and burins invariably lack grinding, except perhaps in the late stages of the Denbigh Flint Complex. The quality of flaking in both cases is quite high, with fine parallel, oblique and collateral patterns being commonly found on certain tool classes.

Additional parallels can be made between the Denbigh Flint Complex and the ASTt sites of the Beaufort-Amundsen region, on the basis of apparent economic orientation. In contrast to the highly specialized Barrenlands Pre-Dorset, the people who used the southwest Anderson Plain appear to have had access to and exploited both coastal and inland resources, much as did the Denbigh Flint Complex of Alaska. Both Engigstciak and Dismal-2 are inland sites.

When D.Clark (1976) re-examined the Engigstciak collection, he noted the same kinds of parallels with the Denbigh Flint Complex as well as the significant differences with materials further east. Clark also noted what appeared to be local peculiarities of the Engigstciak ASTt collection that he felt sufficient to permit the definition of a separate "phase" of ASTt, namely the New Mountain phase, a concept originally proposed by MacNeish. It is now apparent that more than one ASTt "phase" is actually represented at that site. The continued use of the term "New Mountain Phase", other than as an historical reference, may be confusing.

Clearly, recent data strengthens the distinctiveness of the ASTt history in the Beaufort-Amundsen region. It is also evident that there is more than likely a few centuries of Palaeoeskimo prehistory which was acted out in this region.

For example, when I accompanied W.E.Taylor on a survey of Stapylton Bay, at the eastern end of Amundsen Gulf in 1989, we found two early Palaeoeskimo sites on old limestone boulder beach ridges (NfPn-1, NfPn-3). At one of these sites (NfPn-1) at least ten oval or circular tent rings were recorded, some of which included classic Independence-style midpassage structures. Such features have not been recorded for the Barrenlands Pre-Dorset.

This information reinforces the notion that the Arctic Small Tool tradition in the Beaufort-Amundsen region stands apart from that of the Barrenlands Pre-Dorset. Further it seems apparent that strong links can be made with both the early Alaskan ASTt (Denbigh Flint Complex) and even the closely related early High Arctic ASTt (Independence I). On this basis, I propose that the Beaufort-Amundsen region ASTt sites be grouped under the Inuvik Phase of the Arctic Small Tool tradition.

Within this region there were more than likely economy-based distinctions between the north Yukon, Anderson Plain and Amundsen Gulf sub-regions, much as there were between late prehistoric and historic Inuit groups, much as Sutherland (in press) has proposed for Northern Ellesmere Island. We might also expect to find chronological distinctions which might reflect local cultural dynamics between the ASTt and other neighbouring cultural manifestations.

The Inuvik Phase thus appears as a regional expression of the early Arctic Small Tool tradition with strong links with the Alaskan Denbigh Flint Complex which existed between about 4300 B.P. and 3400 B.P. In some areas such as the north Yukon, it may have persisted until later times. Although possibly overlapping with the Pre-Dorset presence in the nearby Barrenlands, evidence of diffusion between the two groups has yet to be clearly identified.

By extending the effective range of Alaskan ASTt influence, the Inuvik Phase, bridges the vast territory which the first people into the High Arctic had to cross. Further research in key areas like the eastern extremity of Amundsen Gulf, could help us to better understand the conditions under which this movement took place and the processes which operated in pushing the geographical and adaptive limits of the Arctic Small Tool tradition into the far reaches of the Canadian Arctic and Greenland.

Acknowledgements

The ASTt remains discussed in this article were gathered during the field activities of the Canadian Museum of Civilization's Northern Oil and Gas Action Plan (NOGAP) Archaeology Project. I am grateful to my NOGAP colleagues at the Archaeological Survey of Canada for their help and support over the many years of the project, namely Luc Nolin, Jane Dale, Ken Swayze, David Morrison, Raymond Le Blanc and Jacques Cinq-Mars. Excavations at the East Point of the Vidiitshuu site only took place because of Luc Nolin's insistence of systematically testing this area. His perseverance paid off quite nicely. I would like to further recognize the different members of field crews who helped expose the ASTt remains: Willie Simon Modeste, Verna Mae Firth, Ken Stark, Bruce Jamieson, Phil Woodley, Arianne Burke, Deanna Ludowicz, Diane Cockle, Fulgence Belcourt, Michael T.G.Jackson, and Bob Humen. The very important support made available by the Inuvik Research Centre is thankfully recognized. While readily acknowledging full responsibility for the ideas presented in this article, I would nonetheless like to recognize the valuable comments of Pat Sutherland, Don Clark, David Morrison and William Fitzhugh, who reviewed earlier drafts. Finally, I would like to thank Abbie Kwong Pilon for her continuing support and understanding.

References

Anderson, D.D. 1988. Onion Portage. An Archaeological Site on the Kobuk River, Northwestern Alaska. Anthropological Papers of the University of Alaska, 20(1-2).

Arnold, C.D. 1981. The Lagoon Site (OjRl-3): Implications for Paleoeskimo Interactions. National Museum of Man, Mercury Series, Archaeological Survey of Canada Paper 107.

Cinq-Mars, J., C.R. Harington, D.E. Nelson and R.S. MacNeish. 1991. Engigstciak Revisited: A Note on Early Holocene AMS Dates from the "Buffalo Pit". In, NOGAP Archaeology Project: An Integrated Archaeological Research and Management Approach, J. Cinq-Mars and J.-L. Pilon, eds. Canadian Archaeological Association, Occasional Paper, 1: 33-44.

Clark, D.W. 1976. Progress Report on a Reexamination of the Engigstciak Site Collections. MS on file with the Canadian Museum of Civilization, Hull.

Clark, D.W. 1987. Archaeological Reconnaissance at Great Bear Lake. Canadian Museum of Civilization, Mercury Series, Archaeological Survey of Canada Paper 136.

Dumond, D.E. 1977. The Eskimos and Aleuts. London: Thames and Hudson.

Giddings, J.L. 1951. The Denbigh Flint Complex. American Antiquity,16(3): 193-203.

Giddings, J.L. 1964. The Archaeology of Cape Denbigh. Providence: Brown University Press.

Gordon, B.C. 1970. Arctic Yukon Coast: Including a Description of the British Mountain Complex at Trout Lake. In, Early Man and Environments in Northwest North America. Calgary: The University of Calgary Archaeological Association, pp. 67-86.

Gordon, B.C. 1975. Of Men and Herds in Barrenland Prehistory. National Museum of Man, Mercury Series, Archaeological Survey of Canada Paper 28.

Greer, S.C. 1991. The Trout Lake Archaeological Locality and the British Mountain Problem. In, NOGAP Archaeology Project: An Integrated Archaeological Research and Management Approach, J. Cinq-Mars and J.-L. Pilon, eds.Canadian Archaeological Association, Occasional Paper, 1: 15-31.

Harp, E., Jr. 1958. Prehistory in the Dismal Lake Area, N.W.T., Canada. Arctic, 11(4): 219-249.

Harper, J.R., P.D. Reimer and A.D. Collins. 1985. Final Report. Canadian Beaufort Sea Physical Shore-Zone Analysis. Geological Survey of Canada. Open File 1689.

Knuth, E. 1967. Archaeology of the Musk Ox Way. École Pratique des Hautes Études. Contributions du Centre d'Études Arctiques et Finno-Scandinaves, 5.

Le Blanc, R.J. 1986. Report of Field Activities—NOGAP 1985: Northern Yukon-Western Mackenzie Delta. MS on file with the Canadian Museum of Civilization, Hull.

Le Blanc, R.J. 1991a. New Data Relating to the Prehistory of the Mackenzie Delta Region of the NOGAP Study Area. In, NOGAP Archaeology Project: An Integrated Archaeological Research and Management Approach, J. Cinq-Mars and J.-L. Pilon, eds. Canadian Archaeological Association, Occasional Paper, 1: 65-76.

Le Blanc, R.J. 1991b. Prehistoric Clinker Use on the Cape Bathurst Peninsula, Northwest Territories, Canada: The Dynamics of Formation and Procurement. American Antiquity, 56(2): 268-277.

MacNeish, R.S. 1956. The Engigstciak Site on the Yukon Arctic Coast. Anthropological Papers of the University of Alaska, 4(2): 91-111.

Maxwell, M.S. 1985. Prehistory of the Eastern Arctic. Orlando: Academic Press.

McCartney, P.H. and J.W.Helmer. 1989. Marine and Terrestrial Mammals in High Arctic Paleoeskimo Economy. Archaeozoologia, III(1,2): 143-160.

McGhee, R. 1969. Field Notes. MS on file with the Canadian Museum of Civilization, Hull.

McGhee, R. 1970. Excavations at Bloody Falls, N.W.T., Canada. Arctic Anthropology, VI(2): 53-72.

McGhee, R. 1976. Paleoeskimo Occupations of Central and High Arctic Canada. In, Eastern Arctic Prehistory: Paleoeskimo Problems, M.S. Maxwell, ed. Memoirs of the Society for American Archaeology, 31: 15-39.

McGhee, R. 1979. The Palaeoeskimo Occupations at Port Refuge, High Arctic Canada. National Museum of Man, Mercury Series, Archaeological Survey of Canada Paper 92.

McGhee, R. 1987. Eskimo Origins: An Alternative Proposal. MS on file with the Canadian Museum of Civilization, Hull.

McGhee, R. and J.A. Tuck. 1976. Un-Dating the Canadian Arctic. In, Eastern Arctic Prehistory: Paleoeskimo Problems, M.S. Maxwell, ed. Memoirs of the Society for American Archaeology, 31: 6-14.

Morrison, D.A. 1989. Radiocarbon Dating Thule Culture. Arctic Anthropology, 26(2): 48-77.

Noble, W.C. 1971. Archaeological surveys and sequences in the central district of Mackenzie, N.W.T. Arctic Anthropology, 8(1): 102-134.

Nolin, L. 1992. Compte-rendu des fouilles archéologiques effectuées sur les sites MlTk-2 de Vidiitshuu et MlTk-16 du lac Lure situés dans la partie sud-ouest de la plaine d'Anderson, district de Mackenzie, Territoires du Nord-Ouest. MS on file with the Canadian Museum of Civilization, Hull.

Pilon, J.-L. 1985. Mackenzie Valley Archaeological Survey, Field Report. MS on file with the Canadian Museum of Civilization, Hull.

Pilon, J.-L. 1987. Reconnaissance archéologique dans le sud-ouest de la plaine d'Anderson et dans la vallée du fleuve Mackenzie. MS on file with the Canadian Museum of Civilization, Hull.

Pilon, J.-L. 1988. Report of the 1987 NOGAP Archaeological Field Activities in the Southwest Anderson Plain, District of Mackenzie, Northwest Territories. MS on file with the Canadian Museum of Civilization, Hull.

Pilon, J.-L. 1989. Report of the 1988 NOGAP Archaeological Field Activities in the Southwest Anderson Plain and in the Mackenzie Valley, District of Mackenzie, N.W.T. MS on file with the Canadian Museum of Civilization, Hull.

Pilon, J.-L. 1990. *Vihtr'iitshik*: a Stone Quarry Reported by Alexander Mackenzie on the Lower Mackenzie River in 1789. Arctic, 43(3): 251-261.

Pilon, J.-L. 1991. Report of the 1990 NOGAP Archaeological Field Activities in the Southwest Anderson Plain and in the Mackenzie Valley, District of Mackenzie,N.W.T. MS on file with the Canadian Museum of Civilization, Hull.

Pilon, J.-L. 1992. Report of the 1991 NOGAP Archaeological Field Activities in the Southwest Anderson Plain and in the Mackenzie Valley,District of Mackenzie, Northwest Territories. MS on file with the Canadian Museum of Civilization, Hull.

Rainey, F. and E.K. Ralph. 1959. Radiocarbon Dating in the Arctic. American Antiquity, 24: 365-374.

Schledermann, P. 1990. Crossroads to Greenland. Arctic Institute of North America, Komatik Series, 2.

Stewart, A. 1991. Recognition of Northern Plano in the Context of Settlement in the Central Northwest Territories: Developing a Technological Approach. Canadian Journal of Archaeology, 15: 179-192.

Stewart, H. 1989. The Arctic Small Tool tradition and early Canadian Arctic Palaeo-Eskimo cultures. Études/Inuit/Studies, 13(2): 69-101.

Stuiver, M. and P.J. Reimer. 1993. Extended ^{14}C Data Base and Revised CALIB 3.0 ^{14}C Age Calibration Program. Radiocarbon, 35(1): 215-230.

Sutherland, P.D. in press. Continuity and Change in the Palaeo-Eskimo Prehistory of Northern Ellesmere Island. In, Proceedings of the conference "Palaeo-Eskimoiske kulturer i Gronland - Nye perspektiver i Gronlandsarkaeologien". Copenhagen: University of Copenhagen Press.

Swayze, K. 1993. The Tuktoyaktuk Interior Archaeology Project: Summer 1992. MS on file with the Canadian Museum of Civilization, Hull.

Taylor, W.E., Jr. 1972. An Archaeological Survey Between Cape Parry and Cambridge Bay, N.W.T., Canada in 1963. National Museum of Man, Mercury Series, Archaeological Survey of Canada Paper 1.

Tuck, J.A. 1975. Prehistory of Saglek Bay, Labrador: Archaic and Palaeo-Eskimo Occupations. National Museum of Man, Mercury Series, Archaeological Survey of Canada Paper 32.

Tuck, J.A. and W.W. Fitzhugh. 1986. Palaeo-Eskimo Traditions of Newfoundland and Labrador: A Re-Appraisal. In, Palaeo-Eskimo Cultures in Newfoundland, Labrador and Ungava. Memorial University of Newfoundland, Reports in Archaeology, 1: 161-168.

Vogel J.S., T.A. Brown, J.R. Southon and D.E. Nelson. 1991. Accelerator Radiocarbon Dates from the NOGAP Archaeology Project. In, NOGAP Archaeology Project: An Integrated Archaeological Research and Management Approach, J. Cinq-Mars and J.-L. Pilon, eds. Canadian Archaeological Association, Occasional Paper, 1: 143-148.

The Crane Site and the Lagoon Complex in the Western Canadian Arctic

Raymond J. Le Blanc
University of Alberta
Edmonton, Alberta

Abstract

The Crane site (ObRv-1), dated to between 2400 and 2800 years ago, presents a diverse assemblage of lithic and organic remains. These distinctive artifacts compare quite well with similar items found at the slightly younger Lagoon site (OjRl-3) on Banks Island. These considerations suggest the existence of a late Pre-Dorset manifestation in the western Canadian Arctic; the Lagoon Complex. The presence of Alaskan ASTt traits alongside Canadian ASTt influences betrays the geographic position of the Lagoon Complex, while the identification of both Pre-Dorset and Dorset elements among the artifacts is a clear indication of the transitional nature of this cultural manifestation.

Résumé

Le site Crane (ObRv-1), dont l'occupation remonterait entre 2400 et 2800 ans avant aujourd'hui, présente une grande diversité d'objets lithiques et organiques. Ceux-ci se comparent très bien avec des artefacts un peu plus récents, retrouvés au site Lagoon (OjRl-3), sur l'île Banks. Ces données suggèrent l'existence d'une manifestation culturelle prédorsetienne tardive, dans l'Arctique canadien occidental, que nous appelons le Complexe Lagoon. La présence de traits culturels alaskiens de la tradition microlithique de l'Arctique, parallèlement aux influences prédorsétiennes canadiennes, reflètent la situation géographique du Complexe Lagoon. L'identification d'éléments prédorsetiens et dorsétiens, nous offrent une indication de la nature transitionnelle de cette manifestation culturelle.

Introduction

Over a decade ago, Charles D. Arnold (1980, 1981a, 1981b) described a rather enigmatic Palaeoeskimo assemblage from the Lagoon site on the southwest coast of Banks Island in the western Canadian Arctic. Its distinctiveness was reflected in an assemblage whose organic artifacts were Pre-Dorset in character, a lithic collection that had strong Dorset overtones, specific elements of both raw material categories that were reminiscent of Alaskan Norton, and a late date of ca. 400 B.C. At the time, Arnold proposed a hybridization model to account for the eclectic nature of the Lagoon site. The model argued that the Lagoon site may have represented a peripheral vestigial, late Pre-Dorset population that had been influenced by Dorset groups expanding out of the "core-area" in the eastern Arctic, and by weaker Norton influences coming from the west.

Threads of Arctic Prehistory: Papers in Honour of William E. Taylor Jr., David Morrison and Jean-Luc Pilon, eds. Canadian Museum of Civilization, Mercury Series, Archaeological Survey of Canada Paper 149. 1994.

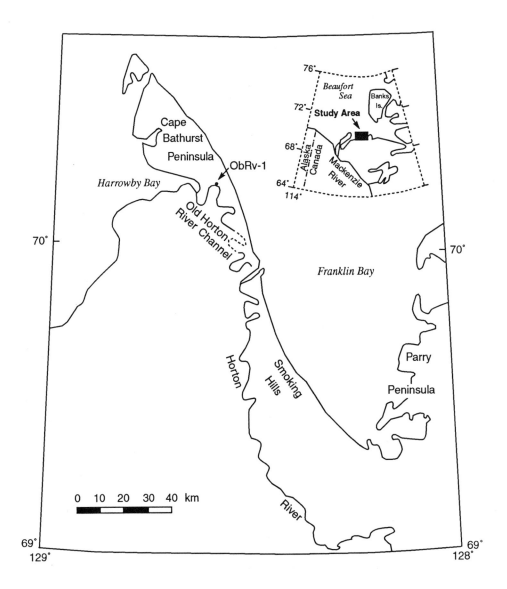

Figure 1 Map of Cape Bathurst Peninsula.

Arnold (1981a) was suitably cautious in his evaluation of the Lagoon site material, largely because the data base at that time, and on which these suggestions was made, was inadequate at best. In particular, the Lagoon site was the only representative of this variant, its relationship to earlier Pre-Dorset sites in the western Canadian Arctic was unclear, and the notion of Norton influences was limited and somewhat conjectural. Some of these limitations can now be addressed by recent field work that I have completed on the Cape Bathurst Peninsula on the mainland opposite Banks Island.

This relates generally to survey and test excavations on Cape Bathurst Peninsula (Le Blanc 1987, 1988, 1991a, 1991c), and more specifically, to the discovery in 1987 and the excavation in 1989 of the Crane site (ObRv-1), which has a Palaeoeskimo component that is virtually identical to the Lagoon site. In this paper I summarize the results of this work, and suggest that there is sufficient evidence to propose a regional late Pre-Dorset complex.

Location and Setting

The Crane site is located in the interior of the Cape Bathurst Peninsula about 250 km east of Tuktoyaktuk (Figure 1). Notable features on the peninsula include the meandering Old Horton River Channel, Harrowby Bay, and the Smoking Hills. The channel, which now is composed of a series of broad interconnected, meandering oxbow lakes, was originally the lower Horton River before it broke through to Franklin Bay on the east side of the peninsula about 400 years ago (Mackay and Slaymaker 1989). The well-known Smoking Hills are naturally burning organic-rich shales of the Smoking Hills Formation that are susceptible to spontaneous combustion when suddenly exposed to the atmosphere. Burnt and burning areas are called *bocannes* (Yorath *et al.* 1975; Yorath and Cook 1981; Mathews and Bustin 1982),and when active are marked by plumes of smoke with a strong

Figure 2 ObRv-1 is between the gullies (between tents); excavations in front of the left-most tent.

sulphurous odour; extinct examples are highly conspicuous because of their brilliant yellow, violet, and brick-red colours. *Bocannes* are found along the east shore of Cape Bathurst Peninsula north and south of the mouth of the Horton River and along the lower 80 km of the same river. The burning rock has cultural importance, because under certain conditions the burning process can create a basalt- to obsidian-like fused rock that was used by prehistoric people on Cape Bathurst Peninsula and elsewhere to manufacture a wide range of tools (Le Blanc 1991b).

Archaeological Research on Cape Bathurst Peninsula

The work at the Crane site was conducted within the context of broader study on Cape Bathurst that has resulted in the discovery of more than 80 sites (as of 1992). The majority of these, including Crane, occur along high terraces on the right bank of the Old Horton River Channel. These flat-topped, steep-sided terraces are cut by numerous gullies and a few ephemeral stream channels. The Crane site is located at one of the latter (Figure 2). The presence of the site was originally indicated by a surface scatter of quantities of bleached-white caribou and seal bone, lithic detritus, and fire-cracked rock. Excavations have revealed that this cultural debris comes from an occupational surface buried by more than 30 cm of aeolian sediments that originated from the bare terrace face. Strong

Figure 3 Intact cultural layer: note dessication cracks.

updrafts created this cliff-top dune with a lens-like configuration thickest at the terrace edge. Fortunately, this accumulation of sediment allowed the permafrost to rise, thus contributing to the excellent preservation of the organic component of the Crane assemblage.

Although intact in a number of areas of the site (Figure 3), the cultural layer was often disturbed and artifacts were found dispersed throughout the profile. This is due to the effects of cryoturbation, desiccation cracking and rodent disturbance, particularly near the terrace edge. Slumping is also occurring as we recorded a 20 cm movement at the edge of the slope in two years. We also observed a dramatic increase in the same period in retrogressive thaw flow failures along the channel. These slump features may reflect the effects of global warming (e.g. Edlund 1989), and over time they will likely be responsible for destroying many archaeological sites here and in other areas of the Mackenzie Delta region.

No evidence of dwellings was found in areas of the site where the occupational layer was intact, but we were able to recognize two hearths, one a small basin-shaped example, the other roughly oval-shaped, and two middens; the latter were indicated by dense accumulations of bone and fire-cracked rock.

Chronology

In view of the chronic problem of dating Palaeoeskimo sites, a major concern of the work at the Crane site was establishing a reasonable if not reliable chronology. Two samples of caribou bone from the 1987 work returned dates of 2805 ± 140 (S-2999; NMC-1393) and 2535 ± 140 (S-3036; NMC-1394) B.P. After the 1989 season an additional five samples of caribou bone were selected to overlap the major area of excavation on the west end of the site. These were processed by a different lab than the first and yielded a tight cluster of dates around 2500 B.P. (Table 1). When calibrated (Stuiver and Reimer 1993), the dates extend from 924 B.C. to 409 B.C., and the one sigma calibrated range is 1127 B.C. to 388 B.C. However, a closer examination of these dates using various techniques summarized in Shott (1992), suggests that the seven dates can be used to calculate a pooled weighted average of 2512.8 ± 40.9 B.P., yielding a calibrated age of occupation at some point in the period between the early eighth to the late seventh centuries B.C. (Table 1). It is not possible, however, to determine whether the site was occupied once, or periodically over a number of decades during this time.

Assemblage

The collections from the site include substantial numbers of lithic, bone and antler artifacts, as well as a faunal collection of 39 233 specimens.

Table 1 Radiocarbon dates from the Crane (ObRv-1) and Lagoon (OjRl-3) sites.

LABORATORY NUMBER	DATE	CALIBRATION*
CRANE SITE		
S-2999; NMC-1393	2805 ± 140	cal BC 1127 (924) 811
S-3036; NMC-1394	2535 ± 140	cal BC 816 (769) 406
AECV–1104C	2530 ± 110	cal BC 805 (768) 413
AECV–1105C	2410 ± 90	cal BC 761 (409) 391
AECV–1106C	2410 ± 100	cal BC 763 (409) 388
AECV–1107C	2540 ± 100	cal BC 805 (771) 427
AECV–1108C	2540 ± 100	cal BC 805 (771) 427
Average	2512.8 ± 40.9	cal BC 782(764, 617, 604) 533
LAGOON SITE		
RL–765**	2320 ± 120	cal BC 511 (390) 202
RL–2290**	2290 ± 120	cal BC 408 (380) 193
RL–767**	2390 ± 110	cal BC 760 (400) 376
Average	2360.4 ± 65.6	cal BC 474 (400) 382

* 1 sigma maximum, (cal. ages), 1 sigma minimum; all calibrations were made using
   CALIB rev 3.0 (Stuiver and Reimer 1993) using method A
**Lagoon site (OjRl-3) dates (Arnold 1981a: Table 22)

Organic

The organic artifacts include tools made of antler, bone, wood, and ivory.

Bone/Antler

The bone and antler materials can be broken into major categories of production material and a number of pseudo-functional categories of implements.

Production material

Production material includes a limited range of items such as antler cores, one of which is also a percussor; a few partially worked antler blanks; and various pieces of waste material such as transversely cut and snapped tines. The only evidence of bone core production relates to the manufacture of sewing needles. This includes five cores and 12 pieces of production waste. A good deal of the needle production material was found in the same area as the majority (n=13, 72.2%) of the needles themselves.

Implements

A) Weaponry and Fishing Gear

Weapons and related items include harpoons, foreshafts, a lance-head, and an arrowhead. The harpoons form a consistent group of seven complete (n=4; Figure 4*a-d*) and fragmentary examples, including one that appears to be a toy or model (Figure 4*d*). The complete specimens are bilaterally barbed, with open sockets opposed by multi-scored lashing beds, central bilaterally-gouged line holes, and single lateral spurs. Three are self-bladed (Figure 4*a,b,d,* not counting the toy), but the fourth has a shallow bed, presumably for the attachment of an end-blade (Figure 4*c*). What I believe to be foreshafts (Figure 5*j*) are represented by three broken, rather heavy duty triangular-shaped antler specimens, which also have central bilaterally-gouged line holes. The single lance-head (Figure 4*e*), which is decorated with parallel lines and chevrons, has an open socket and shallow distal bed similar to one of the harpoons. The arrowhead (Figure 4*f*) is a broken unilaterally barbed specimen, and the fishing gear is represented by an antler leister prong barb (Figure 5*c*).

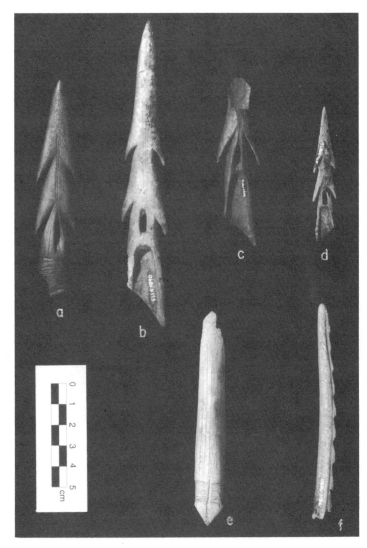

Figure 4 Harpoons (*a-d*), lance-head (*e*), arrowhead (*f*).

B) Hide Working Implements

A variety of tools could be considered as hide working implements. These include a rather large sample of awls. Some of these are made of caribou long bone splinters, others of rod-like pieces of antler, but the majority are bipointed antler examples (Figure 5*f,g*). Elsewhere in the Canadian Arctic, bipointed specimens like the Crane awls have been called leister centre prongs, arrowheads

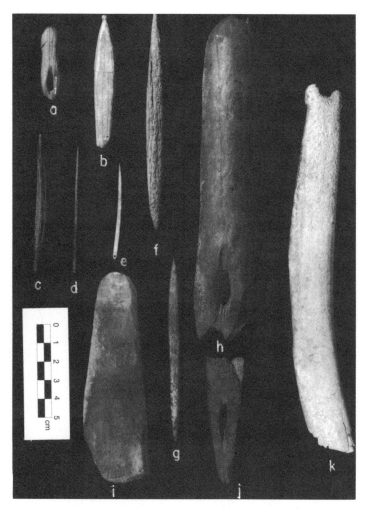

Figure 5 Ornaments (*a,b*), leister prong (*c*), needles (*d,e*), awls (*f,g*), adzes (*h,i*), foreshaft (*j*), flaker (*k*).

(Arnold 1981a: 76), or gorges used for fishing (Maxwell 1985: 91). However, at the Crane site they are found mainly in association with bone needles and typically they exhibit a high degree of polish on the tips that is most effectively explained as being the result of intensive rotary use of the type one would associate with making holes in hide.

Needles (Figure 5*d,e*) are also abundant and made invariably of large bird long bones (e.g. tundra swan). They have flattened cross-sections with rounded edges, blunt ends and drilled eyes.

Finally there are several rather large, thinned sections of antler cortex with convex distal ends, that are usually referred to as split antler scrapers, and may have been used in hide preparation.

C) Ornaments

An effigy of a seal swimming in the water (Figure 5*b-d*) and another object with phallic connotations (Figure 5*a*) represent the only vestiges of non-utilitarian decorative items in the assemblage.

D) Lithic Tool Production and Woodworking Tools

There were a variety of antler tools associated with lithic tool production. This includes a large percussor made from a recycled antler core that has a battered proximal end with microchips (visible at 25-50X) of local raw materials embedded in the antler matrix. There is also a morphologically divergent range of implements that were apparently used as flakers (Figure 5*k*), because they too have microchips embedded in rounded, worn working ends.

Two adze-like implements (Figure 5*h*), one of which appears to have been a blade used in some type of composite haft (Figure 5*i*), and a chisel-like piece of antler made from tine, appear suited to woodworking, an activity indicated by the presence of wood chips and shavings in several areas of the site.

E) Miscellaneous Bone and Antler

A variety of tool fragments and other items defy classification, among them is an impressive 45 cm long antler knitting needle-like object with a bilaterally gouged hole in one end.

Ivory and Wood

Ivory use is represented by a single specimen that may be a knife handle fragment. Wood artifacts include a small handle with a shallow bed on the distal end suitable for one of the small notched end-blades in the collection; a fragment of decorated wood; two sharpened stakes or pegs; various pieces of production material, which exhibit various combinations of cutting and whittling; and a large number of stick and twig fragments.

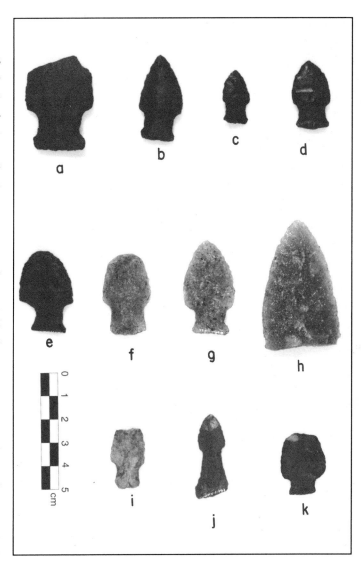

Figure 6 Endblades.

Lithics

All of the lithic artifacts at the Crane site were made of local materials obtained from two major sources. The predominant material is clinker from small, ephemeral *bocanne*-quarries located in the Cape Bathurst Peninsula area (Le Blanc 1991b). The other materials, include chert, quartzite, and various siltstones, all of which come from glacially derived lag gravel in the Old Horton River Channel.

Production Material

Lithic production by-products included several cores (34), core fragments (155), and several thousand (7566) flakes and pieces of shatter. An analysis of this debitage revealed differences in the use of clinker versus the other materials. For example, chert and quartzite cores were collected as waterworn pebbles and apparently brought to the site in this form. Core attributes indicate the use of the bipolar technique on more than half of the core sample, although very few bipolar flakes were actually observed. In contrast, the clinker was brought to the site in the form of rough and semi-finished bifacial preforms. Some of these served as sources of flakes for various small tools and others were further reduced into some of the bifaces that appear in the collection.

Figure 7 Side-scrapers (*a-c*), transverse-oblique scrapers (*d-f*), burins (*g,h*), end-scrapers (*i,j*), gravers (*k,l*), adzes (*m,n*).

Implements

The lithic implements include a variety of bifaces, including side- and corner-notched end blades, stemmed end-blades (Figure 6), side-blades, and a range of large and small bifaces that likely represent cutting implements. Scrapers were next in importance with end (Figure 7*i,j*) and side examples, side-notched side-scrapers (Figure 7*a-c*), and side-notched transverse-oblique scrapers (Figure 7*d-f*). Four flake burins (Figure 7*g,h*), all of which are spalled with no evidence of grinding, and two burin spalls represent the only evidence of this often ubiquitous technology. Finally, there were four gravers (Figure 7*k,l*); six adzes and adze fragments (Figure 7*m,n*); a few abraders, one of which has grooves that suggest use as a sharpening stone for awls and needles; hammerstones, and two pièces esquillées. Blade technology is minimally indicated by a few macroblades (9) and microblades (8), and there are just over 300 edge modified flakes and shatter.

Faunal Remains

A preliminary report on the results of the analysis of the 1987 collection has been reported elsewhere (Nagy 1990). An approximately 12% sample of the more than 33,000 bones from the 1989 collection amplifies and complements the findings of the earlier study. Very briefly, the compiled results of the two analyses indicate the use of a variety of birds (Canada goose, mallard, loon, ptarmigan, snow goose, tundra swan), terrestrial (caribou, domestic dog, moose, muskox, snowshoe hare, ground squirrel, Arctic fox, and muskrat) and sea mammals (bearded, ringed, harp seals, and seal sp.). The faunal sample is dominated by caribou (NISP=4204, %NISP=56.3%; MNI=29, %MNI=34.5%); seal (NISP=1148; %NISP=15.4%; MNI=15; %MNI=17.9%) and snow goose (NISP=237, %NISP=3.2%; MNI=9, %MNI=10.7%) (data abstracted from Le Blanc n.d. Table 9). Seasonality indicators suggest a minimum spring-summer occupation.

Discussion

On many levels the Crane site is directly comparable to the Lagoon site. Typologically, this can be seen in the artifacts where there is a virtually identical range of harpoons and lance-heads, as well as close similarities in such things as needles, bipointed awls, end-blades, scrapers, minimal evidence of a microblade industry, use of quartzite for several varieties of tools and the large size of some of the lithic tools. There are of course differences between the two assemblages, but overall the specific similarities are compelling. In other aspects such as the faunal assemblages, the two sites are alike in species composition but differ in emphasis, with caribou predominating at Crane and snow geese at Lagoon. Seasonality indicators are the same, however, in spite of the different topographic (coastal versus interior) settings of the two sites. There are also parallels in terms of chronology. The calibrated dates on the three muskox bone samples from Lagoon extend from 380-390 B.C, and have a one sigma range of 511 B.C. to 193 B.C. (Table 1). The calculated average yields a date of 400 B.C. (one sigma range: 474-382 B.C.). This represents about 200 years between the two sites, although their ranges overlap at two sigma. However, because of the strong typological similarities, it would appear reasonable to assume that the two suites of dates represent a segment in the developmental history of the same regional cultural expression.

Based on the foregoing, I believe that there is sufficient justification to support the establishment of a regional Palaeoeskimo late Pre-Dorset cultural entity called the Lagoon Complex. This complex would include the Crane and Lagoon sites, and perhaps a site reported briefly by Taylor (1964) from McCormick Inlet on Melville Island. This distribution of sites represents a geographic range of nearly 1000 km northeast-southwest, but with an as yet unknown lateral extent. The 10 calibrated radiocarbon dates from the Crane and Lagoon sites, all of which are on terrestrial mammal bone, span the middle centuries of the last millennium B.C., during the so-called transitional period of Pre-Dorset to Dorset cultural development. The genesis of this complex is presently unknown. However, there are earlier Palaeoeskimo remains in the same area as the Crane site (ObRw-11; Le Blanc 1991a) and there are other early Palaeoeskimo sites in the region, including Banks Island (e.g. Shoran Lake area: Müller-Beck 1977, Taylor 1967), and Ekalluk River on Victoria Island (Taylor 1967, 1972). These remains suggest that the Lagoon Complex was part of an in situ regional Palaeoeskimo developmental history, influenced by trait diffusion from the west and east, rather than one characterized only by periodic colonization from the east (cf., McGhee 1976). A similar pattern of cultural development seems to have prevailed in the High Arctic on the North Devon Lowlands (Helmer 1991), and, to a certain degree on the Bache Peninsula of Ellesmere Island, although migration also played an important role in the latter area (Schledermann 1990). However, unlike the North Devon Lowlands and the Bache Peninsula regions, there is no clear regional successor to the Lagoon Complex. As a site that straddles the period of Palaeoeskimo culture change, logic would imply an eventual evolution into something recognizable as being clearly Dorset in character. On current evidence, there does not appear to be a regional representation of Dorset.

In the broader context of Palaeoeskimo development, the Lagoon Complex remains something of an amalgam. Arnold outlined this in his analysis of the Lagoon site materials, noting elements of Pre-Dorset, Dorset, and Norton traits in the Lagoon site assemblage; by extension, the same is true of the Crane site. The relationship with Dorset and Pre-Dorset is clearly strong, and I think it reflects sustained inter-group contact in one way or another with Palaeoeskimo bands further to the east. The Norton connection was perhaps the most tenuous when Arnold made his comparisons, and this is still the case. The nearest Norton culture occurrences in the Mackenzie Delta region continue to be in the Trout Lake area on the Yukon Coastal Plain (Greer 1991), about 470 km by air from the Cape Bathurst Peninsula region.

However, the lower age limit of around 800 B.C. for the Lagoon Complex suggests that influences could have also included Choris, and indeed, elements of this stage of the Norton Tradition (Dumond 1987) appear to have penetrated into the eastern Mackenzie Delta region. The evidence for this presence is suggested by surface finds of a mid-section of a ripple-flaked lanceolate biface from a site (NkTm-7; Le Blanc 1988) off Hutchinson Bay on the Tuktoyaktuk Peninsula, 180 km by air to the west, and a similarly worked broad-stemmed biface from a site on the Old Horton River Channel (OaRu-1), about 30 km southeast of the Crane site. Sutherland (pers. comm., 1993) has also found a surface scatter of Choris material at a site on Richards Island that has produced, among other things, linear-stamped pottery and a double-ended burin. As yet, the only clear Lagoon Complex similarities to Choris include the bone needles (Giddings and Anderson 1986: Plate 109) and a side-notched end-blade from the "Choris Cache" (Giddings and Anderson 1986: Plate 124z) on Cape Krusenstern that is remarkably like some of the Crane site examples. Nonetheless, a Choris presence in the Mackenzie Delta region at 1000 B.C., or slightly earlier, may reflect the beginnings of increasing western influences on the periphery of the Palaeoeskimo domain. Moreover, the timing of this presence indicates that these potential influences overlap the beginning of the transition from Pre-Dorset to Dorset in the Eastern Arctic, suggesting, perhaps, a greater role for the extreme western Arctic on events in the east (Sutherland pers. comm., 1993).

Acknowledgements

Many individuals contributed to the Cape Bathurst Peninsula project. Permission to conduct the fieldwork on the peninsula was kindly granted by the people of Tuktoyaktuk through a landuse license granted by the Inuvialuit Land Administration. Thanks to Jane Bicknell at the ILA for her help the last several seasons. Funding for various parts of this project were provided by the Northern Oil and Gas Action Plan Secretariat, Indian and Northern Affairs Canada; the Social Sciences and Humanities Research Council of Canada; the Polar Continental Shelf Project; the former Inuvik Scientific Research Laboratory; and the Endowment Fund for the Future, University of Alberta; and the Department of Anthropology, University of Alberta. I would like to acknowledge the help of the following individuals for various aspects of this project: J. Cinq-Mars, J.-L. Pilon, R. McGhee, D. Morrison, the late S. Presley, D. Laverie, L. Johanis, and G. Eustache, Archaeological Survey of Canada; and J. Dale, J. Garland, J. Tremblay, and J. Marsh formerly of the ASC. Thanks also to V. Rampton, C. Schweger, the late O. Hughes, J. Dixon, J. Wong, T. Barry, W. Mathews, and J. R. Mackay. In Edmonton, several provided valuable assistance including (M. Nagy, J. Woollett, G. Hare, R. Shafiq, D. Cockle, C. Duarte, R. Lello, J. Boyer, and L. Chinery). A special thanks to the staff of PCSP in Tuktoyaktuk, including Eddie, Frank, Debbie and Donna, and J. Ostrick and M. Chapman of the Inuvik Research Lab. The crews who participated for the two seasons deserve a special thanks for putting up with the cold, bugs, and freeze-dried whatever: M. Nagy ('87, '89), T. M. Friesen ('87), D. Webster ('87), J. Woollett ('89), and G. Johnson ('89). Finally, a very special note of appreciation to my family for enduring my many absences from family activities while this project developed and continued.

References

Arnold, C.D. 1980. A Paleoeskimo occupation on southern Banks Island, N.W.T. Arctic, 33(3): 400-426.

Arnold, C.D. 1981a. The Lagoon site (OjRl-3): implications for Paleoeskimo interactions. National Museum of Man, Mercury Series, Archaeological Survey of Canada Paper 107.

Arnold, C.D. 1981b. Demographic process and culture change: an example from the Western Canadian Arctic. In, Networks of the past: regional interaction in archaeology, P.D. Francis, F.J. Kense and P.G. Duke, eds. Calgary: The Archaeological Association of the University of Calgary, pp. 311-326.

Dumond, D.E. 1987. The Eskimos and Aleuts. (Revised edition). London: Thames and Hudson.

Edlund, S.A. 1989. Vegetation indicates potentially unstable Arctic terrain. Geos, 18(3): 9-13.

Giddings. J.L. and D.D. Anderson. 1986. Beach Ridge Archeology of Cape Krusenstern. U.S. National Park Service, Publications in Archeology 20.

Greer, S. C. 1991. The Trout Lake archaeological locality and the British Mountain problem. In, NOGAP Archaeology Project: an Integrated Archaeological Research and Management Approach, J. Cinq-Mars and J.-L. Pilon, eds. Canadian Archaeological Association, Occasional Paper 1: 15-31.

Helmer, J.W. 1991. The Palaeo-Eskimo prehistory of the North Devon Lowlands. Arctic, 44(4): 301-317.

Le Blanc, R.J. 1987. Report of activities—NOGAP 1986: Northern Yukon to Cape Bathurst Peninsula. Final report for Yukon permit #86-2ASR; N.W.T. permit #86-603, and Parks Canada permit #86-46. MS on file with the Canadian Museum of Civilization, Hull.

Le Blanc, R.J. 1988. Archaeological Research in the Mackenzie Delta Region. Final report for N.W.T. permit #87-617. MS on file with the Canadian Museum of Civilization, Hull.

Le Blanc, R.J. 1991a. New data relating to the prehistory of the Mackenzie Delta region of the NOGAP study area. In, NOGAP archaeology project: an integrated archaeological research and management approach, J. Cinq-Mars and J.-L. Pilon, eds. Canadian Archaeological Association Occasional Paper 1: 65-76.

Le Blanc, R.J. 1991b. Prehistoric clinker use on the Cape Bathurst Peninsula, Northwest Territories, Canada: the dynamics of formation and procurement. American Antiquity, 56(2): 268-277.

Le Blanc, R.J. 1991c. Archaeology on the Cape Bathurst Peninsula. Preliminary report for N.W.T. permit #89-656. MS on file with the Canadian Museum of Civilization, Hull.

Le Blanc, R.J. n.d. The Crane site (ObRv-1) and the Palaeoeskimo period in the Western Canadian Arctic. in press, Canadian Museum of Civilization, Mercury Series, Archaeological Survey of Canada.

Mackay, J.R. and O. Slaymaker 1989. The Horton River breakthrough and resulting geomorphic changes in a permafrost environment, Western Arctic Coast, Canada. Geografiska Annaler, 71A(3-4): 171-184.

Mathews, W.H. and R.M. Bustin. 1982. Why do the Smoking Hills smoke? Canadian Journal of Earth Sciences, 21: 737-742.

Maxwell, M.S. 1985. Prehistory of the Eastern Arctic. New York: Academic Press.

McGhee, R. 1976. Paleoeskimo occupations of Central and High Arctic Canada. In, Eastern Arctic Prehistory: Paleoeskimo Problems, M.S. Maxwell, ed. Memoirs of the Society for American Archaeology, 31: 15-39.

Müller-Beck, H.J., ed. 1977. Excavations at Umingmak on Banks Island, N.W.T., 1970 and 1973 preliminary report. Tübingen: Urgeschichtliche Materialhefte 1.

Nagy, M.I. 1990. Faunal Analysis of the Crane site (Horton River, N.W.T.). Paper presented at the 23rd Annual Meeting of the Canadian Archaeological Association. Whitehorse, Yukon.

Schledermann, P. 1990. Crossroads to Greenland. Arctic Institute of North America. Komatik Series, 2.

Shott, M.J. 1992. Radiocarbon dating as a probabilistic technique: the Childers Site and Late Woodland occupation in the Ohio Valley. American Antiquity, 57(2): 202-230.

Stuiver, M., and P.J. Reimer. 1993. Extended ^{14}C data base and revised Calib 3.0 ^{14}C age calibration program. Radiocarbon, 35(1): 215-230.

Taylor, W.E., Jr. 1964. Archaeology of the McCormick Inlet Site, Melville Island, N.W.T. Arctic, 17(2): 126-129.

Taylor, W.E., Jr. 1967. Summary of archaeological fieldwork on Banks and Victoria Islands, Arctic Canada, 1965. Arctic Anthropology, 4(1): 221-243.

Taylor, W.E., Jr. 1972. An archaeological survey between Cape Parry and Cambridge Bay, N.W.T., Canada in 1963. National Museum of Man, Mercury Series, Archaeological Survey of Canada Paper 1.

Yorath, C.J., H.R. Balkwill and R.W. Klassen. 1975. Franklin Bay and Malloch Hill Map-Areas, District of Mackenzie. Geological Survey of Canada, Paper 74-36.

Yorath, C.J. and D.G. Cook. 1981. Cretaceous and Tertiary stratigraphy and Paleography, Northern Interior Plains, District of Mackenzie. Geological Survey of Canada, Memoir 398.

Le Paléoesquimau dans la baie du Diana
(Arctique québécois)

Patrick Plumet
Laboratoire d'archéologie
Université du Québec à Montréal

Résumé

Le premier courant de peuplement de la baie d'Ungava venait de l'est, plutôt que de l'ouest. Le réseau spatial des populations du Paléoesquimau inférieur s'étendait donc au moins du Labrador à la région de Wakeham. La région de la baie du Diana semble avoir été occupée assez tôt au Paléoesquimau inférieur, au Paléoesquimau "moyen", c'est-à-dire pendant la période de transition (Groswatérien ou Dorsétien ancien), au Dorsétien moyen et très tard au Paléoesquimau supérieur. Les occupations s'échelonnent sur presque la totalité du Paléoesquimau, avec un hyatus probable entre 1380±100 et 1090±90 B.P., et deux légères inflexions entre 1660±95 et 1555±80 B.P., et entre 635±90 et 490±80 B.P. Néanmoins, les données archéologiques n'indiquent pas de changements dans l'origine des occupants. Nous proposons un premier mouvement de peuplement venu du Nord (Groenland, Ellesmere, Baffin oriental) vers le Labrador et l'Ungava jusqu'au Cap de Nouvelle-France sur la côte sud du détroit d'Hudson. Par contre, le schéma proposé par Taylor d'un courant de peuplement venu du golfe de Foxe par les îles du détroit d'Hudson, ne peut s'appliquer qu'à la partie occidentale de la péninsule et à l'Hudsonie.

Abstract

The first occupants of Ungava Bay came from the East rather than from the West. Thus, the spatial network of these early Palaeoeskimos extended from Labrador to the Wakeham Bay area. Diana Bay was occupied during the following periods: Early Palaeoeskimo, "middle" Palaeoeskimo or transitional (Groswater or Early Dorset), Middle Dorset period, and quite late in Late Palaeoeskimo times. These occupations span the entire Palaeoeskimo period with a probable hyatus between 1380±100 and 1090±90 B.P., and two slight inflections between 1660±95 and 1555±80 B.P., and between 635±90 and 490±80 B.P. Throughout the entire seqence, there are no apparent population changes. It is suggested that the initial population movement into the region was from the North (Greenland, Ellesmere Island and the eastern portion of Baffin Island), towards Labrador and the Ungava Peninsula as far as Cap Nouvelle-France on the southern shore of Hudson Strait. Taylor's scheme of colonization from Foxe Bassin via the islands of Hudson Strait would only apply to the western part of the Ungava Peninsula and the Hudson Bay coast.

Threads of Arctic Prehistory: Papers in Honour of William E. Taylor Jr., David Morrison and Jean-Luc Pilon, eds. Canadian Museum of Civilization, Mercury Series, Archaeological Survey of Canada Paper 149. 1994.

Introduction

En 1957, William Taylor alla fouiller un site dorsétien découvert en 1948 par Michéa (1950) au lac Payne. À 200 km de la côte, cette occupation dorsétienne était la première connue à l'intérieur des terres. Il effectua ensuite des reconnaissances dans la baie d'Ungava et le long du détroit d'Hudson. Cette mission préliminaire lui permit d'observer la première maison longue signalée dans l'Arctique, celle de Pamiok (Imaha I) à l'embouchure de l'Arnaud, et plusieurs sites paléoesquimaux (Taylor 1958). Par la suite, deux sites insulaires proches des côtes du Québec, Arnapik à l'île Mansel et Tyara à l'île de Salluit, lui permettaient d'établir la continuité d'évolution entre le Prédorsétien et le Dorsétien (Taylor 1968). Cependant, en 1964, dans sa synthèse préliminaire sur la préhistoire de la péninsule du Québec-Labrador, il mentionnait que les seuls gisements prédorsétiens connus dans la péninsule du Québec-Labrador étaient les trois d'Ivugivik et les deux de l'île Mansel (Figure 1).

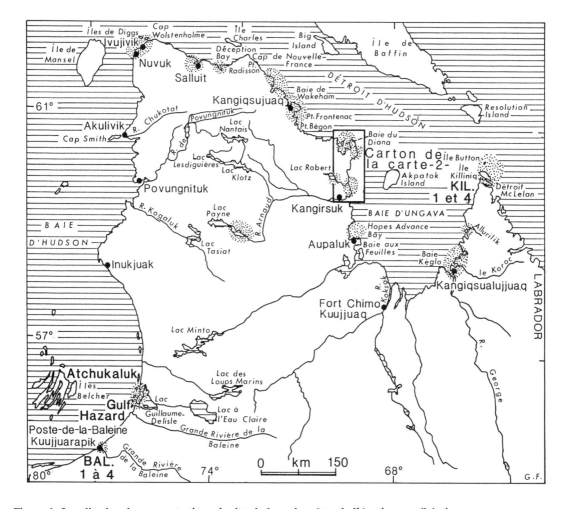

Figure 1 Localisation des concentrations de sites le long des côtes de l'Arctique québécois.

Ayant placé l'extrémité nord-ouest de la péninsule du Québec-Labrador dans l'aire nucléaire du Dorsétien, centrée alors autour du golfe de Foxe, il supposa naturellement que "l'occupation de l'Ungava avant la culture Dorset était le résultat d'une migration de l'île Baffin en passant par l'extrémité ouest du détroit d'Hudson et par les îles Mill, Salisbury et Nottingham". Je repris moi-même cette hypothèse (Plumet 1977) jusqu'à ce que d'autres données me fissent changer d'avis (Plumet 1978, 1986).

En 1964, Taylor pouvait également écrire que dans un territoire deux fois et demie plus grand que la vieille France, «le trait le plus saillant de l'archéologie du Québec est peut-être l'ignorance prodigieuse qu'on en a et qui n'est en somme que la conséquence d'une lamentable pénurie de travaux de terrain» (1964: 1). C'est pour combler cette ignorance que fut conçu le programme Tuvaaluk, subventionné par le Conseil de Recherches en sciences humaines du Canada et l'Université du Québec à Montréal. De 1975 à 1980, il permit d'effectuer de vastes reconnaissances autour de la baie d'Ungava et le long de la côte sud de détroit d'Hudson ainsi qu'à l'intérieur du Nouveau-Québec, aux lacs Klotz et Payne. Trois cent trente-cinq sites furent inventoriés dans ce macro-espace, dont plus de 80 dans la baie du Diana, centre du méso-espace de recherche (Figures 1 et 2). Bien que les recherches archéologiques fussent surtout orientées vers les modes d'établissement dorsétiens, une attention particulière fut portée aux indices d'occupation prédorsétienne dans l'île du Diana, dont l'extrémité sud constituait le micro-espace centré sur le site Tuvaaluk (DIA.4, JfEl-4). Si aujourd'hui toutes les données recueillies au cours de ce programme sont encore loin d'avoir été exploitées, celles qui sont déjà publiées ou disponibles sous forme de rapports préliminaires ou de mémoires de maîtrise permettent d'esquisser un schéma de la mise en place du peuplement paléoesquimau et de

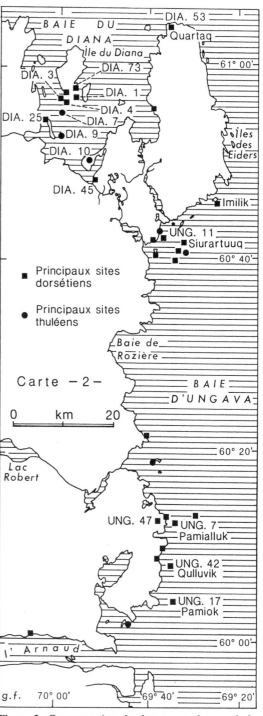

Figure 2 **Concentration de sites au nord-ouest de la baie d'Ungava.**

son évolution assez différent de celui que nous avions à la fin des années quatre-vingt (Badgley 1980; Bibeau 1984, 1986; Desrosiers 1982, 1986; Gauvin 1990; Labrèche 1986; Piérard 1975; Plumet 1986, 1989; Plumet et Badgley 1980; Plumet et Gangloff 1987, 1991).

Nous nous proposons ici, en nous appuyant sur ces données, de tracer les grandes lignes de l'évolution du Paléoesquimau dans la baie du Diana et surtout dans l'île du même nom, depuis la mise en place du premier peuplement jusqu'à la disparition du Dorsétien. Nous insisterons particulièrement sur le Paléoesquimau inférieur, moins étudié jusqu'en 1980 dans la région. Les matières premières nous serviront d'indice pour tenter de retracer le réseau spatial des population de cette période, comme nous l'avons déjà fait pour le Paléoesquimau supérieur (Plumet 1981)

L'île du Diana

L'île du Diana, longue de 15 km et large de 5, est la plus grande des îles de la baie (Figure 2). La toundra de type herbacé ou ligneux bas qui la recouvre est sans doute installée depuis 3 500 B.P., à la suite d'une détérioration climatique (Richard 1981: 136). Son paysage présente une bonne synthèse des conditions géomorphologiques de la région (Figure 3). Constituée, comme les autres îles, de roches précambriennes, la richesse de ses paysages s'explique par la diversité de son relief. Le nord de l'île, prolongement de la «pénéplaine laurentienne», culmine vers 200-225 m d'altitude en un relief heurté aux pentes raides qui contraste avec la partie sud. Celle-ci, correspondant à la surface d'érosion de Quaqtaq fortement dégradée, est riche en dépôts meubles, retravaillés en formations de plages par la mer post-glaciaire d'Iberville. Ces plages sont généralement coincées dans des couloirs structuraux dégagés par l'érosion différentielle (Gangloff 1988). C'est là que se regroupent la plupart des gisements archéologiques (Figure 4). Ils témoignent d'une occupation humaine remontant au début du Paléoesquimau inférieur et qui présente l'intérêt de se poursuivre jusqu'à la fin du Paléoesquimau supérieur, dans un Dorsétien particulièrement tardif. Le Néoesquimau n'y est représenté que par quelques structures de surface, des emplacements de tentes, quelques abris, caches ou affûts, des sépultures et des pièges, généralement d'apparence récente et rarement visibles à proximité immédiate des vestiges paléoesquimaux, sauf au site Gagnon (DIA.73). Par contre, d'autres îles proches, telles que Opingivik (DIA.7, JfEl-7), Pupik (DIA.9), Illutalialuk, ou Ile aux Iglous (DIA.10, JfEl-10), recèlent d'importants habitats néoesquimaux, dont l'un au moins, DIA.10, remonte au début du Thuléen. Les autres sont sans doute moins anciens, celui d'Opingivik étant peut-être contemporain des tout premiers contacts avec les Européens.

L'évolution du milieu physique

S'il y a 6000 ans la baie du Diana communiquait encore avec celle d'Ungava par trois passes, celles-ci allaient se transformer en vallées avant l'arrivée des premiers Paléoesquimaux. Les séries de plages soulevées de l'île du Diana ont été étudiées par Hillaire-Marcel (1979) qui évalue le taux d'émersion à 0,3 cm par an au cours des cinq derniers milliers d'années, soit 30 cm par siècle et 3 m par millénaire. Ce relèvement serait resté très constant pendant toute cette période qui est également

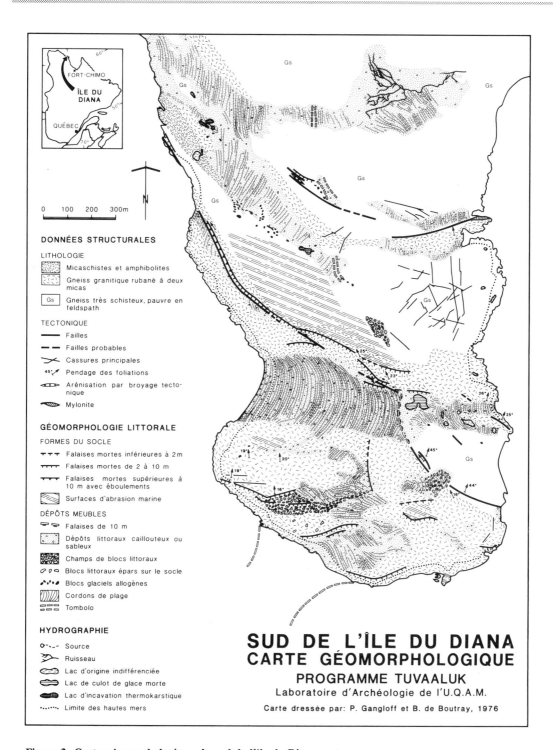

Figure 3 Carte géomorphologique du sud de l'île du Diana.

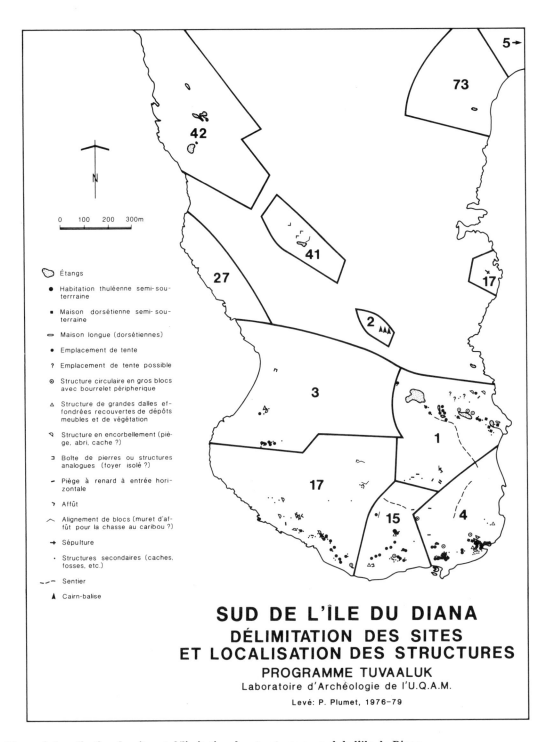

Figure 4 Localisation des sites et délimitation des structures au sud de l'île du Diana.

celle de l'occupation humaine. On peut donc estimer qu'au tout début du Paléoesquimau, le niveau marin pouvait être une douzaine de mètres plus élevé qu'aujourd'hui. Plusieurs indices permettent de croire que l'abaissement du niveau relatif de la mer connut peut-être de brèves inversions: vers 7 m, des dépôts marins apparemment non remaniés recouvrent un niveau archéologique et, vers la même altitude, du matériel lithique a nettement été roulé par l'eau. L'occupation humaine ne connut toutefois pas de transformation importante du paysage, comme il advint pour les premières générations de Paléoesquimaux dans la région de Poste-de-la-Baleine (Plumet 1976). Les terres émergées étaient un peu moins étendues sans être pour autant plus morcelées qu'aujourd'hui; les eaux étaient plus profondes, facilitant l'évolution des gros mammifères marins, mais les courants marins et la topographie générale du littoral devaient ressembler à ce que nous connaissons, n'impliquant donc pas un mode d'établissement différent. Par contre, en 4000 ans, les fluctuations climatiques secondaires ont pu faire varier la disponibilité de certaines espèces animales.

Les ressources animales

La baie du Diana est riche en phoques qui en fréquentent les eaux à l'année longue ou saisonnièrement selon les espèces. Les morses passent devant la baie lors de leur migration entre la région de Wakeham et l'île Akpatok. Les cétacés se rencontrent encore aujourd'hui: rorqual et baleines croisent entre les îles et les bélougas sont chassés jusqu'au fond de la baie. Les os de baleine blanchis qui gisent sur bien des plages attestent l'importance de ces animaux pour les populations locales d'autrefois. Enfin, à la fin des années soixante-dix, le caribou commençait à revenir vers Quaqtaq après avoir délaissé le nord de l'Ungava pendant plusieurs dizaines d'années. Par contre, traces et structures anthropiques témoignent que la chasse au caribou tenait autrefois une place importante dans l'économie esquimaude, même sur l'île du Diana. Les enquêtes ethnographiques ont montré que le souvenir de ces chasses était encore vivant (Piérard 1979; Vézinet 1982).

Les ressources minérales

Les matières premières représentées dans les gisements nous serviront d'indicateurs du réseau spatial des occupants selon les critères établis dans des travaux antérieurs (Archambault 1981; de Boutray 1981; Plumet 1981, 1986) auxquels s'ajoutent des éléments plus récents. Schématiquement, les ressources minérales peuvent être réparties dans les catégories de provenance suivantes:

- Matières premières locales ou sans provenance précise, donc sans valeur heuristique en rapport avec le réseau spatial: les schistes, le métabasalte, le quartz cristallin et certains cherts.

- Matières premières régionales, provenant de la baie du Diana: les quartzites de Diana, enfumés et souvent légèrement bleuté, varicelleux et amphibole. Les affleurements d'où ils proviennent semblent avoir été découverts par un Inuk de Qaqtqaq à l'est de la baie de Hall. D'importants établissements dorsétiens et des indices de chasse au caribou y auraient été repérés (Badgley, comm. pers.). L'analyse pétrographique d'échantillons de ces affleurements qui nous ont été confiés par Badgley, confirme qu'il s'agit bien du type Diana, tel qu'il avait été identifié antérieurement à partir d'échantillons archéologiques (de Boutray 1981; de Boutray et Plumet 1990).

- Matières premières allochtones occidentales provenant probablement du détroit d'Hudson, région de Wakeham: le quartz laiteux et hyalin, deux aspects, plus ou moins laiteux ou translucide, d'une même roche qui n'est qu'une variante de quartz filonien blanc. Toutefois, si le quartz filonien blanc se trouve un peu partout en veines intrusives, il présente très rarement l'homogénéité et les propriétés clastiques qui rendent le quartz laiteux propre au débitage et à la taille. Une carrière de quartz laiteux, exploitée au Dorsétien, se trouverait dans l'île Ukivik, près de Wakeham (Saladin d'Anglure, comm. pers.) et une autre au lac Robert.

- Matières premières allochtones sans doute méridionales et provenant de la fosse du Labrador, peut-être à son intersection avec l'Arnaud: le quartzite ferrugineux, complètement noir et opaque, longtemps confondu avec le quartzite enfumé noir de Ramah. Il domine très largement dans certains sites dorsétiens à l'embouchure de l'Arnaud, mais se trouve aussi dans les sites de la région de Wakeham; il a peut-être plusieurs sources.

- Matières premières allochtones orientales, d'origine labradorienne: le quartzite enfumé de Ramah, les cherts de Mugford, en particulier le chert noir, malheureusement souvent trouvé en petits morceaux difficiles à identifier avec certitude.

Le Paléoesquimau inférieur et le problème de la mise en place du premier peuplement

Les gisements du Paléoesquimau inférieur n'ont fait l'objet de recherches systématiques pendant le programme Tuvaaluk que dans la partie sud de l'île du Diana. Étant très discrets, ils ont peu de chances d'être repérés lors des reconnaissances héliportées. Dans la mesure où maintenant le Groswatérien est placé à la fin de cette période (Tuck et Fitzhugh 1986), nous avons pu recenser dans la baie du Diana au moins 5 gisements bien attestés du Paléoesquimau inférieur, 3 prédorsétiens et 2 groswatériens. D'autres existent sans doute, en particulier sur les hautes plages de l'île Slim. Plusieurs devaient être découverts plus tard par des archéologues d'Avataq autour de Quaqtaq. Nous examinerons rapidement ici les gisements qui ont fait l'objet de fouilles ou de sondages.

Au sud de l'île du Diana, au site du Couchant (DIA.3), sur les hautes plages des sites Cordeau (DIA.1) et Gagnon (DIA.73), des structures du Paléoesquimau inférieur ont été trouvées et étudiées au cours des campagnes de Tuvaaluk (Bibeau 1984; Desrosiers 1982, 1986; Pinard 1980) (Figure 4).

Le site du Couchant (DIA.3, JfEl-3)

Le site du Couchant est situé sur le versant occidental de l'île du Diana, particulièrement exposé aux vents dominants du nord-ouest. Il s'étend sur 800 m en directions est-ouest et 480 m en directions nord-sud, englobant la partie inférieure d'un large cordon de plages soulevées et les affleurements rocheux qui le bordent (Figure 5). À sa lisière sud-ouest, à 17 m au dessus des plus hautes eaux, un sous-espace de ce site est constitué d'un champ de blocs, comme au gisement prédorsétien de Poste-de-la-Baleine (Plumet 1976). Un nombre minimum de 52 structures d'habitation peuvent être discernées à la surface du sol, souvent avec difficulté. Seul un agencement anthropique des blocs et galets locaux permet de reconnaître les structures. Neuf d'entre elles, au moins, présentent les vestiges d'un aménagement axial plus ou moins évident, incorporant, vers le milieu, un aménagement particulier qui pourrait être un foyer. Trois de ces habitations ont été fouillées et deux autres ont fait l'objet de sondages (Pinard 1980). Ces structures à aménagement axial semblent regroupées par trois, sans, toutefois, qu'il soit possible de vérifier leur contemporanéité.

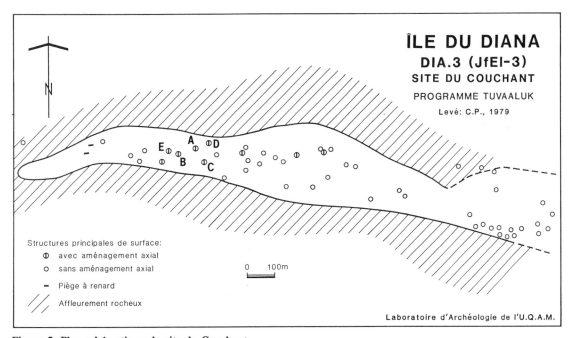

Figure 5 Plan schématique du site du Couchant.

Les objets-témoins sont peu nombreux (n = 274, déchets inclus), mais suffisent cependant pour établir leur appartenance au Paléoesquimau inférieur: un mini-burin en chert, deux petites bipointes foliacées bifaciales en quartz laiteux et quelques fragments proximaux d'armatures distales ou latérales, présentant une légère denticulation (Figures 6 et 7). Ces objets sont répartis plutôt d'un seul côté de l'aménagement axial et près de celui-ci (cf. Figures 8 et 9). La même observation est rapportée par Cox (1978, Figure 3a), Mary-Rousselière (1964) et Plumet (1976).

Contrairement aux autres sites connus de la même période, tant au Labrador (Cox 1978) qu'à l'Ile de Baffin (Maxwell 1973) ou en Hudsonie (Plumet 1980), à l'île Mansel et Ivujivik, (Taylor 1962, 1968), le chert fin n'est pas la matière première dominante: seulement 2% des objets, soit un

Figure 6 Objets du site du Couchant.

mini-burin et 5 éclats et déchets. Ce sont des matériaux régionaux ou allochtones, dont le plus exotique vient du Labrador, qui dominent: quartz laiteux (47%), quartzite enfumé de Diana (36%), quartz

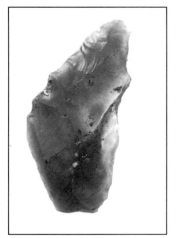

cristallin (5%), enfin, mais en petite quantité, du quartzite enfumé de Ramah (1%). Aucun chert hudsonien ou de l'île de Southampton, tel que le chert zoné caractéristique, n'a pu être identifié.

Deux des trois structures principales fouillées au site du Couchant présentent un caractère rarement signalé jusqu'à maintenant au Paléoesquimau inférieur: elles intègrent à leur périphérie un gros bloc en place, sans doute glaciel, généralement métrique, nettement plus volumineux que les autres. Il est situé latéralement par rapport à l'aménagement axial (Figure 8). La relative rareté de ces blocs à la surface de l'habitat peut expliquer qu'ils ne se retrouvent pas dans toutes les habitations. Par contre, la fréquence relative de leur occurrence permet de croire qu'elle n'est pas aléatoire. La même observation peut être faite pour plusieurs structures dans les champs de blocs de Poste-de-la-Baleine (Plumet 1976: Photo 12). Au Paléoes-

Figure 7 Mini-burin du site du Couchant (long. = 15 mm).

quimau supérieur, nous avons noté que l'insertion de grands blocs en

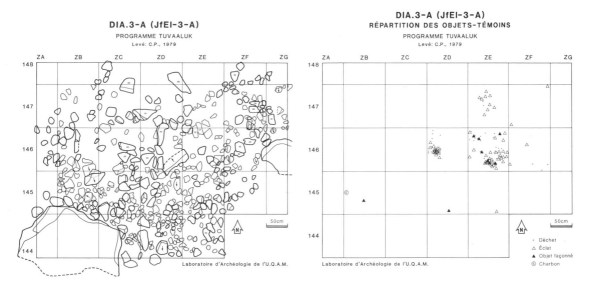

Figure 8 Site du Couchant: plan de la Structure A.

Figure 9 Site du Couchant: répartition des objets dans la Structure A.

place était presque une constante des habitations dorsétiennes, particulièrement nette dans les maisons longues où elle semble avoir perdu toute justification fonctionnelle (Plumet 1985).

Le charbon de bois recueilli dans certaines des structures n'était pas en quantité suffisante pour effectuer une datation. Toutefois, l'altitude du site qui est le plus haut de l'île (à l'exception des structures R et S du site Cordeau), l'outillage et les caractères techniques pourraient indiquer une occupation remontant au début du Prédorsétien, soit un peu avant 3 500 B.P.

Bien qu'aucun vestige osseux n'ait été retrouvé, la situation de l'habitat, autrefois plus près du rivage qu'aujourd'hui, mais toujours sur une élévation permettant de surveiller la mer, semble indiquer une économie orientée vers les ressources marines.

Le site Cordeau (DIA.1, JfEl-1)

Le site Cordeau, au sud-est de l'île du Diana, avait fait l'objet de deux campagnes de fouille avant le programme Tuvaaluk, soit en 1968 et en 1973. Long de plus de 300 m et large de 150 m, il est presque entièrement occupé par deux longs cordons de plages soulevées se rejoignant à partir de 10 m au dessus des plus hautes eaux (Figures 10 et 11). Une trentaine de structures principales, des habitations de divers types, y sont étagées entre 5 et 22 m d'altitude. Les plus basses, en dessous de 13 m, sont probablement toutes dorsétiennes. Une petite maison longue d'une douzaine de mètres s'étend le long d'un affleurement rocheux entre 6 et 7 m au dessus des plus hautes eaux. Au-dessus de 14,50 m, les structures fouillées remontent au Paléoesquimau inférieur (Desrosiers 1982, 1986). Elles se manifestaient avant la fouille par des pierres perceptibles à travers la végétation ou par une très légère dépression que souvent seule une lumière rasante permettait de deviner. Un couvert végétal de 2 à 10 cm d'épaisseur, parfois plus dense à l'emplacement des dépressions, recouvrait la plupart

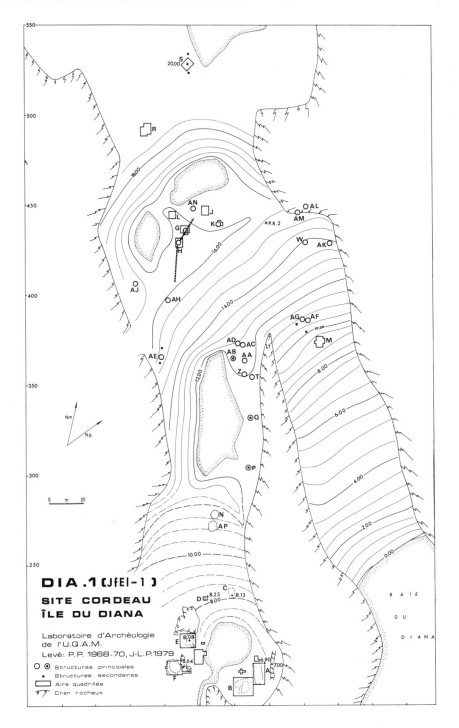

Figure 10 Plan du site Cordeau, localisation des structures et des aires fouillées.

des éléments structuraux. Dessous, une pellicule humique irrégulière, parfois lenticulaire, atteignant exceptionnellement 8 cm d'épaisseur, s'étendait directement sur les matériaux de plage.

Les aires fouillées ne correspondent pas toutes à des habitations. L'aire S, la plus haute de l'île, à 22 m, n'a révélé aucune structure de pierre clairement reconnaissable mais une concentration de vestiges s'étendant sur une surface équivalant à une habitation (3 à 4 m de diamètre). L'idée qu'il

Figure 11 Le site Cordeau vu du tombolo relique séparant les versants est et ouest de l'île du Diana.

pourrait s'agir d'un fond d'iglou vient naturellement à l'esprit. L'aire R, à 20 m, comprend sans doute deux structures secondaires, d'entreposage ou de combustion, dont une boite en pierres, et une autre structure de combustion avec des dalles obliques et du charbon de bois. Desrosiers y perçoit la possibilité de 3 occupations successives. Parmi les aires G, H, J, K et L, toutes à 16 m, deux, J et K ne contenaient aucun vestige mobilier mais seulement une structure de faible creusement, probablement anthropique. Les aires G et L sont des habitations. L'aire L mesure environ 3 m de diamètre et comprend un foyer central en fosse de 1,25 m de diamètre. L'aire G, légèrement ovale (3 x 2,50 m); présente un foyer central intégré à un aménagement axial mal conservé et une structure secondaire de creusement de 80 cm de diamètre occupant une partie du lobe nord. L'aire H n'a révélé qu'une dépression de 10 à 12 cm de profondeur (un foyer selon Desrosiers), bordée de dalles et contenant des galets, mais non associée à une habitation.

Une curieuse structure mérite une attention spéciale. Les aires G et H sont traversées par un alignement discontinu de blocs décimétriques et demi-métriques se poursuivant sur au moins 20 mètres au nord-est et au sud de l'aire H qui se trouve au sommet de l'angle très ouvert formé par cet alignement (Figure 10). Qu'il s'agisse d'une structure ludique (*hopping stone?*) ou d'un mur d'affût pour la chasse au caribou comme il en existe d'autres sur l'île, son association à une occupation prédorsétienne, attestée par l'outillage, indique une continuité de tradition à travers tout l'Esquimau depuis le Paléoesquimau inférieur. Ces deux interprétations, mentionnées par Desrosiers, seront examinées plus loin.

Outillage (Figure 12)

Les quelques outils diagnostiques parmi les 1 026 témoins façonnés recueillis dans les aires S, R, L, G et H, témoignent clairement d'occupations du Paléoesquimau inférieur: couteaux asymétriques à large pédoncule, à base rectiligne et extrémité distale arrondie, armatures latérales et burins. Les quatre burins de chert (long. = 22 à 26 mm) provenant de l'aire R sont en partie ou complètement polis distalement sur les deux faces de la partie active et trois d'entre eux ont été façonnés bifacialement. Les deux burins sur fragments microlaminaires de l'aire G (long. = 15 à 20 mm) sont plus petits, unifacialement façonnés et dépourvus de polissage.

Matières premières

Le tableau de répartition des principales catégories de matières premières (Tableau 1) par aire de fouille permet de faire ressortir les points suivants:

- Le quartzite de Ramah est présent, mais seulement dans l'aire H (16 m d'altitude) sous forme de deux éclats et d'un couteau arrondi à encoches proximales et à base rectiligne (no 811, analogue aux no 679 et 558-587).

- Le quartzite de Diana n'est représenté que dans trois des cinq aires de fouilles, dont S la plus haute: 1,46% pour l'ensemble et de 0,54% à 5,26% selon les aires.

Figure 12 Pointes et fragments de pointes en ardoise ou métabasalte polis du site Cordeau, Structure F.

Tableau 1 Matières premières du site Cordeau (DIA.1, JfEl-1), Structures S, R, G, H et L.

	S (22 m)		R (20 m)		G (16 m)		H (16 m)		L (16 m)		TOTAUX	
	n	%	n	%	n	%	n	%	n	%	n	%
QZTE RAMAH	-	-	-	-	-	-	3	37,50	-	-	3	0,29
QZTE DIANA	10	3,38	3	0,54	-	-	-	-	2	5,26	15	1,46
QZTE FERRU.	-	-	82	14,64	99	71,84	2	25,00	-	-	183	17,84
QZ GROSSIER	16	5,41	88	15,71	3	2,42	-	-	10	26,32	117	11,40
QZ CRISTAL.	3	1,01	3	0,54	-	-	-	-	2	5,26	8	0,78
QZ HYA+LAIT	244	82,43	32	5,71	7	5,65	-	-	23	60,53	306	29,82
CHERTS	19	6,42	58	10,36	8	6,44	3	37,50	-	-	88	8,58
AUTRES	4	1,35	294	52,50	7	5,65	-	-	1	2,63	306	29,82
TOTAUX	296	100	560	100	124	100	8	100	38	100	1026	100

- Le quartz hyalin ou laiteux est globalement le plus abondant (30% des matières premières en nombre d'objet) et constitue la catégorie très largement dominante dans l'aire S (82%) située à 22 m d'altitude.

- le chert fin, beige, gris ou noir, est représenté par 8,58% des objets dans toutes les aires sauf l'aire L.

Les matières premières «autres» comprennent du métabasalte, du schiste ardoisier, mais surtout du schiste argileux qui constitue près de 50% (n = 291) du sous-ensemble et provient sans doute de la même source.

Chronologie (Tableau 2)

Trois fragments de charbon de bois récupérés à différents endroits de l'aire L, sur la plage de 16 m d'altitude, ont été réunis en un seul échantillon daté par radiochronométrie à 3470±160 B.P. (UQ-86). Cette datation, à première vue, s'accorde avec l'estimation chronologique proposée pour DIA.3 à partir des données typologiques. Toutefois, si nous prenons en considération la tendance à un accroissement du polissage et à une plus grande importance du façonnage bifacial des burins avec le temps (Plumet 1980: 238-39), les faibles indices typologiques dont nous disposons à DIA.1-R, incitent à y placer l'occupation après celle du site du Couchant (DIA.3). Cependant, les burins de l'aire G, recueillis sur la même plage que l'aire L d'où provient l'échantillon daté, ne sont ni façonnés

Tableau 2 Dates ^{14}C des sites paléoesquimaux de la baie du Diana et des occupations thuléennes de la région.

	DATES ^{14}C	Calibrée	LOCALISATION Structure ou carré	ALTITUDE (m)	No LABO
CORDEAU DIA.1	3470±160	-1780	L	6	UQ-86
	2070±140	-100	A	7	LV-468
	1860±90	+130	B	7	GIF-1957
	1450±90	+610	E	8	GIF-1352
	1435±70	+620	M	10	UQ-89
	1420±95	+630		6,5	S-931
	1090±90	+970	B	7	GIF-1954
	920±90	+1080	B	7	GIF-1956
TUVAALUK DIA.4	1890±105	+110	A	7	S-933
	1810±110	+210	C	7,4	QC-628
	1770±95	+250	AA-58	6,2	UQ-76
	1715±95	+340	C	7,4	UQ-54
	1660±95	+390	C	7,10	QC-632
	1555±80	+510	AE-52	6,8	UQ-56
	1545±90	+520	ZJ-18	8	UQ-72
	1470±100	+600	C	8,25	QC-633
	1380±100	+640	C	7,4	QC-631
	1080±100	+970	A	7	GIF-3003
	1045±90	+1000	AB-51	6,62	UQ-57
	1000±90	+1020	T	5	QC-627
	955±90	+1020	J	4,40	QC-629
	920±90	+1080	AB-53	6,55	UQ-70
	905±65	+1130	AD-47	7,40	UQ-79
	845±135	+1210	C-62	4,25	UQ-78
	830±100	+1230	J	4,25	UQ-52
	820±75	+1240	T-60	5,75	UQ-73
	815±110	+1240	C	8,50	QC-625
	795±85	+1250	AD-51	6,5	UQ-59
	760±95	+1260	A	7	S-930
	650±100	+1300	W-57	6,3	UQ-82
	635±90	+1310	T	4,7	QC-624
	490±80	+1430	C-62	4,3	UQ-88
	475±70	+1440	E-66	4,1	UQ-83
	470±90	+1440	A	7	GIF-3002
	460±105	+1440	AC-56	6,5	UQ-90
	440±90	+1450	C-59	4,36	UQ-87
	380±85	+1490	AB-58	6,5	UQ-93
ARIANE DIA.45	700±80	+1280	A	12	GIF-4207
ÎLE AUX IGLOUS DIA.10	810±80	+1240	D	15	GIF-4209
POINTE-AUX-BÉLUGAS UNG-11	750±90	+1260	D	9,8	GIF-1948
	680±90	+1280	D	9,8	GIF-1950
	430±90	+1460	D	9,8	GIF-1949

sur les deux faces, ni polis, ce qui pourrait indiquer une plus grande ancienneté. Or cette plage est 4 m plus basse que l'aire R et 1 m plus basse que le site DIA.3. La combinaison des repères chronologiques habituels, typologie et altitude des plages, n'est donc guère concluante. Le site Tuvaaluk (DIA.4) a déjà été l'occasion de montrer qu'il ne fallait pas se fier sans discernement à la chronologie de relèvement isostatique pour dater les établissements du Paléoesquimau (Badgley 1980: 583). La Figure 17 en est une bonne illustration, même si elle reflète une tendance générale des occupations à suivre l'abaissement du niveau marin tout en se dispersant de plus en plus verticalement. Donnant la priorité à la typologie, nous placerons provisoirement les occupations des hautes plages de DIA.1 un peu après celle de DIA.3, c'est-à-dire à partir du milieu du Prédorsétien.

Le site Gagnon (DIA.73, JfEl-30)

Le site Gagnon, à environ 1 km au nord-est des précédents, s'étend sur un espace d'environ 600 m de côté (Figure 13). La fouille en a été confiée à Pierre Bibeau qui en a également analysé les données pour le programme Tuvaaluk dans le cadre de sa maîtrise (Bibeau 1984). Cent trente-cinq structures, dont 71 d'habitations et 64 secondaires, ont été identifiées. Elles s'étagent depuis 1,50 m au-dessus des hautes eaux jusqu'à 16 m, mais sont surtout concentrées entre 2 et 12 m. Le site comprend des vestiges du Paléoesquimau inférieur et supérieur ainsi que du Néoesquimau. Les cinq aires fouillées sont entre 9,75 m et 10,50 m d'altitude. Deux d'entre elles, L et M, distantes de quelques mètres, contenaient des structures principales de surface ovale (L) et sub-rectangulaire (M), sans doute des emplacements de tentes, dans lesquelles semblaient subsister les vestiges assez déstructurés d'un aménagement axial.

Comme au site du Couchant (DIA.3), les structures d'habitation des aires L et M intègrent dans leur aménagement périphérique un ou plusieurs affleurements rocheux de plus d'un mètre de longueur (Bibeau 1984: Plans 7 et 8).

Outillage (Figures 14 et 15)

Si l'aire L n'a pas livré d'objet façonné complet et identifiable, l'aire M contenait une partie mésiale de microlame, une armature latérale asymétrique et un nucléus en quartz laiteux. Un couteau triangulaire à encoches proximales et à base droite est en chert, tandis qu'un fragment proximal d'objet bifacial à encoches larges et bilatérales, dont la base est rectiligne, est en chert fin et lustré, peut-être à la suite d'altération thermique. Enfin un burin à façonnage bifacial, également en chert beige, présente un léger polissage distal sur les deux faces (Figure 15a). Comme au site du Couchant et à d'autres sites prédorsétiens, la répartition des témoins façonnés dans les structures du site Gagnon marquait une nette tendance à se regrouper d'un même côté de l'aménagement axial.

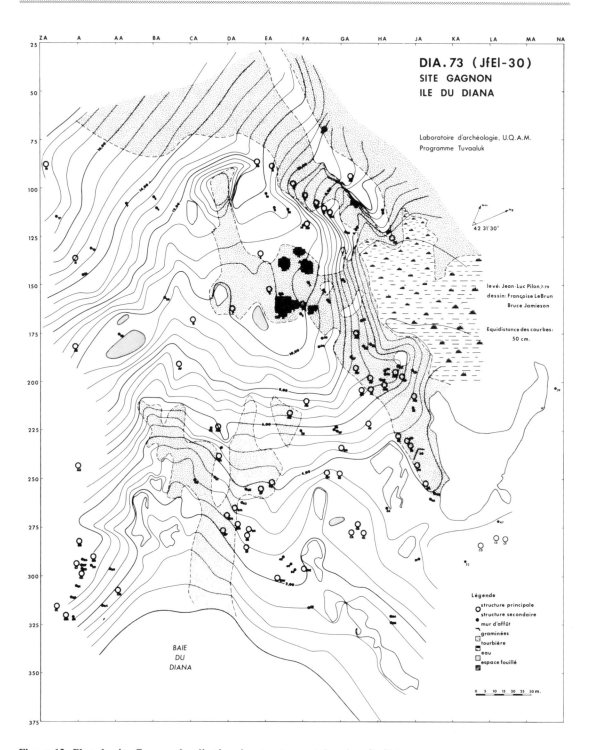

Figure 13 Plan du site Gagnon; localisation des structures et des aires fouillées.

Matières premières

Le Tableau 3, en regroupant les objets des deux aires L et M, montre toujours une présence faible mais certaine de quartzite de Ramah et de quartzite ferrugineux, une absence complète de quartzite de Diana et une prépondérance très forte du chert. Cependant cette dernière doit être pondérée du fait qu'elle correspond à 126 éclats (sur 129 objets) trouvés dans l'aire M, presque tous concentrés dans le même carré (FA-135) (ibid.: 102 Plan 26); elle reflète apparemment une activité de taille d'un petit bloc de chert dans l'aire M, peut-être du couteau ou du burin.

Figure 14 Site Gagnon: *a,b,d*-pointes en chert, *c*-fragment de pointe en ardoise polie, *e*-grattoir.

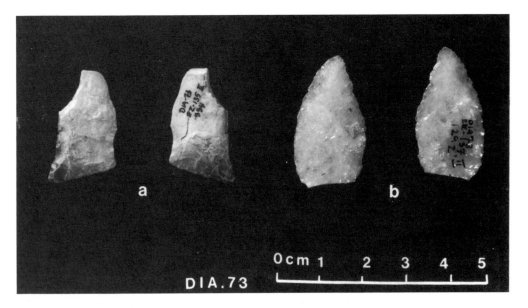

Figure 15 Site Gagnon: *a*-burin, *b*-bipointe.

Chronologie

L'altitude des deux structures des aires L et M—vers 10 m, soit 6 m plus bas que celles du site Cordeau (DIA.1)—et les caractéristiques du burin justifient l'estimation chronologique proposée par Bibeau (ibid.: 137): vers la fin du Prédorsétien, soit vers 3 000 B.P. Toutefois les objets de la structure K (Figure 14) et quelques-uns de M font penser à un Dorsétien ancien ou au Groswatérien.

Tableau 3 Matières premières du site Gagnon (DIA.73, JfEl-30), aires L et M.

	AIRE L		AIRE M		TOTAUX	
	n	%	n	%	n	%
QUARTZITE DE RAMAH	2	15,38	-	-	2	1,32
QUARTZITE FERRUGINEUX	1	7,69	-	-	1	0,66
QUARTZ HYALIN & LAITEUX	5	38,46	8	5,80	13	8,61
CHERTS ET CALCÉDOINE	2	15,38	129	93,48	131	86,75
AUTRES	3	23,09	1	0,72	4	2,66
TOTAUX	13	100,00	138	100,00	151	100,00

Autres sites du Paléoesquimau inférieur - le Groswatérien

Au nord-est de la baie du Diana, près de Quaqtaq, un petit gisement groswatérien, DIA.48 (JgEj-1), est caractérisé par un fragment proximal d'objet fortement denticulé, un burin et une partie proximale de pointe groswatérienne en chert gris-beige, ainsi qu'une microlame de quartzite de Ramah (Figure 16). Il montre que le quartzite de Ramah faisait partie des ressources accessibles. Le grand site DIA.53 (JgEj-3), découvert en 1977 dans le prolongement de la piste d'atterrissage, est apparu par la suite l'un des plus gros habitats paléoesquimaux de l'Ungava qui devait révéler aux archéologues d'Avataq une très importante occupation groswatérienne ainsi que des occupations postérieures. Enfin les reconnaissances de l'organisme culturel inuit ont permis de découvrir autour de Quaqtaq d'autres sites du Paléoesquimau inférieur qui, lorsqu'ils seront publiés, enrichiront considérablement les données sur cette période (Badgley, comm. pers.).

La mise en place du premier peuplement

Dans les sites du Paléoesquimau inférieur que nous venons de passer rapidement en revue, aucune matière première ne permet de supposer des relations directes ou indirectes avec l'Ouest, que ce soit l'Hudsonie ou le golfe de Foxe. Par contre le quartzite de Ramah apparaît dès le début de cette période en petite quantité. Les matières premières dominantes sont le quartz laiteux et le quartzite ferrugineux, le premier venant sans doute de l'île Ukivik près de Wakeham, le second de la région de l'Arnaud. Le quartzite de Diana est utilisé dès le début également. Ces deux dernières matières premières sont macroscopiquement très proches du quartzite de Ramah avec lesquelles nous les avons confondues un certain temps. Il est donc possible qu'elles aient servi de substitut à ce dernier quartzite, très prisé au Labrador. De toute façon, ces éléments indiquent que le premier courant de peuplement de la baie d'Ungava venait de l'est plutôt que de l'ouest. Le réseau spatial des populations du Paléoesquimau inférieur s'étendait donc au moins du Labrador à la région de Wakeham. Selon Ian Badgley (comm. pers.) les nouveaux gise-

Figure 16   DIA.48: *gauche*-burin, *centre*-base de pointe, *droite*-fragments denticulés.

ments du Paléoesquimau inférieur de la région de Quaqtaq ne changent pas ce schéma. D'autre part, dans les différents sites examinés ceux-ci semblent témoigner d'occupations plutôt vers le début et vers la fin du Paléoesquimau inférieur, ce qui, en raison des fouilles très limitées, n'exclut aucunement la possiblité d'occupations intermédiaires et antérieures.

Les modes d'établissement et de subsistance au Paléoesquimau inférieur

En l'absence de vestiges fauniques, c'est la situation de l'habitat qui peut nous fournir des indications sur le mode de subsistance. L'habitat du site du Couchant (DIA.3) est nettement orienté vers la mer qui devait être de 9 à 10 m plus haute qu'aujourd'hui et recouvrir une partie des plages soulevées. Un cran rocheux, vers le sud, gêne la vision vers l'intérieur de l'île dans cette direction. Le champ de bloc était alors le site d'habitat à la fois le moins mal protégé et le plus proche de l'eau. Les habitations prédorsétiennes du site Cordeau (DIA.1) sont également orientées vers la mer, mais sont associées à une structure qui a pu servir à la chasse au caribou. Un sentier bien visible qui pourrait être une piste de caribou, comme nous le verrons plus loin, arrive du sud juste en direction d'alignements de pierres, vestiges probables de murs d'affût. Ce peut être un indice d'une exploitation du caribou par les Prédorsétiens. Certaines de ces structures d'habitation peuvent correspondre à des fonds d'iglous de neige comme Maxwell (1973) en a signalés au sud de Baffin.

Le Paléoesquimau supérieur

Nous avons traité ailleurs de l'occupation dorsétienne dans la baie du Diana et du réseau spatial au Paléoesquimau supérieur (Plumet 1981, 1986). Rappelons cependant qu'après le Groswatérien, le début du Dorsétien est mal connu, même s'il est peut-être attesté au site Gagnon (Figure 14). Les dates fiables les plus anciennes proviennent d'une couche sous-jacente à la petite maison longue et à l'habitation B du site Cordeau (DIA.1), mais dont les quelques outils ne sont pas diagnostiques d'une période: 2180±105 B.P. (S-932 et NMC-723) et 2070±140 (LV-468). Les pointes à cannelures distales trouvées dans la structure M, sur la plage de 10 m, associées à une date de 1435±70 B.P (UQ-89, Desrosiers 1982), les habitations E (1450±90 B.P., GIF-1352) et F, sur une basse plage de 8 m au même site, contenant des pointes à cannelures distales, attestent un Dorsétien moyen et peut-être ancien, également présent au site Tuvaaluk (DIA.4, JfEl-4). L'habitation isolée du site DIA-25, malgré sa date relativement ancienne (1900±110 B.P., GIF-2969, mais rajeunie de plusieurs siècles une fois calibrée) a livré quelques outils plutôt du Dorsétien moyen ou récent ainsi qu'une calotte crânienne qui pourrait être dorsétienne (voir Plumet 1989). Les phases récentes et tardives sont particulièrement bien représentées par l'outillage et confirmées par une série de dates ^{14}C. Elles feront l'objet d'une discussion plus développée.

Les basses plages du site Cordeau (DIA.1, JfEl-1)

Cette partie du site Cordeau fut fouillée en premier à partir de 1968. Au moins 4 habitations semi-souterraines de types différents et une maison longue (long. =12 m) entourent le petit étang situé entre 6 m et 8,50 m au dessus des plus hautes eaux (cf. Plumet 1976: Figures 24, 26 et 28). La maison longue A et l'habitation voisine B furent installées par dessus une occupation antérieure, caractérisée par une couche humique contenant des éclats de quartzite, des fragments de stéatite ocrés, et de la graisse, qui fut datée par le ^{14}C d'un peu avant 2 000 B.P. (cf. Tableau 2 et Figure 17). L'habitation B, très profonde (<50 cm), montre un aménagement axial analogue à celui d'Okak-3 (Cox 1978: Figure 5). Sa moitié ouest était recouverte par un enchevêtrement de dalles métriques constituant autrefois la couverture, alors supportée par des poteaux de bois dont subsistaient des fragments décomposés. L'habitation B a livré un outillage du Dorsétien récent, compatible avec la datation obtenue à partir du charbon de bois prélevé dans le foyer central (920±90 B.P., GIF-1956); la date la plus récente de tout le site DIA.1. Les structures E et F furent creusées à proximité d'un dépôt contenant des pointes à cannelures distales. La structure E (1450±90 B.P., GIF-1352) est clairement précédée d'un couloir courbe et ascendant sur lequel s'ouvre un diverticule riche en déchets organiques (os décomposés, charbon de bois, graisse mêlée d'ocre). Le couloir culmine à sa jonction avec l'aire principale d'habitation marquée par quelques dalle soigneusement disposées, mais à un niveau supérieur par rapport à celui de l'espace intérieur, ce qui est l'inverse d'un sas thermique. L'aménagement axial intérieur comprend deux aires de combustion dont une dalle support de lampe à l'extrémité opposée à l'entrée. La structure F, dépourvue de couloir, a été perturbée par des emplacements de tentes dorsétiens postérieurs. L'outillage est un mélange de Dorsétien moyen et récent, mais de grandes armatures distales polies à encoches angulaires bilatérales pourraient attester

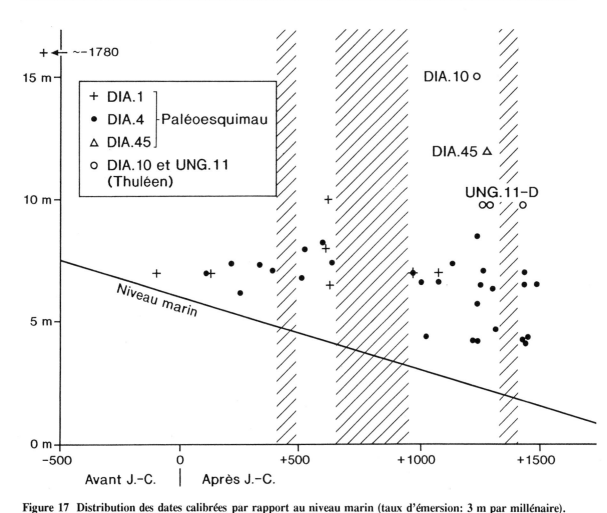

Figure 17 Distribution des dates calibrées par rapport au niveau marin (taux d'émersion: 3 m par millénaire).

un dorsétien ancien (Figure 12). Elles devaient servir à la chasse au caribou dont semblaient témoigner de rares os décomposés et un fragment d'andouiller. Malheureusement les seuls échantillons datés sont essentiellement constitués de graisse carbonisée, mêlée de mousse dans le meilleur cas (GIF-2968, 1350±100 B.P.), ce qui laisse la possibilité d'une contemporanéité des habitation E et F.

Le site Tuvaaluk (DIA.4, JfEl-4) (Figures 18 et 19)

Au cours des trois années de fouille qui s'y déroulèrent, le site Tuvaaluk est apparu beaucoup plus complexe et riche qu'il n'apparaissait au début. En 1978, la fouille d'un ensemble de structures s'étageant entre 7,50 m et 10,50 m d'altitude avait permis de proposer 5 phases d'occupations se succédant de 1470±100 B.P. (QC-633) à 815±110 B.P. (QC-625) (Badgley 1980). En 1979, la dernière année du programme, la fouille du sous espace D avait conduit Badgley à distinguer 24 unités stratigraphiques différentes dans lesquelles étaient réparties 7 structures principales, 3 creusées et 5

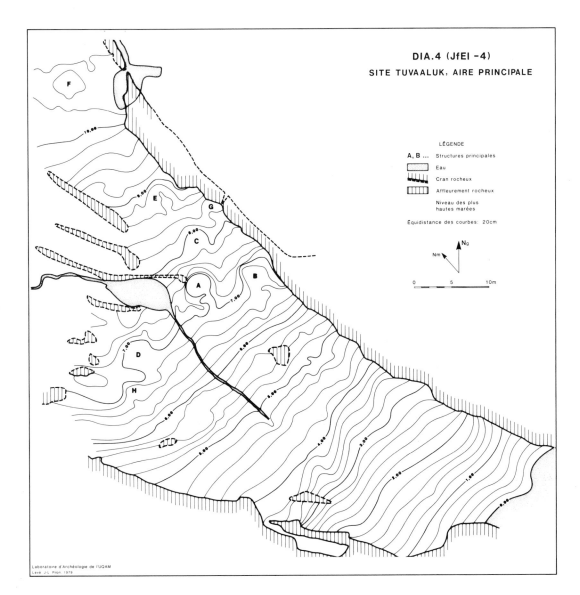

Figure 18 Topographie de l'aire principale du site Tuvaaluk.

de surface, ainsi qu'une vingtaine de structures secondaires (points d'activité spécialisés, fosses, foyers). Douze dates ^{14}C obtenues à partir d'échantillons de graisse ou de mousse brûlées et de charbon de bois prélevés dans 6 de ces unités stratigraphiques, constituaient une séquence allant de 1770 ± 115 B.P. (unité IXA) à 380 ± 85 B.P. (unité I), mais dont la progression ne suivait pas celle des numéros d'unités. Ces dates peuvent être regroupées en trois périodes: 1770 ± 115 à 1555 ± 80 B.P. (3 dates), 1045 ± 90 à 975 ± 85 B.P. (6 dates) et 650 ± 100 à 380 ± 85 B.P.(3 dates).

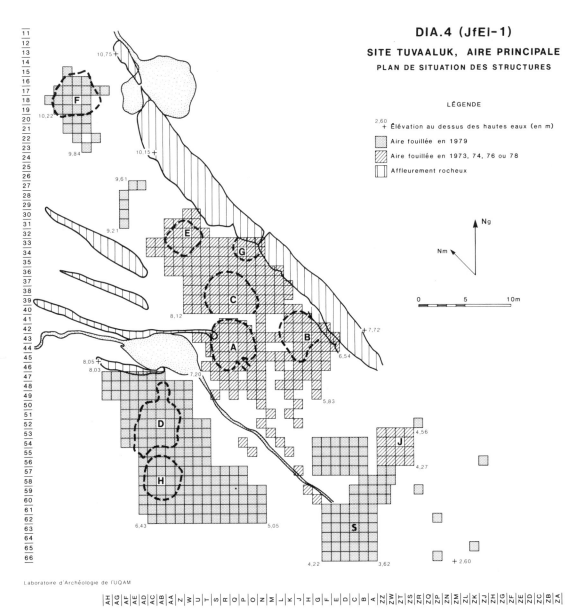

DIA.4 (JfEI-1)

SITE TUVAALUK, AIRE PRINCIPALE

PLAN DE SITUATION DES STRUCTURES

LÉGENDE

2,60
+ Élévation au dessus des hautes eaux (en m)

Aire fouillée en 1979

Aire fouillée en 1973, 74, 76 ou 78

Affleurement rocheux

Laboratoire d'Archéologie de l'UQAM

Figure 19 Plan du site Tuvaaluk: localisation des structures et des sous-espaces dans le carroyage global.

Dans un remarquable travail d'analyse critique et d'interprétation de l'ensemble des données provenant du sous-espace D, Hélène Gauvin (1990) a montré que seules quelques-unes de ces unités stratigraphiques avaient une signification culturelle, les autres n'étant que des lentilles témoignant de rejets ou de déplacement de sédiments par les occupants lors de la construction ou du réaménagement des habitations ou encore de processus taphonomiques. Elle montre que l'occupation du sous-espace

D ne serait en réalité représentée que par un seul sol d'habitat principal dans lequel ne peuvent être distingués clairement que deux «moments» d'occupations et seulement cinq structures d'habitation, dont trois plus ou moins creusées. Une très fine analyse spatiale de variables typologiques et technologiques permet à Gauvin de reconstituer seulement deux «phases» correspondant sans doute chacune à de multiples occupations:

- La première phase commence avant la construction de la première habitation, D. Elle est caractérisée par des objets du Dorsétien moyen et un outillage semblable à celui trouvé au Labrador pour la même période (pointes à cannelures distales, armatures distales polies à encoches proximales multiples, petits grattoirs courts à front très évasé. Les couteaux et les pointes en schiste et en métabasalte polis, caractérisés par des encoches angulaires multiples ou par un pédoncule, pourraient aussi témoigner d'un Dorsétien ancien. Les matières premières dominantes sont les quartzites ferrugineux et varicelleux, le quartz hyalin et laiteux, les quartzites de Ramah et de Diana.

- La seconde phase est celle de la structure D. Elle est caractérisée par des objets de facture différente correspondant au Dorsétien récent et tardif: pointes à pédoncule de taille moyenne, pointes à façonnage unifacial et encoches simples bilatérales, racloirs obliques et simili-burins. Le quartzite de Diana, le chert (en particulier d'Akpatok mais peut-être aussi du Labrador) et le quartz hyalin ou laiteux sont plus importants que dans la phase précédente.

Le fait que seulement deux phases soient reconnaissables n'élimine pas la possibilité, voire la probabilité, qu'il y en eut un plus grand nombre que la fouille n'a pas permis de discerner.

Enfin rappelons qu'en 1973 et 1en 976, la fouille des structures A et B, situées entre 6,50 m et 7,50 m d'altitude, avait permis d'établir une séquence chronologique comparable du sous-espace D, mais plus étendue: de 1890 ± 105 B.P. (S-933) à 470 ± 90 B.P. (GIF-3002). La date la plus récente vient du charbon de bois prélevé dans le foyer de cuisine de l'habitation A, mi-thuléenne mi-dorsétienne par ses caractéristiques architecturales, mais entièrement dorsétienne par son outillage (Plumet 1979). Dans l'ensemble DIA.4-A, les quartzites de Diana sont largement majoritaires (45,5 % du nombre d'objets), suivis par le quartz laiteux ou hyalin, le quartzite de Ramah, puis le quartzite ferrugineux.

Outillage et figurines

Les objets façonnés en os, en ivoire ou en andouiller sont rares au site Tuvaaluk, ce qui contraste avec l'abondance des vestiges de faune, pratiquement absents dans les autres gisements. En dehors de quelques ébauches de têtes de harpon et d'une aiguille à chas buriné (Figure 20), il faut signaler une petite figurine en ivoire représentant un personnage vêtu d'une parka à haut col relevé (Figure 21). Par contre le matériel lithique est riche et varié. D'autres figurines de pierre sont également remarquables. L'une, taillée par retouches marginales dans une lame de quartzite de Ramah a une silhouette humaine qui évoque aussi l'ours (Figure 22). Une autre, n'est qu'une ébauche de la

Figure 20 Site Tuvaaluk: aiguille à chas de section aplatie (long.=51 mm).

même forme, mais sur un éclat de quartzite de Ramah plus mince. Une figurine de même forme et de même facture a été trouvée d'une part à Koliktalik I (Dorsétien ancien) au Labrador (Jordan 1980: Figures 10 et 11), d'autre part au Kamtchatka, au gisement d'Ushki, vers 4000 B.P. (Dikov 1965). Enfin une petite sculpture en stéatite représente nettement un phoque lorsqu'elle est examinée de profile et de dos (Figure 23), mais sa face ventrale semble anthropomorphe et marquée de l'incision fréquente dans l'art animalier dorsétien (Figure 24). Outre les innombrables grattoirs mentionnés précédemment,

Figure 21 Site Tuvaaluk: figurine humaine vêtue d'une parka à grand col relevé (long.=30 mm).

une autre caractéristique du gisement est la grande abondance d'objets en stéatite inachevés et de déchets de taille dans cette

Figure 22 Site Tuvaaluk: figurine humaine ou d'ours (long.= 21 mm).

matière première dont un affleurement existe sans doute dans la baie du Diana, peut-être dans l'île Opingivik, juste au sud du site Tuvaaluk, et peut-être aussi, d'après les Inuit, sur la côte est de la baie. Les analyses des éléments de terre rares de la stéatite semblent montrer qu'une ébauche de récipient était en stéatite de la région de Wakeham, où les carrières sont nombreuses, mais aussi qu'un récipient terminé était en stéatite d'Hébron au Labrador (Archambault 1981). Toutes les ébauches, les lampes et marmites retrouvées sont dorsétiennes et leur forme variable: récipients quadrangulaires à parois évasées, ovales, circulaires. Une fois achevée, l'analyse en cours de cette partie du gisement et celle des remontages des objets en stéatite, apporteront sans doute des précisions intéressantes. Malheureusement, dans le sous-espace A-B la plupart des outils provenaient d'un épais dépotoir fortement remanié par la construction des habitations de sorte qu'il est difficile d'associer les catégories chronologiques d'outils à des structures spécifiques.

Figure 23 Site Tuvaaluk: figurine en forme de phoque, vue de profile.

Figure 24 Site Tuvaaluk: même figurine que dans la Figure 23, mais vue de la face inférieure.

Modes d'établissement et de subsistance

Les gisements du Paléoesquimau supérieur sont généralement à moins de 14 m et le plus souvent entre 8 et 4,50 m au-dessus du niveau marin actuel. Les structures d'habitation sont particulièrement nombreuses et concentrées sur les plages et les affleurements rocheux de la côte sud de l'île du Diana. Les structures semi-souterraines et la maison longue sont toutes orientées vers le sud-est, direction de la mer. Deux d'entre elles ont un couloir d'entrée: l'une, datée de 1450±90 B.P., ce qui correspond à la fin du Dorsétien moyen au Labrador, n'a pas de sas thermique; l'autre, du Dorsétien tardif (470±90 B.P.), en présente un de type thuléen ainsi que divers autres éléments architecturaux typiquement néoesquimaux. Les structures circulaires en gros blocs de chant du site Cordeau et du site Tuvaaluk sont souvent plus éloignées de la mer et plus en hauteur que les maisons semi-souterraines. Par contre les structures de surface qui pourraient être des emplacements de tentes, occupent plutôt les basses plages. Il est difficile d'estimer le nombre d'habitations réellement contemporaines en raison de la superposition et du réaménagement fréquent des structures. Comme dans l'Ungava, les habitats devaient rarement comprendre plus de 4 à 5 maisons occupées en même temps et devaient souvent ne pas dépasser deux habitations contemporaines, comme au site Cordeau.

Nous disposons de meilleurs indices qu'au Paléoesquimau inférieur pour nous faire une idée du mode de subsistance dorsétien. En effet, si les os de phocidés dominent (35,6% dans l'aire C du site Tuvaaluk), c'est le caribou qui vient tout de suite après avec 30% des fragments osseux, suivi par le morse (5,6%) dans l'aire C (Julien 1980). Il est possible que l'abondance des grattoirs reflète le travail des peaux de caribou. La grande baleine apparaît exploitée dès le Dorsétien, sans qu'il soit possible d'établir qu'elle était chassée. Ses os (vertèbres, côtes, crâne) entrent dans la construction de la maison A, mais peut-être sous influence thuléenne.

Cette exploitation du caribou, qui constitue l'originalité du Dorsétien de l'île du Diana, est attestée également par des structures et peut-être des traces. En effet, les traces discontinues d'un sentier, par endroits très net, à d'autres plus ténu, font presque le tour de la partie sud de l'île depuis le lac de congère, en haut de la partie prédorsétienne du site Cordeau, jusqu'à la limite entre les sites DIA.15 et DIA.17 (Figure 4). Ce sentier correspond à l'itinéraire le plus pratique pour se rendre à pied d'un habitat à l'autre et c'est ainsi que nous les avons découverts. C'est le chemin que tout occupant des sites DIA.15, DIA.4 et en partie DIA.1 suivrait pour aller chercher de l'eau de fonte de neige, comme nous le faisions. Nous avons constaté également qu'une vingtaine de personnes vivant et travaillant sur un site tracent de tels sentiers en une semaine car tous les individus, en dépit de quelques variantes, ont tendance à choisir les mêmes facilités offertes par la topographie. L'origine anthropique de telles traces, fréquemment notées autour d'habitats dorsétiens de l'Ungava, n'est donc pas impossible. Toutefois, au site DIA.17, dans le prolongement de l'extrémité ouest du sentier, se trouvent deux murs d'affût, orientés en sens opposés à environ 100 m l'un de l'autre, chacun associé à un affût individuel. Environ 1 km plus au nord, à l'intérieur de l'île et près d'un étang, un autre mur d'affût et trois affûts individuels sont également installés en directions opposées. Enfin des panaches de caribou ont été retrouvés à plusieurs endroits de l'île du Diana (Piérard 1979). Il y a donc bien tout un ensemble de vestiges témoignant de la chasse au caribou selon les techniques connues chez les Esquimaux. Les cairns-balises qui couronnent le plateau au nord des grands cordons de plages soulevées font peut-être partie de ce système. Des restes de lanières de peaux étaient encore attachés aux pierres. Il est probable qu'une partie au moins de ces structures a été utilisée et édifiée au Néoesquimau. Toutefois la présence de ce qui pourrait être un mur d'affût ou une structure ludique (analogue à celle décrite pour le Groenland par Grønnow et al., 1983: 51; Grønnow 1986) associée sans équivoque possible à une occupation prédorsétienne, ainsi que l'abondance des os de caribou au site Tuvaaluk permettent de considérer comme vraisemblable une origine paléoesquimaude pour certaines de ces structures, y compris les grands cairns-balises. Fitzhugh avait déjà établi au nord du Labrador l'association avec des objets dorsétiens de structures liées à la chasse au caribou (Fitzhugh 1981).

Notons enfin que, pour les Dorsétiens de la baie du Diana, le caribou devait tenir une place plus importante que ne laissent croire les données recueillies jusqu'à maintenant. La localisation du site Ariane (DIA.45, JeEl-3), probablement dorsétien, découvert en 1976 tout au fond de la baie, à l'entrée de l'une des vallées conduisant à la baie d'Ungava, s'expliquerait plus facilement par la chasse au caribou que par celle aux mammifères marins. Les 3 habitations rectangulaires qu'il contient sont alignées en haut d'un talus bien marqué et au pied d'une falaise morte d'une dizaine de mètres de hauteur. Un sondage restreint pratiqué à l'entrée de l'habitation A a livré quelques éclats de quartzite enfumé et du charbon de bois (700 ± 80 B.P., GIF-4207). Un peu plus loin vers l'intérieur de la vallée, un affût isolé atteste les activités de chasse au caribou. De plus, selon Ian Badgley (comm. pers.), la carrière de quartzite de Diana découverte par des archéologues d'Avatak à quelques kilomètres de la côte, à l'est de la baie de Hall et à une quinzaine de kilomètres au nord-est du site Ariane, serait un très important lieu de chasse au caribou comprenant aussi des habitations semi-souterraines dorsétiennes.

Essai de synthèse et discussion

Les travaux de Harp en Hudsonie, de Fitzhugh au Labrador aussi bien que les nôtres dans l'Ungava semblent montrer que le Dorsétien se prolongea dans la péninsule du Québec-Labrador jusqu'à la fin du XVe siècle en une phase tardive. Elle semble représentée par un matériel abondant, morphologiquement diversifié et d'assez grandes dimensions. Les dates correspondant à cette phase tardive sont nombreuses et s'étalent presque jusqu'à 1 500 après J.-C. au moins dans la baie du Diana. (Cox 1978; Harp 1976; Plumet 1979). Cette région semble donc avoir été occupée assez tôt au Paléoesquimau inférieur (site du Couchant, hautes plages du site Cordeau), au Paléoesquimau "moyen", c'est-à-dire pendant la période de transition (Groswatérien - Dorsétien ancien) aux sites DIA.73 et DIA.48, au Dorsétien moyen (DIA.1 et 4) et très tard au Paléoesquimau supérieur (sites Ariane et Tuvaaluk). Deux points particuliers méritent d'être discutés: peut-on parler d'une continuité du Paléoesquimau dans la baie du Diana? Les dates les plus récentes associées à des gisements dorsétiens témoignent-elles bien d'une occupation dorsétienne?

La continuité du Paléoesquimau dans la baie du Diana

La série d'une quarantaine de dates ^{14}C (dont les échantillons de graisse carbonisée ont été éliminés: Figure 17) ne permet pas d'affirmer qu'il y eut une réelle continuité d'occupation. Le Paléoesquimau inférieur n'est représenté que par une seule date et le début du Paléoesquimau supérieur par aucune. De plus, le principal ensemble de dates (2070 B.P. à 380 B.P.) présente une césure très nette là où il est le plus dense, soit entre 1380 ± 100 et 1090 ± 90 B.P. ou, en dates calibrées (Stuiver et Kra 1986), entre 640 et 970 après J.-C., soit 330 ans. D'autre part, il n'y a pas, au site Cordeau, de date postérieure à 920 ± 90 B.P.. Deux autres petits intervalles sans date peuvent être notés avant et après la césure principale: entre 1660 ± 95 et 1555 ± 80 B.P., soit 105 ans augmenté à 120 ans après calibration: 390 - 510 après J.-C.; entre 635 ± 90 et 490 ± 80 B.P., mais qui se réduit à 120 ans après calibration: 1 310 et 1 400 après J.-C. Seuls les sites Tuvaaluk et Ariane ont des dates tardives qui se répartissent autour du second intervalle.

En raison du peu de travail effectué sur les hautes plages susceptibles de contenir les gisements du Paléoesquimau inférieur, il est difficile d'interpréter l'absence de date entre 3470 ± 160 B.P. et 2070 ± 140 B.P. comme une discontinuité d'occupation. Il est seulement permis d'estimer que la première date indique que les paléoesquimaux étaient présents au moins dès ce moment-là. Les quelques repères donnés par les très rares outils laissent croire qu'il y eut d'autres occupations avant les premières manifestations dorsétiennes. Espérons que les nombreux sites trouvés par Avataq contribueront à combler cette lacune. Ils témoignent en tout cas d'une importante présence groswatérienne au nord-est de la baie du Diana.

La longue période sans date en plein milieu de la séquence dorsétienne ne peut être interprétée de la même façon. Elle peut refléter une diminution ou un arrêt complet des occupations aussi bien au site Cordeau qu'au site Tuvaaluk. Malheureusement à ce dernier endroit, en raison de l'enchevêtrement des habitations, elles-mêmes aménagées dans les anciens dépotoirs, il n'a pas été possible d'associer globalement des ensembles d'outils chronologiquement diagnostiques à des couches stratigraphiques ou à des structures. La fine analyse effectuée par Gauvin (1990) a très partiellement et localement pallié cette lacune. Si d'autres analyses sont effectuées elle continueront peut-être de décrypter les données de fouille mais sans jamais retrouver la séquence que Badgley avait crû discerner (Badgley 1980).

Les deux autres petits intervalles sont bien courts, compte tenu de l'erreur statistique, pour être interprétés comme un indice d'abandon de la région. Là encore, une comparaison avec les données chronologiques d'Avataq serait utile. Notons toutefois que s'ils se confirmaient, ils pourraient servir de repères aux subdivisions du Paléoesquimau supérieur qui se dessinent dans la région: Dorsétien ancien - Dorsétien moyen pour le premier, Dorsétien récent - Dorsétien tardif pour le second. La grande césure de trois siècles séparerait les phases moyennes et récentes. En dépit des mélanges, l'outillage témoigne de ces différentes phases, les dernières étant les mieux attestées. Ce sont là des hypothèses qu'il reste à confirmer.

Si la baie du Diana a pu connaître des périodes d'occupation moins intense et peut-être même d'abandon au cours du Paléoesquimau, les données archéologiques n'indiquent pas de changement dans l'origine des occupants. Les mêmes matières premières allochtones dominantes se retrouvent du début à la fin du Paléoesquimau, indiquant des relations privilégiées avec l'est, l'Ungava et le Labrador. Il est d'ailleurs intéressant de noter qu'à l'île du Diana le quartzite de Ramah est utilisé au début du Prédorsétien alors qu'au Labrador, à la même période il n'apparaît qu'occasionnellement et ce sont les cherts qui prédominent très largement (Cox 1978).

La prédominance, lors des plus anciennes occupations, du quartz laiteux, dont la source serait près de Wakeham, et du quartzite ferrugineux, provenant sans doute de la fosse du Labrador près de l'Arnaud, tous deux représentés par de nombreux éclats de débitage et de façonnage, semble montrer que les groupes fréquentaient ces deux régions, mais ne pouvaient compter sur un approvisionnement régulier et abondant des matières premières labradoriennes. Quelques rares indices de relations avec l'ouest existent cependant pour le Paléoesquimau supérieur, sous la forme du chert zoné de l'île de Southampton, au nord de la baie d'Hudson, et peut-être de quelques éclats de cherts hudsoniens. Une étude systématique de ces rares témoins reste à effectuer.

L'augmentation de la représentation du quartzite de Ramah au Dorsétien, puis des quartzites de Diana au détriment de celui de Ramah qui se maintient cependant toujours, semble montrer une exploitation croissante des gisements de la région proche, surtout de ceux dont les roches ressemblent à celles de Ramah par leurs enfumures, donc d'une adaptation plus large au milieu étendu, sans toutefois que cessent les relations avec le Labrador. Il est possible que la présence thuléenne ait ralenti les communications entre groupes dorsétiens éloignés. Quelques fragments d'os de castor témoignent d'expéditions lointaines vers les espaces forestiers ou d'échanges avec leurs habitants amérindiens, mais avant l'arrivée des Thuléens.

Les dates les plus récentes sont-elles bien dorsétiennes?

Dans un récent article, Park (1993) défend l'idée que le Dorsétien aurait en réalité disparu de tout l'Arctique avant l'arrivée des Thuléens et que les quelques influences paléoesquimaudes que les préhistoriens ont cru discerner chez ces derniers peuvent mieux s'expliquer par la simple observation et la récupération des vestiges matériels encore très frais abandonnés par les Dorsétiens. D'autre part, il souligne la nette diminution du nombre de dates «dorsétiennes» dans tout l'Arctique canadien entre 700 et ±1000 après J.-C., ce qui correspond à la principale césure de notre séquence chronologique. Il attribue toutes les dates postérieures à une présence thuléenne dans les sites dorsétiens, mais qui n'aurait pas laissé d'autre trace que des témoins de combustion, naturellement attribués au Dorsétien par les archéologues. Le fait que dans l'Ungava les objets façonnés dans des matières organiques soient généralement très mal conservés semble appuyer l'hypothèse de Park puisqu'une grande partie des objets thuléens étaient en os et en ivoire et de ce fait peuvent avoir disparu. Enfin la maison A du site Tuvaaluk, mi-dorsétienne mi-thuléenne (Plumet 1979) est un excellent argument appuyant l'idée d'une réoccupation thuléenne d'une habitation dorsétienne.

Les stimulantes remarques et l'hypothèse de Park méritent d'être prises sérieusement en considération. Il n'est pas question ici d'y répondre longuement ni de les discuter dans tout leur fondement et leurs implications. Ce serait prématuré et trop long. J'en tiendrai cependant compte dans l'interprétation en cours (depuis longtemps malheureusement) du sous-espace A-B du site Tuvaaluk. Dans le cas de la structure A (470±90 B.P.), l'hypothèse d'un réaménagement d'une ancienne

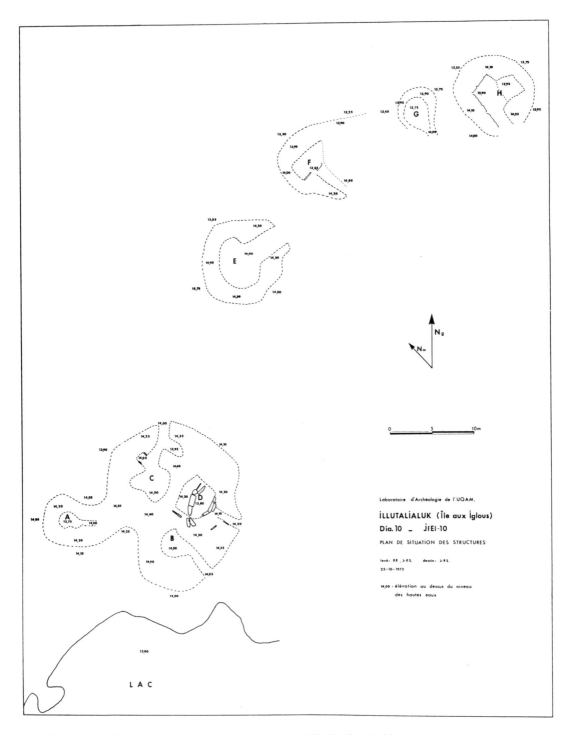

Figure 25 L'ile aux Iglous: plan de situation des structures d'habitation thuléennes.

Figure 26 Site de l'île aux Iglous: exemples d'objets thuléens.

habitation dorsétienne par des Thuléens ne peut être écartée à priori. Les vestiges témoignent au moins d'une connaissance précise du mode de construction des Thuléens et de l'organisation de la partie antérieure de leur espace domestique (entrée, cuisine), surtout telle qu'elle se manifeste au début du Néoesquimau dans la phase de l'île aux Ruines (fin du XIIe et début du XIIIe siècle), au nord-ouest du Groenland et au nord-est d'Ellesmere, (Holtved 1944, 1954; McCullough 1989). Cette connaissance peut aussi bien venir d'une mixité culturelle (une thuléenne ayant épousé un Dorsétien par exemple) que de l'observation d'un village thuléen au cours d'une visite de bon (ou mauvais?) voisinage, ou encore après le départ de ses occupants. On remarquera que la date obtenue à partir du charbon de bois prélevé dans le foyer de cuisine de l'habitation D au site purement thuléen de l'île aux Iglous (DIA.10, JfEl-10, Figures 25 et 26) est pratiquement contemporaine de la phase de l'île aux Ruines: 810 ± 80 B.P. (GIF-4209), soit 1140 après J.-C (ou 1210 après J.-C. calibrée selon Stuiver et Kra, 1986). Au nord-ouest de la baie d'Ungava, à la Pointe-aux-Bélougas (UNG.11, JeEj-7) les dates attribuées aux réoccupations thuléennes de la maison longue D, corrigées selon les mêmes tables, se situent à l'intérieur de l'intervalle maximum 1260 - 1460 après J.-C. (calibrations MASCA: 1220 - 1430 dans Plumet, 1985: 267). Ces réoccupations sont d'ailleurs attestées par plusieurs objets diagnostiques (ibid.: 270, Photo 117). En dépit de leur petit nombre, ces dates thuléennes sont non seulement contemporaines de celles attribuées au Dorsétien, mais se placent aussi de part et d'autre du plus récent intervalle.

Après la lecture de l'article de Park j'ai procédé à la vérification du contexte structural et stratigraphique des échantillons ayant donné des dates contemporaines du Thuléen. Je n'ai rien retrouvé qui pourrait indiquer une réoccupation non dorsétienne. Plusieurs échantillons (UQ-83, 87, 93) étaient associés à une structure de combustion typiquement dorsétienne, d'autres se trouvaient sous une succession de couches d'humus et de cailloutis, jusqu'à 30 cm de profondeur (UQ-82, 90, QC-625). Mais comment contrer l'argument d'une présence thuléenne «fantôme» (c'est-à-dire indiscernable) sur des sites dorsétiens. Comment prouver qu'un événement qui n'aurait pas laissé de trace ne s'est pas produit? C'est l'un des points faibles (et un peu faciles) de l'argumentation de Park. Il est possible qu'un nouvel examen des collections du site Tuvaaluk permette de reconnaître quelques éléments éventuellement thuléens. Ils ne suffiront sans doute pas pour vérifier l'hypothèse que les dates récentes proviennent de différentes réoccupations néoesquimaudes. Park fait valoir que l'inflexion de la distribution bimodale des dates attribuées au Dorsétien dans l'Arctique canadien, entre 700 ou 800 et 900 ou 1200 après J.-C. (calibrées) selon les régions, refléterait la disparition du Paléoesquimau, les dates postérieures étant en réalité thuléennes. Dans la baie du Diana, les premières dates qui suivent cette césure, dès 970 après J.-C. (calibrée), sont antérieures à l'arrivée des Thuléens.

Conclusion

Les données recueillies par le programme Tuvaaluk permettent de proposer quelques hypothèses concernant l'origine du premier peuplement, l'orientation du réseau spatial, le mode de subsistance et d'adaptation au milieu. Elles conduisent aussi à esquisser une hypothétique subdivision du Paléoesquimau supérieur de la baie du Diana en 4 phases: ancienne, moyenne, récente et tardive.

Les premiers occupants venaient sans doute de l'est, plus particulièrement du Labrador, en suivant les côtes de la baie d'Ungava. Les analyses de provenance de la stéatite, bien qu'effectuées sur des échantillons isolés pour chaque carrière, indiquent des relations croisées entre l'est et l'ouest de l'Ungava (Archambault 1981). Les caractères de l'outillage et des structures d'habitation conduisent le plus souvent à constater des affinités avec le Labrador et le Groenland. Des affinités semblables sont également observées pour le matériel du Paléoesquimau inférieur du Labrador (Desrosiers 1982; Pinard 1980; Tuck 1975).

La séquence des dates ^{14}C de la région, les caractères de l'outillage et la permanence du réseau spatial permettent d'estimer que les occupations de la baie du Diana s'échelonnent sur presque la totalité du Paléoesquimau, avec un hyatus probable entre 1380 ± 100 et 1090 ± 90 B.P. (640-970 calibrées) et deux légères inflexions entre 1660 ± 95 et 1555 ± 80 B.P., (390-510 après calibration) et entre 635 ± 90 et 490 ± 80 B.P. (1310-1430 calibéres). Cette séquence se prolonge de plusieurs siècles après le développement du Néoesquimau dans la même région. Pour le moment, aucun indice ne permet d'attribuer les dates récentes à une réoccupation discrète de sites dorsétiens par des Thuléens, comme le croit Park (1993). Cette séquence confirme, s'il en était encore besoin, la continuité d'évolution du Prédorsétien au Dorsétien que Taylor avait établi à partir des gisements de Tyara et d'Arnapik.

À une plus large échelle, les affinités souvent mentionnées entre les éléments culturels paléoesquimaux de l'Ungava et du Labrador d'une part, du Labrador, de Baffin et du Groenland d'autre part, conduisent à proposer un premier mouvement de peuplement venu du Nord (Groenland, Ellesmere, Baffin oriental) vers le Labrador et l'Ungava jusqu'au Cap de Nouvelle-France sur la côte sud du détroit d'Hudson. Par contre, le schéma proposé par Taylor en 1964, d'un courant de peuplement venu du golfe de Foxe par les îles du détroit, ne peut s'appliquer qu'à la partie occidentale de la péninsule et à l'Hudsonie. La région de Wakeham et la côte sud du détroit jusqu'au cap de Nouvelle France recèle peut-être des éléments de transition qui permettront de nuancer cette coupure ou de mieux en comprendre les raisons. L'intérieur de la péninsule, vers le lac Payne, où le quartzite de Ramah est abondant, constitue aussi une extension de l'aire Ungava-Labrador. Dans cette région où prévalait la chasse au caribou, des contacts avaient peut-être lieu avec les populations hudsoniennes. Les lacs et cours d'eau reliant les grands lacs de Payne, Klotz et Minto aux versants ungavien et hudsonien devraient constituer une aire de recherche prioritaire maintenant que les moyens de communications sont grandement facilités.

Ouvrages Cités

Archambault, M.-F. 1981. Essai de caractérisation de la stéatite des sites dorsétiens et des carrières de l'Ungava, Arctique québécois. Géographie physique et Quaternaire, 35(1): 19-28.

Badgley, I. 1980. Stratigraphy and habitation features at Dia.4 (JfEl-4), a Dorset site in Arctic Québec. Arctic, 33(3): 569-584.

Bibeau, P.1984. Etablissements paléoesquimaux du site Diana 73, Ungava. Laboratoire d'archéologie, Université du Québec à Montréal. Paléo-Québec 16.

Bibeau, P. 1986. Présences paléoesquimaudes au site Gagnon. In, Palaeo-Eskimo Cultures in Newfoundland, Labrador and Ungava. Memorial University of Newfoundland. Reports in Archaeology 1: 27-39.

Boutray, B. de. 1981 Étude comparative de quartzites enfumés utilisés par les Paléoesquimaux de l'Arctique québécois. Géographie physique et Quaternaire, 35(1): 29-40.

Boutray, B. de et P Plumet. 1990. L'origine du quartzite de Diana. Manuscrit déposé au laboratoire d'archéologie de l'Université du Québec à Montréal.

Cox, L. 1978. Paleo-Eskimo occupations of the North Labrador coast. Arctic Anthropology, 15(2): 96-118.

Desrosiers, P. 1982. Paleo-Eskimo occupations at Diana.1, Ungava Bay (Nouveau-Québec). Mémoire de maîtrise, Département d'anthropologie, Université McGill.

Desrosiers, P. 1986. Pre-Dorset surface structures from Diana-1, Ungava Bay (Nouveau-Québec). In, Palaeo-Eskimo Cultures in Newfoundland, Labrador and Ungava Memorial University of Newfoundland. Reports in Archaeology 1: 3-25.

Dikov, N.N. 1965. The stone age of Kamchatka and the Chukchi Peninsula in the light of new archaeological data. Arctic Anthropology, 3(1): 10-25.

Fitzhugh, W.W. 1981. A prehistoric caribou fence from William Harbour, Northern Labrador. In, Megaliths to Medecine Wheels: boulder structures in archaeology, M. Wilson, K.L. Road et K.J. Hardy, éds. The Archaeological Association of the University of Calgary, pp. 187-206.

Gangloff, P. 1988. Géomorphologie de la région de Tuvaaluk. Rapport manuscrit déposé au laboratoire d'archéologie de l'Université du Québec à Montréal.

Gauvin, H. 1990. Analyses spatiales d'un site dorsétien: le sous-espace D de DIA.4. Mémoire de maîtrise ès-sciences, Département d'anthropologie, Faculté des arts et des sciences, Université de Montréal.

Grønnow, B. 1986. Recent archaeological investigations of West Greenland caribou hunting. Arctic Anthropology, 23(1-2): 57-80.

Grønnow, B., M. Meldgaard et J.B. Nielsen. 1983. Aasivissuit - The Great Summer Camp. Archaeological, ethnographical and zoo-archaeological studies of a caribou-hunting site in West Greenland. Man & Society 5. Meddelelser om Grønland.

Harp, E., Jr. 1976. Dorset settlement pattern in Newfoundland and southeastern Hudson Bay. In, Eastern Arctic Prehistory: Paleoeskimo Problems, M.S. Maxwell, éd. Memoirs of the Society for American Archaeology, 31, pp. 119-138.

Hillaire-Marcel, C. 1979. Les mers post-glaciaires du Québec: quelques aspects. Thèse de doctorat d'état ès-Sciences naturelles présenté à l'Université Pierre et Marie Curie, Paris.

Holtved, E. 1944. Archaeological Investigations in the Thule District, I-II. Meddelelser om Grønland, 141(1, 2).

Holtved, E. 1954. Archaeological Investigations in the Thule District, III. Nûgdlît and Comer's Midden. Meddelelser om Grønland, 146(3).

Jordan, R.H. 1980. Dorset art from Labrador. Folk 21-22: 397-417.

Julien, M. 1980. Étude préliminaire du matériel osseux provenant du site dorsétien DIA-4 (JfEl-4) (Arctique oriental). Arctic 33(3): 553-568.

Labrèche, Y. 1986. Interprétation d'un assemblage lithique dorsétien de l'Ungava. In, Palaeo-Eskimo Cultures in Newfoundland, Labrador and Ungava. Memorial University of Newfoundland, Reports in Archaeology, 1: 39-49.

McCullough, K.M. 1989. The Ruin Islanders. Early Thule Culture Pioneers in the Eastern High Arctic. Museé canadien des civilisations, Série Mercure, Commission archéologique du Canada Dossier 41.

Mary-Rousselière, G. 1964. Palaeo-eskimo remains in the Pelly Bay region, N.W.T. National Museum of Canada Bulletin 193, Part. 1, pp. 162-183.

Maxwell, M.S. 1973. Archaeology of the Lake Harbour District, Baffin Island. Musée National de l'Homme, Série Mercure, Commission archéologique du Canada Dossier 6.

Michéa, J. 1950. Exploration in Ungava Peninsula. Musée National du Canada Bulletin 118, pp. 54-57.

Park, R.W. 1993. The Dorset-Thule succesion in Arctic North America: assessing claims for cultural contact. American Antiquity 58(2): 203-234.

Piérard, J. 1975. Archéologie du Nouveau-Québec: étude du matériel ostéologique provenant des sites UNG.11 et DIA.1. Laboratoire d'archéologie, Université du Québec à Montréal. Paléo-Québec 6.

Piérard, J. 1979. Le caribou dans la préhistoire et la photohistoire du Québec. Recherches amérindiennes au Québec, 9(1-2): 9-16.

Pinard, C. 1980. DIA3 (JfEl-3). Communication présenté à la rencontre annuelle de l'Association canadienne d'archéologie, Saskatoon, avril 1980. Déposée au Laboratoire d'archéologie de l'UQAM, Université du Québec à Montréal.

Plumet, P. 1976. Archéologie du Nouveau-Québec; habitats paléo-esquimaux à Poste-de-la-Baleine. Laboratoire d'archéologie, Université du Québec à Montréal. Paléo-Québec 7.

Plumet P. 1977. Le peuplement préhistorique du Nouveau-Québec - Labrador. Géographie physique et Quaternaire, 31(1): 185-199.

Plumet, P. 1978. Le Nouveau-Québec et le Labrador. Recherches amérindiennes au Québec, 8(1): 99-110.

Plumet, P. 1979. Thuléens et Dorsétiens dans l'Ungava (Nouveau-Québec). In, Thule Eskimo Culture: an Anthropological Retrospective, A.P. McCartney, éd, Musée National de l'Homme, Série Mercure, Commission archéologique du Canada Dossier 88, pp. 110-121.

Plumet, P. 1980. Essai d'analyse descriptive: les témoins façonnés pré-dorsétiens de Poste-de-la-Baleine, Québec, (1975). Laboratoire d'archéologie, Université du Québec à Montréal. Paléo-Québec 12.

Plumet P. 1981. Matières premières allochtones et réseau spatial paléoesquimau en Ungava occidental, Arctique québécois. Géographie physique et Quaternaire, 35(1): 5-17.

Plumet, P. 1985. Archéologie de l'Ungava : le site de la Pointe aux Bélougas (Qilalugarsiuvik) et les maisons longues dorsétiennes. Laboratoire d'archéologie, Université du Québec à Montréal. Paléo-Québec 18.

Plumet, P. 1986. Questions et réflexions concernant la préhistoire de l'Ungava. In, Palaeo-Eskimo Cultures in Newfoundland, Labrador and Ungava. Memorial University of Newfoundland, Reports in Archaeology, 1: 151-160.

Plumet, P. 1989. Thuléens et Dorsétiens à l'île d'Amittualujjuaq, baie du Diana, Arctique québécois. Géographie physique et Quaternaire, 43(2): 207-221.

Plumet, P. et I. Badgley. 1980. Implications méthodologiques des fouilles de Tuvaaluk sur l'étude des établissements dorsétiens. Arctic, 33(3): 542-552.

Plumet, P. et P. Gangloff. 1987. Contribution à l'étude du peuplement préhistorique des côtes du Québec arctique et de son cadre paléogéographique. Etudes/Inuit/Studies, 11 (1): 67-89.

Plumet, P. et P. Gangloff. 1991. Contribution à l'archéologie et l'ethnohistoire de l'Ungava oriental: côte est, Killiniq, îles Button, Labrador septentrional. Laboratoire d'archéologie, Université du Québec à Montréal. Paléo-Québec 19.

Richard, P. 1981. Paléophytogéographie postglaciaire en Ungava par l'analyse pollinique. Laboratoire d'archéologie, Université du Québec à Montréal. Paléo-Québec 13.

Stuiver, M. et R.S. Kra. 1986. 12th International Radiocarbon Conference. June 24-28, 1985. Trondheim, Norway. Radiocarbon, 28:2A.

Taylor, W. E., Jr. 1958. Archaeological work in Ungava, 1957. The Arctic Circular, 10(2): 25-27.

Taylor, W.E., Jr. 1962. Pre-Dorset occupations at Ivugivik in Northwestern Ungava. In, Prehistoric Cultural Relations Between the Arctic and Temperate Zones of North America, J.M. Campbell, éd. Arctic Institute of North America Technical Paper, 11: 80-91.

Taylor, W.E., Jr. 1964. La préhistoire de la péninsule du Labrador. Musée National du Canada, Études anthropologiques 7.

Taylor, W.E., Jr. 1968. The Arnapik and Tyara Sites. Memoirs of the Society for American Archaeology 22, 33(4) Part 2.

Tuck, J.A. 1975. Prehistory of Saglek Bay, Labrador: Archaic and Paleo-Eskimo Occupations. Musée National de l'Homme, Série Mercure, Commission archéologique du Canada Dossier 32.

Tuck, J.A. et W. Fitzhugh. 1986. Palaeo-Eskimo tradition of Newfoundland and Labrador: a re-appraisal. In, Palaeo-Eskimo Cultures in Newfoundland, Labrador and Ungava. Memorial University of Newfoundland, Reports in Archaeology, 1: 161-167.

Vézinet, M. 1982. Occupation humaine de l'Ungava. Perspective ethnohistorique et écologique. Laboratoire d'archéologie, Université du Québec à Montréal. Paléo-Québec 14.

A Groswater Site at Blanc-Sablon, Quebec

Jean-Yves Pintal
Municipalité de Blanc-Sablon
Blanc-Sablon, Quebec

Abstract

The Groswater occupation of the Lower North Shore of Quebec seems to have involved a pattern of seasonal exploitation of coastal resources in the Gulf of St.Lawrence and the Strait of Belle-Isle. Moreover, the area was apparently shared between the Groswater people and Archaic Amerindians.

Résumé

L'occupation groswatérienne de la Basse-Côte-Nord du Québec semble avoir été axée sur l'exploitation saisonnière des ressources côtières du golfe du Saint-Laurent et du détroit de Belle-Isle. Il y aurait apparemment eu coexistence entre les Groswatériens et les Amérindiens de l'Archaïque.

Introduction

Until recently, archaeological work on the Lower North Shore of Quebec and the northern coast of the Strait of Belle Isle had played a more modest role in defining Palaeoeskimo assemblages than has research in Newfoundland and Labrador. This can partly be explained by the limited number of sites discovered in the Lower North Shore/northern Strait of Belle Isle region and by the fact that these sites had been studied on the basis of surface finds alone (Harp 1951, 1964a, 1964b; Lévesque 1976; Martijn 1974; McGhee and Tuck 1975). Until the mid-1980s, no Palaeoeskimo sites had been excavated extensively or dated in this region.

An inital chronological framework was established for the area through typological analysis (Fitzhugh 1976, 1980; Tuck 1984). Various studies indicated that Palaeoeskimo occupation did not begin until the late Pre-Dorset period (around 3000 B.P.) and it continued throughout Middle Dorset times (Fitzhugh 1980; Lévesque 1976; Tuck 1986). However, sites associated with the latter period seem to be much more rare than those of the Groswater complex, a situation which contrasts with that observed in Newfoundland. Researchers have tried to explain this difference through conflicts between Amerindian groups of the Archaic period and the Palaeoeskimo, which would have turned the Strait of Belle Isle into a kind of no man's land (McGhee and Tuck 1975). According to another hypothesis, the Groswater and Dorset populations had different ways of life (Renouf 1988), with the latter exploiting coastal resources more intensively than Groswater groups. These resources were more readily accessible throughout the year in Newfoundland than on the northern coast of the Strait of

Belle Isle.

A major archaeological survey has been underway on the Lower North Shore since 1984. A number of Palaeoeskimo sites, some of which are *in situ*, were discovered as a result of this program. Preliminary research has provided the first radiocarbon dates for late Pre-Dorset on the Lower North Shore and in the Strait of Belle Isle (Table 1). These dates have confirmed the chronological sequence already established. However, Dorset sites are still much less common than Groswater ones. Therefore, we do not have enough data to deal seriously with questions related to the Pre-Dorset/Dorset transition.

Table 1 List of radiocarbon dates for late Pre-Dorset sites of the Groswater complex on the Lower North Shore.

SITES	DATES	LABORATORY	ALTITUDE	REFERENCE
EiBg-43A	2420±60	Beta-19637	8 m	Pintal 1987
EiBg-43A	2570±90	Beta-40350	8 m	Pintal 1991
EiBi-14	2400±100	Beta-19633	9 m	Groison et al. 1985
EiBg-29A	2430±80	Beta-23004	7 m	Pintal 1988
EiBg-29A	2300±150	UQ-1753	7 m	Plumet 1990

Nevertheless, Palaeoeskimo occupation of the Groswater complex may be described on the basis of data from approximately a dozen sites identified to date, in particular EiBg-43A. This large site of over 800 m² was discovered on the west bank of the mouth of the Blanc-Sablon River. Intensive test pitting and partial excavation (10%) revealed the presence of an intact settlement in which a number of activities seem to have been carried out simultaneously around various types of hearths.

Biogeographical Framework

The region under study corresponds to a part of Quebec where relatively warm water from the Gulf of St. Lawrence comes into contact with cold water from the North Atlantic Ocean in the Strait of Belle Isle (Figure 1). It has a cold continental climate, that is, short wet summers and long winters with little snow. However, the sea affects weather conditions on the coast by substantially reducing seasonal temperature differences. As a result, summers are colder, and winters warmer than further inland (Lavoie 1984). The region is sometimes exposed to strong winds, especially in the area where the Strait of Belle Isle narrows near Blanc-Sablon. Storms can develop at any time of the year except summer, and fog is frequent, especially in July. Ice covers most of the Strait of Belle Isle from early January until the end of April.

Compared with the rest of the Lower North Shore, the Brador/Blanc-Sablon area forms a kind of enclave in which the bedrock is of Palaeozoic origin. This has affected the landscape which consists of widely spaced, tiered hills overlooking a gradually descending series of sandy terraces that attest to the decline in sea level. Long beaches of fine sand provide easy access to the water. Islands are rare in this area.

Further west, the bedrock is of Precambrian origin, and the landscape is characterized by rolling hills that descend toward the sea. The coast is rocky and often bordered by steep cliffs; however, immense archipelagos create a buffer zone between the sea and the mainland and offer a

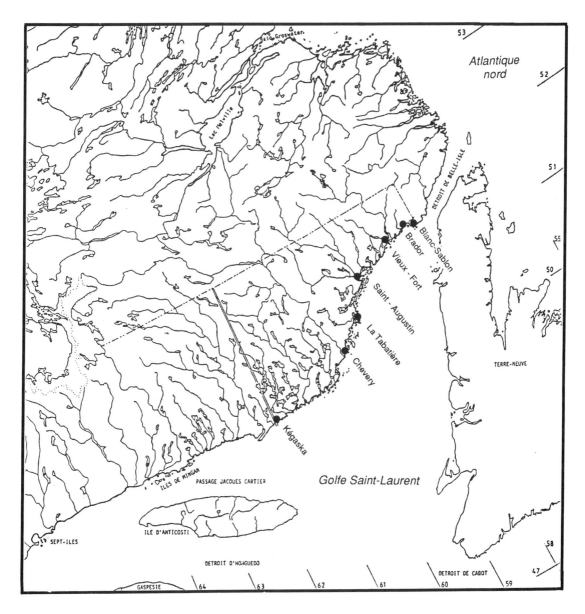

Figure 1 The eastern Lower North Shore and the Strait of Belle-Isle.

multitude of sheltered harbours.

A coastal band measuring 30 kilometers wide is covered by maritime hemi-arctic forest tundra. Further inland, towards the north, this vegetation gradually gives way to subarctic black spruce and fir forest. The intensive, even industrial, modern exploitation of seals, whales, birds (eggs), fish (herring, capelin, cod, salmon) and molluscs readily attests to the abundant marine resources in this area. Inland biological resources seem to have been more fragile, as shown by the impact of hunting activities over the past 100 years. However, freshwater fish abound in the many lakes and rivers, and fur-bearing mammals, hare, grouse, and ptarmigan are still plentiful. The caribou population was larger during the historical period; a few herds were even found in the main river valleys (Folinsbee 1979).

Site Description and Analysis

EiBg-43A is located about 200 m west of the Blanc-Sablon River and 400 m from the Strait of Belle-Isle. It occupies a sandy terrace situated 8 m (Figure 2) above sea level, which is the average altitude of sites of the Groswater complex in this region. Based on their radiocarbon dates (Table 1), the altitude of these sites is perfectly in keeping with the uplift curves for Blanc-Sablon (Bigras and Dubois 1987). When EiBg-43A was occupied, the Blanc-Sablon River must have been slightly wider and the sea a bit closer. In short, the landscape would have been very similar to what it is today.

The surrounding vegetation is typical of that found on terraces in Blanc-Sablon. Moss and lichen are abundant, but krummholz occasionally predominates. Analysis of plant remains from the occupation layer revealed that the vegetation has changed very little since the emergence of the terrace following the decline in sea level (Larouche 1988).

Late Pre-Dorset (Groswater) Palaeoeskimo occupation coincides with a relative deterioration in climatic conditions (Lamb 1980). Temperatures fell slightly and ambient humidity rose. This probably explains why organic matter accumulated fairly rapidly without really decomposing and created a thick organic layer that sealed EiBg-43A.

The two radiocarbon dates for this site were obtained through the analysis of spruce charcoal found in two separate hearths: 2590 ± 70 B.P. (Beta-40350) and 2420 ± 60 B.P. (Beta-19637). These dates clearly situate the site in the period associated with the Groswater complex—2800 to 2100 B.P. (Fitzhugh 1980). However, even though there is a fairly wide gap between the two dates, we do not believe that there is more than one main occupation on the site. This conclusion is based on the fact that the various remains are quite spread out, that none of the structures are superimposed, that all are remarkably intact, that the occupation layer is not very thick, and, in particular, that all the remains are in the same layer. Typologically the material founded on EiBg-43A is late Groswater by Central Labrador coast standards (Cox, 1978) meaning that the more recent date is in closer conformity with the age of that site.

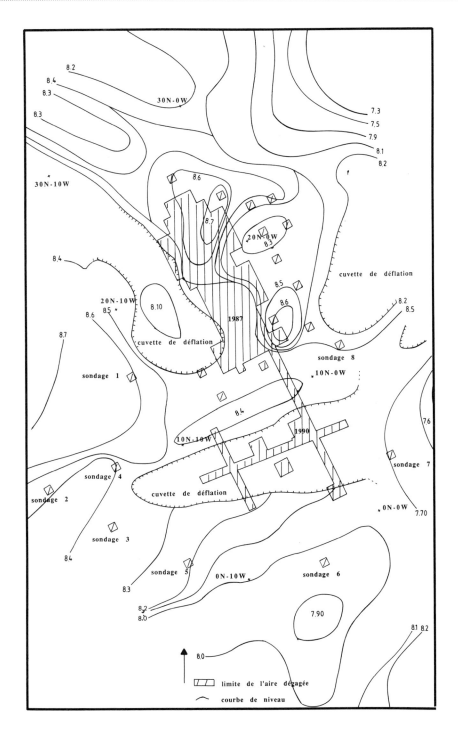

Figure 2 EiBg-43A, site plan.

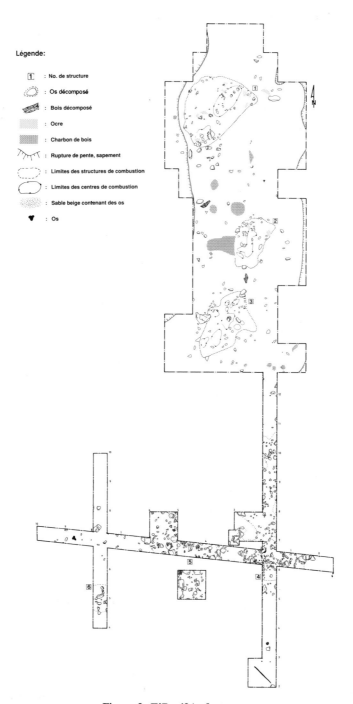

Légende:

- 1 : No. de structure
- : Os décomposé
- : Bois décomposé
- : Ocre
- : Charbon de bois
- : Rupture de pente, sapement
- : Limites des structures de combustion
- : Limites des centres de combustion
- : Sable beige contenant des os
- ▼ : Os

Figure 3 EiBg-43A, features.

Hearths

At least six hearths served as focal points for various activities (Figure 3). Three of these structures (Nos. 1, 2 and 3) consist of low (5 cm), oval-shaped mounds of sand (around 2.00 m x 1.00 m) containing only a limited amount of charcoal. A large quantity of burnt and heat-fractured stones are associated with these mounds or with their perimeters. In two instances, zones of red-ochre-stained sand are located on the perimeter. In addition, the remains of uncooked bone in an advanced state of decay and pieces of rotten wood were found in areas immediately surrounding these structures.

A fourth structure (No. 4) consists of a thin (3 cm), circular layer (0.75 m in diameter) of charcoal almost completely covered with heat-fractured rocks. Based on test pit data, other similar hearths may be located on the periphery of the excavated zone.

Structures 5 and 6 are the most imposing. They are large structures (5.00 m x 1.50 m, 4.00 m x 2.50 m, oriented NNW/SSE) that consist of thin (5 cm), but dense layers of charcoal almost totally buried in rocks, some of which have been subjected to intense heat. In one case, a number of stone slabs surround a concentration of ashes, heated rock and discoloured earth which suggest the existence of an axial feature.

Hearths 1, 2 and 3, which are made of sand, are located in the northern part of the site, while hearths 5 and 6, which are larger, occupy the central area. The smallest hearths are spread out around the periphery of this large group. The hearths in the north section are separated from those in the centre by a long (3.00 m), thick (10 cm) layer of coniferous bark associated with a small axe of polished nephrite (plate 1). In all probability, this was a specialized work area in which Palaeoeskimos removed bark from trees to prepare poles for dwelling frames, or for other domestic or technological purposes.

A small quantity of burned bone, too fragmentary to be identified, was found in hearth 3, which consisted of a mound of sand. However, two pieces of bone from the appendicular skeleton of a young seal were found in an area with only a low artifact density (a few microblades).

Artifacts

There was a substantial amount of chipping debris in the central and northern part of the site. Such debris was more widely dispersed in the area around the small hearths located on the periphery. Over 7000 flakes were collected of which 95 percent are made from fine-grained chert. No chert deposits are know to exist in this area. Opaque and mat, they vary in colour from reddish brown to greenish beige. Geologically, this chert belongs to the St. George group bordering the west coast of Newfoundland (Bostock et al. 1983; Marquis 1988; Nagle 1985). The other raw materials include Ramah quartzite (1.5%), crystal quartz (0.2%) and sandstone (3.0%).

On EiBg-43A flaking was used to trim bifacial objects rather than cores. This conclusion is based on the fact that the weight-size distribution of chipping debris is unimodal and concerns only flakes smaller than 200 m^2 (Figure 4). Trimming activities seem to have been carried out everywhere on the site. However, the discovery of two large concentrations of flakes representing over 50 percent

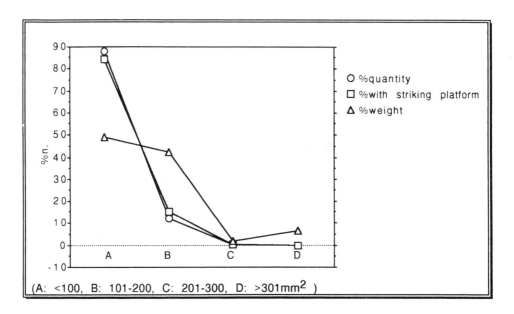

Figure 4 Weight percentage for each size class of Newfoundland chert flakes.

of all such objects found on the site suggests that the occupants used some kind of flexible material, perhaps a piece of animal skin, to gather up and dispose of this waste.

In addition to flakes, the collection is comprised of four cores (including one microblade core), one preform, and around 20 biface trimming/resharpening flakes. The proportion of tools (n=118) to flakes is relatively low: around 1.7 %. The collection is quite varied, however, and includes a large number of utilized flakes, microblades and knives (Table 8).

Endblades

The two endblades (Table 2), both of which are made of chert, correspond exactly to the Groswater type: they have a plano-convex cross-section with the distinctive high side-notches, and are box-based and steeply bevelled. The tip and the notches of both objects have been finely adjusted bifacially.

Table 2 Pooled Groswater endblade measurements.

Mean length	27.75 mm	(s=1.00 mm)
Mean width	12.20 mm	(s=1.41 mm)
Mean thickness	3.45 mm	(s=0.70 mm)
Mean weight	1.25 g	(s=0.2 g)
Mean notch depth	2.50 mm	(s=0.30 mm)
Mean notch width	4.45 mm	(s=0.05 mm)
Mean basal height	7.85 mm	(s=0.02 mm)

s = standard deviation

Triangular Points

Of the three points recovered (two of chert, one of fine quartzite) only one is complete (Table 4). The blade is triangular and symmetrical in form with a bi-convex cross-section. The sides have

Table 3 Triangular point measurements.

Length	36.20 mm
Width	18.30 mm
Thickness	3.00 mm
Weight	2.00 g
Notch depth	2.00 mm
Notch width	3.35 mm
Basal height	4.00 mm

Table 4 Pooled knife measurements.

Mean length	47.20 mm	(s=26.16 mm)
Mean width	24.13 mm	(s=6.78 mm)
Mean thickness	4.20 mm	(s=0.85 mm)
Mean weight	5.7 g	(s=5.1 g)
Mean notch depth	2.00 mm	(s=0.70 mm)
Mean notch width	5.30 mm	(s=1.40 mm)
Mean basal height	6.91 mm	(s=1.20 mm)

been carefully sharpened, and low shallow side notches surmount a linear polished base. The distal part of the two other points has a distinctive chevron pattern with central ridge flaking.

Knives

The knives from EiBg-43A vary in size (Table 4). Almost all have (8/10 identifiable) shallow low side-notches with a well thinned or polished base. The blade of these leaf-shaped knives is usually thin and asymmetrical in both sections, one side being more convex and thinner than the other. They are all made of Newfoundland chert except one, which is of Ramah quartzite. The basal parts of two broken knives each represent a specific type: one is trapezoidal, while the other has multiple basal notches.

Burin-Like Tools

None of the burin-like tools are complete. Nevertheless, we can describe them as being triangular or trapezoidal in shape, with an asymmetrical traverse section. The notches resemble the ones observed on points or knives; they are low and shallow with a linear base. All of these tools are made from Newfoundland chert, and were first chipped and then ground. The amount of grinding on the blade varies from minimal to maximal, except on the notches and the proximal end. Two ground burin spalls were found.

Table 5 Pooled microblade measurements.

Mean length	31.03 mm	(s=15.52 mm)
Mean width	9.54 mm	(s=2.80 mm)
Mean thickness	2.62 mm	(s=0.91 mm)
Mean weight	1.02 g	(s=0.76 g)

Microblades

Microblades represent an important part of the tool collection. While most of them, 80.5%, are made of chert, 16.7% are made of crystal quartz and 2.8% (only one) of Ramah quartzite. Their size follows a bimodal distribution (0.2 g < X < 0.6 g, 1.0 g < X < 2.2 g). They usually have either one or two central ridges; only one specimen has three. A good proportion (20%) were modified for hafting.

Scrapers

The scrapers from EiBg-43A are all made of chert, and most are (6/10) trapezoidal in shape (Table 6). Two are widely flared and one has a distinct quadrangular form. With one exception, they all possess one or two spurs or ears.

Table 6 Pooled scraper measurements.

Mean length	25.50 mm	(s=8.18 mm)
Mean width	23.55 mm	(s=3.63 mm)
Mean thickness	6.00 mm	(s=0.91 mm)
Mean weight	4.02 g	(s=1.78 g)
Mean distal edge angle	64.00°	(s=9.66°)

Utilized Flakes

Used flakes are common on EiBg-43A (Table 7). All are made of chert except one, which is made of Ramah quartzite. Some have a distinct concave side or a spur.

Table 7 Pooled utilized flake measurements.

Mean length	25.10 mm	(s=14.90 mm)
Mean width	21.72 mm	(s=8.71 mm)
Mean thickness	4.44 mm	(s=3.98 mm)
Mean weight	5.3 g	(s=11.38 g)

Some of the tools collected are represented by only one or two specimens. This is the case of the awl formed by the natural pointed part of a chert flake. The only sidescraper found seems to have been used as a spokeshave. The collection also contains two sideblades (one complete), both of which are ovate and made from chert. The two sandstone abraders are incomplete. The small axe is of nephrite, and only its distal part has been polished (length: 43.10 mm; width: 31. 50 mm; thickness: 7.10 mm, weight: 17.20 g).

Interpretation of EiBg-43A

These tools occur in different concentrations throughout the area excavated (Figure 5). Most of the utilized flakes (87.9%), endscrapers (66.7%, Figure 6), abraders (66.7%), and burin-like tools or ground burin spalls (71.0%, Figure 7) are concentrated around the small hearths 1, 2 and 3. There is less variation, however, in the tools around the larger hearths (Nos. 5 and 6). On the other hand, 53.3% of the knives (Figure 7), 56.6% of the microblades, the two sideblades, and the awl (Figure 6) were found around these two structures.

Most of the objects found in the vicinity of the structure identified as an axial feature (No. 6) are cutting implements (knives, microblades, sideblades), while those located around the small hearths (Nos. 1, 2 and 3) are associated with the production of other tools or of wooden or bone tool shafts (endscrapers with spurs, burin-like tools, abraders). There seems to be a clear distinction between areas of a more domestic nature and those of a more technological one. It should also be mentioned

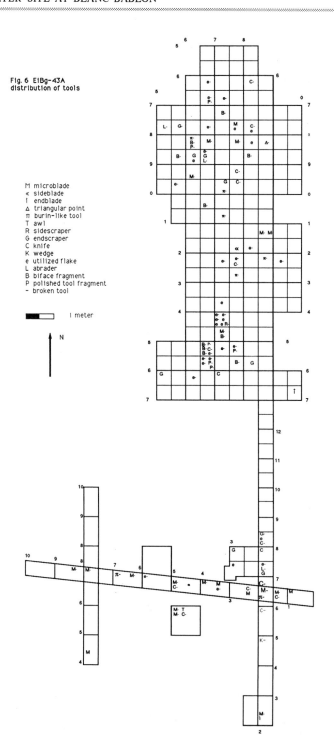

Fig. 6 EiBg-43A
distribution of tools

M microblade
« sideblade
↑ endblade
Δ triangular point
π burin-like tool
T awl
R sidescraper
G endscraper
C knife
K wedge
e utilized flake
L abrader
B biface fragment
P polished tool fragment
- broken tool

1 meter

N

Figure 5 EiBg-43A, distribution of tools.

Figure 6 EiBg-43A: *a*-small polished nephrite axe, *b*-end-blade, *c*-burin-like tool.

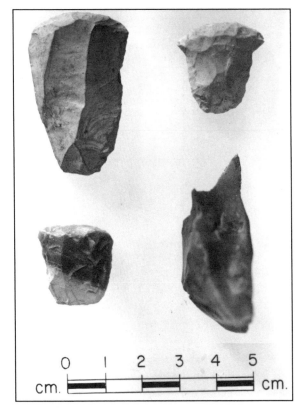

Figure 7 EiBg-43A: scrapers (*a-c*), awl (*d*).

Figure 8 EiBg-43A: bifaces.

that only a small percentage of tools may be related to hunting (2,5%, Figure 7), which is surprising given the number of categories associated with the working of animal skins, bone and wood, or with butchering activities (83.0%).

The specific distribution of artifacts around wide-spread, non-ovelapping, hearths suggest the presence of a single occupation. The rarity of faunal remains seems to reflect the presence of a relatively short term settlement. Young seal has been identified among the faunal remains, and it would suggest a spring occupation, considering the fact that young seals gather in the area mostly at this time.

Table 8 Tool types found on EiBg-43A.

	n	%
SCRAPERS	10	8.5
UTILIZED FLAKES	33	28.0
KNIVES	15	12.7
ABRADERS	3	2.5
MICROBLADES	22	18.6
BURIN-LIKE TOOLS	5	4.2
BURIN SPALLS	2	1.7
ENDBLADES	2	1.7
TRIANGULAR POINTS	1	0.8
WEDGES	1	0.8
SIDEBLADES	2	1.7
AWLS	1	0.8
POLISHED TOOL FRAGMENTS	5	4.2
BIFACE FRAGMENTS	10	8.5
SIDESCRAPERS	1	0.8
AXES	1	0.8
CORES	4	3.4
TOTAL	118	100.0

Discussion

EiBg-43A is an important site for the interpretation of Groswater occupation. It provides the first insights into a Groswater site structure on the north shore of the Strait of Belle-Isle, establishing possible points of comparison between the Central Labrador coast and Newfoundland. As was mentioned in the introduction, approximately a dozen Groswater sites are now known on the Lower North Shore of Quebec. A brief evaluation of these sites will allow us to outline the settlement pattern.

The occupational pattern revealed on EiBg-43A, illustrating the contrast between large hearths associated with domestic tools and small hearths associated with tools of a more technological nature, reflects what seems to be a characteristic of Palaeoeskimo sites of the Groswater complex on the eastern Lower North Shore. In fact, even the limited data from sites EiBj-4, a large domestic camp in Salmon Bay—up to now the western most Groswater occupation on the Lower North Shore (Martijn 1974)—and EiBg-29A, a smaller domestic unit discovered on île à Bois, facing Blanc-Sablon (Groison et al. 1985; Plumet 1990), seem to corroborate the model established for EiBg-43A. The distribution of tools excavated or collected by zones on the surface of these two sites demonstrates the same contrast observed on site EiBg-43A, that is, between scrapers and burin-like tools, on the one hand, and microblades and knives, on the other (Tables 9, 10, 11).

This occupational pattern, which represents the spatial organization established while the camp was being set up, seems to be valid for all large late Pre-Dorset (Groswater) sites located in coastal zones, regardless of whether they occur on the mainland (EiBg-43A, EiBj-4) (Tables 9 and 10), or

Table 9 EiBg-43A: breakdown of tools by zone.

	Zone1	Zone 2	Zone 3	Zone 4	Zone 5	Zone 6	Zone 7
ENDSCRAPERS	4	3	2	0	0	0	0
UTILIZED FLAKES	9	4	15	1	0	0	4
KNIVES	4	8	2	0	0	0	1
ABRADERS	2	1	0	0	0	0	0
MICROBLADES	5	9	1	4	1	0	2
BURIN-LIKE TOOLS	2	1	0	1	0	0	3
ENDBLADES	0	0	0	0	1	1	0
TRIANGULAR POINTS	1	0	0	0	0	0	0
WEDGES	0	1	0	0	0	0	0
SIDEBLADES	0	1	0	0	0	0	1
AWLS	0	1	0	0	0	0	0
POLISHED FRAGMENTS	2	0	3	0	0	0	0
BIFACE FRAGMENTS	5	0	5	0	0	0	0
SIDESCRAPERS	0	0	2	0	0	0	0

Table 10 EiBj-4: breakdown of tools by zone.

TYPES	ZONE 1	ZONE 2	ZONE 3	ZONE 4	ZONE 5
SIDEBLADES	0	1(100.0)	0	0	0
BURIN-LIKE TOOLS	0	6 (85.7)	0	0	1 (14.3)
TRIANGULAR POINTS	1 (50.0)	0	0	1 (50.0)	0
ENDSCRAPERS	0	0	0	1(100.0)	0
ENDBLADES	1 (100.0)	0	0	0	0
UTILIZED FLAKES	0	4 (66.7)	0	2 (33.3)	0
MICROBLADES	13 (44.8)	11 (37.9)	0	5 (17.2)	0
KNIVES	0	1 (20.0)	2 (40.0)	2 (40.0)	0
BIFACE FRAGMENTS	4 (44.4)	3 (33.3)	1 (11.1)	1 (11.1)	0

on an island (EiBg-29A) (Table 11). Other types of sites also exist, however, and, as a whole, they seem to reflect the settlement pattern of late Pre-Dorset groups. Some small sites containing only a few flakes and tools that are scattered over a limited area, without or with small hearths, have been identified on Île Verte (EiBh-80, EiBh-81), facing Blanc-Sablon, (Pintal 1989, 1991), and at

Belles-Amours Point (EiBi-14, EiBi-16), between Blanc-Sablon and Salmon Bay (Groison et al. 1985). Since little data are available for these sites, it is difficult to identify their functions. However, their limited size, strategic location, and relatively high proportion of harpoon endblades or triangular points suggests that they served as hunting sites and look-outs.

Without question, the settlement pattern of the Groswater complex on the Lower North Shore is characterized by the exploitation of the coastal environment, including the islands in the Brador/Blanc-Sablon area which were not utilized by the Amerindians of the Archaic period. Two main types of sites (hunting and look-outs sites, and domestic units with processing activity areas) are located in distinct zones that seem to indicate a pattern of land use based on the exploitation of coastal resources (seal, seabirds, etc.). Although one domestic unit appear to have been established on an island (e.g. EiBg-29A), most of the large sites are located on the mainland coast: EiBj-4, EiBh-36 (Lévesque 1976), EiBh-5 (Mills 1980), and EiBg-43A. On islands or points

Table 11 EiBg-29A: breakdown of tools by zone.

TYPES	ZONE 1	ZONE 2
SIDEBLADES	3 (100.0)	0
BURIN-LIKE TOOLS OR GROUNDED BURIN SPALLS	1 (10.0)	9 (90.0)
ENDSCRAPERS	0	3 (100.0)
ENDBLADES	0	1 (100.0)
UTILIZED FLAKES	0	1 (100.0)
MICROBLADES	3 (42.8)	4 (57.1)
KNIVES	1 (50.0)	1 (50.0)
BIFACE FRAGMENTS	0	1 (100.0)

facing the ocean, we mostly encountered small hunting and look-out sites. The faunal data, even though fairly limited, suggest that these sites were occupied during the spring, or more precisely from April to June, when both adult and young seals were found in large numbers in the Strait of Belle Isle, in particular close to its northern shore.

The remarkable repetition in the occupational pattern of the larger sites seems to indicate that their occupants engaged in a seasonal round involving frequent changes of location—Binford's (1980) opposition between fine-grained and coarse-grained assemblages. From the Lower North Shore point of view, the Groswater settlement pattern seems to correspond to a foraging strategy, involving frequent changes of location over a wide area (Binford 1980, 1990). Comparisons with Groswater occupation in Newfoundland and Labrador may allow us to determine whether this only reflects a seasonal and/or a functional aspect of a particular settlement pattern which predominated in those two areas.

Conclusion

The annual round of the late Pre-Dorset (Groswater) Palaeoeskimo occasionally included the eastern Lower North Shore and the northern coast of the Strait of Belle Isle, or more precisely the Blanc-Sablon/Brador area, which contains the highest concentration of sites of this type in the region. The landscape is very open and provides a clear view not only of the Strait of Belle-Isle, but also of

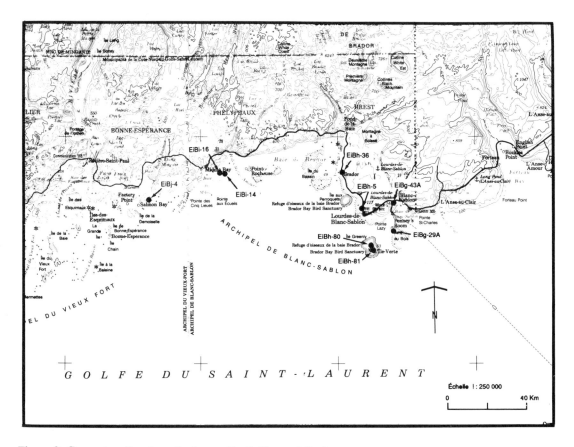

Figure 9 Groswater sites along the Lower North Shore of Quebec.

the Newfoundland coast, and the Gulf of St. Lawrence, from where the seals arrive in spring time.

It is interesting that Renouf (this volume) and Auger (1984, 1986) have found Groswater material on the west coast of Newfoundland which is similar to EiBg-43A. The sites in these two areas differ, however, especially with regard to their site structure and to their respective percentages of different categories of tools. Newfoundland sites have a higher proportion of tools associated with hunting, that is, triangular points and harpoon endblades. These differences should be studied more closely to determine whether they reflect seasonal occupation patterns or site functions.

Lower North Shore sites seem to exhibit more lithic artifact curation than Newfoundland sites where preforms and cores are more abundant (Renouf 1988). This might be due to the fact that Newfoundland sites were closer to geological deposits. In fact, the obvious preference of Groswater people for high quality Newfoundland chert must have affected their annual round and/or their contact with other groups as they sought to secure an abundant and constant supply of this raw material. The occupants of sites on the Lower North Shore used this chert more carefully; an indication of both their preference for the material and their distance from supply sources in Newfoundland.

Based on our research, the exploitation of coastal resources played an important role in the annual round of the Groswater complex. These Palaeoeskimos occupied this region for only a short time compared with Amerindian groups, who used the territory for several millenia (8000 years B.P. to contact period). However, it is becoming more evident that these two groups co-existed (Figure 8). Therefore, the hypothesis that the Strait of Belle Isle became a sort of no man's land, in the wake of power struggles between the Amerindians of the Archaic period and the late Pre-Dorset Palaeoeskimos, is no longer tenable. Amerindians definitely continued to use the Strait of Belle Isle despite the presence of Palaeoeskimos. Nevertheless, the eventual emergence of conflicts between these two cultural groups may still be one of the possible explanations for the scarcity of later Dorset sites in this region.

Ackowledgements

This project was funded by the Ministère des Affaires culturelles, Direction de la Côte-Nord, Baie-Comeau and by the Municipalité de Blanc-Sablon. Many individuals offered criticism of earlier drafts of this paper. I would like to express my thanks to Charles A. Martijn of the Ministère des Affaires culturelles, Québec, and to Denis Roy from the Ministère des Transports, Québec. The English translation is by Alison McGain, Ile d'Orléans.

References

Auger, R. 1984. Factory Cove: Recognition and Definition of the Early Palaeo-Eskimo period in Newfoundland. Unpublished Master's thesis, Department of Anthropology, Memorial University of Newfoundland.

Auger, R. 1986. Factory Cove: An Early Palaeo-Eskimo Component From the West Coast of Newfoundland. In, Palaeo-Eskimo Cultures in Newfoundland, Labrador and Ungava. Memorial University of Newfoundland, Reports in Archaeology, 1: 111-118.

Bigras, P. and J-M. M. Dubois, 1987. Répertoire commenté des datations ^{14}C du nord de l'estuaire et du golfe du Saint-Laurent, Québec et Labrador. Département de géographie, Université de Sherbrooke, bulletin de recherche nos. 94-95-96.

Binford, L R. 1980. Willow Smoke and Dogs' Tails: Hunter-Gatherer Settlement Systems and Archaeological Site formation. American Antiquity, 45(1): 4-20.

Binford, L R. 1990. Mobility, Housing, and Environment: A Comparative Study. Journal of Anthropological Research, 46(2): 119-152.

Bostock, H.H., L.M. Cumming, H. Williams and W.R. Smyth. 1983. Geology of the Strait of Belle-Isle area, Northwestern insular Newfoundland, Southern Labrador, and adjacent Quebec. Geological Survey of Canada, Memoir 400.

Cox, S.L. 1978 Palaeo-Eskimo Occupations of the North Labrador Coast. Arctic Anthropology, XV(2): 96-116.

Fitzhugh, W.W. 1976. Palaeo-Eskimo Occupations of the Labrador Coast. In, Eastern Arctic Prehistory: Paleoeskimo Problems, M. Maxwell ,ed. Memoirs of the Society for American Archaeology, 31:.103-118.

Fitzhugh, W.W. 1980. A Review of Paleo-Eskimo culture history. Études/Inuit/Studies, 4(1-2): 21-32.

Folinsbee, J.D. 1979. Distribution et abondance passées et présentes du caribou (Rangifer tarandus) au Labrador méridional et dans les régions adjacentes du Québec. Recherches amérindiennes au Québec, IX(1-2): 37-46.

Groison D, L. Litwionek, J.Y. Pintal and S. Perras, 1985. Recherche archéologique sur la Basse-Côte-Nord, Rivière St-Paul / Blanc-Sablon. MS on file with the Ministère des Affaires culturelles du Québec.

Harp, E., Jr. 1951. An Archaeological Reconnaissance in the Strait of Belle-Isle. American Antiquity, 16: 203-220.

Harp, E., Jr. 1964a. Evidence of Boreal archaic cultures in southern Labrador and Newfoundland. National Museum of Canada, Bulletin 193: 184-261.

Harp, E., Jr. 1964b. The Affinities of the Newfoundland Dorset Eskimo. National Museum of Canada, Bulletin 200.

Lamb, H.F. 1980. Late Quartenary Vegetational History of Southeastern Labrador. Arctic and Alpine Research, XVII(2): 117-135.

Larouche, A. 1988. Analyse des restes végétaux: Secteur Eibg-, Blanc-Sablon Québec. MS on file with la Municipalité de la Côte-Nord du golfe St-Laurent.

Lavoie, G. 1984. Contribution à la connaissance de la flore vasculaire et invasculaire de la Moyenne-et-Basse-Côte-Nord. Québec/Labrador. Provancheria, 17.

Lévesque, R. 1976. Cadre géographique des gisements archéologiques de la région de Blanc-Sablon. Master's thesis, Department of Geography, Université de Sherbrooke.

Marquis, R. 1988. Étude pétrographique d'une collection archéologique provenant de Blanc-Sablon, Québec. MS on file with la Municipalité de la Côte-Nord du golfe St-Laurent.

Martijn, C. 1974. Archaeological Research on the Lower Saint-Lawrence North-Shore, Quebec. In, Archaeological Salvage Projects 1972, W.J.Byrne, comp. National Museum of Man, Mercury Series, Archaeological Survey of Canada Paper 15:112-130.

McGhee, R. and J. Tuck. 1975. An Archaic Sequence in the Strait of Belle-Isle. National Museum of Man, Mercury Series, Archaeological Survey of Canada Paper 34.

Mills, S. 1980. Reconnaissance et fouille archéologique, région Brador-Lourdes de Blanc-Sablon, travaux en archéologie préhistorique. MS on file with the Ministère des Affaires culturelles du Québec.

Nagle, C.L. 1985. Lithic Raw Materials Resource Studies in Newfoundland and Labrador: A Progress Report. In, Archaeology in Newfoundland and Labrador, 1984, J.S. Thomson and C. Thomson, eds. Historic Resources Division, Department of Culture, Recreation and Youth, Government of Newfoundland and Labrador. Annual Report, 5: 86-121.

Pintal, J.Y 1987. Recherches en archéologie préhistorique sur la Basse-Côte-Nord: région de Blanc-Sablon et de St-Augustin. MS on file with the Ministère des Affaires culturelles du Québec.

Pintal, J.Y 1988. Recherches en archéologie préhistorique sur la Basse-Côte-Nord: région de Blanc-Sablon. MS on file with the Ministère des Affaires culturelles du Québec.

Pintal, J.Y 1989. La préhistoire de Blanc-Sablon: l'intervention de 1988. MS on file with the Ministère des Affaires culturelles du Québec.

Pintal, J.Y 1991. Blanc-Sablon: les travaux archéologiques de 1990. MS on file with the Ministère des Affaires culturelles du Québec.

Plumet, P. 1990. Mission archéologique préliminaire dans la région de Blanc-Sablon. Laboratoire d'archéologie, département des Sciences de la Terre, Université du Québec à Montréal. MS on file with the Ministère des Affaires culturelles du Québec.

Renouf, M.A.P. 1988. Phillip's Garden East: A Re-Examination of Groswater and Middle Dorset Palaeoeskimo Occupations in Western Newfoundland. MS on file with the author.

Tuck, J.A. 1984. La préhistoire de Terre-Neuve et du Labrador. Montréal: Fides.

Tuck, J.A. 1986. Excavations at Red Bay. In, Archaeology in Newfoundland and Labrador, 1985, J.S.

Thomson and C. Thomson, eds. Historic Resources Division, Department of Culture, Recreation and Youth, Government of Newfoundland and Labrador. Annual Report, 6: 150-158.

Two Transitional Sites at Port au Choix, Northwestern Newfoundland

M.A.P. Renouf
Memorial University of Newfoundland
St. John's, Newfoundland

Abstract

This paper presents data from two Groswater Palaeoeskimo sites at Port au Choix, northwestern Newfoundland. Site function and seasonality are discussed. A comparison is made between these Groswater sites and one Dorset site in the same area, and implications are drawn for the two time periods on the island of Newfoundland. Particularly striking is the fact that both the Groswater Phillip's Garden East site and the Dorset Phillip's Garden site are situated at the same spot for the same subsistence function, spring harp seal hunting, but are nevertheless very different kinds of sites.

Résumé

Cet article présente les données archéologiques de deux sites groswateriens de Port au Choix, à Terre Neuve. On y discute particulièrement de la fonction et de la saison d'occupation des sites. Ces sites groswateriens sont aussi comparés à un site dorsétien du même endroit, afin d'examiner la relation entre ces deux périodes culturelles à Terre-Neuve. Il est particulièrement frappant qu'en dépit d'une fonction similaire—la chasse printanière du phoque du Groenland—le site groswaterien Phillip's Garden East diffère de façon importante du site dorsétien Phillip's Garden.

Introduction

The purpose of this paper is to present data from two Groswater Palaeoeskimo sites on the island of Newfoundland. "Groswater" refers to the transitional Pre-Dorset to Dorset period in Newfoundland, Labrador, and Quebec which traditionally has been dated from 2800-2100 B.P., although there are a few new radiocarbon dates in the 2000-1900 B.P. range (Table 1). The transitional period is given different names according to geographical expression: "Independence II" in northern Greenland and elsewhere in the High Arctic, "late Saqqaq" and "Dorset I" in southern Greenland and, more simply, "transitional" on Ellesmere Island (Schledermann 1990) and Devon Island (Helmer 1991).

Groswater material was first identified on the island of Newfoundland in 1974 with the excavation of the Norris Point site (DjAl-2) in Bonne Bay, at the base of the Northern Peninsula (Bishop 1977). While the excavator called the site early Dorset, he recognized its affinity with the Groswater material that was described by Fitzhugh (1972) for Groswater Bay, central Labrador. In

Table 1 Radiocarbon dates from Phillip's Garden East and Phillip's Garden West.

Lab No.	Site and Parks Provenience	Descriptive Provenience	C14 Years B.P. Uncalibrated	C14 Years B.P. Calibrated*
Beta 23979	Phillip's Garden E. 7A383D377+371	Level 3, immediately northwest of house Feature 2	2760 ± 90	2997-2776
Beta 15375	Phillip's Garden E. 7A382B2	Level 2, Feature 1: in 1984 defined as a hearth but re-defined in 1986 as part of the large secondary deposit of fire-cracked rock that covered most of the excavated area. This level was above but contemporary with Level 3a below.	2660 ± 70	2845-2743
Beta 49759	Phillip's Garden W. 7A711A650	Feature 21, a dump within the hillside midden (Feature 5), in Level 2, possibly thrown up from the lower terrace	2540 ± 160	2837-2359
Beta 19086	Phillip's Garden E. 7A383D403	Level 3A, north of, or on, the wall of house Feature 2. Associated with Groswater end-blades	2510 ± 90	2746-2363
Beta 50021	Phillip's Garden E. 7A385A173	Feature 55, storage pit in Level 3, east of house Feature 12	2500 ± 60	2740-2384
Beta 49761	Phillip's Garden W. 7A711D177	Feature 18, a dumping episode within the hillside midden (Feature 5), in Level 3, thrown down from the upper terrace.	2460 ± 120	1739-2349
Beta 42971	Phillip's Garden E. 7A394A426	Level 2, immediately outside house Feature 12, associated with wide side-notched Groswater end-blades.	2420 ± 110	2719-2339
Beta 19089	Phillip's Garden E. 7A383D613	Level 3A, house Feature 2	2370 ± 160	2719-2163
Beta 42972	Phillip's Garden E. 7A394A727	Level 3, directly underneath wall of house Feature 12	2350 ± 100	2702-2314
Beta 49758	Phillip's Garden W. 7A701B386	Feature 16, a hearth in the centre of proposed tent structure (Feature 25), on upper terrace	2350 ± 80	2465-2335
Beta 50023	Phillip's Garden E. 7A393D384	House Feature 12, Level 3	2350 ± 90	2693-2331
Beta 49760	Phillip's Garden W. 7A711D166	Feature 18, a dump episode in the midden (Feature 5), in Level 3, probably thrown down from the upper terrace	2340 ± 100	2693-2212
Beta 19087	Phillip's Garden E. 7A383D539	Level 3A, immediately southwest of house Feature 2	2320 ± 100	2456-2182
Beta 42970	Phillip's Garden E. 7A384C41	Level 2, the central area of house Feature 12	2310 ± 90	2361-2207
Beta 50022	Phillip's Garden E. 7A385B-1193	Feature 53, storage pit west of house, Feature 12	2260 ± 70	2348-2159

Beta 42973	Phillip's Garden W. 7A702A79	Directly associated with hearth Feature 11 and a number of finely made, serrated end-blades and bifaces	2200 ± 110	2349-2061
Beta 49756	Phillip's Garden W. 7A701B236	Feature 23, "spiral" on upper terrace	2190 ± 100	2339-2061
Beta 49757	Phillip's Garden W. 7A701B302	Feature 14, poorly defined hearth on upper terrace	2090 ± 70	2291-1951
Beta 19088	Phillip's Garden E. 7A383D555	Level 3A, immediately northwest of house Feature 2, associated with two pieces of a thick rectangular soapstone vessel	1910 ± 150	2042-1634
Beta 19085	Phillip's Garden E. 7A382C66	Level 2, extension of Feature 1: in 1984 defined as a hearth but re-defined in 1986 as part of the large secondary deposit of fire-cracked rock that covered most of the excavated area. This level was above but contemporary with Level 3a below.	1930 ± 140	2039-1720
Beta 23980	Phillip's Garden E. 7A383D475	Level 3, floor of house Feature 2	1730 ± 200	1890-1410

*Intercept Method, 1 sigma (Stuiver and Becker 1986)
All dates are on charcoal and based on a half-life of 5568 radiocarbon years.

Table 2 Artifact frequencies, Phillip's Garden East and Phillip's Garden West.

LITHIC ARTIFACTS	Phillip's Garden East	PHILLIP'S GARDEN WEST
END-BLADES	300 (10.97%)	227 (11.16%)
BIFACES	506 (18.51%)	573 (28.16%)
BURIN-LIKE TOOLS	79 (2.89%)	47 (2.31%)
BURIN SPALLS	6 (0.22%)	7 (0.34%)
SIDE-BLADES	26 (0.95%)	63 (3.10%)
SCRAPERS	244 (8.92%)	140 (6.88%)
MICROBLADES	857 (31.35%)	126 (6.19%)
RETOUCHED + UTILIZED FLAKES	384 (14.05%)	461 (22.65%)
AXES	12 (0.44%)	2 (0.10)
GROUND SLATE	42 (1.54%)	6 (0.30)
SOAPSTONE	10 (0.37%)	
CORES	181 (6.62%)	342 (16.81%)
OTHER	87 (3.19%)	41 (2.02%)
TOTAL	2734 (100.12%)	2035 (100.02%)

All categories include both complete specimens and fragments.

1976 and 1978 Tuck (1978) recognized similar material from Bands 5 and 6 at Cow Head (DlBk-1), 50 kilometres north of Norris Point (Figure 1). This was followed in 1981 by Auger's excavations at

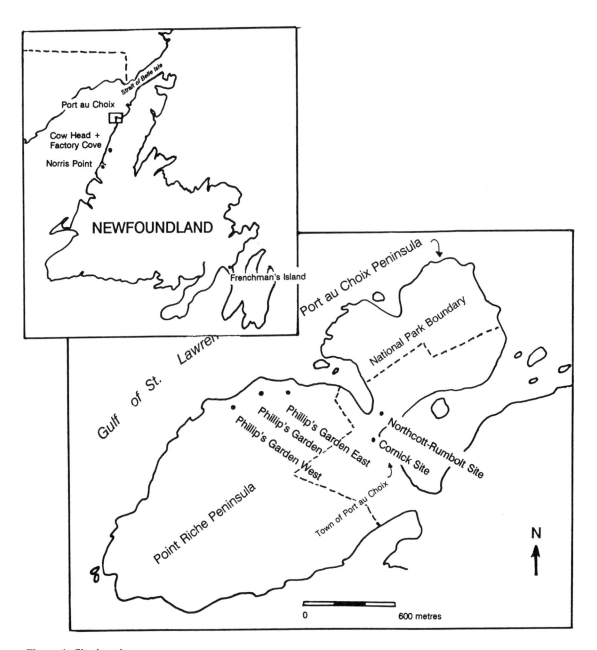

Figure 1 Site locations.

the Factory Cove site (DlBk-3), nearby on the Cow Head Peninsula (Auger 1982, 1984, 1986).

Factory Cove was the first large single component, multi-occupation, Groswater site where excavation went substantially beyond testing pitting and trenching. Perhaps the major contribution of this site, which was analyzed and described in detail (Auger 1984), is that it provided the basis for the first comprehensive description of Groswater material culture in Newfoundland. Subsequently, and not surprisingly, Groswater material has been recognized after the fact in most previously excavated Dorset Palaeoeskimo sites island-wide. Groswater components have been recognized on most recently excavated multi-occupation Palaeoeskimo sites in Newfoundland.

Four transitional period sites have been found on the Point Riche Peninsula (Figure 1). The Point Riche Peninsula juts out into the Gulf of St. Lawrence immediately south of the Strait of Belle Isle and, together with the Port au Choix Peninsula, forms a neck of land where the town of Port au Choix is located today. The Port au Choix Archaeology Project has been active in the area since 1984 and its main focus has been the excavation of a number of Groswater and Dorset Palaeoeskimo sites. Of the four Groswater sites found, two are in the town and have been badly disturbed by house construction. Fortunately the two others are located within the boundaries of the Port au Choix National Historic Park and therefore have been protected from expanding modern settlement. Both sites are found on raised terraces on either side of the two hectare Dorset Palaeoeskimo site of Phillip's Garden (EeBi-1), first reported and tested by Wintemberg (1939, 1940), later excavated by Harp (1964, 1976) and, most recently, excavated as part of the Port au Choix Archaeology Project, which is supported by the Canadian Parks Service (Renouf 1985, 1986, 1987, 1991, 1992). The two transitional period sites are Phillip's Garden East (EeBi-1) and Phillip's Garden West (EeBi-11), and the chronological order of the three neighbouring sites is Phillip's Garden East, Phillip's Garden West and Phillip's Garden. Phillip's Garden and Phillip's Garden East have the same Borden number because they are so close that they originally were considered to be the same site.

Phillip's Garden East

Phillip's Garden East is a fairly large site, at approximately 1500 m^2. This is similar in size to Factory Cove and larger than the Postville Pentecostal site in central Labrador, the only other large Groswater site excavated in the province (Loring and Cox 1986). Phillip's Garden East is contiguous to Phillip's Garden and both share the same terrace. However, they are separated by different vegetation, with Phillip's Garden East characterized by heath vegetation and Phillip's Garden a grassy meadow (Figure 2). Since Phillip's Garden is considerably larger than Phillip's Garden East, it encompasses the lower terrace as well. The terrace at Phillip's Garden East is approximately 12.5 m above the present high water mark.

The site lies under a thick blanket of peat that obscures any indication of the cultural remains below, and it was discovered in 1984 only as a result of systematic test pitting of the coastal perimeter of the Point Riche and Port au Choix Peninsulas (Renouf 1985). In 1984 a 4 m^2 test area was excavated which was expanded to 47 m^2 in 1986 (Renouf 1987; Kennett 1990). A second area was excavated in 1990 and 1991, increasing the total area excavated to 127 m^2 (Renouf 1991, 1992).

Like all the Port au Choix sites, Phillip's Garden East has excellent bone preservation. There are over 2700 lithic artifacts (Table 2), 74 bone, ivory or antler artifacts, somewhere in the region of 75 000 animal bones, and over 35 000 flakes. Two house structures and six pit features have been

Figure 2   Phillip's Garden East in the foreground, with the lower terrace of Phillip's Garden in the background.

recorded. At least one area of the site is stratified, indicating two distinct periods of occupation. Throughout the site, lithic and faunal material is very jumbled within one or both cultural levels, indicating repeated and overlapping use. The radiocarbon dates span 2760±90 B.P. to 1930±140 B.P., reflecting use over several centuries (Table 1).

House and pit features

The two house features found at Phillip's Garden East expand the known range of Groswater dwellings, which up until now has been restricted to versions of the mid-passage, or axial-hearthed structure. The two house features are different both from the mid-passage dwelling and from each other. Feature 2 was a small, circular, well-defined depression, the outline of which was traced by a 20-25 cm drop in elevation (Figure 3) and emphasized by a perimeter of built-up material which was interpreted as walls (Figure 4). A possible entrance-way was in the northeast where there was a break in this built-up material. The internal diameter of the structure was approximately three metres and it was virtually free of debris, in contrast to the abundance of fire-cracked rock, artifacts, charcoal and flakes in the walls and the cultural level outside the depression. The stratigraphy in this part of the site indicated that the house had been excavated through an already existing cultural deposit, which was then thrown to one side to form a layer of debris above, but contemporaneous with, the original undisturbed deposit. A cache of two harpoon heads and a pair of associated side-notched end-blades was found in one of the wall areas, and was dated to 2510±90 B.P. (Figure 6a-b; Figure 7c-d). A small bone-filled pit occurred in the western wall area and another larger and better defined pit occurred just outside the same wall. The dwelling structure's small size, along with the absence of any

Figure 3 One quadrant of house, Feature 12, at Phillip's Garden East, showing depression.

hearth feature or fire-cracked rock suggests warm-weather occupation; however, this contrasts with the fact that it was recessed into the ground which normally indicates cold-weather use. In view of the small size of Feature 2 and its clean interior space, a logical alternative interpretation cannot be ignored, i.e. that it was not a dwelling at all.

The second, larger house, Feature 12, was located seven metres to the south, and was filled with debris. It was on the surface of the ground rather than dug into it. Roughly circular (Figure 5), it was approximately five metres in diameter, and its outline was traced by a slight mound of debris which consisted mainly of fire-cracked rock, along with lesser amounts of flakes and bone. Although this raised area could have been a low wall, it was irregular rather than continuous and consisted of smaller rather than larger fire-cracked rock, which suggested that it was the result of sweeping. If the structure was a tent, and the tent was not rigidly anchored at all points, the debris could have been swept out underneath areas of the skin wall, resulting in the irregular outline of small, broken-up material. Alternatively, it could represent material unintentionally swept up against the inside of a firmly anchored tent wall which, when dismantled, left a ring of debris behind. Within the structure there was an area of large unburned rocks to one side, which was relatively free of fire-cracked rocks, flakes, artifacts and bone. This was probably a sitting or sleeping platform, the large rocks raising people off the damp ground and a covering of boughs or skins resulting in little or no debris falling below.

Within the house, there was one rock-capped pit containing seal cranial elements and some bird bone. Three more capped pits lay outside the house, each containing abundant seal bone along with lesser amounts of fish and bird. Presumably these were storage pits.

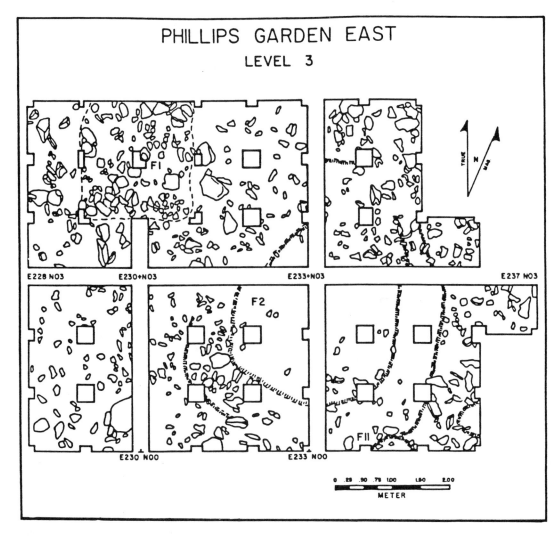

Figure 4 House, Feature 2, Phillip's Garden East, showing wall outline.

Artifacts

Currently, Groswater material culture is characterized by plano-convex side-notched end-blades, chipped and ground chert burin-like tools, a low proportion of true burins, a high proportion of microblades, circular and ovate side-blades, rare use of soapstone for lamps, finely made bifaces, the use of high quality cherts, and the presence of mid-passage structures (Tuck and Fitzhugh 1986). On the basis of his Factory Cove excavations, Auger subdivided the scrapers and burin-like tools into separate formal categories and hypothesized a seriation of end-blade forms (Auger 1984, 1986). Analysis of the artifacts from Phillip's Garden East is in process, and the 1984 and 1986 collection has already formed the basis of one master's thesis (Kennett 1990).

Harpoon heads

Eight nearly complete and five fragmentary harpoon heads were found. Most are self-pointed, two are distally slotted, and one has a side slot for an inset side-blade (Figure 6b). The two most consistent characteristics of the harpoon heads are an open-socketed base (where a base is present) and the fact that virtually no two harpoon heads are alike (Figure 6). On at least three specimens there is some form of transverse basal lashing groove. One of the most interesting specimens has a distal platform against which the characteristic Groswater box-based end-blade can be placed, lashed to the harpoon head through the end-blade's side-notches and the harpoon head's transverse dorsal hole, or "nose" (Figure 6f)—a shallow lashing groove slightly indents the lateral margins next to the "nose". The line hole is gouged from both sides, and two parallel lines are shallowly incised on the ventral surface and extend from the platform to the line hole.

Other organic artifacts

These include a haft with a side slot for a large and thin circular or oval side-blade, and a centrally placed line or lashing hole. Other organic tools are a large cut piece of bone or antler which is probably another handle, two

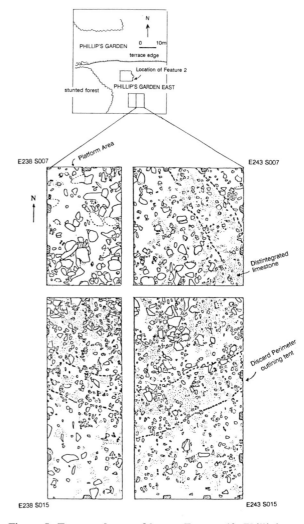

Figure 5 Two quadrants of house, Feature 12, Phillip's Garden East, showing outline of discard perimeter.

foreshafts, two needle fragments lacking the eye, two awls, five flaking punches, ten whole or incomplete expedient points (Figure 8f-g), and several pieces of cut bone.

Lithic raw material

Most of the Phillip's Garden East chert is from the Cow Head area, approximately 115 km to the south (Botsford pers. comm., cf. Botsford 1987). There is a wide range of colour variation in these cherts which can be found in beds, but which are more easily available as cobbles along the beach (Auger 1984). On some of the flakes and artifacts from Phillip's Garden East there are remnants of weathered cortex, confirming cobbles as a source. Despite the colour variation available, which

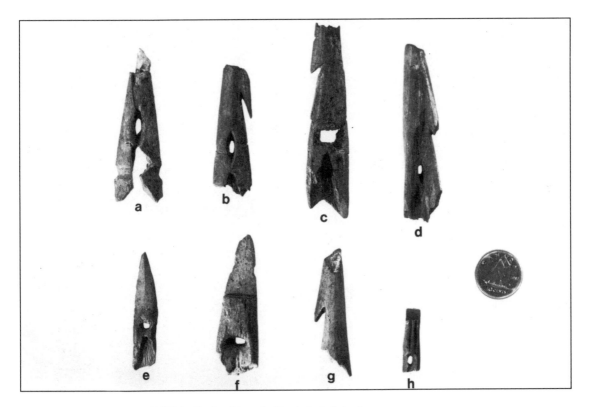

Figure 6 Harpoon heads, Phillip's Garden East: *b* **side-slotted,** *h* **toy harpoon.**

includes blues, greens, blacks, yellows, and reds, the brown-grey and grey-blue segments of the range predominate in the assemblage. In addition to the Cow Head chert, there is a small but regular occurrence of quartz crystal, which can be obtained locally, and a small proportion of Ramah chert, from northern Labrador.

Surface grinding

Many of the lithic artifacts display small or large areas of surface grinding, in particular end-blades, bifaces, side-blades and burin-like tools. Grinding might have functioned to smooth out any irregularities on the surface of the tool and it also might have been fore aesthetic purposes.

End-blades

The typical side-notched Groswater end-blade is characterised by a plano-convex cross-section and a distinctive unifacially bevelled straight base (Figure *7a-d*). These attributes make perfect sense when the end-blade is fitted to the "nosed" harpoon head described above. The plano-convex cross-section allows the blade to rest firmly against the ventral platform, the unifacially bevelled base virtually snaps in, and the end-blade is lashed by its side-notches through the transverse lash hole. Characteristically, the end-blade is made on a flake or a microblade, making it curve in slightly towards the harpoon head, which in turn gives the entire head an incurvate thrust.

Fitzhugh (1972) divided the Groswater end-blades into three length classes, which Auger (1984) followed for Factory Cove. Fitzhugh and Auger also distinguished between low and high side-notches, the latter called box-based. Kennett (1990) took a different approach to the Phillip's Garden East end-blades from the 1986 excavation area. Since she couldn't find any clustering of blade length or notch height, she categorized the end-blades on the basis of basal elements, finding that 28 out of 64 bases could fit the "nosed" harpoon head, described above. She found that a fit did not correlate with length.

In addition to the side-notched end-blades there are two categories of un-notched end-blades. One is roughly triangular with a concave base and a bi-convex cross-section, and a couple of examples are ventrally tip-fluted. The other is lanceolate and straight-based, and looks like a box-based end-blade prior to side-

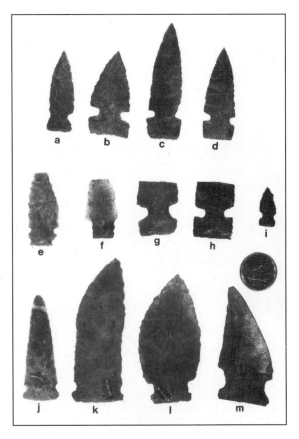

Figure 7 Phillip's Garden East; *a-i* end-blades and *j-m* bifaces.

notching. However, the finished edge retouch suggests that this is the final form.

On the basis of a dated cluster of un-notched end-blades at Factory Cove, Auger (1984; 1986) tentatively suggested a seriation of Groswater end-blades. At the oldest end of the proposed sequence are un-notched end-blades, along with end-blades which are slightly indented where notches would be. Both forms are elongated and have a bi-convex transverse cross-section. These are followed in the series by a less bi-convex, more plano-convex form with well-defined side-notches. The youngest form has a triangular blade and a well-defined plano-convex transverse cross-section.

The Phillip's Garden East end-blades do not reinforce this stylistic sequence since their range is more variable and the dates indicate contemporaneous rather than sequential variability. Some side-notches are very small, others are wide and deep (Figure 7*g-h*), and tiny flake end-blades are common (Figure 7*i*). Three of the most extremely variable forms are a stemmed end-blade (Figure 7*f*), a crudely double side-notched and almost-serrated example (Figure 7*e*), and a third specimen which has such broad side-notches that it is almost contracting-stemmed. The one attribute shared by all end-blades, regardless of variability, is a straight base. The second most common attribute is a plano-

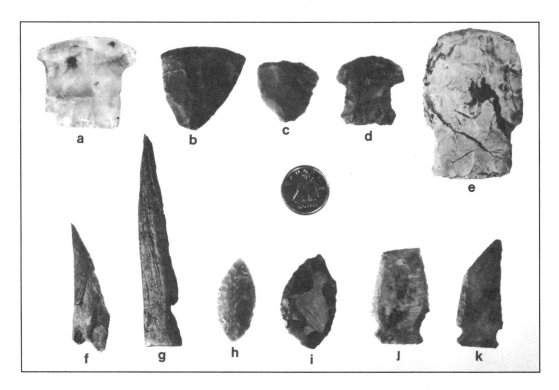

Figure 8 Phillip's Garden East: a-e scrapers; *f,g* expedient bone points; *h,i* side-blades; *j,k* burin-like tools.

convex transverse cross-section.

Bifaces

Variability in form is also common amongst the Phillip's Garden East bifaces, which are un-notched, side-notched, corner-notched and stemmed (Figure 7*j-m*). Many are thin, with fine surface flaking, and they are often made on colourful cherts. Most are asymmetrical, a result of either the shape of the flake on which a specimen was made, or the irregularity of re-sharpening, or a combination of both. The blades of two specimens are almost totally ground (Figure 7*m*). Of the 506 biface fragments and complete bifaces, 65 are preforms.

Burin-like tools

All the burin-like tools are of chipped and ground chert. Specimens are side-notched and the hafting element is always chipped. The amount of grinding on the blade varies from minimal to almost complete. The side-notches are always wide, and there is always at least one chipped lateral margin. Usually the lateral margin which would have rested against a haft was blunted by grinding. No true burins have yet been found at Phillip's Garden East, and only a single specimen was found with a

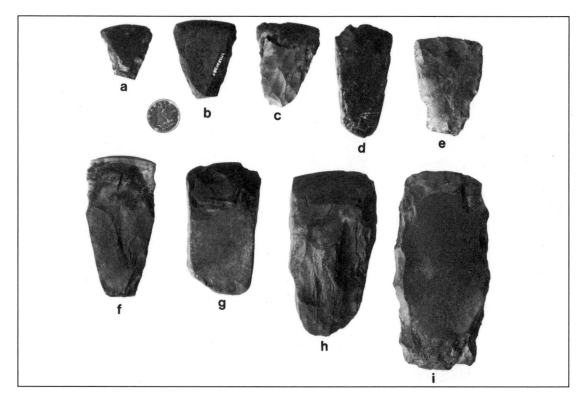

Figure 9 Phillip's Garden East: range of axes.

burin spall removed. Six burin spalls were found. Auger (1984) divided Groswater burin-like tools from Factory Cove into four categories based on blade shape: rectangular, triangular, angled-tip and windswept. Although the burin-like tools from Phillip's Garden East are also reducible to these categories, the rectangular form predominates (Figure 8*j*).

Side-blades

Side-blades are ovate, circular, and triangular (Figure 8*h-i*). Most are thin, surface flaking is not particularly fine, and some specimens have ground areas. Although most are small enough to have functioned as inset side-blades for harpoon heads, three are large enough for use as knife blades.

Scrapers

End scrapers are variable in shape (Figure 8*a-e*); some are on flakes, some are stemmed, some are rectangular, and some are triangular. Many of the stemmed and rectangular scrapers have pronounced distal "ears". There are two very large scrapers, 56 mm and 49.5 mm long, respectively. In addition to these end scrapers, there are two concave side scrapers, both of which appear to have

Figure 10 Phillip's Garden East, Feature 12, netsinkers.

been altered from their original function as burin-like tools.

Expedient stone tools

Microblades constitute approximately one third of the Phillip's Garden East lithic assemblage (Table 2). Most are of Cow Head chert, although there are a small number of quartz crystal and Ramah chert specimens. A fraction of all the microblades are clearly modified for hafting, usually with notches, but sometimes with a stem. A small proportion of the microblades show deliberate retouch. Retouched and utilized flakes together comprise 14% of the total lithic assemblage.

Axes

As with bifaces and harpoon heads, virtually no two axes are alike (Figure 9). Twelve specimens were found ranging in size from 29.96 mm to 110.72 mm in length. The extent of grinding varies from almost entire (Figure 9a-b) to grinding at the bit only (Figure 9f,i). Resharpening facets can be seen at the bit of a number of examples. One specimen is stemmed and does not have the ground bit, which is instead bifacially retouched (Figure 9e). Raw material varies; most seem to be banded rhyolite, silicified slate, basalt, and micaceous siltstone (Dean pers. comm.).

Soapstone

Fragments of three ovate and one rectangular soapstone vessel were found. One ovate specimen is made of fine soapstone, and is from a relatively small and thin bowl which in thinness (8.4 mm), rim shape, and quality of soapstone is very similar to the nearly complete sub-rectangular specimen from the Postville Pentecostal site (Loring and Cox 1986: 76). The other examples are coarser soapstone and are from thicker (13.72-14.32 mm), curved bowls. A fourth fragment is gabbro (Dean pers. comm.), and is also from a thick (20.12 mm), curved vessel. In addition, we have a corner from a fat-encrusted rectangular vessel which is identical to the large rectangular vessels from the adjacent Dorset site, Phillip's Garden. This is one of the few indicators of a more recent component at Phillip's Garden East.

Ground slate

Over three dozen fragments, one large segment, and one nearly complete ground slate specimen were found. A number of these show either unifacially or bifacially ground edges, and these have predominantly unidirectional surface striations. A single specimen has one bifacially bevelled lateral edge opposite a blunted edge, suggesting hafting.

Other

Two grooved stones were found. Both are round, fist-sized, and have distinct one centimetre wide grooves pecked on opposite ends, presumably for binding (Figure 10). This form suggests a netsinker and it might have been used in sealing.

Artifact summary

Phillip's Garden East has expanded what we know about the Groswater tool assemblage, especially with regard to harpoon heads. Harpoon head form is variable; most are open-socketed, and at least three have some kind of transverse basal lashing groove. The range of axes has been increased, the presence of ground slate has been established, as has the use of soapstone on the island of Newfoundland. However, the use of soapstone is limited, and there is no widespread deposit of burned fat as is found at later Dorset sites. Also absent is the use of whalebone for tool-making, common on Port au Choix Dorset sites and elsewhere.

Interpretation of Phillip's Garden East

The general jumble of lithics, organics and fire-cracked rocks at the site reflects repeated occupation, and the abundant faunal material suggests that this was on a regular seasonal basis. The bones are presently being identified by Darlene Balkwill of the Canadian Museum of Nature. She has identified the material from one area of the site, totalling 29 745 bones identifiable at least to class.

Kennett (1990) used this collection as part of her master's thesis. Greater than 90% of this assemblage is seal, most of it presumably, although not demonstrably, harp. This is no surprise since Port au Choix has always been known as a good sealing area, jutting out into the path of the winter and spring harp seal migrations. In the winter, large herds of harp seals migrate from Greenland southward to their breeding grounds off the southern Labrador coast (the Front herd), or further south to the Gulf of St. Lawrence (the Gulf herd). The Gulf herd passes by Port au Choix in December, and it is likely that some stayed in the Port au Choix area to breed (Mosdell 1923; Sergeant 1991). At this time the seals are in the water ahead of, but tied into, the southward movement of the ice. In early spring, the harp begin their return journey northward, travelling with the receding pack ice. In March and April, the females and juveniles (pups) are available on the ice off Port au Choix, with the adult males and immature animals nearby in the water. The small amount of fetal and large amount of juvenile seal found at Phillip's Garden East, if harp, reflects this spring period. Establishing December occupation is more problematic, although it is not unlikely. If the two netsinkers were used for weighting down seal nets, this would suggest open water, which in turn would suggest the possibility of a December hunt. Both netsinkers were associated with house Feature 12.

Table 3 Debitage frequencies, Phillip's Garden East and Phillip's Garden West.

FLAKES	PHILLIP'S GARDEN EAST	PHILLIP'S GARDEN WEST
PRIMARY	1458 (3.8%)	3979 (7.83%)
SECONDARY	7771 (20.23%)	8126 (15.99%)
TERTIARY	29 180 (75.98%)	38 727 (76.19%)
TOTAL	38 418 (100.01%)	50 832 (100.01%)

Primary = those flakes with some cortex remaining
Secondary = those flakes neither primary or tertiary
Tertiary = small retouch flakes

A function-specific occupation is also reflected in the lithic material (Table 2) which includes a high proportion of processing tools, such as microblades and scrapers which together comprise 40.27% of the lithic artifacts, and also a high proportion of hunting tools, i.e. end-blades, at 10.97%. In contrast, there is a low proportion of items related to tool manufacturing, such as cores, hammerstones, abraders, and preforms, which together comprise 9% of the total lithic artifacts. The same pattern is reflected in the debitage (Table 3), where primary flakes are 3.8% of the total flakes, as compared to secondary, 20.23%, and retouch, 75.98%.

Both faunal and artifactual lines of evidence support the interpretation of Phillip's Garden East as a seasonally re-occupied site, and the two different house structures suggests that seasonal re-occupation might have been variable.

Phillip's Garden West

Phillip's Garden West is located on, and covers most of, a 500 m² terrace a few hundred metres west of Phillip's Garden, at about 13 m above the current high water mark (Figure 11). The site was located by Fitzhugh in 1982 (Fitzhugh 1983) and was subsequently tested by the Port au Choix Archaeology Project in 1984 (Renouf 1985), with excavations in 1990-1992 (Renouf 1991, 1992). Although the original expectation was that Phillip's Garden West would be a Groswater site similar to Phillip's Garden East, it contained a number of surprises.

Figure 11 Upper terrace and hillside midden at Phillip's Garden West.

In stark contrast to Phillip's Garden East, the cultural level on the terrace was fairly bare. Artifacts were relatively sparse, there was little lithic debitage other than retouch flakes, and there was no charcoal stained mix of fire-cracked rock.

There was no organic material on top of the terrace, since faunal remains and other debris had been thrown over the edge, forming an overlapping set of midden deposits down the steep slope. Faunal material was abundant and identification is in the early stages. In contrast to Phillip's Garden East, there are some cetacean teeth, some wolf teeth, and a piece of walrus; there is also a much greater frequency of cut bone (Balkwill pers. comm).

In addition to hypothesized differences in function and seasonality between the two sites, there are notable differences in certain elements of the artifact assemblage. First and foremost, the end-blades and some of the other lithics from Phillip's Garden West are unique, as described below.

Dwelling Feature

One dwelling feature, a tent, was found at the edge of the terrace. It was defined by five post-holes and a centrally-placed hearth (Figure 12). The posts probably supported some kind of covering, such as skins, and the large rocks that outlined part of the structure probably held down the edges. The post-holes defined an area 3.48 m north-south and 2.95 m east-west and were evenly spaced from the hearth and from each other, except in one area where a sixth was missing. The absence of a sixth post-hole to close the area in the southwest suggested that this may have been the opening, although it would have faced away from the sea. Nevertheless, if the structure did face southwest, it would have been protected from the prevailing northwest winds. There was an external workshop to the southeast, as defined by a high concentration of micro-debitage, larger flakes, and artifacts, and there were two hearths to the north of the dwelling, which might have been associated with it.

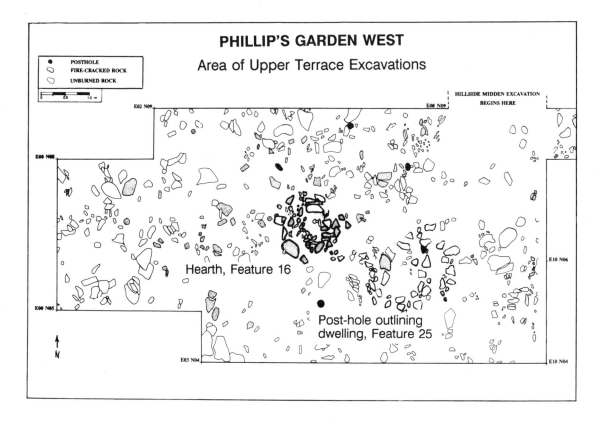

Figure 12 Post-holes outlining dwelling, Feature 25, Phillip's Garden West.

Artifacts

Lithic raw material

Like the Phillip's Garden East cherts, most of the Phillip's Garden West cherts fall within the brown-grey and grey-blue range of the Cow Head beds. However, there are also many end-blades, bifaces, side-blades, and microblades made on colourful cherts, all of which fall within the range of variation known for Cow Head (Dean pers. comm.). There are red, yellow, and dead black specimens, as well as brown-grey and grey-blue examples with various interesting mottling and banding effects. On one grey-blue end-blade there are two parallel bands of muted yellow running diagonally across the base, suggesting deliberate concern with colour and effect (Figure 13*a*). Ramah chert and quartz crystal is limited to a few microblades; there is no soapstone.

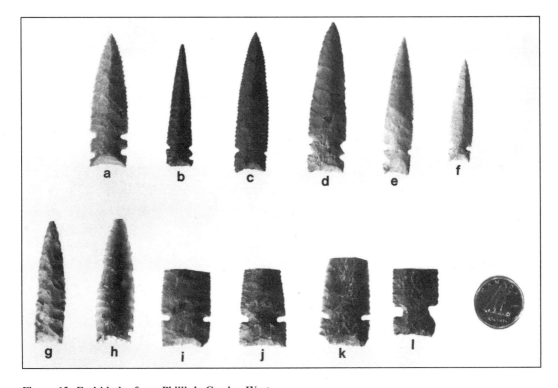

Figure 13 End-blades from Phillip's Garden West.

Grinding

As at Phillip's Garden East, grinding is a prevalent characteristic of several chert tool categories, in particular end-blades, bifaces, side-blades and burin-like tools. In some cases there is also polishing.

End-blades

A total of 227 complete or fragmented end-blades were recovered. All have a plano-convex transverse cross-section, and many are elongated and beautifully made, with extremely fine serrations. Grinding is present on most end-blades, and two specimens have a polished longitudinal facet on the ventral surface. Most of the end-blades have a single set of side-notches. However, some examples have a double set, or else two notches on one side and one on the other. Most side-notches are high and well-defined, similar to the Phillip's Garden East box-based end-blades. However, the notches are narrower and more deeply indented, and the unifacially bevelled base, recognizably Groswater, is concave rather than straight, almost with a tang at both basal edges. Both the basal concavity and the tanged basal edges prevent the Phillip's Garden West point from fitting the "nosed" harpoon head from Phillip's Garden East, described above.

There is a wide range of variation within these side-notched forms. Some much smaller in size (Figure 13*f*), others wider and thicker with slightly larger serrations (Figure 13*i-l*), and a very few cruder, examples that would be at home at Phillip's Garden East, were it not for the concave base and the serrations (Figure 13*l*). There are also several complete or fragmented un-notched unserrated lanceolate end-blades which look like preforms for side-notched end-blades (Figure 13*g-h*). Two impressionistic end-blade categories appear to have some spatial significance: 1) the exquisite Phillip's Garden West points (Figure 13*a-f*) and 2) a larger and less finely made version of it (Figure 13*i-k*). The ratios of these two categories was calculated for three areas of the site: the upper terrace, the upper hillside midden, and the lower hillside midden. The division of the midden into upper and lower is based on a rock ledge three quarters of the way down the slope, which seems to have been a physical separation between dumping episodes. These ratios are approximations, since the categorization of specimens was impressionistic and both categories represent ends of a range. Nevertheless an interesting pattern emerges. The greatest number of the fine examples occurred on the upper terrace, where the ratio between categories 1 and 2 is 1:76. In the upper part of the hillside midden the ratio falls to 1:53, and below the rock ledge the fine forms are even rarer, with the ratio falling to 1:16. These differences may be connected to curation of fine examples compared to the discarding of more everyday ones. Or the pattern may have some chronological significance. So far, seven overlapping dates suggest a span of site occupation from 2090 ± 70 B.P. to 2540 ± 160 B.P., with upper terrace at the recent end of the range and the lower hillside at the older (Table 4).

Table 4 Radiocarbon dates, Phillip's Garden West.

UPPER TERRACE	UPPER HILLSIDE	LOWER HILLSIDE
2090 ± 70 B.P.	2340 ± 100 B.P.	2540 ± 160 B.P.
2190 ± 100 B.P.	2460 ± 120 B.P.	
2200 ± 110 B.P.		
2350 ± 80 B.P.		

Side-blades

There are 63 whole or incomplete side-blades (Figure 14). Many of these are as finely made as the serrated side-notched end-blades, and they range in size from a mere 11.58 mm to 32.44 mm in length. Most are serrated, some have small areas of grinding, and virtually all are crescent shaped. There is a small number of larger ovate and triangular side-blades similar to those from Phillip's Garden East.

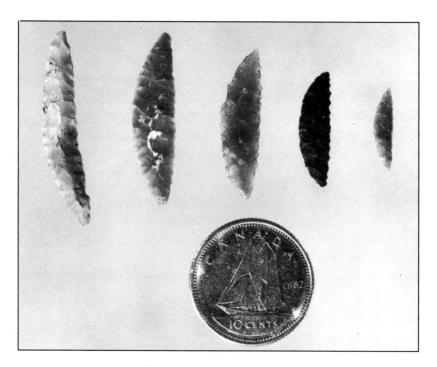

Figure 14 Side-blades from Phillip's Garden West.

Bifaces and unifaces

Most of the 573 biface fragments and complete bifaces overlap in form with those from Phillip's Garden East, being thin, finely flaked, side-notched and asymmetrical. Unlike Phillip's Garden East, there are a number of sickle-shaped unifaces (Figure 15b-c), many of which are made on colourful cherts. Of the biface fragments and complete bifaces, 128 are preforms.

Scrapers

Most of the 140 end-scrapers are triangular (Figure 15i-k), although there are a few flake scrapers and two "eared" examples. Distinct from Phillip's Garden East, there are 14 sickle-shaped

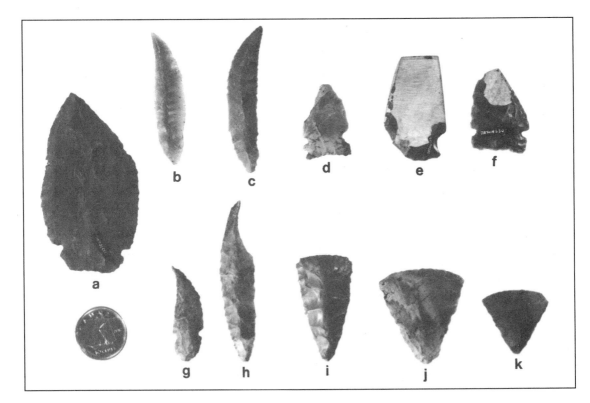

Figure 15 Phillip's Garden West: *a* biface; *b,c* unifaces; *d-f* burin-like tools; *g,h* concave side scrapers; *i-k* scrapers.

concave side scrapers (Figure 15*g-h*).

Burin-like tools

All 47 burin-like tools are similar to those from Phillip's Garden East, with side-notches and a chipped and ground blade. However, in contrast to Phillip's Garden East, the notches are narrower and there is a preponderance of the angle tipped (Figure 15*f*) blade over the rectangular form (Figure 15*e*). There is a small number of unground burin-like tools (Figure 15*d*) and seven burin spalls.

Expedient tools

Microblades constitute only 6.2% of the total lithic assemblage, which is far fewer than at Phillip's Garden East. They are made on the same range of Cow Head cherts as the end-blades, along with a small proportion of quartz crystal and Ramah chert. Although the range of widths overlaps with those at Phillip's Garden East, a greater proportion of the microblades from Phillip's Garden West are wider, especially those from the upper terrace. Together, retouched and utilized flakes are 28.86% of the lithic assemblage, a somewhat higher proportion of the lithics than at Phillip's Garden East.

Axes and gouges

There is a single fragment of a ground bit of an axe (Figure 16*b*), and a fragment of the same red stone, probably silicified slate. There is also a small silicified slate gouge (Figure 16*a*).

Figure 16 Phillip's Garden West: *a* gouge; *b* axe.

Ground slate

A single piece of tabular ground slate was found, along with five slate fragments.

Whetstone

A complete pink quartzite whetstone was found, along with a fragment from a similar specimen. Long and thin, it has three grinding facets and would have been used actively, as opposed to passively. A comparable example was found at Factory Cove (Auger 1984: 195).

Organics

No bone, antler or ivory artifacts have been found that are comparable in careful execution to the lithic artifacts. The only harpoon head found was a modified seal third phalanx (Balkwill pers. comm.). Other organics include four whalebone sled runner segments, a well made bone point, and a needle fragment. Twenty-four flakers were found in the lower midden area, and over 730 pieces of cut bone have come from the faunal remains so far identified. Many of these appear to be expedient points since they are cut to a strong point, and in cases the point is further modified to shape the piercing end. Most of the cut bone appears to be debitage, and the regularities in the patterns of points and V-shaped indentations indicate tool making rather than breakage in butchery. Since less than half the faunal bags are processed, the frequency of bone debitage will greatly increase.

Artifact summary

The Phillip's Garden West artifacts further expand the Groswater repertoire of material culture. Although attributes of end-blade technology such as side-notches, a unifacially bevelled base and a plano-convex transverse cross-section are clearly similar to Phillip's Garden East and other Groswater material, other aspects are unique. For instance, many of the artifact classes, in particular the end-blades and side-blades, are extremely finely made, with parallel surface flaking and tiny well-defined edge serrations. The elongated shape of the end-blades, the crescent shaped unifaces, the occasional surface polishing and the use of colourful, banded or mottled chert suggests a strong aesthetic component to tool-making. The organic component at the site is impoverished by comparison, limited mostly to unformalized, i.e. expedient, tools.

Interpretation of Phillip's Garden West

The location of Phillip's Garden West on a high, exposed, terrace commanding a splendid ocean view, the temporary nature of the dwelling structure, the low frequency of fire-cracked rock on the upper terrace and in the hillside midden, and the absence of soapstone for lamps suggest that it was a warm weather site. The relative sparseness of flakes and artifacts on the upper terrace indicates that the occupation was short term. The overlapping dump episodes in the midden and the wide range of radiocarbon dates demonstrate that the location was used on a number of occasions over a minimum of 220 radiocarbon years, and perhaps as many as 560 (Table 4). The absence of a winter house on the terrace, which was intensively tested and almost completely excavated, suggests that the various site occupations took place at roughly the same time of year. However, the occupations were clearly of a lesser intensity, and were perhaps less regular, than those of Phillip's Garden East.

Differences in function of the two sites are reflected in their tool frequencies (Table 2). At Phillip's Garden East the high frequency of end-blades, microblades, and scrapers, not to mention seal bones, demonstrates that it was a winter-spring site for procurement and processing of harp seal. In contrast, Phillip's Garden West yielded far fewer microblades and scrapers, indicating that there was not the same narrow focus on harvesting and processing. Our own use of a microblade to flense and dismember a young porpoise carcass at Port au Choix showed how extremely efficient microblades are for the task and on this basis I conclude that microblades rather than bifacial knives were the prime sea mammal butchering tool. Nevertheless, hunting did go on at Phillip's Garden West, as indicated by a high proportion of both end-blades and tiny inset side-blades, the latter perhaps indicating a particular hunting technology. If so, it was a different technology than that used at Phillip's Garden East, where side-blades are relatively few. A final difference between the sites is seen in tool manufacturing activities. Whereas at Phillip's Garden East the narrowly focussed range of activities virtually excluded tool manufacture, at Phillip's Garden West cores, preforms and abraders are significantly better represented. However, contrary to this, primary lithic debitage is poorly represented at the site (Table 3).

The cultural-historical position of Phillip's Garden West is more problematic. While certain artifact forms and attributes are comparable to material from Phillip's Garden East, Factory Cove, and other Groswater sites, the serrated end-blades, the tiny serrated side-blades, the crescent shaped unifaces and side scrapers, and the use of colourful cherts resemble Pre-Dorset, suggesting that Phillip's Garden West might belong to an early phase of Groswater. However, the series of seven charcoal-based radiocarbon dates place it between 2540 ± 160 B.P. and 2090 ± 70 B.P. (Table 1), putting the site at the end of the Groswater period.

In addition, this material is limited to a small number of contexts. Harp (1964: 45,47) found some of this material from two houses at Phillip's Garden and noted that they were "exquisitely-made" (Harp 1964: 46). His dates from one of those two houses fit within the Dorset period, at 1580 ± 54 B.P. and 1641 ± 56 B.P. (Harp 1976), which, unless the artifacts were curated, calls into question the contemporaneity of the houses and the "Phillip's Garden West" artifacts. Harp also found tiny side-blades and crescent-shaped unifaces similar to Phillip's Garden West forms at his Port au Choix-5 site (EeB1-5). Also called the Northcott-Rumbolt site (Renouf 1985), this is one of the two heavily disturbed Groswater sites in the town of Port au Choix (Figure 1).

Outside Port au Choix, "Phillip's Garden West" material is so far known only from two multi-component sites. At the Cow Head site (Tuck 1978) some specimens from Bands 5 and 6, and Upper Terrace Feature 40, are similar, although not identical, to material from Phillip's Garden West. At the Frenchman's Island site (ClAl-1) in Trinity Bay, Evans (1982: 225) found a thin, curved serrated knife and a small crescent-shaped side-blade, both of which would be at home at the upper terrace of Phillip's Garden West. More isolated occurrences of "Phillip's Garden West" artifacts might be found by a look through extant Dorset collections from the province. But for the present, this material is limited to the island of Newfoundland, and within the island it is virtually restricted to Port au Choix.

The Groswater Occupation of Newfoundland

Phillip's Garden East and West are important sites for the definition of Groswater material culture in Newfoundland, and are an important comparative case for Labrador. Both Phillip's Garden East and West broaden the range of known Groswater material culture, especially the organic component and dwelling structures. These, and other Groswater sites at Port au Choix, along with the

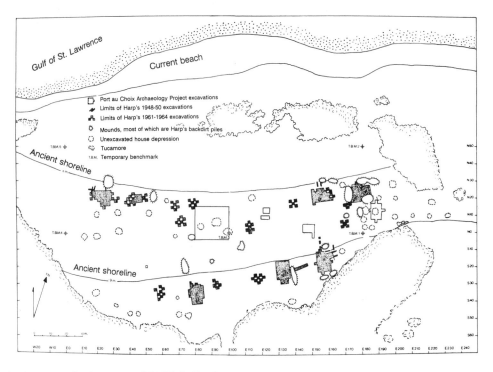

Figure 17 Surface map of Phillip's Garden.

occurrence of Groswater components in most Palaeoeskimo sites on the island, demonstrate the substantial nature of the initial Palaeoeskimo population expansion southward from Labrador into and throughout the island. Groswater's widespread distribution and the size of at least the west coast sites, reflects a successful occupation of what at the time was the southernmost frontier of Palaeoeskimo occupation.

Groswater settlement and subsistence is highlighted by a comparison with the Dorset pattern, and the comparison is best made between Phillip's Garden East and Phillip's Garden at Port au Choix. Both sites were located at the same spot for the same reason, namely the exploitation of the migrating harp seal herds, yet this activity was carried out in very different ways, as reflected in their respective site size and layout. As argued above, Phillip's Garden East was a narrowly focussed, recurrently occupied seasonal site. In contrast, on the basis of size alone, the two hectare Phillip's Garden (Figure 17) was a location of more complex occupation. The entirety of the upper two terraces, and parts of an upper third, overgrown by stunted spruce, is covered in cultural material, most notably a minimum of fifty house depressions and large areas of midden which probably filled-in additional depressions. The cultural material is more spread out than the occupational debris at Phillip's Garden East and there is no overlapping mix. At Phillip's Garden there is greater seasonal and functional variability, with a wide range of house structures and midden deposits. Although the collection from one midden indicates occupation in winter and spring, a smaller collection from one of the houses suggests fall/winter (Murray 1992), and a small collection from a test unit in another midden is clearly the result of a spring seal hunt. Although no summer faunal assemblage has yet been found, there is one definite warm weather structure, an external axial hearth.

It is difficult to generalize from this comparison to Groswater and Dorset settlement patterns island-wide since large excavations have been undertaken at only three Groswater sites, all of which are on the west coast. However, a few comments can be made. Although Auger (1984, 1986) interpreted Factory Cove as a year round residential base, my interpretation of the faunal and artifactual material is that it, like Phillip's Garden East and West, is a seasonally specialized site. All contrast with later Dorset sites which are generally larger (Pastore 1986). Although both the Newfoundland Groswater and Dorset were seasonally mobile throughout the year, the Port au Choix sites suggest that there was an important difference between the two patterns of annual mobility. Whereas both the Groswater and Dorset groups moved from site to site, only the Dorset had the addition of a large permanent central site, which in a sense acted as a pivot to the otherwise mobile annual round.

Not only was the Groswater annual round mobile, but it probably covered a wide geographical area. Tuck and Pastore (1985) point out that the island of Newfoundland's terrestrial resources are few and unreliable. Although marine resources are generally abundant, they too can be unpredictable in the face of changing short term ice conditions. Studies of modern hunter-gatherers demonstrate that in the face of unreliable resources, they employ a wide array of mechanisms to offset the risk. Although there may be alternative subsistence activities for each season, or periodic surpluses might be harvested and processed for storage, the most important mechanism for reducing risk is sharing. This can be expressed in many ways. Territorial boundaries may be permeable and flexibly defined. There may be long distance information exchange so that the behaviour of a migratory resource is monitored in one segment of its route and the information transmitted to groups situated elsewhere along its course of migration. There may be active maintenance of wide-spread social networks, including consanguineal and affinal relatives, and those non-kin who are brought into the network of relationships by formalized means such as, for example, partnerships. These connections entail reciprocal obligations, whereby either ends can be called on to provide hospitality and access to resources. Thus, in the face of the island of Newfoundland's relatively unreliable animal resource base it is likely that hunter-gatherer groups would have maintained connections with the mainland. Some of these could have been direct, such as exploiting areas of the Quebec North Shore and the Labrador side of the Strait of Belle Isle as part of an annual round. In this regard, it is interesting that Pintal (this volume) has found Groswater material on the Quebec North Shore which is strikingly similar to that from Phillip's Garden East. It is also interesting that the pattern of hearth features that Pintal describes for the EeBg-43A site in Blanc Sablon is unlike anything from Newfoundland Groswater, as if the regions were functionally separate. As for more indirect connections, it is likely that Quebec North Shore and west coast Newfoundland Groswater would have maintained sharing and information networks with groups farther to the north.

Were these wide-ranging Groswater populations eventually replaced by Dorset, a distantly related people with a different emphasis on sea mammals and a different kind of mobility, who moved southward from northern Labrador (Fitzhugh 1980; Tuck and Pastore 1985; Tuck and Fitzhugh 1986)? Or, alternatively, were Groswater groups part of a widespread economic shift towards increasing marine specialization that is seen in the archaeological record of Newfoundland at around 1900 B.P., and Labrador at about 2200 B.P., that we call Dorset? Although I think that it is unlikely that Groswater hunter-gatherers would have been so maladapted as to die out, there are presently insufficient data to argue a convincing case either way. Phillip's Garden West could be a crucial piece in the puzzle, since it is chronologically sandwiched between Groswater and Dorset and therefore could represent either continuity between them, or Groswater's last gasp. However, the essential problem with interpreting the significance of this site is that its lithic assemblage is unique and therefore it is not possible to know if it is representative of an individual, a function, a season, a time period or a region. At this point, Phillip's Garden West raises more cultural-historical questions than it answers. However, together the Groswater sites from Port au Choix provide information on settlement and subsistence which, aside from their intrinsic importance, provide important contexts for understanding these and other cultural-historical connections.

Acknowledgements

This project has been funded in large part by the Canadian Parks Service. It has also been funded generously by the Social Sciences and Humanities Research Council of Canada, the Historic Resources Division of the Government of Newfoundland and Labrador, Memorial University of Newfoundland, in particular the Institute of Social and Economic Research, the Office of the Dean of Arts, and the Office of Research, and both Federal and Provincial Governments' student employment programs. I am indebted to Michael Meadows, crew chief of the 1991 excavations of Phillip's Garden East, for the interpretation of the discard perimeter outlining the house feature, Feature 12. Thanks to Trish Dunphy, Deea Linehan and Patty Barefoot who in 1992 butchered a porpoise carcass using a Dorset microblade. I would also like to thank Paul Dean, Department of Mines, Energy and Resources, Government of Newfoundland and Labrador, for identifying the lithic material.

References

Auger, R. 1982. A preliminary report on Early Dorset occupations on the west coast of Newfoundland. In, Archaeology in Newfoundland and Labrador, 1981, J. Sproull Thomson and C. Thomson, eds. Historic Resources Division, Department of Culture, Recreation and Youth, Government of Newfoundland and Labrador. Annual Report, 2: 130-151.

Auger, R. 1984. Factory Cove: Recognition and Definition of the Early Palaeo-Eskimo period in Newfoundland. Unpublished Master's thesis, Department of Anthropology, Memorial University of Newfoundland.

Auger, R. 1986. Factory Cove: An Early Palaeo-Eskimo Component From the West Coast of Newfoundland. In, Palaeo-Eskimo Cultures in Newfoundland, Labrador and Ungava. Memorial

University of Newfoundland, Reports in Archaeology, 1: 111-118.

Bishop, P. 1977. Final Report: 1973 Excavations at Norris Point, Gros Morne National Park. MS on file with the Archaeology Division, Canadian Park Service, Halifax.

Botsford, J.W. 1987. Depositional History of Middle Cambrian to Lower Ordovician Deep Water Sediments, Bay of Islands, Western Newfoundland. Unpublished PhD thesis, Department of Earth Sciences, Memorial University of Newfoundland.

Evans, C.O. 1982. Frenchman's Island Site (ClAl-l) preliminary field report. In, Archaeology in Newfoundland and Labrador, 1981, J. Sproull Thomson and C. Thomson, eds. Historic Resources Division, Department of Culture, Recreation and Youth, Government of Newfoundland and Labrador. Annual Report, 2: 210-225.

Fitzhugh, W.W. 1972. Environmental Archaeology and Cultural Systems in Hamilton Inlet, Labrador. Smithsonian Contributions to Anthropology, 16.

Fitzhugh, W.W. 1980. Preliminary report on the Torngat Archaeological Project. Arctic, 33(3): 585-606.

Fitzhugh, W.W. 1983. Archaeological surveys in the Straits of Belle Isle. In, Archaeology in Newfoundland and Labrador, 1982, J. Sproull Thomson and C. Thomson, eds. Historic Resources Division, Department of Culture, Recreation and Youth, Government of Newfoundland and Labrador. Annual Report, 3: 118-132.

Harp, E., Jr. 1964. The Cultural Affinities of the Newfoundland Dorset Eskimo. National Museum of Canada Bulletin 200.

Harp, E., Jr. 1976. Dorset settlement patterns in Newfoundland and southeastern Hudson Bay. In, Eastern Arctic Prehistory: Palaeoeskimo Problems, M.S. Maxwell, ed. Memoir for the Society for American Archaeology, 31: 119-138.

Helmer, J. W. 1991. The palaeo-eskimo prehistory of the North Devon Lowlands. Arctic, 44(4): 313-317.

Kennett, B.L. 1990. Phillip's Garden East: A New Perspective on Groswater Palaeoeskimo. Unpublished M.A. thesis, Department of Anthropology, Memorial University of Newfoundland.

Loring, S. and S. Cox. 1986. The Postville Pentecostal Groswater Site, Kaipokok Bay, Labrador. In, Palaeo-Eskimo Cultures in Newfoundland, Labrador and Ungava. Memorial University of Newfoundland. Reports in Archaeology, 1: 65-94.

Mosdell, H.M., ed. 1923. Chafes Sealing Book. St. John's: The Trade Printers and Publishers, Ltd.

Murray, M.S. 1992. Seasonal and Spatial Analysis of Faunal Material from House Feature 1, Phillip's Garden, Port au Choix, Northwestern Newfoundland. Unpublished Masters thesis, Department of Anthropology, Memorial University of Newfoundland.

Pastore, R. T. 1986. The spatial distribution of late palaeo-eskimo sites on the island of Newfoundland. In, Palaeo-Eskimo Cultures in Newfoundland, Labrador and Ungava. Memorial University of Newfoundland. Reports in Archaeology, 1: 125-134.

Renouf, M.A.P. 1985. Archaeology of the Port au Choix National Historic Park: Report of 1984 Field Activities. MS on file with Archaeology Division, Canadian Parks Service, Halifax.

Renouf, M.A.P. 1986. Report of 1985 Excavations at the Point Riche and Phillip's Garden sites, Port au Choix National Historic Park. MS on file with Archaeology Division, Parks Canada, Halifax.

Renouf, M.A.P. 1987. Archaeological Investigations at the Port au Choix National Historic Park: Report of 1986 Field Activities. MS on file with Archaeology Division, Canadian Parks Service, Halifax.

Renouf, M.A.P. 1991. Archaeological Investigations at the Port au Choix National Historic Park: Report of the 1990 Field Activities. MS on file with Archaeology Division, Canadian Parks Service, Halifax.

Renouf, M.A.P. 1992. The 1992 Field Season at the Port au Choix National Historic Park. MS on file with Archaeology Division, Canadian Parks Service, Halifax.

Sergeant, D.D. 1991. Harp Seals, Man and Ice. Department of Fisheries and Oceans. Canadian Special Publications of Fisheries and Aquatic Sciences, 114.

Schledermann, P. 1990. Crossroads to Greenland. The Arctic Institute of North America, Komatic Series, 2.

Stuiver, M. and B. Becker. 1986. High precision decadel calibration of the radiocarbon time scale, AD 1950-2500 BC. Radiocarbon, 28(2B): 869-910.

Tuck, J.A. 1978. Excavations at Cow Head, Newfoundland: an interim report. Études/Inuit/Studies, 2(1): 138-141.

Tuck, J.A. and W.W. Fitzhugh. 1986. Palaeo-eskimo traditions in Newfoundland and Labrador: A Re-Appraisal. In, Palaeo-Eskimo Cultures of Newfoundland, Labrador and Ungava. Memorial

University of Newfoundland. Reports in Archaeology, 1: 161-168.

Tuck, J.A. and R.T. Pastore. 1985. A Nice Place to Visit...But: Prehistoric Extinctions on the Island of Newfoundland. Canadian Journal of Archaeology, 9(1): 69-80.

Wintemberg, W. 1939. Eskimo Sites of the Dorset Culture in Newfoundland, Part ll. American Antiquity, 5(3): 83-102.

Wintemberg, W. 1940. Eskimo Sites of the Dorset Culture in Newfoundland. American Antiquity, 5(4): 309-333.

Qeqertasussuk - the Archaeology of a Frozen Saqqaq Site in Disko Bugt, West Greenland

Bjarne Grønnow
Institute of Archaeology and Ethnology
Copenhagen

Abstract

Between 1984 and 1990, interdisciplinary investigations were carried out by the Qasigiannguit Museum at an early Arctic Small Tool tradition site (Saqqaq Culture) on the island of Qeqertasussuk, Disko Bugt, West Greenland. Spanning the period from 3900 to 3100 BP, the permanently frozen cultural deposits have yielded unique organic finds, such as wooden artifacts. These layers have also provided a wealth of contextual information which has shed light on the early ASTt, as well as the palaeo-environment in West Greenland during this time period. Additionally, human bones–the earliest known in the Arctic–have been found. In this article, some results of the Qeqertasussuk Project are presented (Saqqaq technology, subsistence and chronology), and the paper concludes with remarks on the much debated "disappearence" of the Saqqaq Culture in the first millennium BC.

Résumé

Entre 1984 et 1990, des recherches multidisciplinaires furent effectuées par le Musée Qasigiannguit sur un site ancien de la Tradition microlithique de l'Arctique (culture Saqqaq), de l'île Qeqertasussuk à Disko Bugt, au Groenland occidental. S'étalant sur une période de 3 900 à 3 100 BP, les dépôts culturels contenus dans le pergélisol, ont fourni des restes organiques uniques, tels que des artefacts en bois. Ces couches culturelles ont aussi révélé une abondance d'informations contextuelles jettant ainsi un nouvel éclairage sur la période ancienne de la Tradition microlithique de l'Arctique. Elles founissent également des données sur le paléoenvironnement du Groenland occidental durant cette période. Des os humains, qui sont les plus anciens connus dans l'Arctique, s'ajoutent à ces découvertes. Cet article présente certains des résultats du projet Qeqertasussuk (technologie, mode de subsistance et chronologie de la culture Saqqaq), et conclut avec des remarques concernant la polémique de la "disparition" de la culture Saqqaq durant le premier millénaire avant notre ère.

Introduction

During the past ten years, the main focus of archaeological research in Greenland has been the earliest part of the prehistory of this easternmost portion of the New World Arctic. This was due to the rapidly growing interest among Greenlanders of their deep cultural roots–it is no coincidence that practically all municipalities now have established their own local museum–and a renewed interest in

Threads of Arctic Prehistory: Papers in Honour of William E. Taylor Jr., David Morrison and Jean-Luc Pilon, eds. Canadian Museum of Civilization, Mercury Series, Archaeological Survey of Canada Paper 149. 1994.

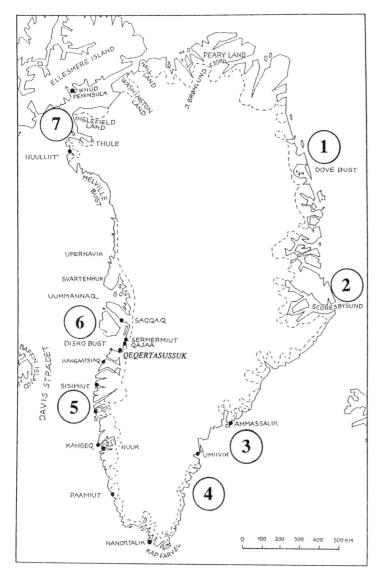

the Palaeoeskimo period among the younger generation of Danish/Greenlandic archaeologists. Several surveys and excavations focussing on Palaeoeskimo sites were conducted during this "wave", or are still in progress (Figure 1). Much emphasis has been placed on the presentation of results through publications and exhibits in Greenland and Denmark. Thus, only limited information about this recent archaeological research effort in Greenland has reached the international literature. The present paper on one of the major projects concerning the earliest Arctic Small Tool tradition in West Greenland, the Saqqaq Culture, will hopefully bridge this information gap.

The Qeqertasussuk Project

Two discoveries in Disko Bugt initiated the present "Palaeoeskimo wave": the Qajaa site and the Qeqertasussuk site. Both sites contained massive frozen cultural deposits relating to the Saqqaq Culture, i.e. within the period from 2400 to 9-800 BC (calibrated). To date, they are the only

Figure 1 Main areas of current Palaeoeskimo research in Greenland: 1-NE Greenland (Andreasen and Elling 1991), 2-Scoresby Sound (Sandell and Sandell n.d.), 3-Ammassalik (Møbjerg 1986, 1988), 4-Skjoldungen (Gulløv et al. 1990), 5-Sisimiut/Kangerlussuaq (Kramer and Jones 1992; Kapel n.d.), 6-Disko Bugt (Grønnow and Meldgaard 1991; Hansen and Jensen 1991; J. Meldgaard 1991; Petersen n.d.), 7-Thule (Madsen and Diklev 1992).

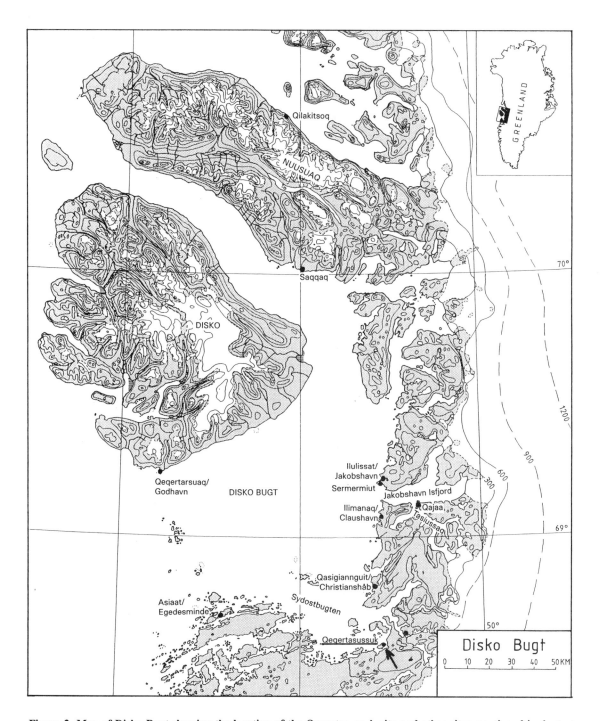

Figure 2 Map of Disko Bugt showing the location of the Qeqertasussuk site and other sites mentioned in the text.

known Saqqaq sites with such excellent organic preservation conditions.

The Qajaa site, re-discovered by Jørgen Meldgaard, was surveyed and investigated in 1982 (J. Meldgaard 1983; Møhl 1986). This was in fact about 100 years after the first archaeological investigations at this historically known site in central Jakobshavn Isfjord. Meldgaard's work showed a 1-2 metre deep Saqqaq sequence spanning the time period from ca. 3600 BP to 2700 BP, an overlying Dorset layer dated to between ca. 2200 BP to 1600 BP, covered by heavy Thule culture and historic Inuit middens and winter houses (J. Meldgaard 1991: 108-109). The excavation of a small portion of the frozen cultural layers yielded excellently preserved wooden and bone artifacts. A new picture of the Palaeoeskimo pioneers of West Greenland began to emerge.

In 1983, attention turned 100 km to the south when two archaeologists, Aappaa Magnussen and the present author, sent out by the Qasigiannguit/Christianshåb Museum, found another frozen Saqqaq site, Qeqertasussuk, in Sydostbugten, which is the southernmost part of Disko Bugt. Here, preservation conditions were as fine as those at Qajaa. The site was easily accessible, being on a small island, only 35 km, as the crow flies, from the town of Qasigiannguit. Furthermore, excavation was facilitated by the fact that the Saq-qaq layers were not disturbed or covered by younger occupations. Being aware of the potentials of the Qeqertasussuk site, the then curator of the local museum, Torben Simonsen, entered into collaboration with the National Museum of Greenland and the University of Copenhagen, and consequently the Qeqertasussuk Project was initiated in 1984. Directed by the present author and quarternary zoologist, Morten Meldgaard, a Greenlandic/Danish interdisciplinary team investigated the site between 1984 and 1990. Other members of the research team were Jens Böcher (palaeo-entomology), Bent Fredskild (palaeo-botany), Charlie Christensen (quarternary geology), Bruno Frølich, Niels Lynnerup and J.P. Hart Hansen (biological anthropology), Anne Marie Rørdam and Eileen Jensen (pharmacology), Gerda Møller, Flora Heilmann and Jeppe Møhl (skin analyses, conservation

Figure 3 Excavations at the Qeqertasussuk site; the mainland in visible across the strait.

technique), Nancy Eskildsen (wood identification), and Pieter van de Griend (knots).

Given the quite unique character of the site, the aim of the Qeqertasussuk Project was to intensively study a single site; to shed light upon as many aspects of the site and it's palaeo-environment as possible. The perspective of such a detailed case study was that it could provide a firm comparative background against which to evaluate and interprete the material from Saqqaq sites where only stone tools are preserved.

In particular, the finds from Qeqertasussuk have yielded new information on Saqqaq technology, subsistence and palaeo-climate. As the settlement at Qeqertasussuk spanned the period from about 3900 BP to 3100 BP, or about two thirds of the Saqqaq period in West Greenland (3900 BP - 2700 BP), we have been able to study changes through time within these research topics. At present, analyses have been completed. A series of English language publications beginning with the palaeo-environmental investigations (pollen and macrofossil analyses, and entomology) by Fredskild and Böcher will soon appear in "Meddelelser om Grønland".

The present paper proposes to introduce the reader to the case study, Qeqertasussuk. Selected results of the archaeological investigations will be presented, and emphasis will be placed upon the technological, economic and chronological aspects of the Saqqaq Culture at the site.

Finally some considerations on the disappearence of the Saqqaq Culture based on the latest archaeological information from Greenland will be reviewed.

The Environment, the Site and the Excavations

Environment and Site Location

The Qeqertasussuk site is situated on a small island in the archipelago of Sydostbugten (Figures 2 and 3). Present-day Sydostbugten is a rich environment in spring and summer when large whales and migrating harp seals follow schools of *ammassat* (capelin), and are channeled through the strait separating Qeqertasussuk Island from the mainland. Bird cliffs housing alcids, cormorants and gulls are found on the mainland coast right across the strait, and terns hatch on every island in the archipelago. The small rivers flowing into Sydostbugten attract spawning char. The mainland still houses a small population of caribou. Winter resources are more scarce, consisting mainly of ringed seal, but fish such as cod and halibut are also present.

Traces of Saqqaq activities at Qeqertasussuk are found all over a series of raised beaches forming a promontory, crowned by a cliff at the easternmost part of the island. The site commands a perfect view over the strait towards the mainland and the archipelago to the North. This is a typical situation for a West Greenland Saqqaq site. During excavations, particularly in early July, we often watched hundreds of *ammissut* (harp seals) and large whales (minke and fin whales) pass the promontory at close range.

Excavations

Based on the results of test excavations, three areas were chosen for more intensive investigations (Figure 4). Area A was laid out around one of the exposed fireplaces and mid-passages on the highest part of the raised beaches (ca. 11 m.a.s.l.). Area B consisted of 10 square metres of the heavy, frozen midden layers in the turf-covered northwest corner of the site. Area C, where remains of mid-passage dwellings were investigated, covered about 45 square metres of a plateau at the centre of the northern half of the site. A series of small test pits, and a 15 metre long trench connecting the "dwelling area" (Area C) with "the midden area" (Area B) provided supplementary information on site structure and stratigraphy.

Due to the complicated strati-graphy, the frozen state of the cultural layers, and the discovery of many organic finds, excavation had to proceed very carefully. This effort resulted in about   25 000 artifacts, 100 000 faunal specimens, and comprehensive contextual information.

Stratigraphy

A portion of the 20 m long Section C is briefly presented here as a typical example of the stratigraphy at the site. This segment, called Section C', cuts North through the culture layers from the front part of the plateau at Area C (Figure 5). Shifts from midden deposits to dwelling floors and traces of other activity areas can be seen.

The series of frozen organic layers rests on beach gravels. The earliest traces of a human presence—a few flakes—are found in Layer 18, which is a black, completely humi-fied peat. Layer 15a is a dense grass turf with a high number of artifacts, including excellently-preserved orga

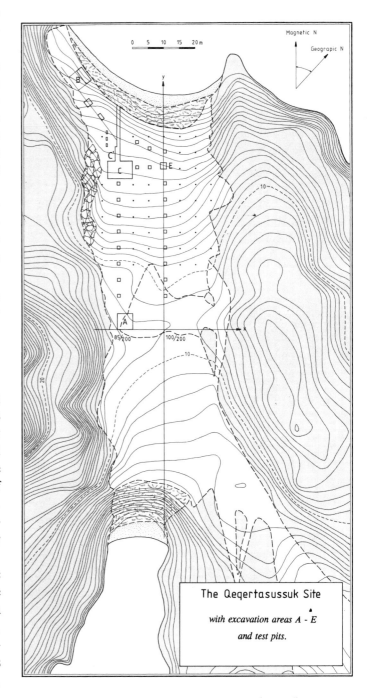

Figure 4 Qeqertasussuk site map (50 cm contour interval).

nic tools and faunal remains. The mid-passages and other stone features of Layer 16 rest on top of Layer 15a. At the southern end of the section (252.5 - 253.5) the flag stones of mid-passage A9 are visible.

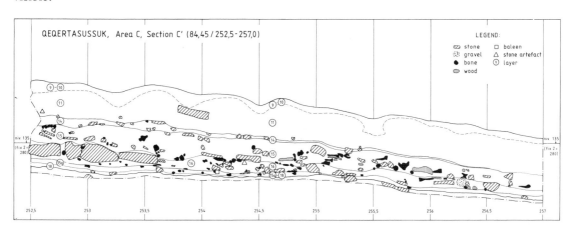

Figure 5 Stratigraphic profile (C'); flagstones of mid-passage structure A9 are visible from 252.5 to 253.5.

Layer 16 consists mainly of twigs and heather (floor and platform material), organic artifacts and faunal remains. Layer 15 is a dense grass turf sealing Layer 16. It contains artifacts and bones, but no well-defined structures. In some places, as in this part of the section, Layer 14 is a black stripe with a high charcoal content, faunal remains and fire-cracked stones. Elsewhere, Layer 14 is up to 50 cm thick, representing large heaps of fire-cracked stones intermingled with large numbers of seal bones. In some areas, the cultural layers are completely soaked with blubber from activities carried out in Layer 14.

The upper limit of permafrost is in the overlying, partly cryoturbated turf and silt layer. In this heavy Layer 11, organic artifacts and faunal remains are not preserved, but stone artifacts are found in great numbers. Several irregular stone features are seen. The finds from Layer 11 represent the latest Saqqaq phase at the site. The present topsoil (Layer 9 - 10) consists of silt and roots, and fragments of the present vegetation (willow, birch, heather and grass).

Analysis of the many layers and sub-layers in the different sections at the site has led to the definition of five stratigraphic units. The artifact contents from these units have been grouped into five archaeological components. Component 5 is the earliest assemblage at the site while Component 1 is the latest. The stratigraphic units have been radiocarbon-dated in this area through eleven datings: Layer 18 (bottom) - 3980±85 BP (turf, K 4823); Layer 15a (upper part) - 3780±85 BP (herbaceous turf, K 4819); Layer 16 - 3640±75 BP (heather, K 4822), 3760±80 BP (heather, K 4821), 3650±85 BP (heather, K 4818); Layer 15 (lowermost part) - 3680±85 BP (herbaceous turf, K 4817); Layer 15 (upper part) - 3310±80 BP (herbaceous turf, K 4816), Layer 14 (lowermost part) - 3570±80 BP (seal bones, K 5127); Layer 14 (upper part) - 3500±80 BP (seal bones, K 5126), 3400±80 BP (seal bones, K 5128); Layer 11 (lower part) - 3150±80 BP (herbaceous turf, K 4820). The seal bone dates are normalised by Henrik Tauber, Copenhagen, according to C-13 measurements and the reservoir effect in West Greenland. They can be directly compared with the dates on terrestrial samples.

Structures

Stone structures were found throughout the exposed parts of the site area. Mid-passage structures and box hearths filled with fire-cracked stones were observed on the surface of the highest part of the "saddle" formed by the fossil beach ridges. Most information, however, relates to the mid-passages excavated in Area C, Layer 16. This "activity surface" was probably formed during a short period between 3900 and 3700 BP (Figure 6). Analyses of this complicated surface are still in progress, but it is apparent that some structures are well-defined: the three mid-passages A3, A8 and A9, the circular fireplace, A1 and the "dumps" of fire-cracked rocks A2, A6 and A7. Stones from the somewhat spoiled southern part of mid-passage A8 have probably been re-used elsewhere. Several wooden stakes were found which probably represent broken tent poles. Some were still vertically anchored in the turf.

Along the sides of A8, the surface was covered with a compact layer of birch brushwood and heather. On either side of this small floor a slightly raised platform (the western one covered by A1) consisted of alternating layers of grass turf and heather. The A8 structure is interpreted as the central

Figure 6 Stone features of Layer 16, Area C.

part of a mid-passage dwelling measuring about 7 by 4 metres. In total, there are probably the remains of two or three dwellings partly overlapping each other and partly disturbed by re-use.

Some characteristics of the artifact distributions support this interpretation. Complete household utensils like spoons, ladles and trays made from driftwood, caribou antler and sperm whale teeth were found close to mid-passage A8. Near the edge of the eastern platform, a cache of complete, hafted hand tools (a double scraper and a couple of burins) was found.

New Aspects of Saqqaq Material Culture and Subsistence

As a result of the permanently frozen condition of the cultural layers at Qeqertasusuk, we are afforded an entirely new and fresh picture of the range of ASTt technology. Saqqaq material culture, previously known almost exclusively through it's stone artifacts, is far more complex than expected. The pioneers of West Greenland posessed a highly developed, functional and flexible tool kit. The people of the Saqqaq culture were able to cope with every change in the resource base with a varied tool kit which remained practically unchanged for 1000 to 1500 years. As we shall see, some "typically Eskimo" material culture attributes, such as *kamiks*, can now be dated to the oldest part of the ASTt. It must be stressed, however, that many "Saqqaq solutions" differ significantly from the Neoeskimo technology.

Rather than presenting the finds in categories based on typology or raw material, a functional approach was chosen.

Hand tools and household utensils

Saqqaq hand tools include a variety of knives, end and side-scrapers, adzes, borers, awls, saws, grinding stones, hammers, wedges, flint flakers and needles.

About twenty hafted knives with bifacial blades of *killiaq* (a grey, silicified slate, earlier called *angmaq*) were found at the site, in particular in the "dwelling area" (Figures 7, 8, 9). The driftwood hafts are split into halves which hold the proximal end of the blade. Traces of lashing (of baleen string) are seen on all knife hafts. Some hafts have been lashed all over to provide a good grip (Figure 10). The knives vary from short, "heavy duty" tools with rounded bifacial blades to slender, pointed bifaces in long hafts. Traces of knife edges have been found on stakes, shafts and other wooden objects.

The burins are hafted in a different way (Figure 11). The hafts of the characteristic Saqqaq burins are split in the distal end, just enough to hold the burin base. Some slightly bent hafts are very carefully made while others seems more casual.

A pair of end-scrapers were found still in place at each end of a bow-shaped double haft made from juniper (Figure 12). These scraper blades belong to the most common "fan shaped" type on the site. Metric analyses show that at least five different types of end-scrapers were used—a fine example of the complexity of Saqqaq material culture.

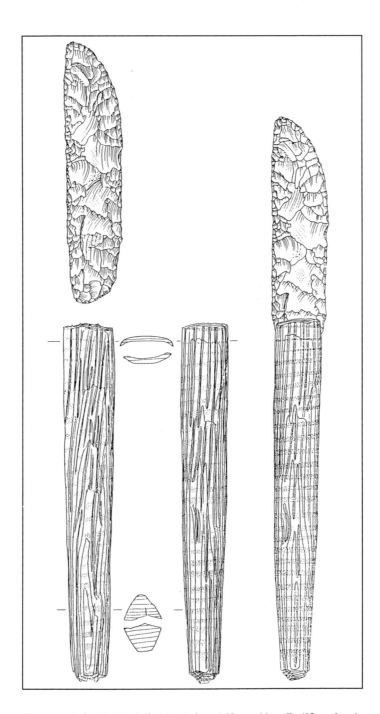

Figure 7 Hafted knife; *killiaq* blade in a driftwood handle (19 cm long).

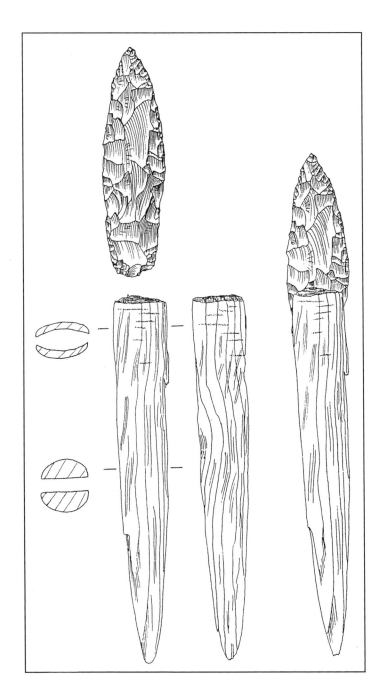

Figure 8 Hafted knife; *killiaq* **blade in a driftwood handle (15.5 cm long).**

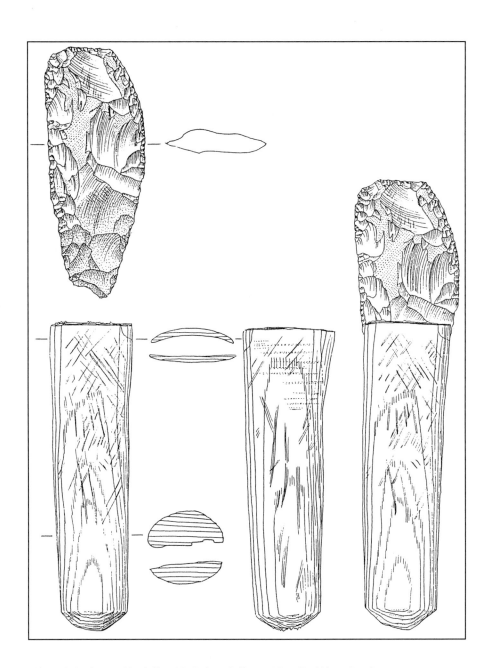

Figure 9 Hafted knife; *killiaq* blade in a driftwood handle (14 cm long).

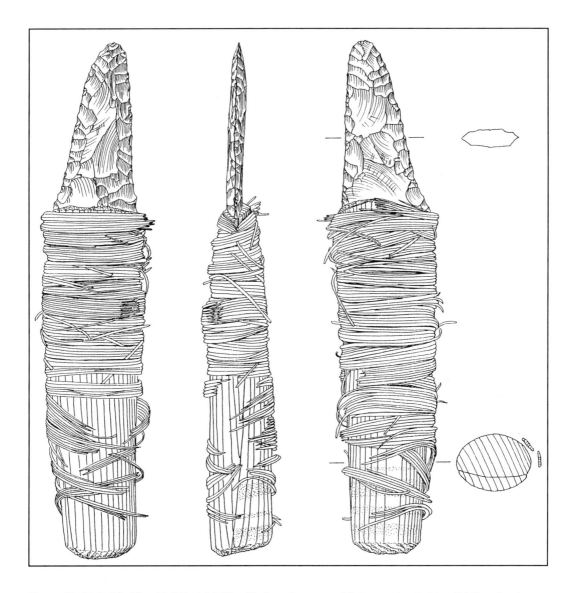

Figure 10 Hafted knife with bifacial *killiaq* blade and preserved baleen string lashing (16.5 cm long).

Two side-scrapers (Figure 13) and three microblades (Figure 14) (agate and quartz crystal) are also among the hafted hand tools, while adzes, saws and borers have not yet been found in their original hafts. Figure 15 provides an impression of the basic elements of the Saqqaq hand tool kit, as it can be assessed from the finds.

Among the artifacts which have been classified as "household utensils", various trays, bowls, spoons and ladles were found. The spoons and ladles are often very elegantly made from whale bone or tooth, caribou antler or hard driftwood, whereas the bowls, representing Saqqaq wood working at it's best, generally are carved from driftwood with broad rings (Figures 16, 17, 18, 19).

Analyses of the driftwood artifacts at the site (by Nancy Eskildsen, The National Museum of Denmark) have shown that spruce (*Picea*) and larch (*Larix*) from Sibiria are by far the most frequent, but pine (*Pinus*) and aspen (*Populus*) were also utilized. Local wood (i.e. probably originating from southern Greenland) such as juniper (*Juniperus*) and willow (*Salix*)were used for a few tool hafts.

Saqqaq hunter's gear and his prey

Seal bones make up over 50% of the roughly 100 000 faunal remains from Qeqertasussuk (Grønnow and Meldgaard 1991a: 137). The primary species was the harp seal. Analysis of harp seal canine thin sections shows that most of these seals were caught during the spring migration in June-July. Ringed seal bones—representing about two thirds the number of harp seal bones—and thin sections, show that this species served as a food source during winter, and, primarily, early spring.

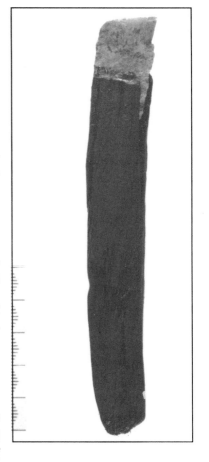

Figure 11 *Killiaq* burin in its original driftwood handle (13 cm long).

Seals were caught with harpoons which were remarkably light in comparison to the well known hunting gear of the historic Inuit of Greenland. In fact the closest ethnographic analog to the Saqqaq harpoon (and bird hunting) technology is found far to the west in the historic Alaskan material culture (e.g. Nelson 1899).

Both the "male" and the "female" harpoon principle were used in Saqqaq Culture. About 50 complete or fragmentary small harpoon heads (mean length about 6.5 cm) were found at the site (Figure 20). All have an individual touch. The most common main type, however, is the tanged harpoon head with a two-spured distal barb and a blade slot parallel to the line hole. Close parallels are known from a couple of other Saqqaq sites, in West Greenland and from several Canadian Pre-Dorset sites, as are variants of the open-socketed main type (e.g. Helmer 1991; McGhee 1979).

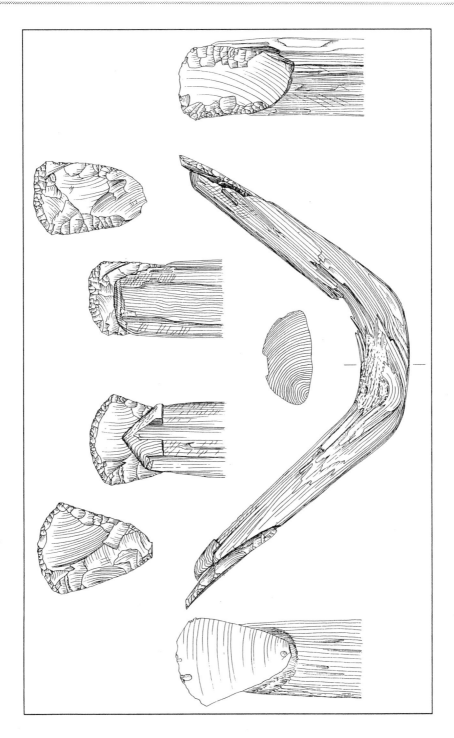

Figure 12 End-scrapers hafted in a bent double-ended handle (16.5 cm long).

Figure 13 Hafted *killiaq* side-scraper in a short, heavy handle (12.5 cm long).

Time is not "responsible" for the harpoon head variation at Qeqertasussuk. Rather function and personal identification marks must be taken into consideration. Slender foreshafts for the small open-socketed harpoon heads add to the picture of the Saqqaq harpoon complex.

Like his historical counterpart, the Saqqaq hunter possessed lances and spears of many different "calibres" (Figure 21). The frequency distribution of wooden shaft diameters (Figure 22) documents that the lances/spears, like the harpoons, were very light weapons (shaft diameters from 12 to 19 mm). All Saqqaq lance foreshafts show an open blade bed for a bifacial, tanged projectile point. Whereas none of the harpoon heads seem heavy enough for whale hunting, some of the lances with broad blades (shaft diameters 22 to 27 mm) might have served this purpose.

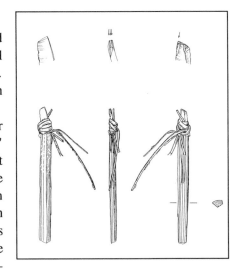

Figure 14 Microblade lashed to haft with baleen string (6.5 cm long).

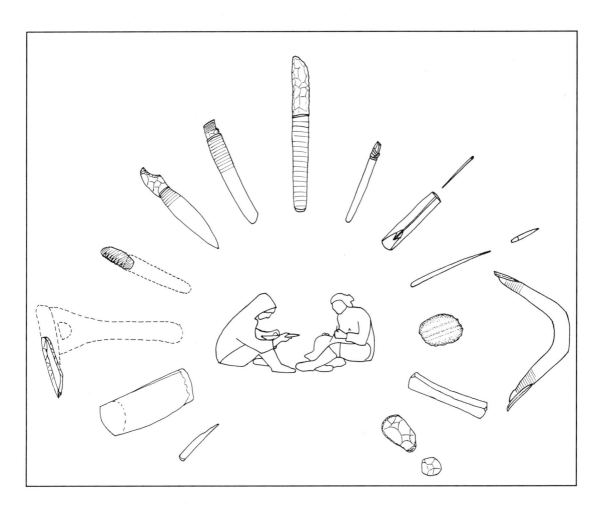

Figure 15 Reconstruction of the Saqqaq hand tool kit (clockwise): flint-flaker, wedge, adze, saw, side-scraper, burin, knife, microblade knife, needle case and needle, bodkins, double scraper, rasp (pumice), grinding stone, and tinder (*killiaq* and pyrite).

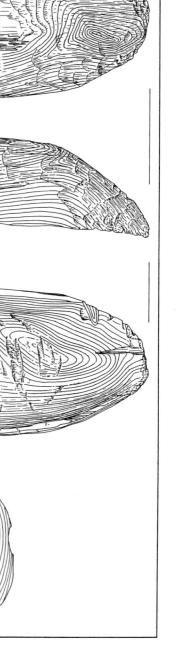

Figure 16 Driftwood ladle (20.1 cm long).

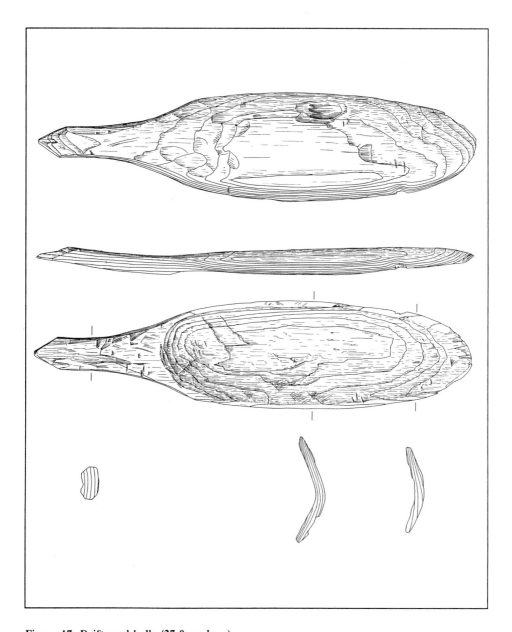

Figure 17 Driftwood ladle (27.0 cm long).

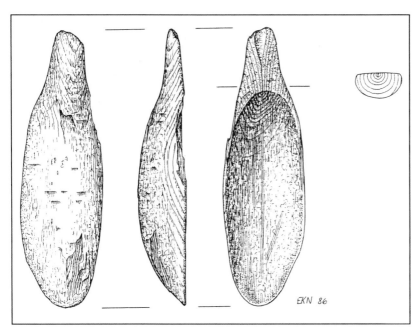

Figure 18 Sperm whale tooth spoon (13.2 cm long).

In any case, six to eight different species of whales are represented in the faunal material: the Bowhead or Right Whale (*Balena mysticetus/glacialis*), the Sperm Whale (*Physeter macrocephalus*), the Minke Whale or Sei Whale (*Balaenoptera acutorostrata/borealis*), the Narwal (*Monodon monoceros*), the Killer Whale (*Orcinus orca*) and the Porpoise (*Phocoena phocoena*).

As expected, a kind of skin boat was used in connection with sea hunting. Several fragments from the frames of slender kayak-like crafts and a couple of oar fragments have been found in the deepest layers at the site representing the earliest known water-crafts in the Arctic (Figures 23, 24).

Birds played a surprisingly important role in the Saqqaq diet at Qeqertasussuk. Thirty-nine percent of the bone material represents birds. Guillemot, fulmar, different species of seagulls and little auk were caught in large numbers, in particular during their late summer and autumn migrations. Also the finding of great auk bones in the midden must be mentioned (M. Meldgaard 1988). Intensive fowling is also reflected through the unilateraly barbed prongs, which were lashed three at a time to the end of a slender wooden shaft (diameter about 12 to 16 mm) (Figure 25).

In spite of the excellent preservation conditions and sieving of the sediments, the material shows the usual bias towards fish bones. However, the bones indicate that large cod (60 to 120

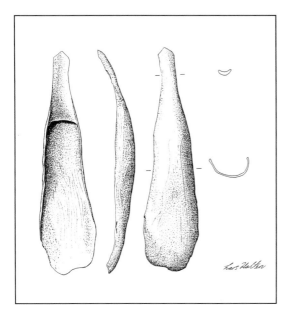

Figure 19 Caribou antler spoon (15.2 cm long).

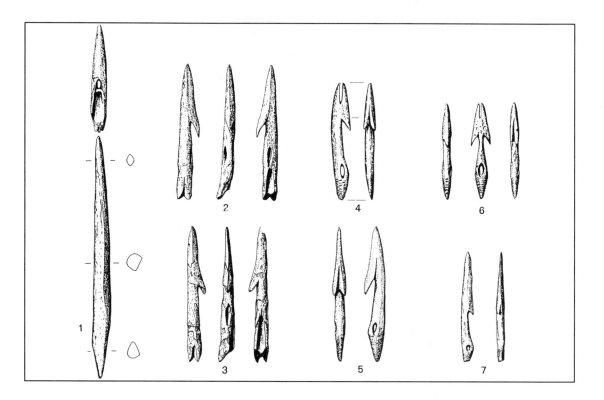

Figure 20 Saqqaq harpoon heads: *1-3* toggling harpoon heads, *4-7* tanged harpoon heads (5 is 7.8 cm long).

cm long) and other fish species like sculpin, capelin, *uuvaq* and char were eaten. The artifacts do not add significantly to our knowledge of the importance of fishing unless some of the harpoon heads, barbed prongs and bone points, are in fact fishing implements.

A small number of caribou bones and worked antler, arrow points of *killiaq* and quartzite, and several fragments of arrow shafts and bows reflect the hunting of caribou on the mainland. The Saqqaq arrow was long, about 75 cm, slender and had a round cross section in contrast to the Neoeskimo arrow (Figure 26). The bow fragments show that bows were reinforced by backing with sinew.

To complete the picture of Saqqaq economy, the hunting of fox, hare and ptarmigan must be mentioned. In particular the arctic fox—hunted primarily during the winter season according to the thin sectioning of canines—was important. Traps have not been found, but baleen strings with loop knots might represent snares used for hunting these small game species.

In conclusion, Saqqaq subsistence economy and the technology connected with it was extremely broad-based (Figure 27). About 45 different mammal, bird and fish species (Table 1) were exploited, as were vegetable resources (seeds of crowberries and mountain sorrel [*Oxyria digyna*] were found in human faeces in the culture layers [Fredskild 1991]).

Table 1 Faunal species found at Qeqertasussuk (all layers compiled).

MAMMALS
Arctic hare (*Lepus arcticus*)
Domestic dog (*Canis familiaris*)
Arctic fox (*Alopex lagopus*)
Caribou (*Rangifer tarandus*)
Whalrus (*Odobenus rosmarus*)
Common seal (*Phoca vitulina*)
Ringed seal (*Phoca hispida*)
Harp seal (*Phoca groenlandica*)
Bearded seal (*Erignathus barbatus*)
Hooded seal (*Cystophora cristata*)
Sperm whale (*Physeter macrocephalus*)
Killer whale (*Orcinus orca*)
Porpoise (*Phocoena phocoena*)
Narwhal (*Monodon monoceros*)
Minke whale or sei whale (*Balaenoptera acuto-rostrata/-borealis*)
Bowhead or right whale (*Balaene mysticetus/glacialis*)

BIRDS
Red-throated loon (*Gavia stellata)*
Great northern loon (*Gavia immer*)
Fulmar (*Fulmarus glacialis*)
Great shearwater (*Puffinus gravis*)
Mallard (*Anas plathyrhyncha*)
Eider (*Somateria mollisima*)

King eider (*Somateria spectabilis*)
Red-breasted merganser (*Mergus serrator*)
White-fronted goose (*Anser albifrons*)
Ptarmigan (*Lagupus mutus*)
Iceland gull (*Larus glaucoides*)
Glaucous gull (*Larus hyperboreus*)
Black-legged kittiwake (*Rissa tridaktyla*)
Great auk (*Pinguinus impennis*)
Little auk (*Plotus alle*)
Thick-billed murre (*Uria lomvia*)
Black guillemot (*Cepphus grylle*)
Raven (*Corvus corax*)

FISH
Salmon (*Salmo salar*)
Arctic char (*Salvelinus alpinus*)
Capelin (*Mallotus villosus*)
Cod (*Gadus morhua*)
Uvaq (*Boreogadus saida*)
Sea scorpion (*Cottidae* or *Cottunculidae*)

MOLLUSKS AND SNAILS
Common mussel (*Mytilus edulis*)
Hiatella byssifera
Scallop (*Pecten islandicus*)
Periwinkle (*Littorina saxatilis*)

The extremely flexible economy allowed the Saqqaq people to live in and exploit the area for a millennium. There is, however, evidence of change in the seasonality of the site through time. Whereas the Qeqertasussuk site served as a year-round base camp during the first four centuries, it later became a summer camp. Unfortunately the latest developments in the subsistence economy at the site cannot be documented due to a lack of preserved faunal remains from the latest cultural layers at the site.

Skin fragments and knotting

Various pieces of seal, caribou and bird skin, some obviously waste while others were finely worked, were found in the frozen layers. They have been analysed by Gerda Møller (1991).

Fine traces of processing are still preserved on the skin fragments. Made with a sharp edge, marks left from working the meat side of the skins reflect a technique which differs from the Neoeskimo as represented by the Qilakitsoq find of the 15th century AD (Møller 1989). One piece

from Qeqertasussuk has been identified as the foot of a kamik-stocking (Møller 1991: 146-147) while others are probably garment fragments.

The thin, twisted two-stranded senew thread is of a remarkably high quality as are the seal skin and baleen thongs showing a variety of knots. Eight different kinds of knots have been identified: sheet bend, clove hitch, lark's head, reef knot, granny knot, overhand knot, noose and fisherman knot (van de Griend n.d.).

Saqqaq Human Remains

Four human bones found in the earliest midden layers (3900-3700 BP) and two tufts of hair represent the earliest known human remains from the Eastern Arctic.

Osteological analyses (Frøhlich et al. 1991) indicate that the two fibulae and the tibia found close together belonged to a female aged 30 to 40 years, and about 150 cm high. The humerus fragment probably belonged to an adult male. The bones and the hair are still in the process of being analysed.

As to the question of why the bones ended up in the midden there is not much supplementary evidence. No cut marks or gnawing are visible, but two tiny spots of red ochre have been found on the tibia.

The hair tufts, which were identified through microscopic investigation (Rørdam and Jensen 1991), seem to be have been cut off. A fine bird bone needle was stuck into the largest tuft,

Figure 21 Heavy *killiaq* lance blade in a wooden shaft (19 cm long).

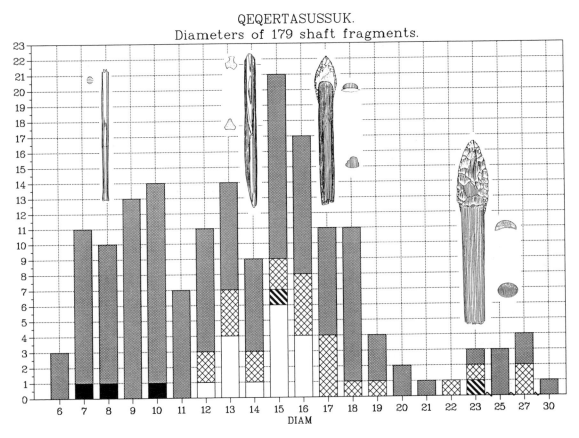

Figure 22 Distribution of shaft diameters: *black*-arrows; *white*-leisters; *cross-hatched*-lances with blade beds; *heavy hatched*-hafted lance blades; *grey*-unidentified shaft fragments with round cross-sections.

indicating that this was the hair of a Saqqaq female. Historic Inuit women sometimes kept their needles in characteristic topknots (J.Rosing pers.comm.).

Chronological Trends

The undisturbed, stratified cultural layers at Qeqertasussuk, covering the period from 3900 BP to at least 3100 BP, hold a potential for detailed chronological studies. Even though we are dealing with a fairly large time span, the find material from the site show a significant stability. Variations in the artifact frequencies, measurements or style ascribed to chronology as opposed to function are few or not statistically reliable. This is as valid for bone artifacts, such as harpoon heads, as it is for stone implements. However, some chronological trends within raw material use and artifact size have been identified, and a few examples will be presented here.

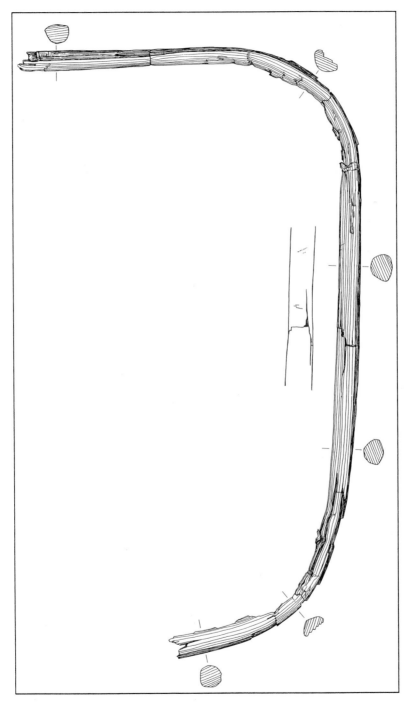

Figure 23 Kayak-like vessel frame made from a piece of split driftwood (35 cm wide).

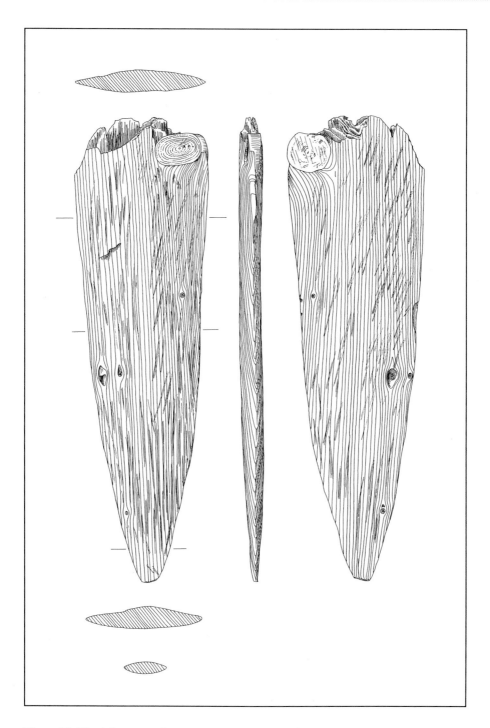

Figure 24 Distal fragment of a slender oar or paddle (28 cm long).

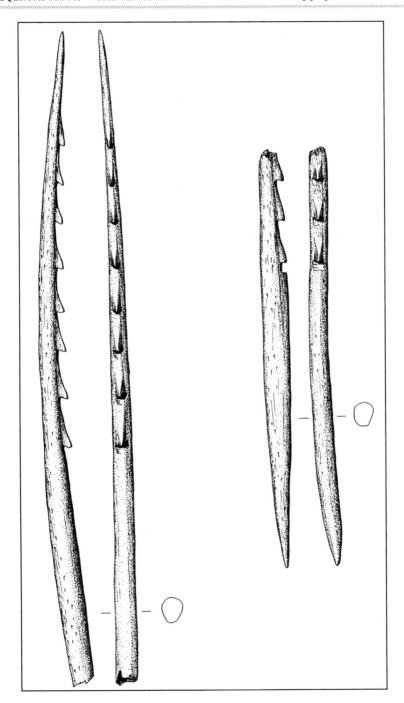

Figure 25 Leister end-prongs (specimen on the left is 27 cm long).

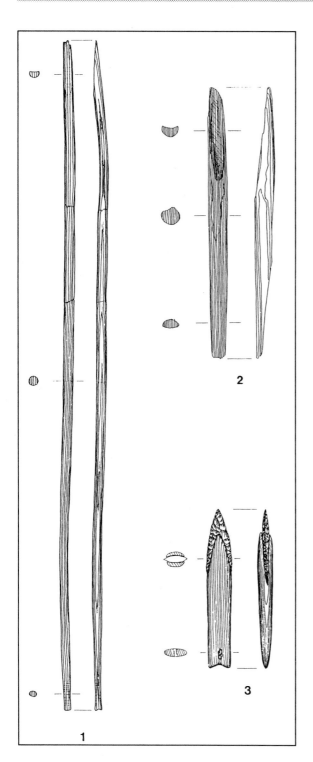

2

3

1

Figure 26 Complete arrow hind-shaft (*1*), tanged arrow head foreshaft (*2*), light spear foreshaft (*3*).

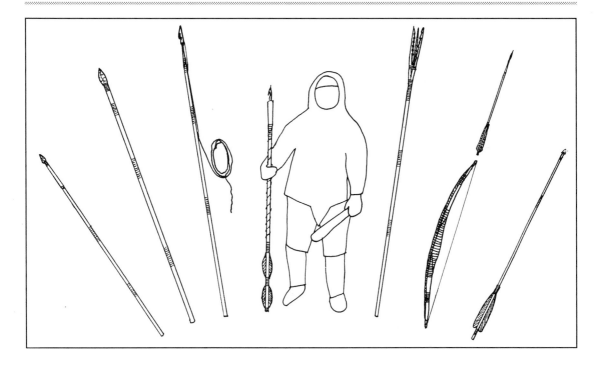

Figure 27 Reconstruction of the basic Saqqaq hunting tool kit (*l* to *r*): light lance, heavy lance, harpoon with toggling head, light throwing harpoon, atlatl, bird spear, bow and arrow, light throwing spear.

Lithic raw material preferences through time

Figure 28 (Table 2) is based on counts of all stone artifacts (tools and waste) from Area C, where chronological control is optimal. Here, the many different lithic raw materials have been lumped under five categories: *killiaq* (grey, silicified slate), agate (including chalcedony), quartz crystal, pumice and others. As can be seen, *killiaq* is the by far the most preferred raw material (70-90%). This trend is also valid when only the tools are examined (Figure 29, Table 3). However, a tendency from a high frequency of agate (about 20%) in Components 5 and 4 towards a low representation in Components 3, 2 and 1 is noted. It is especially obvious when we consider the tool inventory alone.

In conclusion, there is a trend towards uniformity in lithic raw material preferences from the earliest phase towards the later phases at the site.

The impression of greater uniformity through time is supported by analysis of preferences within the *killiaq* variants. Figure 30 (Table 4) shows how the homogeneous *killiaq* (Variant 1) almost completely outnumbers the striped and spotted variants (Variants 2 and 3) in the younger phases.

Within the artifact classes, microblades and burins show the most reliable chronological tendencies in connection with raw material preferences. Whereas about 90% of the microblades

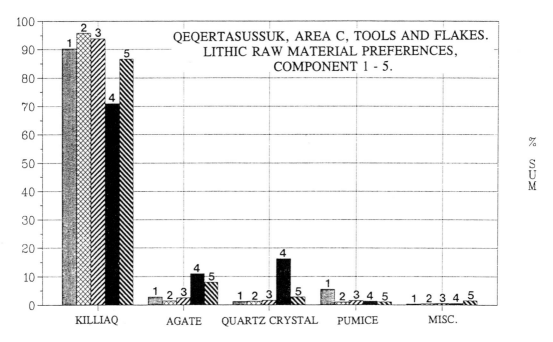

Figure 28 Percentages of different lithic raw materials, Area C (flakes and tools, n ≈ 12 000).

Table 2 Qeqertasussuk, Area C lithic raw material by component (all lithic tools and flakes).

	KILLIAQ	AGATE	CRYST.	PUMICE	MISC.	TOTAL
COMP.1	4193	127	54	254	17	4645
COMP.2	3202	48	44	31	15	3340
COMP.3	1470	38	26	24	9	1567
COMP.4	1290	198	295	24	10	1817
COMP.5	771	71	25	10	13	890
TOTAL	10 926	482	444	343	64	12 259

from Component 5 (Figure 31, Table 5) are made of agate, the proportion drops to roughly 25% in Component 1. This correlates with an increase in the use of quartz crystal as the raw material of choice in the manufacture microblades through time. Variations in raw materials selected for burin manufacture are shown in Figure 32 (Table 6). Here a significant decrease in the use of spotted *killiaq* (Variant 3) and agate (Variants 4-6) is documented.

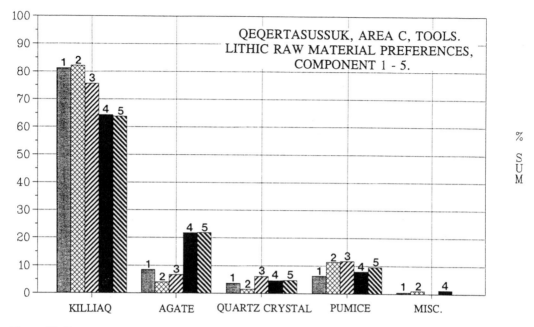

Figure 29 Percentages of raw materials, Area C (tools only, n ≈ 1300).

Table 3 Lithic raw material by component, Area C, (tools only).

	KILLIAQ	AGATE	CRYST.	PUMICE	MISC.	TOTAL
COMP.1	419	35	15	26	2	497
COMP.2	225	11	4	31	3	274
COMP.3	136	12	11	21	0	180
COMP.4	198	66	14	24	4	306
COMP.5	67	23	5	10	0	105
TOTAL	1045	147	49	112	9	1362

Chronological evidence from the metric analyses of burins

Metric analyses on the roughly 2500 stone tools were conducted in order to identify types within main tool categories, and to search for chronological trends within these. However, most of the metric variations, such as the five different end-scraper types mentioned above, are independant of chronology. Rather, they appear determined by function and/or the abilities and preferences of the individual flint knappers (e.g. McGhee 1980).

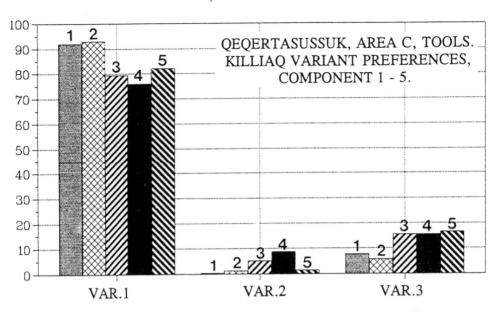

Figure 30 *Killiaq* variant preferences (tools only): *1*-light grey, *2*-striped, *3*-spotted.

Table 4 *Killiaq* variant preferences by component, Area C (tools only).

	KILLIAQ, VARIANT 1	KILLIAQ, VARIANT 2	KILLIAQ, VARIANT 3	TOTAL
COMP.1	309	1	26	336
COMP.2	209	3	13	225
COMP.3	108	7	21	136
COMP.4	148	17	30	195
COMP.5	55	1	11	67
TOTAL	829	29	101	959

One of the only statistically significant metric variations reflecting a chronological trend, is found within the burins. In order to avoid variations due to resharpening, only the proximal ends were measured (maximum length, width, angle between lateral sides). It turned out that the average width of the burin base decreases incrementally from 14 mm (Component 5 and 4) to 11 mm (Component

QEQERTASUSSUK, AREA C, <u>MICROBLADES</u>.
LITHIC RAW MATERIAL PREFERENCES, COMPONENT 1 - 5.

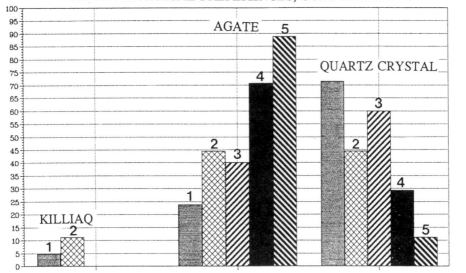

Figure 31 Raw material preferences (microblades).

Table 5 Microblades raw material preferences by component, Area C.

	KILLIAQ	AGATE	CRYST.	TOTAL
COMP.1	1	5	15	21
COMP.2	1	4	4	9
COMP.3	0	6	9	15
COMP.4	0	29	12	41
COMP.5	0	16	2	18
TOTAL	2	60	42	104

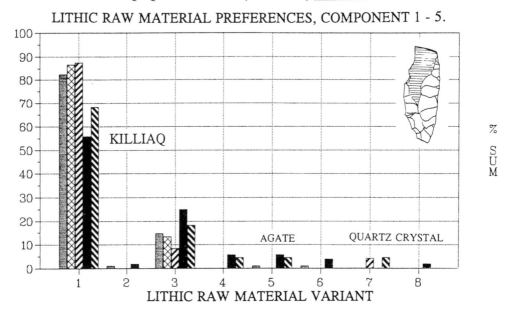

Figure 32 Raw material preferences (burins only).

Table 6 Raw material preferences by component, Area C, (burins).

	KILLIAQ VAR1	KILLIAQ VAR2	KILLIAQ VAR3	AGATE VAR4	AGATE VAR5	AGATE VAR6	CRYST. VAR7	QUA VAR8	TOTAL
COMP.1	84	1	15	0	1	1	0	0	102
COMP.2	39	0	6	0	0	0	0	0	45
COMP.3	21	0	2	0	0	0	1	0	24
COMP.4	29	1	13	3	3	2	0	1	52
COMP.5	15	0	4	1	1	0	1	0	22
TOTAL	188	2	40	4	5	3	2	1	245

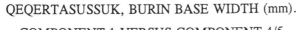

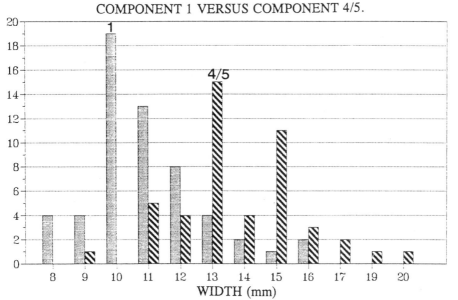

Figure 33 Distribution of burin proximal widths.

Table 7 Burin base width measurements (mm), Area C.

	COMP.1	COMP.2	COMP.3	COMP.4	COMP.5	TOTAL
n	57	26	16	35	12	146
$\bar{x}$	11	12	12	14	14	12
s	1.8	1.7	1.5	2.1	2.1	2.2
s^2	3.1	3.1	2.3	4.2	4.4	4.9

1) (Figure 33, Table 7). This fact supports the subjective impression that burins are larger and have "square" proximal ends in the earliest phases whereas later burins are slender with tapering bases.

Conclusions of the Case Study

Detailed insights into Saqqaq culture, the West Greenland ASTt branch, were provided by the wide range of artifacts contained in the frozen layers of Qeqertasussuk, dating to between 3900 and 3100 BP. The interdisciplinary investigations at the site have yielded a lot of information pertaining to dwellings, material culture, resources and the palaeo-environment. This paper has focused on some aspects of the results concerning technology and subsistence.

Finds of hafted stone tools and implements of wood, baleen, ivory and bone demonstrate that the Saqqaq people possessed a very complex tool inventory, which they saw no reason to change for over a millennium.

The broad-based subsistence economy is directly reflected in the faunal remains which represent about 45 different species. Harp and ringed seal remains predominate, but waterfowl also played a significant role. The site was used all year round during the first settlement phases. In later times, it seems to have been used only as a summer camp.

Some significant differences emerged when compared to Neoeskimo technology. For example, Saqqaq hunting gear was characterized by very light harpoons, which by means of an atlatl (Helmer 1991: 307, Figure 8*h*; J. Meldgaard 1991: 200), could be thrown over a considerable distance. Lances and bird spears are also remarkably light. Artifacts indicative of a "bladder complex", which are common at Neoeskimo sites, are absent. Every component of Saqqaq technology is made with precicion and gives, with an ethnocentric term, an impression of sheer functionality. No "superfluous" ornamentation is seen on the artifacts.

Very little change is seen in the material culture during this long time span. All tool types are present right from the pioneering phase. However, raw material preferences seem to change somewhat through

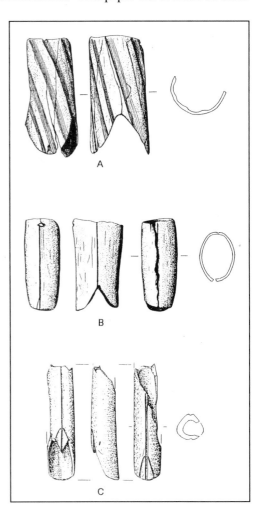

Figure 34 Small object containers: *a*-narwhal tusk (6.5 cm long), *b*-antler, *c*-dog bone.

time. As *killiaq* becomes even more dominant through time, the role of exotic raw materials like agate is reduced. Some characteristic chronological trends are also related to the raw materials used for microblades and burins. Furthermore, burin shape and size changes through time.

While artifacts such as pieces of skin garments, and the human bones and hair bring us closer to Saqqaq people themselves, certain important aspects of the culture are completely missing in the Qeqertasussuk find. Figurines, dools and any other depictions of people or animals are absent, and ornamented objects are significantly few (Figure 34). Furthermore, Saqqaq burial tradition is still unknown. The only clue is provided by the discovery of human extremity bones with traces of ochre in the kitchen midden deposited sometime just after 3900 BP.

One of the purposes of going into detail with the Qeqertasussuk site was to create a background against which finds from sites with more usual preservation conditions could be evaluated, both in functional and chronological terms. Thus, in the near future, comparative analyses will be carried out involving materials from the other Disko Bugt Saqqaq sites, and eventually, early Palaeoeskimo collections from other regions of the Eastern Arctic.

Some Considerations on the "Disappearance" of the Saqqaq Culture in West Greenland

The last traces of human activity at the Qeqertasussuk site are dated to about 3150 BP. Elsewhere in the Disko Bugt region, Saqqaq culture is known to have thrived until about 2700 BP (J. Meldgaard 1991: 204-205). The same is true for the Sisimiut area where investigations into late Saqqaq culture have been carried out over the last three years (Kramer and Jones 1992). No site in West Greenland has yet been radiocarbon-dated to the four centuries following 2700 BP. The earliest West Greenland Dorset culture (Dorset I) dates are around 2400 BP. These are still very few in number. A more coherent series of Dorset I dates begins around 2300 BP. It must be borne in mind, however, that these radiocarbon dates should not be too rigoriously adhered to given the plateau on the calibration curve between 2500 BP and 2400 BP (Stuiver and Pearson 1986).

The fact that a culture changes radically or even disappears from the archaeological record after a long period of stability has always required an explanation. Thus, the change from Saqqaq to Dorset culture in Greenland has been discussed for many years (e.g. Meldgaard and Larsen 1953). W.E. Taylor (1968) has also contributed to this discussion. The question of continuity versus discontinuity between these cultures is still unresolved, and the problem is as relevant as ever.

New evidence suggests that we should approach the problem on a regional scale. For the Disko Bugt area, the present author is in agreement with Jørgen Meldgaard. We are quite convinced that the development is discontinous. This is based primarily on two elements. The first is the stratigraphic evidence at several Disko Bugt sites (Møbjerg 1986) which show a break between Saqqaq and Dorset I layers. The second is the coherent series of radiocarbon dates on the large sites of Sermermiut and Qajaa (J. Meldgaard 1983 and 1991).

Kramer and Jones' research in the Sisimiut area, however, might suggest another regional development, even though this is not yet fully confirmed by radiocarbon dating and typology. In this region, they were able to document a correllation between site elevation above present sea level—a probable "age scale" due to land upheaval during the Palaeoeskimo period—and lithic raw material frequencies. In particular, this applies to the frequency of *killiaq* versus other materials. *killiaq* frequency falls systematically from about 70 - 100% (total material including flakes) on sites situated at about 15 to 20 metres above sea level, to lower than 30% on Dorset sites located right at the present sea level. These conclusions are based on observations from over 100 sites in the district. The results from Sisimiut underlines the fact that what goes for one region might not be true for the rest of Greenland. As may be recalled, the opposite tendency in lithic raw material frequencies through time was documented at Qeqertasussuk.

The following senario is proposed. Cultural and demographic change between Saqqaq and Dorset I in West Greenland was triggered by external factors such as <u>drastic changes and decline in the resource base</u> due to changing sea currents and ice conditions. Fluctuations in important marine game species (Grønnow and Meldgaard 1991b; Vibe 1967) and caribou populations (Meldgaard 1986) are documented in detail for the historic period in West Greenland. The rare coincidence of several of these "minima on the resource curves" might have caused the abandonment of some regions, such as Disko Bugt, during late Saqqaq. Thus, an important link in a chain of territories, social and exchange networks along the West Coast—as reflected by the wide distribution of lithic raw materials from Disko Bugt—would break down. It is important to bear in mind that the *killiaq* and agate, which are found in great quantities on Saqqaq sites all over West Greenland, occur naturally only in the Disko and Uummaanaaq areas (Henderson et al. 1976). Here access to quaries can be controlled by a few local groups.

It is suggested that the demographic situation in West Greenland in the centuries between the Saqqaq and the Dorset cultures is generally comparable to the late 19th/early 20th century settlement of East and North-East Greenland, i.e. a few populated regions separated by vast areas without permanent settlement.

Even though the archaeological sources are biased—many Dorset I sites are exposed to erosion from the sea—the tendency in the centuries after the "transitional period" is also quite clear: Dorset I sites in West Greenland are considerably fewer and most of the sites are significantly smaller as measured both in terms of numbers of artifact, and the overall site size in comparison to Saqqaq sites (e.g. Møbjerg 1986: Table 3).

In contrast to the scarce or totally absent remains from the "transitional period" in West Greenland, recent investigations in North-East Greenland and on Ellesmere Island—the "gateway" to Greenland—point to an increasing number of sites dating to this and the Early Dorset period (Andreasen and Elling 1991; Schledermann 1990). The finds are referred to as Independence II, "transitional phase" or "the younger Palaeoeskimo culture", such as the Ile de France site found by Eigil Knuth (pers.comm.) in North-East Greenland with its more than 400 dwelling remains. Resources must have been abundant in this part of Greenland during these centuries.

In conclusion, after one and a half millennia of significant stability during the Saqqaq period, West Greenland became marginalized. The country was not completely depopulated, but the demographic and cultural "centre" moved to North and North-East Greenland in close connection with the developments in High Arctic Canada.

The next phase of radical change in Greenland's Palaeoeskimo prehistory seems to be even more severe. After the disappearence of Dorset I from the archaeological record in the third century

AD no traces of human activity are found until late Dorset (Dorset II) remains from about AD 700 appear sporadically on the scene. This lacuna is yet another unexplained phenomenon in the prehistory of Greenland which must be adressed in the future.

Acknowledgments

The author is grateful to the research team members and to the many foundations, institutions and persons who have supported the Qeqertasussuk Project through all the years in the field and in the laboratories. All information on the subsistence species is based on Morten Meldgaard's comprehensive analyses of the faunal material at the site and on his work on resource utilization in Disko Bugt. The Qasigiannguit/Christianshåb Museum and the citizens of the town are thanked for their unique support. This paper is dedicated to the memory of master carpenter Egon Geisler (1931 - 1991), Qasigiannguit, whose enthusiasm inspired and encouraged us all during the field work in Greenland.

References

Andreasen, C. and H. Elling. 1991. De arkæologiske undersøgelser. In, Naturbevaring i Grønland (Nature Conservation in Greenland), C. Andreasen et al., eds. Atuakkiorfik. pp. 55-65.

Fredskild, B. 1991. Planterester og klimaændringer. Qeqertasussuk set med botanikerens øjne. Tidsskriftet Grønland, 4-7: 172-180.

Frølich, B., N. Lynnerup and J.P. Hart Hansen. 1991. Menneskeknoglerne fra Qeqertasussuk. Tidsskriftet Grønland, 4-7: 150-154.

Griend, P. van de n.d. The Qeqertasussuk Knots. MS prepared for Meddelelser om Grønland.

Grønnow, B. 1990. Prehistory in Permafrost. Investigations at the Saqqaq Site, Qeqertasussuk, Disco Bay, West Greenland. Journal of Danish Archaeology, 7: 24-39.

Grønnow, B. and M. Meldgaard. 1991a. De første vestgrønlændere. Resultaterne fra 8 års undersøgelser på Qeqertasussuk-bopladsen i Disko Bugt. Tidsskriftet Grønland, 4-7: 103-144.

Grønnow, B. and M. Meldgaard. 1991b. Hvor blev de af? Tidsskriftet Grønland, 4-7: 206-209.

Gulløv, H.C. and H.Kapel. 1988. De palæoeskimoiske kulturer i Nuuk Kommune. In, Palæoeskimoisk forskning i Grønland, T. Møbjerg, B. Grønnow & Schultz-Lorentzen, eds. Aarhus Universitets-forlag. pp. 39-58.

Gulløv, H.C., M. Meldgaard and M. Rosing. 1990. Skjoldungen - et paradis bag Storisen. Feltrapport fra et tværvidenskabeligt projekt i Sydøstgrønland. Naturens Verden, 11-12: 377-400.

Hansen, K.M. and J.F. Jensen. 1991. Orpissooq - en sommerfangstplads fra Saqqaq-kulturen. Tidsskriftet Grønland, 4-7: 181-190.

Helmer, J.W. 1991. The Palaeo-Eskimo Prehistory of the North Devon Lowlands. Arctic,44(4): 301-317.

Henderson, G., A. Rosenkrantz and E.J. Schiener. 1976. Cretaceous-Tertiary sedimentary rocks of West Greenland. In, Geology of Greenland, A.Escher and W. S. Watt, eds. The Geological Survey of Greenland, pp. 340-363.

Kapel, H. n.d.. The Saqqaq site at Angujaartorfik, Kangerlussuaq. To be published in Proceedings from a conference at the University of Copenhagen, May 1992.

Knuth, E. 1967. Archaeology of the Musk-ox Way. Ecoles Practiques des Hautes Etudes, Centre d'Etudes Arctiques et Finno-Scandinaves, Contributions 5.

Kramer, F.E. and H.L. Jones. 1992. Nipisat I - en boplads fra den yngre Saqqaq-kultur. Tusaat/-Forskning i Grønland, 1: 28-38.

Larsen, H. and J. Meldgaard. 1958. Paleo-Eskimo Cultures in Disko Bugt, West Greenland. Meddelelser om Grønland, 161(2).

Madsen, B. and T. Diklev. 1992. Arkæologisk berejsning i Thule 1991. MS on file with Avanersuup Katersugaasivia, Thule.

McGhee, R. 1980. Individual Stylistic Variability in Independence I Stone Tool Assemblages from Port Refuge, N.W.T. Arctic, 33(3): 443-453.

McGhee, R. 1979. The Paleo-Eskimo Occupations at Port Refuge, High Arctic Canada. National Museum of Man, Mercury Series, Archaeological Survey of Canada Paper 92.

Meldgaard, J. 1983. Qaja, en køkkenmødding i dybfrost. Feltrapport fra arbejdsmarken i Grønland. Nationalmuseets Arbejdsmark 1983: 83-96.

Meldgaard, J. 1991. Bopladsen Qajaa i Jakobshavn Isfjord. Rapport om udgravninger 1871 og 1982. Tidsskriftet Grønland, 4-7: 191-209.

Meldgaard, M. 1986. The Greenland Caribou - zoogeography, taxonomy, and population dynamics. Meddelelser om Grønland, Bioscience 20.

Meldgaard, M. 1988. The Great Auk, Pinguinus impennis (L.) in Greenland. Historical Biology, 1: 145-178.

Møbjerg, T. 1988. De palæoeskimoiske kulturer i Ammassalik. In, Palæoeskimoisk forskning i Grønland. T.Møbjerg, B.Grønnow and Schultz-Lorentzen, eds. Aarhus Universitets-forlag, pp. 81-94.

Møbjerg, T. 1986. A Contribution to Paleoeskimo Archaeology in West Greenland. Arctic Anthropology,23(1&2): 19-56.

Møhl, J. 1986. Dog Remains from a Paleoeskimo Settlement in West Greenland. Arctic Anthropology, 23(1&2): 81-89.

Møller, G. 1991. Verdens ældste kamik. Om skindstykkerne fra Qeqertasussuk. Tidsskriftet Grønland, 4-7: 145-149.

Møller, G. 1989. Eskimo clothing from Qilakitsoq. In, The Mummies from Qilakitsoq -Eskimos in the 15th Century, Hansen, J.P. Hart and Gulløv, H.C. editors. Meddelelser om Grønland, Man & Society 12, pp. 23-46.

Nelson, E.W. 1899. The Eskimo about Bering Strait. Eighteenth annual report of the Bureau of American Ethnology, 1896-97, pp. 3-518.

Petersen, E.B. n.d. A Saqqaq tent ring from the Disko Bugt. To be published in Proceedings from a conference at the University of Copenhagen, May 1992.

Rørdam, A.M. and E. Jensen. 1991. Hår fra Qeqertasussuk - stammer de fra mennesker eller dyr? Tidsskriftet Grønland, 4-7: 155-158.

Sandell, B. and H. Sandell. n.d. Paleo-Eskimo sites and finds in the Scoresby Sund area. To be published in Proceedings from a conference at the University of Copenhagen, May 1992.

Schledermann, P. 1990. Crossroads to Greenland. The Arctic Institute of North America, Komatic Series, 2.

Stuiver, M. and G.W.Pearson. 1986. High-precision calibration of the radiocarbon time scale, AD 1950-500 B.C. Radiocarbon, 28(2B): 805-838.

Taylor, W.E., Jr. 1968. The Arnapik and Tyara sites: an Archaeological Study of Dorset Culture Origins. Memoirs of the Society for American Archaeology , 22.

Vibe, C. 1967. Arctic Animals in Relation to Climatic Fluctuations. Meddelelser om Grønland, 170(5): 1-227.

Staffe Island 1 and the Northern Labrador Dorset-Thule Succession

William W. Fitzhugh
Smithsonian Institution
Washington, D.C.

Abstract

The Dorset-Thule transition is one of the least studied issues in Eastern Arctic archaeology. Lack of clear evidence of Dorset-Thule contact and cultural exchange has often been taken as *de facto* evidence that Thule people rapidly replaced Dorset people throughout the region. However, the evidence from Hudson Bay, Ungava, and Labrador suggests late persistence of Dorset people here and raises questions about the rapid replacement model. This paper addresses evidence from northern Labrador where radiocarbon dates indicate several centuries of overlap between Late Dorset and early Thule cultures. Evidence of an early Thule settlement on Staffe Island, Killinek region, is presented. This site appears to be part of the first Thule migration into Labrador in the thirteenth century. Dorset culture disappears in central-northern Labrador only in the fifteenth century. Throughout this period of slow Thule expansion, little evidence of acculturation is noted on either side of this cultural divide.

Résumé

La transition du Dorsétien au Thuléen est un des problèmes les moins étudiés de l'archéologie de l'Arctique de l'est. L'absence de preuve manifeste d'un contact ou d'un échange culturel entre ces deux groupes a porté à conclure que les Thuléens avaient rapidement succédé aux Dorsétiens partout dans la région. Toutefois, de nouvelles indices provenant de la Baie d'Hudson, de l'Ungava, et du Labrador permettent de constater la présence tardive du peuple dorsétien dans cette région. Des dates obtenues par l'analyse du C14, effectuée sur des témoins provenant du Labrador septentrional, indiquent un chevauchement de plusieurs siècles entre le Dorsétien supérieur et le Thuléen inférieur. D'autres preuves, telle la présence de vestiges de structures d'habitation thuléennes observés sur l'île de Staffe dans la région de Killinek, seront présentées dans cet article. Ce gisement, datant du treizième siècle, témoignerait de la première migration thuléenne au Labrador. Or, la disparition de la culture dorsétienne dans cette région a été fixée au quinzième siècle. Il n'existe néanmoins aucune preuve d'acculturation pendant toute cette période d'expansion thuléenne en le Labrador.

Introduction

Sometime in the thirteenth century a small group of Thule culture pioneers established a foothold on Killinek Island at the northernmost tip of Labrador. Where they came from has not been

Threads of Arctic Prehistory: Papers in Honour of William E. Taylor Jr., David Morrison and Jean-Luc Pilon, eds. Canadian Museum of Civilization, Mercury Series, Archaeological Survey of Canada Paper 149. 1994.

determined, but Baffin Island via the Button Islands (known as *tutjat*, or "stepping stones" [Hutton 1912: 28]) was their likely homeland. At the time northern Labrador was occupied by a Late Dorset people whose settlement area extended south to Okak and Nain, west across northern Ungava, and may have included those parts of south Baffin not already occupied by Thule people. The Labrador coast south of Nain was occupied by Point Revenge people, a proto-Innu group. Adding to northern Labrador's unusual degree of cultural diversity at this time were the occasional probings of Norsemen who were also exploring new lands and opportunities.

The presence of two resident Native American populations in addition to Thule pioneers and Norse visitors transformed northernmost Labrador from what previously had been an homogeneous Dorset realm into a zone of multicultural contact. This paper explores this dynamic period in Labrador's pre- and proto-history primarily from the Thule perspective. More personally, it is dedicated to two individuals who challenged classical concepts of Thule archaeology and stimulated the author's education in Thule archaeology. William E. Taylor, Jr. encouraged my early gropings at understanding the Dorset-Thule transition (1967), and his pioneering work on economy moved Thule archaeology toward a broader study of prehistoric society. My second debt is to the late Richard H. Jordan whose research at Inuit sites in Hamilton Inlet focussed attention on processes that transformed Thule culture into Labrador Inuit culture. Jordan's (1978) efforts, as expanded by Susan Kaplan (Jordan and Kaplan 1980; Kaplan 1983, 1985a, 1985b), made the last 500 years of Labrador Inuit development a model archeological study of Native American-European contact and created new opportunities for scholarship relevant to Inuit interests. Thanks to these two pioneers, my own interest in this subject evolved significantly.

Background and Previous Research

In 1977 and 1978 members of the Torngat Project investigated a large sod house village site at the south end of Staffe Island that was visited in 1967 by Patrick Plumet (Plumet and Gangloff 1991). Referred to as "Imittumavik" ("where one eats men") in oral historical accounts speaking of famine and cannibalism (Vezinet 1982: 140), Staffe Island 1 (JaDb-2; Plumet's LAB-10) is notable as one of the largest Neoeskimo village sites in northern Labrador. Our interest was sparked by the site's fifteen well-preserved sod house foundations, of two types: small (4 x 5 m) shallow rectangular structures without entrance passages, and somewhat larger (5 x 6 m) and deeper structures with entrance passages and internal rock construction. Both types contained Dorset and Thule materials with no evidence of stratigraphic separation. This, and the fact that Labrador Middle Dorset sites often had entrance passages, suggested that the site might yield important information on Dorset-Thule contact and succession. This possibility was strengthened by a late thirteenth century coniferous-wood date (Table 3) from a Thule floor that was two centuries earlier than an A.D. 1415 date on sterile moss separating Dorset and Thule levels at the Nunaingok site in McClelan Strait only 25 km from Staffe Island. Was Staffe Island occupied by Dorset and Thule peoples sequentially, its components having become mixed by "Thule-turbation"; or did architectural similarities and mixed assemblages result from contact and acculturation?

Here as in other areas of the Eastern Arctic the question first raised by Collins (1937: 315) and Rowley (1940: 498) of possible interaction between Dorset and Thule cultures based on similarities in harpoon styles, soapstone vessel use, and house forms is one many archaeologists have considered (e.g. Collins 1957: 514; W. E. Taylor 1959; Fitzhugh 1967; Bielawski 1979; Maxwell 1985: 241-245; Park 1993; and Plumet, this volume, to cite those most directly concerned; for others see Park 1993: 204). Such contact is suggested by a broad array of data including radiocarbon chronology, settlement patterns, culture areas, material culture, and oral history. Dorset and Thule dates overlap especially in Labrador-Quebec, where Late Dorset dates fall between AD 900-1500 or later, early Thule dates are rare, and Norse artifacts have been found in Dorset sites (Harp 1974). Thule culture seems not to have established early bridgeheads in Labrador-Quebec, and its expansion and replacement of Dorset culture here occurred over a period of several hundred years. While claims of Dorset-Thule contact at some sites like Mill Island (O'Bryan 1953) do not stand scrutiny, Sadlermiut architecture and lithics (Collins 1957; W. E. Taylor 1959), Amagssalik art (Meldgaard 1960a), and various material culture exchanges (e.g. Meldgaard 1960b, 1962) raise questions about Dorset-Thule interaction that are not easily dismissed, as Park (1993) has done. The problem is that Dorset-Thule contact has been judged by standards requiring material culture transfer, and few such instances have been accepted. Park's argument suffers most from the assumption that Labrador-Quebec radiocarbon overlaps result from mistaken stratigraphic contexts and makes this the keystone of his negative assessment.

Labrador data are particularly interesting in this regard. Data from the Torngat Project surveys in 1977-78 suggested possible Dorset-Thule contact in a number of areas. In addition to evidence for Dorset-Thule co-existence implied by overlapping radiocarbon dates between AD 1200-1350 (Table I; Fig. 1) and Middle Dorset use of sunken entrance passages (Fitzhugh 1976; Cox 1978), both Dorset and Thule used rectangular "Sculpin Island" structures (Cox 1978: 111; Fitzhugh 1980b: 600-601; Kaplan 1980, 1983: 500-512). In addition, the abandonment of winter sod houses for *sina*-edge snowhouse dwellings in Late Dorset times (Fitzhugh 1980b: 600) parallels a Thule settlement pattern. But did Dorset snowhouses precede or follow Thule arrival? Rowley (1940) and Meldgaard (1962: 93) cite evidence of pre-Thule Dorset snowknives from the Igloolik region, and a snowknife has recently been found in an Early Dorset site in Frobisher Bay (Odess 1993). The question of the Dorset Parallel harpoon type remains moot in Labrador due to poor preservation and limited excavation. Additional evidence of Dorset-Thule co-occupation in northern Labrador is suggested by oral history. Labrador Inuit stories of the "giant" of Hebron (Hawkes 1916: 148) tell of early Inuit ancestors mixing with an ethnic group with markedly different customs. It remains to be seen whether "Tunit" stories from Labrador refer to Dorset or to Neoeskimo peoples, Thule or others, who built the large Thule stone structures with which Tunit are associated in these stories. Perhaps the giant Tunits of Labrador also wielded the mammoth-sized slate ulus, knives, and harpoons that were collected from Inuit graves by early explorers and are now in the Newfoundland Museum and Nain Moravian Museum. Such data imply, and human nature guarantees, that the meeting and mixing of Inuit ancestors with earlier peoples in the Eastern Arctic must have been more complex than Park's isolationist reconstruction permits.

However, the purpose this paper is not to present a full review of the Dorset-Thule contact

Table I Radiocarbon dates from Labrador Late Dorset sites.

Site	Borden	Prov.	Locale	Lab #	Material	BP Age	AD date	Calib. Range (2 sigma)
Newell Sd-4	KgDl-4	H1	Frobisher	B-61068	wood(pine)	800±70	AD 1230-1256	AD 1030-1280
Amity Is-1	JcDc-2	L3, TP1	Killinek	SI-3367	charred wood	725±100	AD 1278	AD 1040-1410
Avayalik-1	JaDb-10	HI	Home Is.	SI-3864	wood (conif.)	670±60	AD 1283	AD 1232-1410
Big Head-6	IiCw-8	H2	Seven Is.	SI-3893	charcoal[1]/fat	1045±60	AD 882	AD 784-1153
Big Head-6	IiCw-8	H2	Seven Is.	SI-3894	char.(conif)/fat	1225±65	AD 776,794,797	AD 660-980
Peabody Pt-1	IiCw-1	H1	Seven Is.	SI-3372	char.(conif)	1315±95	AD 674	AD 540-943
Peabody Pt-1	IiCw-1	H1	Seven Is.	SI-3869	wood (spruce)	1335±70	AD 667	AD 580-865
Beacon Is.-5	IiCv-6	H2	Seven Is.	SI-3373	charred fat	1160±60	AD 886	AD 686-1000
Tinutjarvik Cove-2	IgCv-3	L3	Nachvak	SI-3375	charred grass, moss, betula	665±95	AD 1284	AD 1190-1430
Okak-3	HjCl-3	H1	Okak	SI-2154	charcoal	1005±95	AD 1002-1018	AD 780-1220
Okak-3	HjCl-3	H1	Okak	SI-2506	charcoal	895±85	AD 1157	AD 980-1280
Central Is-1	HdCh-32	H1	Nain	SI-4828	charred fat	685±60	AD 1282	AD 1220-1405

[1] - coniferous, vaccinium

issue but to describe a restricted aspect of that problem - the appearance of early Thule culture in northern Labrador. This is a subject about which almost nothing is known. Previous research (Bird 1945; Leechman 1950; J. G. Taylor 1974; Jordan 1978; Jordan and Kaplan 1980; Kaplan 1980, 1983, 1985a, 1985b) investigated only the historical phase of Labrador Inuit archaeology and history. Thule archaeology in Labrador is known only from Schledermann's (1971: 34-69) analysis of the Ikkusik site collections in Saglek. Unfortunately this site's Thule component was considerably disturbed by later occupations. Torngat Project survey data also provide Thule data (Kaplan 1980, 1983).

Recently Thule history in Labrador has been complicated by the discovery of a prehistoric Thule component at Red Bay (James Tuck, personal communication). These finds hundreds of miles south of Thule core areas in northern Labrador require reconsideration of the dynamics and capabilities of the Thule adaptation in Labrador. The Red Bay site and Auger's (1985, 1991) later contact period sites at Chateau Bay are the first concrete archeological evidence bearing on the debate on Inuit appearance in the Strait of Belle Isle region (Clermont 1980; Martijn 1980; J. G. Taylor 1980).

Some indication of the undeveloped state of Thule/Labrador Inuit archaeology is indicated by the many major research questions relating to this field. These include: (1) the source (Ungava? Baffin?) and date of Thule arrival; (2) the chronology and geography of Thule expansion in Labrador; (3) the role of Dorset culture as an element in this expansion; (4) the ethnicity of Labrador "Tunit"; (5) relationships between Thule and Point Revenge Indian groups on the central coast; (6) the role of Europeans as catalysts of Thule expansion; (7) Norse contacts and the identity of Labrador "skraelings"; (8) origins of the Labrador communal house; (9) relationships between central coast

Christian Inuit and their epi-historic ("heathen") relatives in northern Labrador; and finally (10) the problem of *in situ* Thule-Labrador Inuit continuity versus multiple migration origins. This paper touches upon only the first four of these questions.

During the decade preceding the Torngat Project the chronology of Dorset culture in Labrador was established by excavations at many sites on the central coast from Hamilton Inlet to Okak (Fitzhugh 1972, 1976, 1980a; Cox 1977, 1978; Nagle 1984; Tuck and

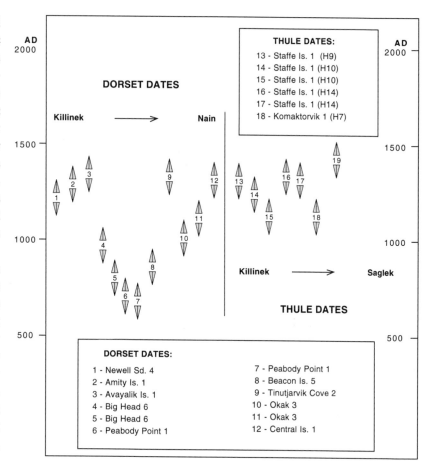

Figure 1 Selected Late Dorset and Thule radiocarbon dates.

Fitzhugh 1986). In addition to a time-transgressive shift, with limited culture contact or exchange between Groswater (2800-2200 B.P.) and an in-migrant Early Dorset culture (2400-1800 B.P.), we defined a northern and central coast Middle Dorset phase consistently dating to 2200-1500 B.P. Middle Dorset was also time-transgressive, earlier in northern Labrador than in central or southern Labrador, where few sites were known, presumably because of Indian occupations in these regions. This was followed by a gap in Dorset radiocarbon dates and Dorset lithic types between 1500-1000 B.P. This gap, which extends throughout northern Labrador, has been interpreted as evidence of a possible hiatus in Dorset occupation in Labrador, and probably in Newfoundland also (Cox 1978: 99; Fitzhugh 1980a; Tuck and Fitzhugh 1986: 166). This is also a time when Daniels Rattle and Point Revenge proto-Innu complexes were present on the central Labrador coast (Fitzhugh 1978: 167; Loring 1988, 1992). Although sites of these complexes have not been found in northern Labrador, both complexes made extensive use of Ramah Chert, and a trail of isolated artifacts leading to the Ramah Chert quarries suggests that these groups visited them occasionally. Dorset people again appear in Labrador sometime before A.D. 1000, taking up residence at sites from Killinek to Nain. Our Late Dorset sample (excluding Saglek [Thomson 1988, 1993]) includes 10 sites, six of which date within the Thule period (Table I; Fig. 1). None of these Late Dorset sites have Thule components as possible sources of dating error. As a result Late Dorset is one of the most distinctive and well-dated phases in Labrador. One of its characteristics is the absence of the sod house winter villages that are a feature of Middle Dorset settlement patterns (Fitzhugh 1976; Spiess 1978). Instead, Late Dorset people used shallow rock-walled *qarmats* during fall and early winter and in mid/late winter seem to have shifted into snowhouses to take advantage of productive *sina* open-water resources (Fitzhugh 1976, 1980a, 1980b: 601; Cox and Spiess 1980). A similar pattern has been noted in Lake Harbour (Maxwell 1985: 235-238).

Considering the overlapping radiocarbon dates during the Dorset-Thule transition ca. AD 1200-1350, Staffe Island 1 excited interest because its Thule houses were early and better preserved that at other sites, Late Dorset materials were present, radiocarbon dates indicated contemporaneity with Dorset sites, and similarities in dwelling types existed. The site seemed an ideal one for investigating the problem of Dorset-Thule succession in Labrador.

Setting

Staffe Island is located on the western end of a large shallow bay between Cape Kakkiviak and Killinek Island (Fig. 2). To the south an emerged beach of marine-washed till separates the bay from Williams Harbour; to the west is a complex of smaller bays and fjords; and to the north lies McClelan Strait, a narrow fifteen-mile channel that connects Ungava Bay and the Labrador Sea, separating the tip of the Labrador peninsula, Killinek (meaning "where pack ice stays some distance off shore"), from the mainland. To the east Home and Avayalik Islands and numerous skerries and shoals shield Home Island Bay from ice pressure and marine storms. Numerous channels, islands, and fjords create an ideal setting for human occupation. Staffe Island 1 is only one of many sites in the area; large Dorset and Neoeskimo sites have also been found in Martin Bay and on Avayalik Island (Jordan 1980).

The dominant resources of the region are marine mammals, seabirds, and waterfowl (Hantzsch 1928-1932; Val 1976; Cox and Spiess 1980; Vezinet 1982: 55-80; Spiess 1986). Fulmars, shearwaters, ducks, and geese are available seasonally. The Galvano Islands lying to the east are heavily populated by eiders, whose nests were regularly utilized by nineteenth century Inuit for egg and down collecting. In earlier times the waters surrounding Staffe Island were populated with walrus, beluga, and possibly large whales. Today polar bears and harp, bearded, and ringed seals are common, especially in late winter and spring, while the turbulent, ice-free waters around Killinek have whales, walrus, birds, and huge harp seal runs in the fall. Salmon and char were important enough to support a commerical fishery in the 1960s. Small land game is relatively scarce, except for foxes. Caribou, at least in 1978, were only available far to the south. When we returned in 1989, ten years after the town of Burwell had been closed, caribou were plentiful on Killinek Island, and were frequently seen swiming between the mainland and the bay islands. The Williams Harbour caribou drive system (Fitzhugh 1981) demonstrates that caribou hunting was practiced by both Dorset and Thule groups. That few caribou bones were recovered from Dorset and Thule middens at Avayalik, Staffe Island, and Akulialuk suggests these animals were not present here in winter and spring. Avayalik Dorset fauna suggests a late winter-early summer occupation empha-sizing walrus, seal, and bird exploitation in *sina* or open-water conditions (Cox and Spiess 1980: 664).

Data presented by Cox and Spiess suggest that Middle Dorset people living in the Home Island-Killinek region may have utilized a settlement pattern requiring seasonal shifts between Avayalik and Killinek sites. While faunal evidence indicates Avayalik was occupied from late winter through early summer, the Akulialuk site contains fall and winter fauna. Absence of semi-subterranean founda-tions at Avayalik suggests

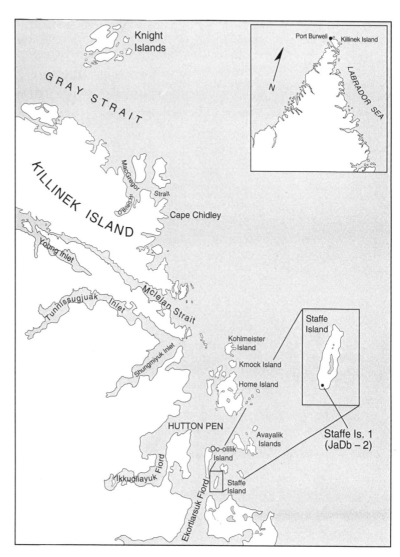

Figure 2 Staffe Island 1 site location and environs.

that its Middle Dorset occupants utilized skin or snow-walled *qarmats* rather than deep full sod houses. It is possible that these sites were not been occupied by a single group but by two groups whose alternate seasonal sites lie elsewhere. Late summer and early fall sites have not been identified but must have involved char fishery and caribou hunting.

Although the presence of numerous sites indicates that the area around Staffe Island has been occupied periodically for at least 2000 years, these sites generally consist of only one or two sod houses, probably accommodating 15-20 persons in the Dorset period and 30-40 persons in the Inuit communal house period. Site densities and house sizes during the recent Inuit period suggest Staffe

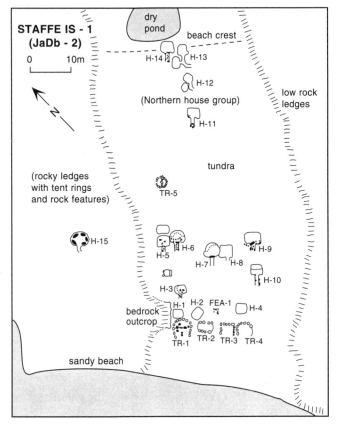

Figure 3 Staffe Island 1 site sketch map.

Island faunal resources did not support the large populations known to have occupied the Jackson and Killinek Islands during late fall and winter. The Staff Island region appears to have been an important seasonal complement in a regional subsistence-settlement pattern. Its waters are especially productive in late winter and spring when walrus and seal can be hunted from a stable late winter *sina*, among the open pack in spring, and in early summer open water. Spring brings huge influxes of bird life. As the season progresses, char and caribou become abundant. But as the bay waters froze over people would have to move to Killinek to hunt harp seals in the open waters of McClelan Strait and around Killikek Island, storing seal meat for mid-winter use. Whale hunting capabilities at Staffe Island were modest or nil because large whales do not frequent the region. The resource base at Staffe Island would be suitable for supporting groups of 4-5 families but not 15. Hence while Staffe Island would have been an important winter-spring sea mammal hunting site, local resources could not have been the sole sustainer of the larger Thule populations of the Killinek area.

In addition to faunal resources, the early Thule population in the Killinek-Home Island region needed a wider universe of social contacts to obtain non-local lithics (soapstone, silicified slate, nephrite) and other materials. Problems in procuring lithic materials would have been solved by trading with Thule people to the north or with Dorset populations in Labrador and Ungava. High-quality slates are not known from the Torngat region.

Site Description

Torngat Project fieldnotes and Kaplan's (1983: 789-795) description provide the basis for the following summary of our original 1977-78 work. The houses and associated tent rings, caches, and rock features are located on a sandy raised beach slope at the south end of the island facing Iselin Bay and Williams Harbour (Fig. 2). The site is bounded by low ridges to east and west and to the north by an ephemeral beach-crest pond whose waters feed a water-logged marshy turf and collect in the interiors of the houses in the upper portion of the site. In this area we found excellent wood preservation, but no bone or ivory. The sandy, drier soils at lower elevations were unfriendly to all but lithics and robust animal bones.

The site plan and architectural patterns of the Staffe Island houses suggest three settlement groups (Fig. 3). The **Lower Group** consists of three structures (Houses 1, 2, and 4) placed near the shore at an elevation of 1.7 m. These structures have 5 x 4 m rectangular depressions and lack entrance passages. Test pits in these structures revealed Late Dorset and a few Thule artifacts and debitage upon paved floor slabs. Four tent rings located between these houses and the shore appear to be of recent Inuit origin. The **Middle Group** includes seven rectangular sod foundations (Houses 3, 5-10) with 4-6 m long entrance passages (except House 8), rear sleeping platforms, and (again excepting H-8) use of heavy rock construction, including rock roof pillars and post-and-lintel doorways. House 8 appeared Dorset-like, lacking pavement, entrance passage, and rock construction, but contained Thule implements. House 9 produced a date with a mid-point average of A.D. 1283. Test pits in these houses revealed predominately Late Dorset artifacts and Ramah Chert flakes associated with Thule slate and nephrite tools and debitage. Most of the slate varieties were "hard" types of dark and light green slate, banded green and grey slate, with softer varieties of red, grey, and black slate being less common. Kaplan notes that Nachvak Thule sites contain soft slates of local origin and had relatively small amounts of high-grade foreign silicified slates and nephrite. Whale, walrus, bearded seal, and polar bear bones were recovered, despite rather poor preservation. The **Upper Group** includes Houses 11-14 located in the wet soil region below the pond near the crest of the beach. These houses include two house types, H-11 and 14 resembling Middle Group houses in form, while H-12 and 13 are either double houses sharing a single entrance passage or bilobed houses similar to houses at the Ikkusik site and in Frobisher Bay and Cumberland Sound. Like the Middle Group houses, these have heavy stone internal construction with post-and-lintel doors and rear sleeping platforms. House 13 was free of water and was tested: small bone preservation was poor; wood and whalebones were recovered, but no artifacts. West of a low rock outcrop lies a cluster of recent-looking tent rings and a sod house (House 15) different from those described above (see below).

1989 Investigations

In 1989, while conducting a trial run with the Pitsiulak for our forthcoming Frobisher project, we returned to Staffe Island for four days to isolate Dorset and Thule levels and to search for deeper deposits and wood/bone-bearing middens. We completely excavated House 10, tested wet soils in the upper area of the site, and mapped House 15.

Midden Test

Four 50 x 50 cm test pits were excavated in the wet soils of the Upper Group area. Three of these were located a few meters south of House 14 and a fourth (Test Pit 3) east of the House 13 entrance. Test Pit 2 (4 m south of the House 14 entrance passage) revealed a 5 cm-thick Thule level in which we found a wood spear-thrower, a wick-trimmer, a knife handle, the base of a drilled slate whaling lance or harpoon point fragment, and charcoal (Fig. 4). This level overlay a 1 cm layer of sterile peat below which was a Dorset level with wood remains, charcoal, and a variety of Late Dorset implements. Test pit 1 (7 m south of House 14 entrance) revealed similar stratigraphy but lacked diagnostic implements. Here the absence of a distinct sterile sod level between the Dorset and Thule deposits suggested a relatively rapid cultural succession. Radiocarbon data confirm the rapid sequence of events indicated in this stratigraphy: the Dorset level in Test Pit 2 yielded a charcoal sample dating to A.D. 1283, while a wood sample from the Thule level in Test Pit 1 produced a date of A.D. 1340 (Table 3).

House 10 Excavation

During the 1978 Torngat Project James Savelle mapped House 10 and excavated two 1 x 1 m test pits, one in the entrance passage and another in front of the sleeping platform. Dorset and Thule implements, including a slate harpoon endblade, and 21 walrus bones were recovered. A low sod wall rising 10-15 cm above the level of the surrounding beach enclosed the structure. At its highest, the wall was 80 cm above the working floor of the house, which had been excavated into the beach and had a thick sod-covered slab rock pavement. Portions of a paved sod-covered sleeping platform were also evident, set 20 cm above the level of the floor and sloping up to the rear (north) end of the house. A metre-high upright stone pillar had been erected on the sleeping platform just inside the rear wall as a roof support. Upright lintel posts stood at the door and a number of large rocks were exposed lining the walls of the entrance passage. It appeared that some rocks, including the door lintel, had been removed from House 10 for

Figure 4 Staffe Island 1 House 14 Thule level Test Pit 2 finds.

Figure 5 Staffe Island 1 house 10 interior.

use in other houses at the site.

When we returned in 1989 we selected House 10 for excavation (Fig. 5) because its interior lacked a large jumble of rocks and could be excavated quickly with few complications. Artifacts, flakes, bones, and rocks were recorded three-dimensionally. As expected for the houses in the lower part of this site, where the soil was sandy and well-drained, organic preservation was poor.

The deposits encountered in House 10 were similar to those noted in the 1977 and 1978 test excavations. The interior of the house had a thin 5-10 cm thick cultural level beneath a 5 cm thick level of surface vegetation. Thule cultural materials were associated with a dark sandy soil, under which lay a sterile tan sandy beach deposit. In some areas the Thule deposits contained bone, but this was rare except in a few patches on the house floor and in the east wall deposit. House floor deposits were usually free of Dorset flakes and artifacts, but Dorset deposits were often found intact beneath the Thule floor slabs. Outside the west wall, a 10-15 cm thick and generally boneless Dorset midden, containing both Middle and Late Dorset artifacts, was overlain by Thule deposits. This Dorset midden had been cut by the excavation of the Thule house pit. Most of the faunal remains from both Dorset and Thule levels consisted of walrus and large seal or whale bones. It was apparent that smaller bones rarely survived the site's acidic soils. Charcoal samples were carefully selected from Thule floor deposits.

Raw Materials

Slate, soapstone, nephrite, and mica were the only lithic materials definitely associated with Thule deposits at this location. As noted in tests at other Staffe Island structures, most of the Thule artifacts from House 10 were made of "hard" slates or nephrite, of several varieties: green or black nephrite, banded green slate, dark green slate, light green slate, and red slate with yellow or orange-green inclusions. These materials are not characteristic of Thule sites in more southern regions of

Labrador and appear to have northern origins, whereas soft grey and black slate, which is found at Staffe Island House 10 in lower frequencies, is probably of local Torngat origin (Kaplan 1983: 797). Mica, whose function is not known, occurred sporadically in the deposit. The only piece of Thule soapstone was a small corner fragment from a lamp. By contrast many Dorset soapstone vessel fragments were recovered from the House 10 area, together with 133 grams of Ramah Chert (324 flakes). Dorset debitage included 15 grams of quartz, five quartz crystal fragments (1.5 g total), 7 pieces of red chert (10.9 g), 12 pieces of schist (5 g), and 1 chunk of "Groswater Dorset" chert (2.4 g).

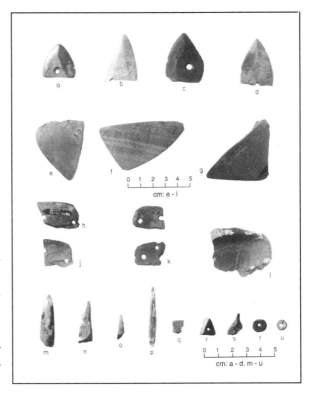

Figure 6 Staffe Island 1 House 10 Thule artifacts.

Small flake size, the small amount of debitage, and extensive tool recycling demonstrate that the Thule people living in House 10 used care to maximize the life of their lithic tools and raw material supplies.

Collection Description

The excavated collection (Fig. 6) from House 10 in 1989 includes 123 catalogued artifacts, of which 71 are Thule and the remainder are Dorset. The 71 Thule implements are described here and in Tables 2 and 4. Nearly the entire assemblage consists of endblades and knives, accounting for .38 and .27 of the entire assemblage, in the following classes:

Endblades

Of the 27 Thule endblades, 14 (the largest tool class) were complete or fragmentary harpoon point endblades, of which only two were complete and undamaged. All have a single perforation for a peg or line attachment, usually off-centre (outside the haft, for line attachment rather than for pegging), and have asymmetric blade outlines. A triangular patch of unpolished surface marks the

Table 2 Thule Artifact Assemblage from Staffe Island 1 House 10.

Artifact		no.	freq.
ENDBLADES		27	.38
harpoon endblade		14	.20
harpoon endblade preform		4	.06
large perforated endblade		3	.04
small arrowhead		1	.01
misc. endblade frags		3	.04
large endblade preform		2	.03
KNIVES		19	.27
pocketknife		3	.04
large knife		3	.04
large flensing knife		1	.01
ulu		4	.06
flake ulu		2	.03
side knife, oval		2	.03
straight edge flake knife		4	.06
SKIN-SOFTENERS		3	.04
AWL		1	.01
DRILL		1	.01
BEADS		2	.03
LAMP		1	.01
CORE		4	.06
GROUND FRAG		11	.15
MICA		2	.03

portion of the blade covered by the haft whereas the exposed portions of the blades are facetted from sharpening attrition. The width of the striated surface shows that these endblades were used in harpoons with 12-15 mm wide tips. All perforations were made with a twist drill except for #244 whose hole was triangular. All specimens have their greatest thickness in the centre of the blade and thin toward the base for use in tapered hafting slots. The majority of the points are made from hard green slate; two are of nephrite. Most were found on the west side of the sleeping platform or outside the southwest corner of the house. Details are presented in Table 4. In addition to finished blades four harpoon blanks were recovered on the west side of the sleeping platform near the majority of the harpoon points.

Among other tools were recovered three large perforated endblades, the base of a small side-notched point, probably used for an arrow, three miscellaneous endblade fragments, two endblade preforms of hard green slate, three small knife blade fragments, three large multiply-perforated knife fragments, one fragment of a large flensing knife blade, four ulu fragments, three of which are from large ulus and the fourth (#251) from a small ulu with multiple perforations, two flake ulus, two side knives for mounting in a multi-bladed, slotted butchering implement (cf. Thomson 1986), four straight-edge flake knives, three blunt-tipped skin-softening tools, two of which are flat and one of pyramidal form, possibly boot-creasers, an awl made of fibrous green nephrite, found in the sod north of H-10, a twist drill of green nephrite with an expanded head for hafting insertion, two flat disc beads, one of soapstone and the other, of red slate, having been refashioned from a broken harpoon endblade (cf. #245; see Maxwell [1960: 63] on Thule use of amber beads at Lake Hazen), a corner fragment of a thick soapstone lamp, four chunks from slate cores or discarded celt fragments, eleven pieces of otherwise unclassified slate flakes with polished or modified surfaces, and two small plates of mica.

Faunal Remains and Economy

The faunal collection from House 10 comes primarily from the interior of the house rather than from external middens. In fact, our testing failed to reveal the presence of an external midden. Few whale bones were present. The majority of the bone material was found in the centre and southeast floor and consisted of walrus remains. A secondary component consisted of bearded seal. Bones from animals smaller than this generally were not preserved. If whalebones had been used as structural elements in the house, neither they nor their traces were found. Such remains may have been removed for use in other houses, or had been consumed by caribou, which we have seen eating architectural whalebones at Neoeskimo sites on a number of occasions.

The absence of whale bones and whaling gear and the presence of walrus and sealing harpoon blades suggests that the latter were the primary economic resources of the Staffe Island 1 Thule occupation. Undoubtedly smaller seals and other small mammals and birds were utilized but have not been preserved. Not surprisingly this economy is similar to that noted for the Avayalik Island Middle Dorset site: late winter, spring, and early summer *sina* and open-water hunting for walrus, seals, waterfowl, and seabirds.

Radiocarbon Dating

Dates from Staffe Island (Table 3) indicate two periods of Dorset occupation: Middle Dorset

Table 3 Radiocarbon dates from Staffe Island I (JaDb-2) and other Thule sites in northern and central Labrador.

Lab. no.	Unit	Year	Material	Culture	B.P. Age	Calib. Range (2 sigma)	Average
SI-3396	SI House 7	1977	char. (conif.)	Dorset	1560±95	AD 256-650	AD 475
B-33047	SI House 10	1989	char. (conif.)	Thule	870±70	AD 1000-1280	AD 1170
B-33046	SI House 10	1989	char. (conif.)	Thule	740±50	AD 1208-1384	AD 1277
SI-3891	SI House 9	1978	wood (conif.)	Thule	675±70	AD 1220-1410	AD 1283
B-40406	SI H14, TP2	1989	char. (con.)[1]	Dorset	670±130	AD 1039-1450	AD 1283
B-33045	SI H14, TP 1	1989	wood	Thule	630±60	AD 1263-1420	AD 1340
SI-3365	Nunain. mid.	1977	moss[2]	Thule	520±110	AD 1280-1650	AD 1415
SI-3898	Komaktor. H7	1978	charcoal[3]	Thule	420±80	AD 1329-1650	AD 1443
B-22400	Snack Cove Area 1	1986	char. (conif.)[4]	Thule	360±100	AD 1333-1490	AD 1440
B-40401	Snack Cove Area 3	1987	char. (conif.)[4]	Thule	300±80	AD 1430-1637	AD 1552, 1637
----	Ikkusik H21	1972	char. (willow)[4]	Thule	275±90	AD 1440-1955	AD 1643

[1] blubber contamination present

[2] moss lens separating Dorset and Thule levels in midden between Houses 4 and 10

[3] Picea, salix, alnus; possible Dorset contamination

[4] Fitzhugh 1986: 168, Fitzhugh 1987a

ca. A.D. 475 (calibrated) from a test pit in House 7, and Late Dorset ca. A.D. 1283 from the midden outside House 14. On the basis of these dates and stratigraphic evidence from Test Pit 2 in the House 14 midden, Late Dorset occupation appears to have continued virtually until the arrival of Thule people. Thule houses and levels at Staffe Island date to A.D. 1283 (House 9), A.D. 1170-1277 (House 10), and A.D. 1340 (House 14 midden). The 2-sigma range for all Thule dates from Staffe Island falls between A.D. 1039 and 1410.

House Structure and Spatial Patterns

The House 10 floor plan is similar to early Thule dwelling plans known from other areas of the Eastern Arctic. Its single inner room is subrectangular in shape, measures 4 x 4 m, and had been excavated to a depth of 50-70 cm below the surrounding ground surface. Access to the house was from the southwest via a 2.5 m long flagstone-paved entrance tunnel. All internal areas of the house were covered with paving slabs, loosely placed on the platform but more carefully laid on the floor. The floor and passage had two and sometimes three pavement levels. Large rectangular blocks lined the passage walls while inclined slabs served as house wall retainers. A jumble of slabs found above the west side of the passage appeared to have lined a small niche in the wall. The most clearly defined internal feature was the carefully paved front edge of the sleeping platform and the 80 cm high roof support pillar found inside the rear wall. No niches were found under the sleeping platform. Charcoal stains on a raised soil platform in the southwest corner suggested a lamp-stand or hearth. Walrus and bearded seal bones were mostly confined to the southeast corner

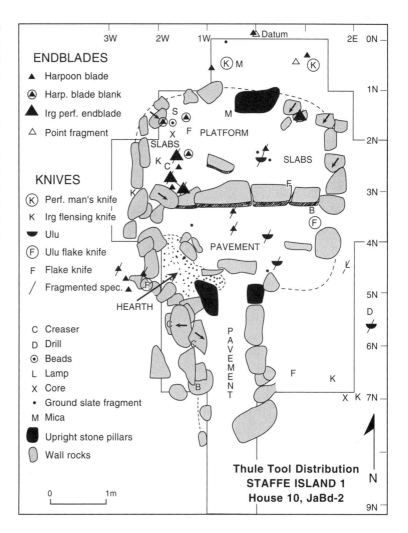

Figure 7 Staffe Island 1 House 10 distribution map.

of the house above and beneath slab pavements. A pile of large rocks outside the east wall of the passage, with bone inclusions, was probably a meat cache. On the whole the house was remarkably intact, with little evidence of rock scavenging or post-occupation disturbance common at Thule settlements. A thin boneless midden containing intermingled Thule and Dorset materials lay outside the entrance passage.

The distribution of artifacts and debitage (Fig. 7, 8 and 9) gives a clear idea of construction history and use. With few exceptions, Thule artifacts and slate debitage were confined to the interior, except for a group of harpoon endblades outside the southwest wall and points and knives outside the rear wall. Dorset artifacts and Ramah Chert flakes were found sporadically in the Thule occupation layer, but were encountered mostly near the walls, suggesting their origin from the Dorset midden into which the house had been excavated. It seems likely that the Thule house had been prepared by

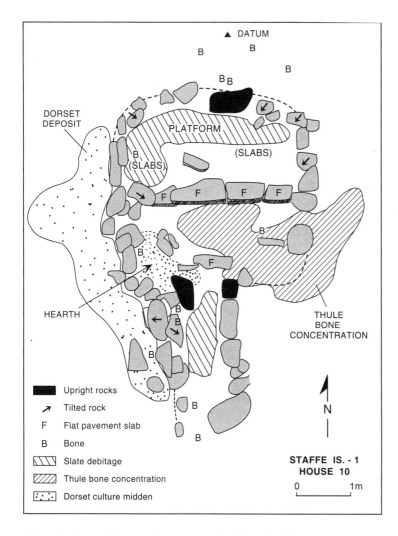

Figure 8 House 10 excavation plan and artifact distribution.

deepening a shallow Dorset structure and using artifact-rich Dorset sods as construction material for the wall's low foundation. Few artifacts were found in the shallow Thule midden outside the entrance passage. This, together with the general paucity of Thule finds inside, suggests that House 10 was occupied by a single small family for a brief period, perhaps only a season or two.

House 10 was probably part of a small thirteenth to fourteenth century early Thule settlement that included four or five houses of the Middle Group house cluster. A number of architectural features suggest it was not a fall-early winter village site. In addition to the seasonality and faunal evidence cited above, House 10 is shallow; lacks sod and rock walls and a cold trap; has thin floor deposits and low densities of artifacts, lithic production debris, and soapstone vessel remains; and lacks extensive bone deposits, heavily oil-stained hearth and lamp areas, and deep middens. While these features could result from a brief occupation they suggest this house may have been a skin-covered *qarmat* and not a sod and earth-covered structure early winter structure. As such it could have been a winter-spring phase of a regional settlement pattern that included fall and winter dwelling at sites in the Killinek region.

Social and Technological Patterns

The following spatial patterns reflect the organization of some work activities at House 10 Staffe Island: (1) Food-processing activities seem to have been confined largely to the east floor as evidenced by the concentration of bone remains and ulu fragments. This may have been the principal domain of the mistress of the house. (2) One would expect the lamp-stand to be on the woman's side of the house. We were unable to ascertain its location, but a fragment of a Thule lamp was recovered in the southeast house corner near the ulu fragments. Charcoal stains in the southwest corner may indicate a cooking or lamp area. (3) Almost without exception, harpoon and lance points, flensing knives, and slate blanks were recovered on the west platform. Here we also found the highest concentration of slate debitage, broken implements, and slate raw materials. Why a group of harpoon points was found outside the southwest wall is more difficult to explain. (4) Two of the three boot-creasers recovered came from a niche-like area in the west wall of the passage that may have served as a "mud room". (5) The absence of large volumes of slate debitage or grindstones suggests that this home was not the scene of primary implement production. Rather, the slate debitage occurred as small flakes (n=428) and in small quantities (788 g), indicating tool rejuvenation rather than primary production. The weight of an average slate flake was 1.8 grams. Only three slate cores were recovered, two of soft red slate and one of soft black slate. Flakes of hard silicified slate and nephrite were rarely found. Tool maintenance rather than tool production is indicated.

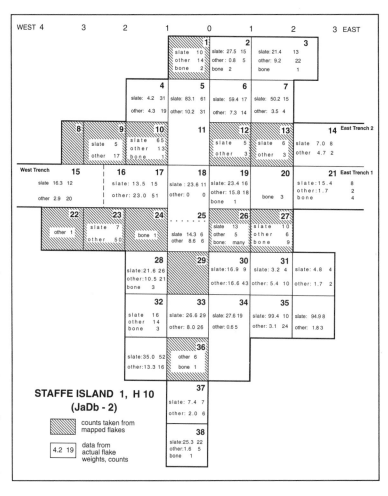

Figure 9 House 10 debitage distribution.

Comparisons

Comparison of House 10 with other Thule sites in Labrador is difficult because no other Thule houses have been fully excavated. Staffe Island dwellings, with their rectangular shape and short entrances, closely resemble the earliest houses excavated by Bird in Hopedale (Bird 1945). General parallels are also found with Thule houses in Saglek (Schledermann 1971), along the Torngat coast (Kaplan 1983: 216-230, 1985a, 1985b), and in eastern and southern Baffin Island (Schledermann 1975; Stenton 1987; Sabo 1991; Gullason et al. 1993). None of these sites exhibit the rounded forms of the earliest Thule houses in the Eastern Arctic (e.g. Holtved 1944, 1954; McGhee 1984; McCullough 1989). Lacking harpoon heads to provide typological dating, we may only note that the radiocarbon dates appear reasonable for an occupation that on the basis of architecture and lithic artifact assemblage should be assigned to the Classic Thule phase. The presence of stone beads is unusual in a Thule site.

Comparison of radiocarbon dates with Thule dates from the Central Arctic assembled by Morrison (1989) suggests the Staffe Island sites were occupied toward the end of the Classic Thule period. The little artifactual and architectural (e.g. Hopedale) evidence available supports this view. Hence Thule people appear to have entered Labrador rather late compared to other areas of the Eastern Arctic.

An unexpected discovery in 1989 was that House 15 departed considerably from the form of other winter structures at this site (Fig. 10). This house lies apart from the rest of the village, west of a low rock ridge. Although techniques of construction - low sod walls, slab pavement, lintel door construction - were similar, its shape was oval, with the long axis perpendicular to the entrance tunnel. No platform lamp-stands or hearths were noted, and flat stone benches encircled the inside wall of the

structure. The most significant difference was the absence of a sleeping platform. The floor seemed to be more or less completely paved. The inner dimensions of the structure measured 4 x 4.5 m. A stone pillar (lamp-stand? roof support?) was placed at the rear of the house.

This house appears to be a dance hall (*kashim/karrigi*) similar to structures identified by McCartney (1977: 161) at Kamarvit, by McCullough (1989: 245) on Ellesmere Island, by Susan Rowley (personal communication) at Ungayuat in Igloolik, and by Susan Kaplan (personal communication) at a Thule spring whaling camp at Skull Island near Nain in 1987. Historical evidence of the use of *kashim* by Labrador Inuit has been presented by J. Garth Taylor (1990). The Skull Island

Figure 10 House 15 ceremonial structure.

house had high multi-tiered boulder walls, unlike the house at Staffe Island, but its interior bench arrangement and shape are similar. The presence of slate implements and debitage at the Skull Island house suggested it had been used for making implements as well as for holding rituals and ceremonies. Such functions are known for ethnographically described men's houses in Alaska and the Central Arctic (Nelson 1899: 285; Lantis 1946: 251). While we cannot predict what will be found in the Staffe Island dance house, we can imagine its importance in the social life of this early Thule community. J. Garth Taylor (1990: 52) reports that snowhouse *kashim* continued in use among Labrador Inuit until the early Moravian period (AD 1771-1800), often for feasting and ceremonies following hunting success and at least once at a time of starvation.

Conclusions

Summarizing 1977-78 work at Staffe Island 1, Kaplan (1983: 789-796) concluded that this site contained the remains of several short-lived early Thule villages that had been occupied long before the beginning of the historical era. Evidence of brief occupations included low tool densities, thin middens, lack of bone preservation, and thin house floor deposits. She noted that Dorset finds had become mixed with Thule deposits when Dorset houses had been remodelled by Thule people. The predominance of what appear to be exotic high-quality slates and nephrite suggested that Staffe Island Thule people retained access to Central Arctic or Baffin Island lithic sources through contacts with Thule groups in their original homelands. By the time Thule people had settled in the Nachvak area high-quality slates and nephrite were replaced largely by softer local materials. Kaplan also noted that Staffe Island's location was ideal for walrus, seal, and marine bird hunting, but lacked whaling potential and back-up resources for times of scarcity or bad weather. Building on her interpretation it now seems likely that the Staffe Island Thule economic adaptation was seasonal and specialized and represented a winter-spring walrus, seal, and bird-hunting camp whose fall-early winter settlements may lie in the McClelan Strait-Killinek-Bush Island region. Alternatively, Staffe Island may be part of a settlement system paired with the Nunaingok early winter site, with a second group occupying the Killinek-Bush Island region.

Analysis of the Staffe Island 1 settlement pattern provides new information about its history and use. The site's first occupants appear to have been Middle Dorset people who built a number of semi-subterranean sod houses here ca. AD 500. Late Dorset people occupied the site sometime between AD 1000-1300, building *qarmat* structures and creating midden dumps. Thule people appeared ca AD 1250, and between then and A.D. 1450 occupied a series of three Thule settlements corresponding to the major house groups at the site, each of which had three to five single-family dwellings. The absence of any sign of European material suggests that occupation of the site terminated before A.D. 1500-1550 when Thule sites with metal appear at Iglosiatic Island south of Nain (Susan Kaplan, personal communication) and in Hopedale. It is not possible at this time to establish the sequence of these occupations, but the Upper Group houses, with their multiple-roomed or "double" houses, are the best-preserved and probably latest.

The House 10 excavation sheds little light directly on the problem of Dorset-Thule relations in northern Labrador. Dorset implements found in the Thule level clearly originated from the surrounding Dorset midden or from recycled sod. No Dorset tools are made of "Thule" raw materials, and no Thule tools are made from identifiable "Dorset" materials like Ramah Chert or schist. If Dorset and Thule groups were in contact, there is as yet no evidence to support this from Staffe Island. Similarly, our work detected no evidence of contact with Point Revenge, or Late Prehistoric Period Indian groups, or with the Norse. This is expected, perhaps, since Point Revenge (prehistoric Innu) peoples lived south of the tree-line; and as for the Norse, the thirteenth century was not a time of frequent Vinland voyages. Nevertheless, future excavations at Staffe Island should be prepared for possible evidence of Norse contact.

Since at least six Late Dorset sites in northern Labrador have been dated to the period of Thule expansion south, ca. AD 1250-1500 (Kaplan 1983: 215-230), Dorset-Thule contacts must have been a factor in local Dorset-Thule succession. Even though direct evidence of such contact is slim and has not yet been identified at Staffe Island, overlapping radiocarbon dates from Late Dorset and Thule sites indicate that these cultures shared regions of northern Labrador for several hundred years before the Dorset culture disappeared archaeologically. The only evidence to date of direct contact is a Thule cache from Saglek containing both Late Dorset and Thule implements (Thomson 1993). In the absence of more evidence of culture exchange it appears Dorset and Thule people lived largely separate lives and interacted principally over territorial rights and resource use.

Detecting evidence of periods in prehistory when cultures meet and change, either by dramatic events such as warfare or by more gradual processes, may be more difficult to perceive than we might imagine, especially in the absence of organic preservation. Evidence from Labrador prehistory demonstrates many dramatic shifts in cultures and populations over thousands of years (Fitzhugh 1977, 1987a). For the most part, these changes are detected, not by battlefields, trade goods, or material evidence of acculturation, but as territorial gains or losses when one group expands and another retreats or "disappears". Perhaps this is the type of behaviour - territorial movements with little material culture transfer - to be expected of contacts between hunting peoples when their interests lie principally in increased access to territory and resources rather than to technology or economic, social, or political opportunities. Even though the Indian and Eskimo frontier was a highly dynamic one, with many territorial advances and reversals over a 4000 year period, acculturation does not become easily identifiable in Labrador archaeology until the beginning of the European era.

On the other hand, territorial shifts can be among the most rapid of all types of culture change and often require little or no technological and social innovation or intervention and few adjustments in pre-existing lifeways. The Thule expansion into Arctic Canada and Greenland are often cited in this regard (W. E. Taylor 1963; McGhee 1969/70; Maxwell 1985: 250; Morrison 1989). The movement of Thule culture south in Labrador appears slower by this scale, reaching Saglek by A.D. 1500 and Nain and Hopedale by ca. A.D. 1550. However, instances of rapid, deep southern Inuit probes are indicated by the Red Bay finds. That these incursions did not produce permanent residence in southern regions is probably due to the presence of Indian peoples who resisted Thule encroachment. When Thule/Inuit culture did appear on the central coast it is in the context of an oral history expressing Inuit-Tunit and Indian-Inuit avoidance, antagonism, or warfare reflecting the legacy of Inuit expansion from Killinek into central and southern Labrador by the early 1500s.

The Staffe Island excavations, although limited in extent, support the interpretation of a pioneering, technologically-advanced and economically diverse culture that established a bridgehead in Killinek ca. A.D. 1250 and soon afterward expanded southward. Staffe Island people themselves may not have been the first Thule pioneers to reach Killinek but they probably were among the first to utilize the rich resources south of McClelan Strait in Labrador. Staffe Island people may have been among the first Killinekers to seek new lands and whaling places in the south, as Kaplan (1983: 797) has suggested. Factors contributing to southern expansion may have involved the need to find new

Table 4   Staffe Island 1 (JaDb-2) Artifact Measurements.

Cat no.	Type no.	Length (mm)	Width (mm)	Thickness (mm)	Weight (g)	Material	Comments
Endblades							
164	1			2.5	0.5	gs	
173	1	24.5	24	3.5	2.4	bn	
177	1	(3)	27	3.2	3.4	gs	
182a	1		21.5	2.3	0.4	gs	
189	1	35.4	24.5	4.0	4.1	gs	
207	1			2.5	0.6	gs	
213	1			2.8	0.9	hgs	
223	1	36	28.5	3.5	4.3	hgs	
227	1	(34.5)	24.5	3.0	2.8	gs	
232	1				0.9	hgs	
244	1	(23)	31	3.0	3.1	hgs	
245	1				0.6	rs	
249	1			4.0	2.2	hgs	
255	1	(26.3)	21	3.5	2.4	hgs	
Mean:		31.97	25.25	3.15	3.6		
Harpoon Endblade Blanks							
175	2	42.5	4.5	28.0	7.3	gs	flaked
218	2	46.4	5.0	30.0	7.0	hgs	flaked
231	2	41.5	4.0	25.5	6.3	bn	
276	2	45.5	4.2	32.0	6.8	gs	flaked
Mean:		43.98	4.43	57.75	6.85		
Large Perforated Endblades							
202	3			4.5	6.4	hgs	lance blade
203	3				2.3	bgs	lance blade
229	3				2.8	hgs	lance blade
Mean:				4.5	3.83		
Arrowhead							
210	4	(10)	9	2.2	0.3	hgs	
Misc. Endblade Fragments							
245	5					gn	edge fragment

Cat no.	Type no.	Length (mm)	Width (mm)	Thickness (mm)	Weight (g)	Material	Comments
196	5					gnsl	edge fragment
192	5					rs	edge fragment
Endblade Preforms							
253	6	(35)	(41)	7.5	11.9	hgnsl	
256	6	(44)	16.2	(32.5)	9.5	hgnsl	stem fragment
Mean:	6		16.2	7.5	10.7		
Pocket Knives							
171	7	(26.8)	19.2	3.2	2.7	gs	
214	7	(26.2)	20.0	2.8	2.2	gs	
185	7	(38)	20.0	2.8	4.4	bksl	blank
Mean:	7		19.73	2.93	3.1		
Butcher Knives							
176	8			tapers	3.6	hgs	
187	8			tapers	2.2	gs	
188	8			6.0	6.7	gs	
Mean:	8				4.17		
Large Flensing Knife							
217	9	(53)	(51)	(9)	25.1	rs	.
Ulus							
234	10	(18.8)	(18.5)	3.5	1.3	hgs	corner fragment
235	10	(71.5)	(38.3)	3.8	14.2	bgs	half
240	10	(38.8)	(50.0)	4.0	9.9	hgs	
251	10	(35.7)	(22)	3.7	3.1	bks	3 perforations
Mean:				3.75	7.13		
Flake Ulu							
224	11				5.7	hgs	made on spall
226	11				13.1	hgs	made on spall
Mean:					9.4		
Sideblade Knives							
226	12	35	22	2.7	2.9	gs	
233	12	(34)	18	3.0	3.1	gnsl	
Mean:		35	20	2.85	3.0		
Straight Edged Flake Knives							
237	13	41	23.3	4.0	3.9	bksl	

Cat. no.	Type no.	Length (mm)	Width (mm)	Thickness (mm)	Weight (g)	Material	Comments
246	13	81	35	7.0	26.7	bksl	
258	13	50.5	31.5	2.8	5.2	hgnsl	
275	13	51.8	29.3	3.5	4.6		
Mean:		56.08	29.78	4.33	10.1		
Skin Working Tools							
159	14	19	5.0	4.5	0.5	gn	
161	14	38.5	10.5	3.8	2.3	gsl	
186	14	30.5	10.8	3.5	1.6	gnsl	
Mean:		29.33	8.77	3.93	1.47		
Needle							
293	15	45.6	6.0	3.0	1.0	gn	tip broken
Drill							
225	16	17.6	10.0	3.6	0.5	gn	tip broken
Perforated Beads							
205	17	8	8	3.8	0.3	soapstone	
247	17	11	10	3.6	0.7	rs	
Mean:		9.5	9.0	3.7	0.5		
Lamp							
200	18	50	39.9		32.4	soapstone	corner fragment
Cores							
206	19	104	60	40	280.5	rs	
242	19				595.2	bs	2 fragsments
280	19	180	51	11.2	102.1	gs	
281	19	90	55	21	149.8	rs	
Mean:		124.7	55.3	72.2	281.9		

Key

Material: bn (black nephrite); gn (green nephrite); hgs (hard green slate); gs (grey slate); bgs (banded green slate); dgs (dark green slate); rs (red slate); gnsl (green slate).

brackets (): incomplete measurement, specimen is broken; not included in statistics.

hunting grounds for a growing population and replacement sources for materials like soapstone, slate, nephrite, wood, and other products obtained previously through northern Thule networks; or perhaps just the thrill of exploring new lands. Social fragmentation and community fission, the need for new whaling grounds, and European trading opportunities have been stressed as factors in the rapid expansion of Labrador Thule culture (J. G. Taylor 1974: 89; Jordan and Kaplan 1980; Kaplan 1983). It is easy to imagine that, having rounded Cape Kakkiviak and perceiving the amazing rows of superimposed headlands receding southwards, cape after marvellous cape, the urge to explore this new land would have been irresistible for a group of enterprising Thule explorers even if this meant competition and challenge. While these early Labradorians must have had knowledge of northern Labrador Dorset people, they could not have imagined their travels would lead them far south into forested Innu lands, and beyond, to discover the pioneering settlements of an even stranger people, European Basques, who had travelled nearly as far from Europe as Thule people had from Bering Strait, both following whales.

Acknowledgments

Excavations at Staffe Island were made possible by grants from the Smithsonian Institution Scholarly Studies Program and funds from the Arctic Studies Program. Excavation permits were granted by the Newfoundland Museum/Division of Historic Resources. Thanks is due to our project team of Mark Allston, Bruce Bourque, Peter Clark, Carolyn Maybee, Andris Slapins, and Pitsiulak skipper, Perry Colbourne and crew Sophie Morse. Drawings were prepared by Marcia Bakry; photgraphs by Victor Krantz. Analytical assistance was provided by Carla Favreau. Tori Oliver assisted manuscript preparation. Stephen Loring contributed to subsistence and settlement ideas. I also thank the volume editors for comment and suggestions on improving the initial draft.

References Cited

Auger, R. 1985. The Inuit in the Strait of Belle Isle. In, Archaeology in Newfoundland and Labrador, Annual Report, 5, J. Sproull Thomson, ed. Historic Resources Division, Government of Newfoundland and Labrador, pp. 272-293.

Auger, R. 1991. Labrador Inuit and Europeans in the Strait of Belle Isle: from the written sources to the archaeological evidence. Quebec: Centre d'Etudes Nordiques.

Bielawski, E. 1979 Contactual transformations: the Dorset-Thule succession. In, Thule Eskimo Cutlure: an anthropological retrospective, A. P. McCartney, ed. National Museum of Man, Mercury Series, Archaeological Survey of Canada Paper, 88: 100-109.

Bird, J. B. 1945. Archaeology of the Hopedale area, Labrador. Anthropological Papers of the American Museum of Natural History, 39(2).

Clermont, N. 1980. Les Inuits du Labrador meridionale avant Cartwright. Etudes/Inuit/Studies, 4(1-2): 147-166.

Collins, H. B. 1937. Archaeology of St. Lawrence Island, Alaska. Smithsonian Miscellaneous Collections, 96(1).

Collins, H. B. 1957. Archaeological investigations on Southampton and Walrus Islands, N.W.T. National Museum of Canada Bulletin, 147: 22-61.

Cox, S. 1977. Prehistoric settlement and culture change at Okak, Labrador. Unpublished PhD dissertation, Department of Anthropology, Harvard University. Cambridge.

Cox, S. 1978. Paleo-Eskimo occupations of the north Labrador coast. Arctic Anthropology, 15(2): 96-118.

Cox, S. and A. Spiess. 1980. Dorset settlement and subsistence in northern Labrador. Arctic, 33(3): 659-669.

Fitzhugh, W. 1967. The Dorset-Thule transition: studies in culture change. Seminar paper, Department of Anthropology, Harvard University.

Fitzhugh, W. 1972. Environmental Archeology and Cultural Systems in Hamilton Inlet, Labrador. Smithsonian Contributions to Anthropology, 16.

Fitzhugh, W. 1976. Preliminary culture history of Nain, Labrador: Smithsonian Fieldwork for 1975. Journal of Field Archaeology 3: 123-145.

Fitzhugh, W. 1977. Population movement and culture change on the central Labrador coast. Annals of the New York Academy of Sciences, 288: 481-497.

Fitzhugh, W. 1978. Winter Cove 4 and the Point Revenge occupation of the Central Labrador Coast. Arctic Anthropology 15(2):146-174.

Fitzhugh, W. 1980a. A review of Paleo-Eskimo culture history in southern Labrador and Newfoundland. Etudes/Inuit/Studies, 4(1-2): 21-31.

Fitzhugh, W. 1980b. Preliminary report on the Torngat Archaeological Project. Arctic, 33(3): 585-606.

Fitzhugh, W. 1981. A prehistoric caribou caribou fence from Williams Harbour, northern Labrador. In, Megaliths to Medicine Wheels: Boulder Structures in Archaeology, M. Wilson, K. Roads and K. Hardy, eds. Calgary: University of Calgary Archaeological Association, pp. 187-206.

Fitzhugh, W. 1986. Hamilton Inlet and Cartwright Reconnaissance. In, <u>Archaeology in Newfoundland and Labrador, Annual Report</u>, 7. C. Thomson and J. Sproull Thomson, eds. Historic Resources Division, Government of Newfoundland and Labrador, pp. 164-181.

Fitzhugh, W. 1987a. Archaeological ethnicity and the prehistory of Labrador. In, <u>Ethnicity and Culture</u>, R. Auger, M. Glass, S. MacEachern, and P. McCartney, eds. Calgary: University of Calgary Archaeological Association, pp. 141-153.

Fitzhugh, W. 1987b. Surveys on the Central Labrador Coast, 1987. MS on file with the Newfoundland Museum, St. John's, Newfoundland.

Gullason, L., A. Henshaw and W. Fitzhugh. 1993. Preliminary report on excavations at Kuyait (JfDf-2) and Kamaiyuk (KfDe-5), Frobisher Bay, Baffin Island, N.W.T. In, <u>The Meta Incognita Project: contributions to field studies</u>, S. Alsford, ed. Canadian Museum of Civilization, Mercury Series, Directorate Paper, 6: 176-198.

Hantzsch, B. 1928-1932. Contributions to the knowledge of the avifauna of north-eastern Labrador; and Contributions to the knowledge of extreme north-eastern Labrador. <u>Canadian Field-Naturalist</u>, 41-46.

Harp, E. 1974. A Late Dorset copper amulet from southeastern Hudson Bay. <u>Folk</u>, 11-12: 109-124.

Hawkes, E. W. 1916. <u>The Labrador Eskimo</u>. Department of Mines, Geological Survey Memoir 91.

Holtved, E. 1944. Archaeological investigations in the Thule District. <u>Meddelelser om Gronland</u> 141.

Holtved, E. 1954. Archaeological investigations in the Thule District (Part 3): Nugdlit and Comer's Midden. <u>Meddelelser om Gronland</u> 146.

Hutton, S. K. 1912. <u>Among the Eskimos of Labrador</u>. London: Seeley Service.

Jordan, R. 1978. Archaeological investigations of the Hamilton Inlet Labrador Eskimo: social and economic responses to European contact. <u>Arctic Anthropology</u>, 15(2): 175-185.

Jordan, R. and S. Kaplan. 1980. An archeological view of the Inuit/European contact period in Central Labrador. <u>Etudes/Inuit/Studies</u>, 4(1-2): 35-45.

Kaplan, S. 1980. Neoeskimo occupations of the Northern Labrador coast. <u>Arctic</u>, 33(3): 646-658.

Kaplan, S. 1983. <u>Economic and social change in Labrador Neoeskimo culture</u>. Unpublished PhD dissertation, Bryn Mawr College.

Kaplan, S. 1985a. Eskimo-European contact archaeology in Labrador, Canada. In, <u>Comparative studies in the archaeology of colonialism</u>, S. Dyson, ed. British Archaeological Reports, International Series, 233: 53-76.

Kaplan, S. 1985b. European goods and socio-economic change in early Labrador Inuit society. In, Cultures in Contact: the European impact on Native cultural institutions in Eastern North America, A.D. 1000-1800. W. Fitzhugh, ed. Washington: Smithsonian Institution Press, pp. 45-69.

Lantis, M. 1946. The social culture of the Nunivak Eskimo. Philadelphia: The American Philosophical Society.

Leechman, D. 1950. Eskimo Summer. Toronto: Museum Press.

Loring, S. 1988. Keeping things whole: nearly two thousand years of Indian (Innu) occupations in northern Labrador. In, Boreal Forest and Sub-Arctic Archaeology, C.S. Reid, ed. Occasional Publications of the London Chapter, Ontario Archaeological Society, 6,: 157-182.

Lorsing, S. 1992. Princes and Princesses of ragged fame: Innu (Naskapi) archeology and ethnohistory in Labador. Unpublished PhD dissertation, University of Massachusetts.

McCartney, A. P. 1977. Thule Eskimo prehistory along northwestern Hudson Bay. National Museum of Man, Mercury Series, Archaeological Survey of Canada Paper, 70.

McCullough, K. 1989. The Ruin Islanders: early Thule culture pioneers in the Eastern High Arctic. Canadian Museum of Civilization, Mercury Series, Archaeological Survey of Canada Paper, 141.

McGhee, R. 1969/70. Speculations on climate change and Thule culture development. Folk, 11/12: 153-184.

McGhee, R. 1984. The Thule village at Brooman Point, High Arctic Canada. National Museum of Man, Mercury Series, Archaeological Survey of Canada Paper, 125.

Martijn, C. 1980. La presence Inuit sur la Cote-Nord du Golfe St. Laurent a l'Epoque historique. Etudes/Inuit/Studies, 4(1-2): 105-125.

Maxwell, M. 1960. An archaeological analysis of eastern Grant Land, Ellesmere Island, Northwest Territories. National Museum of Canada Bulletin 180: 20-55.

Maxwell, M. 1985. Prehistory of the Eastern Arctic. New York: Academic Press.

Meldgaard, J. 1960a. Origin and evolution of Eskimo cultures in the Eastern Arctic. Canadian Geographical Journal, 60(2): 64-75.

Meldgaard, J. 1960b. Prehistoric culture sequences in the Eastern Arctic as elucidated by stratified sites at Igloolik. In, Selected Papers of the Fifth International Congress of Anthropological and Ethnological Sciences, A. Wallace, ed. Philadelphia: University of Pennsylvania Press, pp. 588-595

Meldgaard, J. 1962. On the formative period of the Dorset culture. In, Prehistoric relations between the Arctic and Temperate zones of North America, J. M. Campbell, ed. Arctic Institute of North America Technical Paper, 11: 92-95.

Morrison, D. 1989. Radiocarbon dating Thule culture. Arctic Anthropology, 26(2): 48-77.

Nagle, C. 1984. Lithic raw materials procurement and exchange in Dorset culture along the Labrador coast. Unpublished PhD dissertation, Brandeis University.

Nelson, E. W. 1899. The Eskimo Around Bering Strait. Eighteenth Annual Report of the Bureau of American Ethnology for the Years 1896-1897.

O'Bryan, D. 1953. Excavation of a Cape Dorset Eskimo house site, Mill Island, West Hudson Strait. National Museum of Canada Bulletin, 128: 40-57.

Odess, D. 1993. Paleoeskimo research in outer Frobisher Bay, 1993. Appendix to, Meta Incognita Project: Archeology of the Frobisher Voyages. Field Report for 1993, W. Fitzhugh, ed. Washington: Arctic Studies Center, Smithsonian Institution.

Park, R. 1993. The Dorset-Thule succession in arctic North America: assessing claims for culture contact. American Antiquity, 58(2): 203-234.

Plumet, P. and P. Gangloff. 1991. Contribution a l'archeologie et l'ethnohistoire de l'Ungava Oriental. Paleo-Quebec, 19.

Rowley, G. 1940. The Dorset culture of the Eastern Arctic. American Anthropologist, 42(3): 490-499.

Sabo, G. 1991. Long term adaptations among Arctic hunter-gatherers: a case study from southern Baffin Island. New York: Garland Press.

Schledermann, P. 1971. The Thule tradition in northern Labrador. Unpublished MA thesis, Memorial University of Newfoundland.

Schledermann, P. 1975. Thule Eskimo prehistory of Cumberland Sound, Baffin Island, Canada. National Museum of Man, Mercury Series, Archaeological Survey of Canada Paper, 38.

Spiess, A. 1978. Zooarchaeological evidence bearing on the Nain area Middle Dorset settlement-subsistence cycle. Arctic Anthropology, 15(2): 48-60.

Spiess, A. 1986. The biological basis for archeological fauna interpretation in Labrador. MS on file with the Arctic Studies Center, Department of Anthropology, Smithsonian Institution.

Stenton, D. 1987. Recent archaeological investigations in Frobisher Bay, Baffin Island, N.W.T. Canadian Journal of Archaeology, 11: 13-48.

Taylor, J. G. 1974. Labrador Eskimo settlements of the early contact period. National Museum of Man, Publications in Ethnology, 9.

Taylor, J. G. 1980. The Inuit of southern Quebec-Labrador: reviewing the evidence. Etudes/Inuit/Studies, 4(1-2): 185-194.

Taylor, J. G. 1990. The Labrador Inuit kashim (ceremonial house) complex. Arctic Anthropology, 27(2): 51-67.

Taylor, W. E. 1959. The mysterious Sadlermiut. The Beaver, 290: 26-33.

Taylor, W. E. 1963. Hypotheses on the origin of Canadian Thule culture. American Antiquity, 28: 456-464.

Thomson, C. 1986. Caribou Trail Archaeology: 1985 investigations in Saglek Bay and inner Saglek Fiord. In, Archaeology in Newfoundland and Labrador, Annual Report, 6. C. Thomson and J. Sproull Thomson, eds. Historic Resources Division, Government of Newfoundland and Labrador, pp. 9-53.

Thomson, C. 1988. Late Dorset shamanism at Shuldham Island, Northern Labrador. Unpublished MA thesis, Bryn Mawr College.

Thomson, C. 1993. Culture change in Saglek Bay, Northern Labrador. MS in possession of the author.

Tuck, J. and W. Fitzhugh. 1986. Palaeo-Eskimo traditions of Newfoundland and Labrador: a reappraisal. In, Palaeo-Eskimo Cultures in Newfoundland, Labrador and Ungava. Reports in Archaeology, 1: 161-168. Memorial University of Newfoundland.

Val, E. 1976. Inuit Land Use in the Port Burwell Area. In, Inuit Land Use and Occupancy Report, M. Freeman, ed. Ottawa: Department of Indian and Northern Affairs, vol. 1, pp. 121-124.

Vezinet, M. 1982. Occupation humaine de l'Ungava: perspective ethnohistorique et ecologique. Paleo-Quebec, 14.

The Importance of Wood in the
Early Thule Culture of the Western Canadian Arctic

Charles D. Arnold
Prince of Wales Northern Heritage Centre
Yellowknife, N.W.T.

Abstract

The Nelson River site on southern Banks Island is a Western Thule site dating to late in the first millennium A.D. The artifact assemblage from the site includes an abundance of well-made wooden tools. An examination of pottery and chipped stone tools show that these traits also have strong links to the availability and use of wood in the Western Arctic.

Résumé

Le site Nelson River, situé au sud de l'île Banks, represente une occupation thuléenne occidentale datant de la fin du premier millénaire A.D. L'assemblage d'artefacts provenant de ce site comprend une abondance d'outils en bois de bonne fabrication. Un examen de la poterie et des outils en pierre taillée révèle que ces traits distinctifs sont étroitement liés à l'usage du bois et à la facilité de s'en procurer dans l'ouest de l'Arctique.

Introduction

The archaeological record shows quite clearly that the Thule culture developed out of a Birnirk culture base in northern Alaska approximately 1000 years ago, although the processes involved in that transition are not well understood (Ford 1959; Stanford 1976; Giddings and Anderson 1986). Soon thereafter an eastward migration of people carried the Thule culture into the Canadian Arctic. Much of what is known of early Thule in the Canadian Arctic comes from archaeological sites situated at considerable distances from the Alaskan homeland, and in quite different environments. It is reasonable to suspect that these new environments quickly stimulated changes in economy, technology and perhaps even society, causing the early Canadian Thule to diverge from the culture of northern Alaska, where at least in its early phase it is referred to as Western Thule (Larsen and Rainey 1948; Giddings 1967). An important point along this trajectory of change which until recently has been missing from the archaeological record is evidence of early Thule culture in the western part of the Canadian Arctic. Archaeological sites in that area and from the appropriate time period could be expected to provide important details on changes that occurred as this ancestral Inuit culture began its eastward journey.

Threads of Arctic Prehistory: Papers in Honour of William E. Taylor Jr., David Morrison and Jean-Luc Pilon, eds. Canadian Museum of Civilization, Mercury Series, Archaeological Survey of Canada Paper 149. 1994.

In 1980 and 1981 excavations carried out near the mouth of the Nelson River on southern Banks Island on the western edge of the Canadian Arctic Archipelago provided information on the early post-expansion Thule culture (Arnold 1986). The archaeological remains from the site derive from people whose Birnirk roots were still strongly evident, and who differed in several significant ways from the Thule people who became established in the more easterly regions of the Arctic. Apart from stylistic elements, many of the traits which link the Nelson River assemblage to the Western Thule culture of Alaska and which distinguish it from eastern Canadian Thule are associated with a reliance on wood in the former area.

The Nelson River Site

Along the northern Yukon coast and continuing eastward for several hundred kilometres the earth's crust is gradually subsiding. Throughout much of this area ocean waves and currents are eroding the coastline, and at the same time removing the archaeological remains of people who lived close to the ocean's shore. This is in contrast with most areas in the Eastern Arctic where isostatic rebound resulting in the emergence of new coastlines from the ocean is more the norm. On Banks Island there is little evidence either for subsidence or rebound. Archaeological fieldwork was undertaken on the southern part of the island in 1980 and 1981 on the assumption that not only would the expansion of the maritime Thule culture have encompassed this area, which is rich in terrestrial and marine resources, but also that it is one of the most westerly regions in the Canadian Arctic where coastlines are stable enough to have preserved their archaeological remains. The Nelson River site (OhRh-1) is situated adjacent to the river of that name which empties into Amundsen Gulf on the southeastern coast of Banks Island (Fig. 1). The remains of a single house were found buried in a low sand ridge just above the reach of the high tides. The site was remarkably rich in archaeological remains, with more than 1400 artifacts and approximately 20,000 faunal elements recovered during the excavation of the structure and its associated midden.

Four radiocarbon dates, two of these on sedge matting from the house and two on associated terrestrial mammal bone, range from A.D. 820 $\pm$ 110 to 1060 $\pm$ 110. The four assays have a two-sigma average, calibrated for atmospheric C-14 fluctuations, of A.D. 991$\pm$101 which is very near the estimated date for the transition from Birnirk to Thule (Morrison 1989: 59). The close temporal proximity of the Nelson River archaeological site to Birnirk indicated by these radiocarbon dates is supported by stylistic attributes of certain artifacts, including harpoon heads, arrowheads and a needle case.

Several varieties of harpoon heads were found at the Nelson River site. Most are early Thule types, while a few are reminiscent of earlier time periods. Two are of the Sicco type (Ford 1959: 83). These harpoon heads flare slightly above and below the position of the line hole, giving them a constricted waist, and the body above the line hole is facetted when viewed in cross-section. One specimen is plain (Fig. 2, a), but the surface of the other although badly pitted has traces of decoration in the form of raised lines (Fig. 2, b). Sicco harpoon heads were once thought to be a hallmark of the earliest immigrants to the Canadian Arctic. They are now more properly recognized as being

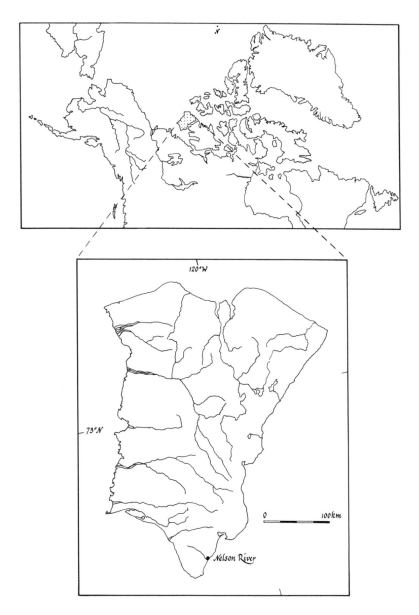

Figure 1 Location of the Nelson River archaeological site.

indicative of recent emigrants from Alaska, where this style is first found in sites which date to late in the first millennium AD and where it persisted for several centuries (Stanford 1976: 109; Giddings and Anderson 1986: 61). Two harpoon heads belong to the Natchuk type (Ford 1959: 83) which is defined by the presence of a single barb (Fig. 2, c). The edge opposite the barb on one of the Natchuk heads has a shallow groove. This is often interpreted to be an ornamental slot which provides continuity from earlier Neoeskimo harpoon heads that had stone blades inserted in their edges. The Natchuk harpoon head is most likely an ancestral form of the Thule type 2 head, one that is characteristic of Birnirk (Ford 1959: 83). Thule 2 harpoon heads are well represented in the assemblage, including one which has a bifurcated toggling spur and a vestigial third spur (Fig. 2, d) and the base of another with the vestige of a second spur (Fig. 2, e). Both bifurcated spurs and vestigial or ornamental spurs are traits which are reminiscent of pre-Thule forms found in Alaska (Ford 1959; Stanford 1976). Only a few arrowheads were recovered, but all have the rounded shoulders and knobbed tangs which were common through most of the Birnirk period and in early Thule (Stanford 1976: 112, Fig. 2, f). Included in the small collection of needle cases from the site is a decorated specimen with a 'winged' form which provides another link to Alaskan cultures (Fig. 2, g). The only other reported occurrence of this particular style in the Canadian Arctic is in Ruin Island phase sites on Ellesmere Island which are quite likely the remains of a

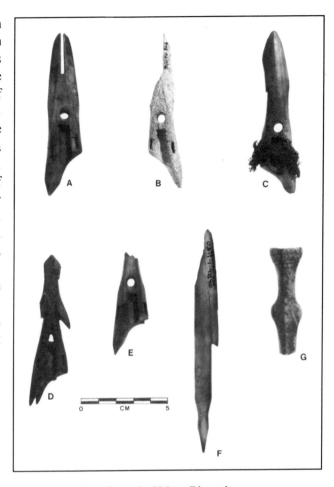

Figure 2 Artifacts from the Nelson River site.

later migration from Alaska (McCullough 1989). In Alaska winged needle cases have a considerable time depth, although McCullough (1989: 251) suggests that they originated in Birnirk.

In North Alaska, Birnirk and Thule are not sharply divided on stylistic grounds (Stanford 1976: 109). One of the functional traits that serves to separate the two cultural periods in that area and which was likely instrumental in the eastern expansion of Thule culture was the increased importance that hunting large whales played in the economy (McGhee 1969/70). In this respect the Nelson River assemblage should be considered allied to Thule culture since a preform for a whaling harpoon head was found, along with numerous artifacts made from baleen. However, there are a number of traits in the Nelson River assemblage which serve to distinguish it from the Thule culture as it is represented in the Central and Eastern Canadian Arctic. The most apparent of these traits are the architecture of the Nelson River house, pottery, a chipped stone tool industry and wood working.

Architecture

Beneath as much as a metre of overburden which had accumulated on top of the archaeological deposits were well-preserved architectural elements. These, together with the distribution of cultural debris and differences in soil texture, defined the configuration of a multi-roomed dwelling (Fig. 3).

The largest room of the dwelling complex had an earthen sleeping platform at the rear which was slightly elevated above the level of its planked floor. A small alcove situated at the front of the room on one side of the entrance may have been designed for a lamp. At the front on the other side was a jumble of fire-cracked rocks and charcoal cemented together by oil which appeared to be the floor of a cooking area, possibly a tent-like addition judging from the lack of structural supports surrounding it. A similar feature, also interpreted to be the remains of an attached tent used as a kitchen because of an outlining ring of stones, has been observed at the Co-op site on Victoria Island (Le Mouel 1987). Keeping the kitchen area separate from the main room is logical when burning driftwood in an open hearth for cooking. Not only would this have prevented smoke from polluting the main living chamber, it would also have reduced the risk of sparks setting fire to the wood used

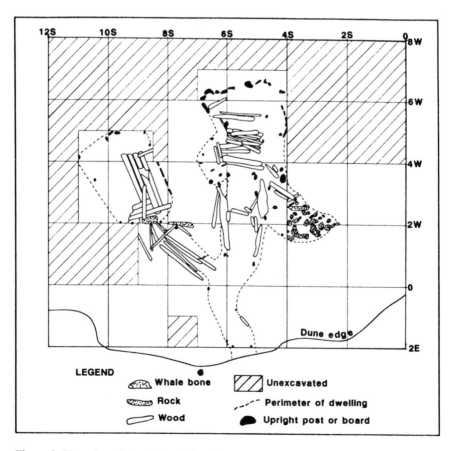

Figure 3 Plan view of the Nelson River house.

in the house.   Houses with separate kitchens are known from Alaska, but are rare in the Canadian Arctic.   One exception is the Ruin Island phase houses of northeastern Ellesmere Island and Greenland.   As was noted earlier, the Ruin Island remains probably relate to later emigrants from Alaska who found Siberian driftwood on the High Arctic shores when they first moved into that area (McCullough 1989).

Joining the sunken entrance way of the main chamber was the entrance to a smaller room which had no evidence of a raised sleeping bench.   Giddings and Anderson (1986: 110) suggest that similar features found in early Thule houses at Cape Krusenstern in western Alaska may have been workrooms, representing a variant of the *kagzi* associated in other areas with *umealiks*, or whaling captains, where men from several households would gather.   If so, this indicates that the Nelson River site may indeed have been part of a larger settlement, and that other houses formerly at the site have washed away.

Embedded below the original ground level were remnants of driftwood posts used as structural elements in the dwelling, and adzed planks set on end which formed the walls.   Layers of rotted timbers in the upper levels of the excavation were probably from the collapsed roof.   There was no evidence of whale bone having been used in the construction.   Extrapolating from historic period architecture, the driftwood shell of the Nelson River house was probably covered with an insulating layer of sod.   Fist- to head-sized boulders which do not occur naturally in the sandy matrix surrounding the archaeological site were common in the upper excavation levels, and may have been placed on the roof to weigh down the sod blocks.

Houses constructed from driftwood are the norm along the arctic coast of Alaska and in the western reaches of the Canadian Arctic where rivers flowing from the interior carry wood to the ocean.   In the Central and Eastern Arctic other materials, most commonly whale bone, were used for structural supports.   Whalebone houses from a slightly later time period are found within a few kilometres of the Nelson River site, showing that Banks Island was an area of overlap between these house building traditions.

Pottery

Pottery was used at the Nelson River site both for blubber lamps and for pots.   Two virtually complete lamps which were excavated are triangular in shape (Fig. 4).   No whole pots were found, but sherds indicate that at least some of the vessels had slightly flattened bases and flaring sides curving in to vertical necks and straight rims.   Surface decoration was limited to slight burnishing on some of the pots.

The Nelson River pottery was of poor quality.   Gross attributes of the pottery indicate that it had been fired at low temperatures and thin section analysis of the grain size, texture and internal formation of the clay used shows that it was lean and poorly developed.   The integrity of the pottery was further weakened by the addition of large quantities of organic and inorganic temper (Arnold and Stimmel 1983).

These attributes are characteristic of most Neoeskimo pottery in the Western Arctic.   The generally poor quality probably results from the lean clays found in most areas and from the necessity

Figure 4 Pottery lamp.

of having to use driftwood, which burns hot but not long, for firing the clay. Pottery was introduced by Thule people into the central and eastern regions of the Arctic during the initial and later expansionary phases from Alaska, but in those areas clays and driftwood are rare and pottery was quickly replaced by the more durable steatite which had been used by earlier Dorset and Pre-Dorset peoples for containers and lamps.

Chipped stone tools

Throughout the Neoeskimo period there was a general decline in technological skills for producing chipped stone tools, so that by the time the Thule culture had established itself in most parts of the Canadian Arctic stone tools were fashioned almost entirely by grinding. The Nelson River assemblage represents a point well along this trajectory, but the ability to make chipped stone tools was still part of the technological repertoire. Most are quite simple tools, and in most cases the process of making them was ruled more by expediency than concern for adhering to style; however, a close look shows that they probably served a number of important functions in the tool assemblage.

A large number of unaltered flakes, decortication spalls, and cores are present in the assemblage. One flake which would likely have escaped detection as a tool were it found alone remains hafted for use as a graver (Fig. 5, a). Some stone tools are evident only by the presence of use wear on the edges of flakes and cores (Fig. 5, b); on others there has been intentional retouch along their margins (Fig. 5, c). Some of these utilized and marginally retouched flakes and cores have rounded edges which may have been used for some of the steps involved in working hides. Others which have sharp edge angles ranging from acute to nearly 90 degrees had likely been used for various cutting and scraping functions.

Formed tools, which exhibit flaking directed towards modifying their overall shapes in addition to their edges, are less common in the Nelson River assemblage. Included are a variety of unifacial and bifacial scrapers (Fig. 5, d,e), and adzes

Figure 5 Artifacts from the Nelson River site.

which have been roughly chipped to shape from thick flakes and split cobbles (Fig. 5, f). A few adzes had been produced entirely by flaking, but most have been ground along their working edges.

In most Canadian Thule sites chipped stone tools were replaced by functional equivalents made by grinding slate. Slate tools are also well represented in the Nelson River assemblage, which suggests that the chipped stone tools may have been more efficient than ground slate for specific tasks. One possibility is that they were preferred for working wood.

Woodworking

An emphasis on woodworking is another of the traits that links the Nelson River assemblage to the Birnirk and Thule cultures of the Western Arctic, and one which distinguishes it from Thule in most eastern arctic locations. In the west, wood could have been obtained through trade or directly

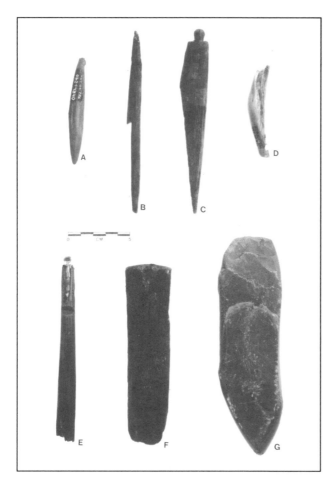

Figure 6 Artifacts from the Nelson River site.

from forests which in some areas closely approach the mainland coast, or from driftwood deposited on beaches. In most central and eastern arctic regions wood from any source is a rare commodity. On the mainland south of Banks Island the tree line dips sharply away from the coastal areas as one moves toward the east, and southern Banks Island is near the eastern limit of driftwood carried north by the Mackenzie River.

The importance of wood to the people who occupied the Nelson River site is indicated by the large number and variety of tools fashioned from that material. The assemblage includes artifacts such as sled runners, tool hafts and harpoon shafts which are relatively common throughout the Thule area. In addition there are items which in the Eastern Arctic were more commonly fabricated from harder organic materials, including leister barbs (Fig. 6, a), projectile points (Fig. 6, b) and harpoon heads. Some of these may have been made as toys or models, but there is no reason why some could not have been used as functional tools.

The value placed upon wood at the Nelson River site is also indicated by the skill with which it was worked. A good example of the superb wood working craftsmanship is seen in the manufacture of recurved bows, which required selection of strong, straight-grained wood, careful shaping, bending and joining. Most of the bows found at the site were made from several pieces of wood which had been mated along precisely cut splices (Fig. 6, c) that would have been extremely difficult to produce using modern tools, let alone the technology available to the Thule.

As mentioned, many of the chipped stone tools may have been related to woodworking. The adze blades are obvious examples, but some of the other utilized and retouched stone pieces may have been used for this purpose as well. In particular, blocky pieces or core fragments with steep edge angles displaying use retouch such as that shown in Figure 5, b would have been useful for fashioning wood artifacts. The edges of this and similar pieces are sharp enough to reduce wood to shape, yet would not blunt easily nor are they sharp enough to bite into the grain of the wood which could ruin the tool being fabricated. A variety of organic artifacts were probably also used for woodworking, including tools made from bear teeth which may have served as chisels or gravers (Fig. 6, d). These come in a variety of forms, the common attribute being ground facets at their working ends. Although there is no direct indication what these were used for, as a softer organic material wood seems to be a likely candidate. Caribou tooth chisels also were found (Fig. 6, e), as well as bone (Fig. 6, f), antler and stone (Fig. 6, g) wedges which quite likely had been used for working wood.

Taylor's Contributions to an Understanding of Early Thule Culture

In an article published thirty years ago, William E. Taylor (1963) predicted that important clues to the origin of the Thule culture were to be found in the western Canadian Arctic. To develop this thesis, Taylor presented a series of linked hypotheses expressing the idea that Thule culture did not appear fullblown in the Canadian Arctic, but instead developed out of an earlier Birnirk phase which extended east from Alaska along the Beaufort Sea coast as far as Amundsen Gulf.

Taylor's ideas were based more on intuitive reasoning than on hard data, as the archaeology of the western Canadian Arctic was poorly known at that time. However, the Nelson River assemblage demonstrates that Taylor was not far wrong in his thinking. The archaeological evidence from the site shows that the people who lived there were temporally and culturally close to Birnirk, and were it not for evidence of whaling Nelson River might as easily be considered a late Birnirk as an early Thule site. Taylor predicted correctly that the early Neoeskimo intrusions into the Canadian Arctic would differ in several important ways from the Thule culture that became established in the central and eastern regions. Data from the Nelson River site give a glimpse at those differences, which include driftwood architecture, pottery, chipped stone tools and a highly developed woodworking technology. All of these traits are predicated on the abundant presence of driftwood.

Perhaps in part due to coastal erosion, sites demonstrating continuities in Western Thule in the western Canadian Arctic are rare. The Jackson and Vaughn sites near Cape Parry excavated by Taylor (1972) in 1963, the as-yet unreported Pearce Point site which he investigated more recently, and the Co-op site on Victoria Island (Le Mouel 1987) are among the few other candidates for Western Thule sites, but the trail leading from there to the historic Inuit occupants of the western Canadian Arctic remains obscure. Meanwhile, the continued eastward expansion took the Thule people into areas where wood was more difficult to obtain. As access to wood diminished pottery, wooden tools and woodworking technology decreased in importance and new traits were adopted in their place. These processes contributed in no small way to the differences which developed between Western and Canadian Thule cultures.

References

Arnold, C. D. 1986. In search of the Thule pioneers. In, Thule Pioneers, E. Bielawski, C. Kobelka and R. Janes, eds. Occasional Papers of the Prince of Wales Northern Heritage Centre, 2: 1-93.

Arnold, C.D. and C. Stimmel. 1983. An analysis of Thule pottery. Canadian Journal of Archaeology, 7(1): 1-21.

Ford, J. A. 1959. Eskimo Prehistory in the Vicinity of Point Barrow, Alaska. Anthropological Papers of the American Museum of Natural History, 47(1).

Giddings, J.L. 1967. Ancient Men of the Arctic. New York: Alfred A. Knopf.

Giddings, J.L. and D. D. Anderson. 1986. Beach Ridge Archaeology of Cape Krusenstern. National Parks Service Publications in Archaeology, 20.

Larsen, H. and F. Rainey. 1948. Ipiutak and the Arctic Whale Hunting Culture. Anthropological Papers of the American Museum of Natural History, 42.

Le Mouel, J.-F. 1987. Co-op Project: The 1986 summer campaign. MS on file with the Prince of Wales Northern Heritage Centre, Yellowknife.

McCullough, K. 1989. The Ruin Islanders. Canadian Museum of Civilization, Mercury Series, Archaeological Survey of Canada Paper, 141.

McGhee, R. 1969/70. Speculations on climatic change and Thule culture development. Folk, 11-12: 173-184.

Morrison, D. 1989. Radiocarbon dating the Thule culture. Arctic Anthropology, 26(2): 48-77.

Stanford, D. J. 1976. The Walakpa Site, Alaska. Smithsonian Contributions to Anthropology, 20.

Taylor, W. E., Jr. 1963. Hypotheses on the origin of Canadian Thule culture. American Antiquity, 28(4): 456-64.

Taylor, W. E., Jr. 1972. An archaeological survey between Cape Parry and Cambridge Bay, N.W.T., Canada in 1963. National Museum of Man, Mercury Series Archaeological Survey of Canada Paper, 1.

Thule Inuit Bowhead Whaling: A Biometrical Analysis

James M. Savelle
McGill University
Montreal, Quebec

and

Allen P. McCartney
University of Arkansas
Fayetteville, Arkansas

Abstract

Bowhead whale bones associated with Thule Inuit archaeological sites in the central Canadian Arctic are the focus of an ongoing study to compare hunted whales with those of the Davis Strait stock from which they were derived. In 1978 and 1988, we recorded all bowhead bones and measured crania, mandibles, scapulae, and cervical vertebrae at Thule sites on six adjacent islands near the western terminus of the Davis Strait bowhead summer range. This data set was expanded in 1990-1993 to include additional measured whale bones from Thule sites and from natural stranding localities. The overall bowhead mortality profiles based on the measurements are compared with modern live and Holocene stranded bowhead populations. Further, regional variation in Thule-derived mortality profiles are examined through the delineation of three whaling zones: core, intermediate, and peripheral. The results suggest that (a) Thule bowhead exploitation was based on active hunting as opposed to scavenging of drift/beached carcasses, (b) hunting tended to be selective (for smaller, primarily yearling, whales) rather than random, and (c) the degree of selectivity was influenced by local environmental conditions, with the greatest selectivity evident in the core whaling region and the least in the peripheral whaling region.

Résumé

Les ossements de baleines boréales associés aux sites archéologiques d'Inuit thuléens dans le centre de l'Arctique canadien font l'objet d'une étude continue visant à comparer les baleines chassées à celles du détroit de Davis dont elles étaient issues. En 1978 et 1988, nous avons fait l'inventaire de tous les os de baleines boréales et mesuré les crânes, les mandibules, les omoplates et les vertèbres cervicales dans les sites thuléens qui se trouvent sur six îles adjacentes, près du point d'aboutissement ouest du banc estival de baleines boréales du détroit de Davis. Cet ensemble de données fut augmenté en 1990-1993 de manière à inclure d'autres ossements mesurés de baleines qui provenaient des sites thuléens et des lieux naturels d'échouage. Les courbes générales de mortalité de la baleine boréale qui

Threads of Arctic Prehistory: Papers in Honour of William E. Taylor Jr., David Morrison and Jean-Luc Pilon, eds. Canadian Museum of Civilization, Mercury Series, Archaeological Survey of Canada Paper 149. 1994.

sont basées sur ces mesures se comparent aux populations modernes de baleines boréales vivantes et à celles qui ont échoué durant la période holocène. En outre, la variation régionale qui marque les courbes de mortalité des populations issues de la période thuléenne est étudiée par le biais de la délimitation de trois zones de chasse à la baleine : centrale, intermédiaire et périphérique. Les résultats laissent supposer : a) que l'exploitation thuléenne de la baleine reposait sur une chasse intensive par opposition à la récupération de carcasses dérivées ou échouées; b) que la chasse avait tendance à être sélective (petites baleines, surtout baleineaux d'un an) plutôt qu'à se faire au hasard; c) que le degré de sélectivité était influencé par les conditions de l'environnement local, la sélectivité maximale étant manifeste dans la zone centrale de chasse à la baleine et minimale dans la zone périphérique de chasse à la baleine.

Introduction

Bowhead whales have been considered an integral part of Thule Inuit subsistence since Mathiassen (1927) initially described this arctic culture 65 years ago. However, Bill Taylor, in whose honour we contribute this paper, played an instrumental role during his own northern archaeological career in refining our understanding of Thule subsistence patterns. He located, excavated, and analyzed a number of Thule and other Neoeskimo sites throughout the Canadian Arctic (Taylor 1960, 1972; Taylor and McGhee 1979, 1981), sought the origins and described the nature of Thule Inuit occupations (Taylor 1963, 1968), and aided the investigation of Thule sites by others through his two principal administrative positions, Director of the National Museum of Man (now Canadian Museum of Civilization) and President of the Social Sciences and Humanities Research Council of Canada.

Of Taylor's many contributions to northern archaeology, we call attention to his 1966 article, "An Archaeological Perspective on Eskimo Economy," since it strongly influenced his own as well as subsequent generations of northern anthropologists. In that seminal paper, Taylor (1966) offered a number of observations on prehistoric Inuit subsistence and society. Of particular concern to the present study were the following points: (a) the Thule Inuit diet was varied, or "omnivorous," with the exploitation of different species reflecting environmental characteristics rather than an economic heritage (especially an inland or coastal adaptation), (b) flexibility was a fundamental characteristic, and this quality may have pervaded other aspects of Thule Inuit culture including social organization and religion, (c) Thule Inuit were rarely specialists, but rather were versatile in exploiting many ecological niches, (d) dependency upon or use of bowhead whales varied from region to region, and (e) food surpluses and a means of preserving and storing them were required.

We have attempted to incorporate these and related general points about the prehistoric Inuit economy into our own Thule research, especially that regarding bowhead whale hunting and use. For example, we have examined the articulation between the arctic environment, bowhead whale ranges, and Thule Inuit subsistence (McCartney and Savelle 1985), surplus production and storage (McCartney 1980a), subsistence-related factors shaping settlement, social organization, and, to an extent, religious aspects of Thule society (Savelle 1987; Savelle and McCartney 1988, 1990), specialist versus generalist Thule subsistence strategies (Savelle and McCartney 1988, 1991), and the creation and comparison of natural and human-derived bowhead mortality profiles (Savelle and McCartney 1991; for a chronological review of these Thule-bowhead studies, see McCartney and Savelle 1993).

While we recognize, with Taylor, that Thule Inuit were not specialists in the sense that they focused on only one or a very few species or focused on a coastal rather than an inland environment, we wish to emphasize here that Thule subsistence did require specialist knowledge and hunting techniques as these applied to the successful hunting of particular animals. Further, we hope to demonstrate that selective rather than random hunting took place in pursuing bowhead whales. We suggest that whaling, by virtue of the huge animals hunted, the bulk of food and materials derived from them, the logistic requirements and constraints imposed in harvesting, beaching, and processing individual whales, and transporting whale meat, muktuk, blubber, baleen and bones to caches and winter settlements, is a "specialist" or "collector" strategy in contrast to a "generalist" or "foraging" strategy (Winterhalder 1981; Binford 1980; for a discussion of Thule bowhead hunting as a "specialist" pursuit, see Savelle and McCartney 1988:37-39).

In this paper, we present multiple site data relating to Thule Inuit whaling in the central part of the Canadian Arctic Archipelago, north and south of Barrow Strait (Fig. l). Specifically, we examine the nature of the archaeological whale bone assemblages, quantities and sizes of bowheads used, and how these assemblages reflect Thule harvesting strategies. We have previously published overviews of some of these bowhead data (McCartney and Savelle 1985, 1993; Savelle and McCartney 1991). This paper updates these previous summaries through the addition of new data, and also presents for the first time site-by-site information which potentially would be of use to other northern archaeologists. In addition, while we have stressed the general relationship between central Canadian Arctic site locations and the historic bowhead range, and have described "core" versus "peripheral" bowhead summer ranges (Savelle and McCartney 1991), in this paper we use synoptic sea ice patterns to distinguish three rather than two zones for bowhead presence and Thule Inuit whaling: core, intermediate, and periphery.

Bowhead Whales in the Central Canadian Arctic

Bowhead or Greenland right whales (*Balaena mysticetus*) are the largest arctic sea mammals, growing to lengths of up to 18-20 m and weighing in excess of 60 tons (Eschricht and Reinhardt 1866; McVay 1973; Nerini et al. 1984; Reeves and Leatherwood 1985; Reeves 1991). Bowheads are often found near shore, are slow swimmers, and therefore may be approached by umiak or kayak. In addition, bowheads float well when killed, and thus are relatively easily towed to shore or the ice edge for processing. Finally, large amounts of meat, blubber, baleen, and bones may be taken from even small bowheads.

Bowheads seasonally migrate close to the ice edge, moving north into Davis Strait and Baffin Bay in May and June and continuing further west through Lancaster Sound, Barrow Strait, and Prince Regent Inlet in July (Ross and MacIver 1982; Reeves et al. 1983). As sea ice forms in the fall, the bowheads reverse their route, with southern Davis Strait and the Labrador Sea serving as the wintering grounds. The western terminus of the Davis Strait stock range is roughly along western Somerset and

1. Mount Oliver (PaJs-2)
2. Ditchburn Point (PaJs-3)
3. Hazard Inlet south (PaJs-4)
4. Hazard Inlet north (PaJs-13)
5. Cape Garry (PcJq-5)
6. Idlout Point south (IPS)
7. Idlout Point north (IPN)
8. Learmonth (PeJr-1)
9. Near (PeJr-2)
10. Quoak (PeJq-1)
11. Beaches; Bellot Strait - Creswell Bay (BS-CB)
12. Batty Bay (Bt.By.)
13. Port Leopold (Pt.Lp.)
14. Aston Bay south (ABS)
15. Aston Bay north (ABN)
16. Back Bay 2 (BB2)
17. Back Bay 3 (BB3)
18. Back Bay 1 (BB1)
19. Cape Walker (Cp.Wk.)
20. Northeast Prince of Wales Is. beaches (Ne.PW.)
21. Radstock Bay (Rd.By.)
22. Resolute M-1 (Res.B.)
23. Porden Point (Pd.Pt.)
24. Port Refuge (Pt.Rf.)
25. Brooman Point (Br.Pt.)
26. Deblicquy (DeBq)
27. Black Point (Bk.Pt.)
28. Southeast Bathurst Island beaches (BP.Bch)
29. Cape Evans (Cp.Ev.)
30. Fellfoot Point (Ff.Pt.)

Suggested whaling zones: C = core;
I = intermediate; P = peripheral.
Borden designations or abbreviations
in brackets are used in Tables 1-6.

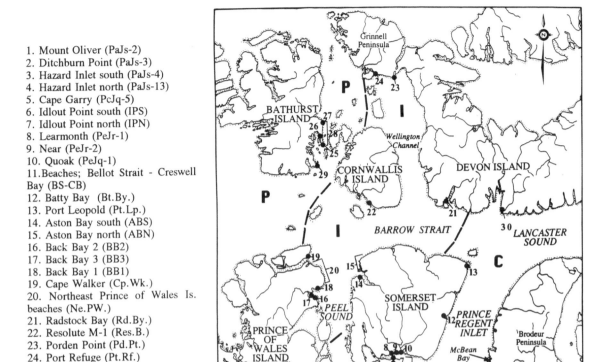

Figure 1 Thule whale bone sites in the central Canadian Arctic.

Cornwallis islands, with the confluence of Lancaster Sound, Barrow Strait, Prince Regent Inlet, Peel Sound, McDougall Sound, and Wellington Channel (Fig. 1). North, south and west of this area, the channels commonly remain covered with pack ice year-round, preventing bowheads from entering them.

The modern Davis Strait stock is estimated to be several hundred whales only, while the precommercial whaling population (prior to the early 19th century) is estimated to have been between 6,000 and 12,000 animals (Mitchell and Reeves 1982; Reeves et al. 1983). Nineteenth century whaling logbooks indicate that bowheads were common along the Lancaster Sound-Barrow Strait-Prince Regent Inlet corridor, that this corridor was known as a "nursery" area where calves/young bowheads were found, and that essentially all of the bowheads taken were from the core or intermediate areas, as described below (Lubbock 1937; Ross 1979; Ross and MacIver 1982; Reeves et al. 1983).

Detailed studies of Western Arctic bowhead migrations indicate that "runs" of immature, dams and calves, and large adult whales take place in the Bering-Chukchi Sea region (Maher and Wilimovsky 1963; Durham 1979; Cubbage and Calambokidis 1987). For the Eastern Arctic, 19th century whalers made frequent reference to "young fish," "females and mature whales," "suckers," and "nursery fish" congregated into groups (see Reeves et al. 1983:57 for examples). Accordingly, there is reason to believe that such segregation occurred among bowheads of the past millennium in the Eastern Arctic as well. Unfortunately, any attempt to investigate this in detail is constrained by the severe reduction of this stock during the historic period.

Sea Ice and Whaling Zones

For the purposes of this study, we define three whaling zones according to sea ice patterns and historic whaling records: core, intermediate and periphery (Fig. 1).

Sea ice patterns are useful predictors of whale abundance and predictability, because bowheads typically favour open water and loose conditions up to 3/8ths-4/8ths loose pack cover (Braham et al. 1980; Brueggeman 1982; Reeves and Leatherwood 1985). The three zones identified here are defined

Figure 2 Collapsed Thule dwelling showing roof supports of bowhead mandibles and maxillae, Deblicquy site, Bathurst Island.

Figure 3   Excavated dwelling at Hazard Inlet, southeast Somerset Island, showing <u>in situ</u> whale bone elements.

Figure 4   Bowhead whale processing and caching area, Hazard Inlet, southeast Somerset Island.   Arrows indicate bowhead crania.

in part on the basis of longitudinal studies of central and eastern Canadian Arctic sea ice patterns described by Lindsay (1977, 1982) and especially Markham (1981).

The core whaling zone is the area of summer open water and loose ice that occurs in Lancaster Sound, eastern Barrow Strait, and Prince Regent Inlet. Other channels and inlets such as Admiralty Inlet and Eclipse Sound on northern Baffin Island are also ice-free for much of the summer but they lie outside the study region. The intermediate zone also is characterized by summer open water and loose ice, but such conditions occur for a shorter period, as in western Barrow Strait, Peel Sound, and Wellington Channel. Finally, the peripheral zone is the area of even shorter periods of open water and loose ice, to the point where open water may rarely occur; in the study area these include channels and inlets west of Barrow Strait and north and west of Cornwallis Island.

According to Markham's 15-year (1959-1974) weekly averages, sea ice clears to 4/8 or less in the core zone by August 6, in the intermediate zone by August 20, and in the peripheral zone only by August 27. In the fall, sea ice aggregation to greater than 4/8 occurs in the peripheral zone by September 24, in the intermediate zone by October 1, and in the core zone by October 8.

Since bowheads are ice-adapted and follow the retreating ice margins during the summer migration, it follows that they (a) enter the core zone earlier, (b) probably spend up to twice as long in this zone compared to the intermediate and peripheral zones, and, (c) because of the period over which migrations take place, occur in far greater numbers in this zone.

The annual breakup of sea ice is largely dictated by seasonal temperature warming, and also by local variables such as surface area, water depth, tides and currents, and orientation of sea bodies with relation to prevailing winds (Dunbar and Greenaway 1956: 415ff; Stirling and Cleator 1981). Whereas the period of breakup and clearing will vary each year, depending on these factors, the pattern of how the ice breaks up and

Figure 5   Early Holocene naturally beached bowhead whale remains, northwest Baffin Island.

Figure 6 Measuring early Holocene bowhead whale remains, Fitzgerald Bay, Broduer Peninsula, northwest Baffin Island.

clears will be fairly consistent for the same locale year after year. Finally, while the scheduling of breakup may have changed since the Thule period due to climatic change, it is unlikely to have altered clearing and reforming patterns to the extent that the three zone distinctions cannot be made.

Methods

Archaeological Bowhead Bone Sample

We have counted and measured bowhead elements at coastal Thule Inuit sites and adjacent beach locales since 1978 (see McCartney and Savelle 1993). In 1978, a field crew visited sites in the southeastern Somerset Island area in order to collect whale bone data. During 1988, this initial study was expanded to northern Somerset, Prince of Wales, Bathurst, Cornwallis, and western Devon islands. Approximately 10,500 bones were recorded during these two field seasons, representing approximately 1000 individual whales (based on a regional aggregation method; see e.g. Grayson 1984). An additional 28 mandibles were measured in 1990 and 1992 at Hazard Inlet, southeastern Somerset Island, and six mandibles and ten crania at Fellfoot Point, southern Devon Island, in 1993. These recently measured bones are included in this study. A total of 441 crania, 798 mandibles, 217 scapulae, and 122 cervical vertebrae have been measured from these Thule sites and beaches. Of this number, 354 crania, 784 mandibles, 213 scapulae, and 120 cervical vertebrae produced sufficient measurements to enable original whale size to be estimated.

The sampled Thule sites and beach areas are indicated on Figure 1. Most radiocarbon dates for these sites for which we have dated materials fall between A.D. 900 and 1500 (Morrison 1989); we believe that most whale bone-related sites actually date to between A.D. 1100 and 1500. Bone elements were recorded at four different site types: (a) permanent winter residential sites, consisting primarily of semisubterranean whale bone/stone/sod dwellings; (b) whale flensing sites, (c) whale product caching sites (often combined with flensing sites), and (d) seasonally occupied summer and/or fall tent camp sites. Examples of winter whale bone dwelling sites and flensing/caching sites are shown in Figures 2-4. With the exception of previously excavated whale bone dwellings, all bones measured were on the surface or protruding through features. In the case of previously excavated semisubterranean dwellings, measurements were made on bones found piled adjacent to them.

Previously excavated or tested sites include those at Cape Garry (PcJq-5; McCartney 1979), Creswell Bay (PeJr-1, PeJr-2; Taylor and McGhee 1979; McCartney 1979), Resolute Village M-1 (Collins 1951), Brooman Point (QiLd-1; McGhee 1984), Deblicquy (QiLe-1; Taylor and McGhee 1981), Porden Point (RbJr-1; Park 1989), and Port Refuge (McGhee n.d.). In addition, Savelle's recent excavations at several sites at Hazard Inlet (including PaJs-4 and PaJs-13) produced additional whale bones which were measured. Bowhead bones have been removed from some of the excavated and unexcavated sites over the years for Inuit carving material and for zoological comparative specimens.

Naturally Stranded Early Holocene Sample

Naturally stranded bowhead whale remains occur throughout the Eastern Arctic, especially on Brodeur Peninsula on Baffin Island, Somerset Island, Prince of Wales Island, and Devon Island (Dyke 1979, 1980; Dyke and Morris 1990; Dyke et al. 1991). Using unpublished information supplied by Arthur Dyke (Geological Survey of Canada), in 1990 we relocated approximately 75 bowhead localities (each with one or more bowhead bones) recorded by him, and discovered an additional 25 at McBean Bay and Fitzgerald Bay, western Brodeur Peninsula (see Fig. 1). A further 180 stranded bowheads were recorded on the east coasts of Brodeur Peninsula and Somerset Island in 1992. These remains date to as early as 10,000 years B.P., and are typically found embedded within raised beach ridges up to 3 km inland (Fig. 5). We measured all appropriate bowhead elements at these bowhead localities (Fig. 6), and were able to derive lengths for 231 individual whales. (In Savelle and McCartney [1991:Fig. 10.3] we illustrate a histogram of Holocene stranded whale lengths based on cranial measurements taken by Dyke on 129 specimens. The estimated sizes of the 231 specimens we deal with here are based on our own measurements, using the Mitchell schedule; see below).

Bowhead Osteometric Data

Beginning in 1975, McCartney recorded bowhead bones at central Canadian Arctic Thule sites in order to determine the importance of whales in Thule subsistence and feature construction patterns (McCartney 1979). While we have recorded total numbers of bowhead elements at various sites during that and later studies, the osteometric analyses have focused specifically on crania, mandibles, scapulae, and cervical vertebrae, since these single or paired bones are usually the most abundant and thus represent the highest minimum number of individual whales for most sites.

Traditional techniques for determining the age at death of mammalian archaeofauna, such as those based on tooth eruption and wear and dental annuli, are not appropriate for bowhead whales, since they lack teeth. Instead, they feed through a series of baleen plates. Accordingly, an osteometric approach was employed that focused on the four elements noted above. The osteometric measurement schedule was initially designed in 1975 by E.D. Mitchell, a cetacean biologist and paleontologist then with the Department of Fisheries and Oceans (Canada). This schedule, slightly modified in 1976, has subsequently served as the standard schedule for all age/size determinations by us. Details of the techniques have been described elsewhere (McCartney 1978, 1980b).

The bone measurements selected were those that were (a) indices of animal growth, (b) based on osteological measurement points that nonbiologists could recognize in the field, and (c) suitable for bowhead bones in an archaeological context. These included 16 cranial, 12 mandibular, five scapular, and five cervical vertebral measurements. A control sample, consisting of skeletal elements from 14 Alaskan bowhead whales of known size collected by Dr. Floyd Durham for the Los Angeles County Museum, was measured by McCartney in 1980. Measurements on individual bones in this control sample were used to generate a series of multiple linear regression models that were, in turn, applied to the archaeological samples to estimate original whale length.

Whale age from whale length was determined through comparison with recently killed bowheads in Alaska (e.g., Nerini et al. 1984; Breiwick et al. 1984). That is, calves = 4.0-6.0 m; yearlings = 6.0-9.4 m; subadults (2-5 years) = 9.4-12.0 m; and adult males = 12.0+ m and adult females 14.0+ m. These age/size characteristics introduce a potential problem in the use of mortality profiles in the traditional attritional versus catastrophic models (Klein 1987; Stiner 1990, 1991), since whale age is not linearly correlated with whale size. Growth rates are fastest immediately following birth and decrease throughout life. Furthermore, the full potential life span of bowheads is not known. Accordingly, our interpretations will be based primarily on comparison of whale length and only secondarily on whale age.

Mandibles and crania were found to offer the most precise estimates for whale length, and thus will be the only elements treated here. Comparison of size profiles based on these two elements indicates that relative frequencies according to estimated derived whale length are remarkably consistent (see Fig. 7), and statistical T-tests corroborate this relationship (see Table 7). Since mandibles are the most abundant element, whether considered as minimum number of individuals (MNI) or minimum animal units (MAU), whale lengths based on them will be used for comparisons with the stranded and live populations.

Results and Discussion

Results of the size/length determinations for the archaeological populations are summarized in Tables 1-6. For each site or coastal survey region, the total number of a particular element (cranium or mandible) observed, the total from the observed population that could be measured, and the total from the measured population for which reliable length estimates could be calculated are given. Comparisons of the resulting mortality profiles are presented in Figures 7-11.

Thule Assemblage vs. Stranded Assemblage

One objection that has been previously raised concerning equating bowhead bones at Thule sites with active whale hunting is that such bones may instead derive primarily from the remains of

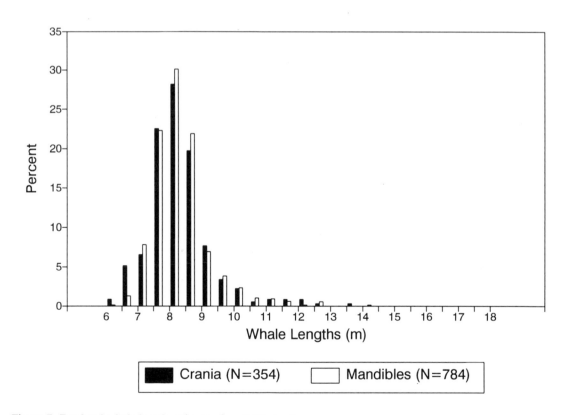

Figure 7 Bowhead whale length estimates for all Thule sites.

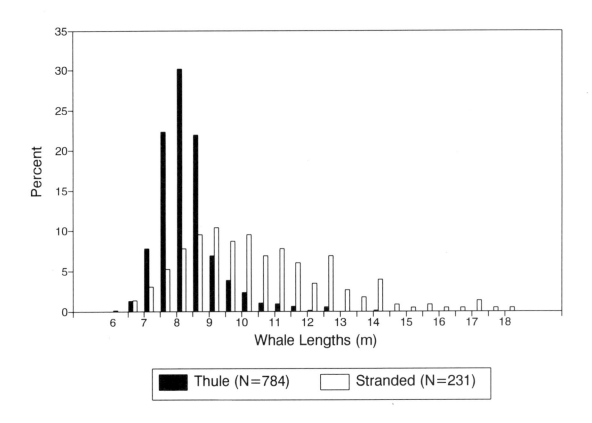

THULE vs. STRANDED POPULATIONS
Comparison of Estimated Whale Sizes

Figure 8 Comparison of lengths of Thule whales (mandibles) and naturally beached Holocene whales.

naturally stranded or beached animals (e.g., Freeman 1979). A direct implication of bone/carcass scavenging, as opposed to active hunting, is that the Thule age/size profile should resemble that represented by naturally stranded bowheads.

The age/size profile for all Thule sites is compared with the stranded population size profile in Figure 8. There are clearly significant differences between the two, strongly suggesting that Thule Inuit were acquiring very few, if any, bone elements from naturally stranded whales. Although the stranded assemblage is admittedly smaller than the Thule assemblage (231 vs. 784), the differences, especially in the larger whale categories, are nevertheless striking.

Thule Assemblage vs. Live Bowhead Population

The overall Thule age/size profile (based on mandibles) is compared with a modern, live Beaufort Sea bowhead population in Figure 9. The Alaskan bowhead population is used for comparison here, since the stock that entered the central Canadian Arctic (Davis Strait stock) has been severely depleted by commercial whaling, and we do not have accurate census data that could be used to characterize the precommercial whaling stock. The Beaufort Sea bowhead profile was generated by Koski et al. (1988) from photogrammetric measurements made during aerial surveys in the 1980s. Assuming that growth rates and population demographics for Eastern and Western Arctic bowheads are essentially the same, the live animal profiles of Western Arctic populations may be considered to represent the profiles of Eastern Arctic bowheads during the Thule occupation period.

Using the Breiwick et al. (1984) length-age groupings discussed earlier, it is immediately

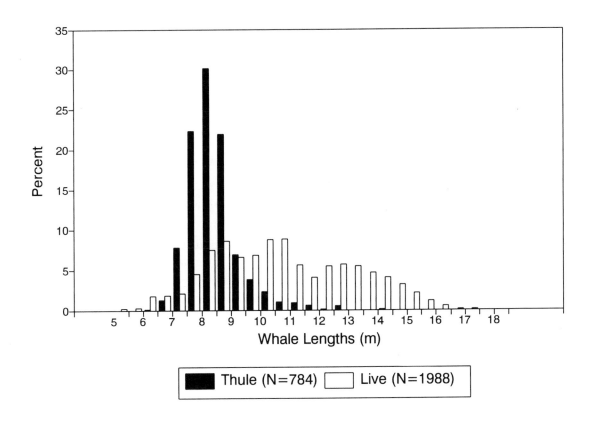

Figure 9 Comparison of lengths of Thule whales (mandibles) and a live population (Beaufort Sea).

WHALES BY ZONE (MANDIBLES)
Comparison of Estimated Whale Sizes

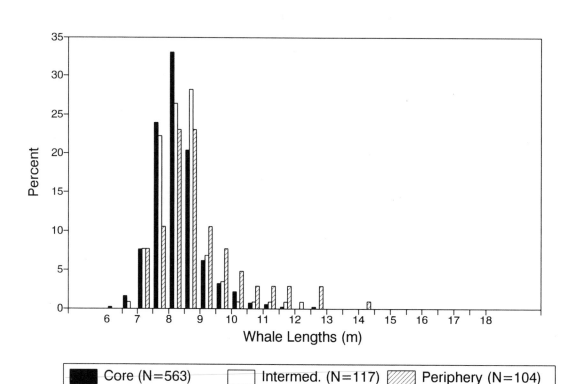

Figure 10 Estimated Thule whale lengths from core, intermediate, and peripheral zones (mandibles).

evident that yearlings (6-9.4 m) are represented in far greater proportions in the archaeological sample (91%) than in the live population (approximately 30%), whereas calves (4-6 m) and adults (12.5+ m; less than 1%) are almost totally excluded.

These results, then, clearly demonstrate a definite selection for smaller whales, especially yearlings, in contrast to random hunting strategies, wherein animals would be harvested from the living population in direct proportion to their abundance. Based on our comparative sample from which the regression models were derived, we feel confident that this selectivity is not a function of the models themselves, nor do we feel that taphonomic factors resulted in the differential destruction of calf bone elements. Further, although mention was made previously of potential age/sex segregation during the summer migration, calves and mature whales are well documented throughout the study area. Rather than lack of availability, older animals were probably ignored because of the increased danger in their actual pursuit and the increased logistical difficulties of handling the larger carcasses. Calves, although probably highly desired, would have been very difficult to hunt because of their close physical association with their mothers during their first year. Yearlings, on the other hand, are not closely associated with their mothers, and, in addition, can be expected to be relatively inexperienced compared to older whales when confronted by predators. Thus, logistical manageability and whale behaviour are probably both operative in age/size selection.

Interregional Variation

Age/size profiles of both mandibles and crania for the core, intermediate, and peripheral whale zones are compared in Figures 10 and 11. It is evident that while there is an overall selection for smaller whales within the three zones, the relative proportion of larger whales increases from the core

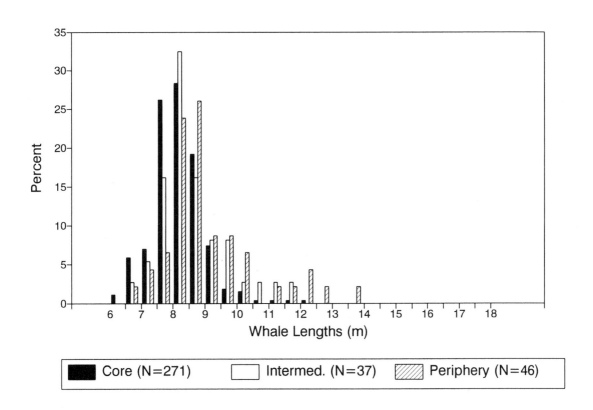

WHALES BY ZONE (CRANIA)
Comparison of Estimated Whale Sizes

Figure 11 Estimated Thule whale lengths from core, intermediate, and peripheral zones (crania).

Table 1 Estimated whale lengths based on crania for core zone sites.   Numbers refer to site locations in Figure 1.

Whale length (m)	(1) PaJs-2	(2) PaJs-3	(3) PaJs-4	(4) PaJs-13	(5) PcJq-5	(6) IPS	(7) IPN	(8) PeJr-1	(9) PeJr-2	(10) PeJq-1	(11) BSCB	(12) Bt.By.	(13) Pt.Lp.	(30) Ff.Pt.	Total
6.0-6.5	-	-	-	-	-	-	-	-	-	-	2	-	1	-	3
6.5-7.0	-	-	1	1	-	-	-	-	-	-	12	-	1	1	16
7.0-7.5	-	-	3	1	-	-	1	-	2	-	11	-	1	-	19
7.5-8.0	3	1	2	4	7	2	1	-	11	1	32	1	2	4	71
8.0-8.5	1	-	-	6	6	1	1	2	29	2	27	-	1	1	77
8.5-9.0	2	-	1	8	8	-	-	1	11	1	18	-	2	-	52
9.0-9.5	1	-	-	3	-	-	-	1	3	2	7	-	2	1	20
9.5-10.0	-	-	-	-	-	-	-	-	-	1	3	-	1	-	5
10.0-10.5	-	1	-	-	-	-	-	-	2	-	-	-	-	1	4
10.5-11.0	1	-	-	-	-	-	-	-	-	-	-	-	-	-	1
11.0-11.5	-	-	-	-	-	-	-	-	1	-	-	-	-	-	1
11.5-12.0	1	-	-	-	-	-	-	-	-	-	-	-	-	-	1
12.0-12.5	-	-	-	-	-	-	-	-	-	-	-	-	-	1	1
12.5-13.0	-	-	-	-	-	-	-	-	-	-	-	-	-	-	-
13.0-13.5	-	-	-	-	-	-	-	-	-	-	-	-	-	-	-
13.5-14.0	-	-	-	-	-	-	-	-	-	-	-	-	-	-	-
14.0-14.5	-	-	-	-	-	-	-	-	-	-	-	-	-	-	-
14.5-15.0	-	-	-	-	-	-	-	-	-	-	-	-	-	-	-
Total	9	2	7	23	21	3	3	4	59	7	112	1	11	9	271
Measured	16	7	8	38	33	3	3	5	81	18	123	1	12	9	357
Observed	19	22	25	50	78	7	3	12	86	31	147	1	19	10	510

Table 2 Estimated whale lengths based on crania for intermediate zone sites. Numbers refer to site locations in Figure 1.

Whale Length (m)	(14) ABS	(15) ABN	(16) BB2	(17) BB3	(18) BB1	(19) CpWk	(20) NePW	(21) RdBy	(22) ResB	(23) PdPt	(24) PtRf	Total
6.0-6.5	-	-	-	-	-	-	-	-	-	-	-	-
6.5-7.0	-	-	-	-	-	-	-	-	-	1	-	1
7.0-7.5	-	-	-	-	-	1	-	-	-	1	-	2
7.5-8.0	-	6	-	-	-	-	-	-	-	-	-	6
8.0-8.5	1	7	1	-	-	-	-	2	-	-	1	12
8.5-9.0	-	3	-	-	-	-	-	1	-	2	-	6
9.0-9.5	-	-	-	-	-	1	1	-	-	1	-	3
9.5-10.0	-	1	-	-	-	-	-	1	-	1	-	3
10.0-10.5	-	1	-	-	-	-	-	-	-	-	-	1
10.5-11.0	-	-	-	-	-	-	-	1	-	-	-	1
11.0-11.5	-	1	-	-	-	-	-	-	-	-	-	1
11.5-12.0	-	-	-	-	-	-	-	1	-	-	-	1
12.0-12.5	-	-	-	-	-	-	-	-	-	-	-	-
12.5-13.0	-	-	-	-	-	-	-	-	-	-	-	-
13.0-13.5	-	-	-	-	-	-	-	-	-	-	-	-
13.5-14.0	-	-	-	-	-	-	-	-	-	-	-	-
14.0-14.5	-	-	-	-	-	-	-	-	-	-	-	-
14.5-15.0	-	-	-	-	-	-	-	-	-	-	-	-
Total	1	19	1	0	0	2	1	6	0	6	1	37
Measured	1	19	1	0	0	2	1	6	0	6	1	37
Observed	9	42	1	0	0	2	1	11	1	6	1	74

Table 3 Estimated whale lengths based on crania for peripheral zone sites. Numbers refer to site locations in Figure 1.

Whale Length (m)	(25) BrPt	(26) DeBq	(27) BkPt	(28) BPBch	(29) CpEv	Total
6.0-6.5	-	-	-	-	-	-
6.5-7.0	-	-	-	1	-	1
7.0-7.5	-	1	-	1	-	2
7.5-8.0	-	2	-	1	-	3
8.0-8.5	-	7	-	4	-	11
8.5-9.0	-	6	-	5	1	12
9.0-9.5	-	2	-	1	1	4
9.5-10.0	-	1	-	3	-	4
10.0-10.5	-	1	-	2	-	3
10.5-11.0	-	-	-	-	-	-
11.0-11.5	-	-	-	1	-	1
11.5-12.0	-	-	-	1	-	1
12.0-12.5	-	-	-	2	-	2
12.5-13.0	-	-	-	1	-	1
13.0-13.5	-	-	-	-	-	-
13.5-14.0	-	-	-	1	-	1
14.0-14.5	-	-	-	-	-	-
14.5-15.0	-	-	-	-	-	-
Total	0	20	0	24	2	46
Measured	0	20	0	24	2	46
Observed	1	26	1	24	2	54

Table 4 Estimated whale lengths based on mandibles for core zone sites. Numbers refer to site locations in Figure 1.

Whale Length (m)	(1) PaJs-2	(2) PaJs-3	(3) PaJs-4	(4) PaJs-13	(5) PcJq-5	(6) IPS	(7) IPN	(8) PeJr-1	(9) PeJr-2	(10) PeJq-1	(11) BSCB	(12) Bt.By.	(13) Pt.Lp	(30) Ff.Pt.	Total
6.0-6.5	-	-	-			-	-	-	-	-	1	-	-	-	1
6.5-7.0	8	-	-		-	-	-	-	-	-	-	-	1	-	9
7.0-7.5	21	1	-	3	-	2	-	4	-	2	8	-	2	-	43
7.5-8.0	26	6	1	8	3	4	-	25	14	17	16	8	6	1	135
8.0-8.5	19	4	1	10	8	3	3	42	21	35	16	7	13	4	186
8.5-9.0	3	3	1	7	4	1	-	31	5	34	10	9	7	-	115
9.0-9.5	1	-	-	-	3	1	-	9	2	13	2	1	3	-	35
9.5-10.0	1	1	2	-	-	-	-	9	2	3	-	-	-	-	18
10.0-10.5	-	-	-	-	-	-	-	3	-	7	1	1	-	-	12
10.5-11.0	-	-	-	-	-	-	-	2	-	2	-	-	-	-	4
11.0-11.5	-	-	-	-	-	-	-	2	-	1	-	-	-	-	3
11.5-12.0	-	-	-	-	-	-	-	-	-	-	-	-	-	1	1
12.0-12.5	-	-	-	-	-	-	-	-	-	-	-	-	-	-	-
12.5-13.0	-	-	-	-	-	-	-	-	-	-	-	-	1	-	1
13.0-13.5	-	-	-	-	-	-	-	-	-	-	-	-	-	-	-
13.5-14.0	-	-	-	-	-	-	-	-	-	-	-	-	-	-	-
14.0-14.5	-	-	-	-	-	-	-	-	-	-	-	-	-	-	-
14.5-15.0	-	-	-	-	-	-	-	-	-	-	-	-	-	-	-
Total	79	14	4	30	18	11	3	127	44	114	54	26	33	6	563
Measured	79	19	4	37	18	11	3	127	46	114	54	26	33	6	577
Observed	368	35	21	68	133	17	8	209	46	251	99	52	48	6	1361

Table 5 Estimated whale lengths based on mandibles for intermediate zone sites. Numbers refer to site locations in Figure 1.

Whale Length (m)	(14) ABS	(15) ABN	(16) BB2	(17) BB3	(18) BB1	(19) CpWk	(20) NePW	(21) RdBy	(22) ResB	(23) PdPt	(24) PtRf	Total
6.0-6.5	-	-	-	-	-	-	-	-	-	-	-	-
6.5-7.0	1	-	-	-	-	-	-	-	-	-	-	1
7.0-7.5	-	5	-	-	-	-	-	2	1	-	1	9
7.5-8.0	3	11	-	-	-	4	-	5	2	-	1	26
8.0-8.5	3	6	-	-	-	1	-	12	3	1	5	31
8.5-9.0	2	11	-	-	-	1	-	7	1	3	8	33
9.0-9.5	1	2	-	-	-	1	-	-	1	1	2	8
9.5-10.0	-	-	-	-	-	-	-	-	-	3	1	4
10.0-10.5	-	-	-	-	-	-	-	1	-	-	-	1
10.5-11.0	-	-	-	-	-	-	-	-	-	1	-	1
11.0-11.5	-	-	-	-	-	-	-	1	-	-	-	1
11.5-12.0	-	-	-	-	-	-	-	-	-	1	-	1
12.0-12.5	-	-	-	-	-	-	-	-	-	1	-	1
12.5-13.0	-	-	-	-	-	-	-	-	-	-	-	-
13.0-13.5	-	-	-	-	-	-	-	-	-	-	-	-
13.5-14.0	-	-	-	-	-	-	-	-	-	-	-	-
14.0-14.5	-	-	-	-	-	-	-	-	-	-	-	-
14.5-15.0	-	-	-	-	-	-	-	-	-	-	-	-
Totals	10	35	0	0	0	7	0	28	8	11	18	117
Measured	10	35	0	0	0	7	0	28	8	11	18	117
Observed	36	72	1	2	0	10	0	91	55	20	28	315

Table 6. Estimated whale lengths based on mandibles for peripheral zone sites. Numbers refer to site locations in Figure 1.

Whale Length (m)	(25) BrPt	(26) DeBq	(27) BkPt	(28) BPBch	(29) CpEv	Total
6.0-6.5	-	-	-	-	-	-
6.5-7.0	-	-	-	-	-	-
7.0-7.5	4	2	-	-	2	8
7.5-8.0	4	4	2	-	1	11
8.0-8.5	9	8	2	2	3	24
8.5-9.0	6	15	3	-	-	24
9.0-9.5	2	8	1	-	-	11
9.5-10.0	3	5	-	-	-	8
10.0-10.5	-	4	1	-	-	5
10.5-11.0	-	3	-	-	-	3
11.0-11.5	1	-	-	1	1	3
11.5-12.0	-	1	-	1	1	3
12.0-12.5	-	-	-	-	-	-
12.5-13.0	-	2	1	-	-	3
13.0-13.5	-	-	-	-	-	-
13.5-14.0	-	-	-	-	-	-
14.0-14.5	-	-	1	-	-	1
14.5-15.0	-	-	-	-	-	-
Totals	29	52	11	4	8	104
Measured	29	52	11	4	8	104
Observed	37	119	26	13	14	209

Table 7: T-test statistics for mandible and crania comparisons.

a) Whale lengths derived from crania vs. whale lengths derived from mandibles for all zones.

Element	N	Mean	Standard Deviation	Pooled Variance	Probability
Crania	354	8.380	1.020		
				-0.899	0.369
Mandibles	784	8.434	0.909		

b) Whale lengths derived from core zone crania vs. whale lengths derived from intermediate zone crania

Zone	N	Mean (metres)	Standard Deviation	Pooled Variance	Probability
Core	271	8.211	0.833		
				-2.925	0.004
Intermediate	37	8.655	1.085		

c) Whale lengths derived from intermediate zone crania vs. whale lengths derived from peripheral zone crania.

Zone	N	Mean (metres)	Standard Deviation	Pooled Variance	Probability
Intermediate	37	8.655	1.085		
				-1.701	0.093
Peripheral	46	9.152	1.486		

d) Whale lengths derived from core zone crania vs. whale lengths derived from peripheral zone crania.

Zone	N	Mean (metres)	Standard Deviation	Pooled Variance	Probability
Core	271	8.211	0.833		
				6.185	<0.001
Peripheral	46	9.152	1.486		

e) Whale lengths derived from core zone mandibles vs. whale lengths derived from intermediate zone mandibles.

Zone	N	Mean (metres)	Standard Deviation	Pooled Variance	Probability
Core	563	8.329	0.771		
				-1.362	0.174
Intermediate	117	8.438	0.863		

f) Whale lengths derived from intermediate zone mandibles vs. whale lengths derived from peripheral zone mandibles.

Zone	N	Mean (metres)	Standard Deviation	Pooled Variance	Probability
Intermediate	117	8.438	0.863		
				-3.736	<0.001
Peripheral	104	9.000	1.346		

g) Whale lengths derived from core zone mandibles vs. whale lengths derived from peripheral zone mandibles.

Zone	N	Mean (metres)	Standard Deviation	Pooled Variance	Probability
Core	563	8.329	0.771		
				7.104	<0.001
Peripheral	104	9.000	1.346		

through the intermediate to the peripheral zone. T-test results (Table 7) indicate that, with the exception of core versus intermediate zone whale lengths based on mandible measurements, these increases are statistically significant at the 99 % confidence level (four out of six cases), or at least the 90 % confidence level (one out of six cases). Even in the case of the exception, however, the trend is still toward an increase in whale length from core zone to intermediate zone.

While various factors may affect human harvesting strategies, prey species demographic characteristics, accessibility, and abundance (cf. Stiner 1990) are probably the most important in the context of Thule whaling. Since, as noted above, there is no definite evidence for summer age/size segregation between these three regions, we suggest that probable differences in absolute abundance and/or predictability of bowheads are reflected in differences in the degree of selectivity. That is, the more abundant and/or accessible the whales within any given area, the more likely the "luxury" of selective harvesting for animals of a particular age or size. By corollary, the fewer animals available and/or accessible, the less selective the harvesting strategies may be.

Finally, while not a central concern in this paper, it should also be noted that there are differences in both absolute (total whale MNI) and relative (whale MNI/dwelling) abundances of whales represented at Thule sites in the core zone versus those sites in the intermediate and peripheral zones (see Tables 1-6; cf. Savelle 1987, 1990). While there are several factors that could account for this, these differences are consistent with limited access to whales in the intermediate and peripheral zones relative to the core zone.

Conclusions

As discussed by Stiner (1991), the analysis of mammalian mortality profiles in zooarchaeological assemblages represents an important dimension in understanding ecological relationships between prehistoric human predators and their prey species. Typically, archaeologists (e.g., Klein and Cruz-Uribe 1984; Klein 1987; Stiner 1990, 1991 and references therein) utilize mortality profiles to distinguish natural versus cultural assemblages, active hunting from scavenging, and opportunistic versus specialized hunting strategies.

While we only briefly address active hunting versus scavenging here (this topic is covered in considerable detail in Savelle and McCartney 1990, 1991), the primary focus of this paper has been the determination of opportunistic in contrast to specialized hunting strategies and whether these strategies varied according to differing ecological contexts. Our results suggest that Thule hunting strategies were selective (specialized) rather than random (generalized), but that the degree of selectivity varied according to whale abundance and accessibility. In the study region, selectivity is interpreted to have been weakest in the peripheral zones, and we would expect similar results in other peripheral regions such as southern Peel Sound, the Gulf of Boothia, and eastern Amundsen Gulf.

The study we have summarized here is, in many respects, coarse-grained. We have not dealt with individual site size profiles (although these may be constructed from Tables 1-6) or with intraregional variation, for example. However, we believe the study does demonstrate that mortality profiles offer a useful approach to the investigation of Thule whaling practices.

In his 1966 Eskimo economy paper, Taylor suggested that flexibility was fundamental to the Inuit economy. In the context of the present study, the demonstrated variability in Thule whale harvesting strategies may be considered part and parcel of this flexibility.

Acknowledgements

We gratefully acknowledge the sponsoring institutions, field assistants, and principal colleagues who assisted the studies summarized here.

The 1978 survey was sponsored by the Northern Environmental Protection Branch, Department of Indian and Northern Affairs. In addition to McCartney, the field crew consisted of Allen Clarke, Michelle McLaughlin, and David Sudlovenick (Resolute Bay). Field advisors and facilitators were Bryan Kemper and Ed Mitchell. The 1988 fieldwork was conducted under the sponsorship of the Social Sciences and Humanities Research Council of Canada; in addition to Savelle and McCartney, the field crew consisted of Karen Digby, Elisa Hart, and Terry Manik (Resolute Bay). The 1990 and 1992 Brodeur Peninsula surveys were funded by the Geological Survey of Canada, the National Sciences and Engineering Research Council of Canada, and the Social Sciences and Humanities Research Council of Canada; in addition to Savelle (1990, 1992) and McCartney (1990), field crew members were Ruth Edelstein, Colin Grier, and Elisa Hart. Art Dyke (Geological Survey of Canada) and Tom Smith (Department of Fisheries and Oceans) were instrumental in the design and implementation of this fieldwork. Sandra Parker, Susan Houston, Brian Schnarch, Matthew Sturgess, and Robert Rosenswig have, variously, assisted in the data analysis since 1978.

The Polar Continental Shelf Project, Department of Energy, Mines and Resources (Canada), assisted us with logistical support and aircraft and helicopter service during all of the fieldwork described here; we especially wish to thank the staff of the Resolute PCSP base for their invaluable assistance.

Finally, we thank the two anonymous referees and David Morrison for their many valuable comments and suggestions on an earlier draft of this paper.

References

Binford, L. 1980.   Willow smoke and dogs' tails: hunter-gatherer settlement systems and archaeological site formation. American Antiquity, 45: 4-20.

Braham, H. W., W. M. Marquette, T. Bray and J. Leatherwood, eds. 1980. The bowhead whale: whaling and biological research.   Marine Fisheries Review, 42 (9-10): 1-96.

Breiwick, J. M., L. Eberhardt and H. Braham. 1984.   Population dynamics of western arctic bowhead whales (Balaena mysticetus). Canadian Journal of Fisheries and Aquatic Sciences, 41: 484-496.

Brueggeman, J. J. 1982. Early spring distribution of bowhead whales in the Bering Sea. Journal of Wildlife Management, 46: 1036-1044.

Collins, H. B. 1951. Excavations at Thule Culture sites near Resolute Bay, Cornwallis Island, N.W.T. National Museums of Canada Bulletin, 123: 49-63.

Cubbage, J. and J. Calambokidis. 1987. Size-class segregation of bowhead whales determined through aerial stereophotogrammetry.   Marine Mammal Science, 3: 179-185.

Dunbar, M. and K. Greenaway. 1956.   Arctic Canada from the Air.   Ottawa: Defense Research Board of Canada.

Durham, F. 1979.   The catch of bowhead whales (Balaena mysticetus) by Eskimos, with emphasis on the Western Arctic.   Natural History Museum of Los Angeles County, Contributions to Science, 313: 1-14.

Dyke, A. 1979. Radio-carbon dated Holocene emergence of Somerset Island, central Canadian Arctic. Current Research, Part B, Geological Survey of Canada Paper, 79-1B: 307-318.

Dyke, A. 1980.   Redated Holocene whale bones from Somerset Island, District of Franklin. Current Research, Part B, Geological Survey of Canada Paper, 80-1B: 269-270.

Dyke, A. and T. Morris. 1990. Postglacial history of the bowhead whale and of driftwood penetration; implications for paleoclimate, central Canadian Arctic. Geological Survey of Canada Paper, 89-24.

Dyke, A., T. Morris and D. Green. 1991. Postglacial tectonic and sea level history of the central Canadian Arctic. Geological Survey of Canada Bulletin, 397.

Eschricht, D. and J. Reinhardt. 1866. On the Greenland right whale (*Balaena mysticetus*, Linn.), with special reference to its geographic distribution and migrations in times past and present, and to its external and internal characteristics. In, Recent Memoirs of the Cetacea by Professors Eschricht, Reinhardt and Lilljeborg. London: Published for the Ray Society by Robert Hardwicke.

Freeman, M. 1979. A critical view of Thule Culture and ecological adaptation. In, Thule Eskimo Culture: An Anthropological Retrospective, A.P. McCartney, ed. National Museum of Man, Mercury Series, Archaeological Survey of Canada Paper, 88: 278-285.

Grayson, D. 1984. Quantitative Zooarchaeology. New York: Academic Press.

Klein, R. 1987. Reconstructing how early people exploited animals: problems and prospects. In, The Evolution of Human Hunting, M.H. Nitecki and D.V. Nitecki, eds. New York: Plenum Press, pp. 11-45.

Klein, R. and K. Cruz-Uribe. 1984. The Analysis of Animal Bones from Archaeological Sites. Chicago: University of Chicago Press.

Koski, W., G. Miller and R. Davis. 1988. The potential effects of tanker traffic on the bowhead whale in the Beaufort Sea. Indian and Northern Affairs Canada, Environmental Studies, 58.

Lindsay, D. 1977. Sea Ice Atlas of Arctic Canada 1969-1974. Ottawa: Dept. of Energy, Mines and Resources, Canada.

Lindsay, D. 1982. Sea Ice Atlas of Arctic Canada 1975-1978. Ottawa: Dept. of Energy, Mines and Resources, Canada.

Lubbock, B. 1937. The Arctic Whalers. Glasgow: Brown, Son and Ferguson.

Maher, W. and N. Wilimovsky. 1963. Annual catch of bowhead whales by Eskimos at Point Barrow, Alaska, 1928-1960. Journal of Mammalogy, 44:16-20.

Markham, W. 1981. Ice Atlas: Canadian Arctic Waterways. Ottawa: Supply and Services Canada.

Mathiassen, T. 1927. Archaeology of the Central Eskimos. Report of the Fifth Thule Expedition 1921-24, 4.

McCartney, A. P. 1978. Study of archaeological whale bones for the reconstruction of Canadian Arctic bowhead whale stocks and whale use by prehistoric Inuit. Preliminary MS report prepared for the Northern Environmental Protection Branch, Dept. of Indian and Northern Affairs, Ottawa.

McCartney, A. P. 1979. ed. Archaeological Whale Bone: a Northern Resource. University of Arkansas Anthropological Papers, 1.

McCartney, A. P. 1980a. The nature of Thule Eskimo whale use. Arctic 33: 517-541.

McCartney, A. P. 1980b. Study of archaeological whale bones for the reconstruction of Canadian Arctic bowhead whale stocks and whale use by prehistoric Inuit. Final MS report prepared for the Northern Environmental Protection Branch, Dept. of Indian and Northern Affairs, Ottawa.

McCartney, A. P. and J. M. Savelle. 1985. Thule Eskimo whaling in the Central Canadian Arctic. Arctic Anthropology, 22: 37-58.

McCartney, A. P. and J. M. Savelle. 1993. Bowhead whale bones and Thule Eskimo subsistence - settlement patterns in the central Canadian Arctic. Polar Record, 29: 1-12.

McGhee, R. 1984. The Thule village at Brooman Point, High Arctic Canada. National Museum of Man, Mercury Series, Archaeological Survey of Canada Paper, 125.

McGhee, R. n.d. Archaeological excavations at Port Refuge and Porden Point, Devon Island, N.W.T. (Summer 1977). MS on file with the Canadian Museum of Civilization, Hull.

McVay, S. 1973. Stalking the arctic whale. American Scientist, 61: 24-37.

Mitchell, E. and R. Reeves. 1982. Factors affecting abundance of bowhead whales, *Balaena mysticetus*, in the eastern Arctic of North America, 1915-1980. Biological Conservation, 22: 59-78.

Morrison, D. 1989. Radiocarbon dating Thule Culture. Arctic Anthropology, 26: 48-77.

Nerini, M., H. Braham, W. Marquette and D.J. Rugh. 1984. Life history of the bowhead whale, *Balaena mysticetus* (Mammalia: Cetacea). Journal of Zoology, 204: 443-468.

Park, R. 1989. Porden Point: An intrasite approach to settlement system analysis. Unpublished Ph.D. dissertation, University of Alberta.

Reeves, R. 1991. The Bowhead Whale. Ottawa: Dept. of Fisheries and Oceans.

Reeves, R. and S. Leatherwood. 1985. Bowhead whale, *Balaena mysticetus* Linnaeus, 1958. In, Handbook of Marine Mammals: the Sirenians and Baleen Whales, S.H. Ridgway and R.J. Harrison, eds. London: Academic Press, pp. 305-344.

Reeves, R., E. Mitchell., A. Mansfield and M. McLauglin. 1983. Distribution and migration of the bowhead whale, *Balaena mysticetus*, in the eastern North American Arctic. Arctic, 36: 5-64.

Ross, W. G. 1979. The annual catch of Greenland (bowhead) whales in waters north of Canada 1919-1915: a preliminary compilation. Arctic, 32: 91-121.

Ross, W. G. and A. MacIver. 1982. Distribution of the kills of bowhead whales and other sea mammals by Davis Strait whalers 1820-1910. Prepared for the Arctic Pilot Project.

Savelle, J. M. 1987. Collectors and foragers: subsistence-settlement system change in the central Canadian Arctic, A.D.1000-1960. British Archaeological Reports (Int. Series), 358.

Savelle, J. M. 1990. Information systems and Thule Eskimo bowhead whale harvesting. Paper presented at the Annual Meeting of the Canadian Archaeological Association, Whitehorse.

Savelle, J. M. and A. P. McCartney. 1988. Geographical and temporal variation in Thule Eskimo subsistence economies: a model. Research in Economic Anthropology, 10: 21-72.

Savelle, J. M. and A. P. McCartney. 1990. Prehistoric Thule Eskimo whaling in the Central Canadian Arctic: current knowledge and future research directions. In, Canada's Missing Dimension: Science and History in the Canadian Arctic Islands, C.R. Harington, ed. Canadian Museum of Nature, pp. 695-723.

Savelle, J. M. and A. P. McCartney. 1991. Thule Eskimo bowhead whale procurement and selection. In, Human Predator and Prey Mortality, M. Stiner, ed. Boulder: Westview Press, pp. 201-216.

Stiner, M. C. 1990. The use of mortality patterns in archaeological studies of hominid predatory adaptations. Journal of Anthropological Archaeology, 9: 305-351.

Stiner, M. C. 1991. Introduction: actualistic and archaeological studies of prey mortality. In, Human Predators and Prey Mortality, M. Stiner, ed. Boulder: Westview Press, pp. 1-14.

Stirling, I. and H. Cleator, eds. 1981. Polynyas in the Canadian Arctic. Canadian Wildlife Service Occasional Paper, 45.

Taylor, W. E. 1960. A description of Sadlermiut houses excavated at Native Point, Southampton Island, N.W.T. National Museum of Canada Bulletin, 162: 53-100.

Taylor, W. E. 1963. Hypothesis on the origin of Canadian Thule Culture. American Antiquity, 28: 456-464.

Taylor, W. E. 1966. An archaeological perspective on Eskimo economy. Antiquity, 40: 114-120.

Taylor, W. E. 1968. Eskimos of the north and east shores. In, Science, History and Hudson Bay, vol. 1, C.S. Beals and D. Shenstone, eds. Ottawa: Dept. of Energy, Mines and Resources, pp. 1-26..

Taylor, W. E. 1972. An Archaeological Survey Between Cape Parry and Cambridge Bay, N.W.T. National Museum of Man, Mercury Series, Archaeological Survey of Canada Paper, 1.

Taylor, W. E. and R. McGhee. 1979. Archaeological Material from Creswell Bay, N.W.T., Canada. National Museum of Man, Mercury Series, Archaeological Survey of Canada Paper, 85.

Taylor, W. E. and R. McGhee. 1981. Deblicquy, a Thule Culture site on Bathurst Island, N.W.T., Canada. National Museum of Man, Mercury Series, Archaeological Survey of Canada Paper, 102.

Winterhalder, B. 1981. Optimal foraging strategies and hunter-gatherer research in anthropology: theory and models. In, Hunter-Gatherer Foraging Strategies, B. Winterhalder and E. A. Smith, eds. Chicago: University of Chicago Press, pp. 66-98.

An Archaeological Perspective on Neoeskimo Economies

David Morrison
Canadian Museum of Civilization
Hull, Quebec

Abstract

The excavation of Gutchiak and several other late pre-contact and early contact Inuvialuit sites in the western Canadian Arctic has revealed an interior occupational focus during the summer-autumn period which is not documented in the ethnographic literature. It appears that while some Inuvialuit were whaling on the main Arctic coast, other groups or social segments spent this same crucial time of year exploiting fish and caribou in the near-interior of the Eskimo Lakes. This type of dual exploitative pattern is comparable to the Nunamiut-Taremiut situation in northern Alaska and may be typical of the Western Eskimo in general. It has implications when considering the spread of Thule culture from the richer environments of Alaska and the Mackenzie Delta (which allow different economic strategies during the same season) to the much poorer environments of the Central Arctic.

Résumé

Les fouilles de Gutchiak, ainsi que plusieurs autres sites inuvialuit datant de la fin de la période du précontact et du début de celle du contact dans l'ouest de l'Arctique canadien, ont révélé une tendance à séjourner à l'intérieur des terres durant l'été et l'automne que la documentation ethnographique ne vient nullement confirmer. Il semble que, tandis que certains Inuvialuit passaient cette période cruciale de l'année à chasser la baleine sur la côte de l'Arctique en bordure immédiate de l'océan, d'autres groupes ou cellules sociales exploitaient le poisson et le caribou dans les lacs Eskimo non loin de la côte. Ce type de double structure d'exploitation se compare à la situation des Nunamiut-Taremiut du nord de l'Alaska, et caractérise vraisemblablement les Esquimaux de l'ouest en général. Cette structure a des implications si l'on considère l'étendue de la culture thuléenne, depuis les milieux plus riches de l'Alaska et du delta du Mackenzie (qui permettent diverses stratégies économiques au cours d'une même saison) jusqu'aux régions beaucoup plus pauvres de l'Arctique central.

Introduction

In 1966, William E. Taylor Jr. published a short article in the journal *Antiquity* entitled "An Archaeological Perspective on Eskimo Economy" (Taylor 1966). In it, he pursued one of his persistent themes in the 1960s; an attack on the old ethnological model of Eskimo prehistory, as promulgated most recently by Kaj Birket-Smith (1959). In other articles, Taylor argued for direct cultural continuity between Canadian Thule culture and the cultures of the historic Central Inuit (Taylor 1963, 1965, 1972, etc.). In his *Antiquity* article he attacked the intellectual underpinnings of the ethnological model; the dichotomy between maritime and terrestrial economies and their arrangement in a unilinear evolutionary scheme. Taylor argued that Eskimo societies were above all omnivorous and flexible, their economies more an adaptation to local conditions than the products of their historical heritage. This paper picks up on some of these themes with particular reference to the Inuvialuit or Mackenzie Inuit of the westernmost Canadian Arctic.

The Gutchiak Site

The Eskimo Lakes is one of the major topographic features of the western Canadian Arctic, a long, shallow arm of the Beaufort Sea stretching southwest from Liverpool Bay almost as far as the Mackenzie River. Although part of the ocean, the name reflects the basic configuration of four lake-like basins separated by inter-digitating narrows (Fig. 1).

In 1991 the author excavated an Inuvialuit archaeological site on the Eskimo Lakes, as part of the Canadian Museum of Civilization's continuing NOGAP Archaeology Programme. The site - Gutchiak (NhTn-1) - was found and originally tested by Charles Arnold in 1984 and 1985 (Arnold

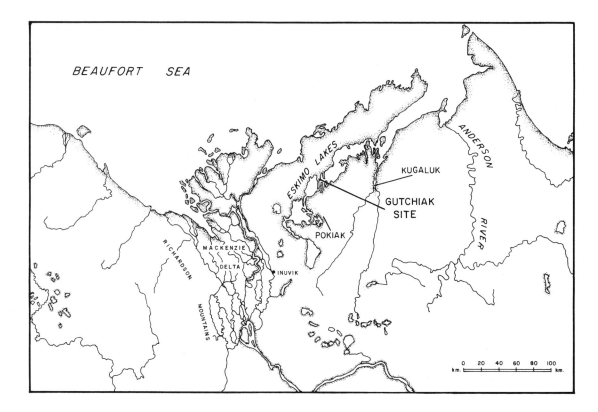

Figure 1 Location of the Gutchiak site in the western Canadian Arctic.

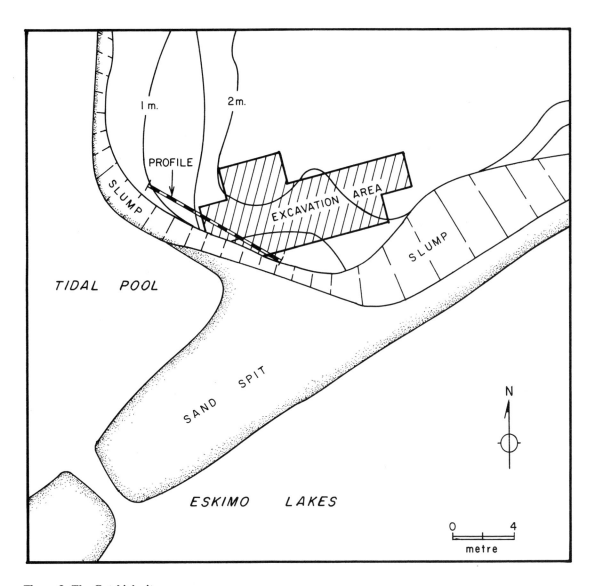

Figure 2 The Gutchiak site.

1986). It is located on the northern shore of the narrowest of the Eskimo Lakes' narrows, where the gap between coasts closes to a mere 200 metres. The location is reflected in the Inuvialuktun place-name, Gutchiak, which means "like a river" and describes the fast tidal current in the area.

The site environment is Low Arctic tundra; the nearest trees (spruce) approach to within about 10 km to the immediate south. The topography is low and rolling and the vegetation cover dense and complete, dominated by thick stands of brush willow, with sedges and grasses on the more exposed slopes. Important resources in the area include caribou, waterfowl, and both anadromous and

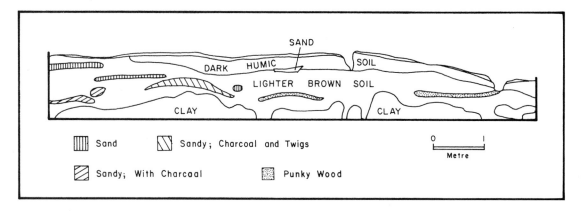

Figure 3 Gutchiak site profile.

freshwater fish.   Seals and beluga whales occasionally enter the Eskimo Lakes, but are not abundant. Because of the fast current, Gutchiak is a particularly good fishing spot.

The Gutchiak site occupies a nearly two-metre high mound on the east side of a sandspit and lagoon at the tip of the Narrows peninsula (Fig. 2). At first it was thought to represent an unusually large house mound, but this proved not to be the case. Altogether an area of about 50 square-metres was excavated to a maximum depth of 90 cm, before work was halted by permafrost and the shortness of the digging season.   Cutting a profile through the erosion face on the seaward side of the site revealed a cultural deposit extending to a depth of about 125 cm, resting on a frost-rolled sterile clay (Fig. 3).

The site produced a large number of artifacts typical of pre-contact Inuvialuit, which in turn suggests bracketing dates of about A.D. 1400 and

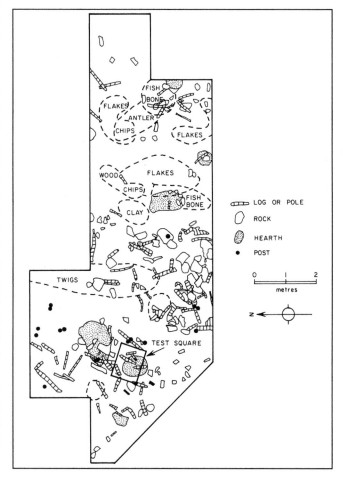

Figure 4 Gutchiak site, 20-40 cm.

1800 (see McGhee 1974). Two open-socket harpoon heads and a few antler arrowheads with weak shoulders and knobbed tangs hint at the possibility of an earlier Thule-culture occupation at the base of the mound, but this is still uncertain. Excavated artifacts represent the whole range of traditional Inuvialuit tools, from bone sewing needles to harpoon heads. Not surprisingly, fishing equipment was particularly well represented.

Although most of the site mound is of cultural origin, it is not a simple midden. The shallow, eastern side of the excavation area revealed a series of sometimes overlapping out-of-door activity areas, centred around ill-defined hearths (Fig. 4). These activity areas took the form of scatters of lithic debitage and of wood and antler chips resulting from adze work. The comparable upper layers of the deeper western half of the excavation area yielded two large, dense hearths. One of the hearths (the one beneath Arnold's 1985 "test square") yielded, as well as ash and fish bone, several handfuls of unburned twigs and even leaves. The bases of six wooden posts arranged around this hearth strongly suggest that it functioned as a meat or fish-smoking area, with a smudge fire surmounted by a conical smoking rack. During July and early August, local summers are warm enough that such fires are necessary to preserve meat and fish, and particularly to keep them from becoming fly-blown.

Remains of a more substantial sort were encountered at deeper levels (Fig. 5). A jumble of wooden poles and *in situ* posts seem to represent one or more small structures of some sort. Although badly disturbed, they were evidently quite small and had vertical pole walls. There was no evidence of a roof or floor, or a defined entrance, and they were comparatively flimsy in construction. One seems to have been built around a large hearth. Many of the wall poles were of adzed lumber, sometimes identifiable as boat or *komatik* sled parts apparently broken up or scavenged for construction purposes, perhaps since the local coastline is without driftwood. The structures seem to be too small to represent archaeological examples of the driftwood windbreaks still used by Mackenzie Inuvialuit in their summer and fall camps on the Beaufort coast. They may represent meat or fish smoking structures of a heavier type than those found in the upper layers.

The site presented a rich faunal assemblage. It is dominated by fish, mainly the various whitefish (subfamily Coregoninae), lake trout, and herring (Table 1; from Still 1992). Our own summer netting at the site yielded almost exclusively crooked-back and broad whitefish (*Coregonus clupeaformis* and *C. nasus*), in about equal portions, and it is likely that these two species make up the great majority of the Coregoninae

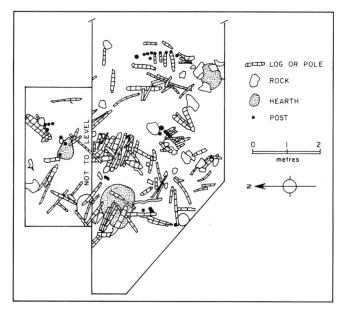

LOG OR POLE
ROCK
HEARTH
POST

0   1   2
metres

N

Figure 5 Gutchiak site, 50-90 cm.

Table 1 Fish Bones from the Gutchiak site

TAXON	NISP	%NISP	MNI
Pacific herring (*Clupea harengus*)	4169	34.11	191
lake trout (*Salvelinus namaycush*)	1010	-	146
arctic char/lake trout (*Salvelinus alpinus/S. namaycush*)	1387	-	-
salmon/trout/char (subfamily Salmoninae)	581	23.37	-
inconnu (*Stenodus leucichthys*)	518	-	17
whitefish (Coregonus/Prosopium sp.)	1566	-	148
whitefish/inconnu (subfamily Coregoninae)	1456	28.96	98
trout/whitefish (family Salmonidae)	156	1.28	-
northern pike (*Esox lucius*)	26	.21	4
cod sp. (family Gadidae)	982	8.03	100
sculpin sp. (family Cottidae)	371	3.04	52
unidentified fish	18017		
Totals	30239	99.0	

in the archaeological sample. The abundance of herring may be misleading, since they may have been imported into the site as stomach contents of the larger fish, particularly trout and inconnu. Judging by the associated artifacts, fish were caught using all of the traditional techniques of spearing, jigging and especially netting, mainly in open water to judge by the 50 or so bark net floats recovered.

Aside from the fish, faunal analysis from Gutchiak is not yet complete. However canid, waterfowl and especially caribou bone were all encountered in reasonable frequencies. Sea mammal remains were rare, limited to the occasional seal and beluga bone.

The determination of the season or seasons during which an archaeological site was occupied is usually dependent on the identification of seasonally specific, migratory fauna. In the Arctic this method is extremely unreliable, because of the absence of winter indicators and the ease of food storage in a generally cold climate. However there is good evidence that Gutchiak was primarily occupied during the summer and fall. The best data are architectural; the absence of a winter house, the outdoor activity areas, and the meat and fish smoking structures. The fairly abundant presence of immature bird bone in the faunal assemblage also points to this conclusion.

Maritime and Terrestrial Summer Options

The Gutchiak site adds a new perspective on traditional Inuvialuit socioeconomic patterns around the Eskimo Lakes. It is one of three sites the author has excavated in the immediate area (see Fig. 1). The other two - Kugaluk (Morrison 1988) and the Pokiak site (Morrison 1992) - differ from Gutchiak in several obvious ways. They are primarily caribou-hunting rather than fishing sites, to judge by the faunal material, and share that most visible of archaeological features, the semi-subterranean sod "winter" house. But at the same time, both share with Gutchiak fairly unambiguous evidence of a summer/fall occupation, in the form of in-ground cache pits, smoking pits, and outside activity areas associated with hearths and tool manufacture. All of these summer/fall caribou-hunting and fishing sites share a common response to a fundamental scheduling conflict between the exploitation of maritime and terrestrial resources, and between the main coast and the near interior.

The summer/fall maritime option is well documented along the main Arctic coast, both by 19th century travellers and by more recent archaeological work. The village site of Kittigazuit is an important example, scene of an annual beluga hunt of major proportions (McGhee 1974). Bowhead instead of beluga whaling was the main summer/fall activity at other large and equally visible villages on the coast of the Tuktoyaktuk Peninsula and at Cape Bathurst (Richardson 1851: 257, 267; Armstrong 1857: 176-183; M'Clure 1969: 87, etc.). These villages generally included a number of winter houses (Stefansson 1914: 166, 326; Franklin 1971: 215; Miertsching 1967: 59), but the main season of occupation evidently occurred during the whaling season. As Stefansson (1914: 323) describes it, "Kittegaryuit (sic) was a large village only in summer. In winter the people scattered...."

The largest of the coastal villages seem to have functioned as important social centres, integrative locations where most members of a particular local group or "society" met at least once a year (cf. Burch 1980: 271). At the time of European contact in the early nineteenth century, the Inuvialuit were divided into at least six territorially and politically distinct societies (McGhee 1974; Morrison 1990). Each seems to have taken its name from the name of its largest village, with a "miut" ("people of") suffix. Thus we have the Gupukmiut based at Gupuk, the Kittegaryumiut, with their capital at Kittigazuit, the Nuvorugmiut at Nuvurak (Point Atkinson), the Avvaqmiut at Avvaq (Cape Bathurst), and so on. The largest was probably Kittigazuit, where up to 1000 people congregated each year for the summer beluga hunt.

Nineteenth century accounts consist largely of observations made by officers of the British Royal Navy, and are inevitably limited not only to the summer sailing season but to the main Arctic coast. They neglect what has been referred to above as the "near-interior," an area centring on the Eskimo Lakes. The first European to hear of the Eskimo Lakes was Alexander Mackenzie in 1789 (Mackenzie 1970: 197). Yet throughout the nineteenth century the very existence of the Eskimo Lakes was hotly debated and often denied, despite persistent Native accounts and even deSainville's explorations of 1889 (Richardson 1851: 250, Stone 1900: 38, Castonguay 1979: map 497, deSainville

1984). There is essentially no ethnographic information on the area prior to Stefansson's visit in 1906 (Stefansson 1914, 1990; see also Harrison 1908), by which time traditional Inuvialuit life had been nearly overwhelmed. Even Stefansson's description refers only to winter life. References to a summer occupation prior to 1900 are few, brief and second-hand (Mackenzie 1970: 197; Franklin 1971: 203).

Although ignored by early European travellers, the near-interior was potentially a very important area during the summer and fall. Several key terrestrial resources were most readily available here. Among the most important were caribou, valued for their meat and especially for their hides, which were necessary for winter clothing. The primary season for caribou hunting was August and September when the animals were fat, the hides were prime, and animals were bunched together in migrating herds (Stefansson 1914: 149). Of equal importance were the main cisco and whitefish runs, again in August and September (Martell et al. 1984: 154, 158).

There is a direct scheduling conflict between these terrestrial resources and the whaling season on the main arctic coast, which runs from July through September for beluga and from August to September or early October for bowhead. Recent archaeology in the Eskimo Lakes makes clear that not all Inuvialuit chose the coastal option. While some Nuvorugmiut were hunting bowhead whales from coastal villages at Pt. Atkinson and Warren Point, others of their countrymen were intercepting caribou at Kugaluk (Morrison 1988). And Gutchiak was repeatedly occupied and re-occupied at about the same time of year as the beluga hunt at nearby Kittegazuit.

A close and complementary relationship must have existed between those who chose the terrestrial and those who chose the maritime summer/fall hunting option. Stefansson (1914: 356) reports that "Only those of the Kittegaryuit (sic) who neglected the white whale hunt, and they were few, got any considerable number of deer during the season of suitability for clothing; hence, their need to buy skins." In exchange interior people presumably received whale meat, muktuk, beluga skins (see Stefansson 1914: 348, 355), and especially the blubber necessary for their lamps.

By the full historic period we are almost certainly dealing with different members of the same societies, and a variety of individual subsistence choices (Morrison 1988). By the latter half of the nineteenth century, if not earlier, both the coastal Kittegaryumiut and the Nuvorugmiut had ranges which together included the whole of the Eskimo Lakes (see Morrison 1990: Fig. 10). However, this may not have been the case in earlier times. There is a strong oral tradition in Tuktoyaktuk of a now-extinct Inuvialuit society which in pre-contact times lived around the Eskimo Lakes. They were known as the Inuktuiut, a people whose former existence has also been briefly noted by Stefansson (1914: 145, 356). By all accounts they were the people who lived at Gutchiak, even though historically the area was occupied (at least during the winter) by Kittegaryumiut. In the oral accounts there was bad feeling between the Inuktuiut and the coastal people. In one version this was because of a trading inbalance, in another it was because the coastal people used to steal caribou hides from the Inuktuiut. The result was bloodshed and ritual cannibalism ("Inuktuiut" has been translated as "cannibals"). Eventually the Inuktuiut fled their home, going all the way to Greenland, it is said, out of fear and disgrace (Lemeur 1984, personal communication; Pokiak 1991, personal communication; Anon. 1991: 35). This story suggests that at one time the relationship between the near-interior and the coast was probably between independent societies.

Subsistence Options and Neoeskimo Economies

The ideas of scheduling conflict, subsistence diversity and complementary maritime and terrestrial options underlines the comparative environmental richness of the greater Mackenzie Delta area. They also suggest a basic economic difference between the Inuvialuit of the Mackenzie area and the Central Inuit of much of the rest of Arctic Canada. Among most Central Inuit there was very little real subsistence diversity, either during the crucial summer/fall period or at any other time of the year. The Copper Inuit can stand as an example. Among the Copper Inuit, according to all ethnographic accounts (Stefansson 1914; Jenness 1922; Damas 1969; etc.), everyone spent the winter in snowhouse villages hunting ringed seals at their breathing holes. Summer and fall were spent wandering the interior in small groups, hunting caribou and fishing. There were slight variations due to minor environmental differences, such as the Kanghiryuarmiut emphasis on polar bear hunting during the winter, or a greater than usual emphasis on fishing by the Ekaluktomiut living around Cambridge Bay. There might also be individual variations in the timing of certain activities, but the basic homogeneity of the system seems clear. Among the Copper and most other Central Inuit, the maritime and terrestrial aspects of the regional economy were sequential rather than complementary. Their economy could be characterized as simple or unstructured in comparison with that of the Mackenzie Inuvialuit.

On the other hand something very similar to the Mackenzie pattern can be seen among many other Inuit groups. Perhaps the best ethnographic example comes from northwestern Alaska, where the well-known if over-simplified dichotomy between Nunamiut and Taremiut points to a regional economy based on the strong inter-dependence of interior and coastal subsistence patterns (see Spencer 1959). As Burch (1976, 1980) has forcefully pointed out, the terms "Nunamiut" ("people of the land") and "Taremiut" ("people of the sea") are relative geographic terms only. Northwestern Alaska was the home of twenty-six individual Inupiat societies, not just two, each following its own distinctive subsistence round. Yet some of those subsistence rounds were based on harvesting interior resources (caribou, sheep, fish) at a particular season, while others were based on harvesting maritime resources (whales, walrus, seals). And all were linked by various mechanisms of exchange, including institutionalized trading partnerships, the potlatch-like Messenger Feast, and major regional trade fairs.

All of these mechanisms of exchange were greatly affected by access to Euro-American trade goods, beginning in the late eighteenth century. Indeed the major regional trade fairs date only to this period (Ray 1975: 98ff; Morrison 1991), although they probably grew from smaller local antecedents. But as well as dealing with luxury and exotic trade goods, it is striking how much northwest Alaskan trade was based on traditional subsistence commodities. Chief among these were sea mammal oil and caribou hides, each so important to arctic life and each subject to potential problems of access and scheduling. The volumes involved seem to have been considerable. At the Nirliq fair at the mouth of the Colville River, Spencer (1959: 203) describes how "the peoples of the coasts loaded their umiaks with sealskin pokes filled with oil, a single umiak carrying as many as fifty such...." Conversely, the "nuunamiut came with umiaks fully loaded with caribou hides. These were packed into bundles, about fifty hides to each...." A "Nunamiut" group like the Kukpigmiut (see Burch 1980:

287) thus had access to the seal oil necessary for their winter lamps, while their Central Inuit counterparts - the Caribou Inuit (Birket-Smith 1929) - did without.

A complex structured economy based on a diversity of subsistence pursuits during, especially, the summer-fall period seems to distinguish both Alaskan and Mackenzie Inuit from their countrymen in the central Canadian Arctic. The distinction seems to be an important one, mirroring a range of other cultural differences. Diversity clearly reflects a generally richer environment, with greater economic security and higher population densities. This in turn implies more coherent social groups; the kinds of well-defined societies Burch (1980) describes for the northwest Alaskan Inupiat, as opposed to the small, fluid, and relatively inchoate bands of the Central Inuit (see Jenness 1922: 32-43; Damas 1969). Finally, the incipient social ranking characteristic of Western Inuit has a firm economic basis not only in the kinds of surpluses which complex economies can produce, but also in the prestige implications inherent in different kinds of economic choice (see Morrison 1988). Coastal whalers would normally be of a higher individual or family status than more humble caribou-hunters and fishermen of the interior.

This line of argument can be pursued one step further. Structured, diverse regional economies may have some antiquity in the Western Arctic. In northwestern Alaska, for instance, they may date to at least early Thule times, with the coastal Inuit penetration of riverine, interior environments like the Kobuk River valley (Giddings 1952). A "Western Arctic" economic ideal might have been among the cultural expectations of the first Thule immigrants into the Central Arctic. What happened when these Western Arctic pioneers began moving into the far more austere environments to the east? Do we see an attempt to maintain the old structured, mixed summer-fall economy of the Western Arctic, or instead the kind of homogeneous, simplified economy of the historic period?

This is an idea for future investigation, and not one which can be dealt with in detail here. However, preliminary impressions do suggest that Thule pioneers attempted to maintain a mixed summer-fall economy in their new, often far more rigorous homes in the Central Arctic. The western part of Coronation Gulf, for instance, is the locational setting for much of the basic ethnographic description of the Copper Inuit (Stefansson 1914; Jenness 1922). It presents an environment as rigorous as most, with lake-like winter ice conditions and a sea-mammal fauna reduced to essentially one species - ringed seal. Historically the area supported a population density of fewer than one person per 250 square-kilometres, less than one-tenth the population density among historic Inuvialuit (Morrison 1990: 1). Yet the Thule period occupation of the area suggests a diversity of same-season subsistence pursuits which contrasts markedly with the homogeneity of the historic pattern. Unfortunately, our knowledge of the area is almost entirely restricted to coastal winter villages. However, subsistence at some coastal villages - like Clachan and Beulah (Morrison 1983a, 1983b) - seem to have depended overwhelmingly on ringed seal, stored from the open-water summer/fall season. At other villages, like Lady Franklin Point (Taylor 1972), winter subsistence seems instead to have been based almost entirely on caribou. This kind of information is a long way, it is true, from what we know of regional diversity and interaction in north Alaska. But within the limits of archaeology it is possible that the Coronation Gulf data weakly reflect the same kinds of organizational priorities.

Conclusions

In recent years, there have been several studies contrasting the economic patterns of Thule and historic Inuit in Canada. Morrison (1983a, 1983b), working around Coronation Gulf, and McCullough (1986), working on eastern Ellesmere Island, have both argued for a much greater reliance on stored food during the winter than was the case historically, suggesting that Thule Inuit were not adept breathing-hole seal hunters. In a similar vein, Savelle (1987) has contrasted Thule "collectors" with historic Inuit "foragers" in the bowhead whaling area around Somerset Island.

This paper suggests another way in which Thule immigrants into Canada may have differed from their historic descendants. Analysis and comparison based on the Gutchiak site illustrate the kind of subsistence diversity characteristic of Western Arctic Inuit. Different local groups with complementary economic specializations were integrated within regional economies which were much more complex and dynamic than those of Central Inuit, where the basic homogeneity of the system limited exchange essentially to raw materials such as wood, copper and soapstone (see Morrison 1991). Some version of the basic Western Arctic economic system may have been imported into the Central Arctic by incoming Thule pioneers nearly a thousand years ago. Sites in the western Coronation Gulf area suggest a regional economic strategy which was at least more complicated, more diverse and more structured than that documented historically in the same area.

As Taylor stressed twenty-five years ago, Inuit cultures are undoubtedly omnivorous and opportunistic (Taylor 1966). At the same time, they are also the products of their own history. In the long run, adaptation to the Central Arctic required a number of fundamental economic changes to the old "Neoeskimo" (Steensby 1917) pattern developed in the much richer West. One of these changes seems to have been a reorganization and simplification of the scheduling relationship between the harvesting of maritime and terrestrial resources.

Acknowledgements

Work at the Gutchiak site was funded by the NOGAP Archaeology Programme of the Canadian Museum of Civilization. I wish to thank Ken Swayze and my field crew (Claire Alix, Wayne Thrasher, Rita Elias and Mark Diab), Randall Pokiak and all the people of Tuktoyaktuk, the Inuvik Science Lab, and the Polar Continental Shelf Project. Analysis of the Gutchiak fish remains was carried out under contract by Leslie Still (1992). Maps and other art work are products of the pen of Dave Laverie.

References

Anon. 1991. Inuvialuit Pitqusiit: the culture of the Inuvialuit. Yellowknife: Northwest Territories Education.

Armstrong, A. 1857. A Personal Narrative of the Discovery of the North-West Passage. London: Hurst and Blackett.

Arnold, C. 1986. Archaeological Investigations in the Mackenzie Delta and Eskimo Lakes area. MS on file with the Canadian Museum of Civilization, Hull.

Birket-Smith, K. 1929. The Caribou Eskimos; Material and Social Life and Their Cultural Position. Report of the Fifth Thule Expedition 1921-24, 5.

Birket-Smith, K. 1959. The Eskimos, revised edition. London: Methuen.

Burch, E. S. 1976. The "Nunamiut" concept and the standardization of error. In, Contributions to Anthropology: The Interior Peoples of Northern Alaska, E. Hall, ed. National Museum of Man, Mercury Series, Archaeological Survey of Canada Paper, 49: 52-97.

Burch, E. S. 1980. Traditional Eskiomo societies in north Alaska. In, Alaskan Native Culture and History, Y. Kotami and W. Workman, eds. Senri Ethnological Series, 4: 253-304.

Castonguay, R. 1979. L'Occupation Territoriale Chez les Amerindiens du Nord-Ouest Canadien au XIXe Siecle Selon Emile Petitot. Ottawa: Dept. of Indian Affairs and Northern Development.

Damas, D. 1969. Characteristics of Central Eskimo band structure. National Museum of Canada Bulletin, 228: 116-134.

deSainville, Edouard. 1984. Journey to the mouth of the Mackenzie River (1889-1894). Fram: The Journal of Polar Studies, 1(2): 541-550.

Franklin, J. 1971. Narrative of a Second Expedition to the Shores of the Polar Sea in the Years 1825, 1826, and 1827. Edmonton: Hurtig.

Giddings, L. J. 1952. The Arctic Woodland culture of the Kobuk River. Philadelphia: Museum Monographs, University Museum .

Harrison, A. 1908. In Search of a Polar Continent, 1905-1907. London: E. Arnold.

Jenness, D. 1922. The Life of the Copper Eskimos. Report of the Canadian Arctic Expedition 1913-18, Vol. 12.

Lemeur, R. 1984. Personal communications, Roman Catholic Mission, Tuktoyaktuk, NWT.

Mackenzie, A. 1970. The Journals and Letters of Sir Alexander Mackenzie, W. Kaye Lamb, ed. Toronto: Macmillan.

Martell, A., D. Dickinson and L. Casselman. 1984. Wildlife of the Mackenzie Delta Region. Boreal Institute for Northern Studies, Occasional Publication, 15.

McCullough, K. 1986. Neo-Eskimo diet and hunting strategies on eastern Ellesmere Island, N.W.T. Paper presented to the 19th Annual Chacmool Conference, Calgary.

M'Clure, R. 1969. The Discovery of the North-West Passage, S. Osborn, ed. Edmonton: Hurtig.

McGhee, R. 1974. Beluga Hunters: An Archaeological Reconstruction of the History and Culture of the Mackenzie Delta Kittegaryumiut. Memorial University of Newfoundland, Newfoundland Social and Economic Studies, 13.

Miertsching, J. 1967. Frozen Ships: The Arctic Diary of Johann Miertsching, L. Neatby, trans. Toronto: Macmillan.

Morrison, D. 1983a. Thule Culture in Western Coronation Gulf, N.W.T. National Museum of Man, Mercury Series, Archaeological Survey of Canada Paper 116.

Morrison, D. 1983b. Thule sea mammal hunting in the western central Arctic. Arctic Anthropology, 20(2): 61-78.

Morrison, D. 1988. The Kugaluk Site and the Nuvorugmiut. Canadian Museum of Civilization, Mercury Series, Archaeological Survey of Canada Paper 137.

Morrison, D. 1990. Iglulualumiut Prehistory: The Lost Inuit of Franklin Bay. Canadian Museum of Civilization, Mercury Series, Archaeological Survey of Canada Paper 142.

Morrison, D. 1991. The Copper Inuit soapstone trade. Arctic, 44(3):239-246.

Morrison, D. 1992. Inuvialuit archaeology at 500 Lakes and the Old Horton Channel: the 1992 NOGAP season. MS on file with the Canadian Museum of Civilization, Hull.

Pokiak, R. 1991. personal communications, Eskimo Lakes and Tuktoyaktuk, NWT.

Ray, D. J. 1975. The Eskimos of Bering Strait, 1650-1898. Seattle: University of Washington Press.

Richardson, J. 1851. Arctic Searching Expedition, Vol. 1. London: Longmans, Brown, Green, and Longmans.

Savelle, J. 1987. Collectors and Foragers: Subsistence-Settlement System Change in the Central Canadian Arctic, A.D. 1000-1960. British Archaeological Reports, 358.

Spencer, R. 1959. The North Alaskan Eskimo: A Study in Ecology and Society. Bureau of American Ethnology Bulletin, 171.

Steensby, H. P. 1917. An anthropogeographical study of the origin of Eskimo culture. Meddelelser om Gronland, 53: 39-288.

Stefansson, V. 1914. The Stefansson-Anderson Arctic Expedition: Preliminary Ethnographic Results. Anthropological Papers of the American Museum of Natural History, 14(1).

Stefansson, V. 1990. Hunters of the Great North (orig. 1922). New York: Paragon House.

Still, L. 1992. Bony Fish Remains from the Gutchiak site NhTn-1. MS on file with the Canadian Museum of Civilization, Hull.

Stone, A. J. 1900. Some results of a natural history journey to northern British Columbia, Alaska, and the Northwest Territory. American Museum of Natural History Bulletin, 13: 31-62.

Taylor, W. E. 1963. Review of J.W. Van Stone's "An Archaeological Collection from Somerset Island and Boothia Peninsula." Arctic, 16(2):144-145.

Taylor, W. E. 1965. The fragments of Eskimo prehistory. The Beaver, Spring, 4-17.

Taylor, W. E. 1966. An archaeological perspective on Eskimo economy. Antiquity, 40:114-120.

Taylor, W. E. 1972. An Archaeological Survey between Cape Parry and Cambridge Bay, N.W.T., Canada in 1963. National Museum of Man, Mercury Series, Archaeological Survey of Canada Paper 1.

Nadlok and the Origin of the Copper Inuit

Bryan C. Gordon,
Canadian Museum of Civilization
Hull, Quebec

Abstract

Nadlok is the only site presently known which clearly spans the transition between Thule and Copper Inuit culture in the western Central Arctic. Radiocarbon dates and the absence of European trade goods support an occupation for the site over several centuries, between about A.D. 1450 and 1750. An interior site with abundant evidence of caribou hunting, Nadlok may document an occupational shift away from the coast during the Little Ice Age.

Résumé

Nadlok est le seul site connu à ce jour qui englobe nettement la transition entre la culture des Thuléens et celle des Inuit du cuivre dans l'ouest de l'Arctique central. La datation au radiocarbone et l'absence de marchandises commerciales européennes vient appuyer la thèse selon laquelle le site aurait été occupé pendant plusieurs siècles, entre environ 1450 ap. J.-C. et 1750. Site se trouvant à l'intérieur des terres, où les signes de la chasse au caribou sont légion, Nadlok révèle que la population s'est éloignée de la côte au cours du Petit âge glaciaire.

Introduction

Nadlok or "crossing-place-of-deer" is an island water-crossing on the Burnside River in the Mackenzie District of northern Canada (Figs. 1 & 2). Located on the main migration route of the Bathurst caribou herd, Nadlok is in the centre of a gently sloping basin of open tundra commanding a magnificent view in all directions. Up and downstream from the island are two crossings presently used by migratory caribou, and presumably extensively used in the past. The upstream crossing is narrow with fast water but no rapids, an ideal place for kayakers to tire and lance caribou by making them swim against the current. The downstream crossing has wide shallow rapids entering a deep pool with many lake trout, arctic char and grayling. During site excavations in July of 1985 and 1986, herds numbering up to an estimated thirty thousand caribou each passed through both crossings.

Caribou bone and antler blanket the island and pave the shallows around it, extending into the river as far as visibility permits. Bones were also found buried in our food cache, post holes and test pits. Evidently, caribou provided the people of Nadlok with a huge supply of meat, which was probably dried by draping strips over antler racks. Nadlok's openness and constant northwest breeze facilitated meat-drying in a relatively insect-free environment. Caribou may also have provided skin

Threads of Arctic Prehistory: Papers in Honour of William E. Taylor Jr., David Morrison and Jean-Luc Pilon, eds. Canadian Museum of Civilization, Mercury Series, Archaeological Survey of Canada Paper 149. 1994.

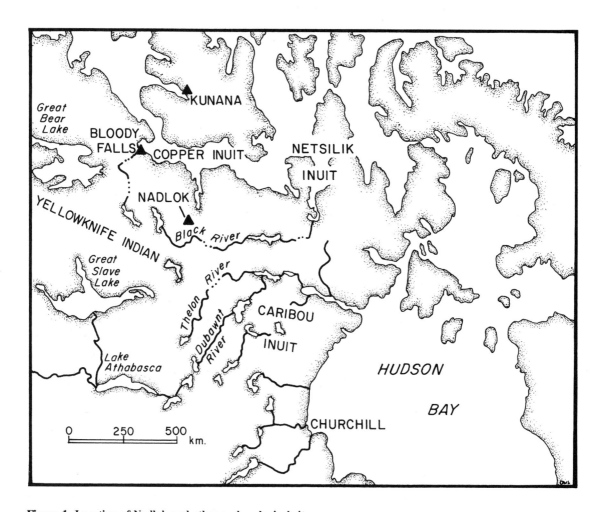

Figure 1 Location of Nadlok and other archaeological sites.

clothing, hut covers, sinew for sewing, and bone and antler tools. These uses are expected in a people dependent upon one primary game species. But at Nadlok, the people also used antler for architectural purposes, as seen in five partially buried 5 m diameter rings. Two antler rings twenty-five metres apart were dug in 1985-6 using a metre string grid and overhead bipod photography.

Each ring contained hundreds of intertwined bull caribou racks, with a few dagger-like cow antlers, most with adhering skull fragments. The Bathurst herd presently calves along the eastern side of Bathurst Inlet, to the northeast of Nadlok. Considering that cows cast their antlers at the calving grounds several weeks after parturition in June, the rarity of cow antler suggests a late summer to autumn hunting focus at Nadlok. Not only are caribou in poor nutritional shape earlier in the season, but the frozen Burnside River at the time of the spring migration would tend to cancel the strategic

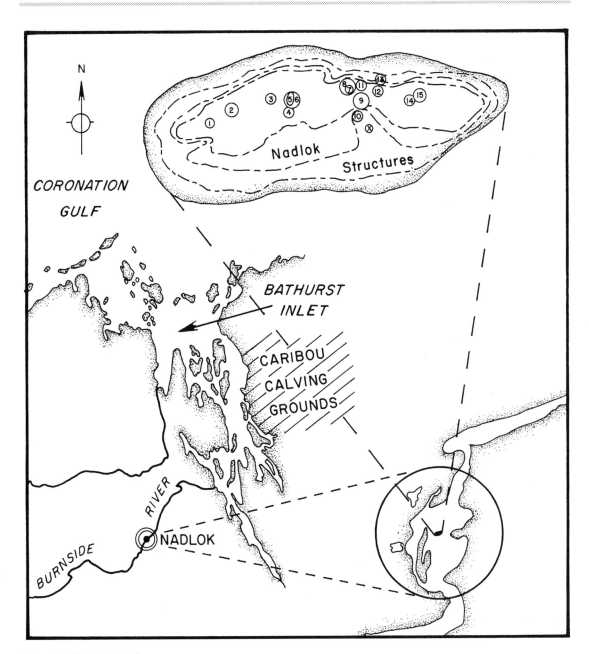

Figure 2 The Nadlok site.

advantages of a water crossing.

When cleared, each of the two excavated ring features enclosed a flagstone floor. Further digging revealed deeper rings encircling deeper floors, each progressively smaller than the one above it. The uppermost rings (Floors 1 and 2) of the second feature, for instance, contained 1167 and 1006 antlers, respectively, each enclosing an area of about eight square metres. The third ring contained 328 antlers, while bottom ring with only 170 antlers enclosed a floor only four square metres in extent. Feature one presented a similar picture. These antler rings and associated floors are interpreted as a superimposed series of antler-walled huts. When occupied, they were presumably roofed with hides.

The door of each hut is represented by a meter-wide break in the antler ring delineated by two upright stones. Within each door and extending about a metre from the hut is a flagstone patio leading to a semi-subterranean stone house of generalized Thule Inuit type. Each house is only 2 by 3 m, but has a stepped entrance passage and lateral sleeping platform. Separating each house from the lake is a second but lower paved area likely used for storing kayaks and performing outdoor activities.

Nadlok has five pairs of antler huts and stone houses, with a trail joining their upper patios. At the east end of the island are four separate unpaved tent-rings (Fig. 2). Stone house 2 and its hut were excavated in 1985 (structures 4-5), while stone house 3 and its hut were dug in 1986 (nos. 7-8). Structure 6 is a simple round wall rebuilt from stone from no. 5. Unexcavated stone houses include structures 3, 9, 12, 14 & 15, while undug antler huts include structures 2, 11 and 13. Structures 14 and 15 at the east end of the island are big deeply-inset boulder tent-rings without antlers.

The pavement floors of Huts 2 and 3 tilt. Summer thawing of supporting frozen clay and sand caused the floors to sink gently away from their doorways on the island spine. Settling floors were levelled by adding new flagstones, creating a wedge-shaped profile of southward thickening floors, each a separate occupation. Under the turf, Huts 2 and 3 had 3 and 4 floors, respectively, with many subfloors separated by thinner flagstones. Where possible, charcoal samples were collected from each floor for radiocarbon dating.

Climate, Dating and Seasonality

Nadlok's radiocarbon dated floors and levels indicate it was occupied in the period 1450-1750 A.D. This coincides with the Neo-Boreal climatic episode or Little Ice Age, a time of deteriorating climate when ocean temperatures dropped 1-3 deg. C and the Arctic summer front retreated four to five degrees south (Bryson & Wendland 1967; Lamb 1966; Ball 1986). Sea ice remained into summer and likely stayed all year round in sheltered places such as Bathurst Inlet and eastern Coronation Gulf. This would inevitably have disrupted the habitat of sea-mammals and their hunters, but the cold, dry air may have had little affect on caribou and muskox habitat.

An unpaved basal level underlies all structures, extending into the lake as an exposed bone layer. Its dates of 1425±130 under one hut and 1470±95 A.D. at a one meter depth at the east end of the island (S-2724 and S-2845) represent the first occupation of the site, evidently in the form of a seasonal tent camp. The first semi-permanent hut was built at about 1540±105 A.D., based on a date from hut 2 floor 3 (S-2775). Later, occupants resided on Floor 2 at about 1560 A.D., and Floor 1 above at about 1580±130 A.D. (S-2725). Hut 3 may have been built somewhat later than Hut 2, as its Floor 3 dated 1625±90 A.D. (S-2846), but sigma errors do not preclude concurrent occupancy.

Upper Floors 2 and 1 presumably date to about 1625-1800 A.D., with occupation terminating sometime, probably, in the eighteenth century. Possible evidence of European trade goods are limited to a single ulu handle with a stain suggesting an iron blade.

Time limits prevented the complete excavation of the stone winter houses, but at least the uppermost floor was revealed, along with faunal and cultural material.

Thin-sections of caribou teeth (Gordon 1982) from several floors substantiate the impression given by the architecture that Nadlok was occupied from summer through winter. A winter occupation is particularly significant since historic Copper Inuit wintered exclusively on the sea ice and never in the interior (Jenness 1922), while even Thule culture winter houses are known only from coastal or near-coastal locations (McGhee 1972; Taylor 1972; Morrison 1983).

Nadlok was apparently abandoned at the beginning of a mild warming trend after about 1750 A.D., when turf began to grow on the outer collapsed walls of the huts. Later, it was sporadically visited in the 1930's by Bathurst Inlet Kingaunmiut who used it as a location for trapping. Turf on the trail crossing the upper pavement of hut 3 yielded fox traps, matches and a Winchester 38-55 carbine and cartridges, while wooden box slats were found on a lookout east of Nadlok .

Artifacts

Diagnostic artifacts illustrating Nadlok's age and cultural position are emphasized in the artifact descriptions which follow, as are trade items. Bone and antler arrowheads (Fig. 4, b, c, f, h), whetstones, soapstone vessel fragments, and slate knives common to most Inuit sites, including Nadlok, will be the subject of a more comprehensive report.

Harpoon heads

Two open and five closed-socket harpoon heads were found. The open socket specimens include single examples of Thule type 2 (Fig. 3, d) and Thule type 3 (Fig. 3, b) (Mathiassen 1927). The former lacks a line hole and may have been a toy. Three of the closed socket specimens are small and barbless, like Thule type 3 in having the endblade slit parallel to the line hole (Fig. 3a, c). The final two specimens are bilaterally barbed (Fig. 3, e). There was no clear stratigraphic separation between presumably early "Thule types" and presumably later closed socket forms.

Projectile points

Projectile points recovered include the tip and half of the basal tang of a broken black chert arrowhead from Hut 2 Floor 3, and a hafted triangular copper arrowhead from Floor 1b of Hut 3. The latter is very ground, sharp and rivetted to a socketed foreshaft (Fig. 3, f).

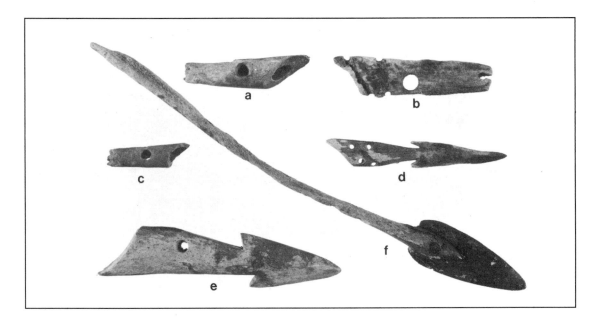

Figure 3 Nadlok arrow and harpoon heads.

Knives and Adzes

A finely engraved man's knife handle from Hut 3 Floor 3 (Fig. 4, e) has a row of nubbins on each of its four edges, while the intervening sides are inscribed with three parallel lines. Its round butt has a drilled line-suspension hole, while the opposite end has a deep rectangular socket for inserting a metal blade and a small side hole for attaching a separate sharpener (the blade shown with this specimen is a recreation). Except for the decoration it closely resembles the "men's" knives used by early twentieth-century Copper Inuit (Jenness 1946: Fig. 107).

Another man's knife is represented by a handle piece from Hut 3 Floor 2 (Fig. 4, a). An undepicted whittling knife with socketed antler handle and semi-lunar copper blade from Hut 2 Floor 3 is, stratigraphically, the earliest knife from Nadlok.

A nephrite adze blade is represented by a Floor 1 spall, probably detached through use.

Fishing tools

Copper fishhooks occur in several floors, the largest in Hut 2 Floor 1 (Fig. 5, a). A separate antler shank has seven holes and a spoon-like profile.

Ulus

Three untanged and two tanged ulu handles were found (Fig. 6), along with a copper blade

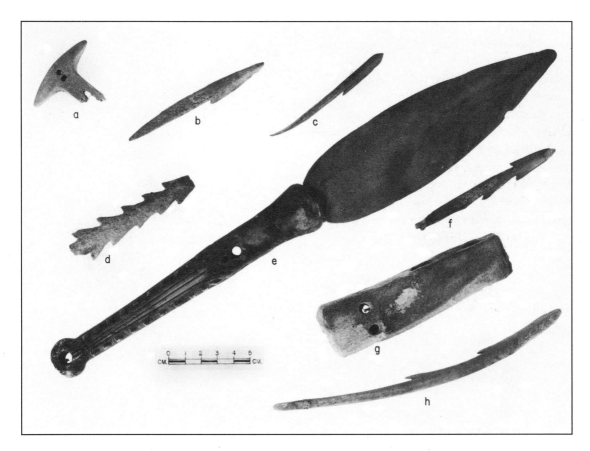

Figure 4 Nadlok site artifacts.

(Fig. 6, b). In Hut 2, where the two forms were found in stratigraphic relation it was the upper floor (floor 2) which produced the tanged form while the lower floor produced the untanged handle.

Sewing Equipment

A needlecase made on a bird bone tube with paired peripheral lines at the middle and both ends was found in Hut 2 Floor 1 (Fig. 7, g). A similarly decorated bird bone drinking tube was also found, along with gull-winged thimble-holders (Fig. 7, d, e, f).

Cooking and Eating Utensils

A bifurcated meat fork or marrow spatula was found in Hut 2 at the edge of the pavement, allowing no floor assignment. There are tiny spurs are on the outside of each tang, and on the side of the blade just up from the tang (Fig. 6, g).

Several crude pottery sherds from Hut 2 include a heavily encrusted rim sherd from Floor 1c and two body sherds from the sand above the first floor. Since the earliest soapstone pot fragments were found in Hut 3 floor 5 - dating to about 1500 A.D. - it is apparent that both ceramic and soapstone vessels were used at the same time at the site. Both lamps and pots are represented, the latter with both lugged and simple rim profiles.

Birchbark basket fragments were also ubiquitous. Several were found painted with red cinnabar lines (Fig. 7).

Transportation Gear

An antler kayak lance rest was found in Floor 1.

Ornaments and Amulets

Pendants with drilled suspension holes were made from teeth, including a dog or wolf canine (Fig. 7, m), a caribou incisor (Fig. 7, n) and a canid carnassial (Fig. 7, o). A canid metapodial was also drilled for suspension (Fig. 7, p). Also found was a bilaterally carved bone object, apparently drilled for suspension at one end (Fig. 7, l).

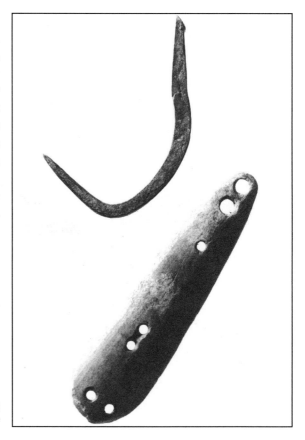

Figure 5 Nadlok site fish hook and shank.

Subsistence

The faunal assemblage was overwhelmingly dominated by caribou. In one analyzed sample of 5170 specimens from Hut 3 Floor 1, 98.8% of identified bone was caribou (Still 1987: Table 1), with comparable figures in the floors of other huts. In total each hut yielded about 30,000 caribou bones and fragments, distributed mainly on either side of the door for each occupation level. Unfortunately the sheer volume of caribou bone precluded air shipment of more than a representative sample, so precise MNI (Minimum Number of Individuals) or NISP (Number of Identified Specimens) counts are not available.

A study of caribou bone epiphyseal fusion and tooth eruption based on 622 elements from Hut

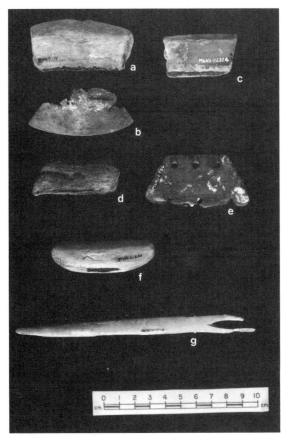

Figure 6 Nadlok site artifacts.

3 Floor 1 found that 15% were from animals at least 13 months old, 30% at least 25 months old, 34% at least 37 months old, 8% at least 49 months old, and 13% at least 61 months old (Still 1987: 17). This suggests the selective hunting of young adults between two and three years of age.

Non-caribou bone included 788 elements shipped to Ottawa for further analysis. Of these, 563 elements (71.5%) were identified to order, including; 62.4% mammalian, 35.3% avian and 2.3% fish (O'Sullivan 1987). Hut 2 bone by NISP includes muskox (52), dog or wolf (17), wolf (5), dog (3), arctic fox (4), wolverine (7), arctic hare (5), arctic ground squirrel (8) and brown lemming (1). Hut 3 bone by NISP includes muskox (59), moose (1), dog or wolf (20), wolf (3), wolverine (9), ermine (2), red squirrel (1), arctic ground squirrel (5) and brown lemming (125). The red squirrel specimen is entirely out of range, and its presence in the site is unexplained.

Bird bones, mostly shaft fragments, include red-throated loon, swan, Ross and white-fronted goose, northern pintail, green-winged teal, oldsquaw, red-breasted merganser, duck family, herring gull, jaeger, short-eared owl, lesser golden plover, and rock and willow ptarmigan. Only ptarmigan are permanent residents of the Nadlok area, the rock variety inhabiting elevations where caribou spotters congregated, and the willow variety in the low wet areas adjoining the site.

Only 2.3% of non-caribou bone are fish, and include lake trout, grayling, arctic char, round and lake whitefish and least cisco. We were able to catch the first three species in the deep pool at the lower caribou crossing using casting rods and spinners or plugs.

Comparisons

Thule culture sites from nearby Coronation Gulf, such as Clachan, Beulah, and Lady Franklin Point (Taylor 1972; Morrison 1983) provide the cultural background for a site like Nadlok, but are themselves too early for close comparison. The very late Thule site of Bloody Falls (McGhee 1972), in the lower Coppermine valley, provides probably the closest similarities. Like Nadlok, it has

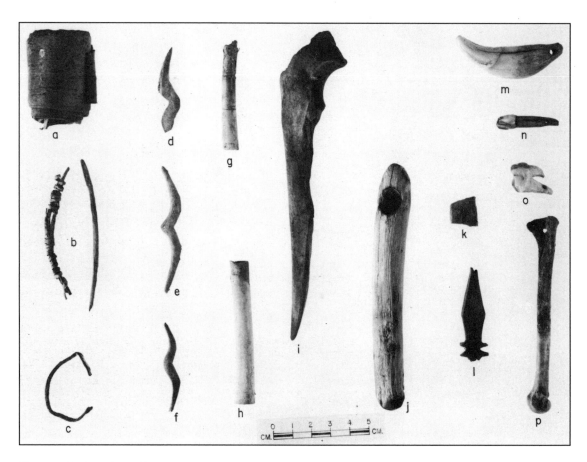

Figure 7 Nadlok site artifacts.

dwellings with slightly sunken pavement floors, untanged copper ulus, both pottery and soapstone vessel fragments, copper arrowheads, and a single open-socket harpoon head. The remarkable antler walls seen on Nadlok structures, however, are clearly absent from Bloody Falls. The occupation at Bloody Falls probably overlaps the earlier portion of the occupational sequence at Nadlok.

Dating after the abandonment of Nadlok are nineteenth-century coastal Copper Inuit sites such as Kunana (McGhee 1972) and Naliqaq (Morrison 1981), both of which have produced abundant European material in the form, primarily, of metal scrap. Some specific similarities persist, including the rare appearance of pottery (Naliqaq). Confusingly, harpoon heads from Kunana are markedly different from those known from other sites. However, the Naliqaq harpoon heads closely resemble closed-socket Nadlok specimens, and duplicate the form described by Jenness (1946) in the early twentieth century. Other similarities, including copper arrowheads and gull-winged thimble holders, also have close counterparts in the material culture of the twentieth-century Copper Inuit (Jenness 1946). A significant difference in tool assemblages is the exclusive use of tanged ulus from the later Copper Inuit sites .

Figure 8 Nadlok site stone house and antler hut (reconstructed).

Nadlok antler huts have few analogies anywhere. They can exist only at water-crossings where hundreds of antlers were available. More may be found at crossings on the Bathurst herd migration path and on the trade route between the Copper and Caribou Inuit (Stefansson 1914). Caribou Inuit tent rings with fallen spruce tent poles are clearly quite different, while Late prehistoric-early historic Copper and Caribou Inuit houses on Coronation Gulf and Hudson Bay are surface dwellings (Linnamae and Clark 1976; McGhee 1972: 66). Since abundant antler was available to the Caribou Inuit, its non-utilization may be explained by readily available wood, a raw material rare at Nadlok.

Nadlok semi-subterranean houses (Figs. 8 and 9) resemble Thule culture houses at Baker Lake (Gordon 1974) and in coastal locations throughout the Arctic. They may also resemble so-called *qarmats* at the Buliard, Nichol, and lower Coppermine sites (McGhee 1972: 67), with low entrance passages and tiny sleeping platforms. More suited to migratory caribou hunters, *qarmats* are smaller and less permanent than coastal Thule houses. Nadlok families probably vacated them in the spring, moving to the drier warmer antler surface huts.

Another island crossing like Nadlok is located just upstream. In 1986, six stone-walled structures were found but remain untested. Antler rings were either absent or buried in the willows. Other historic Inuit sites were found upstream towards Contwoyto Lake, but no structures occur. Downstream, several unusual but untested mounds are near the Mara River, a tributary of the Burnside.

Discussion

Nadlok's occupation seems to span the transition from local Thule to Copper Inuit culture, from about A.D. 1450 to 1750. Thule origins are best seen in the open-socketed harpoon heads, tangless ulus, and in the persistent if rare use of pottery for vessel manufacture. Later Copper Inuit traits include the common use of copper staples (Fig. 7, c) and rivets (Fig. 6, e) for joining the parts of composite tools (Morrison 1987), the tanged ulus (cf. Jenness 1946: Fig. 82), decorated bone-tube needlecase (cf. Jenness 1946: Fig. 94), thimble-holders, the meat fork or marrow spatula (cf. Jenness 1946: Fig. 102), the copper-bladed whittling knife (cf. Jenness 1946: Fig. 114) and "man's" knife (cf. Jenness 1946: Figs. 107), and the closed-socket harpoon heads (Jenness 1946: Fig. 140).

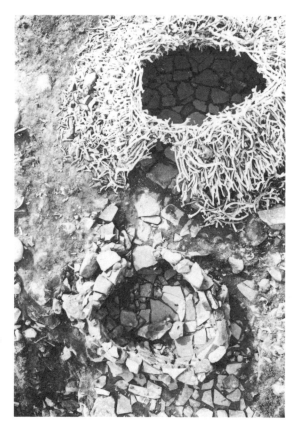

Figure 9 Nadlok site stone house and antler hut (reconstructed), from above.

Comparisons can be made beyond the territory of the coastal Copper Inuit. The crudely retouched unground black chert arrowhead with wide shoulders resembles specimens from post-1600 A.D. levels at Kittigazuit (McGhee 1974: Table 2), Okat (Morrison 1990: Pl. 12e-m) and Cape Krusenstern in northwestern Alaska (Giddings and Anderson 1986: 48). Nephrite adzes have previously been found in Arctic Canada, but only in the Mackenzie Delta area (Gordon 1970; McGhee 1974) and are possibly traceable to the Kobuk River in Alaska (Giddings 1952). The decoration on the finely engraved man's knife handle has close parallels on a specimen from Langton Bay, between Coronation Gulf and the Mackenzie Delta (Morrison 1990: Pl. 19, c).

A few items point to possible trade or other connections to the south. Nadlok is located close to a traditional trade route linking Bathurst Inlet and the Thelon River area, and it may be that some of the abundant wood found in the site came from the latter area. During the nineteenth and early twentieth centuries, there was a trading rendezvous on the Thelon River at a place called Akilinek, where Copper Inuit met Caribou Inuit who in turn were trading with the Hudson's Bay Company

(Stefansson 1914). Before the fur trade era the Thelon area may already have been used by eastern Copper Inuit as source of wood. Notable wooden pieces at Nadlok include a bow fragment, a number of blackened spruce fire-hearths and several charred fire spindles (Fig. 7, j). The birchbark vessel fragments were taken from trees with diameters of about 15 to 20 centimetres, and may suggest trade or other connections with the forested interior to the south. A birchbark basket of similar size was found even further north at the Beulah site on Coronation Gulf (Morrison 1983: Fig. 20).

Conclusion

Since the 1960s it has become apparent that the Copper Inuit, like all Inuit, have an origin in coastal Thule culture (Taylor 1972; McGhee 1972). Yet there may be merit in the suggestion by earlier ethnographers, including Birket-Smith (1929) and Jenness (1923), that their more immediate ancestry lay, at least in part, in the interior. Nadlok is the only excavated site thus far known which spans the crucial transitional period between Thule and Copper Inuit culture. Coastal sites dating to this period are unknown, or essentially so (cf. McGhee's [1972] "Intermediate Interval"), and it has been suggested that coastal regions such as Coronation Gulf suffered a nearly complete population collapse at the end of the Thule period, some 300 or 400 years ago (McGhee 1972; Morrison 1983). Reasons remain uncertain, but may have had much to do with the deteriorating climatic conditions of the Little Ice Age. Certainly, the persistence of multi-year ice would have had very serious effects on the local seal population, upon which in turn local Thule people depended. There may have been a population shift from coastal locations to more secure inland areas where caribou hunting predominated. The occasional presence of seal bones at Nadlok suggests that they were not entirely cut off from the sea, but continued to make seasonal forays there. But only with the warming climatic conditions of the nineteenth century did the focus of occupation return to the coast, leading directly to the development of historic Copper Inuit culture as documented in the early twentieth century.

At a time of climatic stress, Nadlok was established where the Bathurst caribou herd crosses the Burnside River on its July migration to the southern forest north of Great Slave Lake. It became an important site because here people were able to draw upon this huge seasonal reservoir of food, drying and freezing a great deal of meat and fat for winter. They occupied Nadlok over a period of several hundred years between about A.D. 1450 and 1750. After living in autumn tent camps in the early period, occupation became more permanent, with the building of both semi-subterranean winter houses and paved antler-walled autumn huts.

By the early twentieth century the Nadlok area was little used by Copper Inuit (Freeman 1976: Map 22). Yet an echo of the Nadlok occupation may be found in the traditional Yellowknife Indian name for the Burnside River on which the site is located. They called it the *Annatessey*, or "River of Strangers" (Franklin 1969: 405).

Acknowledgements

I thank David Morrison for interpreting the significance of many of the artifacts, he and Marjory Gordon for editorial assistance and Richard Morlan for identifying the canid tooth.

References

Ball, T. F. 1986. Historical evidence and climatic implications of a shift in the boreal forest tundra transition in central Canada. Climatic Change, 8: 121-134.

Birket-Smith, K. 1929. The Caribou Eskimos: Material and Social Life and their Cultural Position. Report of the Fifth Thule Expedition 1921-24, 5(1).

Bryson, R. A. and W. M. Wendland. 1967. Tentative climatic patterns for some late glacial and post-glacial episodes in central North America. In, Life, Land and Water, W. Mayer-Oakes, ed. University of Manitoba, Dept. of Anthropology, Occasional Paper, 1: 271-298.

Freeman, M. 1976. Inuit Land Use and Occupancy Project, Vol. 3: Land Use Atlas. Ottawa: Dept. of Indian and Northern Affairs.

Franklin, J. 1969. Journey to the Shores of the Polar Sea. New York: Greenwood Press.

Giddings, L. J. 1952. The Arctic Woodland culture of the Kobuk River. Philadelphia: Museum Monographs, University Museum .

Giddings, L. J., and D. Anderson. 1986. Beach Ridge Archaeology of Cape Krusenstern. United States Dept.of Interior, National Park Service, Publications in Archaeology, 20.

Gordon, B. 1970. Recent archaeological investigations on the arctic Yukon coast, including a description of the British Mountain complex at Trout Lake. In, Early Man and Environments in Northwestern North America, J. Smith and R. Smith, eds. Calgary: University of Calgary Archaeological Association, pp. 67-86.

Gordon, B. 1974. Thule culture investigations at Baker Lake, N.W.T. Canadian Archaeological Association , 6: 218-24.

Gordon, B. 1982. Tooth sectioning as an archaeological tool. Archaeological Survey of Canada, National Museum of Man, Canadian Studies Report 14e.

Jenness, D. 1922. The Life of the Copper Eskimos. Report of the Canadian Arctic Expedition 1913-18, Vol. 12.

Jenness, D. 1923. Origin of the Copper Eskimos and their copper culture. The Geographical Review, 13: 540-551.

Jenness, D. 1946. Material Culture of the Copper Eskimos. Report of the Canadian Arctic Expedition 1913-18, Vol. 16.

Lamb, H. H. 1966. The changing climate. London: Methuen .

Linnamae, U. and B. Clarke. 1976. Archaeology of Rankin Inlet, N.W.T. The Muskox, 19: 37-73.

Mathiassen, T. 1927. Archaeology of the Central Eskimo. Report of the Fifth Thule Expedition 1921-24, 4.

McGhee, R. 1972. Copper Eskimo Prehistory. National Museum of Man, Publications in Archaeology 2.

McGhee, R. 1974. Beluga hunters: an archaeological reconstruction of the history and culture of the Mackenzie Delta Kittegaryumiut. Memorial University of Newfoundland, Newfoundland Social and Economic Studies, 13.

Morrison, D. 1981. A preliminary statement on Neo-Eskimo occupations in western Coronation Gulf, N.W.T. Arctic, 34(3): 261-269.

Morrison, D. 1983. Thule culture in western Coronation Gulf, N.W.T. National Museum of Man, Mercury Series, Archaeological Survey of Canada Paper, 116.

Morrison, D. 1987. Thule and historic copper use in the Copper Inuit area. American Antiquity, 52(1): 3-12.

Morrison, D. 1990. Iglulualumiut Prehistory: the lost Inuit of Franklin Bay. Canadian Museum of Civilization, Mercury Series, Archaeological Survey of Canada Paper, 142.

O'Sullivan, A. 1987. Final faunal report of the Nadlok Island site, MbNs-1. MS in the author's possession.

Stefansson, V. 1914. Prehistoric and present commerce among the Arctic coast Eskimo. Geological Survey of Canada, Museum Bulletin, 6: 1-29.

Still, L. 1987.   Where the caribou cross the river: a faunal examination of a late prehistoric Copper Inuit summer hunting camp. MS on file with the Zoological Identification Centre, National Museum of Natural Sciences, Ottawa.

Taylor, W. E.. 1972. <u>An archaeological survey between Cape Parry and Cambridge Bay, N.W.T., Canada in 1963</u>. National Museum of Man, Mercury Series, Archaeological Survey of Canada Paper, 1.

Protohistoric Settlement Patterns in the Interior District of Keewatin: Implications for Caribou Inuit Social Organization

T. Max Friesen
McGill University
Montreal, Quebec

and

Andrew Stewart
Royal Ontario Museum
Toronto, Ontario

Abstract

Inuit of the interior District of Keewatin were named "Caribou Eskimo" by Birket-Smith in 1929, due to their profound reliance on caribou for food, clothing, shelter, weapons, and tools. In part because of this adaptation, they have generally been portrayed as among the most primitive and simple societies in the Canadian Arctic. This portrait is based on ethnographic research conducted after major epidemics and drastic reductions in caribou populations had decimated Inuit societies of the Keewatin. This paper, based on two recent archaeological projects in the District of Keewatin, presents Inuit site distributions for two areas: Aberdeen Lake on the Thelon River, and the lower Kazan River. Both areas yielded settlement patterns characterized by significant variability in site size, complexity, and function. These data indicate that Inuit societies of interior Keewatin were able to maximize their social interaction in ways more complex than are indicated by the ethnographic record.

Résumé

En 1929, Birket-Smith baptisa «Esquimaux du caribou» les Inuit de l'intérieur du district de Keewatin parce qu'ils dépendaient énormément du caribou pour leur subsistance, leur habillement, la construction de leur gîte, ainsi que pour la fabrication de leurs armes et de leurs outils. Cette adaptation, entre autres, a valu à ces Inuit d'être représentés parmi les sociétés les plus primitives et les plus simples de l'Arctique canadien. Ce portrait est fondé sur des recherches ethnographiques menées après que de graves épidémies et des réductions considérables des populations de caribous eurent décimé les sociétés inuit de Keewatin. Ce document, basé sur deux recherches archéologiques entreprises récemment dans le district de Keewatin, présente la répartition des sites inuit dans deux régions : le lac Aberdeen sur la rivière Thelon, et le cours inférieur de la rivière Kazan. Ces deux régions offrent des modèles d'implantation qui se caractérisent par la variabilité des dimensions, de la complexité et de la fonction du site. Ces données indiquent que les sociétés inuit de l'intérieur du district de Keewatin étaient en mesure de maximiser leur interaction sociale de manière plus complexe

Threads of Arctic Prehistory: Papers in Honour of William E. Taylor Jr., David Morrison and Jean-Luc Pilon, eds. Canadian Museum of Civilization, Mercury Series, Archaeological Survey of Canada Paper 149. 1994.

que les documents ethnographiques ne l'indiquent.

Introduction

Inuit of the interior District of Keewatin were named "Caribou Eskimo" by ethnographers due to their profound reliance on caribou for food, clothing, shelter, and tools. In part because of this adaptation, they were portrayed as a particularly simple society, extremely high in mobility and low in social and cultural sophistication. It has recently become clear, however, that the principal ethnographers failed to understand Caribou Inuit society within its historical context. In particular, they failed to fully explore the effects of major epidemics and drastic reductions in caribou populations which had decimated Inuit societies just prior to their period of observation in the early 1920s (Burch 1986, 1988).

This paper will present archaeological evidence from two regions of interior Keewatin; Aberdeen Lake on the lower Thelon River and the lower Kazan River below Angikuni lake (Fig. 1). Both regions yielded more complex community patterns than are indicated in the "ethnographic present" which was created by the comprehensive descriptive work of the Fifth Thule Expedition. In particular, evidence for large, seasonal aggregations and more elaborate architecture at several sites could have provided the conditions for a greater degree of social complexity than is evident in the ethnographic record. These data reinforce the work of Burch (1986, 1988), who emphasizes the higher regional Inuit population and more stable resource base in the Keewatin interior during the period prior to the 1920s.

The Ethnographic Present in the Interior District of Keewatin

Current knowledge of the "ethnographic present" for the Caribou Inuit is based largely on the work of Kaj Birket-Smith and Knud Rasmussen of the Fifth Thule Expedition. Their reports, based on fieldwork conducted in 1922 and 1923, illustrate a fragmented and highly mobile people, living in small camps, with a material culture which seemed "primitive" or "archaic" to the ethnographers (Birket-Smith 1929b, 1959; Rasmussen 1930a,b). Rasmussen's (1930a: 6) statement that "we had not been long among the Caribou Eskimos before we became aware that we had before us a primitive culture that had originated in the interior" indicates that he and Birket-Smith became convinced very early that the Caribou Inuit were survivals of a "proto-Eskimo" stage of development, and were the primitive forbears of later, more advanced, coast-adapted Inuit cultures.

The hypothesis that the Caribou Inuit represent a holdout of an ancient inland Inuit group was initially questioned by Mathiassen (1927: 200), and has since been thoroughly discredited. Anthropological literature on the Caribou Inuit has, however, incorporated other observations and conclusions of the Fifth Thule Expedition, such as the small scale and impermanence of settlements, simple, flexible social and residential organization, and generally marginal existence in contrast to coastal Thule and post-contact societies (eg. Damas 1968: 111). In certain extreme cases, Caribou Inuit are described as "primitive" or "degenerated", as when Harper (1964) wrote that "the Padlimiut in general are said to be the most primitive of all the Eskimos" (cf. also Clark 1977).

In order to understand the Inuit cultures observed by Birket-Smith and Rasmussen, however, their historical context must be examined. This context included famines resulting from a drastic reduction in the caribou population which began in 1915 (Burch 1986; Csonka 1991). In interior Keewatin, Inuit economies were subject to annual change as variation occurred in the timing of caribou migrations and the size of the herds. Changes in the level of the caribou supply affected people's ability to procure food as well as equip themselves with skins for clothing and tents and raw materials for tool production. In addition, caribou meat provided food for dogs, which allowed Inuit to travel to Hudson's Bay Company

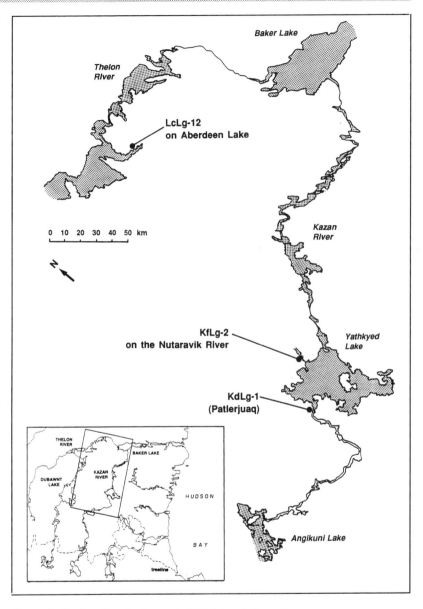

Figure 1 Site locations in the central District of Keewatin.

posts that supplied other important goods such as guns and ammunition. Weather conditions were an important source of annual variability, to some extent controlling the availability of caribou and affecting conditions generally for fishing, hunting, and travelling. For example, freeze-thaw cycles during a series of winters beginning in 1915 or 1917 drastically reduced the availability of caribou over the following decade (Burch 1986: 129; Csonka 1991: 182-194), permanently altering the Caribou Inuit way of life. Thus, "hard times" (cf. Amsden 1979) were the norm by the time

Birket-Smith visited the Caribou Inuit in 1922 and wrote that starvation was a regular event every winter.

Superimposed on this pattern of annual variability were longer-term background sources of change. They included a declining musk-ox population during the later 19th century, once a mainstay of Caribou Inuit subsistence (Burch 1977), culminating in near-extirpation by the early 20th century. Another source of steady change was the high rate of population growth within southern and central Keewatin throughout the 19th and early 20th centuries, from a low of less than 500 in 1790 to a high of about 1375 in 1890 (Burch 1986; cf. Csonka 1991). New societies formed and territory expanded as a result of this population increase (Burch 1986). A third source of change was the fur trade, with its most important effect being an increased availability of guns. Eurocanadian technology became increasingly common as new trading venues were established, beginning with whaling ships along the northwest coast of Hudson Bay from 1860 to 1915 (Ross 1975), followed by Hudson Bay Company ships after 1880, and finally interior trading posts after about 1910 (Usher 1971). These changes suggest that economic and social life was in a constant state of adjustment and that the situation during the 1920s cannot be expected to accurately represent earlier periods.

Caribou Inuit Social Organization

This section presents two aspects of the ethnographic portrait of Caribou Inuit social organization that can be approached using archaeological evidence: aggregation and sophistication of architecture. Other aspects of social organization are more difficult to observe in the archaeological record. For example, the ethnographically recorded leadership role, held by a senior hunter, or *ihumataq*, of each extended family (Birket-Smith 1929a: 259; Burch 1986: 119), will probably never be visible archaeologically, because there is no indication that he would have occupied a larger tent, or that he would have had the opportunity to amass much material wealth. By contrast, settlement behaviour, including the extent to which people aggregated and the effort invested in construction of dwelling and community structures, can be inferred more directly from archaeological evidence.

Seasonal population aggregations were related to the distribution of different kinds of resources. Along the coast, overwintering whaling vessels provided centres for aggregation during the late 19th century (Ross 1975), as did trading posts during the early 20th century. In the Keewatin interior, however, the largest aggregations were associated with communal caribou hunts, especially at water-crossings where large herds could be intercepted. These hunts occurred from late August to early October and meat resulting from successful hunts was stored near these sites. Even during the hard years of the 1920s, meat resulting from fall hunts supported at least some residents until mid to late winter.

On the Kazan River, Birket-Smith (1929a: 74) recorded 423 people in 24 camps, with an average camp size of 17.6 people, and a maximum of 54. Rasmussen's (1930a: 37) maximum observed aggregation, at a winter camp near Yathkyed Lake, was 47. Other early authors have recorded scattered data on camp sizes, with an unfortunate lack of consistency as to whether they recorded the population, the number of tents, or both. The largest reported population of a single inland site is 54 (Birket-Smith 1929a: 74); while the largest number of tents recorded at one site is the count of 10-12 tents at the west end of Baker Lake (J. B. Tyrrell 1897: 74), and one of 16 tents at the east end of Baker Lake (Hanbury 1904: 65). This latter aggregation was related to the availability of marine resources and Eurocanadian trade goods on Hudson Bay, and therefore cannot be considered a result of a full-time inland adaptation. More recent synthesists reinforce the small size of camps, with a figure of 50 or fewer people often cited, except at places of trade with Eurocanadians (Arima 1984; Damas 1968).

This perception of small aggregation size is reinforced by observations of a high degree of mobility, as indicated by frequent moves and short periods of aggregation. Although specific data are scarce, Birket-Smith (1929a: 70) wrote that "the most conspicuous thing about the settlements on the Barren Grounds is their temporary character, which is further emphasized by the perishable material, snow, of which the winter dwellings are built". This picture was further summed up by the statement that they "spend their whole lives travelling" (Birket-Smith 1929a: 153).

The second category of data which can be derived from the ethnographic record is the relative sophistication of architecture. Simple architecture has been cited as an indication of the relative simplicity of Caribou Inuit society (Birket-Smith 1959: 198). According to ethnohistoric sources for inland areas (Birket-Smith 1929a: 76-84), dwellings are restricted to tents and snow houses, with the occasional use of snow *qarmat*, which are constructed of snow block walls with a skin roof (Hanbury 1904: 75). All of these seasonal dwelling types are extremely temporary, and reinforce the idea of a high level of residential mobility. There is no ethnographic record of the use of stone houses by Inuit inhabiting the interior, although records exist for their use on the coast in the 18th century (Burch 1978: 19).

A second architectural category which can be used to infer social organization consists of special constructions for dances and community activities. In the ethnographic record, Caribou Inuit summer dances or meetings occurred in the largest tent, and not in a specially constructed feature (Burch 1986: 123; Rasmussen 1930a: 66). In winter villages, a large communal snow-house was sometimes built (Birket-Smith 1929a: 269). More permanent constructions for communal gatherings are not, however, mentioned in any ethnohistoric text.

This ethnographic record of an unchanging, highly mobile, simply organized society existing in small camps, except along the coast where trade with Eurocanadians occurred, should not be accepted uncritically. Rather, it can be tested against oral histories and the ethnohistoric record, as Burch (1986, 1988) is currently doing, and against the archaeological record.

Data Presentation

The ethnographically derived generalizations discussed above will be assessed on the basis of two archaeological surveys which were conducted along the Thelon and lower Kazan rivers between 1988 and 1991 (see Fig. 1). The Kiggavik Archaeological Project was conducted during the summers of 1988, 1989, and 1991 (Friesen 1990). This project was designed as an archaeological impact assessment for the proposed Kiggavik mine site which is located east of Aberdeen Lake. The scale of the mining project necessitated extensive survey in a region extending from Chesterfield Inlet to northeast Aberdeen Lake. Initial helicopter survey was followed by more intensive foot surveys of areas which yielded significant archaeological sites. In total, 70 archaeological sites were recorded, a majority of which result from Inuit occupations. For the present discussion, a series of 21 sites on the north shore of the southeast arm of Aberdeen Lake will be used to infer aspects of Inuit settlement patterns.

The second project, which occurred in 1988, was a reconnaissance of the lower Kazan river between Angikuni and Baker Lakes by foot and canoe, a distance of about 450 river kilometres (Stewart 1991). This project involved selective survey of river narrows, prominent landforms, eroded shorelines, and places associated with cultural activity mentioned by previous travellers such as Tyrrell, or identified in Inuit accounts or maps (e.g. Freeman 1976; Rasmussen 1930b). The survey included a five kilometre excursion up the Nutaravik river, a tributary of the Kazan on Yathkyed Lake, the location of KfLg-2, one of the sites discussed in this paper. A total of 190 sites were noted. Only about 30 of these sites date to the precontact period based on assemblages that contain exclusively stone tools.

Although the archaeological record of Keewatin contains evidence of Palaeo-Indian, Archaic, Arctic Small Tool tradition, and Taltheilei peoples, most of the 260 sites encountered during the two surveys were occupied by Inuit. These sites can be attributed with certainty to Inuit occupation on the basis of 1) the presence of specific Inuit feature types such as kayak rests; 2) the presence of Inuit artifact types such as kayak parts, snow beaters and women's hair sticks (Birket-Smith 1929a); or 3) reported visits by Tyrrell (n.d., 1895, 1897) to Inuit camps at the locations of some of these archaeological sites. However, precise chronological determination is made difficult by the probable reuse of some sites, which could result in the deposition of recent artifacts on earlier features, and by the fact that certain sites contain almost no visible diagnostic artifacts. The Neoeskimo culture history of this vast region is not yet fully understood, and the probability of some prehistoric Inuit occupation has been raised by the interpretation of several sites as Thule (Gordon 1974; Harp 1961).

Regional distributions of large sites are presented here in order to provide context for the specific site descriptions which follow. Inuit sites encountered during these surveys range in size from a single feature, such as an isolated tent ring or hearth, to over 100 features, including tent rings, meat caches, inuksuit, hunting blinds, graves, kayak stands, and fox traps. Sites are distributed widely throughout the study area, however they tend to occur more frequently in areas of east-west trending river channels or lake margins, due to the tendency of these landforms to concentrate caribou movements. The locations of 23 sites with more than 15 features each are shown in Figure 2. The frequency of dwelling features at these sites, which should more closely approximate actual population sizes, ranges from one to 52, with a median of nine. Large sites may, of course, result from reoccupation during successive years. They may even result from small scale shifts in residence within a small area during a single season. During the summer, for instance, frequent changes in camp location were sometimes prompted by the stench of rotting caribou (Harper 1964: 10).

The problem of distinguishing aggregations from other processes resulting in large sites, such as reoccupation, may be approached from several directions. First, the presence of more than one seasonal type of dwelling feature may, under certain circumstances, indicate stable occupations of more than one season's duration, providing a context for aggregation. In several Alaskan cases, for example, families moved between different seasonal dwellings which were constructed adjacent to one another within a single settlement (eg. Nelson 1899: 247; Spencer 1959: 60). Second, the spatial

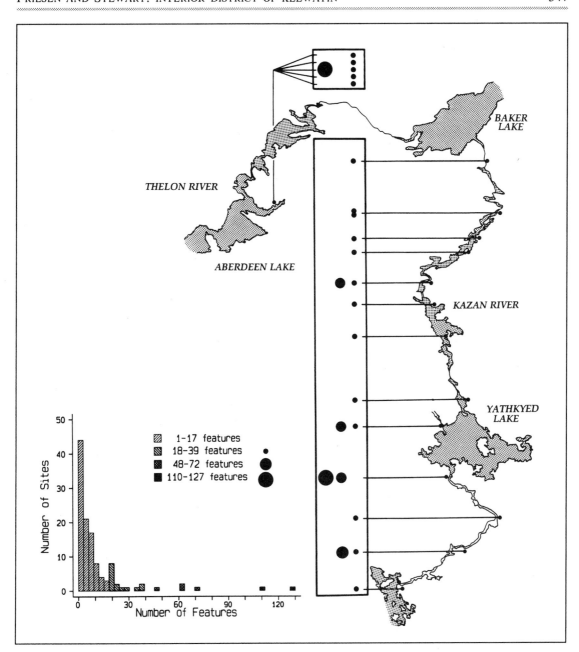

Figure 2 Distribution of sites by size in the study area.

arrangement of residential features may provide a clue to the relative number of people occupying the site. In a cross-cultural ethnographic survey, Whitelaw (1991: 165) reports that clustered and linear patterns of dwellings at large sites are associated with aggregations of people. In an archaeological context, features conforming to these patterns would have to be discrete, or non-overlapping, to support the idea of simultaneous occupation by a large number of people (eg. Deaver 1989: 259). Finally, oral testimony is relevant to the question of reoccupation. Direct information from Inuit elders in Greenland, published by Gronnow (1986: 78), and Baker Lake, in the context of the present research, supports the inference that all surface dwelling features at a given site were occupied contemporaneously. In both cases, elders indicated that Inuit who reoccupied a site would use preexisting tent rings or other dwelling features, rather than building new ones, supporting the premise that the observed number of tent rings tends to represent the maximum occupation of a site, rather than sequential occupation by smaller groups.

These criteria for identifying simultaneous occupation of dwellings at large sites will be used to assess evidence for the presence of large aggregations at three sites in the study area. Two sites are located in the Kazan River basin and one on Aberdeen Lake, which is a part of the Thelon River system. These sites are interpreted as having been occupied during the period prior to 1915, based on the nature and scarcity of historic artifacts observed on the surface. However, precise dates cannot be determined on the basis of currently available information, and some of the sites could be up to several centuries in age. Of greatest importance to the argument advanced here is the fact that they represent Inuit adaptations to the interior District of Keewatin during the period before direct

Figure 3 *Qarmat* at site KfLg-2.

ethnographic observation.

KfLg-2

KfLg-2 is located on the Nutaravik River, which flows into the north end of Yathkyed Lake. This site consists of a dense concentration of at least 60 features, including 18 tent rings and 17 substantial house features (*qarmat*) with paved or sub-surface floors. Individual habitation structures do not appear to overlap, though some borrowing of rock from one tent ring suggests a limited amount of re-working of tent rings during different occupations. Figure 3 illustrates one of the most substantial *qarmat*, located in a boulder field adjacent to the river bank. Its two metre thick walls were formed by the clearing of boulders from a five metre diameter area within the boulder field. The floor, overgrown with willow, is partly paved with flat boulder slabs. Two wood pole fragments protrude from the top of the wall, likely indicating that the structure once had a skin roof. These large house features suggest a residential function involving a relatively large family or group of families during the cold season, perhaps during freeze-up or break-up when neither tents nor snow houses were practical.

The slightly overlapping but discrete zones occupied by tent rings, on the one hand, and *qarmat*, on the other (Figure 4), support the idea that they represent two seasonal aspects of the same occupation. *Qarmat* are generally found to the south and east, close to the river's edge. Tent rings are found to the north and west. These areas are roughly equal in size, about 50 metres in diameter, with outlying features scattered to the

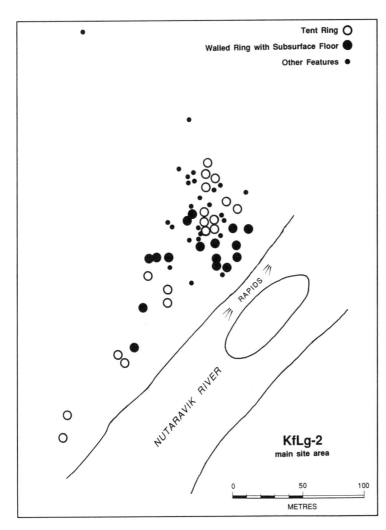

Figure 4 Plan of site KfLg-2.

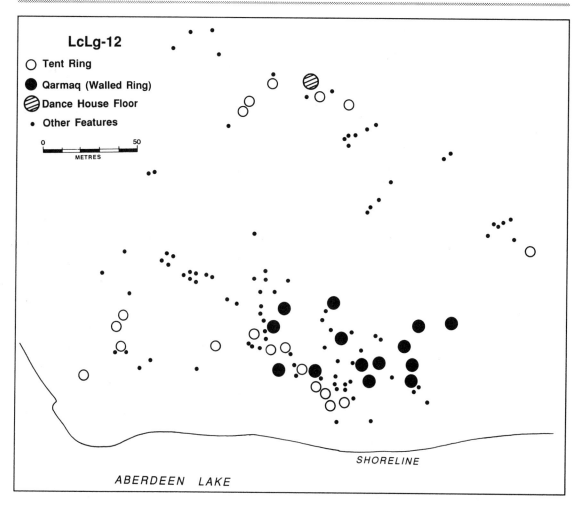

Figure 5 Plan of site LcLg-12.

south along the west bank of the river. Approximately equal numbers of tent rings and *qarmat* suggest that a seasonal shift in settlement occurred involving a single large group of people moving from 15 to 20 warm-season tents, located in a relatively high, exposed part of the site, to a similar number of cold-season dwellings, located in a more protected area next to the river.

LcLg-12

The second site which contains evidence for a large aggregation of long duration is LcLg-12, located on the southeast arm of Aberdeen Lake on the Thelon River. At this site, a total of 127 features were mapped including dwelling features, kayak rests, caches, inuksuit, and a special, large dance-house (Fig. 5). Dwelling features included 14 *qarmat* and 19 tent rings, four of which were constructed as two sets of adjoining, double tent rings. The stone *qarmat* are constructed mainly of

Figure 6 *Qarmat* at site LcLg-12.

large stone slabs placed on edge, and are much more substantial constructions than the simple tent rings reported in the ethnographic record (Fig. 6). They range in shape from round to oval, with the maximum internal dimension ranging from 3 to 4.5 metres. None of the dwelling features overlaps, and none was observed to have had stones removed for construction of other, later features. The dwelling features are concentrated in two primary clusters, with a northern cluster consisting of five tent rings and the dance-house, and the southern cluster containing 13 tent rings and 14 *qarmat*. These two clusters may be contemporaneous, however this inference is impossible to assess given current archaeological methods. In this regard, it should be noted that although ethnographic sources do not describe spacing of dwellings within a community, a number of early photographs indicate significant unoccupied gaps within large camps (eg. Hanbury 1904: opp. 76).

As with site KfLg-2, the zones occupied by the *qarmat* and tent rings are relatively discrete, but overlap slightly (see Figure 5). In addition, the two dwelling types in the main site cluster are roughly equal in number, with 13 tent rings and 14 *qarmat*. These facts are interpreted to indicate that a single group of people occupied this site over a relatively long-duration occupation, during which a seasonal shift of dwelling type occurred.

Figure 7 Communal structure at site LcLg-12.

LcLg-12 also contains a special feature which is clearly a dance-house (Figure 7). This feature is 6.5 metres in interior diameter, and 7.5 metres in exterior diameter, making it almost double the floor area of any other feature on the site. It is also more carefully constructed than other features, being almost perfectly circular, with a central floor area paved with large stones, two niches in the rear wall, and relatively precise construction of the walls in several courses of stone slabs. Finally, and most convincing, is the fact that this feature was immediately identified as a dance-house by Barnabus Piryuaq, an elder from Baker Lake who visited the site during the survey.

KdLq-1 (Patlerjuaq)

Both sites described above lie at one end of a continuum of size and complexity, as measured by the number of tent rings, the presence of more than one seasonal type of dwelling, and the spatial patterning of dwellings. Not all large sites in the study area are equally complex. The site of Patlerjuaq, located at the effluence of the Kazan River into Yathkyed Lake, contains a total of about 110 features, including 23 tent rings (Fig. 8). The evidence of size, alone, might suggest the presence

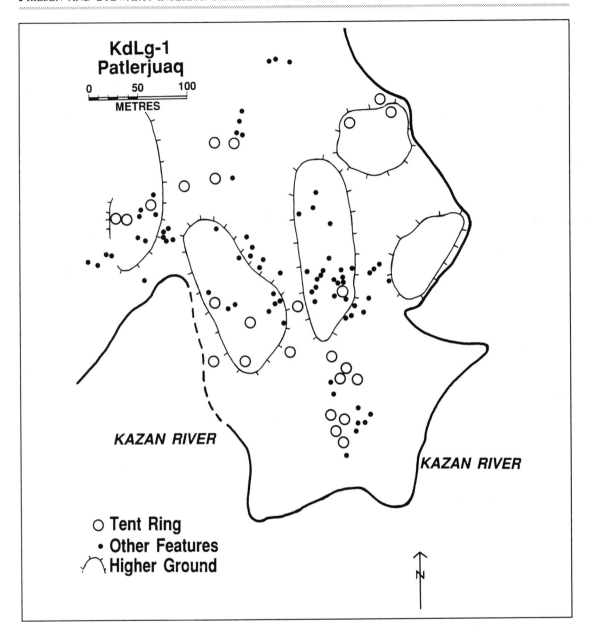

Figure 8 Plan of site KdLg-1 (Patlerjuaq).

of a large aggregation of people during summer or early fall. A number of factors other than size suggest, however, that reoccupation was an important process in the formation of this site.

First, the high proportion of non-residential features observed at this site is consistent with the idea of reoccupation. This conclusion is based on the fact that residential features, such as tent rings, tend to be reused (see discussion above), whereas other kinds of features, particularly caches and graves, are more likely to be constructed in response to specific needs during each new occupation. Thus, a site which is subject to repeated episodes of reoccupation should show an increase in non-residential features in relation to residential features over time (Stewart 1993). Second, although winter occupation cannot be ruled out, as snow houses might have been located on the river ice, leaving no trace, there is no evidence of heavier rings or *qarmat* that might otherwise suggest prolonged use during the fall caribou hunting season. Third, a cluster of 8 tent rings is found at the south end of the small peninsula where Patlerjuaq is located, but the remaining rings and other features are generally distributed throughout the peninsula and on the mainland to the north. This pattern suggests changing circumstances of occupation - different weather conditions, for example, or different sizes of camp during occupations in different years. For these reasons, Patlerjuaq is interpreted as the result of a series of summer-fall occupations, some of which probably also represented larger aggregations of people. Thus, despite its size and the fact that aggregation must have contributed to its formation, Patlerjuaq does not appear to represent a complex, single occupation on the scale of the previous two sites.

Discussion

Sites KfLg-2 and LcLg-12 contain evidence for population aggregations larger than 50 people, an upper limit commonly mentioned when Caribou Inuit camp size is estimated (e.g. Arima 1984: 454). Exact populations cannot be defined, however an approximation can be calculated using information collected by J. B. Tyrrell (n.d., 1895, 1897) on the number of tents and people at camps that he visited on the Dubawnt and Kazan rivers in 1893 and 1894. Tyrrell recorded at least 128 people in 20 tents at seven camps, yielding a mean of 6.4 people per tent (Table 1). If this figure is multiplied by the number of same-season dwellings at sites KfLg-2 and LcLg-12, each was occupied by at least 90 people. Not only were these aggregations relatively large, but they are also interpreted as being of long duration. In both cases, two types of dwelling feature, appropriate for different seasonal conditions, were present in roughly equal numbers. If the aggregations had been brief, only one dwelling type would be expected.

Both of these aggregations did not occur at places of trade with Eurocanadians, and therefore can reasonably be considered to be associated with other aspects of the interior subsistence-settlement system. The specific context for these aggregations is probably the fall caribou hunt, an inference which is supported by the presence of large caches at both sites, as well as their proximity to inuksuk systems which may have served to direct caribou movements. In addition, the presence of secondary resources probably contributed to large-scale occupation of specific settlements, due to the fact that an increase in the number of harvestable resources should decrease the risks produced by failure of a specific resource, such as caribou. KfLg-2, for example, is situated in a region along the north shore of Yathkyed Lake that was favourable to musk-oxen and which became a refuge for this species in the early 20th century (Burch 1977: 145). Moreover, the site's location at rapids on the Nutaravik River would have provided opportunities for relatively easy fishing at open water until late in the fall season. Both types of resource could have supplemented caribou, which migrate through the area

Table 1 **Demographic information for seven Inuit camps** visited by J.B. Tyrrell in 1893 and 1894. In cases where J.B. Tyrrell (1895, 1897, nd) and J.W. Tyrrell (1908) report more than one population estimate for a single camp, the lowest reported number is used here.

CAMP LOCATION, NAME OF LEADING HUNTER, AND REFERENCE.	NUMBER OF TENTS	NUMBER OF PEOPLE	PEOPLE PER TENT
Below Yathkyed Lake, Kazan River (Tyrrell n.d., 1897:136)	1	3	3.0
Below Grant Lake, Dubawnt River (Tyrrell 1897:11)	1	8	8.0
Hallo's camp, above Angikuni Lake, Kazan River (Tyrrell n.d., 1897:20).	2	16	8.0
Elrayuk's camp, between Angikuni and Yathkyed Lakes, Kazan River (Tyrrell n.d., 1897:131).	2	12	6.0
Ungaluk's camp, between Angikuni and Yathkyed Lakes, Kazan River (Tyrrell n.d., 1897:131).	3	20	6.7
Aunah's camp, between Angikuni and Yathkyed Lakes, Kazan River (Tyrrell n.d., 1897:133).	4	27	6.8
Pasamut's camp between Angikuni and Yathkyed Lakes, Kazan River (Tyrrell n.d., 1897: 132).	7	42	6.0
Totals	20	128	6.4

twice a year.

This demonstration of relatively large aggregations has implications for the interpretation of Caribou Inuit society. Studies of social organization repeatedly indicate a general correlation between population density and social complexity (eg. Cohen 1985; Mellars 1985; Price and Brown 1985b; cf. Carneiro 1967). In the context of foraging societies, a greater degree of social complexity can be manifested in a number of ways, from management of storage facilities (Woodburn 1982) to increased differentiation of social roles (McGuire 1983). The evidence for a greater degree of aggregation along the lower Kazan and Thelon rivers suggests that Caribou Inuit society was more complex, in some respects, than previously believed.

This interpretation of a greater degree of social complexity has been partially tested against two classes of settlement data. First, a greater elaboration of architecture is evident in the presence of stone *qarmat*, or substantial cold-weather house features, at both sites as well as others in the study area. These features have not previously been reported for the Inuit of interior Keewatin (Burch 1978:

19; Csonka 1991: 138), and are very different from the small, overnight shelters of boulders and sod which Rasmussen (1930a: 31) described.

Second, at least one substantial communal structure (Caribou Inuit *kadgek* [Birket-Smith 1929a: 269; Thibert 1970: 95]) was identified at LcLg-12, based on its size and quality of construction. The ethnographic record indicates that communal Caribou Inuit activities occurred primarily during the winter in snow houses (Birket-Smith 1929a: 269; Gilder 1881: 41-44). Present evidence, however, suggests that in some instances more effort was expended in the production of relatively substantial and durable communal structures during a warmer season, perhaps coinciding with the crucial fall caribou hunt.

This combined evidence suggests a degree of social complexity beyond that expected from ethnographic accounts. The nature of this complexity cannot be defined more precisely on the basis of current information. Clearly, however, larger and longer aggregations imply more frequent and possibly more structured personal interactions (Bamforth 1988; McGuire 1983). This interaction may involve an increased degree of community organization and leadership, either to facilitate cooperative productive activities, or to reduce stress in situations where resource concentrations produce localized crowding (Cohen 1985: 108-9; Riches 1982: 31-47). Organization does not, however, imply the development of a social hierarchy. Rather, decision-making that involved large numbers of people could have occurred within traditional units of kinship integrated in a number of ways, including, for instance, alliances (Guemple 1972), larger regional societies (Burch 1986), and in the context of feasting and ceremony (Johnson 1982). The communal structure at LcLg-12 can be interpreted as physical evidence of just such an additional level of community integration.

Conclusions

This paper has presented direct evidence for significantly more complex settlement patterns in the interior District of Keewatin than are evident in the ethnographic record. This complexity is evident in larger and longer-lasting population aggregations, more sophisticated and varied architecture, and more energy devoted to construction of special community structures than is indicated in the Fifth Thule Expedition reports.

Clearly, prehistoric and protohistoric Inuit of the interior District of Keewatin were not as sedentary and heterogeneous as were societies labelled "complex hunter-gatherers" (Price and Brown 1985a), or as complex as certain densely populated Arctic societies such as northwest Alaskan Inupiat, who manifested a degree of ranking, formalized leadership, and redistributive economic structures (Spencer 1959). However, neither was the course of their history as fragmented and simple as is implied in the ethnographic record. Data presented here confirm and expand Burch's (1986, 1988) contention that the ethnographic present, particularly as represented by Birket-Smith and Rasmussen, is a distorted and in many ways inaccurate portrait of Inuit societies which inhabited this region. As such, they reaffirm the status of archaeology as an integral part of research into recent protohistoric and historic societies, and not simply as a limited study of the distant, prehistoric past.

Acknowledgements

Both authors are pleased to present this paper in a volume which honours the many contributions of William E. Taylor, Jr. to arctic archaeology. Friesen wishes to thank a number of individuals from Baker Lake: archaeological crew members Moses Kayuryuk, Lucy Scottie, Robert Tookoome, and Deborah Webster; elders and town council members who came out to public meetings and contributed their knowledge and interest; and in particular Barnabus Piryuaq, an elder who visited many of the sites and interpreted them for the project. The Kiggavik Archaeology Project was conducted as part of an environmental impact assessment for Beak Consultants Ltd. and Urangesellschaft Canada Ltd. Stewart wishes to thank the 31 members of the Operation Raleigh expedition who recorded information on sites along the Kazan river in the summer of 1988, in particular David Pelly who coordinated this effort, and the people of Baker Lake and their mayor at the time, David Simailak, who contributed their support and interest.

References

Amsden, C. 1979.   Hard times: a case study from northern Alaska and implications for arctic prehistory. In, Thule Eskimo Culture: an Anthropological Retrospective, A.P. McCartney, ed. National Museum of Man, Mercury Series, Archaeological Survey of Canada Paper, 88: 395-410.

Arima, E. 1984. Caribou Eskimo. In, Handbook of North American Indians, Vol. 5: Arctic, David Damas, ed. Washington: Smithsonian Institution, pp. 447-462.

Bamforth, D. 1988. Ecology and Human Organization on the Great Plains. New York: Plenum Press.

Birket-Smith, K. 1929a. The Caribou Eskimos: Material and Social Life and their Cultural Position, Descriptive Part. Report of the Fifth Thule Expedition 1921-24, 5(1).

Birket-Smith, K. 1929b. The Caribou Eskimos: Material and Social Life and their Cultural Position, Analytical Part. Report of the Fifth Thule Expedition 1921-24, 5(2).

Birket-Smith, K. 1959. The Eskimos, revised edition. London: Methuen.

Burch, E. S. 1977. Muskox and man in the central Canadian subarctic, 1689-1974. Arctic, 30: 135-154.

Burch, E. S. 1978. Caribou Eskimo origins: an old problem reconsidered. Arctic Anthropology, 15: 1-35.

Burch, E. S. 1986. The Caribou Inuit. In, <u>Native Peoples, the Canadian Experience</u>, R. Morrison and C. Wilson, eds. Toronto: McClelland and Stewart, pp. 106-133.

Burch, E. S. 1988. Knud Rasmussen and the "original" inland Eskimos of southern Keewatin. <u>Etudes/Inuit/Studies</u>, 12: 81-100.

Carneiro, R. 1967. On the relationship between size of population and complexity of social organization. <u>Southwestern Journal of Anthropology</u>, 23: 234-243.

Clark, B. 1977. <u>The Development of Caribou Eskimo Culture</u>. National Museum of Man, Mercury Series, Archaeological Survey of Canada Paper, 59.

Cohen, M. 1985. Prehistoric hunter-gatherers: the meaning of social complexity. In, <u>Prehistoric Hunter-Gatherers</u>, T.D. Price and J.A. Brown, eds. Orlando: Academic Press, pp. 99-119.

Csonka, Y. 1991. Les Ahiarmiut (1920-1950) dans la perspective d'histoire des Inuit Caribous. Unpublished Ph.D. dissertation, Université Laval.

Damas, D. 1968. The diversity of Eskimo societies. In, <u>Man the Hunter</u>, R. Lee. and I. DeVore, eds. Chicago: Aldine, pp. 111-117.

Deaver, K. 1989. Identifying ring site occupations. In, <u>Households and Communities</u>, S. MacEachern, D. Archer and R. Garvin, eds. Calgary: University of Calgary Archaeological Association, pp. 256-265.

Freeman, M. 1976. <u>Inuit Land Use and Occupancy Project</u>. Ottawa: Dept. of Indian and Northern Affairs.

Friesen, T. M. 1990. Archaeological Investigations in the Vicinity of the Kiggavik Uranium Mine Project, District of Keewatin, Northwest Territories. MS on file with the Canadian Museum of Civilization, Hull.

Gilder, W. H. 1881. <u>Schwatka's Search: Sledging in the Arctic in Quest of the Franklin Records</u>. New York: Charles Scribner's Sons.

Gordon, B. 1974. 1974 Thule culture investigations at Baker Lake, N.W.T. <u>Canadian Archaeology Association Bulletin</u>, 6: 218-224.

Gronnow, B. 1986. Recent archaeological investigations of West Greenland caribou hunting. <u>Arctic Anthropology</u>, 23: 57-80.

Guemple, D., ed. 1972. Alliance in Eskimo Society: Proceedings of the American Ethnological Society for 1971. Seattle: University of Washington Press.

Hanbury, D. 1904. Sport and Travel in the Northland of Canada. New York: Macmillan.

Harp, E. 1961. The Archaeology of the Lower and Middle Thelon, Northwest Territories. Arctic Institute of North America Technical Paper, 8.

Harper, F. 1964. Caribou Eskimos of the Upper Kazan River, Keewatin. University of Kansas Museum of Natural History, Misc. Publications, 36.

Johnson, G. A. 1982. Organisational structure and scalar stress. In, Theory and Explanation in Archaeology, C. Renfrew, M. Rowlands and B. Seagraves, eds.. New York: Academic Press, pp. 389-421.

Mathiassen, T. 1927. Archaeology of the Central Eskimo. Report of the Fifth Thule Expedition 1921-24, 4.

McGuire, R. 1983. Breaking down cultural complexity: inequality and heterogeneity. Advances in Archaeological Method and Theory, 6: 91-142.

Mellars, P. 1985. The ecological basis of social complexity in the Upper Paleolithic of southwestern France. In, Prehistoric Hunter-Gatherers, T. Price and J. Brown, eds. Orlando: Academic Press, pp. 271-298.

Nelson, E. W. 1899. The Eskimo about Bering Strait. Report of the Bureau of American Ethnology for the Years 1896-1897.

Price, T. and J. Brown, eds. 1985a. Prehistoric Hunter-Gatherers. Orlando: Academic Press.

Price, T. and J. Brown. 1985b. Aspects of hunter-gatherer complexity. In, Prehistoric Hunter-Gatherers, T.D. Price and J.A. Brown, eds. Orlando: Academic Press, pp. 3-20.

Rasmussen, K. 1930a. Observations on the Intellectual Culture of the Caribou Eskimos. Report of the Fifth Thule Expedition 1921-24, 7(2).

Rasmussen, K. 1930b. Iglulik and Caribou Eskimo texts. Report of the Fifth Thule Expedition 1921-24, 7(3).

Riches, D. 1982. Northern Nomadic Hunter-Gatherers: A humanistic approach. New York: Academic Press.

Ross, W. G. 1975. Whaling and Eskimos: Hudson Bay 1860-1915. National Museum of Man, Publications in Ethnology, 10.

Spencer, R. 1959. The North Alaskan Eskimo: a study in ecology and society. Bureau of American Ethnology Bulletin, 171

Stewart, A. 1991. Report on an Archaeological Survey of the Lower Kazan River and Test Excavations at KdLg-1 and KdLh-9, 1988. MS on file with the Canadian Museum of Civilization, Hull.

Stewart, A. 1993. Caribou Inuit Settlement Response to Changing Resource Availability on the Kazan River, Northwest Territories, Canada. Unpublished Ph.D. dissertation, University of California, Santa Barbara.

Thibert, A. 1970. Eskimo-English dictionary, revised edition. Ottawa: Canadian Research Centre for Anthropology, Université Saint Paul.

Tyrrell, J. W. 1908. Across the Sub-Arctics of Canada, 3rd edition. Toronto: William Briggs.

Tyrrell, J. B. n.d. Unpublished Field Notes, 1894. Thomas Fisher Rare Book Library, University of Toronto.

Tyrrell, J. B. 1895. A second expedition through the barren lands of northern Canada. The Geographical Journa, 1 6: 438-448.

Tyrrell, J. B. 1897. Report on the Doobaunt, Kazan and Ferguson rivers, and the north-west coast of Hudson Bay. Ottawa: Geological Survey of Canada.

Usher, P. 1971. Fur Trade Posts of the Northwest Territories, 1870-1970. Ottawa: Northern Science Research Group, Dept. of Indian Affairs and Northern Development.

Whitelaw, T. M. 1991. Some dimensions of variability in the social organisation of community space among foragers. In, Ethnoarchaeological Approaches to Mobile Campsites, C. Gamble and W. Boismier, eds. Ann Arbor: International Monographs in Prehistory, pp. 139-188.

Woodburn, J. 1982. Egalitarian societies. Man (n.s.), 17: 431-451.

The Sadlermiut: Mysterious or Misunderstood?

Susan Rowley
6660 Forest Glen Rd.,
Pittsburgh, Pennsylvania, U.S.A.

Abstract

The Sadlermiut were a small and isolated Inuit group living on Southampton Island, to the north of Hudson Bay. During the winter of 1902-03 they disappeared, victims of disease, unstudied and essentially unknown. Who were the Sadlermiut? Is it possible, as some have suggested, that they were the last survivors of the ancient Dorset culture of the Eastern Arctic? Or were they an aberrant group of Thule Inuit? Our desire to perceive the Sadlermiut as one or the other - as intrinsically mysterious - has coloured our interpretation of the data. This paper presents archaeological and documentary evidence to argue that the Sadlermiut were neither a remnant nor an aberrant group, but another example of the Inuit ability to adapt to different environmental and historical constraints.

Résumé

Les Sadlermiut constituaient un petit groupe d'Inuit qui vivaient isolés dans l'île Southampton, au nord de la baie d'Hudson. Durant l'hiver de 1902-1903, ils disparurent, victimes de maladies, sans jamais avoir fait l'objet d'études et en étant pour ainsi dire inconnus. Qui étaient les Sadlermiut? Est-il possible, comme d'aucuns l'ont suggéré, qu'ils fussent les derniers survivants de l'ancienne culture dorsétienne de l'est de l'Arctique? Ou formaient-ils un groupe marginal d'Inuit thuléens? Notre désir de classer les Sadlermiut dans l'un de ces deux groupes - aussi mystérieux l'un que l'autre - a teinté notre interprétation des données. Ce document présente des faits archéologiques et documentaires qui permettent d'affirmer que les Sadlermiut n'étaient ni un groupe survivant, ni un groupe marginal, mais plutôt un autre exemple de l'aptitude des Inuit à s'adapter à diverses contraintes environnementales et historiques.

Introduction

In the spring of 1903 a dog team left the Scottish whaling station at Cape Low on Southampton Island for the Sadlermiut (In this paper the term Sadlermiut is used to refer to the extinct indigenous population of Southampton and Coats Islands) camp at Tunirmiut (Native Point). In the winter of 1902 several Sadlermiut had visited the station and while there had contracted a disease. In fact, they had been so ill that the Aivilingmiut working for the whalers had had to take them home. Since that voyage, nothing had been heard from the Sadlermiut and the whalers feared something had happened.

Threads of Arctic Prehistory: Papers in Honour of William E. Taylor Jr., David Morrison and Jean-Luc Pilon, eds. Canadian Museum of Civilization, Mercury Series, Archaeological Survey of Canada Paper 149. 1994.

362 THREADS OF ARCTIC PREHISTORY

As they approached the settlement their suspicions were confirmed - something was dreadfully wrong. No light glowed from the *qarmat* (sod, stone and whale bone houses) and no one came to greet them. The scene the visitors discovered was gruesome. Inside the *qarmat* people were curled up on the sleeping platforms, lying where they had died, victims of an introduced disease. From an estimated population of 56 Sadlermiut there were only five survivors, one woman and four children.

In his 1977 article Gill Ross argued convincingly that this introduced disease was most likely a form of dysentery carried by a sailor on board the whaling ship <u>Active</u>. In 1902 this ship called in at several ports in the Eastern Arctic. At almost every port the Inuit contracted the disease and many died. In Lyon Inlet the Inuit believed that the "people of another tribe have cast evil spell over them." (Ross 1977: 6)

From this time the Sadlermiut have entered our imaginations. Their very disappearance prior to extensive Euro-American contact has made them a mystery - a mystery compounded by their seemingly "primitive" material culture and the disrespect with which they were viewed by other Inuit

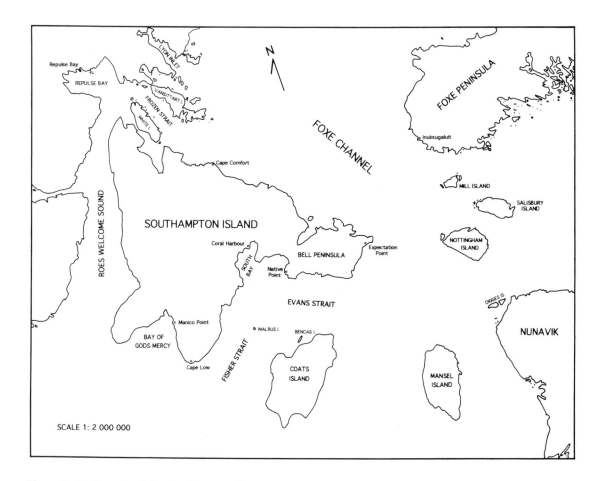

Figure 1 Southampton Island and surrounding area.

groups. As a result anyone writing on the prehistory of the Eastern Arctic has felt obliged to spill some ink on the Sadlermiut and to offer up new interpretations of who they were.

In this paper the various theories postulated by archaeologists as to the origins of the Sadlermiut are reviewed. This is followed by a discussion of the sources of our knowledge about the Sadlermiut and possible biases inherent in these sources. This information is then used to compare and contrast Sadlermiut culture with that of neighbouring Inuit groups and archaeological cultures. Finally, a different interpretation of the origins of the Sadlermiut is presented.

On the Origins of the Sadlermiut

From the beginnings of archaeological research in the Eastern Arctic the Sadlermiut have been considered an aberrant population. Their fortunes have been firmly tied to explanations of the origins of the current Inuit occupants of the region. In Table 1 archaeologists' and physical anthropologists' explanations of the origins of Sadlermiut culture are presented in chronological order.

In *Archaeology of the Central Eskimos*, Mathiassen (1927) argued that the Thule culture had been replaced recently by immigrants from the interior. Mathiassen devoted many pages to the Sadlermiut and concluded:

> ... we have thus been able to follow the Sadlermiut right from the time when, at the Thule culture phase, they built their first whale bone houses at Kuk, trace how their cultures changed, by isolation, separate development, by slight influences from west and east; but all the time the Thule elements were the bases of their culture - like a relic of an older stratum of culture that lasted even until the present time on their inhospitable island. But we have also seen how they gradually became fewer, how they disappeared from the northern part of the island and finally, how an epidemic carried them away in 1902 from their last settlement on the south coast. *Southampton Island is now in the possession of the Aiviliks; the last redoubt of the Thule culture in the Central Eskimo region has fallen!* The Sadlermiut are already on the way to inclusion among the legends of the Aiviliks as the last Tunit in the country (Mathiassen 1927: 287, emphasis mine).

Mathiassen's views were challenged almost immediately by other archaeologists who recognized that the Inuit were the direct descendants of the Thule culture. In conjunction with this theory a new interpretation was put forward to explain the Sadlermiut: they became the last remnant of the Dorset population (deLaguna 1947: 9; Collins 1955a, 1956a). This view was championed by Collins following his 1954 and 1955 excavations on Southampton, Coats and Walrus Islands.

Table 1: Opinions on Sadlermiut Origins

Author	Year	Dorset	Thule	?	Comments: the Sadlermiut were...
Hrdlicka	1910			X	an inherent part of the general Inuit population.
Jenness	1923		X		a possible small first wave of inlanders who soon became isolated.
Mathiassen	1927		X		the last of the Thule culture.
Jenness	1933		X		a remnant Thule group in contrast to the Inuit who were recent migrants from the interior.
Jenness	1934		X		a modified form of the old Thule culture.
Manning	1942	X			a remnant Dorset culture population (refers to the people of Coats Island).
Manning	1942		X		derived from the Thule culture (refers to the people of Southampton Island).
Holtved	1944		X		part of the eastern Thule culture.
Popham & Bell	1951			X	long isolated, based on an analysis of their skulls.
Bell	1951		X		the last of the Thule, driven onto Southampton by hostile Inuit tribes.
Collins	1955a &b	X			merely influenced by the Thule culture.
Collins	1956a			X	made a conscious but crude copy of a found Dorset harpoon head (hence not Dorset themselves?)
Collins	1956b	X			in fact the last of the Dorset population.
Collins	1958	X			influenced by the Thule culture.
Taylor	1959			X	not enough information to decide.
Merbs and Wilson	1962		X		an Inuit isolate.
Taylor	1960			X	more information is needed.
Collins	1975	X			the last Dorset
McGhee	1978			X	probably Inuit - only further excavation will tell.
deLaguna	1979	X			more Dorset than Thule.
Mayhall	1979		X		Sadlermiut and Thule one people from dentition.
Utermohle and Merbs	1979		X		a possible remnant of Thule culture.
Clark	1980	X	X		an in situ Thule isolate with some Dorset cultural affiliations.
Maxwell	1985			X	We still don't know.

> There was undoubtedly a connection of some kind between
> Sadlermiut and Thule. However, from our work on Southampton
> and Walrus Islands it seems more likely that the Sadlermiut had
> merely been influenced in some ways by Thule culture and that they
> were actually the descendants of the prehistoric Dorset Eskimos,
> who were the other, and principal object of study by the expedition
> (Collins 1956a: 342).

Beginning in 1960 archaeologists began to explain regional differences in Inuit culture as a result of *in situ* development (cf. Meldgaard 1960; VanStone 1962). The Sadlermiut then became an extreme example of this theory. However, they were unable to shake the air of mystery surrounding them. Discussions of the Sadlermiut almost always contained a reference to possible Dorset affinities (cf. Taylor 1959; McGhee 1978; Clark 1980).

> Considering all lines of evidence available at the present, it appears
> likely that Sadlermiut culture developed *in situ* from a Thule culture
> ancestry not unlike that represented at the Lake Site. The Thule
> culture on Southampton Island rapidly took on a distinctive flavour,
> however, and some positive affiliations with the Dorset culture
> cannot be ignored. Directly or indirectly the Dorset culture must
> have had some strong influences on local Thule development. The
> nature of this influence is not presently understood (Clark 1980:
> 78-9).

Furthermore, these discussions generally concluded with a suggestion that only further archaeological research would resolve this issue.

> There has been much speculation about the Sadlermiut, especially
> about the possibility that they were a remnant Dorset population.
> This speculation is based on only two clues: the Sadlermiut used
> chipped-stone tools instead of the ground-slate tools used by other
> Thule peoples, and the claim by neighbouring groups that the
> Sadlermiut spoke a strange dialect. On the other hand, their houses
> and most of their artifacts are firmly based in a Thule ancestry,
> indicating that the Sadlermiut were probably Inuit. Only further
> archaeological work will reveal the history of this enigmatic group
> (McGhee 1978: 110).

Taylor even volunteered to undertake this research:

As Collins has pointed out (1958, p.539), the solution of these Sadlermiut problems do not lie in the recently excavated sites of late Sadlermiut peoples but in older sites representing developmental stages. With the easy travel and numerous sites on the south shore of Southampton Island the task could be a pleasant one (Taylor 1960: 87).

Who were the Sadlermiut?

Our knowledge of the Sadlermiut comes from many different sources. These include: eyewitness accounts (both the written accounts of explorers and whalers and Inuit oral testimony); oral history testimony of Inuit who learned about the Sadlermiut from their elders; archaeological collections; and ethnographic collections (Table 2 lists known Sadlermiut archaeological and ethnographic collections in museums).

While it is possible that Luke Foxe and William Coats met Sadlermiut on their voyages into Hudson Bay in the seventeenth and eighteenth centuries, the first confirmed meeting between the Sadlermiut and Europeans took place on the south coast of Coats Island in 1824 (Lyon 1825; see Fig. 2). Lyon's description as well as that of a crew member, John Paton (1825) are the earliest known accounts of the Sadlermiut. Lyon conversed with the Sadlermiut using the Inuktitut he had learned from the Aivilingmiut and Iglulingmiut during his sojourn in the north from 1821-23. He was astonished by the hairstyle of the men, who wore their hair braided and tied in a knot on their crown and by the paucity of trade goods in their possession. During his visit he saw only one piece of painted and planed wood (possibly from a Hudson's Bay Company shipwreck) and a few pieces of lead. He recorded that the Sadlermiut used tools made from chert and cooked in pots made from limestone slabs held together with a mortar of blood, hair and ground limestone. Lyon gave all the people iron implements and later, when he stopped at a seasonally abandoned Sadlermiut site, he left still more iron tools.

In 1836 during the drift of the H.M.S. Terror, George Back recorded that some of his men saw a human foot print at Cape Comfort when they walked to shore one day (Back 1838). Following Back's voyage the British Navy turned their attention to Lancaster Sound and northern Hudson Bay and Foxe Basin were not visited. Then, in 1860 American whalers began exploiting the bowhead whale hunting grounds off the west coast of Hudson Bay. The only known contact in the early period of whaling was noted by Boas, who wrote: "About 1865 an American whaling vessel found some natives on Manico Point living in five tents. Even then they had scarcely any iron, but used the old stone implements; this proves the want of all communication with the natives of the mainland" (Boas 1888: 451).

In 1878 and 1879 the men of the whaler Abbie Bradford traded with the Sadlermiut. Ferguson, one of the sailors on board, wrote an account of his visits with these people. In contrast with all other informants, Ferguson reported that the Sadlermiut were very clean and their clothing was extremely well made. While Lyon had been able to converse with the Sadlermiut, Ferguson noted that the Aivilingmiut they had on board could not converse with the Sadlermiut nor could he (he spoke the

Table 2 Collections of Sadlermiut Material Culture.

COLLECTOR	YEAR	LOCATION	MUSEUM	TYPE
?????	17**	Southampton?	BM - Sloane coll.	Ethno
?????	18**	Southampton?	AMNH - Sturgis coll.	Ethno
?????	19**	Southampton	CMC - Borden coll.	???
Lyon, George	1824	Coats	Pitt-Rivers, RSM	Ethno
Comer, George	1899-1915	Southampton	CMC, AMNH, UM, Berlin, MAI	Ethno
Comer, George	1900-1913	Southampton	UM	Ethno
Low, A.P.	1904	Southampton	CMC	?
Hawkes, E	1914	Coats	CMC	Arch
HBC	1920-21	Coats	CMC, UM	Arch
Munn, H.T.	1921	Southampton	B.M.	Arch
Birket-Smith	1922	Southampton	CMC	Arch
Freuchen, P.	1922	Southampton	CMC	Arch
Mathiassen, T.	1922	Southampton, Kuk, Duke of York Bay	CMC, Nationalmuseet	Arch
Burwash, L.	1924	Coats	CMC	Arch
Bird, J.	1933	Southampton: Hut Point, Neakuktoktuyok	MAI	Arch
Bird, J.	1933	Bear Island	MAI	Arch
Leechman, D.	1934	Southampton: Coral Harbour	CMC	Arch
Manning, T.	1934	Southampton: Kirchoffer River, Gibbons Point	CMC	Arch
Rowley, R.	1936	Southampton: Kirchoffer River, Gibbons Point	UMAE	Arch
Rowley, G.	1936	Walrus	UMAE	Arch
Rowley, G.	1936	Coats	UMAE	Arch
Nichols, D.A.	1937	Southampton: Native Point	CMC	Arch
Dutilly, A.	1938	Southampton	CMC, Churchill?	Arch
Manning, T.	1938	Southampton: Expectation Point	CMC	Arch
Stewart &Nichols	1938	Coats	CMC	Arch
Bell, D.	1950	Southampton: Native Point, Prairie Point, Expectation Point, Liver Creek, Kirchoffer River	CMC	Arch
Collins, H.B.	1954	Southampton: Native Point	CMC	Arch
Collins, H.B.	1954	Coats	CMC	Arch
Collins, H.B.	1955	Southampton: Native Point, Lake Site	CMC	Arch

Collins, H.B.	1955	Walrus	CMC	Arch
Taylor, W.	1956	Southampton: Native Point, Lake Site	CMC	Arch
Laughlin, W.	1959	Southampton: Native Point (KkHh-1), Prairie Point (KlHj-1)	CMC	Arch
Laughlin, W.	1959	Coats: North shore (KfHh-1)	CMC	Arch
Laughlin, W.	1959	Walrus (KhHk-1)	CMC	Arch
Smith, N. G.	1960	Southampton: east side of Hansine Lake (LjHq-1)	CMC	Arch
Freeman, M.	1962	Southampton: Ruin Point (KkHk-1)	CMC	Arch
Czuboka, W.	1967	Coats: Southampton Point	CMC	Arch
Wright, J. V.	1970	Southampton: Native Point	CMC	Arch
Clark, B.	1970	Southampton: Lake Site (KkHh-2)	CMC	Arch

AMNH - American Museum of Natural History, New York
Berlin - Museum fur Volkerkunde, Berlin
BM - British Museum, London
Churchill - Eskimo Museum, Churchill, Man.
CMC - Canadian Museum of Civilization, Ottawa.
MAI - Museum of the American Indian, New York/Washington, D.C.
Nationalmuseet - Nationalmuseet, Copenhagen
Pitt-Rivers - Pitt-Rivers Museum, Oxford
RSM - Royal Scottish Museum, Edinburgh
UM - University Museum, Philadelphia
UMAE - University Museum of Archaeology and Ethnography, Cambridge

Aivilingmiut, Netsilingmiut and Padlirmiut dialects) or the captain, Elnathan Fisher (who in addition could speak Greenlandic: Ferguson 1938: 43, 156). In this respect Ferguson's information contradicts later sources who noted that the Aivilingmiut and Sadlermiut could converse (Comer in Sutton 1932-36: 40). Perhaps Ferguson's comments reflect more on his and Fisher's proficiency in Inuktitut!

Most of our ethnographic knowledge of the Sadlermiut comes from the whaling Captain George Comer. Comer, in addition to his duties as a whaling captain, collected information on the Inuit for Franz Boas. This included taking casts of people's faces, taking photographs, interviewing people about shamanism and collecting both ethnographic and archaeological material. Comer first met the Sadlermiut in 1896 and his association with them continued on an intermittent basis until their demise (Boas 1901-07; Comer 1906, 1910, 1921; Ross 1984)

The final outsider from whom we have an eyewitness account is Captain John Murray. Murray was the station manager at the Cape Low whaling station from 1899 until 1901. Murray's description

Figure 2 Neeakoodloo paddling out to greet Captain G. F. Lyon in 1824 (from Lyon 1825: f.p. 243).

of the Sadlermiut is brief but important because it corroborates that of both Comer and Angutimmarik (an Aivilingmio) that relations between the Sadlermiut and the Aivilingmiut were mistrustful (Clark 1986).

Inuit eyewitness accounts of the Sadlermiut are scattered throughout the literature, in some cases the informants' names are given and in others they are not. The best known and most detailed account is that of Angutimmarik (also known as "Scotch Tom"), an Aivlingmio who worked with the whalers at Cape Low (Mathiassen 1927; Manning 1942). Angutimmarik stressed how different the Sadlermiut were from the Aivilingmiut. He commented on their inability to build proper snow houses, their poorly tended lamps that gave off vast quantities of soot so the people were always filthy, their poorly softened hides, and their use of polar bear skin trousers and consequent greasing of their legs to prevent chafing. Angutimmarik also told Mathiassen that the Sadlermiut were Tuniit rather than Inuit.

Another of Mathiassen's informants was Saorre. He corroborated much of Angutimmarik's testimony but related that the Sadlermiut were migrants from southwestern Baffin Island. Saorre continued to explain that upon their arrival the Sadlermiut had met Tuniit who were living on Southampton Island (Mathiassen 1927: 283). When reaching his conclusions about the origins of the

Sadlermiut, Mathiassen chose to ignore Saorre's story and instead concluded that the Sadlermiut were the last of the Tuniit.

The Tuniit Question

Archaeologists in an unusual and uncritical acceptance of oral history have generally accepted that the Tuniit traditions of the Eastern Arctic refer to Neoeskimo peoples meeting the Palaeoeskimo, or more specifically the Late Dorset people. Therefore, when the Aivilingmiut called the Sadlermiut "Tuniit" this gave credence to the theory that the Sadlermiut were indeed the last of the Dorset people. While this interpretation of Inuit traditional knowledge is the simplest is it necessarily correct?

In order to examine this question we must first examine the specifics of Inuit oral history concerning the Tuniit. In 1981 Inuit elders in five Baffin communities were interviewed about the Tuniit. The following information is compiled from the data they shared with me. All accounts agree that the Tuniit occupied the land prior to the arrival of the Inuit. While the Inuit could understand the language spoken by the Tuniit they referred to it as similar to baby talk. Some examples of the language of the Tuniit were apparently kept alive in Inuit songs and shamanic language. Another common feature of Inuit accounts concern the relative strength of Tuniit. Physically, the Tuniit were much stronger than the Inuit. Houses built with heavy stones and the many huge rocks found on the land that people today are unable to move attest to this strength. Whether the Tuniit were taller or shorter than the Inuit depends on the region of the north. In southern Baffin Island the Tuniit are considered shorter than Inuit. In contrast, Inuit in northern Baffin Island call the Tuniit "Tunijuat" - meaning large people. In neither case, however, is this height difference large. The Tuniit were neither dwarfs nor giants.

The Tuniit were frequently but not always denigrated in the history. They were incapable of preparing and softening skins properly. As a result they needed to grease their legs to prevent the stiff skins from chafing. Apparently, the Tuniit were unconcerned about this and other habits that the Inuit considered filthy. For example, they prepared *igunaq* (aged meat) in an interesting way. The women would place the meat next to their thighs and leave it until it ripened. These habits led the Inuit to look down on the Tuniit.

Does the fact that the Tuniit occupied the land prior to the arrival of the Inuit and were so different from the Inuit demonstrate an equivalence to the archaeologically defined Late Dorset culture? What do Inuit report about the technology and life styles of the Tuniit that we could compare with archaeological collections? Housing styles of the Tuniit vary from region to region and are described either as circular sod and whalebone houses or as rectangular stone structures. All other material culture indicators are also inconclusive. These include hunting weapons, soapstone lamps, kayaks and clothing.

What about Inuit claims that the Tuniit were dirty and that their language was baby talk? These remarks are typical of the comments people use to describe their neighbours, people they fear, people they are unfamiliar with and people they look down upon. This last is the classic example -- everyone knows jokes that are used to denigrate specific groups of people who are considered inferior.

The most critical information linking the Tuniit with the Dorset culture comes from Inuit statements that the Tuniit occupied the land prior to the arrival of the Inuit. However, this is only accurate if one accepts that the Inuit stayed in one place and rarely migrated into new regions. In fact, this is not the case. Perhaps the most famous of these movements is the migration of Qitdlarssuaq and his followers from Baffin Island to northern Greenland in the mid-1800s (Mary-Rousseliere 1980). There are many other examples of similar migrations in the historic record (Rowley 1985a and b). Also, Inuit testimony suggests that southern assumptions about the Tuniit may be too simplistic. For example, people in Arctic Bay know that when Ulluriaq and her family migrated into the Admiralty Sound region they saw the last of the Tuniit running away in fear. This migration took place at the turn of the twentieth century and certainly has little to do with the carriers of Late Dorset culture.

When Inuit migrated they took their traditions with them and anchored them in the new landscape. After the death of the Sadlermiut the island was repopulated by Aivilingmiut from the west coast of Hudson Bay ca. 1910 and later by the Oqomiut who came to the island in 1928 with the Hudson's Bay Company. By the time Junius Bird visited Southampton Island in 1933 on the Morrissey the site of Neakuktoktuyok (the "Place of Skulls," located on the west coast of South Bay) had become the scene of a battle between Aivilingmiut and Okomiut complete with bleached human skeletal remains! Bartlett wrote that, "None of the Eskimos can remember how long ago this happened, and they always shun the place, but eight human skulls on the ground testify to the story's truth" (1934: 289).

The answer to the question, Who were the Tuniit? is not an easy one. While some of the traditions undoubtedly refer to memories of interactions with Dorset people and locations where Dorset people lived others do not. Inuit used these and other traditions, which form an important part of their history, to recreate their intellectual landscape and legitimate their claim to a new territory when they migrated. Therefore, Aivilingmiut claims that the Sadlermiut were Tuniit should be seen in a different light. This interpretation is corroborated by Sadlermiut statements. Peter Pitseolak, a Sikosuilarmio from southwestern Baffin, wrote:

> When asked if they [the Sadlermiut] were tooniks they said in their
> baby voices, 'We have only heard of tooniks; we are not tooniks,'
> But they were the only people who ever talked that way. The people
> from this side didn't believe them. They don't believe them even
> today (Pitseolak and Eber 1975: 33).

Trait Comparisons

This brings us to the nexus: Just how different were the Sadlermiut from other Inuit groups and from the Dorset culture? In order to examine this problem a simple element comparison was performed. The results of this comparison are presented in Table 3. It demonstrates quite clearly that the Sadlermiut, in terms of their material culture, hunting practices, and belief system are most closely affiliated to ethnographically known Inuit groups. While the Sadlermiut were generally reviled by the Aivilingmiut there is evidence that they held at least two Sadlermiut shamans in great respect (Comer

Table 3 Element Comparison

ITEM	DORSET	THULE/ H. INUIT	SADLERMIUT
Architecture			
House type - circular, semi-subterranean, with elevated sleeping platforms and cold trap entrance		X	X
Mattocks		X	X
Snow houses	X	X	X
Composite snow knives		X	X
Festival houses		X	X
Mushroom caches		X	X
Burial style (cache type)		X	X
Burial - coiled bodies		X	X
Transportation			
Large sleds		X	X
Baleen sled		X	X
Dog sled traction equipment		X	X
Dogs	?	X	X
Kayak	X	X	X
Kayak stands		X	X
Umiak	?	X	?
Clothing			
Clothing - had tails	?	X	
Bear skin trousers	?	X	X
Long women's boots		X	X
Combs		X	X
Tooth pendants		X	X
Hair ornaments		X	X
Hair in a top knot		X	X
Facial tattoos	X	X	X
Needle cases - moss form		X	X
Domestic Objects			
Baleen pails		X	X

ITEM	DORSET	THULE/ H. INUIT	SADLERMIUT
Ladles		X	X
Lamp - semi-circular		X	X
Ulu		X	X
Hunting Equipment			
Avataq - mouthpieces		X	X
Chert end blades	X		X
Accomplished whale hunters		X	X
Snow goggles with visor		X	X
Nets - baleen		X	X
Wound plugs		X	X
Bolas		X	X
Bows and arrows		X	X
Fish weirs	?	X	X
Kakivak (fish spear)	X	X	X
Tools			
Chipped stone tools	X	X	X
Flaker - walrus rib		X	X
Drill bows		X	X
Pegs (joinery)	?	X	X
Games			
Ajajaq		X	X
Gaming pieces (bird)		X	X
Nuglutaq		X	X
Thule style dolls		X	X
Ornamentation			
Dot design		X	X
Society			
Shamanic practices	X	X	X
Land/Sea mammal restrictions	?	X	X
Speak Inuktitut	?	X	X

1906: 484, 1910: 89). The comparisons with the Dorset culture are limited and will be discussed in more detail below.

Architecture

Sadlermiut winter houses were constructed from locally abundant limestone slabs, whale bones, and sod. They were circular and contained elevated sleeping platforms with cold trap entrances. Collins (1955a: 342, 1956b: 686) argued that similar structures excavated on Walrus Island (located between Southampton and Coats Islands) were constructed by Dorset people and indicated an affiliation between the Dorset and the Sadlermiut. He based this interpretation on the finds from the Walrus Island site - a few Sadlermiut tools and some Dorset material in the cracks of the house floors. Unfortunately, the houses Collins was excavating had previously been partially excavated and cleared of most of their Sadlermiut artifacts. Earlier excavations on Walrus Island had been undertaken by both T. Manning and G.W. Rowley when they were shipwrecked on the island in 1936. Collins was aware of their work at the time of his excavation (Collins 1955c), however, he appears to have ignored the extent of their excavations when publishing his results (Collins 1958: 32). In addition, Walrus Island is a small rocky granite outcrop at the junction between Fisher and Evans Straits. There is only one good camping spot on the island. The few stones on the island that were suitable for building would have been used and reused throughout time. It is therefore not surprising to find a mixed assemblage at this site.

Apparently the Sadlermiut could build snow house shelters when travelling but these were very poorly built and were a source of ridicule (Mathiassen 1927: 270).

Festival houses or *qaggiq* are a well known feature of Neoeskimo sites in the Canadian Arctic. They consist of a large central boulder with a surrounding circle of stones used as a bench. Often there was another circle of stones outside this inner circle that was higher and acted as a partial windbreak. These structures are not known from Palaeoeskimo contexts. There is a large *qaggiq* at the Sadlermiut site at Expectation Point on the southeast coast of Southampton Island (Bell 1951).

To compare burial features is almost impossible as so little is known of Dorset burial practices. However, Sadlermiut practices were identical to other ethno-graphically known Inuit groups. This included both the simple placement of a circle of rocks around the body and the use of a cache type burial with concomitant coiling of bodies. The deceased were often placed on ridges overlooking the sea.

Transportation

It is in this area that the differences between the Sadlermiut and the Late Dorset people are most striking. The Sadlermiut had long heavy sleds constructed from whale bones. These sleds were pulled by large dog teams. The faunal collections from Sadlermiut sites always contain numerous dog bones. This is in marked contrast to Dorset sites where evidence for the use of dogs is ambiguous at best.

The most frequently used illustration of the Sadlermiut is Figure 2. The implication of this drawing of the man paddling sealskin floats is that the Sadlermiut were unfamiliar with kayaks. However, many Sadlermiut sites have kayak rests (Lyon 1825; Bell 1951), kayak lances were collected by Comer (Boas 1901-07: 69), and Mathiassen reported that the Sadlermiut had a special kayak dress (1927: 274) In addition, the Sadlermiut were considered by both the whalers and the Aivilingmiut as superior bowhead whale hunters. These whales were hunted both from the ice (Comer 1910: 89) and from kayaks (Mathiassen 1927: 277) by the Sadlermiut. We have no evidence the Palaeoeskimo were ever able to exploit the bowhead population other than to make use of stranded carcasses.

Clothing

The Sadlermiut are often differentiated from the Inuit by their clothing. The most commonly mentioned distinguishing feature is the wearing of polar bear skin pants by the men. Although the Sadlermiut and Polar Inuit were the only people to wear bearskin trousers regularly they were not unique to these groups. Among the Iglulingmiut, the Baffin Inuit and the Inuit of Northern Quebec this style was common. Polar bear clothing is both light and extremely warm; its problem is the natural stiffness of the skin that makes it somewhat uncomfortable to wear. Southampton Island is well known as having a high concentration of polar bears. It is therefore unsurprising that the Sadlermiut used the abundant bear skins for clothing.

Another clothing difference is the lack of fringes on Sadlermiut parkas. This makes their clothing more similar to that of the people of south-east Baffin and northern Quebec. Interestingly, this similarity was noted by both the explorers and whalers who met the Sadlermiut. Lyon (1825) noted that the parka style of the natives of the Savage Islands was very similar to the Sadlermiut style; a view also held by Comer (1910: 88).

Women's boots among the Sadlermiut were very long, reaching almost to the hip. Although these boots were unusual in this region, they were similar to the boots worn by Copper Inuit women in the early 1900s (Jenness 1922: frontispiece) and by Labrador and southern Baffin women at the time of contact. See for example the "John White" painting of an Inuit woman brought to England by Sir Martin Frobisher in 1577 (Fitzhugh 1993: 3) or the painting of an Inuit woman from Labrador by Angelica Kauffman ca. 1773 (Driscoll 1983: 30). In suggesting a relationship between the Sadlermiut and the Thule culture, Holtved noted that one of Mathiassen's dolls from Qilalukan seemed to be wearing similar boots (Holtved 1944: 159).

While certain aspects of Sadlermiut clothing differ from their neighbours, they do not fall outside the range of well known Inuit clothing styles. In fact, clothing styles were used in the north as markers of group identification (Rowley 1985a) and differences between neighbouring groups are to be expected.

Technology

Perhaps the most perplexing fact about Dorset culture tools is that holes were never drilled; they were always gouged. Collins considered that the overabundance of drilled holes on Sadlermiut artifacts was indicative of their unfamiliarity with this technique; like children discovering a new toy they overused it (Collins n.d.). However, the technique of drilling a series of holes in order to fracture a bone occurs in many Neoeskimo sites.

For cooking vessels and lamps the Sadlermiut used limestone slabs held together with baleen and a blood, hair and ground limestone mortar. The Sadlermiut constructed their vessels from these materials because there is no source of soapstone on Southampton Island. At Brooman Point the same technique was used by the Neoeskimo population when faced with a lack of soapstone (McGhee 1984: 70). Likewise, it was also employed by Neoeskimo on Somerset Island (McCartney and Savelle 1989). As far as is known, there is no evidence that Dorset people employed this technique. The form of lamps made by the Sadlermiut is identical to the most common semi-lunar form of Neoeskimo lamps and bears no similarity to the oval form of Late Dorset lamps.

Collins noted that one form of Sadlermiut harpoon head style was undoubtedly developed from the Dorset Parallel type (Collins 1956a: 84, 1975: 65). However, the derived form of this type is common across the Eastern Arctic. Stylistic variations in its design can be used to distinguish Inuit regional groups (Rowley 1985a).

The strongest statements of Dorset-Sadlermiut continuity always emphasize Sadlermiut use of chert rather than slate for their lithic tools. Clark (1980: 76) pointed out that Sadlermiut tools are similar to Late Dorset tools sharing a tendency towards a convex dorsal surface and flat ventral surface. If the Sadlermiut were a remnant Late Dorset population we might expect to find the following traits: fine edge serration on chipped stone tools; microblades; thumbnail end scrapers; and burin like implements. None of these traits exist. Instead, the reason for Sadlermiut use of chert rather than slate is the abundance of the former on Southampton Island. In fact, there is no slate source on Southampton Island, and the Sadlermiut were forced to turn to another material. Other examples of Neoeskimo using chert also exist. One of the most striking is a late precontact Mackenzie Inuvialuit site recently excavated by D. Morrison where nearly all the lithic tools were made from chert or quartzite (Morrison 1993).

To conclude this section: while some differences do exist between the Sadlermiut and other Inuit groups these differences are no more pronounced than the differences one would expect to find between Inuit groups due to adaptation to differing environmental conditions and regional stylistic expression.

Contact with Other Groups

The most obvious point of contact between the Sadlermiut and other Inuit groups would appear to be with the people living along the west coast of Hudson Bay. In fact, there is only one recorded instance of such a visit. The Aivilingmiut told Comer of a visit to Wager Bay made by the Sadlermiut before 1800. The five Sadlermiut met five male Nuvukmiut and entered friendly combat. One of the Sadlermiut was wounded:

He called to his father, who reassured him, saying that this

encounter would establish amicable relations between the two tribes.
... Later the Saglern returned to their own island, and so far as is
known, this was their first and only contact with the mainland Innuit
(Comer 1910: 88).

There were two reasons why contact with the west coast of Hudson Bay was infrequent. First, Roes Welcome Sound, the body of water separating Southampton Island from the mainland, is an extremely difficult waterway to cross. In the winter it rarely freezes firmly enough to provide a reliable route to the island. Second, although the Sadlermiut occasionally visited the west coast their seasonal round was concentrated on the southeastern half of the island. The richest resources of the island are found in the area of South Bay and Bell Peninsula. Therefore, anyone wishing to visit the Sadlermiut would not only have to cross Roes Welcome Sound they would also have to make a long and arduous trip over the rough limestone of Southampton Island. The main reason for making such a trip would be to trade. However, the Aivilingmiut were part of a major trade route along the west coast of Hudson's Bay. This trade route brought European goods to the Aivilingmiut from the Hudson's Bay Company posts at the "bottom of the bay." Therefore, as early as 1700 there was no need to trade with the Sadlermiut because more desirable goods were available in a different direction.

This brings us to the east. In this direction there are two possible points of contact: Northern Quebec and the islands of Hudson Strait and Foxe Peninsula. There is no published Inuit testimony about the Sadlermiut from northern Quebec. Therefore any suggestions must rest on a comparison of material culture. There are several items that point to possible contact and sharing of traits. These include similar combs (Jenness 1941: 203), hair ornaments (Jenness 1941: 204), snow goggles (Rowley 1985a), needle cases (Rowley 1985a), and mushroom shaped caches. These caches are a well known feature of Sadlermiut material culture, narrower at the bottom than they are at the top. Sticks or bones are placed inside from which birds, fish and caribou are suspended to dry. As Lyon (1825) noted the shape of these caches and the suspension of the meat protected the contents from foxes. These caches are known from northern Quebec. They were first noted by Abacuk Prickett, one of the mutineers on Henry Hudson's ill fated trip (Asher 1860). They were also occasionally built on the Foxe Peninsula (Hallendy 1992, personal communication). While the evidence of contact between northern Quebec and Southampton Island is admittedly slim the material culture suggests that this link merits further investigation.

What about Foxe Peninsula? We know that extensive contact occurred between the Sadlermiut and the Sikosuilarmiut and Kingakmiut. The Sadlermiut told the Aivilingmiut employed by Comer that they used to cross to King's Cape on Foxe Peninsula. "It is said that the last man to go over to King's Cape never returned and it is thought that he was killed" (Comer 1910:89). Likewise, the Sikosuilarmiut remember the Sadlermiut whom they used to call the Pujait (meaning "dried up oil").

Years before, it is said, South Baffin people used to go over in their
skin boats to visit these people who talked in such a strange manner.
South Baffin islanders called them then "takoogatarak," meaning
"we are shy with them" because before the skin boats got to shore,
the men there would try to trade wives with them and say in their

baby voices, "They don't want it; they don't want it." But before
the whalers arrived no one had been to them for years (Pitseolak in
Eber 1989:79).

Contact between the two groups was not confined to harmonious relations. Mathiassen was
told of battles (1927: 283-285) and the people of South Baffin have their own account of the demise
of the Sadlermiut:

> South Baffin people believed that the Pujait died out because of
> enmity between the shamans. The Pujait had two chiefs, the first
> chief Kamakowjuk (perhaps Comer's Cumercowyer, who saw
> whales under the water) and his brother, the second chief, Avalak,
> who astonished the ordinary Inuit with his great strength. Avalak
> and Pitseolak Oojuseelook, who was a powerful shaman from South
> Baffin Island, had a test of strength, and "Pitseolak just went down
> immediately and flipped over a couple of times." People thought
> that Pitseolak killed all the Pujait because he lost in the strength
> game (Eber 1989:82).

There is also material evidence of contact between the Sadlermiut and the people of Foxe
Peninsula. All the early Europeans noted that Sadlermiut clothing reminded them, not of the west coast
of Hudson Bay but of south Baffin Island. Another piece of evidence comes from the remarkable site
at Inuksugalait. At this site there are several alignments of *inuksuit*, one of which pointed the way to
Southampton Island. This alignment was non-functional (Hallendy, this volume). Not only did the Inuit
know where Southampton Island was but also, the island often had a large cloud over it. This cloud
was visible from southwest Baffin Island (Hallendy 1992, personal communication). The Inuit of Foxe
Peninsula knew how to get to Southampton Island and also knew the Sadlermiut.

As mentioned above, Pitseolak states that contact with the Sadlermiut ceased long before the
advent of the whalers. Why did this happen? The Sadlermiut were at the end of the trade route that
ran along the south coast of Baffin Island. As long as this trade route was maintained they had access
to small amounts of slate and soapstone (a few pieces of each of these is generally found at Sadlermiut
sites). However, in 1823 British whalers began whaling on the southeast coast of Baffin Island. This
led to a major population shift. Inuit began to cluster around the whalers and the resources they
offered. By 1840 the whalers were firmly ensconced in Cumberland Sound and were using Inuit crews.
Inuit full time employment combined with the decimation of the population through introduced diseases
disrupted the traditional trade routes. As an example of this, in 1862 a group of Sikosuilarmiut visited
Frobisher Bay. Charles Francis Hall noted that these people were using stone tools unlike the
Frobisher Bay people who were well supplied with iron (Hall 1860-62). As the Sikosuilarmiut had
little access to iron in the early and mid-1800s, it seems hardly surprising that the Sadlermiut had
almost no iron when they encountered whalers in the 1860s and 70s.

The isolation of the Sadlermiut was exacerbated in the late 1870s when Captain James Spicer opened a whaling station at Spicer's Harbour on the south coast of Baffin Island. Spicer's station attracted the Foxe Peninsula population to the east. This change in the Sikosuilarmiut seasonal cycle made contact with the Sadlermiut unlikely.

In 1899 Scottish whalers established a station at Cape Low on Southampton Island. The station managers imported Aivilingmiut, who had already been working for the whalers since 1860, as crew and station personnel. The Aivilingmiut were better equipped than the Sadlermiut having access to iron, wooden boats, and guns. They were thus able to disregard Sadlermiut cultural restrictions. When travelling in the area occupied by another group, Inuit would follow not their own taboos but those of the groups whose region they were traversing. Failure to do this was seen as showing disrespect to the local people (Rowley 1985a:62-4).

> ...what hastened their end was the bringing in to their country a large number of Natives of at least three different tribes, even these mistrusted each other and the Southampton natives disliked them all for these new people made a butt of the Southampton natives and could do so without fear, being more numerous and well armed.... with Rifles and knives and many other comforts (and) carried themselves in an independent way and disregarded the Tabboos of the land.... I mention these different things to show how their minds must have been affected by their land being run over by what to them must have seemed a lawless set of people.
>
> With these ideas in their mind it can be seen how easily they would be discouraged in sickness and when their prayers failed to bring success or health all would be laid to the disrespect for the laws of the Great Spirits which ruled over the Island (Comer 1925).

By 1902 the Sadlermiut were truly isolated; strangers in their own land.

Conclusions

I would like to conclude by making the following points about the Sadlermiut. First, the Sadlermiut are no more or less a Dorset culture population than any other Eastern Arctic group. Of course, the nature of the relationship between the Dorset and Thule populations is still to be determined.   Second, the Sadlermiut were a population well adapted to the environmental and physiographic conditions on Southampton Island. Their use of limestone for vessels and chert for tools replacing unavailable soapstones and slates clearly demonstrates this ability. Our impressions of them as a "backward" group derive from uncritical reading of the ethnographic literature.

Finally, I have always been concerned by the concept of *in situ* regional development to explain the origins of historic Inuit groups (Rowley 1985a). Strict *in situ* development represents a closed system, something that is inoperative in an environment as unpredictable as that of the Arctic. The

Sadlermiut are perhaps the closest of any historic group to representing an *in situ* development. However, their isolation was a recent development, stemming from the changing geo-political arena in the north following the arrival of British and American whalers.

Acknowledgements

I would like to thank the elders of the Eastern Arctic communities of Igloolik, Arctic Bay, Pond Inlet, Clyde River, Broughton Island and Pangnirtung who discussed Tuniit with me in 1981. Phil Goldring of Parks Canada brought Comer's unpublished letter to Dr. Livingstone to my attention. Norm Hallendy provided me with information about Inuksugalait. Henry B. Collins permitted access to the Sadlermiut material he had excavated and to his field notes. My debt to him for his help and kindness can never be repaid. I am only sorry I have to disagree with his conclusions.

References

Asher, G. M. 1860. Henry Hudson the Navigator: The Original Documents in which his Career is Recorded. London: Hakluyt Society.

Back, G. 1838. Narrative of an Expedition in H.M.S. Terror, Undertaken with a View to Geographical Discovery on the Arctic shores . London: John Murray.

Bartlett, R. 1934. Sails over Ice. London: Charles Scribner's Sons.

Bell, W. D. 1951. Archaeological Fieldwork on Southampton Island, N.W.T. MS, used with permission of the author's widow.

Boas, F. 1888. The Central Eskimo. Annual Report of the Bureau of American Ethnology, 6.

Boas, F. 1901-07. The Eskimo of Baffin Land and Hudson Bay. Bulletin of the American Museum of Natural History, 15(1): 1-370.

Clark, B. 1980. The Lake site (KkHh-2), Southampton Island, N.W.T. and its Position in Sadlermiut Prehistory. Canadian Journal of Archaeology, 4: 53-81.

Clark, G. 1986. The Last of the Whaling Captains. Glasgow: Brown Son and Ferguson.

Collins, H. 1955a. Dorset Dwellings. Science, 122: 866-867.

Collins, H. 1955b. Archeological work on Southampton and Walrus Islands, Hudson Bay. Year Book of the American Philosophical Society, 1955: 341-344

Collins, H. 1955c. 1955 Southampton Island Journal. MS on file with the National Anthropological Archives, Smithsonian Institution, Washington, D.C.

Collins, H. 1956a. Archaeological Investigations on Southampton and Coats Islands, N.W.T. National Museum of Canada Bulletin, 142: 82-113.

Collins, H. 1956b. Vanished Mystery Men of Hudson Bay. National Geographic Magazine, 110(5): 669-687.

Collins, H. 1958. Archaeological Investigations on Southampton and Walrus Islands, Northwest Territories. National Museum of Canada Bulletin, 147: 22-61.

Collins, H. 1975. Archaeological Investigations in Hudson Bay, 1954. National Geographic Society Research Reports, 1890-1954, Projects 63-77.

Collins, H. n.d. Sadlermiut-Tunit-Dorset. MS on file with the National Anthropological Archives, Smithsonian Institution, Washington, D.C.

Comer, G. 1906. Whaling in Hudson Bay with notes on Southampton Island. Boas Anniversary Volume: Anthropological Papers Written in Honor of Franz Boas. New York: G.E. Stewart & Co., pp. 475-484.

Comer, G. 1910. A Geographical Description of Southampton Island and Notes upon the Eskimo. American Geographical Society of New York Bulletin, 42: 94-100.

Comer, G. 1921. Notes by G. Comer on the Natives of the Northwestern shores of Hudson Bay. American Anthropolgist, 23(2): 243-244.

Comer, G. 1925. Letter to Dr. Livingstone of the Department of the Interior, on file with the Public Archives of Canada, RG 85, Vol. 815, File 6954, pt. 1.

de Laguna, F. 1947. The Prehistory of Northern North America as Seen from the Yukon. Memoirs of the Society for American Archeology, 3.

de Laguna, F. 1979. Therkel Mathiassen and the Beginnings of Eskimo Archaeology. In, Thule Eskimo culture: An Anthropological Retrospective, A.P. McCartney, ed. National Museum of Man, Mercury Series, Archaeological Survey of Canada Paper, 88: 10-53.

Driscoll, B. 1983. The Inuit Parka. Unpublished M.A. thesis, Carleton University.

Eber, D. 1989. When Whalers Were Up North. Kingston: McGill - Queen's University Press.

Ferguson, R. 1938. Arctic Harpooner: A Voyage on the Schooner Abbie Bradford 1878-1879. Philadelphia: University of Pennsylvania Press.

Fitzhugh, W. 1993. Introduction. In, Archeology of the Frobisher Voyages, W. Fitzhugh and J. Olin, eds. Washington: Smithsonian Institution Press, pp. 1-7.

Hall, C. F. 1860-62. The Unpublished Diaries of Charles Francis Hall. MS on file with the Division of Naval History, Smithsonian Institution, Washington, D.C.

Hallendy, N. 1992. Personal Communication, London, Ontario.

Holtved, E. 1944. Archaeological Investigations in the Thule District. II: Analytical Part. Meddelelser om Gronland, 141(2).

Hrdlicka, A. 1910. Contribution to the Anthropology of Central and Smith Sound Eskimo. Anthropological Papers of the American Museum of Natural History, 5(2): 177-280.

Jenness, D. 1922. The Life of the Copper Eskimos. Report of the Canadian Arctic Expedition 1913-18, Vol. 12.

Jenness, D. 1923. Origin of the Copper Eskimos and their Copper Culture. Geographical Review, 13(4): 540-551.

Jenness, D. 1933. The American Aborigenes: their Origin and Antiquity, D. Jenness, ed.. Toronto: University of Toronto Press, 371-396.

Jenness, D. 1934. Indians of Canada. National Museums of Canada Bulletin, 65.

Jenness, D. 1941. An Archaeological Collection from the Belcher Islands in Hudson Bay. Annals of the Carnegie Museum, 28: 189-202.

Lyon, G. 1825. A Brief Narrative of an Unsuccessful Attempt to Reach Repulse Bay, through Sir Thomas Rowe's "Welcome." London: J. Murray.

Manning, T. 1942. Remarks on the Physiography, Eskimo, and Mammals of Southampton Island. Canadian Geographic Journal, 24(1): 17-33.

Mary-Rousseliere, G. 1980. Qitdlarssuaq - l'Histoire d'une Migration Polaire. Montreal: Les Presses de l'Universite de Montreal.

Mathiassen, T. 1927. Archaeology of the Central Eskimo. Report of the Fifth Thule Expedition, 1921-24, 4 (1).

Maxwell, M. 1985. Prehistory of the Eastern Arctic. New York: Academic Press.

Mayhall, J. 1979. The Biological Relationships of Thule culture and Inuit Populations: An Odontological Investigation. In, Thule Eskimo Culture: an Anthropological Retrospective, A.P. McCartney, ed. National Museum of Man, Mercury Series, Archaeological Survey of Canada Paper, 88: 448-473.

McCartney, A. P. and J. M. Savelle. 1989. A Thule Eskimo Stone Vessel Complex. Canadian Journal of Archaeology, 13: 21-49.

McGhee, R. 1978. Canadian Arctic Prehistory. Toronto: Van Nostrand Reinhold.

McGhee, R. 1984. The Thule Village at Brooman Point, High Arctic Canada. National Museum of Man, Mercury Series, Archaeological Survey of Canada Paper, 125.

Meldgaard, J. 1960. Origin and Evolution of Eskimo cultures in the Eastern Arctic. Canadian Geographic Journal, 60(2): 64-75.

Merbs, C. and W. Wilson. 1962. Anomalies and Pathologies of the Sadlermiut Eskimo Vertebral Column. National Museum of Canada Bulletin, 180: 154-180.

Morrison, D. 1993. The Rita-Claire site: 1993. MS, on file with the Canadian Museum of Civilization, Hull.

Paton, J. 1825. A Journal of a Voyage of Discovery to the Polar Regions, in the Year 1824, in His Majesty's Ship Griper. Paisley: J. Fraser.

Pitseolak, P. and D. H. Eber. 1975. People from Our Side. Edmonton: Hurtig.

Popham, R. and W. Bell. 1951. Eskimo Crania from Southampton Island. Revue Canadienne de Biologie, 10(5): 435-442.

Ross, W. G. 1977. Whaling and the Decline of Native Populations. Arctic Anthropology, 14(2): 1-8.

Ross, W. G. 1984. <u>An Arctic Whaling Diary: the Journal of Captain George Comer in Hudson Bay 1903-1905</u>. Toronto: University of Toronto Press.

Rowley, S. 1985a. The Significance of Migration for the Understanding of Inuit Cultural Development in the Canadian Arctic. Unpublished Ph.D. dissertation, University of Cambridge.

Rowley, S. 1985b. Population Movements in the Canadian Arctic. <u>Etudes/Inuit/Studies</u>, 9(1): 3-21.

Sutton, G. 1932-36. <u>The Exploration of Southampton Island</u>. Memoirs of the Carnegie Museum, 12.

Taylor, W. E. 1959. The Mysterious Sadlermiut. <u>The Beaver</u>, 260: 26-33.

Taylor, W. E. 1960. A Description of Sadlermiut Houses Excavated at Native Point, Southampton Island, N.W.T. <u>National Museum of Canada Bulletin</u>, 162: 53-100.

Utermohle, C. and C. Merbs. 1979. Population Affinities of Thule Culture Eskimos in Northwest Hudson Bay. In, <u>Thule Eskimo Culture: an Anthropological Retrospective</u>, A.P. McCartney, ed.. National Museum of Man, Mercury Series, Archaeological Survey of Canada Paper, 88: 435-447.

VanStone, J. 1962. An Archaeological Collection from Somerset Island and Boothia Peninsula, N.W.T. <u>Royal Ontario Museum. Art and Archaeology Division. Occasional Papers</u>, 4: 1-63.

Inuksuit:
Semalithic Figures Constructed by Inuit in the Canadian Arctic

Norman Hallendy
Tukilik Project,
Carp, Ontario

Abstract

Inuksuit - figures made of stone - are among the many important objects created by the first people known to have inhabited the Arctic portions of Alaska, Arctic Canada, and Greenland. The term inuksuk (the singular of *inuksuit*) means "to act in the capacity of a human." It is an extension of *inuk*; human being. These stone figures were placed on the temporal and spiritual landscapes. Among many practical functions, they were employed as hunting and navigation aids, coordination points, indicators, and message centers. In addition to their earthly functions, certain *inuksuk*-like figures had spiritual connotations, and were objects of veneration, often marking the threshold of the spiritual landscape of the *Inummariit* - the people who knew how to survive on the land living in a traditional way.

Résumé

Les *Inuksuit* - personnages en pierre - comptent parmi les nombreux objets importants qui ont été créés par les premiers peuples connus pour avoir habité les régions arctiques de l'Alaska, du Canada et du Groenland. Le terme *inuksuk* (singulier d'*inuksuit*) signifie «agir à titre d'être humain». Ce terme est une extension d'*inuk*, qui veut dire «être humain». Ces personnages de pierre prenaient place dans les paysages temporels et spirituels. Ils remplissaient un grand nombre de fonctions pratiques : ils servaient d'instruments de chasse et de navigation, de points de coordination, d'indices, et de centres de messages. Outre leurs fonctions terrestres, certains personnages ressemblant à des *inuksuit* présentaient des connotations spirituelles et ils étaient des objets de vénération, qui marquaient souvent le seuil du paysage spirituel des *Inummariit*, ces êtres qui savaient comment survivre sur la terre en respectant le mode de vie traditionnel.

Messages on the Land

In various parts in the Canadian Arctic as late as the mid-1950s, one could meet Inuit who had recently "come off the land" to live their final years in settlements. These were the *Inummariit* - "the people who knew how to survive on the land living in a traditional way." The term *Inummariit* is regarded as an expression of esteem.

Threads of Arctic Prehistory: Papers in Honour of William E. Taylor Jr., David Morrison and Jean-Luc Pilon, eds. Canadian Museum of Civilization, Mercury Series, Archaeological Survey of Canada Paper 149. 1994.

My first encounter with the *Inummariit* occurred when I was a young man, and in the last three decades I have responded to a consuming curiosity about how they perceived their world living on the land under conditions that would be fatal to most of us. My questions to Elders resulted in answers that beguiled me with accounts of places, things, and events beyond the limits of my experience. Whenever possible, I arranged to travel with the Elders, and that experience exposed me in an intimate way to their joy when back on the land, and their respect for it. I learned that it was not unmanly to be moved by the touch, the smell, and the sounds of the land. This sensual communion, this *unganatuq*, is a "deep and total attachment to the land," often expressed in spiritual terms.

The reverence some Elders had for *utirnigiit* - the "traces of comings and goings" of their ancestors was very evident. Most notable was the respect they showed for *inuksuit* built by their predecessors. The hunter/historian Taamusi Qumaq, confided to me that "such was the respect for *inuksuit* built by our ancestors, we would not even think of touching them." It is not difficult to understand the quiet abhorrence experienced by Elders who witnessed outsiders disturbing places or artifacts which attached them to their past.

During my travels in the Arctic, I heard that some *inuksuit* were believed to have spiritual qualities. However, my attempts to learn more from Inuit Elders met with limited success at the outset. Often I received an outright denial that *inuksuit* possessed spiritual qualities. Sometimes I would be given a charming story or scary tale which nourished my imagination, conveniently leaving no opening for questions. More often than not I encountered the side-stepping "*ah-choo?*" meaning "who knows?" When dealing with outsiders, it enables one to avoid risking the consequences of revealing important things, without denying their very existence.

However, now and then I encountered an Elder who would speak of spiritual matters, of objects and places deserving much respect. Over time, this information proved to be invaluable in gathering yet more information from Elders in other settlements. This essay is based on that information; it also outlines my attempts to understand the significance of *inuksuit* upon the earthly and spiritual landscapes.

I was intrigued for a time with the occurrence in other parts of the world of objects similar to *inuksuit* such as the *apashektas* of the Andes, the *chortens* of Nepal, the *seite* of Lapland (Ehrhardt 1964), and the *dorazy chaloveka* of Siberia. Though references to these objects are scant in archaeological texts, illustrations of these stone figures appear increasingly in world travel literature, geographical journals and "popular science" periodicals. Though it was tempting to study *inuksuk*-like figures constructed in other lands, I chose to examine only those found in the Canadian Arctic.

I reviewed bibliographic databases, noted facts, and arranged them in interesting ways. That gave me a feeling of making headway, but contemplating the accumulating piles of information I thought of the Inuktitut expression *angiarivaa* - "he hides it within words." I realized that my arranging and rearranging of facts was conjuring an illusion of progress, but in real terms this work had done little to increase my understanding of what had been revealed to me about *inuksuit* over the years. I was adrift in a sea of detail.

Once again I reviewed all the information I had collected; scores of interviews, hundreds of pages of field notes, thousands of photographs. An invaluable back-drop to the terms and expressions I gathered from Elders was the work of Flint (1991), Peck (1964), Schneider (1985), and Therrien

(1970). It seemed reasonable that if I described the numerous configurations of *inuksuit* and their many functions; if I annotated all the references that had appeared in the literature, I would acquire the insight that had eluded me. I was wrong again, no matter how I arranged and rearranged the data, insight continued to be elusive.

A single expression - *utirnigiit* - "traces of coming and going," appeared often in my notes. It was that word, that expression, that prompted me to examine my data in a new way. By grouping words and expressions related to *utirnigiit*, I created what I learned later is referred to by linguists as a "semantic set." These word groupings were so useful it occurred to me that doing the same thing with *inuksuit* data I had gathered could reveal meanings and relationships that had eluded me thus far. A semantic field (Vassilev 1974) is usually made up of a number of semantic sets whose meanings relate to a common entity. A familiar example is, the names and positions given relatives in a kinship structure. A semantic set may relate to any area of human experience, for example hunting. Semantic sub-sets related to hunting may include observable and non-observable entities such as hunting equipment, techniques, precautions, animal behaviour, religious practices related to hunting, ethics, etc. Thus its possible to describe an entire network of meanings, each offering a particular insight into that transaction between life and death we call hunting.

More relevant to this paper, the semantic field associated with *inuksuit* and *inuksuit*-like figures, emerged from the articulation of the following semantic sets:

1) Levels of abstraction;
2) the term *inuksuit* used in a general manner
3) types of *inuksuit* indicating direction and position
4) *inuksuit* related to hunting and fishing
5) *inuksuit* related to caribou hunting
6) *inuksuit* and other objects related to hunting and fishing
7) *inuksuit*, caches and camps
8) *inuksuit* which are venerated
9) Places of Power
10) Objects of Veneration
11) places on the spiritual landscape.

The terms used in the semantic sets were gathered from a number of sources in various places. For this reason, each term is accompanied by the initial of the place where it is, or was, most commonly used. The following are the abbreviations of place names used in the semantic sets:

A   Arviat (Arviat: "Bowhead Whales")
AQ   Arctic Quebec (Nunavik : "Homeland")
B   Baffin area (Qikiqtaaluk: "Great Island")
C   Coppermine (Quqluktuug: "Place of rapids")
D   Cape Dorset (Kingait: "Mountains")
HI   Holman Island (Uluksaqtuuq: "Where there is copper")

I   Igloolik (Iglulik : "Place of many dwellings")
L   Labrador
PB   Pelly Bay (Aqvilikjuaq : "Place of many Bowhead whales")
RI   Rankin Inlet   (Kangiq&iniq: "The great inlet")
RB   Repulse Bay   (Naujaat: "Where seagulls nest").

Each semantic set illustrates a different but related aspect of *inuksuit* and of objects similar to *inuksuit* that have either utilitarian or spiritual qualities. For example, semantic set 1 begins with the inuktitut expression *utirnigiit* - "traces of coming and going. " It progresses through *nellonaikutak;* "things which are signs, marks and tokens," carries on to *inumivjait*; "things made by Inuit," continues to *ittarnisaq*; "ancient things " (artifacts), then branches to *napataq*; "the precursors of *inuksuit*", while on the other side there is a link with other types of artifacts, such as arrowheads, cutting blades, etc.

Another set picks up from the term *napataq* in the first set and describes the different kinds of *inuksuit* and their purposes. There is a link from the set describing *inuksuit* related to hunting and fishing to another set describing some *inuksuit* related to caribou hunting. An extension of this set is a remarkable drawing of a traditional caribou hunt drawn by the hunter who spoke to me of the spiritual aspect of hunting (Fig. 1). The set dealing with *inuksuit* and *inuksuit* look alikes is linked to the one dealing with places of power, revealing "dreadful and fearful places on the landscape, " and "places where certain *inuksuit* can still be seen. "

An interesting way to view the following semantic sets is to photocopy them and then arrange the copies into a network of meanings.

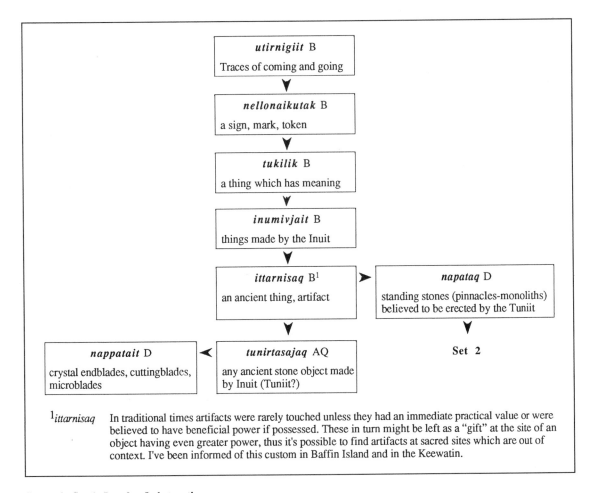

Semantic Set 1 Levels of abstraction.

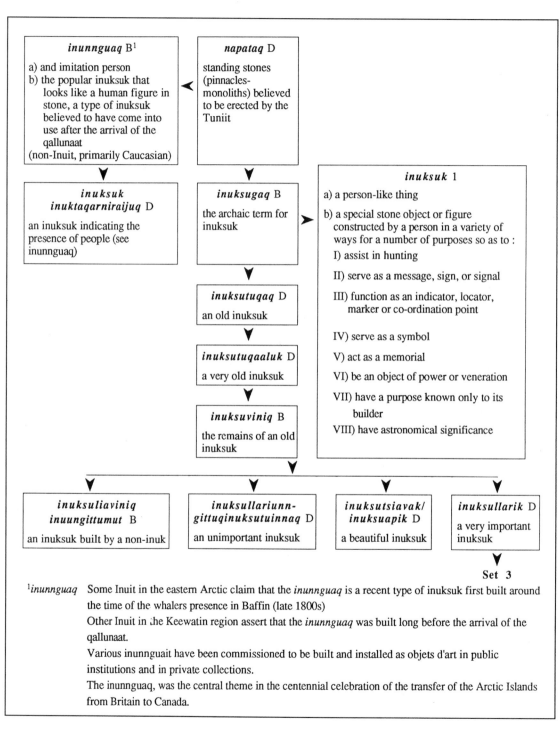

inunnguaq B[1]

a) and imitation person
b) the popular inuksuk that looks like a human figure in stone, a type of inuksuk believed to have come into use after the arrival of the qallunaat
(non-Inuit, primarily Caucasian)

napataq D

standing stones (pinnacles-monoliths) believed to be erected by the Tuniit

inuksuk 1

a) a person-like thing

b) a special stone object or figure constructed by a person in a variety of ways for a number of purposes so as to :

I) assist in hunting

II) serve as a message, sign, or signal

III) function as an indicator, locator, marker or co-ordination point

IV) serve as a symbol

V) act as a memorial

VI) be an object of power or veneration

VII) have a purpose known only to its builder

VIII) have astronomical significance

inuksuk inuktaqarniraijuq D

an inuksuk indicating the presence of people (see inunnguaq)

inuksugaq B

the archaic term for inuksuk

inuksutuqaq D

an old inuksuk

inuksutuqaaluk D

a very old inuksuk

inuksuviniq B

the remains of an old inuksuk

inuksuliaviniq inuungittumut B

an inuksuk built by a non-inuk

inuksullariunn-gittuqinuksutuinnaq D

an unimportant inuksuk

inuksutsiavak/ inuksuapik D

a beautiful inuksuk

inuksullarik D

a very important inuksuk

Set 3

[1]*inunnguaq* Some Inuit in the eastern Arctic claim that the *inunnguaq* is a recent type of inuksuk first built around the time of the whalers presence in Baffin (late 1800s)

Other Inuit in the Keewatin region assert that the *inunnguaq* was built long before the arrival of the qallunaat.

Various inunnguait have been commissioned to be built and installed as objets d'art in public institutions and in private collections.

The inunnguaq, was the central theme in the centennial celebration of the transfer of the Arctic Islands from Britain to Canada.

Semantic Set 2   The term *Inuksuk* used in a general manner.

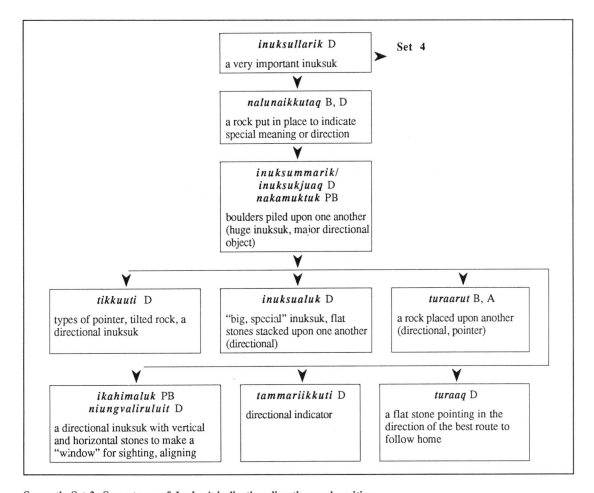

inuksullarik D

a very important inuksuk

➤ **Set 4**

nalunaikkutaq B, D

a rock put in place to indicate special meaning or direction

inuksummarik/ inuksukjuaq D **nakamuktuk** PB

boulders piled upon one another (huge inuksuk, major directional object)

tikkuuti D

types of pointer, tilted rock, a directional inuksuk

inuksualuk D

"big, special" inuksuk, flat stones stacked upon one another (directional)

turaarut B, A

a rock placed upon another (directional, pointer)

ikahimaluk PB **niungvaliruluit** D

a directional inuksuk with vertical and horizontal stones to make a "window" for sighting, aligning

tammariikkuti D

directional indicator

turaaq D

a flat stone pointing in the direction of the best route to follow home

Semantic Set 3 Some types of *Inuksuit* indicating direction and position.

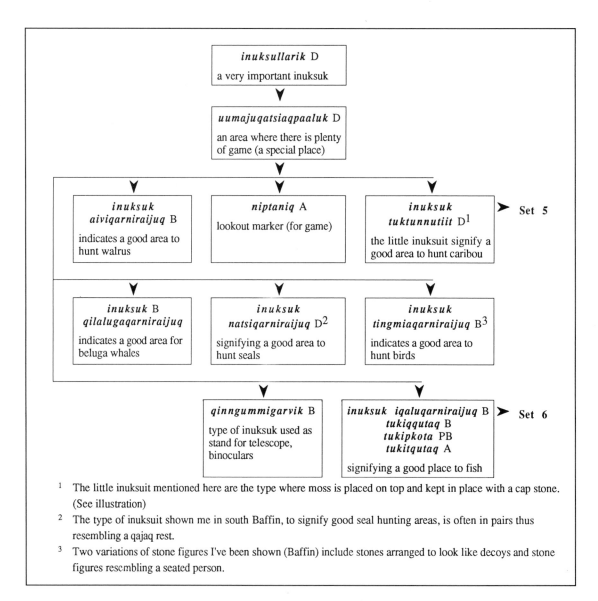

The contents of the diagram:

inuksullarik D

a very important inuksuk

↓

uumajuqatsiaqpaaluk D

an area where there is plenty of game (a special place)

↓

inuksuk aiviqarniraijuq B	niptaniq A	inuksuk tuktunnutiit D[1]
indicates a good area to hunt walrus	lookout marker (for game)	the little inuksuit signify a good area to hunt caribou

➤ Set 5

inuksuk B qilalugaqarniraijuq	inuksuk natsiqarniraijuq D[2]	inuksuk tingmiaqarniraijuq B[3]
indicates a good area for beluga whales	signifying a good area to hunt seals	indicates a good area to hunt birds

qinngummigarvik B	inuksuk iqaluqarniraijuq B tukiqqutaq B tukipkota PB tukitqutaq A
type of inuksuk used as stand for telescope, binoculars	signifying a good place to fish

➤ Set 6

[1] The little inuksuit mentioned here are the type where moss is placed on top and kept in place with a cap stone. (See illustration)

[2] The type of inuksuit shown me in south Baffin, to signify good seal hunting areas, is often in pairs thus resembling a qajaq rest.

[3] Two variations of stone figures I've been shown (Baffin) include stones arranged to look like decoys and stone figures resembling a seated person.

Semantic Set 4 Some *Inuksuit* related to hunting and fishing.

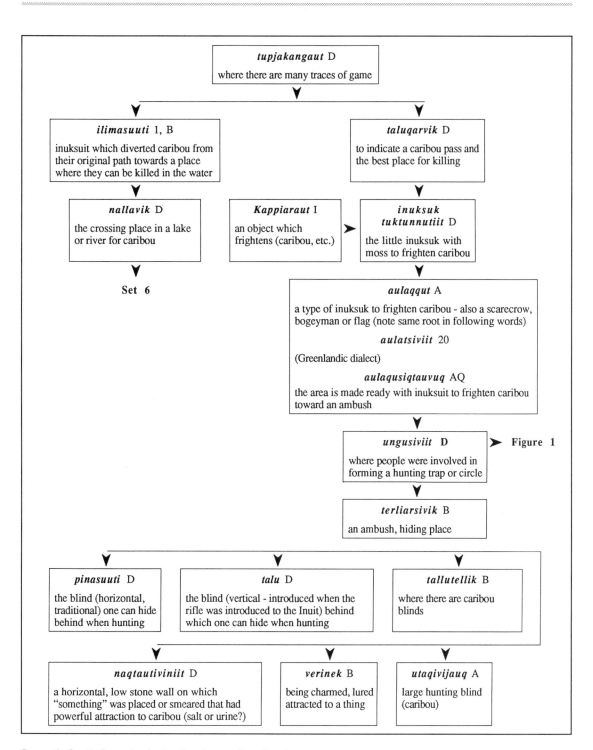

Semantic Set 5 Some *Inuksuit* related to caribou hunting.

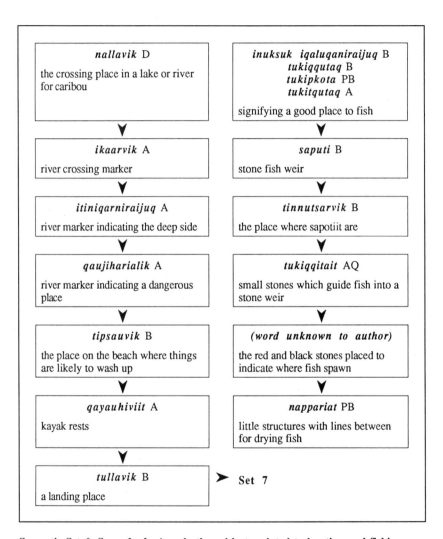

nallavik D

the crossing place in a lake or river for caribou

↓

ikaarvik A

river crossing marker

↓

itiniqarniraijuq A

river marker indicating the deep side

↓

qaujiharialik A

river marker indicating a dangerous place

↓

tipsauvik B

the place on the beach where things are likely to wash up

↓

qayauhiviit A

kayak rests

↓

tullavik B

a landing place

inuksuk iqaluqaniraijuq B
tukiqqutaq B
tukipkota PB
tukitqutaq A

signifying a good place to fish

↓

saputi B

stone fish weir

↓

tinnutsarvik B

the place where sapotiit are

↓

tukiqqitait AQ

small stones which guide fish into a stone weir

↓

(word unknown to author)

the red and black stones placed to indicate where fish spawn

↓

nappariat PB

little structures with lines between for drying fish

➤ Set 7

Semantic Set 6 Some *Inuksuit* and other objects related to hunting and fishing.

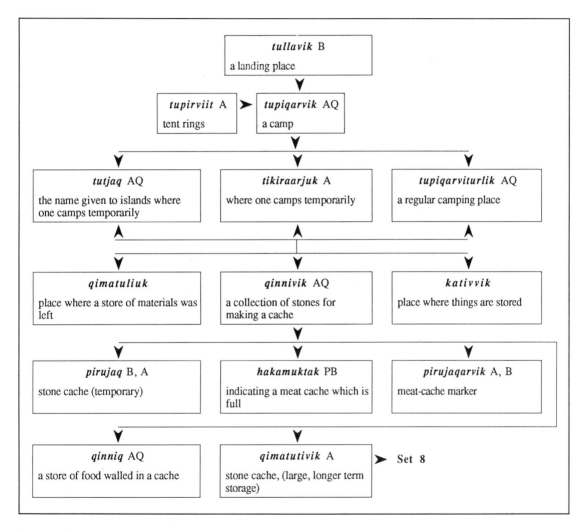

Semantic Set 7 Some *Inuksuit*, caches and camps.

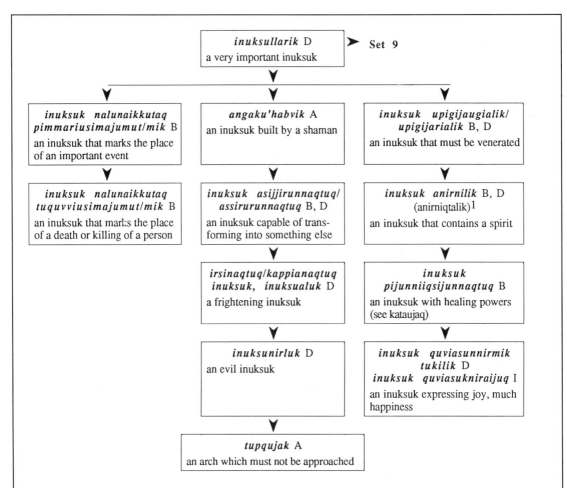

inuksullarik D
a very important inuksuk   ➤ Set 9

*inuksuk nalunaikkutaq
pimmariusimajumut/mik* B
an inuksuk that marks the place
of an important event

angaku'habvik A
an inuksuk built by a shaman

*inuksuk upigijaugialik/
upigijarialik* B, D
an inuksuk that must be venerated

*inuksuk nalunaikkutaq
tuquvviusimajumut/mik* B
an inuksuk that marks the place
of a death or killing of a person

*inuksuk asijjirunnaqtuq/
assirurunnaqtuq* B, D
an inuksuk capable of trans-
forming into something else

inuksuk anirnilik B, D
(anirniqtalik)[1]
an inuksuk that contains a spirit

*irsinaqtuq/kappianaqtuq
inuksuk, inuksualuk* D
a frightening inuksuk

*inuksuk
pijunniiqsijunnaqtuq* B
an inuksuk with healing powers
(see kataujaq)

inuksunirluk D
an evil inuksuk

*inuksuk quviasunnirmik
tukilik* D
inuksuk quviasukniraijuq I
an inuksuk expressing joy, much
happiness

tupqujak A
an arch which must not be approached

[1] "In spring, when there is water between the winter ice and the shore, big shoals of salmon follow along the land just at Nuvuteroq, and they are speared with the leister and caught in large numbers. But one must be careful about fishing like this from the ice if one has no kayak; for once water appears along the shore and the ice in Qûkitlroq (Simpson Strait) begins to drift backwards and forwards before the changing winds, it might easily go out to sea. Once all the men at Kamigluk went hunting for caribou and only the women were left. The men urged them not to fish for salmon from the edge of the ice, but the women did so just the same. with the result that they drifted out to sea with the ice. Suddenly the ice went adrift and they dared not jump ashore; there was only one who took the risk, and she was saved. All the others went out to sea and were lost. so pitiable were their cries and screams out on the drifting ice that from a distance it sounded like the howls of terrified foxes.

But when the men came home they sorrowed so deeply over the loss of their women that they built cairns up on the shore, just as many cairns as there were women lost. They did this because they wanted the souls of the drowned women to be on dry land and not out in the wet sea."

All the cairns at Kamigluk are from this event.

Rasmussen 1930 p. 379.

Semantic Set 8 *Inuksuit* **that are venerated.**

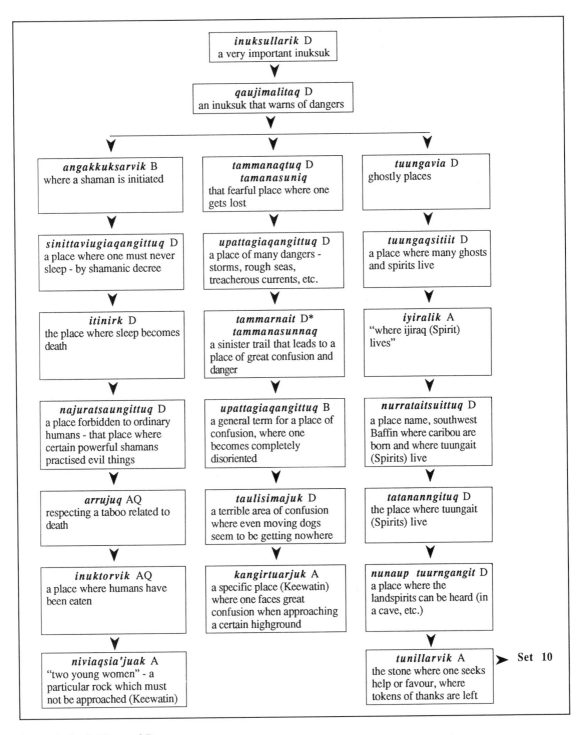

inuksullarik D
a very important inuksuk

qaujimalitaq D
an inuksuk that warns of dangers

angakkuksarvik B
where a shaman is initiated

tammanaqtuq D
tamanasuniq
that fearful place where one gets lost

tuungavia D
ghostly places

sinittaviugiaqangittuq D
a place where one must never sleep - by shamanic decree

upattagiaqangittuq D
a place of many dangers - storms, rough seas, treacherous currents, etc.

tuungaqsitiit D
a place where many ghosts and spirits live

itinirk D
the place where sleep becomes death

tammarnait D*
tammanasunnaq
a sinister trail that leads to a place of great confusion and danger

iyiralik A
"where ijiraq (Spirit) lives"

najuratsaungittuq D
a place forbidden to ordinary humans - that place where certain powerful shamans practised evil things

upattagiaqangittuq B
a general term for a place of confusion, where one becomes completely disoriented

nurrataitsuittuq D
a place name, southwest Baffin where caribou are born and where tuungait (Spirits) live

arrujuq AQ
respecting a taboo related to death

taulisimajuk D
a terrible area of confusion where even moving dogs seem to be getting nowhere

tatananngituq D
the place where tuungait (Spirits) live

inuktorvik AQ
a place where humans have been eaten

kangirtuarjuk A
a specific place (Keewatin) where one faces great confusion when approaching a certain highground

nunaup tuurngangit D
a place where the landspirits can be heard (in a cave, etc.)

niviaqsia'juak A
"two young women" - a particular rock which must not be approached (Keewatin)

tunillarvik A
the stone where one seeks help or favour, where tokens of thanks are left

> Set 10

Semantic Set 9 Places of Power.

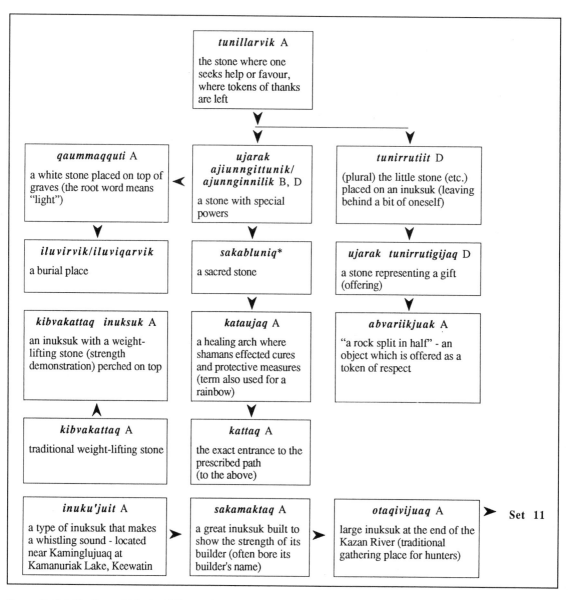

Semantic Set 10 Some Objects of Veneration.

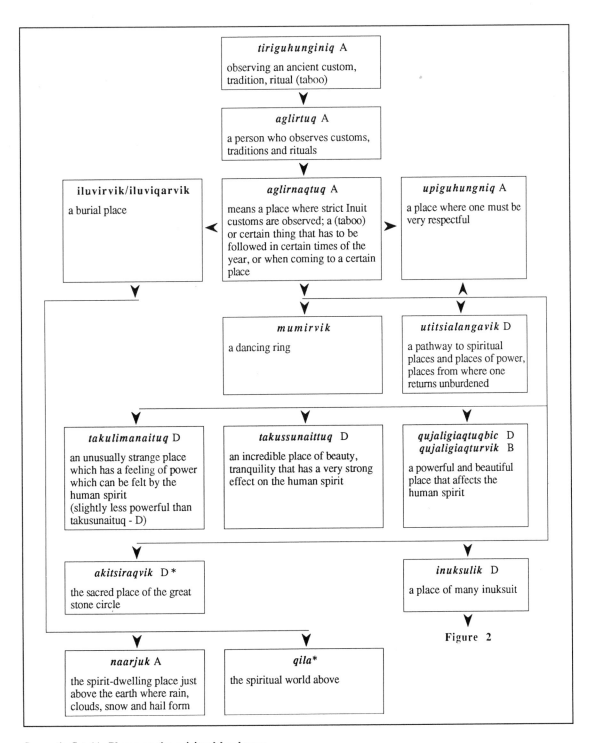

Semantic Set 11 Places on the spiritual landscape.

Figure 1 "Traditional way of caribou hunting," by Osutsiak Pudlat, Cape Dorset, Kingait, 1990.

One of a series of drawings illustrating the use of *inuksuit tuktunnutiit* in directing caribou toward "shooting pits. " Such a place is referred to as *tallutellik* - where there are caribou blinds. The root of the word *tallutellik* is the word for shadow - "one is hidden by a shadow. " Osutsiak has made many drawings of traditional hunting methods and spiritual beings, such as *ijirait*, the caribou spirits who behave like humans.

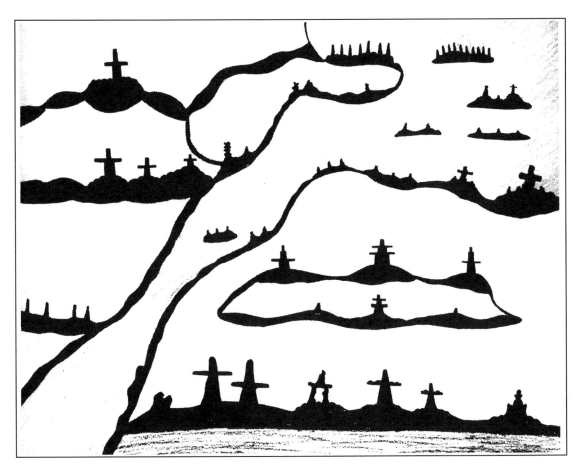

Figure 2 "Mystical Landscape," by Pudlo Pudlat, Cape Dorset, Kingiat, 1990.

Note the horizon placed in the foreground, requiring the viewer to look beyond. One sees landscapes within landscapes. Cross-like *inuksuit* stand at the places of the dead (upper left). Pinnacles are seen on the land and upon a nearby island (upper right) which mark the sometimes dangerous passages along the Baffin coast. We see an "island" (lower middle) prescribed within the landscape by six *inuksuit*. Such "islands" or places of power may be prescribed by a single great dancing circle or may include a large area of several kilometres which is forbidden to all. Pudlo has made many drawings of mystical landscapes; and several have been exhibited at the National Gallery of Canada.

Figure 3 "The coast of southwestern Baffin Island," by Simeonie Qapappik, Cape Dorset, Kingait, 1990.

The upper drawing is of the coast from Cape Dorset (far left) to Simeonie's birthplace near the Amadjuak (far right), some 300 kilometres distant. He identifies the location of whales, square-flipper seals, walrus, small seals, fish, birds, etc. He shows the migration path of geese and the reindeer herd once tended by the Laplanders (the people of the pointed shoes) at the Amadjuak. The *inuksuit* he illustrates in the upper and lower drawing are symbolic characters upon the landscape. They are not meant to show the structure of *inuksuit*, but rather communicate a variety of impressions. The three small *inuksuit* in the lower drawing (far right, top to bottom) are the *inuksuit* used in caribou hunting, as illustrated in the next drawing.

A *Distinct natural objects:* four types - dominant, features, such as a hill or mountain; a rock so unusual in shape it attracts attention; perched boulders; and caves.

B *Placed, shaped, or constructed objects:* Morphology of Inuksuit and related objects.

C *Placement and arrangement of Inuksuit:* Positioning of Inuksuit on the landscape.

Figure 4 The basic types and arrangements of *inuksuit*.

Discussion

The semantic field of Inuktitut words and expressions revealed that I had studied more than 20 different kinds of standing structures, each with a different name, each with a different function but together, constituting a "family" of *inuksuit*. The following illustrates some of the types and functions of *inuksuit*:

aulaqqut	A	*inuksuit* which frightened caribou
ilimasuuti	B	*inuksuit* which diverted caribou
taluqarrik	D	best place for killing a caribou
niptaniq	A	look out marker for game
napataq	D	standing stones, pinnacles
pirujaqarvik	A, B	meat cache marker
hakamuktak	PB	indicator - full meat-cache
nakkatain	C	points to good fishing place
ikaarrik	A	river-crossing marker
itiniqarniraijuq	A	deep side of a river
qaujiharialik	A	dangerous place in river
turaarut	B, A	rock placed upon another - a pointer
turaaq	D	flat rock pointer
tikkuuti	D	tilted rock, type of pointer
niungvaliruluit	D	directional *inuksuk*, vertical and horizontal stones making a "window" for sighting, aligning
inuksualuk	D	image *inuksuk*, major directional object, stacked flat stones
nakamuktuk	PB	huge *inuksuk*, major directional object, piled boulders
tammariikuti	D	directional indicator
nalunaikkutaq	B, D	rock put in place indicating special meaning or direction
inuku 'juit	A	*inuksuit* that make whistling sounds

The following are some, but certainly not all, of the functions related to *inuksuit*:

Indicators
. depth of snow
. where food, etc. is cached
. safe or dangerous crossing places
. deep or shallow side of river
. where ice is dangerous in spring
. direction, or change of direction, of
    hunter communicating to follower
. caribou crossing

. where there is plenty of game (general)
. where fish spawn
. good hunting for seal
. good hunting for walrus
. good hunting for whale
. good egg gathering
. good fishing
. hauling out place for seal
. hauling out place for walrus

- landing sites for boats or kayaks
- the furthest limit of one's journey
- where important resources are found

Inuksuit **venerated, related to places:**
- where traditions must be observed
- where one must not camp
- where one must not trespass
- where shaman(s) was initiated
- subject to violent storms
- treacherous water
- dangerous ice
- falling rocks, etc.
- where spirits reside
- earthly human remains
- where life is renewed (calving, spawning, etc.)
- where judgements/decisions are made
- celebrations, festivals

Inukshuit **venerated, related to objects**
- an object which must never be approached or touched
- an object to which one should give gifts or show respect
- capable of providing safe passage, good fortune

Unknown
- believed to have been made by non-Inuit

Navigation/coordination
- best route home (not necessarily shortest)
- position of mainland from distant island
- direction of significant inland place (eg. fish lake)
- direction of significant place below the horizon
- major transition points between water routes and inland routes
- beacon where fog is prevalent between islands

Hunting instruments for caribou
- drift fences
- direction changers
- sound makers

Hunting instruments for geese
- dummies (look like seated human figures)
- bird decoys

Private
- secret or private cache in vicinity
- hiding place in vicinity

Astronomical
- pointing to pole star
- pointing to mid-winter moon

Memorials
- place of death (natural or unnatural)
- place of tragedy (starvation, violence, etc.)

Symbols
- presence of people
- arrival of people (eg. ship, celebrants)
- warning to intruders
- joy, frivolity, favoured locations
- fertility/virility
- human-like figures (*inunguaq*) for tourist attraction
- spirit figures
- represented in myths, string games, *Ayayait* (songs), etc.
- human-like figures for target practise
- human-like figures for receiving curse (killing) by a shaman

The term *inuksuk* can be used in a generic sense for standing stone objects, whatever their name or particular function that "act in the capacity of a human. " Equally important are what I refer to as "*inuksuk* look alikes," some of which include:

sakamaktaq	A	great inuksuk showing strength of builder, often bearing his name
tupqujak	A	an arch which must not be approached
tunillarvik	A	the stone where one seeks favours, and tokens of thanks are left
angaku 'habvik	A	an *inuksuk* built by a shaman
sakabluniq		a sacred stone

These structures do not include the many cairns and beacons constructed by explorers, whalers, traders, surveyors, or tourists. The *inuksuk* look alikes erected by the Inuit are often found at places of particular importance, or in their vicinity. While they may have the human-like form of an *inunnguaq*, or may look like a *napataq*, a standing stone structure, or a *nakamuktuk*, a huge inuksuk constructed of piled boulders, they do not "act in the capacity of a person. " Their spiritual or religious function was rarely divulged. They are a physical manifestation of spiritual power, and many are objects of veneration. Some served to mark the thresholds of the spiritual landscape for the Inummariit, who felt compelled to build them out of love, loneliness, or fear.

I have been asked, "How old are *inuksuit*? Were they first built within the Palaeoeskimo or Neoeskimo period?" Quite frankly, I do not know. Some old *inuksuit* are constructed of a type of stone or are in an area that repels the colonization of lichens, so they tend to look recent. Some *inuksuit* are favoured roosts of birds whose rich guano encourages a luxuriant growth of the lichen *xanthoria*. These *inuksuit* tend to look old, but may not be.

My questions to Elders about the age of various *inuksuit* and the occurrence of related events were often answered by situating the object or event in one of nine timeframes:

1 Before there were humans   *Suli inutagalautinagu silaqjuaq*
2 The time of the earliest humans   *Inuit sivulliit tamaanigiagnaliqtillugit*
3 The time of the Tunniit   *Tuniqtaqaliqtillugu*
4 The time of our earliest ancestors   *Sivuliriagnavut tamaaniliqtillugit*
5 Before the arrival of whites   *Qallunaat tamaugnallautinagit*
6 After the arrival of whites   *Qallunaat tamaniliqtillugit*
7 Within living memory   *Iqaumalugu taimagnanituqaluk*
8 The time when all Inuit lived on the land   *Inulimaat nunaqaqatatillugit nunaliralagnulutik*
9 When most Inuit moved into settlements   *Ilunagalatik Inuit nuumata nunalinut*

The interval between the first and the most recent timeframe is often referred to as "the traditional time " by Elders with whom I have spoken. They say the building of *inuksuit* began "in the time of the earliest humans - those who prepared the land for our ancestors. "

In a place called Inuksugalait on the southwest coast of Baffin Island, there may be some two hundred *inuksuit*, about fifty of which remain standing. Some face specific directions aligned to the rising sun or to important places below the horizon. Others point heavenward to *nikisuituq*, the star which never moves. Each inuksuk is different; collectively they represent a myriad of forms and structures of *inuksuit*. They range in size from an *inuksuk* no bigger than two fists placed one upon the another, to some much larger than a human figure. I was told some had been built by the *Tuniit*, and that many had been erected by a succession of *Inumnariit* who travelled the entire length of the southwest coast of Baffin Island and across the Hudson Strait to Nunavik - Arctic Quebec. They made numerous voyages to Southampton Island, and travelled up and down much of the west coast of Baffin Island. *Inuksuit* are often found wherever the *Inumariit* travelled. So compelling was the desire of the Inumnariit to create *inuksuit* that the structures appear not only on the temporal landscape but in legends and stories, in figures that emerge from the movements of fingers playing string games; and in a winter-sky constellation.

Many Inuit who lived most of their lives on the land retain a strong attachment to *inuksuit* believed to have been built by their ancestors. Some of these "old" *inuksuit* are mentioned in *aya-yait*, the travelling songs passed from one generation to the next to help travellers remember a series of directions for long trips. Often these old *inuksuit* are venerated regardless of their function. Even today, the appearance of familiar *inuksuit* on the landscape is a welcome sight when one is a long way from home. Whether they symbolized their maker, acted in his capacity, or were the object of veneration, *inuksuit* functioned as semaliths - messages created by the arrangement of stones that were an integral part of the hunters' language, and endure as indelible signatures on the Arctic landscape.

Coming upon an old camp where huts, cairns and graves could be seen, a mid-19th century explorer wrote "Though evidently long deserted, my drivers seemed to know all about them, for they suspended the hunt... to take a close look at these evidences of a bygone generation of their fathers" (Kane 1856: 159).

Acknowledgements

I cannot thank enough the Elders I have met in various parts of the Arctic who have enriched my life in so many ways over the years. I am deeply indebted to them for providing me with the information presented here. In addition I wish to acknowledge the assistance of the Canada Council and the Inuit Culture and Linguistics Section of the Department of Indian and Northern Affairs, Thomas Fotiou, William Cowan, Charles Martijn, Darrell Eagles, and William E. Taylor, Jr.

References

Flint, M. S. 1991. A Workbook for the Study of Innuktetut, (Canadian Eastern Arctic). MS on file with the Indian and Northern Affairs Library, Ottawa.

Kane, E. K. 1856. Arctic Explorations In Search of Sir John Franklin, 1853. Vol. II. Philadelphia: Childs and Peterson.

Peck, E. J. 1925. Eskimo-English Dictionary, compiled from Erdman's Eskimo-German Edition, 1864 AD. The General Synod of the Church of England in Canada.

Rasmussen, K. 1931. The Netsilik Eskimos: Social Life and Spiritual Culture. Report of the Fifth Thule Expedition 1921-24, 8.

Schneider, L. 1985. Ulirnaisigutiit, Inuktitut-English dictionary of Northern Quebec, Labrador and Eastern Arctic Dialects. Quebec: Les Presses de l 'Université Laval.

Therrien, M. 1987. Le Corps Inuit (Québec arctique). Centre National de la Recherche Scientifique del 'Institute National des Langues et Civilisations Orientales du Ministère des Relations Extérieures.

Thibert, A. 1970. Eskimo-English dictionary, revised edition. Ottawa: Canadian Research Centre for Anthropology, Université Saint Paul.

Ehrhardt, K. J. 1964. Aalte Kultsteine und Opferplatze der finnischen Lappen im Gebiet des Inarisees und Iijari. Anthropos, 59: 840-848.

Vassilyev, L. M. 1974. The Theory of Semanic Fields: A survey. Linguistics, An International Review, 137.

Formation Processes and Thule Archaeofaunas

Douglas R. Stenton
Arctic College,
Iqaluit, N.W.T.

and

Robert W. Park
University of British Columbia
Vancouver, British Columbia

Abstract

This paper discusses the integrity of Thule winter house faunal assemblages as influenced by cultural and natural formation processes. It is argued that the assemblages consist largely of mixed, secondary deposits and that existing reconstructions of Thule settlement and subsistence behaviour do not reflect the importance of the varied depositional processes that have shaped the assemblages. If our understanding of Thule social and economic behaviour is to improve, the study of formation processes affecting faunal assemblages must become an explicit dimension of Thule research. In this regard, accurate classification of bone refuse deposits and modified collection techniques will be of special importance.

Résumé

Le présent document traite de l'intégrité des assemblages fauniques retrouvés dans des maisons d'hiver thuléennes, et de la manière dont les processus de formation culturels et naturels les ont influencés. L'auteur soutient que les assemblages consistaient surtout en dépôts mixtes secondaires, et que les reconstitutions existantes de villages thuléens et du mode de subsistance des Thuléens ne reflètent pas l'importance des divers processus de dépôt qui ont modelé ces assemblages. Si notre compréhension du comportement social et économique des Thuléens doit s'améliorer, l'étude des processus de formation qui affectent les assemblages fauniques doit devenir une dimension explicite de la recherche sur la culture thuléenne. Sur ce plan, une classification précise des dépôts de déchets osseux et de nouvelles techniques de collecte revêtiront une importance particulière.

Introduction

The study of subsistence behaviour has been an integral component of Thule archaeology since Mathiassen conducted the first systematic investigation of the culture some seventy years ago

Threads of Arctic Prehistory: Papers in Honour of William E. Taylor Jr., David Morrison and Jean-Luc Pilon, eds. Canadian Museum of Civilization, Mercury Series, Archaeological Survey of Canada Paper 149. 1994.

410   THREADS OF ARCTIC PREHISTORY

(Mathiassen 1927a, 1927b). The attributes of winter house and midden faunal assemblages figured prominently in Mathiassen's assessment of Thule settlement and subsistence behaviour (de Laguna 1979: 20-21; Mathiassen 1927a: 85) and these topics continue to be areas of active research interest. Since Mathiassen's time, however, the orientation of Thule subsistence research has undergone important changes. Site-specific reconstructions based on descriptive summaries of species harvested have been replaced by comparative studies incorporating various analytical techniques designed to address more complex issues such as the number of animals harvested, the procurement strategies employed, the amount of meat and subsidiary materials obtained, and the season and duration of site occupation (Møhl 1979; Morrison 1983; Rick 1980; Staab 1979; Stenton 1983). Most recently, regional ecological approaches incorporating explicit theoretical models have been explored for their potential in developing a more sophisticated understanding of Thule adaptive strategies, particularly systemic responses to environmental changes (Sabo 1991; Savelle 1987; Stenton 1991).

Regardless of the type of approach adopted, archaeologists attempting to reconstruct Thule subsistence and settlement behaviour invariably place special emphasis on faunal assemblages recovered from winter houses. In view of the fundamental importance of this data set, one might logically conclude that formation processes (Schiffer 1972, 1987) that generate and modify these assemblages have been thoroughly investigated. Surprisingly, the effects of natural and cultural formation processes on the integrity of faunal assemblages in Thule winter house ruins have not received systematic study commensurate with their importance. Given the continued importance and increasing complexity of research involving faunal data, in this paper we discuss cultural formation processes that we believe play significant, long-term roles in determining the nature of faunal assemblages from Thule winter houses.

Thule Faunal Assemblages

The importance of faunal data to Thule archaeology is reflected in the range of research problems to which they have been applied. In addition to providing basic information on diet, researchers have used faunal assemblage composition and element frequencies to document changes in subsistence strategy (e.g., Schledermann 1976; Stanford 1976: 113-114), to estimate the duration and intensity of site occupation (e.g., Sabo 1991: 145; Sabo and Jacobs 1980: 500), and even as a basis for establishing chronologies (e.g., Savelle and McCartney 1988: 44).

In assessing the general potential of Thule faunal assemblages for these purposes, researchers traditionally cite the favourable preservation conditions of high latitude environments. As a result of low temperatures and reduced precipitation, skeletal remains and more perishable organic materials (e.g., skin, hair, baleen) are often found in exceptionally good condition. This perspective must be balanced, however, by the recognition of other factors that affect the interpretive potential of the assemblages regardless of their state of preservation. Many Thule winter sites, for example, yield evidence of occupation by earlier Pre-Dorset and Dorset groups, and subsequent use by their Inuit descendents. There exists, therefore, ample opportunity for disturbance and admixture of materials to occur in Thule winter sites. In addition, many Thule houses served a variety of functions through their life histories, with the result that faunal materials from a structure do not necessarily derive from the most "obvious" function inferred from the structure's formal characteristics.

A survey of Thule site reports indicates that while many researchers report evidence of post-occupational human disturbance of Thule winter houses, the broader implications of these and related processes are either not discussed or are addressed in a post-hoc, cursory manner only (c.f.: Maxwell 1985; McCullough 1989; McGhee 1984; Morrison 1988; Park 1989; Sabo and Jacobs 1980; Savelle 1987; Stenton 1983, 1990; Taylor and McGhee 1981). The reasons underlying the relative lack of effort devoted to understanding these processes are unclear, but it may be explained in part by a lack of concensus concerning the significance of post-occupational disturbance of Thule houses and, therefore, of our ability to accurately reconstruct Thule subsistence behaviour. McGhee, for example, has suggested that because most Thule winter houses have been disturbed to some extent, our ability to reconstruct many aspects of ancestral Inuit lifeways using faunal data may be severely compromised (McGhee 1982: 74, 1984: 1). By contrast, in a critical review of approaches to the study of Thule subsistence economies, Savelle and McCartney (1988) suggest that Arctic archaeologists may be constrained more by the limited extent to which they adopt explicit theoretical approaches in their research rather than from limitations inherent in the data base. With the exception of the removal of bowhead whale bone, they characterize post-occupational human disturbance of Thule sites as "generally insignificant" (Savelle and McCartney 1988: 23).

Support for either position could be found in a given site, but the views of most archaeologists probably fall somewhere in between these extremes, and there appears to be general agreement that prior to their excavation, many Thule winter houses underwent some degree of modification as a result of both natural and cultural processes. This consensus is based on empirical data that demonstrate clearly that the value of specific locations to human populations continued over time, in some cases millennia, and is confirmed by ethnographic analyses (Boas 1888: 547; Mathiassen 1927a).

Formation Processes And Faunal Assemblages

There have been comparatively few studies focusing on the behaviours that produce Thule faunal assemblages. With a few notable exceptions (e.g., Maxwell 1981; McCartney 1979), detailed discussion of formation processes affecting Thule winter house assemblages has been restricted to the implications of the recycling of bowhead whale bone during the prehistoric period (largely for structural purposes) and the potential effects of this practice for understanding the importance of Thule bowhead whale hunting (Freeman 1979; McCartney and Savelle 1985). McCartney (1979) has provided the most detailed examination to date of the effects of formation processes on Thule winter houses. He identifies six basic phases of a directional process in which cultural and natural modification of Thule winter houses is driven by changing human needs and perceptions (McCartney 1979: Table 2). Activities characteristic of each phase contribute to patterning of winter house faunal assemblages, but for present purposes we will limit discussion to the following closely related cultural processes that influence the structure and composition of the assemblages: discard and maintenance, abandonment, reoccupation, and change in function. These processes are discussed separately, but they can be expected to operate simultaneously in many cases.

To provide a framework for the discussion, Schiffer's (1987) terminology relating to refuse is employed. Schiffer distinguishes three main types of refuse generated by human activities. Primary refuse is that which accumulates in locations of use. Residual primary refuse consists of small items that are not removed by cleaning or "maintenance" processes, and secondary refuse refers to materials that are deposited away from locations of use (Schiffer 1987: 58-64).

Discard And Maintenance

Discard can be considered to be one of the most important behavioural process affecting the composition and integrity of faunal assemblages from Thule winter houses. Current understanding of Thule discard behaviour has been derived primarily from the observed state of house ruins and middens rather than from descriptions contained in historic or ethnographic sources. This can be explained by the fact that most early European expeditions occurred during the summer months and, moreover, that by the time of sustained contact with Europeans, the predominant form of Inuit winter residence in most of the Canadian Arctic was the snowhouse (see Savelle 1984 for a discussion of formation processes affecting historic Inuit snow houses).

Nevertheless, based on the quantities of animal bones found in the interiors of many Thule houses and on what limited ethnographic information we possess, it seems evident that at least some discard took place within the house. Food preparation, consumption, and storage occurred indoors during the winter season and considerable food waste could accumulate over a period of several months. However, some or all of this primary refuse would presumably have been removed from the house through intermittent or *ad hoc* maintenance (Schiffer 1987).

Ethnographic and archaeological evidence provide only a limited understanding of house maintenance processes. A principle reason for this is the difficulty of assessing the frequency with which food waste and other refuse was removed from activity areas within houses. Factors that could be expected to influence the frequency of maintenance include the number of house occupants, the duration of occupation (i.e., number of weeks or months) and the extent to which food waste and other forms of debris interfered with other activities. In this regard, sleeping platforms and entry passages may have required the most frequent cleaning. It has been suggested that Thule winter houses were cleaned on at least an annual basis, possibly prior to their reoccupation in the late fall (McCartney 1979: 307; McGhee 1984: 16, 78). Bone refuse, if encased by frozen melt water, might have been most easily removed during this season to a midden opposite the house entry (McCartney 1979: 307; cf. Stefansson 1922: 88). The presence of middens in this location at many sites suggests that such cleaning was done, but we have no reliable means of determining the rate of accumulation or the specific source of the debris.

The excavation of a Thule winter house at the Utkiagvik site, Point Barrow, Alaska, provides a tantalizing glimpse of a situation where in-house discard can be assumed to have been the predominant factor shaping an excavated faunal assemblage (Newell 1990: 230-231). This house and its five occupants were apparently crushed by a surge of sea ice (Reinhardt and Dekin 1990: 39) and the only post-occupational disturbance of the house appears to have been the removal from some accessible parts of the house of valued artifacts, presumably not including unmodified animal bones (Dekin 1990: 235-236; Reinhardt and Dekin 1990: 46). Therefore, the quantity of faunal remains should be representative of an occupied house before abandonment. The results of the faunal analysis show that faunal remains were scarce in the floor area of the house (n=125), and only somewhat more abundant in the sub-floor level (n=422) (Reinhardt and Dekin 1990: 75-76, 82, 89-90). Removal of accumulated faunal debris (i.e., maintenance) prior to the house collapsing is included among the explanations offered for the small amount of bone recovered (Reinhardt and Dekin 1990: 76). The Utkiagvik house is instructive concerning the importance of discard and maintenance behaviour in Eastern Thule winter houses in that assemblages from the latter typically contain thousands of bones. This suggests either that house maintenance was not practiced (or relaxed prior to abandonment), or that factors other than discard have contributed substantially to the formation of the assemblages.

Abandonment

Two general abandonment categories can be distinguished for Thule winter houses; seasonal abandonment and final abandonment. These categories simply refer to the intentions of the house's occupants at the time of abandonment, so houses abandoned with the intent of occupying them the following year (i.e., seasonally abandoned) were not necessarily reoccupied. Assuming that unexpected events sometimes altered peoples' plans, archaeologists can expect to encounter houses of both types.

When a house was abandoned at the end of the winter with the intent of reoccupying it the following year it would presumably be left intact or nearly so. In the case of final abandonment, the house superstructure might be taken apart to remove the whale bones forming the roof framework and the skins that would have covered them under a layer of sods. This dismantling could displace secondary refuse into the house interior, particularly from what Morrison (1983: 53) refers to as wall middens or from other deposits abutting the outside wall of the house. If the house was abandoned intact, the gradual collapse of its superstructure could also introduce secondary refuse from middens adjacent to or on the house walls into the house interior by slumping.

As mentioned previously, the frequency of house maintenance is difficult to determine but modern precedents (Schiffer 1987) suggest that houses were unlikely to be cleaned prior to seasonal or final abandonment. If ad hoc maintenance had been practiced during the winter, any refuse left in primary context following abandonment would reflect only consumption that occurred since the last cleaning, and provide a limited view of subsistence.

Reoccupation And Refurbishment

There is abundant archaeological evidence for the repeated use of Thule winter sites over both interannual and longer time intervals. This is demonstrated clearly at several sites in the form of structural modifications, in which new paving stones were set over the main floor of the house, or in which the size of the dwelling was altered (e.g., Collins 1955: 24; Maxwell 1981: 138; McCartney 1977: 113; McCullough 1989: 31; McGhee 1984: 15-16, 22, 24; Park 1984: 17-21, 1989: 76;

Schledermann 1975: 81; Stenton 1987: 18). Repaving of the floor areas can be expected to affect the faunal remains in several ways. If the existing floor debris were not removed or only partially removed prior to the laying of a new floor, food refuse in primary context may be preserved (e.g., McGhee 1984: 24). However, at least one case has been documented where faunal debris appear to have been deliberately deposited prior to repaving a sleeping platform, presumably to provide a solid base for the new slabs (Park 1984: 17). Therefore, those bones represent secondary refuse employed for structural purposes.

Unusual concentrations of faunal remains in particular parts of Thule houses may also result from refurbishment and reoccupation. In the Frobisher Bay area, for example, it is not uncommon to find that a Thule house was reduced in size during its history, presumably in the course of an episode of reoccupation. Considerable amounts of debris are often found in the former living space (e.g., Stenton 1990). Reoccupation, however, need not have involved modifications that would be evident structurally. On the basis of ethnographic information from various areas within the North American Arctic, reoccupation could have been by the same family or families that occupied the house in the previous season, or by a completely different group of people (e.g., Steensby 1910: 286). The interval between occupations may have varied enormously. For example, Mathiassen (1927a: 19) discusses a centuries-old winter house at the Naujan site being refurbished and used as an autumn house in the early 1920s.

Post-Abandonment Functional Changes

Thule winter houses continued to serve important functions subsequent to their final abandonment. The most important of these functions was undoubtedly as concentrated supplies of building materials that could be recycled into new house construction (McCartney 1977: 309; Park 1989: 157). Whale bones are typically cited as the most sought-after commodity, but concentrations of flat slabs used for paving and sleeping platforms appear also to have been exploited (e.g., McGhee 1984: 24). The removal of stone slabs and whale bones from abandoned houses can be expected to result in the displacement and admixture of both primary and secondary refuse.

The use of abandoned winter houses as food caches (Maxwell 1981: 138; Sabo 1991: 118), temporary autumn dwellings (Mathiassen 1927a: 19; Sabo and Jacobs 1980: 500), refuse pits (Schledermann 1975: 84) and locations for hearths (McGhee 1984: 33; Morrison 1988: 25; Stenton 1990) have all been documented. The presence of hearths or fire pits is intriguing. The fact that they contain ash and bone fragments, in some cases fused into a large mass, indicates that a proportion of the faunal assemblage from a given site or dwelling has been destroyed. Morrison (1988: 32) suggests that burning may have been employed as a means of garbage disposal, although in some cases stratigraphic evidence suggests that the hearths post-date residential use of the structures.

Implications For Archaeological Interpretation

While it is clearly problematic to ascertain whether some or all of these processes occurred in a given case, they have obvious implications for the manner in which we reconstruct Thule settlement and subsistence behaviour using faunal evidence. Returning to Schiffer's distinction between primary refuse, residual primary refuse and secondary refuse, and applying these basic concepts uncritically to Thule winter houses, we would classify food waste found in the house interior as primary or residual primary refuse while that found outside the dwelling (i.e., in separate middens as well as in and around the perimeter of the exterior wall) would be classified as secondary refuse.

In practice, this simple scheme might accurately describe the probable context of the faunal bones at the time of final abandonment and before any dismantling of the house. However, the factors that we have outlined can be expected to have altered the composition of the faunal assemblages as encountered by the archaeologist. Therefore, the basic questions that one would want to have answered include: How can we distinguish between various faunal subassemblages from a Thule winter house? Which faunal subassemblages from a house are associated with the particular occupation of interest? How comparable are subassemblages of different kinds (e.g., primary refuse versus secondary refuse) even if they do derive from the same occupation of the structure? To answer these questions it is necessary to consider the nature of the faunal remains as encountered by the archaeologist.

Depositional Patterns Of Food Waste And Refuse Zonation

For discussion purposes we distinguish four basic "zones" of refuse associated with excavated Thule winter houses; dwelling interior, entrance passage, exterior midden (normally opposite the entry), and exterior wall and perimeter. Refuse accumulations in each zone have certain unique characteristics including the source, amount and type of refuse they contain, and raise different issues of interpretation for archaeologists.

Dwelling Interior Refuse

Thule house fill typically consists of a surface vegetation layer overlying an organic matrix of variable thickness which in turn rests on a paved floor or platform surface. The overburden may range in thickness from several centimetres to nearly a metre, with the upper levels often incorporating large amounts of rocks and whale bone. Bone refuse is found in direct or near-direct contact with the paved entry and main floors, as well as in the overburden that fills the house depression.

Refuse found directly on or in clear association with the floor can be considered primary refuse or residual primary refuse, but that contained within the fill above the floor is much more problematic. Realistically, it must be considered secondary refuse, but originating from what source? Several processes would produce secondary refuse in this location, including abandonment, refurbishment, or the use of the house pit as a cache or refuse dump. If the assemblage was the product of abandonment then the secondary refuse might derive from the occupation of that house, but in the latter case (i.e., cache or refuse dump) it would bear no necessary relation to the occupation of that house. The examination of profiles through the house fill might clarify whether it derived from abandonment processes rather than from the use of the house as a dump.

Entrance Passage Refuse

Entrance passage refuse is subject to the same factors outlined for the dwelling interior. However, from ethnographic data we know that entrance passages were sometimes used to house dogs to protect them from the weather or from wolves (Lyon 1824: 156). Therefore, refuse in this location might have been differentially affected (e.g., in volume) by consumption by dogs.

Midden Refuse

Thule middens are conventionally defined as accumulations of secondary refuse situated several metres from, and opposite to, the house entry passage. Morrison (1983: 53) has also distinguished a type he refers to as "wall middens," consisting of domestic midden placed up against the outside of the house wall. Midden refuse consists of food waste and other debris removed from the house by maintenance (cleaning) or rebuilding processes. The volume and condition of midden faunal assemblages is highly variable, ranging from thin lenses of poorly preserved bone to relatively thick and well-preserved deposits (e.g., McGhee 1984: 40; Staab 1979: 351).

Because Thule houses characteristically yield greater numbers of diagnostic artifacts, most Thule site excavations concentrate on house ruins. As a result, the majority of faunal assemblages that have been studied have been derived from house excavations rather than from middens or other extramural site areas. Interpretations based on assemblages recovered from middens must, however, take several factors into account. Midden bones are differentially exposed to mechanical erosion by freeze-thaw processes and subject to scattering and destruction by carnivores (dogs, wolves, foxes, bears). Also, a midden may or may not be referable to a specific house, especially in sites where houses cluster. Equally important is the fact that where houses were used over a long period of time, midden assemblages can rarely be assigned to a particular occupation (although the deposit will generally reflect the order of refuse deposition, stratigraphic breaks can rarely be discerned). Finally, although midden deposits obviously represent secondary refuse, we have little information on how these secondary deposits can be expected to compare with the primary, residual primary and secondary deposits from house interiors. For example, Park (1989: 205-207) has compared seal bone anatomical element representation from two published sources that reported element data from both the interior of a Thule house and from its external midden (Møbjerg 1983: Table 3; Staab 1979: Table 2). In one case the distribution of elements appears to be similar while in the other there are substantial differences between the house and midden. However, the significance of this patterning is unclear, because it is possible to envision processes that should produce differences, and because the faunal remains from the house interiors were treated as a unit for the purposes of the comparison (i.e., no attempt was made to use only primary or residual primary refuse).

Exterior Wall and Perimeter Refuse

In addition to wall midden deposits, other bone refuse is found within the walls and around the exterior perimeter of winter houses. There are several potential sources for this refuse. Bones in these locations might represent byproducts from house construction, domestic waste deposited through maintenance, or bones scattered by animals. The area surrounding a Thule house is rarely excavated extensively and faunal deposits here require greater attention.

Conclusion

Our discussions with colleagues convince us that there is broad awareness of the issues we have outlined, and we have been able to extract examples of formation processes altering the composition of Thule faunal assemblages from field reports and published papers. We argue, however, that the practical and theoretical consequences of factors affecting assemblage composition are not adequately reflected in the literature. Archaeologists have been vigilant in identifying and excluding from analysis faunal assemblages derived from sites where obvious cultural mixing has taken place (such as at Dorset sites re-used by the Thule) but very few Thule site reports recognize explicitly the complexity inherent in the faunal remains associated with all Thule winter houses. Even fewer demonstrate that an effort has been made to deal with these issues by (for example) attempting to analyze primary and secondary refuse separately. Instead, house interior refuse is implicitly (or explicitly) treated as being in primary context and the secondary refuse in middens is treated as directly comparable with the refuse from house interiors. Reconstructions of Thule subsistence behaviour based on faunal analysis rely on those assumptions. We contend, however, that most Thule deposits consist of mixed, secondary refuse, and thus require more careful and thorough analysis.

We offer the following basic suggestions to begin to address this issue. The first is to make formation processes an explicit dimension of Thule research. This is essential for the analysis of all Thule sites, but can be considered especially important for the study of winter sites because these continue to serve as the foundation for most analyses of Thule culture history and socio-economics. The second is to explore ways to identify and measure key characteristics of primary and secondary Thule refuse deposits, and to collect and analyze faunal remains in a manner sensitive to the distinctions in human behaviours they may reflect.

Finally, rather than continue to use faunal data simply to amplify pre-existing models of Thule settlement and subsistence behaviour, we suggest a shift in analytical perspective is required, in which greater emphasis is placed on the relationship between the faunal remains and the associated structure(s). In more concrete terms, faunal data should be used to examine the extent to which life histories of formally similar structures (i.e., winter houses) differ. Accomplishing this requires a much clearer understanding of the ways in which the faunal remains found in houses were deposited and the factors that affected them prior to and following deposition. In practical terms, this need not result in a loss of basic information concerning Thule dietary habits; however, viewing Thule faunal assemblages as the product of varied depositional processes may force us to reconsider existing models, particularly those that interpret differences in faunal assemblages principally as reflections of human responses to environmental change.

We believe this to be especially important because researchers typically give analytical priority to interpretations based on the formal characteristics of structures rather than to conclusions based on faunal analysis. With only a few exceptions (including Taylor's seminal 1966 and 1968 works on Thule adaptation) researchers use faunal data not to evaluate the efficacy of models of Thule adaptive behaviour but simply to reinforce them. In cases where the faunal data contradict expectations, taphonomic or cultural factors are often cited to explain the discrepancy. This relegation of faunal analysis to a secondary, confirmatory role effectively limits its potential for contributing to a fuller understanding of Thule culture.

We believe that the various formation processes outlined above have dramatically but not disastrously shaped the character of Thule faunal assemblages. These processes, rather than presenting an insurmountable barrier to understanding this important dimension of the archaeological record, instead provide us with an opportunity to learn about the diversity of Thule settlement systems. The fact that Thule houses were used in different ways and had complex life histories should not be a reason to ignore or reject the faunal evidence. Rather, the faunal evidence offers opportunities that should permit us to understand better the complex nature of Thule settlement and subsistence systems.

References

Boas, F. 1888. The Central Eskimo. Annual Report of the Bureau of American Ethnology, 6.

Collins, H. B. 1955. Excavations of Thule and Dorset Culture Sites at Resolute, Cornwallis Island, N.W.T. National Museum of Canada Bulletin, 136: 22-35.

de Laguna, F. 1979. Therkel Mathiassen and the Beginnings of Eskimo Archaeology. In, Thule Eskimo Culture: An Anthropological Retrospective, A.P. McCartney ed. National Museum of Man, Mercury Series, Archaeological Survey of Canada Paper, 88: 10-53.

Dekin, A. 1990. Summary and Conclusions. In, The Utqiagvik Excavations Vol. 3: Excavation of a Prehistoric Catastrophe: A Preserved Household from the Utqiagvik Village, Barrow, Alaska, C.R. Polglase and D.F. Cassedy, eds. The North Slope Borough Commission on Iñupiat History, Language and Culture, Barrow, pp. 234-241.

Freeman, M. 1979. A Critical View of Thule Culture and Ecological Adaptation. In, Thule Eskimo Culture: An Anthropological Retrospective, A.P. McCartney, ed. National Museum of Man, Mercury Series, Archaeological Survey of Canada Paper, 88: 278-285.

Lyon, G. 1824. The Private Journal of Captain G.F. Lyon, of H.M.S. Hecla During the Recent Voyages of Discovery under Captain Parry. London: J. Murray.

Mathiassen, T. 1927a. Archaeology of the Central Eskimos: Descriptive Part. Report of the Fifth Thule Expedition 1921-24 , 4 (1).

Mathiassen, T. 1927b. Archaeology of the Central Eskimos: the Thule Culture and its Position Within the Eskimo Culture. Report of the Fifth Thule Expedition 1921-24, 4 (2).

Maxwell, M. 1981. A Southeastern Baffin Island Thule House With Ruin Island Characteristics. Arctic, 34(2): 133-140.

Maxwell, M. 1985. Prehistory of the Eastern Arctic. Orlando: Academic Press.

McCartney, A. P. 1977. Thule Eskimo Prehistory Along Northwestern Hudson Bay. National Museum of Man, Mercury Series, Archaeological Survey of Canada Paper, 70.

McCartney, A. P. 1979. A Processual Consideration of Thule Whale Bone Houses. In, Thule Eskimo Culture: An Anthropological Retrospective, A.P. McCartney, ed. National Museum of Man, Mercury Series, Archaeological Survey of Canada Paper, 88: 301-323.

McCartney, A. P. and J. Savelle. 1985. Thule Eskimo Whaling in the Central Canadian Arctic. Arctic Anthropology, 22(2): 37-58.

McCullough, K. 1989. The Ruin Islanders: Early Thule Culture Pioneers in the Eastern High Arctic. Canadian Museum of Civilization, Mercury Series, Archaeological Survey of Canada Paper, 141.

McGhee, R. 1984a. The Thule Village at Brooman Point, High Arctic Canada. National Museum of Man, Mercury Series, Archaeological Survey of Canada Paper, 125.

McGhee, R. 1982. The Past Ten Years in Canadian Arctic Prehistory. Canadian Journal of Archaeology, 6: 65-77.

Mobjerg, T. 1983. An Ethno-Archaeological Investigation of the Sermermiut Settlement, West Greenland. Folk, 25: 23-50.

Mohl, J. 1979. Description and Analysis of the Bone Material from Nugarsuk: An Eskimo Settlement Representative of the Thule Culture in West Greenland. In, Thule Eskimo Culture: An Anthropological Retrospective, A.P. McCartney, ed. National Museum of Man, Mercury Series, Archaeological Survey of Canada Paper, 88: 380-394.

Morrison, D. 1983. Thule Culture in Western Coronation Gulf, N.W.T. National Museum of Man, Mercury Series, Archaeological Survey of Canada Paper, 116.

Morrison, D. 1988. The Kugaluk Site and the Nuvorugmiut. Canadian Museum of Civilization, Mercury Series, Archaeological Survey of Canada Paper, 137.

Newell, R. R. 1990. On the Theoretical Implications of the Mound 44 Kataligaaq Iglu. In, The Utqiagvik Excavations Vol. 3: Excavation of a Prehistoric Catastrophe: A Preserved Household from the Utqiagvik Village, Barrow, Alaska, C.R. Polglase and D.F. Cassedy, eds. The North Slope Borough Commission on Iñupiat History, Language and Culture, Barrow, pp. 227-233.

Park, R. 1984. Porden Point and Port Refuge: Thule Eskimo Sites from the Grinnell Peninsula, Devon Island, N.W.T. Unpublished Masters thesis, McMaster University.

Park, R. 1988. "Winter Houses" and Qarmat in Thule and Historic Inuit Settlement Patterns: some implications For Thule studies. Canadian Journal of Archaeology, 12: 163-175.

Park, R. 1989. Porden Point: An Intrasite Approach to Settlement System Analysis. Unpublished Ph.D dissertation, University of Alberta.

Reinhardt, G. A., and A. Dekin. 1990. House Structure and Interior Features. In, The Utqiagvik Excavations Vol. 3: Excavation of a Prehistoric Catastrophe: A Preserved Household from the Utqiagvik Village, Barrow, Alaska, C.R. Polglase and D.F. Cassedy, eds. The North Slope Borough Commission on Iñupiat History, Language and Culture, Barrow, pp. 38-112.

Rick, A. 1980. Non-Cetacean Vertebrate Remains from Two Thule Winter Houses on Somerset Island, N.W.T. Canadian Journal of Archaeology, 4: 99-117.

Sabo, G. 1979. Development of the Thule Culture in the Historic Period: patterns of material culture change on the Davis Strait coast of Baffin Island. In, Thule Eskimo Culture: An Anthropological Retrospective, A.P. McCartney, ed. National Museum of Man, Mercury Series, Archaeological Survey of Canada Paper, 88: 212-241.

Sabo, G. 1991. Long Term Adaptations Among Arctic Hunter-Gatherers: A Case Study from Southern Baffin Island. New York: Garland Press.

Sabo, G. and J. Jacobs. 1980. Aspects of Thule Culture Adaptations in Southern Baffin Island. Arctic, 33(3): 487-504.

Savelle, J. 1984. Cultural and Natural Formation Processes of a Historic Inuit Snow Dwelling Site, Somerset Island, Arctic Canada. American Antiquity, 49(3): 508-524.

Savelle, J. 1987. Collectors and Foragers: Subsistence-Settlement System Change in the Central Canadian Arctic, A.D. 1000-1960. British Archaeological Reports (Int. Series), 358.

Savelle, J. and A. P. McCartney. 1988. Geographical and temporal variation in Thule Eskimo subsistence economies: a model. Research in Economic Anthropology, 10: 21-72.

Schiffer, M. B. 1972. Archaeological Context and Systemic Context. American Antiquity, 37: 156-165.

Schiffer, M. B. 1987. Formation Processes of the Archaeological Record. Albuquerque: University of New Mexico Press.

Schledermann, P. 1975. Thule Eskimo Prehistory of Cumberland Sound, Baffin Island, Canada. National Museum of Man, Mercury Series, Archaeological Survey of Canada Paper, 38.

Schledermann, P. 1976. The Effect of Climatic/Ecological Changes on the Style of Thule Culture Winter Dwellings. Arctic and Alpine Research, 8(1): 37-47.

Staab, M. L. 1979. Analysis of Faunal Material Recovered from a Thule Eskimo Site on the Island of Silumiut, N.W.T., Canada. In, Thule Eskimo Culture: An Anthropological Retrospective, A.P. McCartney, ed. National Museum of Man, Mercury Series, Archaeological Survey of Canada Paper, 88: 349-379.

Stanford, D. 1976. The Walakpa Site, Alaska: its Place in the Birnirk and Thule Cultures. Smithsonian Contributions to Anthropology, 20.

Steensby, H. P. 1910. Contributions to the Ethnology and Anthropogeography of the Polar Eskimos. Meddelelser om Grønland, 34: 255-405.

Stefansson V. 1922. Hunters of the Great North. New York: Harcourt and Brace.

Stenton, D. 1983. An Analysis of Faunal Remains from the Peale Point Site, (KkDo-1) Baffin Island, N.W.T. Unpublished Master's thesis, Trent University.

Stenton, D. 1987. Recent Archaeological Investigations in Frobisher Bay, Baffin Island, N.W.T. Canadian Journal of Archaeology, 11: 13-48.

Stenton, D. 1990. Archaeological Investigations at the Tungatsivvik Site (KkDo-3), Baffin Island, N.W.T. Preliminary Report. MS on file with the Canadian Museum of Civilization, Hull.

Stenton, D. 1991. Caribou population dynamics and Thule culture adaptations on southern Baffin Island, N.W.T. Arctic Anthropology, 28(2): 15-43.

Taylor, W. E. 1966. An Archaeological Perspective on Eskimo Economy. Antiquity, 40: 114-120.

Taylor, W. E. 1968. An Archaeological Overview of Eskimo Economy. In, Eskimo of the Canadian Arctic, V. Valentine and F. Valee, eds. Toronto: McClelland and Stewart, pp. 1-17.

Taylor, W. E. and R. McGhee. 1981. Deblicquy, a Thule Culture Site on Bathurst Island, N.W.T., Canada. National Museum of Man, Mercury Series, Archaeological Survey of Canada Paper, 102.